No Telephone to Heaven

To Kat – who shared it all

NO TELEPHONE

TO

HEAVEN

*From Apex to Nadir—Colonial Service in
Nigeria, Aden, the Cameroons and the
Gold Coast, 1938-61*

Malcolm Milne

MEON HILL PRESS

Copyright © Malcolm Milne 1999
First published in 1999 by Meon Hill Press
Little Manor Lodge
Longstock
Stockbridge
Hants SO20 6DS

Distributed by Gazelle Book Services Limited
Falcon House, Queen Square
Lancaster, England LA1 1RN

British Library Cataloguing in Publication Data
A catalogue record for this book is available from the British Library

ISBN 0-9535540-0-7

Typeset by Amolibros, Watchet, Somerset
This book production has been managed by Amolibros
Printed and bound by Professional Book Supplies, Oxford, England

Contents

PART TWO   NADIR

List of Illustrations & Maps

Maps

Illustrations

Nos 1-13 facing page page 102, nos 14-28 facing page 230, nos 29-39 facing page 358.

Acknowledgements

I am deeply indebted to HE Chief Anyaoku for the Preface supplied when he was more than normally pressed by most urgent Commonwealth matters.

In 1939 we cadets were expected to receive our on-the-job training from our expatriate superiors. In fact, these chaps were so busy that apart from the odd titbit passed over with the drinks of an evening we received the bulk of our early training from Nigerian staff, then in the junior service. And very good they were, too. I owe a great debt to such men as H O Nwosu, Sergeant Major Chop Bafutmai, Warder Nwokedi, J R Romaine, J M Onyechi, A E Eronini...the list goes on and on. I thank them one and all for the time and attention they gave me.

And I'm grateful, too, to the staff of the colonial administrative service course at Cambridge all so carefully appointed by Furse. Much of what they taught has remained in my mind and served me well.

Naturally one learnt a lot from one's superiors if only by dint of greater experience but it was also an honour and a privilege to work under such exceptional men as the brilliant Lord Grey, the wise and quietly authoritative Sir James Robertson, the worldly-wise Geoffrey Gardner-Brown, the highly experienced Sir Sydney Phillipson and, at provincial level, the idiosyncratic but basically kindly Dermott O'Connor, Hyaena Smith and so many others.

I am very grateful to Raph Uwechue who hearing that I was writing about West Africa gave me copies of *Africa Today* and *Makers of Modern Africa*—both copious volumes essential to any student of African affairs. Uwechue himself, who as far as I know, hasn't written about his own country since the civil war, will, I sincerely hope, shortly be persuaded to leave his busy desk as the head of Africa Books Ltd and give us his thoughts on the last unsettled thirty years in Nigeria – a subject on which he is refreshingly erudite. Victor Pungong has deeply researched the Cameroons years 1930 to 1962 and has for several years now been very willing to discuss details with me. I am most grateful to him for his help and patience.

Tony Kirk-Greene needs no introduction from me. He is Emeritus Fellow of St Antony's College, Oxford and has recently published a classical history of the colonial service entitled *On Crown Service*. I am much obliged to him for points he helpfully raised when reading the original typescript, and now, of course, I am especially grateful to him for contributing a Foreword.

Jane Tatam is the professional publishing consultant for this book and has done—and continues to do—a magnificent job of work.

I am grateful to the chief librarian of the Foreign and Commonwealth Office library collection for permission to reproduce the photographs used in illustrations nos 11, 14, 22 and 32.

Sally Chilver and Shirley Ardener have both taken time off their intensely busy academic lives in Oxford to read the typescript of this book and I am immensely grateful to them both for the corrections they have made.

Now that the thirty years rule applies and members of the public can secure access to official records at the Public Records Office, Kew and a number of ministry libraries, it is possible to paint a much fairer picture of official dealings of the past. The PRO at Kew, although only moved there recently, manages to provide an efficient and patient service to the large numbers that use it. Many ministry libraries have been helpful. I must particularly thank Peter Bursey head of the Library and Information Service of the Foreign and Commonwealth Office. Not only is he singularly efficient—no query being too difficult for him—but he possesses the gift of positively encouraging his clients, coming up with ideas and helpful suggestions himself.

Lastly, I must go back seventy years and thank Jack and the two Aunts for taking on my two sisters and me in the first place. Without their great generosity there would have been for me no Cambridge, no colonial experiences and *No Telephone to Heaven*.

Preface

The memoirs of colonial servants, especially of British colonial civil servants with which 1 am more familiar-and as distinct from any memoirs of indigenous civil servants who served the colonial master-are coming into their own as a literary kind. And for Africans of my generation for whom these books are partly about our childhood and young adult experience, they stimulate a whole gamut of emotions but remain unendingly a source of fascination. That fascination is for their multi-disciplinary variety as both important historical and political documents, as Anthony Kirk-Greene has noted in his foreword in these pages, as well as the fascination they offer as a human story of considerable depth and a version of our collective memory.

The views expressed in these books will always be a talking point for those who read them and deal with the subject at different levels of interest and intensity. The books that hold the longest interest are likely to do so mainly by the extent to which they have been true and honest to the experience of their authors. The honesty of his narrative is the great strength of Malcolm Milne's book. It is also a very good read. I commend *No Telephone to Heaven*, a title of particular resonance for those familiar with West Africa. Like most of its kind Mr Milne's book is the outsider's tale of the colonised people's most dominant experience of the turn of the outgoing century. Coming at the turn of a new century, it is about a past of which the Commonwealth is the future and a timely contribution to our shared heritage.

Emeka Anyaoku

Commonwealth Secretary-General
Marlborough House
London
October 1999

Foreword

It is generous of Malcolm Milne to invite me to contribute a foreword to such a distinguished and delightful volume of colonial service memoirs. Apart from the normal sense of honour among authors attaching to such requests, this one exercises a particular service atypicality. In colonial service terms, it both originates from one who was by twelve years my senior (and the deep sense of seniority in the service's postings and promotions is constantly alluded to throughout the memoir) and is addressed to one who was not a member of the same regional civil service—a "Northerner", in the idiom of the Nigerian Administrative Service, and never an "Easterner" like Malcolm Milne.

Yet in reading this attractive, important and well-written memoir in its very first draft, I was immediately alerted to the number of colleagues and experiences that we nevertheless seem to have shared. Among the personalities in Malcolm's story, for instance, Geoffrey Gardner-Brown had been Supervisor of the Devonshire Course at Cambridge which I attended in 1949; John Stapleton was a Senior District Officer under whom I worked in Yola in 1953; and Dermott O'Connor and Peter Gunning my parents—and I in due course—knew socially in Tunbridge Wells, where Patricia Gunning was my mixed doubles partner in the annual tennis tournament. As for Nigel Cooke, Malcolm's brother-in-law, he was, as SDO Bida, my number one mentor in the whole of my colonial service career, and I later visited his (and Kat Milne's) mother, Kitty Cooke, at her home outside Jos, on the Plateau. I just missed the opportunity of meeting the "mercurial" Brigadier John Gibbons, Commissioner of the Cameroons, through his illness, when I was seconded to the United Nations Trust Territory Visiting Mission as his ADC for the northern leg of its triennial Cameroons' inspection in 1952, and was Northern liaison officer to Godfrey Allen instead; and had John Field been similarly indisposed at the critical Cameroons session of the UN in 1958/59 when I was attached to the Northern Cameroons delegation led by Abba Habib, it is on the cards that I would have been liaising in New York with his Deputy Commissioner, none other than Malcolm Milne.

In the event, it was to be another thirty-five years before we met. Slight as such links may have been, they were strong enough to engender in me right from the start a "special relationship" dimension to my reading of this attractive and important memoir.

Having at least partially presented my credentials for writing this foreword (I am too small a fry to get away with just the conventional Big Name commendation), I must enter one caveat. I find that, for all my admiration of Malcolm Milne's memoir, I have to express my disagreement with one of his interpretations. Such an option to differ was one we in the colonial service were always open to exercise: as he himself neatly encapsulates the ethos,

> The service was not only eminently fair to us, it took care of us. We, in turn, obeyed the accepted usages of the service: we were encouraged at whatever level we served, to say what we thought but we did what we were told.

In particular, I am far happier over the executive role of the colonial administrative service in the dismantling of empire than he is, with his belief that whereas the pre-war administration represented its apex, its post-war involvement in the mechanics of the transfer of power constituted its nadir. In rejecting such an argument as too negative, I may of course simply be proving the point Milne assiduously and accurately makes, the generational gap:

> Post-war entrants to the service seemed to view this dilemma [of a career colonial service aiding and abetting early decolonisation] more practically; they did not appear, as we pre-war entrants did, to feel as torn by the switch in course…There were differences in outlook and attitude between those recruited before and after World War II, possibly exacerbated by the substitution of the colonial administrative service course by the Devonshire course.

It is a theme he vigorously returns to in Chapter Fourteen, no doubt making this a subject for lively debate.

Nothing in our colonial service "generational" divergence of opinion can detract from the real enjoyment of this thoughtful and stimulating memoir. It does everything one expects from the best of memoirs—and does it effectively and elegantly, with serious intent but a light touch, largely based on the first-hand testimonies of diaries kept by his wife Kat and supplemented by letters home to the two aunts and from the perceptive Uncle Jack. The narrative is skilfully constructed from a series of recollections set within a clear historical framework rather than a straightforward—and likely less readable—monthly chronology. It opens in 1939 (with Chapter Two moving back to his upbringing), when Malcolm sailed from Liverpool on RMS *Accra*, "one of the most expensive hotels in the world", and takes the reader through a basically standard but steadily rising colonial service career on to 1961, when his quasi-gubernatorial post as acting Commissioner of the Cameroons was abolished consequent on the Southern Cameroons' decision to join its francophone neighbour, the Republic of Cameroon. Names—so crucial for the colonial service historian—are scrupulously recorded and their owners often tellingly described, the sole exceptions being the understandable veil drawn over the ebullient cadet Percy X after his behaviour at the ship's fancy dress ball (p 12) and the similar anonymity granted to the procrastinatory senior officer in the Lagos Secretariat (p 335). Anecdotes abound, not merely to amuse but often to illustrate. J S ("Hyena") Smith's putting down of unloved superiors by quoting a Latin tag recalls the story about the legendary Lenox-Conyngham, my first DO, who peppered his correspondence to headquarters with foreign language quotations randomly lifted from the Angostura Bitters labels. Among my favourite anecdotes for the reader to anticipate are the tale of the missionary language-teacher's Ibo-speaking parrot, the dramatic *dénouement* of the local showing of the film *Daybreak at Udi*, and the confidential safe "trap" set by the outgoing Governor, Sir Clem Pleass, for his over-enterprising successors.

The discomforts, anxieties and crises of family life in the colonial service, especially in West Africa, are almost palpably depicted by Milne, and the nature of the work of an administrative officer, whether in bush, provincial headquarters or the central secretariat, is convincingly described. He admits that for him the worst hardship in his career was the long spells spent alone on tour. Given the importance of career motivation, it is interesting to learn why he joined the colonial service, given his comfortable schoolboy's life (apart from his passionate prayer on the eve of St Bees' annual rugger match against their arch-rivals, "Dear God, please let us knock hell out of Sedbergh") in pre-war Cumbria. Having read *The Story of Fergie Bey* at the age of twelve, he told his father he intended to be a DO in the Sudan. In the event, after Cambridge he was accepted for the Sudan Political Service, but turned it down for the Colonial Administrative Service, which not only offered a permanent and pensionable career but also far wider opportunities than a single-territory service like the Sudan. Apart from three years' war service in West Africa and a later secondment to Aden, Milne spent the whole service in Southern Nigeria, moving from the Eastern Region to Lagos in 1955 and then to the Southern Cameroons from 1958 to 1961. Although his memoir does not extend to his subsequent Kenya days, it does conclude with a frank presentation of the personal dilemma officers of his vintage found themselves feeling as their expectedly full career prematurely fell to pieces.

With the wind-down of Her Majesty's Colonial Service as a permanent career since the mid-1950s and the closure of its successor, Her Majesty's Overseas Civil Service, in 1997, the service memoir has over the past decade become a mini-literary genre in its own right. As the last generations of colonial civil servants look back on their life, they realise that they are just that, the final colonial service cohort. Many have been inspired to write up their experiences, to set down what they did in the colonial service, in work and leisure, for the benefit of a new generation for whom the opportunity of such a career in Crown public service has never existed and who consequently know nothing about what the colonial service was or did. For most people born since c1970, the profession of the colonial service (and, of course, the Indian Civil Service, the Indian Political Service, the Sudan Political Service) is beginning to be as outdated, as fading and just occasionally as unbelievable, as other bygone occupations.

Whilst many such recollections are not always meant for publication and not necessarily for an archival posterity, but simply for their family, others have a serious place to occupy in the literature available. In *No Telephone to Heaven*, as well as offering an accessible and entertaining style, Malcolm Milne also provides one dimension to his repertoire which lifts him beyond the commonality of many colonial service memoir-writers. Milne's career, with its culmination of four years of high office in the Southern Cameroons, focuses in its last fifty pages on a rare kind of British colonial responsibility, one with unique international features. Neither Colony nor Protectorate, the Cameroons was legally a Mandated Territory, one of the former German/Ottoman possessions handed to Britain to administer by the League of Nations in 1922 and then restyled a Trust Territory by the United Nations in 1946. While not unique, there were only two other such territories in Britain's colonial empire, that region of the former Togoland administered as part of the Gold Coast and the ex-German East Africa administered (apart from the areas of Rwanda and Burundi which were mandated to Belgium) as Tanganyika Territory.

Thus it is that Milne's final chapters, where he deals with the constitutional and personality problems associated with the emergence of the Southern Cameroons as a self-governing entity and its ultimate reunification with the dominant francophone Cameroun in 1961 to form the new state of the Republic of Cameroon, have considerable historical importance. Standard sources, like Victor Le Vine's *The Cameroons: from Mandate to Independence* (1964), W R Johnson's *The Cameroon Federation* (1970), Neville Rubin's *Cameroun: An African Federation* (1971) and the Introduction to the second edition of my *Adamawa Past and Present: an historical approach to a Northern Cameroons Province* (1969), have already made available to researchers a coherent account of the successive, separate and confusing plebiscites on the future of both the Northern and the Southern Cameroons, the latter revealing a district anti-Ibo sentiment and the former a pro-Kaduna inclination with all that this implied for Nigeria's own political turmoil of 1954-60. But what Milne has added is his rare insider's knowledge, backed up by unusual access to official dispatches, telegrams and correspondence. Here, then, is the eye-witness testimony of one who was not only there but who was very much at the centre of the Southern Cameroons debate and dissension over where it really wanted to go once Nigeria and Cameroun became independent.

Historians will derive as much profit from the last three chapters of Milne's meticulous account as the colonial service and general readers will draw pleasure from the entire narrative. *No Telephone to Heaven* is an informative and important colonial service memoir which I, for one, am already looking forward to having the profound pleasure of *re*-reading. As those Nigerian lorries from which Malcolm Milne has drawn his title used to phrase it in their sometimes delphic mottos, "Let Man Enjoy the Way Ahead".

Anthony Kirk-Greene

Emeritus Fellow
St Antony's College
Oxford
September 1999

Introduction

I try to build up a picture of colonial service life in this book between 1938 and 1961; some would say between the apex and the nadir of the colonial administrative service.

Over eighty young men were recruited to the service in the late summer of 1938. I was one. Approximately half our number attended the Colonial Administrative Service Course at Oxford, the remainder a similar course at Cambridge, for the ensuing academic year. There we were encouraged to believe that we were embarking on a job for our working lives. We understood that our task was to bring the colonial peoples in our care up to the point where they could hold their own politically, culturally and economically with the so-called advanced peoples of the world. This was a pretty presumptuous task for anybody to take on sixty years ago but rightly or wrongly we believed it was within our powers.

However attitudes—both in the UK and the Western World in general—changed much more rapidly in the years immediately following 1945 than most of us had anticipated. Sizeable sections of American opinion, perhaps influenced by memories of their own colonial experience, had always been touchy about, and critical of, the colonial situation. Released from the constraints of the war-time alliance these sections, particularly the universities, became positively hostile. True, other sectors of US opinion, including some official bodies, took up a pro-British stand on the same question but their voice was less than that of the of universities and the media together.

The US lead found ready followers amongst embryonic UNO members, none more eager than the Afro-Asian group some of whom had only recently cut colonial ties themselves. This group, in fact, became a powerful voting body dominating the Trusteeship Council. It did not take them long, for example, to persuade the Council to abolish Trustee Agreements.

Great Britain herself was no longer the affluent country that she had been before the war: she was still paying its enormous costs. Consequently throughout the 1950s matters involving additional expenditure, however small, were viewed with caution by successive

British governments. Another financial consideration intruded. Since well before the war few, if any, colonial territories had run a positive financial balance with the UK. Post-war demands and expectations of colonial territories were rising steadily. So much so that in the early 1950s some members of the British cabinet were prepared to advocate dissolution of the colonial empire on financial grounds alone.

The usual mode of progression from rule by expatriate officials themselves to independence in colonial territories had been by way of the creation of benevolent oligarchies which in turn were transformed into parliamentary democracies, these latter, it was hoped, leading to full democracy. Once the penultimate stage was reached, political parties were formed and politicians proliferated. These politicians were understandably loud in their demands for early and full independence. Dangerous waters were spied ahead. It began to be apparent that, if full independence was not granted rapidly to colonial dependent territories, the danger of violent revolt lay ahead under the leadership of nationalist politicians. This was not to be contemplated.

Taken together these factors—our relative poverty after the war, the steadily increasing demands and expectations by colonial territories, the world-wide hostility to colonialism, the adverse financial balance with colonial countries, the demands by colonial politicians—all constituted good grounds, from the British government point of view, for the early dismantling of the colonial empire.

Other European colonial powers, including the French, Spanish, Portuguese and Belgians, found themselves very much in the same predicament. They reacted each in their own way, some better than HMG others less effectively.

So far as HMG was concerned, the 1950s were the decade of decision. Territory after territory was either given or promised independence. In each case the Colonial Administrative Service would do the job. Our objective had always been to achieve independence for our colonial peoples but I and many of my pre-war colleagues felt vaguely uneasy. There was something wrong. The decision was right but the timing was wrong or wrong in some cases. There were even some territories that didn't want premature independence (SC was one). On the other hand HMG had no real choice in the matter: they were forced to act precisely as they did act...dismantle the colonial empire. Members of my group, those mobilised and trained before the 1939-45 War, had two choices: resign, or stay on to independence loyally obeying our instructions. Most, in West Africa, Nigeria particularly, stayed on at least until 1960. Post-war entrants to the service viewed this same dilemma differently. They didn't appear, as we pre-war entrants to the service did, to feel as torn by the switch in course. I attribute this largely to the teaching on the pre-war colonial administrative courses being replaced by the post-war Devonshire Courses.

To give verisimilitude to the narrative I have tried throughout to stick to the rule of writing always in the light of our *perceived knowledge at the time of the events described*. As I became more senior my "perceived knowledge" of course increased in comprehensiveness. The introduction in this country of the "thirty years' rule" (under which government documents are open to inspection by the public) has proved a great boon. I have given the Kew Public Record reference to a number of documents quoted in the text and bearing out my contentions.

Right up to the 1950s an expatriate officer in the Nigerian service was required to get his Resident's permission to be joined by his wife. Wives with young children were unheard of. The reasons included erroneous analogies with Indian experience and the state of tropical medicine. But by 1942 tropical medicine, inspired by the war, had made tremendous advances. I felt that it was a thoroughly wrong state of affairs whereby some officers went the whole tour without being joined by their wives and equally strongly that those who were apprised of the risks should not have their young children with them. Kat and I owe a great debt to Dermott O'Connor, then Resident, Onitsha, for allowing Kat to bring Jackie with her from South Africa in 1943 and, a year later, to have John with us as well. Rules of this magnitude aren't easily changed but Dermott's action opened the door and others rapidly followed our example. Children soon proved themselves great ambassadors. With their frank, unpretentious approach they were able to forge ties where we adults weren't. I felt much happier and contented when Kat and the family were with me and I am sure my output improved. It certainly did with others whom I closely observed.

In 1995 a delegation from the Cameroons National Council (a body representing sections of the old Southern Cameroons), which included Foncha and Muna amongst its members, visited the UK and the UNO. They maintained that the 1960-61 process of unification with the R of C had been illegally conducted and sought the recognition of UNO and HMG that this was indeed so. In passing they mentioned that the 1961 boundary had shown the Bokasso Peninsula oilfield on the SC side...raising suspicions that oil was perhaps the main reason for their visit.

The delegation asked how I could assist. I could only promise to refurbish my memory of the years 1958-61 and devote two or three chapters of this book—which I was then planning—to the subject.

Chapters Thirteen, Fourteen and Fifteen are the result. I'm afraid the delegation got nowhere in 1961 with their approaches to HMG and UNO.

I have referred in the text to "building the colonial empire". This, of course, does not refer to adding more red to the map. On the contrary I am thinking of the very *raison d'être* of the colonial administrative service at its apex—the construction of institutions and services necessary to a (then) modern state.

There were distinct differences in attitude between differing groups of administrative officers. My brother-in-law, Nigel Cooke, was very impressed by the ill-feeling between the "1915-ers" (who had joined the service in 1915) and those of the same age who had fought throughout the war years and joined the service in 1919. The former enjoyed nearly four years of seniority over the latter. I didn't come across any examples of this apparent injustice but I did, right from my first days in the service remark a difference between those who had endured trench warfare and those who hadn't. There were in Nigeria, as mentioned earlier, differences in outlook and attitude between those recruited before and after World War II, possibly exacerbated by the substitution of the colonial administrative service by the Devonshire course. An officer's first region of posting left a strong imprint on him. Some regional groups found it harder than others to keep pace with the changes demanded by rapidly approaching independence.

Apart from one or two short term assignments the three years of my military service was spent in West Africa. I was in a good position to view the loyalty of Nigerians to the Crown during that period. It was superb. There is no other word for it. And our everyday relationship, from 1939 until 1961 continued to be equally good. Kat and I never locked an outside door during the whole of our period in West Africa. It is sometimes forgotten that during the apex of British administration it was possible, for the only time in the history of the world, before or since, to walk anywhere in the middle of the tropical night armed with no more than a walking stick—and that stick merely used to find the edges of the path in the dark.

British administration can't have been all that bad (as is sometimes alleged).

The title of this book is half explained in the text. The signs on southern Nigerian lorries were generally exhortations addressed by the owner to the driver or vice versa. "No Telephone to Heaven" is, of course, directed at the driver. "It's all very well, my friend, you driving badly, having an accident and telephoning for my help. Wait until you go over the khud and kill yourself. You'll soon find out there is no telephone to heaven." In the way of many West African plays on words it can be extended to a secondary meaning. "The DO is very much on his own when it comes to making urgent decisions. He can't, from the far bush, telephone for help."

A Note to the Reader

Apex to Nadir

The sub-title and the division of this book into two parts, the Apex and the Nadir, require an explanation.

When I joined in 1938, HMG was employing the colonial administrative service to build up the colonial empire.

In 1961 the service was engaged in the rapid dismantlement of the colonial empire by means of the accelerated introduction of independence.

HMG took the decision to employ the colonial administrative service in this revised role in the 1950s. Dr Azikiwe, as the account of the African Continental Bank affair will illustrate, played as notable a part in the turn-around as any West African.

For the purposes of this book I refer to the earlier phase as the Apex of the service and to anything appertaining to the later, scramble for independence phase, as the Nadir.

Independence was still the objective but a different sort of independence to that imprinted on my colleagues and me in 1938.

Views Expressed

This book is my personal account of the years 1938 to 1961 and all the views expressed, unless specifically ascribed to other sources, must be treated as my own.

Malcolm Milne

PART ONE

Chapter One

The Journey Out

From time to time life firmly changes course. One such moment for me was the 26th July 1939. The place…a sloping-floored four berth cabin somewhere near the bows of RMS *Accra*; present were my father, Uncle Jack Walton, the two Walton aunts and my sister, Geraldine.

A bevy of colonial administrative service cadets was about to join the 200 or so first-class passengers en route to the West African territories—the Gambia, Sierra Leone, the Gold Coast and Nigeria. I was one of the twenty-five bound for Nigeria. We were leaving an ordered, sheltered existence—school, the university, the colonial services' course—for an altogether rougher, more basic scene. Presumably those who had selected us thought we were up to the challenge ahead. We, of course, were full of the arrogant excitement of youth and had no doubts. We were merely in a hurry to get on with it.

A fellow cadet, Angus Robin, appeared. He and I had been friends and contemporaries at Cambridge. Jack and the Aunts knew him as he had stayed several times at Lynwood with them when he and I had been climbing in the Lake District.

Jack suggested that we'd find four in a cabin too crowded in the tropics. The assistant purser obligingly amended his berthing list, giving Angus and me an outside cabin for two. We hurried to move our "wanted on voyage" bags.

A boat-train arrived alongside and a steady stream of passengers began to come on board. Angus was much too well-mannered to show any sort of impatience in front of my family but I was anxious to explore the ship, take a look at the senior officials coming aboard and check up on our friends from Cambridge. My father and the Aunts, perhaps with the deeper premonition of age, were in no hurry to go. I began to press them to be on their way…"long partings are so embarrassing"…"It's only a short first tour, we'll be back in fifteen months or so."

So much for a short tour. It was to be six years before I returned to England and saw Geraldine and the Aunts again. My father died in 1942 and Jack in 1944. Jack's thoughtfulness in arranging the change of cabins and my father's heavy sadness as he descended the gangway to be lost to sight on the crowded Merseyside jetty were the last memories I have of either.

It would be touching to say that I have carried those two memories undimmed now for sixty years. But the truth is that memories are not strictly chronological; they are more like a pack of mixed cards, some in black and white, some in colour, indiscriminately assorted. An incident emerges here, a sentiment there, in no settled order. It is only now that I have come to realise that those moments, as the *Accra* lay alongside in Liverpool, were the last that I should spend with Jack or my father.

The *Accra*, too, was not to survive the war. The last convoy in which she sailed was stalked by U34. Her station at the head of the port wing column suggested that she was an armed merchant cruiser. She was torpedoed and sank with the loss of eleven passengers and eight crew, and now lies on the floor of the Atlantic, 450 miles due west of the northernmost point of Ireland. The date of the *Accra*'s loss was 26th July 1940—precisely a year from the day we sailed in her.

A photograph of Korvettenkapitan Wilhelm Rollman, commander of U34, appears in Cowden and Duffy's *History of Elder Dempster Lines*. It depicts an immaculately turned out young U-boat commander, small mouthed and hard-eyed, sporting an Iron Cross over his tie-knot; a proud commander of a proud fleet and a formidable enemy, capable of clinical destruction.

Rollman himself was killed with all hands when U848 he was then commanding was sunk by US aircraft in the South Atlantic on 5th November 1943. Even after this length of time I do not regret his going—how can I for the Battle of the Atlantic nearly brought my country to its knees?—only the manner of it. Vulnerable on the surface, fortuitously surprised by aircraft, and an ally's at that, I would have wished for him to die ship to ship and man to man.

The *Accra* was operated by Elder Dempster Lines, a company that had been founded by Alexander Elder and John Dempster in 1868, (in the same decade that British authority was first established over Lagos) and had served British interests in West Africa in the intervening seventy-one years.

As we were to discover for ourselves, Elder Dempsters operated with considerable style. Not for nothing were the *Accra* and her sister ship, the *Apapa*, referred to as "the two most expensive hotels in the world". The first-class fare for the fourteen-day passage Liverpool—Lagos was of the order of £60—about £1,700 in today's values. For this Elder Dempsters provided accommodation that by the standards of the time was quite excellent and food that in terms of quality and variety was a revelation to us. However great a gourmet one might be it would not have been possible fully to explore the breakfast or luncheon menus in the course of a single trip.

Doubtless the wines were of comparable quality but few of us were interested. Life then seemed to offer so much there was no need for further stimulation. Wits of the day had it, however, that there were no navigational problems along the route to the West Coast. If the navigating officer was in doubt he merely had to check the line of bottles strewn on the floor of the ocean.

The world was a much bigger place in 1939 than it is today. What took us a day by ship then can now be covered in forty minutes by air. I doubt if there was more than a single member of our group of twenty-five cadets on the *Accra* who had visited a continent other than his own. Nowadays in any equivalent group of graduates I doubt whether you would find any single one who had not visited a continent other than his own. So when we sailed on the evening of 26th July it was for me a departure for page seventy of my Bartholomew Atlas, the great fat continent of Africa only lightly and infrequently touched with green, the rest the browns of 3,000 ft and above. Hot plains and cool hills...or so I hoped.

I have a memory of the cold airs of our surprisingly swift passage down the Mersey and of the sun sinking low over the Wirral Peninsular. We'd been told that passengers didn't dress for dinner on the first evening and hunger called. We found our allotted tables. We'd soon see England again. Other goals were now before us.

There is another memory from the early days of that voyage, perhaps the second day out. Several of us had gathered in the bar, some to sample the ship's lager, others merely gregarious. Suddenly I realised we were under inspection. A little posse of colonial wives, most doubtless travelling alone, all in the late thirty to forty age grade which betokened smartness and not a little sophistication, were scrutinising us...openly, even brazenly. It wasn't as though they thought we might enliven the voyage for them. We were far too young and callow for that. It was simply the first manifestation we were to come across of the importance of seniority in the service; they were the wives of chaps our seniors by fifteen years or more. They were merely interested in the calibre of young cadet the colonial office was now sending out.

We called at Madeira four or five days out. Practically every administrative cadet on board, led by a second-tour Department of Mines officer from Northern Nigeria, foregathered at what must have been the island's largest brothel. It was a wooden building, three stories in height, attractive as so many of Madeira's indigenous buildings were.

We were welcomed with dignity by the madame and senior girl. The madame made no impression on me but her adjutant, slim and dark and perhaps in her late twenties, was quite charming. So must have thought our guide for he and she, halfway through our visit, slipped upstairs and were gone for half an hour or so. They were the only couple to leave the room. The rest of us were too hesitant, or just plain scared to follow suit. We sat round the room, boy, girl, boy, girl sipping tea. It was like some Victorian tea party—rather stilted, everybody behaving impeccably.

The girl sitting next to me several times suggested we should go upstairs but, as she appeared to be twelve years old at the most, the very idea seemed absurd. When we left I gave her two English half-crowns which she accepted after some demur.

The nine hundred nautical miles to our next port of call, Bathurst in the Gambia, must have taken nearly four days but we had established a routine of deck cricket, long hours in the portable swimming pool interspersed with hearty luncheons and reading in the breeze-cooled shade. Time slipped by unreckoned.

We entered the Gambia River at dawn and tied up alongside the little Bathurst jetty two hours later. Bathurst was thirteen degrees north of the equator and this was truly tropical West Africa. For a little while I had the boat deck to myself. I leant over the rail enthralled. This was my first view and smell of the continent where perhaps I should spend the whole of my working life. The memory is as vivid today as though the moment was yesterday.

It was a shock to have lost the breeze of the ship's passage. The hot, humid air pressed round me. The banks of the Gambia River were heavily vegetated, brilliant green; the earth where it lay bare was the bright brick red of laterite. There was nothing of the subdued greens, the browns and greys of northern latitudes. This was a different land, strident in its colouring, heavy in the heat. I took note and accepted.

Later that morning four of us made our way to the long, deserted, Atlantic-facing beach. All seemed calm, distance blurred by the haze, yet there was great power there, for the rollers were larger than they seemed and broke steadily into two feet of surf. But we were young and strong and stood against them, not then being skilled at diving into the base of each as it broke.

On our slow and bumpy taxi ride back to the ship we contemplated once more our first West African country. It seemed the people walked rather than drove. Bicycles, even, were few and far between. Walls of compounds and houses were built of sun-dried mud bricks; some houses were whitewashed. Roofs were of corrugated iron or thatched with coarse-stemmed grass. There was an air of well-being amongst the people: none appeared ill-fed; many, particularly the women, were cheerfully, waddingly fat. It seemed to me that there were more signs of grey rib-revealing poverty at that time in Lancashire and Northumberland than there were in Bathurst. We couldn't look on these people—the first true West Africans we had come across—as poverty-stricken savages. They were short, it is true, of European gewgaws and artefacts but they possessed a buoyancy and integrity of their own. I would like to be able to say that the prejudices acquired in twenty-two years in Europe dropped away that first day in a West African country but of course it wasn't so. Such convictions come slowly over the years. Let me be content with saying that the seeds of new thoughts were sown: "Be careful my boy. These people aren't as you were led to believe. Take care. Learn more."

We sailed for Freetown in Sierra Leone that evening, clearing the mouth of the Gambia River just after sunset as the tropic day gave hastily away to the tropic night.

Although the *Accra* lay in the anchorage off Freetown there were opportunities of going ashore. A small group of cadets took a taxi to Lumley beach where once again we swam amidst the breaking surf. There had been a storm out to the west during the previous night and there the waves were larger and more formidable than those on the Bathurst beach. We began to learn about suck-back from one wave to the next and to time our inward progression on the crests of breaking waves, surfing, as it were, without a board. If there is a predominant memory it was one of fear. Never being a good swimmer I was always awed by the power of breaking rollers.

The same afternoon the boat boys of Freetown Harbour put on a wonderful show. Paddling out to the *Accra's* anchorage in a variety of canoes, some so small it seemed a miracle a child could ride them, others large enough to hold twenty gesticulating youths, they begged spectators leaning over the rail above to throw coins into the sea. Their retrieval was spectacular. Some they would follow ten, twelve or even fifteen feet into the depths. One could never be sure they had succeeded in grasping the deepest coins. Others they dived for

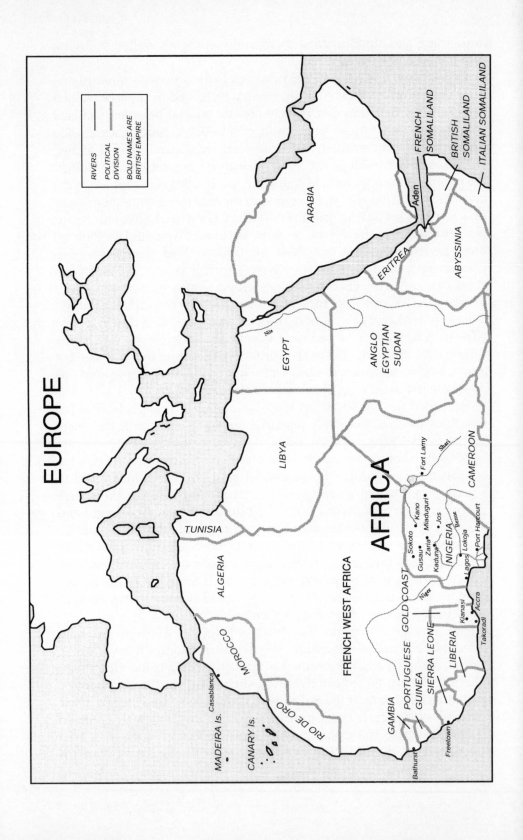

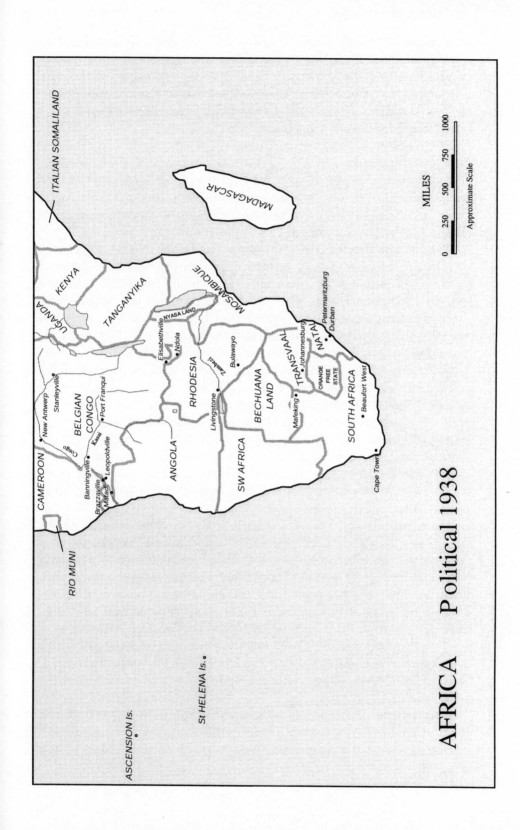

AFRICA   Political 1938

MILES

0   250   500   750   1000

Approximate Scale

immediately after they hit the water and got them before they had zigzagged more than two or three feet towards the depths. Bolder spirits climbed the gangway and, standing poised on the rail, challenged the spectators to throw silver into the sea. Copper coins they didn't deign to dive for. Large silver coins they allowed to go deep before they went after them.

It was about this stage of the voyage that Angus and I had the first of several long talks with Dr G R Griffiths of the Gold Coast Medical Service which we kept up until he left the ship at Takoradi. Griffiths was in his mid-thirties and had completed two tours in West Africa since he had qualified. He talked vividly and had the practical experience to illustrate much of what he said.

Angus came from a medical family. His father was a well-known Edinburgh physician and one of his brothers was to become a prominent London ENT consultant. It surprised me that Angus was as fascinated by all that Griffiths had to recount as I was. But he was.

Tropical medicine and hygiene had been one of the principal subjects of the colonial administrative service course. The lecturers had done their best to alert us to the subject and to help us to protect ourselves. In an examination lasting three hours at the end of the course we had been expected to answer questions involving Ancylostomiasis, Trematode diseases, vitamin content of diet and like matters in considerable detail. The subject hadn't been neglected but, speaking for myself, my imagination hadn't been touched. It took Griffiths, with his exciting mixture of experience and theory to do that. It was he, in fact, who convinced me that tropical disease was the single most important determining agency in the development of West Africa.

I remember particularly a simple little story he told us of his first tour. "A young girl," he said, "aged about eleven, walked unaccompanied into my surgery. Her upper arm was virtually severed by a massive yaws infection. I immediately contemplated amputation. There seemed no other possibility. But something made me hesitate. There was a bismuth treatment that recent reports had said was proving effective. I determined to try it. The wound, massive as it was, soon began to heal. Three weeks' treatment and the girl's arm was saved. She eventually recovered full use of it." And he added: "Marvellous, marvellous; that one patient made my whole tour worthwhile."

Malaria was, of course, endemic to the whole of West Africa. Until 1942, when mepacrine was introduced, the prophylactic was quinine. The recommended dosage was five grains of bi-hydrochloride. We had already started taking this on the first day out and most of us had found it was a bit of an ordeal to take. Few of us had escaped the side effects of buzzing heads and mild nausea. Griffiths laughed at our complaints, saying a little nausea was a cheap price to pay for protection against malaria. He scared us not a little when he told us he was convinced of the link between irregular quinine taking and blackwater fever.

Griffiths was unsparing of the time he would devote to West African medical subjects. Angus and I were a ready audience, it is true. He was perhaps intrigued by our ingenuous interest; he was talking on matters to which he had given a lot of thought. Nevertheless I have, as I write sixty years later, a warming impression that he felt a degree of responsibility to us. Maybe his thoughts ran that here were two young fellows whose usefulness to their country and the country where they were to work would be governed by their ability to avoid tropical disease. It behoved him to do what he could to help us keep clear of what he perceived were major handicaps to a good performance.

Those selected for the administrative service in Nigeria in 1938 had all been sent a copy of the 1936 *Nigeria Handbook*, the first four chapters of which dealt with the history, the climate the ethnology and the government of the country. The excellent short chapter on the history had encouraged many of us to read more widely during the year that the course lasted.

Our first contacts with the smells, the feel and the sights of West Africa in Bathurst and Freetown brought our readings to the fore. Griffiths, we found, was better read than most of us. In addition he had interposed, as it were, a medical filter between readings and interpretation. There was a sound medical reason for much that had occurred. Not only had tropical diseases been a fearsome impediment to exploration of the interior but their presence had affected later social relationships between black and white communities.

Page six of the *Nigeria Handbook* carried the statement: "In Nigeria today the legal status of slavery has been abolished."

This is misleading. What was made illegal was the exaction of labour out of an individual without consent. There were many categories of slave, including agricultural, domestic and *juju*. Over the years a great mass of "native law and custom" (to use a phrase current in 1939) had grown up protecting the rights and place in the

11

community of the slave. Many ex-slaves, technically freed by the Nigerian legislation abolishing the legal status of slavery, didn't want to be free. Some, for instance, preferred the old protected regime where a wife and a place to farm were provided for them.

Most of us destined for the Eastern Region of Nigeria, and a goodly proportion of the others, were to be faced with complex native court cases affecting the status of ex-slaves before we were much older.

Page 243 of the *Nigeria Handbook* made us smile. The advice concerning exercise in the tropics was couched in purely Victorian terms: "A healthy man should get physically tired every day and should experience the sensation of pleasurable fatigue. This, and more, comes in the course of their work to those engaged in an active life; but in the tropics the majority of Europeans lead a sedentary existence, work is often performed in a leisurely fashion and the climatic conditions are not conducive to activity; the tendency to "Slack" is great and, if indulged in, is apt to lead to nostalgia, tedium, isolation and over-indulgence of alcohol. The remedy for all of this is vigorous exercise."

The colonial service selection board saw to it that young men were not appointed to serve in the tropics unless the foregoing advice was plainly superfluous. The *Handbook*, so far as most of the 1939 intake were concerned, might well have saved the space.

There were, as happens with most generalisations, exceptions. One in our batch of cadets was Percy X. He turned round in Lagos and sailed back in the *Accra*. One can only suppose the actuality of the West Coast was too much for him. A wise man, following the precedent of an early divorce or a silly fellow who'd gone through the full year of the colonial service course with eyes closed and ears firmly sealed? It was difficult to judge.

Percy X was tall, stiff-backed, in the sense of denoting a modicum of obstinacy in his makeup, very much his own man; most people would have said that he was plainly unfitted for a career involving a high degree of corporate loyalty and individual discipline. It was puzzling that he'd been appointed in the first place.

He never hesitated to express his dislike of conformity and was always readier to sneer at, rather than praise, the doings and ideas of his fellows. Youth is, however, ever tolerant of the attitudes and eccentricities of its own kind and I am sure none of us positively objected to Percy or his ideas. We regarded him, rather, with amused interest.

He certainly surprised us on the night of a fancy dress dance held as we sailed along the West Coast. We were given the option of appearing at dinner dressed as usual in tropical evening dress—"bum freezer", black evening tie, white shirt, cummerbund, black evening trousers—or wearing some form of fancy dress. Percy sported only an evening shirt with black tie. Pinned to his back was a placard "Gone with the wind" (Margaret Mitchell's mammoth best-selling novel had won a Pulitzer Prize in 1937).

Whether he felt compelled to wear short pants or not I shall never know. The shirt, as was customary in 1939, was lengthy and reached well below the Plimsoll line.

The formidable Sir Arthur Richards (later Lord Milverton) then Governor of the Gambia had boarded the *Accra* at Bathurst on his way to a conference of West African governors in Lagos. Doubtless he observed Percy's performance and duly commented on it to Sir Bernard Bourdillon, the Governor of Nigeria.

It was pretty daring to take one's trousers off anywhere in public in 1939 but to choose a carnival dance on board RMS *Accra* with Sir Arthur Richards a likely spectator seemed to me to be positively foolhardy.

Our voyage on the RMS *Accra* was rapidly coming to an end. We paid brief visits to Takoradi—where we tied up alongside for a few hours—and Accra itself. The former was a stone-built port, albeit small in size but at Accra we anchored a mile off shore. Cargo and a handful of passengers were taken off in surf boats. The latter, manned by strong-muscled crewmen, were paddled furiously through the breaking surf and run up on the long beaches beyond. Passengers were transferred from the deck of the *Accra* to the surf boats by "mammy chair" lowered by one of the ship's davits. No doubt passengers' feet or hands were very occasionally crushed as an unexpected swell flung the surf boat upwards but on the whole the West African crew on the surf boats and the African winchmen on the davits were highly skilled. Extra heavy items of cargo were lowered onto makeshift catamarans: two canoes linked by a raft of heavy planks. Going ashore by mammy-chair was certainly no picnic but passengers and crew were all young. A senior official in his late forties was a rarity. Life in West Africa of those days was far too elemental for the old to visit their working young even if they could afford it. Tourists were unheard of.

The *Accra* made fast alongside the Apapa wharf in Lagos early in the morning of 10th August, fifteen days out from Liverpool. The administrative service cadets aboard were divided into parties of three or four; each party was supplied with an administrative officer working in Lagos as host. I recall that our little party consisted of Reggie Blunt, Bunny Carter, Angus and me. Our host was John

Gibbons, at that time a rapidly rising secretariat officer of thirty-three, recently awarded the MBE for what I described in a letter home written the same day as "a particularly nice bit of report writing". (I hope, at least, "nice" was used in the sense of delicately sensitive.)

During the morning we were taken by our hosts to the secretariat and sworn in by the chief secretary in an impressive little ceremony.

Apart from dinner at Government House that night—the governors of the Gambia, Sierra Leone and the Gold Coast would be there in addition to our hosts, Sir Bernard and Lady Bourdillon—the time was ours.

I say ours. In fact, as far as Reggie, Bunny, Angus and I were concerned, the time was John Gibbons'. I have seldom if ever spent such a tedious night. John Gibbons told us—perhaps not all at once but as the evening progressed—that he felt it his duty to show us every night club and drinking den in Lagos. We trapezed slowly from one to the other. At each Gibbons managed to find some African acquaintance who was prepared to enter into animated discussion with him on subjects obviously dear to the pair of them but utterly incomprehensible to the rest of us. Reggie and—unusually for him—Bunny Carter took refuge in alcohol. As the night progressed they had to be shaken into mobility before we went on to the next port of call. Angus, who drank sparingly if he drank at all and I (I was teetotal until the age of thirty) were just lost. Politeness demanded that we try to understand what was evidently of such importance to Gibbons and his African friends but our attention eventually wandered and we dozed intermittently.

Dawn came; quite suddenly it was full day and to our relief we were all seated round John Gibbons' breakfast table while the Steward, assisted by the "small boy", produced coffee, toast, bacon and eggs.

I don't remember finding our way back to the *Accra* or tumbling into my bunk. We were halfway down the Nigerian coast to Port Harcourt when I awoke. I do recall, however, a change in atmosphere pervading the *Accra*. She seemed to have lost status with the disembarkation of her VIP passengers in Lagos, to have become all of a sudden tired and slightly tatty.

During that night we anchored off the mouth of the Bonny River waiting for the light of day. Angus and I were woken by the busy grunts of the donkey engine as we weighed anchor. Quite suddenly it was full day.

Surely, I thought, a miracle of seamanship would be needed to coax such a large vessel as the *Accra* up the Bonny River to Port Harcourt.

We crossed the bar in company with a fleet of Bonny fishing canoes homeward bound after a night's work in the open sea. Slowly

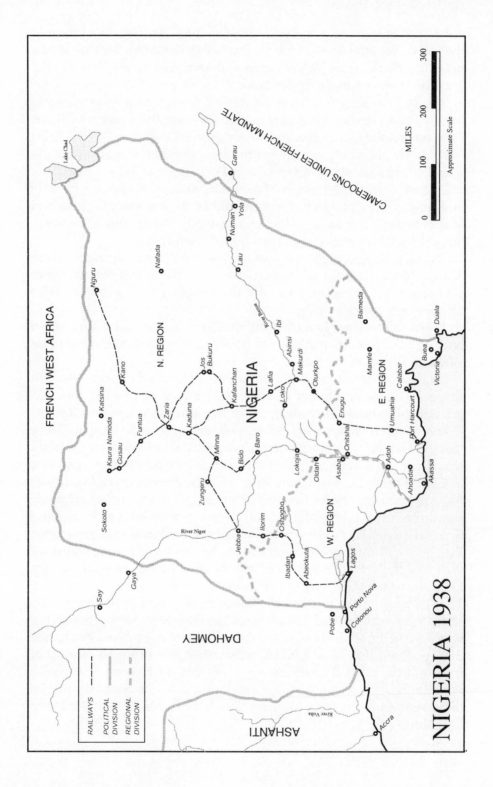

NIGERIA 1938

outstripping them, we moved almost silently up-river, heading into the last of the land-to-sea breeze. The banks closed in. We threaded a maze of small islands each covered with mangrove trees, their roots a mass of hoops rising from the mud.

An Ibo, working for Nigerian Railways, was next to me leaning over the rail. He was nearly home after a six months' course at Crewe. I envied him the excitement and happiness that so obviously possessed him. He would surely receive promotion now that he was more fully qualified. His family awaited him in Port Harcourt where his father still worked in the Nigerian Marine Department. He had one wife and three young children. There would be a great reception for him that evening. He was an achiever and would be acclaimed as such. Something of his excitement transferred itself to me.

By ten p.m. that night we were on the train from Port Harcourt to Enugu. None of us bid goodbye to the *Accra*. We would see her again; perhaps she'd even carry us—by then experienced administrative officers—on our next leave.

Poor *Accra*—if we had but known—in twelve months' time she'd be lying 6,000 feet down in the cold Atlantic, holed by Korvettenkapitan Wilhelm Rollman's torpedo.

And a note about John Gibbons…I never worked closely with him or got to know him better in later years but of course we gossiped assiduously about our colleagues in the administrative service and his name often cropped up. All agreed he had a golden touch. Every task he tackled was marked by a limpidity all of his own. Nobody was surprised that he ended his war service as Mountbatten's Director of Civil Affairs, SE Asia Command, with the rank of brigadier. It was no secret, too, that he had a compulsion to go off from time to time on the most imperial benders. Just after the war he was promoted Secretary, Eastern Provinces. Two years after that it was rumoured that he was in line for the top job in the Eastern Region. The story goes that the brand new Governor of Nigeria made a special journey to Enugu to meet Gibbons and presumably announce the appointment. The morning of the momentous meeting he couldn't be found. His friends guessed the trouble and while His Excellency was kept waiting they searched high and low in the drinking dens of Enugu. They found him, washed him, filled him up with coffee and propped him up in front of HE. Instead of becoming Governor of Eastern Nigeria he became Commissioner of the Cameroons; a lesser post but one he filled, as a Cameroonian Minister was later to comment, "with rare humanity".

CHAPTER TWO

The Child is Father to the Man

When I joined the colonial service in 1938 I had spent half my life with my mother and father and half with the Aunts. Let me now depart from Africa just long enough to paint some sort of picture of those who have influenced me so much.

My father was born in 1868. He was the fourth son and sixth child of Alfred and Ellen Milne. His parents were married in 1854. His older brothers and sisters were born in '55, '56, '58, '60, and 1862. The gap from 1862 to 1868, to my mind, is significant.

A sister to my father, Blanche, was born in 1870. By searching consulate records I discovered the other day that another child Christopher Percy, had been born to Ellen in 1873. The original entry of place of birth read, "In the Pyrenees". This had been amended to "Spain".

When I sailed in the *Accra* in 1939 I really possessed very little factual knowledge of my father and his family. One reason for this is the general one: the young of any generation are so busy living their own lives and building up their own experience that they have no time for the affairs of their elders. Nor do they possess the knowledge of life to permit them to evaluate what they glean. An interest in family antecedents comes later in life.

In my case there was, too, a degree of mystery and a conspiracy of silence.

I sensed that my Milne uncles and aunts, born up to 1862, looked on my father and Blanche as somehow "different". Inferior in some way, a little to be pitied perhaps.

And then on my mother's side—the Waltons—I remember having a real set-to with the younger and more outspoken of the two aunts, Alice. In response to some fierce bit of provocation from me she called my father "a ne'er-do-well", a "rotter". There was hostility here, too.

It is only in the past six years or so that son John and I have done a little research and gathered a few facts. The truth is beginning to

17

emerge, slowly. One of the difficulties is, because my father was forty-nine when I was born, I am dealing now with descendants of Alfred and Ellen who are roughly my age but one or two generations later than I am. Memories have become attenuated, as it were.

Ellen was, of course, a bolter. Family legend, sparse as it is, has it that Ellen's liaisons had steadily grown more outrageous from about 1864 onwards.

A petition was filed in HM Court for Divorce and Matrimonial Causes by my grandfather Alfred citing another barrister, one Robinson Fowler, as corespondent on 13th January 1870. The *decree nisi* was granted on the 8th December 1870. On the same day the marriage settlement was, it seems to me, drastically readjusted in Alfred's favour. The London edition of *The Times* of 9th December 1870 carries a fairly juicy account of the proceedings. Alfred was described by his leading counsel as "a gentleman of very high standing in society and a barrister". No evidence was produced on behalf of the respondent and co-respondent and any imputations against Alfred by Ellen and Robinson Fowler were withdrawn. In spite of this rather lofty suggestion of "we couldn't care less" by Ellen and Robinson Fowler, Alfred had retained no less than three leading Queen's Counsels and a barrister while Sir J Karslake QC and two barristers appeared for Ellen and another QC and a barrister for Robinson Fowler. The divorce, in modern values, must have cost well over three-quarters of a million pounds. It seems, at this range, an awful waste of money but Alfred no doubt was pretty sure of getting his costs and, doubtless in the 1870s, "his position in society" was worth a lot to him.

The divorce petition for good judicial reasons concentrated upon Ellen's recent misdemeanours. I can do no better than quote from *The Times'* account of 9th December 1870:-

> On the 8th April 1869 Mrs Milne left her house, having an engagement, as she said, to dine and sleep at the house of a friend and she was to return on the following day when there was to be a dinner party at Mr Milne's. On the morning of the 9th April Mr Milne was surprised to receive a short note from her, with the postmark of Peterborough upon it, saying, 'Unless you like to have the dinner party without me, write and put off the guests as I shall not be there.'

I must confess that when I first read that message, in the National Newspaper Library at Colindale, my heart went out to my grandmother, naughty girl that she obviously was. It was no small thing in Victorian England for the mother of six in her home patch as it were to kick her heels quite as high as she had. She was fourteen years younger than Alfred. After the divorce he bought Chiddingfold House and lived there until his death in 1899. The Chiddingfold parish magazine and the local press in that part of Surrey carried many references to him in the last twenty-nine years of his life. He was always depicted as an admirable member of the local gentry; generous, full of many good deeds, a man "without an enemy in the world". But I wonder.

My father maintained that he, his sister Blanche and his mother had "been caught in the siege of Paris". Blanche was born sometime in 1870 but up to now I've not been able to discover when or where. It might well have been in Paris. I do know that Ellen, accompanied by Blanche and my father, moved to the Maison Moston, Rue de France, Biarritz, about 1871. I also gathered from Phoebe Verschoyle, a granddaughter of my father's elder sister, Cotty, (and Phoebe had it from Ellen's ex ladies' maid) that Ellen appeared before Alfred round about 1874 and told him that because he had left her relatively poor after the divorce and amendment of the marriage settlement he would have to see to the education of Gerald, my father, and Blanche. This he apparently did.

I remember my father telling me that the first language he spoke was French. After leaving his mother in Biarritz he did not use it again until he found himself in France with the Remounts in 1914 when, so he said, French came back to him quite naturally. Maybe it did but it must have been French largely learned from grooms and servants and his idiom must have sounded a little odd to his slightly more sophisticated French friends.

The conspiracy of silence touched my father, the Aunts, my father's relatives and my sisters and me right up to the time of my departure for Nigeria in 1939. Much of what I recount here derives from the briefest hints dropped by my father confirmed by later enquiries son John or I have made.

For instance I have established that my father and Blanche lived with Alfred from 1873 or 1874 and I have my father's prep school and public school records. He was "supered" from Wellington for failure to get out of his form and finished his public school career at Malvern where he won the Ledbury run and was a member of both cricket and soccer first teams.

He was a natural athlete and I believe that had he wished he could have made his name at any of several disciplines. As it was he chose the role of steeplechase jockey and in the 1890s became one of the

19

leading "Gentlemen Riders"—GRs as amateur jockeys were then known as—in the country. Perhaps his greatest feat was to ride Skedaddle to victory in the Grand Steeplechase de Paris at odds of forty to one. The favourite made most of the running but misjudged the pace. My father was able to cosset Skedaddle until after the last fence and then come with a rush and beat the favourite by a neck. He had had great trouble in making the weight of nine stone twelve in spite of the fact that his natural weight was around ten stone seven pounds. One of the press reports of the race state that he had to be helped onto the scales at the weigh-in, having nearly fainted because of the effort involved in getting down to the requisite weight.

I still have two rather intermittently kept albums of press cuttings concerning his racing career which the Aunts had found on his death in 1942. Amongst them are two short and cryptic letters which by their omissions rather than by what they say seem to illustrate the racing scene of a hundred years ago.

One is from Mrs Child, the owner of Skedaddle. The notepaper is headed 10 and 11 St James's Place, SW. It reads baldly, "Dear Mr Milne, Mind you are in Paris before Sunday. Weight nine stone twelve." The other is headed Melton Lodge, Melton Mowbray; and reads: "Dear Milne, Will you ride Father O'Flynn in the National for me? Please wire me on deciding and don't tell anyone till you see me and till after I have backed him."

My father once told me that he'd had five rides in the National. He'd got round each time but had never done better than fifth and "...that was on the Old Father," he said, referring to Father O'Flynn, "in 1893, the year after he won. He couldn't carry the extra weight," he added; "eleven stone eleven pounds was too much for him. He was only a little horse—fifteen hands and a half an inch."

I asked him if he himself had trained hard before Aintree. "Train...no fear," said he. "After a long, hard season and over Aintree fences what you want is a rest, not training. I used to go off for a day or two to Brighton if I could."

"Was Aintree the most dangerous course you rode?" I persisted. "No, no," said he. "Cheltenham—far more dangerous. Aintree were big fences; you had to stand back and jump them. Cheltenham had small fences, but very solid. You raced over them. Hit one and you were in trouble. I had my worst falls there."

Joshua Slocum, writing in honour of his father, said, "My father was the sort of man who, if wrecked on a desert island, and had he a knife and were there a tree, would sail home." I've carried that attic judgement in my mind with pleasure since I first read it, sixty-five or seventy years ago.

I carry still with equal pleasure a remark my father once made about the National. "You know that after four miles at Aintree man and horse have but one heart," said he.

At the end of his days at Malvern Alfred had said to my father, "You must have a profession, Gerry. What's it to be...the law, army or church?" Apparently Gerry had worn the old man down, after several months of indeterminate discussion, and I gather that the final agreement was roughly as follows: Gerry was to be free to pursue his ambition of becoming the leading GR. Alfred would give him then and there the capital that would otherwise have been Gerry's patrimony when Alfred died. Gerry would attend Cirencester Agricultural College and at the end of the course be free to pursue his racing career.

As Alfred must at that time have had his doubts about Gerry's true paternity—he surely had none about Blanche's who is said in later life to have exclaimed, " I was the first of the true bastards"—I feel it was a generous settlement.

Ellen had died in Biarritz in February 1878 at the age of forty-six.

In 1995 Kat and I spent a day fruitlessly searching the impressive Cimetière St Martin in Biarritz for Ellen's grave.

That evening, ominously, there was a violent storm. The sky blackened, bringing darkness four hours forward and the rain hammered down. In minutes one of the most sophisticated pleasances of Europe was transformed for a short while into the bed of a dangerous stream. Traffic came to a halt in the narrow streets leading up to the high ground overlooking the sea. Visibility was reduced to a few feet. Through the misted, rain-slashed windows of our stationary car I caught a brief glimpse of a cyclist, still grasping his machine like a piece of flotsam, washed rather than floundering past. It seemed almost as though Ellen was prohibiting our search.

But no. The following day was bright and beautiful. The sun lit the sands far down the coast and the Pyrenees stood out, clear and massive, on the southern horizon. We were joined by Joan Selby-Lowndes, the writer (and a relative of mine by marriage as Blanche had married a Selby-Lowndes). We returned to the Cimetière St Martin and searched, each on our own. In no time at all Kat called us over. There, next to the mass grave of fourteen of Wellington's infantrymen, who'd died in Biarritz of wounds received in Spain in 1813, was the grave of Ellen. It was covered by a great stone sarcophagus. How Kat and I had missed it the previous day we could not fathom. The inscription was terse and deeply sad. It read, simply:

"Ellen
Youngest daughter of Samuel Brooks
Died 16th Feb 1878"

Family legend, passed onto me by Phoebe Verschoyle (who in turn had it from Trenfield, one time Ellen's lady's maid) states that Alfred, in spite of the divorce, wanted Ellen buried appropriately. He had the sarcophagus erected over her grave and was responsible for the inscription.

Phoebe, a much more charitable person than I, sees it as an act of goodness of heart, almost of forgiveness, on Alfred's part. I, I'm afraid, am inclined to view that heavy stone structure as a means of battening her down for ever and the inscription as a cold dismissal of an unhappy episode and the final denial of the name Milne to Ellen.

I'd dearly like to unearth much more about the relationship of Ellen and Alfred. Passions must have run very high if he could so reject the mother of at least five of his children.

By about 1897 my father had firmly established himself as one of the two or three leading GRs in the country. This much is clear from press reports of the time. But I wonder—and this is largely conjecture—whether from about 1895 onwards he was not beginning to find the more sybaritic role of showing off horses in the hunting field preferable to the hazards and strain of steeplechasing. Several of the well-known dealers of the time vied with each other to demonstrate their horses with the famous shire packs in this way and who better than a famous amateur steeplechase jock whom everybody knew, who loved hunting and houndwork and was socially acceptable? From the early 1930s onwards, when I first began to talk of these things with him, I always took it for granted that he had an encyclopaedic knowledge of what was really a world within a world—the hunting world.

At the turn of the century the Boer War intervened. My father served in South Africa with his friends in the Leicestershire Yeomanry. He stayed on in South Africa for some three years after the war as a sportsman on the fringe of the intellectual coterie of "Milner's young men". He established, and I believe was secretary, of the first of Jo'burg's two race courses.

After that he travelled in Kashmir, Nepal and Australia and I guess in England continued to show off horses for Sam Haimes and other leading dealers.

A fortnight after the Great War broke out in 1914 he was commissioned in the Remounts with the rank of captain. Shortly afterwards he was promoted major and from then onwards, until the day of his death in 1942, he was always known as "the Major'. In the 1930s he thought this was a little unfair on me and conferred on me the purely family honorific of "the Captain". Many of his letters to me written at the time start "Dear Captain," and I was once told that the Cumberland rugby selectors watching a club match were more than a little nonplussed when he said to them, "That was a good move by the captain just now. Made that try!" I should add that selectors were honey to a bee to him and he would always stand near them whenever I was playing, extolling my virtues. Whether he was silenced when I was playing badly I don't know. But there was one occasion when at least he was momentarily silenced. Bruce Lockhart was Headmaster of Sedbergh. His son, R A B Bruce Lockhart, Oxford and Scotland centre, was persuaded one holiday weekend to turn out for Kendal. He scored seven magnificent tries and was a joy to watch. After the game my father pushed his way into the changing room and asked, "Is RAB ready yet? His father wants to get back to Sedbergh." One of the Kendal hangers-on said, "Nay, Major. He ain't ready. We're keeping him here to do a bit of breeding."

What my father used for money in the years between the Boer War and the Great War I haven't established. Photographs, of which quite a number still survive, show that he visited many of the great country houses of Victorian and Edwardian England and was always impeccably dressed. In my Cambridge days he advised me, quite seriously, "Always wear handmade shoes. Much better, and the mark of a gentleman, ye know." I went into Lobbs in St James's in the late 1950s and they still had one of his lasts and there was an old workman there who remembered him. I'd follow his advice if I could afford it but £2,300 a pair—the present price—is, I'm afraid, for the rich only.

Although I'm sure that Alfred honoured his undertaking to make over some capital to my father in the early 1890s I have not been able to find proof of the amount. When he died in 1899, Alfred left in modern values some three and a half million. A seventh share of this is half a million. I find it hard to credit that he made over the equivalent of this amount but the fact must remain that my father received something between £300 and £500 thousand in modern values in 1890. A substantial sum which I believe he managed to get through entirely by 1915, the year he married my mother.

I've commented on the significance of the six-year gap between my father and his nearest preceding sibling, "Parson Milne" as he was known. With retrospective memory I find it hard to believe that he and my father shared the same sire. When my father and I stayed briefly with him at the Rectory, Compton Valence, about 1930, I remember him as tall and thin and, as I was to learn later, dolicho-cephalic. He was a good horseman but no athlete. My father, on the other hand, was five feet seven inches tall, brachy-cephalic and an outstanding athlete and horseman.

E D Milne's entry in *Who's Who* records his recreations as fox hunting and gardening. I think this might have been more accurately expressed as Master of Hounds. His deepest love almost certainly was for hounds and houndwork and providing good sport for those who hunted with him. He was Master at Cambridge of Trinity Beagles, then, after taking holy orders, of the North Bucks Harriers. He was best known, however, for his mastership of the Cattistock Foxhounds from 1900 to 1931, a task he combined with the rectorship of Compton Valance.

He was understandably known as the Hunting Parson or simply Parson Milne although I believe his relatives and intimates called him Jack. Whether it was no more than the ordinary disdain of an older for a younger brother I can't be sure but I certainly picked up a certain suggestion on that visit in 1930 that he considered my father and their younger sister Blanche as "different". For instance going round the stables before dinner early in our visit, my father had admired a bay mare. "I'd like to have a ride on her tomorrow," he said. Quickly Jack Milne replied, "No. You don't ride that mare, Gerry, you haven't good enough hands."

I was furious. I well knew that my father had beautiful hands. Anything would go for him. I'd heard comments from horsemen all over the place about how good he was. There was something dismissive and hostile about the remark which I felt and didn't understand. Even now, as I write, sixty-seven years after the visit, I still feel my blood pressure rising.

Looking back, however I appreciate that my uncle was rated as no mean character in the sporting world of the 1930s. His name often appeared in the *Horse and Hound*, *The Field* and even *The Pink 'un* of the time as well as in longer biographical works. There were many stories told about him, some perhaps apocryphal such as his alleged remark to the sole communicant at an early morning service: "Hurry up, me dear. Come and get it. Don't you know it's a hunting morning." Apparently the good lady in question was rather slow and wont to take her time. My father told one, of a previous visit on his own to ours in 1930. After dinner he and Jack strolled down the dingle at the bottom of which flowed a small trout stream. They met the curate coming up carrying a rod. "Where have you been, my boy—catching a fish?"

"Yes, parson."

"Very good sport, very good sport. You might see a fox," said Jack.

It was alleged that often on weekday early morning services the toes of his hunting boots could be seen peeping out from under his canonicals.

My mother's immediate family exercised a dominant influence not only on my own life but on the lives of two of my younger sisters, Geraldine and Marie. We owe an immense debt to them. By immediate family I mean Ethel and "the Aunts".

The "Aunts" consisted of Jack Walton who was a sixty-one year old bachelor in 1939 and his two unmarried sisters: Kate, my mother's twin, born in 1880, and Alice, born in 1887.

Jack was the oldest son of John Pears Walton and had gradually taken over management of the numerous small family-owned mines which the Walton family had operated in Cumberland, Durham and Northumberland for five or six generations before JPW assumed control.

JPW himself had inherited Green Ends near Nenthead from a long line of Walton forbears but although the house was large enough to accommodate a Victorian family—extending along the contour of the steep hillside to which it clung—it was austere and very bleak, being over 1,100 feet above sea level. He is said to have courted his future wife, Francis Mary Bellville, for five years before she consented to marry him and then only because he purchased Acomb High House, near Hexham. Brought up in the luxury of Stouton in Leicestershire and 22 Berkeley Square she could hardly have been expected to opt for married life amidst the austerities of Green Ends. When I stayed there with the Aunts in the 1920s (they kept it on as a shooting box) there was no inside WC. Urgent calls during the night involved a thirty-yard trek and then it was a "long drop".

In the middle, and late Victorian years, Harmans of Bromley in Kent became widely known for their "Souvenir de Temps"—small gold engraved cards bearing photographic reproductions of the daily *Times'* entries of births and marriages. The birth column—a touch here which seems quintessentially Victorian—recorded also failures. There is amongst the Walton papers a card announcing the arrival, "stillborn, prematurely" of a little son on 23rd April 1876. As Francis and John were only married on 24th September 1875 the nicety of "prematurely" can be appreciated.

Jack and his twin sister, Ethel, were born in 1878. George, the youngest of the family, was born in 1889, two years after Alice.

Poor George, I cry for him to this day. He was a fine, simple product of his time; good rugger player, sound cricketer, charged high with dictates of duty. He went to France with the Northumberland Fusiliers just after the outbreak of war in 1914 and spent most of the war there apart from three invalidings. He was wounded three times, the last time gravely. However, in mid-1918 he felt more anguish for his men left in France, if possible, than for himself; he forced his way past a medical board to rejoin them. He was killed a month short of the armistice.

Jack, being eleven years older than George, treated him more as a father than a brother. During the years that Jack and the Aunts gave a home to Geraldine, Marie and me, Jack was to tell us much of the war years. He felt it very much that he was refused permission to enlist at first on account of his age and later because his management of the mines was a reserved occupation. When George was killed Jack was inconsolable. He couldn't bear the thought that George had borne so stoically the horrors of trench warfare for so long only to lose his life at the very end of the war.

Robert Graves, in perhaps the greatest of 1914-1918 war books, *Goodbye to All That* confessed that it took him ten years to recover from the horrors of the trenches. I can well believe it. Jack, in his conversations with me between 1929 and 1939, talked coldly and factually about the war. He did not seek to horrify me or be sensational but his recital of the bare facts filled me with terror when, in common with many of my friends, I felt that war with Germany from about 1937 onwards was inevitable. When it came it was, thank God, a war of strategy and movement. Less terrible, but bad enough for all that, than the dreadful killing in the mud of Flanders.

Jack's father and mother both died during the Great War. His twin sister, Ethel, married a cousin, Archie Bellville, as his second wife in 1906. Archie's first wife, Phyllis Brown, had "bolted" taking their two children with her. They had lived at Lawbottle Hall, a Northumberland estate the property of Phyllis' father. Jack, with the thinnest of smiles used to tell me of Archie's fury at Phyllis' behaviour. Apparently just after she'd left and before Archie married Ethel, he said to Jack: "Bring a gun and as many cartridges as you can get your hands on and stay the weekend. We are not going to leave a single damned feather on the estate." Jack went but I am sure he fired well behind any blackbirds that might have got up and I guess Archie didn't fulfil his threat either.

Archie's grandfather had come to England from France in 1790 and with his English partner, Robinson, had made a fortune as a dealer in patent barley and groats operating from 64 Red Lion Street, Holborn. Archie's father, William John Bellville, increased the fortune by manufacturing mustard and subsequently selling out to Colmans. There was enough money in the Bellville family in late Victorian days to provide Archie and his three brothers each with an estate, two in Leicestershire.

My father had hunted with all four of the Bellville brothers in the 'shires and I see from one of his scrap books that he had stayed with Archie at Lawbottle in the days when Archie had still been married to Phyllis. Perhaps this was the occasion when Gerry first met my mother, Winifred Walton, because the Walton young and Archie were first cousins and obviously knew each other.

One of the Bellville brothers, Frank, seemingly on the spur of the moment, did me a service which greatly enlivened my last three years at Cambridge. He lunched with my father in Kirkoswald one day in 1934. I was asked, too. Not trusting my father to provide the right claret Frank sent his chauffeur out to the car to fetch a bottle of his own which "by chance" he had brought along. Or so he said. I think it really was out of kindness. Knowing Gerry was TT and not wanting him to spend money he could ill afford he had brought his own. Later in the meal my father, who could be quite irascible at times, said crossly to me, "Speak up, boy. You mumble."

I replied, "You know very well I speak clearly. It's you who is getting deaf."

Frank B was delighted. "That's right. Stick up to the old devil. I'll leave you a thousand pounds for that." And, by Jove, he did. Two years later he died suddenly. I'd forgotten entirely about being rude to my father but sure enough there came a lawyer's letter and a cheque worth, in today's value nearly £30,000.

With hindsight I realise now it was Frank B's way of being kind to my father whom he realised was very hard up. True, a fifth of the money went on an MG which apart from being an excellent girl trap enabled Angus and me to spend many summer Cambridge weekends climbing in the Lakes and Wales but it did allow me to pass on some to my father which he badly needed.

Although the Waltons only lived in Acomb High House for fifty years, in retrospect there was something entirely appropriate about their occupation. The male members of the Walton family had either farmed or been involved in small mining operations in the hills of Durham, Northumberland and Cumberland for countless generations: a lead working employing ten men here, a small coal seam there. Nothing as large as the London Lead Company's undertaking at Alston, perhaps, and certainly nothing that made the family fortune. But they were local employers employing local men and from what I remember, and from what I have heard since, Jack and his father, and those before them, ran the workings with paternal responsibility and great fairness. When staying with the Aunts at Acomb in the 1920s I used to accompany Jack to the two enterprises near Acomb that still remained in Walton hands: the small Wall Colliery which employed about 150 men and the Fallowfield Fell lead and barytes mine which employed about half that number.

Jack knew the family details of every miner we talked to. And there wasn't a miner who felt the need to talk that Jack didn't talk to. The time he spent in discussing what seemed to me to be the pettiest and most wearisome details of their affairs I know now to have been time well spent.

Sadly both Wall Colliery and Fallowfield Fell ceased to be economic after 1923 and, as the family was losing money on both enterprises, Jack was forced to close both down. They sold Acomb High House and moved to Lynwood, near Penrith, a house built on the edge of the Beacon Hill which dominated the little market town of Penrith. It yielded magnificent views of Saddleback and the western Lakes hills, with Lowther Castle prominent in the middle distance.

Whenever Jack or his sisters had occasion to visit Acomb, which they frequently had in the years up to the outbreak of war in 1939, they were received with affection by every ex-miners' family in the place. I took this for granted at the time but now realise how remarkable it was considering the bitterness that had consumed the mining industry during the general strike and the poverty that had attended the run down and closure of so many mines.

My mother and father were married—secretly as far as the family were concerned—at Shirehampton Registry Office in Bristol on 17th March 1915. My father, posted to the Remount Depot nearby was just short of his forty-seventh birthday and my mother within three weeks of her thirty-fifth. She was doing war work on the land near Bristol. The secrecy was occasioned by the Waltons' opposition to the marriage on grounds of my father's lack of income other than his military pay.

I was born in London on 24th April 1917 and, my father being in France, my mother and I spent the rest of the war with Jack, Alice and

Kate at Acomb; John Pears W and Frances having died in 1915 and 1917 respectively.

The earliest memory that I can date with accuracy is the arrival of my sister Geraldine. I was two years and two months old at the time. We—that is a nursemaid and me in a pram—were at the entrance gates of a large house at the bottom of the hill leading to Acomb village. A carriage pulled into the open space.

I knew—in the way that children just know—that the occasion was one of supreme importance. I was allowed to scramble up the steps and through the open door of the carriage. On the seat, with her arms held out, was my mother. She'd been away and was back. We hugged and laughed, laughed and hugged. On the other seat was a bundle—my new sister, Geraldine. In the middle—or so it seemed—of the same night (certain knowledge tells me it was the same night) lit by the gentle warm light of a candle was my mother pulling up the clothes in a bed alongside mine. I laughed and laughed again with happiness. My mother laughed, too, and happiness flooded the room.

Later in the same year my parents rented a house called Newlands halfway between the villages of Natland and Sedgewick in Westmoreland. Our landlord, I discovered later, was John Fothergill better known for his classic, *An Innkeeper's Diary*. In the twenties he was busy consorting with Shaw, Wells, Rebecca West, David Garnett and artists such as Augustus John, Tonks and John Nash whilst making a name for himself as the cultured but unpredictable proprietor of the Spreadeagle at Thame.

The Fothergills were an old established Lakeland family but I can't remember my father talking much of his landlord. He obviously cared little for horses and didn't hunt and I guess in my father's view was missing out on the best things in life.

My parents never owned a car. At Newlands we used a pony trap for journeys up of to ten miles; for the very occasional longer journey we hired a car. My father was very dismissive of speed. He would often declare, "Man is not meant to go any faster than a horse can gallop."

I remember motoring him up to Cambridge in the MG bought with Frank Bellville's legacy, some twelve years later. We were bowling along at the then respectable speed of fifty miles an hour when he objected quite fiercely. Out came the familiar statement, "Man's not..."

On the other hand at speeds up to thirty-nine miles an hour (which I believe is the fastest a horse can gallop) he was an expert. In his racing days he'd been noted as a fine judge of pace—a gift he apparently extended to his own running.

It might have been 1925—I was about eight at the time—when Charles Fitzroy, the son of an old friend of my father's, brought three young friends to lunch. One had arrived in a two-seater Bugatti. I heard him say to my father, "Come on, Major. I'll show you what real speed is. Come for a spin."

Predictably out came the familiar axiom: "No. Man's not meant to travel faster than a horse can gallop." And then I heard him add, a little gratuitously, I now judge, "You young men should use your legs more."

"Steady on, Major. I know you are an old fellow but I can give you a yard a year in a hundred."

In 1925 my father would have been fifty-seven years old. "No need for that. No need at all. Give me ten in fifty and put your money down." Bets were taken. My father and the young guest flung off their jackets and shoes in spite of my mother's anxious "No, Gerry, no" and took up their positions on the McAdam road that ran past Newlands. The finish and the ten-yard handicap were marked out. The amused chatter died away to a sudden silence as my father adopted a crouch start.

And, of course, he won. Ten yards in fifty is an enormous handicap. Here my memory ends but I know that in later years he used to boast that he bought a pearl hat pin for my mother with his winnings.

One harbours memories for strange reasons. I write seventy-two years after the event but I still carry clearly the feel and the texture of the surface of that McAdam road. It was dry, dusty and kind to horses and stocking-feet. Quite unlike the tarmacadam main road up the hill, skirting the Helm which, wet or dry, was dangerous for horses.

The stables at Newlands were generous. About eighty yards from the house they were built on the four sides of an open square. There were loose boxes for at least a dozen horses and accommodation for two or three grooms above together with tack rooms. My father had persuaded the farmer on the land across the McAdam road to make a gallop with a bank and several fences and he had taken out a training licence about the same time. On the date Charles Fitzroy brought his friends to luncheon my father had five or six horses in training including at least two belonging to Charles' father.

This training enterprise was obviously financially rash. As far as I am able to reconstruct matters at this length of time I doubt if my parents had as much as £500 per annum between them. My father had his salary of about £350 p.a. from his appointment as district remount officer for the NW of England and my mother must have had a small income of about £150 p.a. although I guess she and my

30

father were already digging into the capital. Training 'chasers is a hazardous undertaking at the best of times. I can imagine the concern that must have been felt in the Walton family.

Nor did I greatly care for it myself. Horses—hacks, hunters, racehorses, workhorses…the lot—seem much kinder now than they were seventy years ago. Perhaps it is because they are predominately looked after by women; possibly, too, attitudes have changed; have softened. I remember leaping back as a sixteen and a half hands chaser swung his dangerous end my way in his box. "What are you frightened of?" my father demanded.

"He'll stand on my feet," said I, improvising.

"No, he won't. A horse won't stand on you if he can help it," said my father, and to prove his point made me lie down in the straw in the centre of the box while he had three or four great 'chasers led over me. None of them, of course, touched me.

For one winter, at least, I was required to ride out at exercise what seemed every morning, accompanying the string of horses in training. My mount was Strawberry. Unlike so many equine friends of later years she was a sod of a pony and I hated her. Big barrelled she was too round for a kid to ride with comfort. She had a mouth like iron. Her favourite amusement was to wait until my father was out of sight and then try to rub me off against some stone wall. Maybe she took it out of me in revenge for the hardness of her lot at other times for her real job was to lug us round the district in the pony tub.

On early morning exercise rides my role was gate-shutter. Hammering away at Strawberry I dragged along behind the string. Every gate I had to shut involved a battle…badly hung heavy wood gates I had to get off to shut and fields often holding big-footed gallumping carthorses who liked nothing better than to mob us and put their silly faces to Strawberry's blunt end. Often the only way I could get on again was to slip the reins over her head and tie her to a gate post. And then, once aboard, recover the reins. Several times she made my eyes fill with tears as she gave me a crack in the face with her poll.

And would Strawberry jump anything? Not on your Nelly. I remember one afternoon (memory firmly says "afternoon", strangely) my father was trying to force Strawberry and me up the small bank he had had cut on the gallop. At least once she had me off, refusing. I'm sure I yelled with fear and fury…and I guess my father didn't keep his voice down either.

One thing Strawberry did like, though, was a hedge. The bigger the better. No matter where I tried to steer her she'd find a gap or a weakness on her own and be through it like a rabbit. To this day I can't approach a thorn hedge in winter without inviting a bar of pain across my eyes. Even to write about it hurts.

Most young males, in the animal as well as the human world, seem to go through a period of rebellion against their parents at one stage or another of their development. I rebelled, against my father in particular, at about this time. I had the fiercest passages with him and used quite abominable language much of which I'd picked up in the stables. It wasn't that I resented his pressing me to master Strawberry. I realised that he only wanted me to become "a real man". This was an eminently acceptable goal which I wanted for myself. And I loved him and never resented his pressures. Possibly, as children will, I was picking up vibes which I did not understand but which I felt were alarming, and thus blindly reacting. The point is that he became concerned enough to take me to a friend of his, a GP who lived near Carnforth, and sought his opinion as to whether "I was all right".

The GP turned out to be a short, rather stout, individual with what I judged to be a nasty manner. My father told his story: my frightful language, my abusiveness, my wrong-doings...the old boy listened grimly.

In the surgery there was a glass-front display case which carried a number of antique surgical instruments. Among them were two spiked rollers which my father later told me were for use in bleeding apoplectic patients.

The old GP turned to me with one of the rollers in his hand. "Do you know what I'd do if my son spoke to me as you speak to your father?" he asked me.

"No, what?" I replied.

"I'd run this down his back," he said in a threatening manner.

"Then you are a bloody old fucker," using an expression I'd recently acquired in the stables which seemed appropriate.

"There," said my father, "I told you how he behaves."

About 1926 or 1927 a new element began to permeate life at Newlands. This was a sense of unease, of wrongness. Like any other child of nine or ten I hadn't the experience to judge what was wrong. But signs worrying to a child proliferated: my mother became more serious, more introspective. My father's temper—short at the best of times— showed more often. Unease, verging on the impertinent, could be observed in the behaviour of the two or three hands in the stables.

I began to find my frequent visits to the Aunts, first to Acomb High House, then, after 1924 to Lynwood and always in the autumn to Green Ends, increasingly desirable. True, they used to make a great fuss of me—perhaps because of the Victorian tendency to favour the male—but so much so that I used to refer to myself at this time, half mockingly, as "Little Lord Fauntleroy". Whenever I returned from the Aunts I would shed, in the presence of my mother—generally when she tucked me up for the night—bitter tears of regret. Instead of showing joy at my return here I was crying miserably. I realise now how hurting this must have been for her but, worst omen of all, she seemed almost to sympathise with my predicament. This really worried me. Something about our life at Newlands was wrong, very wrong.

A copy of a letter written by Jack to the Milne relatives in 1928 supports the figures I surmised on page 30. By 1928 my father and mother had virtually exhausted my mother's small capital and they were left with only his income as district remount officer. Educating me and my two sisters was a growing problem. I was due to go to a prep school but the fees were obviously beyond their reach. I can well imagine the Aunts saying, "If only Gerry had not blued the sum given him by his father in 1890." The mounting anxiety and sense of hopelessness about the future must have indeed been intolerable for both my parents. The arrival of our sister, Heather, in 1926, had added to the physical burden on my mother.

It was plain that the financially hazardous training enterprise at Newlands had to stop and my parents' lifestyle had to be drastically cut. Bruce Rigg, real friend to my father and mother, came to the rescue. He was a well-to-do farmer and hotel proprietor in the Windermere area and, in spite of riding at nineteen stones, a very good horseman. He was obviously a sound businessman as well and as soon as he learnt the details of my parents' financial plight he insisted that they move from Newlands into a cottage he offered them rent-free on Orrest Head above Windermere.

Had it not been for Bruce Rigg's quick appreciation of my parents' plight and his generosity at this time I fear my father might well have been faced with bankruptcy.

Memory has us one moment at Newlands and the next at the cottage. Children take such changes of circumstance in their own stride. They judge, if judge at all, by the impact on their own activities. For me there was much that instantly appealed; it must have been summer when we moved for I clearly remember suddenly discovering the joy of sun-warmed rocks.

The cottage was built on the edge of Ellery Wood, some quarter mile from and one hundred feet below the summit of Orrest Head which yielded wonderful views over Lake Windermere and the hills to the west. The steep fields leading up to Orrest Head and the common land of Orrest Head itself had been strongly glaciated and were strewn with partially buried glacial boulders which although ten feet high at the most nevertheless offered wonderful climbs for a child. In the 1920s rock-climbing was rapidly becoming a sport for all classes rather than an esoteric pursuit for a small group of the privileged. After a week or two on those boulders I knew that I would become a rock climber.

There was a public footpath past the foot of the cottage garden leading to the summit of Orrest Head. It was possible, just, to get a car as far as the cottage. I have memories of my mother struggling to push Heather's pram from the streets of Windermere up to the cottage which hurt me today to recollect. I know now that the cottage, although in an ideal situation for young children to adventure away from the dangers of urban streets, was in the 1920s a cruel place for the mother of four to live. There was a walled garden along the contour on which the house was built. This contained a stone-built rondavel which my father used as office for his remount work. It must have been bitterly cold in winter for I remember my mother more than once exclaiming how cold he felt after working there.

Geraldine and Marie shared a governess with a family living near Windermere railway station—within twenty minutes' walk of the cottage. At first a small male friend and I were admitted to the kindergarten section of St Anne's Girls' School but I was sent to Windermere Grammar School and my friend to a prep school as a boarder after Miss Rudyard, the formidable headmistress of St Anne's complained to our respective parents that we were "showing our age and must leave".

There was an enlightened attitude to learning at Windermere Grammar School in the 1920s due, I think now, largely to the personalities of two masters. One was the headmaster himself, Abrahams. He was a mild, reflective man, tall and slightly stooping who possessed the most exquisite handwriting. It was a pleasure to read his helpful and perspicacious comments on one's own work, however elementary it may have been. He drew one along with him, as it were. It was he who introduced me to Lavengro and the writings of Borrow. He may well have seen in himself something of the scholar, the gypsy, the priest.

The other, whom I remember equally vividly in spite of the seventy years that have passed since I last saw him was Knowles. He taught

34

French and taught it very well. I firmly believe that had I stayed on at WGS under Knowles he would have encouraged me to acquire enough of the language to speak it reasonably well in later years—instead of atrociously, as I must confess I do. He was a sharp featured, quick-reacting little man who had built up a strong reputation for himself at the school. He must have lived to a very old age for I remember reading his obituary in a Cumberland paper relatively recently. It was he who taught me, somewhat drastically one morning, a fundamental rule of human relations—the need for circumspection in dealing with others. A group of us, masters and boys, was descending a corridor heading for "big-school" and morning prayers. I was cheerfully flexing my biceps and punching out sideways. A cheeky but "feel good" mode of progression. Suddenly I received an almighty clout on the side of my head. Shaken but furious I swung round to see who had done it. It was Knowles. "That'll teach you, boy, not to be impertinent." He strode on down the corridor. The boys near me laughed.

"What the hell was that for?" I asked, Knowles being safely out of earshot by now.

"You were copying him, you ape. Don't you know he always walks like that?"

And of course the devil of it was I had to admit that Knowles often adopted that particular mannerism. I had imitated him, true, but so often that I'd made it my own. Knowles corrected that misapprehension. It was a lesson.

I suppose if a secondary school master corrected one of his pupils like that today there'd be a great to-do...inquiries by the country education authorities...the works. And how much worse we are for it, too. Knowles was absolutely right and I bear him not the slightest resentment.

———

Late in 1928 my mother suffered what was diagnosed at the time to be a "nervous breakdown". She was taken to a small nursing home in Bowness where she lay, tearful and obviously far from well, in a dark little room facing the hillside. We children visited her under the care either of Nellie (my mother's only domestic help in Ellery Wood Cottage) or my father.

Two or three days later—I have no recollection of time, it might have been longer—Jack and the Aunts and Bruce Rigg, stepped in. Geraldine and Marie were taken by Aunt Alice to Lynwood; Heather, then only two and a half years old, was given a home—at first a temporary one, later a permanent home, by Mabel Milne, wife of a cousin of ours, John Milne. I was sent as a "special guest" by Bruce Rigg to his large Windermere hotel where I would breakfast in the dining room but have supper brought to my room. I continued to attend WGS.

The next chapter in my mother's illness followed swiftly. The Aunts took her to Lynwood where they nursed her themselves under the direction of Dr Mactavish who was both the Aunts' family physician and a tennis-playing friend of theirs. At first all seemed reasonably well then she suddenly developed bowel trouble. Initially Dr Mactavish took it lightly—"an expected consequence of being confined to bed. Nothing to worry about," he said. Three days later peritonitis developed. My father was sent for. When he arrived Jack met him at the foot of Lynwood drive and was forced to say, "Gerry, there's no hope. Win is dying." My father, utterly stunned by the unexpected shock, fainted at Jack's feet. My mother died the same night.

I was sent to Lynwood arriving late on the day of my mother's funeral which we children did not attend. That night I lay in a camp bed in Alice's room watching broken, scattered clouds, one following another, blow over a three-quarter moon. The beauty of that night sky was inextricably bound up with the agony of my mother's loss. The loss was pain that was worse than pain. I couldn't bear it. Neither prayers, nor tears nor fight would bring her back.

Seen now, with the perspective of seventy years, I am convinced that life at Ellery Wood Cottage was quite simply too much for my mother. She experienced a physical struggle every time she descended to Windermere to shop. She had to take Heather—a baby couldn't be left in the cottage—and the struggle required to push the pram up the 800 yards of stony path exhausted her. Domestic labour in those days was a dire chore: dishes had to be washed by hand and dried by hand; cooking ranges had to be constantly fuelled and the ashes removed; stone floors washed and mopped to keep them reasonably clean; clothes washed by hand; there were no washing machines or spin dryers. Lamps burnt paraffin and demanded regular cleaning and adjustment. Even we children were aware that paraffin is one of the most pervasive of fluids—it possesses a nightmare facility to contaminate with smell and taste every article in the vicinity. Add to these heavy domestic chores—with which in her maiden days my mother had had no practice—the physical struggle with Heather's pram and lastly the ever-increasing concern about the financial future and one instantly feels that many a far stronger and tougher person than my mother would have been daunted...would indeed have given up.

Jack and the Aunts were heroic. It is no easy thing for a bachelor of forty-nine and his two younger unmarried sisters to live together in a single household as they had done since their mother's death in 1917. They were, one supposes, just arriving at a *modus vivendi* when my mother became ill. Their joint decision to give a home to Geraldine, Marie and me would involve them in unknown financial risks. They would have all the responsibilities of parental care without even the certainty that we would appreciate what they were doing for us. Some have said to me in later life: "They were living an arid sterile life. You gave them an object for living." But knowing the Aunts as I came to I have never accepted this view. They did what they felt they had to do and put into the task all their joint thought and experience and not a little love.

My father arranged digs in Kirkoswald, a village eight miles from Lynwood. Jack wrote to both Walton and Milne relatives seeking promises for contributions to an educational fund sufficient to send the three of us children to school for a total of seven years. In today's figures he would be talking of a sum of £40,000 per annum—a very considerable amount.

Jack and the Aunts, my mother and my father had all been brought up in the Victorian era. They represented what was best of that period in terms of manners, family coherence and human relations. Anybody can argue anything—white can be shown as yellow with pink spots by the dialectically swift if they are so inclined—but the Victorians did at least recognise perimeters. They knew and believed in a distinction between good and bad; they respected human dignity. They valued human life.

Geraldine and Marie to this day have much that is Victorian in their makeup. I believe that I have, too and I am proud of it.

Although the Aunts bravely took over the care and schooling of my sisters Marie and Geraldine, aged respectively nine and ten when our mother died, and me, they felt that the youngest of the Milne brood, Heather, then aged only three, was too young for them to look after. Mabel Milne, a cousin by marriage, came to the rescue and brought up Heather as one of her own children until Heather, at the age of twenty-one married Wing Commander Gordon Bates.

Mabel Milne had married John Milne, a son of my father's sister, Constance Milne, who had herself married a Milne cousin. John and Mabel had three children (apart from Heather) who were roughly contemporaries of mine.

Mabel was a loving foster mother to Heather and she and Heather remained very close until Mabel's death. Mabel's marriage to John

Milne was a disturbed one and I suspect that from time to time Heather's thoughts turned to her true siblings although we, too, were not living in a father-mother-children relationship in our formative years.

Heather's marriage to Gordon Bates broke down after twenty-seven years and she married, secondly, Philip Howard, a widowed director of ICI Pharmaceuticals. Their marriage was truly happy and it was a great sadness for all when Philip died of a multiplicity of war wounds after seventeen years.

In early 1930, shortly before I went to St Bees, I read a book *The Story of Fergie Bey (Awarquay) told by himself and some of his friends*—published by Macmillan. It was the story of a district officer in the Southern Sudan recounted in his letters—and after his murder by a disgruntled group of Nuers—by a number of his friends. Fergie Bey had joined the Sudan Civil Service in 1919 and had made the pacification of the Nuers—a wild tribe of the Bahr el Ghazal—his main task. One of his grandfathers had been a distinguished surgeon. The other, although a layman, possessed deep medical knowledge. Fergie Bey inherited a strong natural gift for healing and achieved an immense amount of medical development amongst the Nuers. He took his familiar name—Awaraquay—from the name of a bull with black face and white body given him by a neighbouring tribe, the Dinkas, and said to possess magical powers.

Fergie Bey was killed by a small, rebellious section of Nuers who did not like his instructions to them to stop their raids on Dinka cattle.

Sir Reginald Wingate, Governor-general of the Sudan from 1899 to 1916, following Kitchener, wrote a moving and informed foreword to the book.

One day I showed my father the book and said that it had determined me to join the Sudan Administrative Service. He mentioned this to a friend of his—a General Kerr-Montgomery who lived near Corbridge in Northumberland. The latter at once said that he knew, and had served under, Wingate and he would see that I had my wish, provided annual inspections satisfied him that "I was progressing on the right lines". Thereafter my father and I lunched annually with Kerr-Montgomery. He seemed to obtain the right impressions for he supported my application to join the Sudan Political Service in 1938.

The response of the Walton and Milne relatives to Jack's hard work on the educational fund must have been generous because Geraldine was sent to the Royal School, Bath; Marie to Dr William's School, Dolgellau under the stimulating and advanced headship of Miss Nightingale and I to St Bees and St Catharine's College, Cambridge.

In 1929 I was twelve years old. I was to spend a further ten years with the Aunts before leaving for Nigeria. We all change to some degree as life progresses but it is often said that the earlier ten or a dozen years have the larger effect on the sort of character one ultimately becomes. I believe that this is a truism and that the relative stability of life under the Aunts' regime had less effect on me than the turbulent vicissitudes of the years at Newlands.

Of the five years I spent at St Bees, the first two were pretty hellish. I suppose I was arrogant and cocky and got the treatment I deserved. Life became more tolerable after I began to show some promise as an athlete and rugger player. St Bees had long been known as a good rugby football school and in my day rugger had been elevated virtually to the status of a religion: one pursued the good (rugger) life; the highest achievements occurred, *pari passu*, on the rugger field. In my last year I was made captain of rugger.

Sedbergh was in fact the leading Northern rugger school when I assumed the captaincy of St Bees in September 1934. They had at that time a ten year unbeaten record by any other school team.

"My" 1934-35 team decided we would lower Sedbergh's record as well as win all other of our school matches. Lower it we did but only by the thinnest of margins.

Looking back I recall that our 1934-35 side was forced to play (allowing, of course, for changes in the rules over the years) a relatively modern game. We hadn't a particularly heavy pack and our strength lay in our running the ball as a team. Our forwards practised handling and passing as assiduously as scrummaging; the wings were expected to score tries on either side of the field; the full back was ordered to start off movements as often as he kicked in defence. By employing these tactics, as far as one can ever follow a game plan, we won all our school matches up to the last one, that against Sedbergh. They had had a good season and of course, won all matches. Their aggregate of points against the same opponents beat ours but I tried to explain this by pointing out that the Sedbergh pitches were a lot faster and drier that the crease at St Bees which a strong shower of rain could turn into a quagmire.

Sadly the day of the Sedbergh match, in late January, was a filthy day; strong wind and driving rain forecast to persist into the late afternoon. Whenever I had a moment of privacy during the morning I was on my knees praying unashamedly, "Dear God, please let us knock hell out of Sedbergh." I have a team photo hurriedly taken in the shelter of Foundation House veranda which shows me with two black rings on my knees, proof of what I say.

Sedbergh, as guests, went out first. I gave them as long as I dared "to cool down" on the crease. It was, of course, a mud battle. Bob Hanvey, Cumberland and England, was refereeing. At half time he said to me, "I can hardly distinguish the two teams apart," but I merely replied, "Let's cut half time short." The Sedbergh captain agreed and we restarted. The mud fight continued. Neither side scored nor looked like it. The touch lines were thronged with miserable rain-drenched St Beghians (it was compulsory to watch all matches). After some twenty minutes of no score battle, Bob Hanvey blew his whistle and said to me, "It's hopeless, Malcolm. I can't tell you apart." I didn't blame him. Sedbergh played in brown jerseys in any case, while we were in blue. Both were, as he said, wet brown by then.

On no account must he be allowed to give the awful decision: "No side."

"Hang on, hang on," I said and, turning to the spectators, I ordered three sixth formers: "Quick! Each of you get five shirts from the chaps here," pointing at the spectators.

I should explain that the St Bees school uniform consisted of blue knee-length stockings, blue shorts, white flannel shirts, no tie and a blue blazer. I believe jerseys were allowed over the flannel shirts in winter.

In no time at all the St Bees team had discarded their cold wet jerseys and put on the body-warmed shirts. "Now you can tell us apart," I said to Bob and he reluctantly agreed.

Ten minutes later there was a scrimmage on the Sedbergh line. Halstead, scrum half, got the ball and was over in a flash. Three—nil.

The try wasn't converted and we played out the remainder of time without either side scoring again. We'd done it. We'd done it.

I heard later that the school had replaced the shirts the spectators had so generously lent. Later still I learnt the headmaster himself (E A Ball) had actually paid for the flannel shirts turned rugger jerseys. Good for him. One of the reasons we were a strong rugger school was because of his support.

When I returned to St Bees at the end of every school holidays my father had always said goodbye with the axiom "work hard, play hard". I had done my best. I wanted to please both the Aunts and my father and also myself: there was much in my own makeup that was highly competitive. In the holidays I tried to average one hour a day at my books, later increased to four hours a day during the longer Cambridge vacations. As for rugger I used to aim at four miles a day slow work and twenty minutes of sprinting with no formal exercise on the days before and after a match.

The Aunts allowed me to use the Lynwood library for my book work, giving me a large oil stove to make it tolerable in the cold days of winter. There was about eighty yards of grass joining the precious tennis court (which Jack and Ellem, the gardener, had dug out and turfed themselves) to a lawn running the full length of the house. I used to wear a pair of "miler's spikes" for the sprinting and swerving practice. I'm sorry to confess that in wet weather I must have left footmarks on the tennis court for I used to see Jack assiduously easing them out with a small fork he kept for that purpose.

Entry to Cambridge was dependant upon passing the "Little-go" examination in Latin. As I had abandoned Latin during my first year at St Bees I had to undertake a three months intensive course to acquire enough of the language to pass the exam. I judge now that it was a great mistake not to have continued throughout my school days: Latin is, after all, the basis of many of the words used in English scientific, commercial and literary writings. But to write of the past at all involves a myriad "might have beens" and the least that I can usefully say is that I have never regretted those three months of hard work trying to acquire a little Latin.

The pre-school and school years, to my mind, largely form the man. The university is the transition from dual instruction to solo flight; you are on your own, for better or worse. There is little to say about the three years necessary to get a degree save that I presumably did enough academically and in other pursuits (rugger, mountaineering) to convince the selection boards of the Sudan and colonial services to offer me appointments in each service. The Sudan appointment (I am sure influenced by Kerr Montgomery) was to be on a seven year contract, renewable at the end of the seven year period but on non-pensionable terms. The colonial service appointment carried the possibility of transfer anywhere within the colonial empire and was pensionable on generous terms. With Jack's and my father's agreement I chose the latter which required me to spend a further year at Cambridge attending the colonial administrative service course 1938-39.

During the year-long colonial service course at Cambridge in 1938-39 we studied in general perspective a number of subjects which were likely to be of value to us in the service at large: field engineering, colonial systems of accounting, surveying, tropical medicine, the language appropriate to our posting (in my case Ibo), anthropology, education, colonial agriculture, comparative religion, law and first aid. At the end of the course we were expected to pass written examinations on these subjects. I have kept some of the examination papers and I notice that the questions were sympathetically framed:

there was a wide choice and anybody who had done any reading at all on each subject would be able to find something on which to write with reasonable intelligence.

I take off my hat to Major Sir Ralph Furse who was in large measure solely responsible for the colonial service course. He subtly invited us to pursue those areas in which we were most interested. As we took up our postings later on we all found there was scope on the ground to follow our particular interest. I think immediately of Eric Powell and Ibo, Colin Hill and road engineering, Bernard Fagg on antiquities and Angus Robin, government systems and NA accounts. There was so much to do. Best start on what interested us most.

Superficially the course was easy-going and relaxed, a happy contrast to the three previous years' tense pursuit of a degree.

We were all enthusiasts—we wouldn't have been there otherwise—but Furse knew something we didn't: there would be aspects of service, no matter whether on the West Coast of Africa, Malaysia or the Far Pacific which would be worse than our expectations of them. He wanted to instil into our naïve idealism an actuality of things to come.

Furse chose the lecturers carefully. They were all without exception men (there weren't many women about in academic circles in those days) who had pleasing personalities and knew what they were talking about. One or two were odd-balls. One, a retired colonial judge, as batty as a coot but, despite behaviour and opinions pretty near the edge, I remember several of the tips he gave us to this day.

Tall and thin, red-faced, cropped hair still ginger he must have been about fifty-five or so. His every movement was that of a young horse, too full of oats in a high wind. I have a memory of him galloping out from the wings of some Cambridge lecture theatre and launching straight into a characteristic encapsule of advice.

"You've got a chap in front of you in a native court criminal appeal. He's a rogue. You know it; everybody knows it. The court below gave him the maximum. You want to confirm it. What do you do?

"You make a right ruddy fuss of him...that's what you do. Re-hear witnesses, be nasty at every turn to the prosecution, ask hostile questions from the bench. Hang on every word the defence utter. Even laugh at their jokes.

"And at the end confirm judgement. How does he take it? Like a lamb, still loving you."

We weren't long in discovering that he had an area of interest outside his expertise where we could always divert him should his purely legal expositions become a little dry. He was fascinated by tropical medicine. Nothing pleased him more than to amble off into long discussions of such subjects as the horrors of leprosy or the factors affecting the rapid growth of a major epidemic of cholera. And we knew, too, that he had quite a thing about the tropical sun.

On the last occasion of all, just before we all set off to our colonies, some wicked fellow tried his hand:

"Is it true, sir, that if you don't wear a hat in the tropics you go bonkers?" he asked.

"Of course it is. Look at me...I always wore a hat until five o'clock, every day of my life."

Howls of laughter greeted his statement. Such is memory. But looking back, and could I hear that exchange over again, I wonder whose leg I'd think was being pulled by who.

An eminent ex-missionary, who had worked in Eastern Nigeria, did his best on the course to teach us a little Ibo. He possessed an elderly grey parrot called Alfred. Although Alfred had a fairly extensive vocabulary for a parrot he wouldn't learn the four letter f-word which on the missionary's frequent absences from the room we did our best to teach him.

Again, it was near the end of the course. We were alone with Alfred. "Fuck fuck fuck..." said Reggie Blunt to him. But Alfred merely stared silently at Reggie through half a jaundiced eye. At that moment the good missionary returned. He couldn't fail to understand what Reggie was up to.

A note of sadness in his voice, he said, "If only you gentlemen had troubled to learn a little more Ibo you'd be aware that Alfred has an excellent command, in the vernacular, of that word you were trying to teach him."

CHAPTER THREE

Tyro ADO

To return to Eastern Nigeria.

I left our party of cadets on the train from Port Harcourt to Enugu. We arrived in Enugu about an hour after dawn. No sooner had we alighted than John Field, accompanied by five or six porters, arrived. He was to put three of us up and distribute the rest to their hosts' houses. He was then an ADO of four years standing. In a service—as we were soon to learn—where seniority was taken very seriously those four years were to count for much in terms of knowledge and experience. So far as modes of address and behaviour was concerned cadets and ADOs were considered to be members of the same grade. You minded, as it were, your Ps and Qs when addressing a member of a superior grade, ADO to DO, DO to SDO and SDO to Resident.

I was to serve as John Field's deputy twenty years later in the Southern Cameroons. By then he had become a little pompous. When, much later still, I studied his dispatches to the secretary of state for the colonies released under the "thirty year" rule I was mightily impressed by the power and lucidity of his representations and by the degree to which he had influenced United Kingdom policy at the time of Cameroonian independence. Somewhat pompous he might have been but effective and influential he certainly was. When he met us at Enugu station in August 1939 he was a short, slim administrative officer, not at all pompous, friendly and very lucid in all he told us. We were to stay three or four days with him and in that time we could not have wanted a better mentor.

Apropos of seniority there was a story current just before the war of a visiting American diplomat who found the concern of officers serving in the HQ of Northern Nigeria with seniority too much of a good thing. When dinner was announced in his temporary quarters one evening he sat down himself, and throwing a staff list on the table said to his guests, "Sort yourselves out."

44

The Onitsha Native Administration lorry—a 1912 Albion—arrived after a day's delay to take us to our once-again-revised postings. I was to go to Onitsha, Reggie Blunt to Udi, Geoffrey Horne to Awka and Eric Powell to continue to Owerri.

Getting into the lorry I committed the first of the many solecisms that I fear I have been guilty of during my service in Africa—I climbed into the driving seat and loftily ordered the driver to sit in the back.

We diverted some two miles to leave Reggie at Udi, a pleasant station on the edge of the escarpment with fine views from the four government quarters. We stopped again at Awka. I had it in mind to call on Basil Walters and show him what a good ADO he had missed (having originally been posted to Awka myself) but he was out and the district clerk met Geoffrey and showed him to his house.

Slowly ascending a twisting section of road a mile out of Awka, I found that the steering had suddenly become very light; in fact the vehicle hardly answered to the wheel at all. We stopped and discovered that the tie-rod on the near side had become disconnected. Fortunately there was some steering left on the offside front wheel but barely enough to guide the lorry at more than a walking pace. The driver slowly climbed down from the rear and made a make-shift repair with a length of wire produced from the tool box. I asked him to drive the rest of the way to Onitsha.

It was only when I thought about this incident the other day— fifty-seven years after it had occurred, if you please—that I realised that of course I was being punished. It was arrogant cheek to have pushed myself into the driving seat in the first place. I had made the driver lose face by usurping his function and making him sit in the back. He had plainly availed himself of the stop at Awka to loosen the steering link. I'm sure every Ibo passenger in that vehicle—and there were several—knew the whole sequence of events and were eagerly awaiting the moment I should plunge into the bush. If I broke my neck the joke on me would have been all the better. And, I fear, I deserved it.

So strong was the Ibo ability to think simultaneously on two levels—a generalisation I was to make my own—that they were certainly aware that without a steering link they themselves were in just as dangerous a situation as me but the essence of the situation was that I should plunge off the road. They could push the possibility of injury to themselves below deck…to the second level of thought.

We are all to some extent capable of harbouring logically incompatible views. The Ibo, of whom I write, seem to me to take this propensity to greater extremes. Perhaps this is related to his greater religiosity, for he is indeed a more religious being than many educated Europeans and Americans. He has had many thousand years of religious belief. In relatively recent times, three or four hundred years at the most, he has been exposed to a strange system with a new philosophy—Christianity. He is invited to switch from one to the other. The new system, it is true, is based upon persuasive tenets, it has much to appeal to his lively intelligence. But against this is the pull of thousands of years of experience, of the gradual burgeoning of belief, of animistic religious experience. The strain of choosing is intolerable to him. Why should he choose? The conviction grows that choice is unnecessary. He accepts the tenets of *both* systems. He comes in time to hold two sets of religious and philosophic and theological belief: one sometimes logically opposed to the other. He is, in Western eyes, both good and bad, violent and peaceful, cruel and kind. So I thought...

Dr M D W Jeffreys, an administrative officer with considerable anthropological interests, spent some time in the Niger Province of Northern Nigeria in the later 1920s and 1930s, in addition to his ordinary duties, studying the beliefs and behavioural patterns of peoples who although not Ibo were as far removed from the influence of the colonial power as any in Nigeria. He produced a paper on the role played "in the real life of the peoples" by secret societies in which he defined "real life of the peoples" as follows:

"...I mean that inner life where mysticism, reverence for ancestors and tradition, magic and mystery, witchcraft, a primitive conception of religion based upon a little book learning and a vague idea of Christianity, all go to make a pattern of life that is as odd and unintelligible to the average European as it is clear and orderly to the African."

Onitsha was classified as a Second-class Township and had a population in 1939 of around 30,000. It possessed a large market of outstanding interest: even before the war an incredible variety of items could be purchased there, varying from spare parts for cars as rare as Rolls Royce to the skeletons of small mammals bound up as phylacteries—skeletons I should add of some animals unknown to western science (as Julian Huxley was to discover on a visit just after the war). The African township and trading establishments sprawled along the banks of the Niger. The European Reservation, for the customary health reasons, was built on the low hills three-quarters of a mile away from the township. The "European" of the title gave way to "senior service" just after the war as the numbers of Nigerians in the senior service rapidly increased.

I was allocated a T3 quarter—really a very well constructed house for a bachelor. On the ground level was a serving pantry, dining room and storeroom connected by a covered way to a separately built kitchen. Upstairs was a large living room, a large bedroom with adjacent bathroom and separate lavatory. There was also a small separate bedroom which could be used as an occasional guestroom. The ceilings were of plaster board sheets with mahogany divisions. Basic furniture consisting of polished hardwood, iroko chairs, bookcases, occasional tables and beds, together with mattresses, pillows and chair cushions which were current issue. Provisions were kept in meat safes, the sides constructed of wire fly netting. After the war refrigerators were supplied.

The upstairs sitting room in the conditions of Nigeria at that time had much to recommend it. One need never close the windows save in the fiercest of storms so that the breeze was unimpeded and they were more private than the ground floor rooms. I had nothing to complain about so far as my first house was concerned.

Onitsha was both a Provincial and District headquarters and the Public Works Department were fully represented. Many outstations (District and Sub-District Headquarters) lacked PWD staff and the housing had to be constructed, and maintained by the administrative cadre. Most of the DOs' and ADOs' quarters built in these remoter spots were in the main constructed much more simply of local materials, generally mud walls and thatched roofs. However, what they lacked in professionalism of construction they often made up in imaginative design.

Throughout Eastern Nigeria every family between the wars had access to farming land and the possibility of winning a subsistence living by their labour. But the toil was hard and the work monotonous. Paid work was almost always less demanding and produced ready cash for little luxuries. In 1939 native authorities, for instance, could obtain as many road labourers as they required for seven pence a day. These men used often to sell the employment opportunity for three pence a day, the purchaser being prepared to do a day's work for a net four pence a day.

A cook and a steward (Isaac Mbe) had been found for me prior to my arrival in Onitsha. They had been selected, the district clerk told me, from 200 applicants. The cook I was required to pay thirty shillings a month and the steward twenty-five shillings a month. Both turned out to be excellent at their job. I gave the cook ten shillings a week to buy meat, fish and vegetables in the market. He regularly turned out four course luncheons and dinners. The steward, Isaac Mba, was by custom permitted to find a "small boy" to whom I was expected to pay ten shillings a month. His duties were very much those that a "tweeny" might have performed in an English household—largely polishing together with some washing up. A washerman called daily for ten shillings a month. Shirt, shorts and stockings—our regular working clothes—could only be worn once as of course were our games clothes. So the washerman, who like all the other servants did an excellent job, well earned his money.

The nearest "store" where slightly more sophisticated European articles could be obtained, was in Enugu. I placed a regular monthly order there for tinned food and drinks which came to about six pounds a month.

Calculating my annual budget in August 1939 I came up with the following figures:

Wages	£ 60 p.a.
Food & Stores	£ 61 p.a.
Club	£ 43 p.a. including subs, drinks, tennis & swimming
Contributions to Widows and Orphans Pension	£ 24 p.a. (compulsory even for bachelors)
Misc	£ 25 p.a.
	£223 p.a.

In addition to this I still owed money for the cost of my kit supplied by Hawes in London and thirty-four pounds per annum life insurance.

Provided that one travelled regularly—as the dictates of one's job required—I calculated that I should be able to save at least fifty per cent of my salary of £400 p.a. In fact, after several months' experience, I found I was living on my travel allowances and saving virtually the whole of my salary.

Cadets in the administrative service were expected to sit the compulsory examinations in language and law as soon after arrival as possible. I was alarmed to find that the Ibo exam was scheduled for early January 1940. It was necessary to engage a language teacher without further delay. The ubiquitous district clerk, who seemed able to solve most problems, produced a local schoolmaster who said he would take me on for a minimum of two hours a day. At the same time the SDO in charge of the District, J S Smith, ordered that I be allowed two hours a day off normal working hours so that I could study the law syllabus.

Ibo, however, was too much for me as it was, indeed, for most officers. It was a tonal language with no less than six tone levels. Thus a two-syllable word, such as AKWA could bear up to thirty-six meanings depending on the tonal pattern—a sigh, a cry, a piece of cloth...meaning after meaning.

Being tone deaf I couldn't distinguish with certainty between two tone levels, never mind six. I was told that it was possible to scrape a pass in the lower standard without an ability to distinguish tones but it would be a waste of time attempting to secure passes in the intermediate or higher standards. Government appreciated these difficulties in Ibo as they did in the case of other tonal languages spoken in the south of Nigeria. Districts in tonal language areas were supplied with interpreters.

An Ibo lady at a recent meeting in London of the Anglo-Nigerian Society, when I mentioned the Corps of Interpreters to her, smiled and said, "We had a TV series on that subject. It was very humorous. The interpreters always twisted what the white man said in so many ways." I am sure she was right; the system was open to abuse and doubtless the TV series was hilarious. But one of the objects in forcing us to acquire at least the lower levels of a language was to enable us to check if the interpreter was going awry. And this happened quite frequently with even the best of interpreters. There were times when an interpreter with the highest of reputations cut down mercilessly what I had said. I always had to ask myself whether this was because he was hot and tired; whether my point in his view was made unnecessarily; or whether I was just plain wrong.

As time went on I realised that the relationship between the district officer and the district interpreter was of crucial importance. Day after day African interpreter and expatriate district officer would tackle together reviews and appeals from the native courts, hold meetings of native authority councils, deal with miscellaneous difficulties at Village level and lastly, deal together with the daily "complaints" sessions. They would soon come to know one another. Again, it was often possible that one or both parties to a dispute had already been to see the interpreter or possibly the dispute was an old one and a previous DO had already given advice or made a ruling. I often found myself asking the interpreter, "Is this a new matter?" or "Do you know about this?"

I never, as far as I can recall, interfered with the interpreter's translations. It seemed preferable to show, and to be seen to show, complete confidence in him and to allow him as free a rein as possible. In Ibo Districts, even before the war, there were nearly always English-speaking persons in the audience who served as a check on the interpreter and would vociferously question anything they deemed to be a misinterpretation especially if it damaged the case they were supporting.

I was working a lot in 1939-40 with J R Romaine. He was an interpreter of about thirty and I a cadet of twenty-two; our relationship was close to the military one of junior officer and senior NCO—the latter provided the knowledge and experience but called the former "Sir". I like to think that we became friends. If one test of friendship is the ability to give advice which is known to be contrary to the wishes of the recipient then Romaine was truly a friend as well as colleague. In return I used sometimes to pull his leg.

There was a time in 1940 when we were together in Nnewi, a Sub-District of Onitsha. His wife was left in Nnewi—she was an attractive and vivacious Onitsha girl—while he and I spent a couple of nights on tour at Ozubulu. Returning from an evening walk I spotted a younger and even more attractive girl than his wife roasting maize for him. Here I must briefly interpolate; to roast maize in such circumstances is tantamount to a lady being seen today boarding a flight for a weekend in New York with some gentleman not her husband.

The next morning I said to Romaine, "Don't you think it would be a good idea for me to assure Mrs Romaine that when you are on tour in Ozubulu she needn't worry that you aren't being well looked after?" or words to that effect.

He replied, "Sir, man cannot exist on bread alone."

I should add that the family name Romaine was adopted in the nineties of the last century when his grandfather was bought out of slavery by an RC priest called Romaine working at the time in Onitsha.

I have mentioned J S Smith as being in charge of the Onitsha District when I arrived. He was known in the service as "Hyena" Smith to distinguish him from two colleagues, also Smiths, who were known as "Gorilla" and "BG" Smith respectively. "Gorilla" Smith was well named for he was immensely strong and boasted a chest covered in dark hair. "BG" were the third Smith's actual initials. Unfortunately in Northern Nigeria the small constructions housing the latrine pail and built behind the main house were referred to as "Bayan Gida' which was shortened to "BG'. This was unfair for B G Smith was the nicest of chaps who bore no resemblance whatsoever to a latrine.

Hyena Smith was ill-named also. He was called Hyena because of his sudden raucous laugh. Having spent twenty years in Kenya I can vouch that the spotted hyena's eerie, wailing call was nothing like J S Smith's laugh.

Hyena Smith led the life of a confirmed bachelor during his service in Nigeria. On his retirement he duly recovered his many years of compulsory contribution to the Widows and Orphans Pension Fund. He then promptly married the sweetest and most charming of women whom it transpired he'd known since he first joined the service.

He was a classical scholar who throughout his years in Nigeria built up a considerable library of works in the original Latin and Greek. I remember visitors to his house in Onitsha complaining that they'd found it difficult to find anything suitable for bed-time reading.

On leave just after the war, Kat and I spent a fortnight as the guest of Jim (as he was also known) Smith and his sister at an hotel in the Central Highlands of Scotland. Breakfast, by ancient custom was a pretty silent meal but it was entirely silent for Kat and me for whenever Jim or his sister—who was also a classical scholar—conversed they did so by swapping Greek or Latin tags.

I believe that Jim Smith used deliberately to insert Latin quotations in reports to senior officers he disliked. One such was Dermott O'Connor, a very positive, witty and idiosyncratic Irishman who was Resident of Onitsha Province in 1939. It was not difficult to see why Jim Smith and Dermott O'Connor did not hit it off: they had entirely dissimilar backgrounds. Dermott O'Connor had been a regular soldier and loved the army. He served throughout the First World War in France, winning an MC and bar, and being mentioned in dispatches. Late in 1918 he was badly wounded in shoulder and knee and was invalided out of the forces. He joined the colonial administrative service in 1920. He never, in my hearing, once mentioned those four years in France but I have no doubt whatsoever that they scored him very deeply. Jim Smith, on the other hand, had been eighteen when the armistice was declared—an age of comprehension but not of participation. This was, of course, the fundamental difference between them.

Dermott O'Connor was a strong supporter of the then-called European Club in Onitsha. He was frequently to be found there on weekday evenings and whatever he was in the station was a regular participant in the Saturday lunch-time sessions. These normally lasted from 12.30 p.m.—when offices closed—to round about four or five p.m. when members departed for a late luncheon.

With only twenty-three Europeans in Onitsha in 1939, it might be thought that we were expected to conform to a single pattern. But no, far from it. There was an extraordinary tolerance of what we did in our spare time. True, all Europeans joined the club as a matter of course. It provided tennis courts, a swimming pool and a bar and snooker tables. At Cambridge I'd found that my being TT was apt to isolate me from some of my rugger-playing contemporaries but nobody gave a damn if I drank or not in Onitsha. I found that I could order a lemonade and sit at the bar while others already ensconced there behind pink gins would chat with me enthusiastically. The key was, in fact, enthusiasm. We were a small group of Europeans in a very large African country. We were always pleased to meet others of our own kind; their problems and interests intermingled with ours. We possessed a common enthusiasm for the life we were leading.

Europeans...expatriates...non-indigenous...call us by whatever name you will...tended to socialise on our own simply because we preferred it that way. There was absolutely nothing of racial prejudice in the modern sense of the term. We spent our working days dealing with Africans of all classes. Those of us whose work required frequent touring in remote areas often forgot about colour or race. I remember being on tour for three weeks just after the outbreak of war and being surprised by the colour of my own hand—just for a fleeting moment I wondered why it wasn't black—and then remembering I was a European.

Similarly Africans who had been educated in the United Kingdom or other expatriate land tended to socialise with their own people on their return. Louis Mbanefo, son of Chief Mbanefo, the Odu One of Onitsha, was an example. He had read law at London University and had been called to the bar of the Middle Temple in 1935. He then entered King's College, Cambridge, where he completed a history degree. His period at Cambridge overlapped with Angus' and mine. We called on him in his rooms at Kings just before he went down. We thought he was a very mature, likeable chap. We didn't see him again in Cambridge as he left shortly after our visit to set up a legal practice in Onitsha.

When I arrived in Onitsha in 1939 I didn't call on Mbanefo because I was beset with other pressures. It was nice to know, at the back of my mind, that he was there. The war intervened and it was not until 1945 that Kat and I met Louis Mbanefo and his recently acquired wife at their house in Onitsha. We were working at Nnewi, eighteen miles out of Onitsha at the time. We dined with them in the European fashion and had a splendid evening, remembering it particularly because it was the first time we had been asked out to dinner in an African household. I don't believe that at that date the Mbanefos socialised much with the expatriate community for very much the same reasons that the Europeans kept to themselves— namely, both groups preferred to spend their leisure hours with their own kind.

Louis Mbanefo had a distinguished career. He continued in private practice until 1948 when he became a government stipendiary magistrate. By 1952 he had been made a judge of the supreme court of Nigeria; in 1958 he was made a judge of the Federal Supreme Court Of Appeal and in 1959 he became Chief Justice of the Eastern Region of Nigeria. His stature as an eminent international jurist was recognised in 1961 when he was appointed as an ad hoc judge to the International Court of Justice at The Hague. He was knighted by the Queen in the same year. All his working life he did much on behalf of the Anglican Church in Nigeria and, indeed, internationally. In 1972 he became President of the World Council of Churches. He died, a relatively young man, in 1977. I hope he rests easy for during his life of sixty-six years he did much for his country, and for ours whose contacts with his were so many and so close.

The war years, and the gallop to independence of the 1950s, produced many West Africans of acclaimed international eminence. What is interesting, however, is that during the previous 150 years, when tropical diseases largely precluded settlement by Europeans in West Africa, a considerable number of West Africans achieved high renown in Europe. The Macaulays, father and son and Bishop Crowther immediately come to mind.

Our reading of African history, and our later experience in Nigeria, brought me and my contemporaries increasingly to appreciate that Nigeria, in keeping with many other African countries, presented an imbalanced aspect to the outside world. On the one hand there is the great body of the peasantry—animistic in belief, their lives entirely circumscribed by religious beliefs and practices, which the Western world found, and still finds, difficult to understand. On the other hand Nigeria has produced sons and daughters who have penetrated alien cultures and have shown that they possess the highest capacities by any measurement.

One of the main tasks of the administrative officer was to convince the man in the bush that there was need for change, for modernisation. The colonial power looked to the high achievers amongst the indigenous population to assist in the process of change and this many of them were willing to do.

I write of 1939. The whole situation changed rapidly after the war when independence approached at an accelerating pace and we were forced into an Africanised version of parliamentary democracy.

In 1939 we cadet members of the Nigerian Administrative Service were expected to receive the bulk of our on-the-job training under the tuition of our superiors in the station. At that time there were very few African members of the senior service and most expatriate members of the service were hard pressed. Although we learnt a lot from our expatriate seniors we were forced to turn more and more to the senior African officials, members of the junior service. I owe a huge debt to people such as the chief clerk of the Onitsha District Office, to the interpreter stationed there, to the chief warder of the prison (one of the earliest duties given to newcomers was the supervision of the prison) and in my case to the African warden of an island leper settlement which I was required to inspect. Later, when we were on tour alone or posted to an outstation, there were no expatriate staff available and we were entirely reliant for guidance and help on the local Nigerian staff. I remember men such as J R Romaine, Interpreter, H O Nwosu, Chief Clerk of Nnewi NA, and various sergeants of police very clearly although it was fifty-six years ago that I first worked with them.

Experienced administrative officers, such as Dermott O'Connor, Hyena Smith and Paxton Wetherell—to mention only those I worked under in the early months—understood the educative role of members of the junior service very well and adjusted appointments appropriately. I can well imagine Dermott O'Connor, for instance, saying, "Milne is weak on NA finances. Post him to Nnewi and let H O Nwosu teach him a thing or two."

I early made friends with Craddock Randell, the Assistant Conservator of Forests, Onitsha Province. He lived in the Forestry department house built in the Onitsha Forest Reserve some two miles out of the station. It was a lonely spot and his loneliness was exacerbated by the fact that he was a grass widower at the time, his wife being due to join him later in his tour. I remember his saying, apropos of female company and what it portended: "Life's a funny business. When it's not there you want it like hell; when it's there, handed to you on a plate, you really don't want it."

The Ibo diet lacked protein and most species of "bush meat" had to be pretty quick on their feet to survive. Two species that not only survived but flourished were the red forest buffalo and the West African leopard; the former largely by its ability to absorb shot after shot from local hunters' dane guns and the latter by sheer cunning and ferocity.

Craddock gave me an early introduction to the West African leopard. His foresters had complained that a leopard was taking their dogs from the vicinity of their houses on the edge of the reserve. The leopard tracks showed that he'd been on several verandas and they feared that he was becoming bold enough to take a child or attack an adult. Craddock had promised his men that he would try to shoot him. He asked me to help. He'd fix everything. All I had to do was turn up with my sixteen bore loaded with SSG shot.

I can't remember how I got out to his house—presumably I biked but I know it was still early, around nine p.m., when we left on foot for the tree he'd prepared. And prepare it he certainly had. He'd had a machan, large enough to seat the two of us, built about fifteen feet up the tree. A goat, bleating pathetically, was tied to a stake some four yards from the foot of the tree and ten yards from the surrounding jungle. Craddock was armed to the teeth—dangerously so, I felt. He carried a fully loaded .45 revolver, a huge electric torch and nursed a rifle. We clambered up to the machan and made ourselves comfortable.

We'd barely ceased talking when there was a sudden and quite unexpected rush of galloping leopard. He fairly thudded out from the wall of the jungle. "Light…light…" yelled Craddock, forgetting it was he who had the torch. My impression as the light went on was of the leopard coming to a fully braked halt, hind feet dug well into the sand in advance of his forefeet. The goat's reactions were probably the quickest of all for he was nowhere to be seen. We later found he'd sprung away from the charging leopard breaking his tether in the process.

The leopard swung round and, looking very dark coloured in the torch light, galloped back the way he had come. "Shoot the bugger…shoot," commanded Randell but didn't get a shot off himself. I fired just as the leopard plunged into the jungle but missed him clean as a whistle—and I knew I'd missed him as I pulled the trigger. I fired the second barrel where he'd disappeared for good luck and to hasten him on his way.

"That's that," said Craddock as we climbed down. But as my feet touched the ground the goat returned, his tether trailing, and rubbed up against my legs. I picked up the cord and led him.

Before leaving the scene we studied the sand for tracks. The leopard must have encircled our tree two or three times before charging.

We all three walked back to Craddock's house, following a narrow path with high elephant grass on each side. "He won't come again tonight," commented Randell, but he'd no sooner made the remark when there was another rush out of the elephant grass just behind me. The leopard was having a second go at the goat; the latter, once again, was too quick for him. He sprang in front of Randell giving my wrist a fierce wrench with the cord. The leopard passed between Randell and me, touching neither, and darted into the elephant grass.

We didn't see him again that night.

The poor chap was later caught in an Ibo trap consisting of a tunnel of stout logs with a goat imprisoned in a secure chamber at the opposite end to the entrance. In the middle of the tunnel a deep pit, lightly covered over with canes and earth, had been dug. The leopard attempting to seize the goat, had fallen into the pit and, despite his frantic efforts, couldn't escape.

Craddock later told me he'd been invited to inspect the imprisoned leopard and had never seen anything so beset with ferocity in his life. The owners of the trap tried at first to spear the leopard to death but he merely tore at the spears with pads and teeth, smashing several. In the end they'd been obliged to kill him with dane guns.

I was glad I'd missed him with the sixteen bore; he had looked so large, black and beautiful. Craddock's account of his end nauseated me and although I wasn't consciously aware of it at the time I plainly made a sub-conscious pact with myself never to kill one. And in doing so—here's a fact for the psychiatrists to chew over—arrived at a state of accord with the species *Panthera pardus*. Somewhat like the same accord, peaceful co-existence...call it what you will that the Masai of East Africa have for the lion.

Touring administrative officers, as I was soon to discover, were often given presents when visiting outlying villages. These varied from chickens to larger gifts such as a young heifer or sun-dried leopard skin. There were various government circulars laying down the value of return presents that officers were required to make. The figure for leopard skins varied from five pounds to seven depending upon the condition of the original gift...in modern values from £120 to £200.

Over the years Kat and I were given many leopard skins. Sadly only one now survives. Eight were spoiled when our heavy loads got wet on the veranda of a Victoria house awaiting shipment from the Cameroons to Aden. Three months later the packing cases eventually caught up with us in Khormaksar, Aden. When we unpacked the box containing the skins all we found was a mess of gluey leopard hair. However, the interesting fact about all the leopard skins that came into our possession, and others whose history I got from the owners, is that the markings reflected the environment from which the leopard had come. High rain forest skins were black and bright—the dark coloured rosettes being blacker, larger and more heavily marked than the skins from more open country. At the same time the high rain forest seemed to ensure that the lighter coloured background was almost pure white. This gave the impression of "brightness" especially when fleetingly viewed in the wild. Skins from open, savannah country were less bright: the rosettes tended to be dark brown rather than black in colour and the light coloured hair between was off-white. Seen in the wild such leopards lacked the seeming brightness of their high forest relatives.

Early in 1940 I was motorcycling from Enugu to Nnewi, where I was then posted, having attended a meeting of the Masonic Lodge in Enugu. I set off around nine p.m. when the lodge meeting had finished. It was raining heavily and the wet laterite presented innumerable traps for the motorcyclist, the worst being stretches where the road gangs had recently laid a four-inch cover of soil and laterite mix. The machine was German made, a BMW if I remember rightly, and had one snag for night travel—the lights only came on fully when the revs were high. Each tumble, and I'm afraid I had several, ended up in complete darkness. I fell off yet again. As I restarted the machine and the lights came on, a leopard sprang out of the ditch and stood tall in the middle of the road, tail swishing, coat wet, barring my way.

The whole journey by then had become something of a struggle. There was no traffic; I hadn't seen another vehicle since leaving Enugu. Early as the hour was by European standards it was long past bedtime by Ibo practice. The frequent falls and my efforts to right the machine had left me pretty tired; I had reached that near-euphoric stage that comes with prolonged effort. I felt as though I was being absorbed into the wet jungle. Mundane hazards such as leopards in the way didn't seem to matter. The leopard was only four or five yards down the road and I thought lazily how beautiful he looked. I revved up the engine and almost to my regret he sprang into the low bush on the far side of the road and was lost to view.

A very slight incident, really. One that made more impression on me occurred in Nnewi. There was a *juju* there, closely associated with the leopard cult. Locals told me that it was often possible to see leopards in broad daylight in the vicinity of the little hill on the summit of which the *juju* house was built. I never saw one myself although I made several trips to the area when reviewing native court land cases concerning claims by the *juju* priest.

One very hot afternoon I was sitting at a small table placed under a vast "bean' tree laboriously taking evidence in one of these cases. Romaine was interpreting and he plainly felt the heat and humidity as much as I did. A fresh witness came forward. "Witness name?" I asked without looking up.

"Nwolo Okafor," he replied.

"Profession?...what does he do?"

"Lycanthropist," replied Romaine. I should like to say that he said "lycanthropist" smugly, pleased with his command of English but it was too hot to remember how he said it.

"Man into wolf?" I queried, still without looking up.

"No, sir. Man into leopard. He says he can change whenever he wants to."

For the first time I looked up at Nwolo Okafor. He was a short fellow, strongly built. I noticed that unlike most Ibos he had whiskers. His were white, sparse and stood out sideways. Then I looked into his eyes. They weren't black, rimmed with a touch of red, as so many Ibo eyes were. They were green, and round, and, as I stared, grew greener and larger. "Profession: man into leopard," I wrote obediently in the court record and there it remains.

Leopard whiskers were held in much of West Africa to be particularly poisonous. If chopped into very short lengths and mixed with a man's food they would surely kill him. Many doctors agreed that this was a distinct possibility since the whisker hair was strong and likely to penetrate the intestine wall causing a fatal ulcer. Just after the war in the Bamenda District, Kat and I, when travelling, came on several parties of hunters who had killed a leopard and were carrying their victim slung from a stout pole. Invariably the head was entirely covered by a cloth. I was told that this was to make sure that no women saw the whiskers. We noticed also that leopard skins cured with the masks never bore the whiskers—they had been safely removed by some male. All this reflects badly on the good ladies but the dowry (bride price) and marriage customs were such that women found it very difficult to get rid of unsatisfactory husbands and poisoning was a feasible means since one of a wife's duties was to prepare food. It was possibly resorted to more frequently than we, with our European upbringing, suspected.

Leopards possess amazing strength even when cubs. This was brought home to us when we spent the Christmas of 1939 in Angus

Robin's house in Enugu. He had acquired a leopard which at that time was little larger than a domestic tabby. I remember five of us trying to dispossess the little fellow of a ball of tightly-rolled socks that he had seized and refused to part with. It took the five of us—one holding him and one to each leg—to force him to deliver.

Kat and I over the years that we were posted to Eastern Nigeria saw quite a lot of leopards, often on the roads at night; we noticed that they demonstrated two distinct paces which we used to refer to as "high walk" and "low walk". The latter was almost a crouch preceding a charge but not quite for the leopard would keep it up for some considerable distance, as though it were a regular travelling pace. The "high walk" was probably a little faster and performed on much straighter legs. Naturally leopards using the "high walk" looked larger than when "low walking". We never arrived at a logical explanation why they selected either gait; perhaps it was related to the profile they felt it necessary to present.

Leopards always loomed large in the Milne family collective mind. From their very young days the kids, Jackie and John, loved travelling in the dark. They'd stand up in the back of the car peering into the night looking for reflection of the headlights in the eyes of creatures on the road side. Serval cats' eyes seemed big but leopards the largest and brightest of all. Goats and sheep differed from each other and both children soon became expert at identifying what the shining orbs portended; but leopards were always the prize sighting.

Some years after the war—it must have been in the mid-fifties, we received a letter from John at his prep school which greatly puzzled us at the time: "Dear Dad, A jolly good show about that leopard. Did you strangle it? Or what? Sorry so short. Love, John." We were in Lagos at the time and couldn't make head or tail of it. We hadn't seen a leopard for months. However, John came out for the holidays shortly after and we asked him about it.

He hesitated for a little while and then told us the story. Apparently he was at war with a junior master one of whose duties was to check the boys' correspondence. John thought this character was too quizzy by far and determined to give him his money's worth. He therefore submitted the letter. He was a little surprised that the master sent it off without comment.

An enigma of much graver import—even giving rise to international reverberations—was the series of leopard killings which took place in Southern Annang, Opobo and Abak Districts of Calabar Province between 1943 and 1948. During this period over 200 persons were killed seemingly by wild leopards. Leopard pug marks were found at the site of killings together with leopard hairs and occasional droppings. The victims were killed by penetrative wounds on the neck, flesh from the head was "scraped" off and many of the victims were dragged or carried some distance from the point where they had been first attacked. All this was characteristic of real leopard killings.

On the other hand there was a great mass of evidence derived largely from the Negro tribes of West Africa, stretching from Sierra Leone to the Belgian Congo, of killings of humans by men in the guise of leopards. In the Southern Annang area the powerful Idiong Society was alleged to promote such murders. Murders disguised as genuine killings by man-eating leopards could, under expert tutelage, easily be simulated.

Over 200 police rank and file under the command of three expatriate senior police officers were posted to the area in 1946. This force was broken down into detachments of four or five men who were accommodated in the villages of the area and spent their time actively collecting evidence on local killings. A number of confessions were obtained together with sufficient evidence in other instances of murder to support proceedings, by the end of December 1947, in 157 cases. Ninety-seven convictions were obtained. Of these seventy-six men were hanged.

The murder cases were tried by the high court sitting in Calabar. The judges sat with assessors but without a jury. A very high level of proof, in accordance with Nigerian law at the time, was demanded.

Up to 1947 the Nigerian police and officers of the administration worked in harmony. It was generally agreed that a possible trigger mechanism precipitating the "pretend" killings might have been the accumulation of native court reviews and appeals which had built up as a consequence of the war-time shortage of administrative staff. Thwarted in their efforts to secure solution of land, dowry, debt and like claims, some litigants had turned to the Idiong *Juju* for help. At the same time it was alleged that Idiong and other cults were using the situation to secure human flesh required for their own purposes. It was also generally agreed that a number of the killings was the work of man-eating leopards.

However, the DO and ADO serving in the Opobo District in the latter half of 1947 concluded that *all* the murders from 1943 to 1947 attributed to humans under guise of leopards were, in fact, true killings by man-eating leopards. They suggested that their views would be substantiated if the killings stopped following a programme to cull all wild leopards within the area.

The killings did stop in December 1947 and on the 13th of that month a leopard was trapped and shot which, having two broken canines and with part of a fore-paw missing, was almost certainly a man-eater. Twenty-eight leopards were killed in the period from November 1946 to March 1948.

Plainly, if all leopards were eliminated from the area, true man-eater killings would stop. However, killings by men under guise of leopards could also stop at any time for a variety of reasons, not least of which might be the removal of the wild leopard population from the vicinity.

The district officer and his assistant referred to above and who formed the opinion that the killings were all true leopard killings advanced a number of strong general arguments in favour of their contention. They did not, however, take any single one of the ninety-seven convictions and demonstrate that it had been based upon flawed evidence. They simply had not the time or facilities to do this. They were fully occupied with the day-to-day duties of their post. The leopard killings represented but one of many urgent matters demanding their attention. The prolonged efforts of Ludovic Kennedy in this country demonstrate how difficult it is to defend instances of alleged injustice and to set the record straight on the falsely accused and wrongly convicted. It was many times more difficult to do the same thing in the 1947 conditions of Nigeria. Now, fifty years after the events took place, it is quite impossible to reconstruct precisely what happened; nearly all the protagonists are dead, the records are widely dispersed or destroyed.

A Nigerian scholar, Dr Nwaka, wrote a paper on the Man-leopard Killings of Southern Annang 1943-48 published in *Africa* in 1986. Considerable research was involved and he reached the conclusion that the killings were substantially due to human agency. The district officer involved commented in the ensuing article and repeated his 1947 contention that the killings were all by real leopards.

At the end of 1947 there were sixteen convicted persons on man-leopard charges awaiting confirmation of their sentences of death. The district officer, Opobo's contentions were not accepted by the Nigerian government of the day but he had said enough to make confirmation of death sentences, passed after December 1947, unsafe. Lord Caradon as he later became (then Mr Hugh Foot) was acting Governor of Nigeria at the time and he reprieved the sixteen men, substituting a sentence of life imprisonment in each case

---

On the day that war was declared—Sunday, 3rd September 1939—most of the expatriate population of Onitsha gathered in the district officer's house. It was conveniently near drinks' time. Dermott O'Connor had not spoken directly to me since my arrival nearly three weeks before. I don't remember being particularly concerned at this as I accepted he was a very senior official and I was that most insignificant of creatures—a cadet administrative officer. However, on this occasion he deigned to ask the district officer, in my hearing, "Which is the remotest part of your District?"

The DO replied, "Anam and Nzam."

"Send young Milne up there," ordered Dermott, adding, "Give him time to think about the war."

The Nigerian Federal Survey Department 1:1,750,000 scale map of the period didn't give a single detail of the Anam and Nzam area other than to indicate the course of the Anambra River itself but I was sure the chief clerk would work out an appropriate itinerary which in due course he did. I suppose that if one treated a young graduate straight from four years at Oxbridge in that way today you wouldn't see him again. But in 1939 our attitudes were different: we were more disciplined, much more accepting and our expectations were considerably lower. Having read several war books, and having had long conversations with my father and Jack about the horrors of the First World War, I accepted the war had been a terrible and demanding experience for Dermott O'Connor himself. His reaction to World War II hardly surprised me, it certainly didn't upset me.

Of all the adverse factors in an African colonial service career—climate, tropical diseases, absence from familiar cultural facilities, distance from family and friends, roughness of living conditions—the long spells I was forced to spend alone on tour, away from my own kind, came to me as the greatest hardship of all. I was away on that tour for about three weeks and I experienced loneliness such as I'd never experienced before. The fact was, of course, that I'd never been so alone in my previous twenty-two years. Even climbing and in the Arctic (where I had taken part in two Cambridge expeditions) there had always been one's immediate companions. There was a friendly relationship, of course, with my African servants and the African officials who made up the party in Anam and Nzam but these were relatively fleeting. I found myself left to my own resources at the end of each working day. Darkness fell some thirty minutes after sunset which varied from 6.15 to 6.45 p.m. as the year progressed.

The long nights trying to sleep in rudimentary rest houses without doors or windows were a particular ordeal. I found that I was afraid of the dark. I did not know what to expect by way of uninvited visitors—thieves or murderers, perhaps. The sound of the distant drumming…of chanting…an occasional howl of terror…all frightened me. I did not know what they portended. And the violent thunderstorms which raged across the forest on several of the nights of that first tour were, quite simply, terrifying.

The rural Ibo at that time exhibited a continuous and pressing inquisitiveness towards the white man. In the remoter areas the district officer, or one of his ADOs, were practically the only white men that the great number of inhabitants had ever seen. There was no TV or radio and communications were little developed. Consequently a visit to the area by one of the fabled Europeans was an occasion of considerable interest. It was incumbent on all and sundry to have a look, to stand and stare. This they did with no sense of embarrassment whatsoever. To have one's every act observed was for those not used to it an ordeal.

But I, I remember, that first tour, was just as curious as the locals. On my evening walks I stopped and gaped and questioned everything that was going on: the contents of stalls in the markets, particularly the purveyors of "native medicines", a wood-carver busy with a dancing mask, a tin-smith making boxes and other objects from old kerosene tins. Not least I took an interest in the "fatting houses" which were then common in the Anam area. I couldn't resist looking on these establishments as a distorted version of the European Finishing School. In Ibo society to be fat was beautiful. To my eyes some of the inmates were grotesquely fat. Although bare of clothes all wore decorative metal rings on legs, arms and neck. So many and heavy were the rings that some of the girls were barely able to waddle. Whether the curriculum included instruction on the more sophisticated aspects of a wife's role I did not enquire but certainly residence in a fatting house increased the dowry that the father was able to demand in much the same way as the acquisition of an expensive education by the daughters of more affluent township houses doubled or even trebled their dowries.[1]

My cook found it difficult to buy meat "suitable" for a European in the markets of Anam and Nzam. Beef and mutton were unobtainable. He once offered me python steak as an alternative to the usual scrawny chicken and I must say I found it perfectly edible—reminiscent of beef tongue. Fish was plentiful but I forbade him to buy any more after one disgusting experience. I found a worm, about two and a half

---

1   See footnote page 74

inches long, curled up in a pocket in the flesh of a portion of boiled fish.

A doctor to whom I later mentioned this experience denied that worms of the nature I have described infected fish from rivers flowing into the Anambra; but it was there all right.

On my return to Onitsha after the Anam and Nzam tour I found a note from Mrs O'Connor asking me to drinks at the residency. Dermott had apparently decided that he might speak to me after all.

The Nigerian military authorities wrote to all the new recruits into government service who had acquired OTC certificates A and B, asking if we wished to be mobilised into the Royal West African Frontier Force. We all—as I later gathered—replied affirmatively. I got busy on the District Office telephone and learnt that we were likely to be called up in the next few weeks and that the government had agreed in principle to release all who were required and to make up the difference between officers' war-time military pay and what they would receive were they still in civilian employment. My letters home, which the Aunts studiously kept, mentioned the early possibility of military service.

Unsure whether we would be faced with law and language examinations before being mobilised I thought it wise to hasten preparations and arranged for the language teacher to increase the hours he came. I also plagued the chief clerk unmercifully with requests for help in the law examinations. He was very patient in producing government circulars bearing on procedures and in explaining matters which I found difficult to grasp. As all this was on top of his routine work I owe him a considerable debt of gratitude.

In the first week of November I was allowed for the first time to hear daily "complaints" and promptly made a mistake which resulted in an inter-village "war".

"Complaints" were a continuation of the indigenous system where men in positions of power—chiefs and others—permitted members of the public to produce their grievances. In colonial days the matters complained about generally concerned native court proceedings, tax, land and family matters. Occasionally there were surprises.

The mistake I mention arose from the two court system. Serious criminal matters which would normally be tried in the high court were investigated and prosecuted by the Nigerian police. The latter were few in number and both district officers and senior police officers worked closely together to ensure that as many cases as possible were dealt with by the native court system. Sometimes the police would seek the DO's advice: "Ought this case to be investigated by us? Or is it a native court matter?"

A single Orlu man, at complaints time, produced a note from the S of P Onitsha asking, "Shall we investigate this complaint?" Apparently a number of Oba men, on the road linking Orlu via Obosi and Oba to Onitsha, had used force to stop a party of strange men approaching Onitsha. When the Obas discovered they were Orlu men, not Obosi as they had thought, they let them go. However, the Orlus were annoyed at being stopped on the main road and wanted the Obas prosecuted.

Bearing in mind the need to protect the Nigerian police as far as possible and only seek their assistance in matters which the native courts couldn't deal with I replied, "No. Let the Orlus sue in the native court." What I had omitted to ask was why the Obas wanted to interfere with Obosi men in the first place. Had I done so I might have learned that an old Oba-Obosi dispute over ownership of a grove of wine palms was once again coming onto the boil and might result in trouble. An experienced administrative officer would have asked this question automatically.

Two mornings later news came in that both villages were at it hammer and tongs. To my fury the DO ordered me to stay in the District Office "to deal with urgent matters" while he, the SASP and an ASP together with six unarmed constables rushed out to the scene in cars. Apparently they found the young men of both villages drawn up in two long lines facing each other. Every now and then groups from the opposing lines would mingle in combat using machetes and dane guns. The six police constables managed to arrest forty-eight combatants from each side whom they marched smartly into Onitsha. There were 120 wounded in all, ten being quite gravely cut up although we later heard that none had died. Oba was deemed to have won the fight because nearly all the Obosi warriors bore machete cuts on their backs.

I was later told that the forty-eight combatants from each side would probably receive a month's imprisonment for their efforts. The old men who had egged them on, on the other hand, would be lucky to escape with less than two months each.

Dermott O'Connor and above him the Chief Commissioner, Eastern Region called for full reports of the incident which the DO duly supplied. I later learned that he had not mentioned my error when hearing complaints, nor had Dermott who was fully aware of it. This forbearance on their part constituted lesson one for me in the subtle mores of the administrative service. They cheerfully bore the implication that they'd been caught out in order to protect me whom they considered had erred from lack of experience only.

It was essential that the service should be seen to speak with one voice...to be completely solid...and this was achieved by rigid observance of a number of unwritten laws. Discipline and loyalty upwards from the most junior recruit to the top were in general absolute and equally loyalty flowed downwards in return. But more of this later. I was to learn a lot about the integrity of my own service as time progressed.

During the second week in November five administrative cadets were sent to Government College, Umuahia (the college was empty of pupils at the time) for a week's special course in Ibo under the tutelage of Miss Ida Ward. I shared a rest house with Reggie Blunt and remember finding him tiresome as he complained loudly about everything in sight. The others, including Ida Ward herself, were accommodated in one of the senior master's bungalows which happened to be vacant at the time. The college was an exceptionally pleasant establishment. It was built round an open grass-covered area which had been converted into a nine hole golf course which in turn encircled some of the games fields.

Ida Ward, although no young sylph, was a most interesting character. At first appearance she came across as a rather short, stout, matronly figure in her late fifties. Ten minutes later even the dumbest of us realised we were in the presence of a splendid original. She lectured at the London School of Oriental Studies on the "Sudanese" group of languages. Her present visit was primarily to acquire information on Ibo and to run two short courses for administrative cadets in that language.

She had no difficulty in immediately recognising the six tone levels of Ibo and in recording Ibo in the form of the shorthand she had developed for other African languages which recorded both pronunciation and tone level. She spent her first morning recording the conversation of two market "mammies"—as we somewhat crudely referred to the good ladies who ran the market stalls. Just before luncheon she read extracts of the market ladies' conversation to the cook and his cook mate in her quarters. Although she couldn't at that stage understand what the ladies had been saying to each other, so good was her ear and shorthand that the cook and his assistant greeted the reading with howls of delighted laughter. The conversation, apparently, had been thoroughly uninhibited.

"Teach as you learn" is far from a bad method and this is precisely what Ida Ward did with us. The only difference, of course, was that at the end of the week Ida Ward had polished a previously acquired working knowledge of Ibo while we, who had struggled for a year at Cambridge and for many hours since arriving in Nigeria, were making but little progress. She comforted me by agreeing that those like myself who were tone deaf probably faced an insurmountable handicap.

The week was nevertheless well spent. Ida Ward's knowledge of the "Sudan" group of languages had given her a deep insight of the anthropological variations between each tribe. Some of this—as much as we were then capable of absorbing—rubbed off onto us.

We were vaguely aware of the phenomenon of "talking drums". It was she who explained matters more thoroughly. Drums can be constructed in several ways so that they are capable of yielding a range of tones when struck. In the hands of a skilled drummer they can reproduce the tonal pattern of any sequence or phrase. The simpler the phrase the more quickly can its meaning be recognised. Sometimes when the message is intended for an esoteric group only the simple phrase is changed into a bit of "in" colloquialism along the lines of cockney rhyming slang before being translated.

On several occasions later in my service, in the Nnewi area in particular, I witnessed messages being sent and received by tonal means. There was one instance when Interpreter Romaine, two or three NA Messengers, a guide and I had walked for two hours through extensive farmland to the site of an inter-quarter land dispute, only to find on arrival that one of the parties had failed to produce an important witness. I was irritated and told them they were wasting our time. "O' no," they said. "We'll call him." A man holding a small elephant tusk came forward. "He'll call the missing witness," Romaine explained. Three or four blasts on the tusk produced a distant reply. "He's coming," said Romaine and sure enough twenty minutes later the missing witness showed up. On the walk back Romaine told me that the first call had been the tonal pattern of the man's name, say Okeke Okafor, with three highs and three descending lows. He'd duly heard the call and replied interrogatively. The second, longer call had been the tonal pattern of "the white man has come"—"onye ocha ona biyo"—in whatever the correct tonal pattern of the eight syllables was. The last short blast was merely an affirmative understood to mean that he was coming. Both men, caller and called, were members of a society part of whose insignia was an elephant "talking" tusk.

Later in the week we begged Ida Ward to tell us what it was that had been so funny in the market mammies' conversation. "Very vulgar," was all she'd say.

I'd been warned before leaving Onitsha that a posting to Nsukka was likely on my return. A telegram from Dermott O'Connor's office received the day we left confirmed this.

Nsukka, where Nnamdi Azikwe was eventually to make his home and where a university bearing his name was to be built, was sited on a small range of hills forty-four miles north of Enugu.

Kendal Robinson, the DO, was on tour when I arrived but he had left a friendly note welcoming me to the station and detailing a number of jobs I might get on with during his absence. One concerned the admission to the Nsukka prison of persons convicted by the native courts. "Don't let them imprison anyone if you think the court proceedings at all fishy," he wrote. "Just list the case for review and let the accused free on bail." I was flattered that he considered me competent for this job which had not been entrusted to me in Onitsha.

I was anxious to meet Kendal Robinson. We had a tie in that his family were Cumbrian and, although eleven years older than I, he'd been to school at St Bees. I'd also heard from both Africans and expatriates that he was considered to be a very good "bush DO". Sadly, he was sent on leave shortly after my arrival and as he toured assiduously when we were both in the District I saw very little of him. I had to wait until just after the war, when we were serving in Enugu, to get to know him better.

His place was taken by a more senior officer whose name I cannot be certain about. Looking at the 1936 staff list I think it might have been Helbert. There is obviously a psychological factor in this lapse of memory for I heartily disliked H (let us call him) from the outset largely because he treated me as the raw recruit I really was. He drastically cut down the responsibility that had been entrusted to me by Kendal Robinson and gave me the impression that I was more nuisance than help to him overall.

H was a short, stout character with firm and pedantic ideas on how everything should be done. I think he was on his last tour of duty before retirement and I can understand that he was anxious to avoid anything that might jeopardise his pension. If he wrote a confidential report on me at that time I don't doubt it was a bad one for he found it necessary to criticise almost everything I attempted and every initiative I showed. His wife loyally supported him and I didn't find her easy either; perhaps I asked for it but I don't remember trying to upset either of them deliberately.

The only comfort I received came from the district clerk who one day vouchsafed the information that Mr H found it harder to keep order in meetings of NAs than I did. "They like to listen to you, sir," he said, "because you first listen to them." Whether he was complimenting me or more likely merely trying to educate me I can't be sure, but nevertheless it's a good tip: let the other side exhaust their argument first. It renders them more likely to accept yours...if only from intellectual fatigue.

H had criticised me for not having studied the district intelligence reports so I borrowed the key of the secret registry where they were filed and set to.

The title "Secret Intelligence Reports" sounds somewhat grandiloquent. Far from being the exciting secret documents that might be thought, they were in fact, a compendium of the history, the social structure and the customary laws of the clans with whom they dealt. They were classified as "Secret" in the district offices of Nigeria largely out of consideration for the feelings of indigenous staff: African society was changing very rapidly and many behaviour patterns of the recent past were outmoded. It was no longer *comme il faut* to mention them.

H was absolutely right in pressing me to read the district intelligence reports. They were an essential working tool of the district administrative staff.

The primary task before us—as my colleagues and I saw it in 1939—was to assist Nigeria eventually to take her full part, as an independent state, in the economic, social and political life of the developed world. We were not then committed to a timetable for independence. Most of my "age-grade" of administrative staff felt that the task would not be completed before our careers had come to a normal end. At the time we saw the means as being through the further development of indirect rule.

Here, though, we were aware of difficulties. In Eastern Nigeria the warrant chief system had failed. Prior to the outbreak of war in 1939 an attempt was being made to introduce a council regime more closely related to the indigenous system, as revealed in the intelligence reports.

Intelligence reports were a relatively recent innovation; they owed their introduction largely to Sir Donald Cameron, Governor of Nigeria from 1931 to 1935. By the time of our arrival in 1939 much of the hard work of holding the initial inquiries, recording the information and checking and counter-checking had been done. Most members of the provincial administration had, at one time or another, turned social anthropologist. Some, by training or intellectual persuasion, were skilled in investigative techniques. Dr M D W Jefferys, for instance, who headed the "long grade" cadre of district officers in the 1936 staff list, then on a salary of £920 p.a., later became a senior member of the University of Witwatersrand Anthropology Department after retirement from Nigeria. When serving as a district officer he had done some outstanding anthropological work in Nigeria and the Cameroons. In fact he returned briefly to Bamenda between 1959-60 as an acting SDO (special duties) in order to deal with arrears of chieftancy cases.

I was fortunate in the Nsukka District for much of the material for the intelligence reports had been gathered in the first instance by a DO named Lloyd who was particularly adept in anthropological studies. His work had later been reviewed by the Government Anthropologist, C K Meek. The latter demonstrated that the Northern Ibos, who inhabited the Nsukka District, were characteristic of the vast Ibo tribe inhabiting Eastern Nigeria from the vicinity of Port Harcourt in the south to borders of Idah and Idoma in the north.

The native authorities were the principal agents of indirect rule. They ran in theory but not in practice such local services as road maintenance, health centres and dispensaries, some schools, occasional water supply schemes, a cadre of NA police (called NA Messengers), maintenance of buildings, clerical and accounting staff, tax collection staff and native courts throughout their area of jurisdiction.

I write "in theory but not in practice" because in much of Eastern Nigeria in 1939 the NAs were virtually run by the DOs and their supporting staff. There had been too little time to effect the change from the indigenous systems of keeping order along with settlement of dowry, debt, inheritance and like disputes to the more westernised system necessary if Nigeria was to take its place in the modern community of nations. Time had been lost in fruitless experimentation with the warrant chief system. The introduction of services such as roads and health required a westernised form of management both in the initial planning and later day-to-day running. This was a new conception in a society used to clubs, title-taking, *juju* and supernatural sanctions in the conduct of affairs. Council meetings tended to be more educative forums than places for the conduct of council business. We did our best but by 1939, at any rate, had made very slow progress.

The native court system, on the other hand, was popular from its introduction in the 1920s. The courts such as we had in 1939 in the Onitsha Province exercised jurisdiction in native law and custom with the proviso that "matters repugnant to natural law and justice" were excluded. The administrative staff were vested with appellate jurisdiction over all proceedings and could act by way of review of appeal on their own volition or on formal review or appeal demanded by one of the parties. There was formal appeal in the first instance to the resident and above him in certain categories of case to the chief commissioner. Land matters, always of high import, in which native courts had unlimited jurisdiction, could be transferred to the Nigerian high court.

Residents of all the Eastern Region Provinces put great stress on administrative officers in all districts keeping pace with appeals and reviews. There were dangers if arrears built up (such as the Calabar Leopard murders referred to earlier). Most district officers took pride in achieving a good appeals rate: on average about half of one per cent of their decisions were set aside on appeal by the resident's or higher court.

In pre-government days secret societies had played a major role in the enforcement of law and order. Fortunately Jeffreys and Meek had both studied the secret societies of the non-Muslim areas of Nigeria as an important factor bearing on the native court system and had concluded that the two systems were not compatible.

Many of these societies depended for their power on the belief that the ancestors continued to play an important role in society after their death. Meek commented: "…by it social continuity is preserved, hereditary rights are respected and conduct is regulated in a variety of ways. The secret societies are still a powerful factor in the maintenance of law and order. They provide also a useful disciplinary training for the younger members of society and for adult males they constitute a strong band of union, besides fulfilling many of the useful purpose of clubs."

Meek then added the warning that had been assimilated by the provincial administration: "…on the other hand they were frequently used for committing brutal judicial murders and many of the societies have for this reason been suppressed by the government. Moreover they were an unfair means of bullying and exploiting women and keeping them in a state of subjection to men. On this account alone Christian Missions are justified in taking a strong hand against these societies, which are fast losing their power as their secrets are being gradually disclosed…"

The Nsukka Intelligence Reports made a big impact upon my education in the indigenous organisation of the Ibo. I began to think in terms of the extended family, the kindred (a group of extended families) and the group of kindreds which made up a Quarter of a village or town. A village itself did not, as in Europe, consist of a group of dwellings geographically close together but rather the general area of land occupied by the kindreds composing the various quarters—"Quarter", of course, in this sense meaning a part of a town or village.

71

Members of an extended family normally lived within calling distance of each other but there were exceptions, some of which were to cause me considerable puzzlement later when dealing with inheritance appeals in the native courts. In pre-government days one or two members of each extended family were required by the village authorities to live on the perimeter of the village land in order to give early warning of attack by neighbouring villages. Their descendants were thus found to be living in proximity to members of an unrelated extended family. Occasionally there were instances where a somewhat eccentric forebear had lived "where he wanted to"—perhaps near a favourite plot of land. The unwritten rule most of us learnt to follow was "whenever possible in matters affecting land inspect the site".

Whether a child cut its lower teeth before its upper was a matter of considerable importance. Should it cut its upper teeth before the lower it was considered not to be a legitimate member of the extended family. In pre-government days such a child was sold into slavery and the proceeds divided amongst the village elders in shares dictated by custom.

Even in government days a matter of this nature might be decided by the village elders in preference to settlement by the native court, the latter route being considered to be more expensive and to take longer. I appreciate that this is in contradiction to my previous statement that the native courts were popular from the outset and the preferred means of dispute settlement. So they were…in overall trend but the process of change in 1939 was slow.

Grave criminal cases, such as the theft of farm produce, if proved in pre-government times, resulted in the accused person being sold into slavery or if this was not feasible put to death by having a wooden peg driven into his head. (This happened illegally to a poor fellow in Nnewi when I was there at the end of the war.)

My reading of the Nsukka Intelligence Reports did much to increase my growing awareness of the deeply-rooted religiousness of the Ibo. Where, amongst the everyday accoutrements of a Northern European's house would it have been possible to find as many religious objects as in the house of an Ibo family head? The latter's house would have been furnished with a bedstead with a fireplace below, a day couch and perhaps a stool. Apart from these mundane objects there would have been a cache of protective "medicines" near the entrance, a shrine for the owners *chi* and a larger shrine for the *chi* of the Creator. Wife, or wives, would each have a separate hut. There would be huts for adult sons, a kitchen and granary and a house for sheep and goats. Backing this group of huts would be an ancestral shrine the back wall of which would be festooned with palm leaves into which would be stuck the feathers of fowls which had been offered as sacrifices to the ancestors.

The head of a kindred was nearly always regarded as the chief priest of that particular kindred. He always carried a hereditary staff known in Nsukka as "Oho". The ancestors were regarded as being ever-present in the Oho. At night the Oho was hung on a special peg in the kindred head's hut.

Cults such as those of the Sun (called "Anyangu" in Nsukka) and the water spirit "Li" were common in the District. These, too, demanded their special shrines. The symbol of the Anyangu cult, for instance, was a three-foot-high pillar where sacrifices were performed in March and July each year. The symbol of Li was a stone taken from a riverbed where the spirit was assumed to take up temporary abode. Here the head of the family would perform sacrifices particularly in the event of illnesses amongst the kindred members.

It would be possible to extend this account of the interplay of the secular and the spiritual almost indefinitely. Perhaps enough has been said to emphasise the intensely deep spiritual beliefs of the Ibo—his life at every turn being bound up with the spiritual world and every object in the natural world having its spiritual connection.

The Christian missions were very strong in Eastern Nigeria in 1939. They did magnificent work, particularly in the field of health and education in addition to their purely evangelical teachings. Over the years Kat and I made many contacts and a number of admiring friendships with members of Catholic, Anglican and other denomination missions. I had many and frequent official relationships with Missions throughout my service; looking back, though, I felt that Roman Catholic priests serving in the bush were best able to appreciate the dichotomy of the Ibo mind and the degree to which, in spite of church affiliations, the Ibo still clung to basic animistic practices.

The Nsukka Intelligence Reports, as elucidated and expanded by Meek, early brought one lesson home to me: it was invariably unwise to accept too readily any single rule of native law. The exceptions were myriad and must always, when disputes arose, be eliminated before considering a finding based on a general rule. The inheritance of widows provided an example. In general, primogeniture is the rule—if the eldest son is too young at the time of the father's death to inherit, the eldest brother of the deceased will inherit everything including widow(s) and property. Farm land and trees will eventually revert to the deceased's eldest son but the widow will remain the property of the deceased's brother. If the widow wishes to remarry outside the family the inheritor is entitled to demand the bride price.

I was intrigued to read of the freedom of pre-marriage sexual relations permitted by Ibo custom. There seemed to be no stigma to a young girl having sexual relations before the age of puberty not only with her intended husband but with one or two paramours in addition. Some paramours might establish a semi-formal acceptance of their role by giving the girl's mother an appropriate gift. In contrast to this it was considered a grave offence for a married woman to grant favours to any man not her husband. It was held that the husband's rights were being trespassed upon and at the same time the Earth Deity was being insulted and angered.

The intelligence reports held that three types of marriage were recognised in Nsukka in the 1930s: bride price, agriculture service and, thirdly, marriage by exchange.

Bride price (dowry)[2] was by far the most common form. It was a universal mode of contracting marriage throughout Iboland. Generally the agreed bride price would be paid in instalments by the suitor to the girl's parents. The girl would move into the bridegroom's house after reaching the age of puberty and on final payment of the bride price. In rural areas the bride price was a fixed amount but in more sophisticated areas, such as the larger townships, the girl might be the daughter of wealthy parents who had sent her away to a boarding school and in such a case the cost of education might be included in the bride price. In late 1939 I heard of instances in Onitsha where as much as £300 had been agreed between the suitor and the girl's parents. This was a considerable sum...in today's values exceeding £8,000. In rural areas attendance at a "fatting house" sometimes increased the girl's bride price.

Agriculture service and marriage exchange, although mentioned in the Reports, were uncommon. I can't remember dealing with a dispute involving either type.

Writing of Ibo marriage customs of fifty-seven years ago gives rise to two thoughts: time has proved that the colonial power ("we", that is) were wise to interfere as little as we did with Ibo practices and secondly, where are we going ourselves in this country today?

Titles, clubs and age-grades were all important elements in 1939 Ibo society appropriately mentioned in the intelligence reports. In

---

2   I am afraid that in those days members of the provincial administration talked loosely of "bride price" and "dowry", as being synonymous instead, as modern anthropologists would put it, of "dowry" coming with the bride and "bride-price" being paid by the husband or his family.

general titles were obtained by the giving of presents to the existing holders of the title and by sacrifice of a horse, cow, sheep or chicken part of the meat being eaten by the public at large and part by the inner circle of title holders. Certain, minor titles, were restricted to the holder's own kindred. Few titles were hereditary.

In most of the Nsukka District the highest title in a village bore the honorific "Eze". Sometimes the elders were strong enough to remove the powers of Ezeship from a holder who was held to be too autocratic or otherwise unfitted to wield the powers and duties going with the rank. I am reminded here of Elizabeth the First who is reputed to have threatened a Bishop who offended her: "My Lord Bishop, remember what you were before I made you what you are or I will defrock you, by God."

Killing of an enemy or slave (Ogbu Madu), cow killer (Ogbu Efi) and Ogbu Anye (killer of a horse) were all recognised titles in the Nsukka District. The first, of course, was outlawed by the administration in the early days of pacification but the remainder persisted until well after the end of the Second World War. Ogbu Anye was particularly repugnant because it involved great cruelty to the horses involved. Bar-el-Ghazal, Bornu or Kano ponies—many old or damaged in some way—would be bought cheaply in the tsetse-free areas of Northern Nigeria and driven down as fast as possible (before they died of trypanosomiasis contacted on the way) to the Nsukka District where they attracted a high price for horse sacrifices. During the title ceremonies they were either clubbed to death by hordes of excited young men or strung up by a rope round the neck over a stout branch and killed by a mixture of blows and slow strangulation.

Moved partly by my fury with H, who refused even to discuss the subject of horse sacrifices, and partly by horror at the cruelty involved, I went to some pains to record what went on. The Nsukka District staff passed word around and aspirant horse title takers were flattered that a European ADO was interested. I received several invitations to be present at horse-title ceremonies. In a few weeks I had accumulated enough matter—notes and photographs—to write a *Wide World*-type article. This I did and sold it to an American magazine.

Apparently the article, which was as unemotional and as factual as I could make it, produced quite a furore in the States.

In due course I received, via the British Embassy in Washington, the Colonial Office and the Nigerian government, a reprimand for publishing the article without permission. By the time the rocket reached me the wording had plainly been moderated by a succession of kindly officials and I was able to feel that if I had done wrong it wasn't a very wrong wrong.

Clubs—using the term in its strictly anthropological sense—were a much broader institution than groups of title holders. At one extreme they could be no more than gatherings of men or women who joined together at regular intervals to enjoy a feast provided in turn by the members. One of the objects of other clubs was to join together for co-operative farm work. The initial clearing of virgin bush, for instance, was a task beyond the capacity of a single natural family and co-operation was essential. Occasionally the members of a club would assist in the resolution of a dispute concerning a run-away wife. They would investigate the matter and decide who was at fault. If the husband he would be ordered to give his wife a suitable gift. If the wife was found to be at fault she would be advised by members to mend her ways. Another purpose of clubs was as a method of collecting capital for a large undertaking.

Membership of a club was always voluntary. A man's or woman's position in an age grade, on the other hand, was a question of fact. Age grades would normally be formed from members of the same sex born within three years of each other. They often remained unorganised until the fifteen to eighteen year-old level was reached whereupon they would assume a name and appoint some senior person in the community as the grade's captain or father. Meek, in a set of notes on Nsukka published in 1931 by the government printer in Lagos, mentions several examples of names which reveal attitudes at the time; "Egbara" meaning a prickly seed, being one. The name suggests that if anybody is in conflict with the age grade members he will get scratched for his pains. Another is "ola" which means brass. The suggestion here being that the members of the age grade are fine looking young men (and, if one considers it, shining brass is indeed truly redolent of Negro skin in the bright sun).

———————

Although the Hs—man and wife—were the only other Europeans for forty miles I saw little of them. They travelled extensively, using up the District's travel allowance provision. Was it, I wondered, a dutiful desire to keep pace with the outstanding court and council business in the District? Or was it, perhaps, the attraction of the travelling allowance itself? I could understand the latter—it was possible to live on it. Anyway, I was left to my own devices. Every now and then files would be brought in from the bush some containing instructions from

H for jobs that he felt I might tackle. By and large I was left with studying the intelligence reports and hearing complaints. The latter on a busy day took me a couple of hours to dispose of.

I remember one middle-aged man shuffling into the office bearing a sort of sling over his neck and one shoulder and using a staff to help him to move "What can I do for you?" I asked him through Esemaia, the interpreter. In reply he bared his midriff. I discovered that the sling supported his scrotum which was swollen to the size of a soccer ball. Esemaia explained that the condition was common in the District and was caused by elephantiasis. The CMS hospital in Enugu, he said, would operate, removing the excess material surgically, provided the patient would contribute two pounds ten shillings towards the cost. This was explained to the complainant who turned away disappointed saying he could not raise two pounds ten shillings. I happened to have three pounds in my pocket (nearly a hundred pounds in today's values) and said to the man, "I'll lend you this provided you agree to pay me back before I'm mobilised into the army." The chap thought about it for an appreciable time and then said, "Yes."

After he'd gone Esemaia said, "That was a lot of money to *give* him"—he emphasised the "give".

But no. Before I left Nsukka the same chap strode into my office, this time with no stick or sling. He put several strings of one penny pieces on my desk (both penny and half-penny pieces had holes in the centre and could be tied in strings) and said the operation had been successful in every way. Isaac Mba counted the penny pieces and reported there were 720 there.

During my non-office hours I read voraciously, averaging about four hours a day, and in the evenings either went for a walk with a gun after francolin partridge or practised tennis. The tennis court was an excellent one—the surface being a murram/anthill mixture—but there was no one to play until I discovered that there was a warder in the Nsukka Prison, one Odong Wudu, who was really quite a good player. He had a fast natural service but chopped all his ground strokes. On the Nsukka court his chopped returns would sit up awkwardly but they always came back and he could place them to within a foot or two of where he wanted. I'm afraid that he received far more invitations to play than he really desired—doubtless he had far better things to do in his time off than exhaust himself on the tennis court with the ADO— and I noticed that he soon got into the habit of rationing me to some three sessions a week. H got to hear about our playing and objected. "You mustn't invite the junior service to use the tennis court," he wrote. "They'll take it as their right and we will never get a game when we want to." As the Hs never went near the court when they were in the station I thought his note somewhat superfluous.

Warder Odong Wudu and I had used prisoners as ball boys and this gave me the idea of seeking volunteers from the station gang. Their normal role was to cut the grass throughout the station and generally keep the place tidy. The chief warder didn't object and I was never short of a couple of volunteers on the tennis court on days when Odong didn't want to play. The volunteer's task was to throw balls at a handkerchief placed on the court to enable me to practise my ground strokes or, for volley practice, to try and throw a ball past me at the net. I worked out a system of cash rewards. I can't remember what sort of income the volunteers earned but I do know that I was never short of chaps wanting the job.

After the war Stan King told me he did the same thing when practising his bowling at Ahoada. He was a very good medium pace off-spin bowler. Jim Smith, who ran the renowned "Outsiders", counted on him in each of the three or four matches a year that the Outsiders played. Stan never played any proper cricket at all in the remoteness of Ahoada. However, he studiously practised his bowling for a month before each Outsiders' match in a net he arranged on the tennis court. It wasn't enough to bowl at a bare wicket so, possibly remembering what I'd done at Nsukka, he called for prisoner volunteers. A brave fellow offered his services and Stan lent him a pair of army boots to protect his bare toes, padded and gloved him up, and stood him in front of the stumps armed with half a broomstick in lieu of a bat. I don't know how much Stan was exaggerating but he told us in Enugu that this fellow turned out to be a natural cricketer: he watched the ball like a lynx, taught himself the advantages of a straight as opposed to a cross bat, and when he was discharged Stan's bowling suffered considerably.

Punishment for native law and custom offences in pre-government days had tended to be quick, drastic and often terminal. Punishment by means of deprival of liberty for relatively short periods accompanied by regular and sufficient food and mildly exacting labour demands, as introduced by the colonial government, was a new and not at all alarming conception. The Nigerian prisons, throughout my service, were very well run. Discipline amongst the staff was good and the atmosphere I can best describe as light—the opposite of heavy and oppressive. In the late 1940s, in the Bamenda District, our two children spent many hours talking to prisoners working in the station. They heard a lot that I certainly would not have been able to dig out for myself even if I had had the time.

Prisoners in outside working gangs were never shackled as they still were in the Belgian Congo, for instance. There is the much-repeated story of the warder escorting his gang of prisoners back to a district prison, calling out to a slow moving prisoner at the back, "Hurry or we'll leff you." Apocryphal, maybe, but carrying the ring of truth, nevertheless.

Late in the war, when administrative staff were becoming very thin on the ground, Dermott O'Connor, Resident still of Onitsha Province, appointed himself acting DO, Awgu and acting DO, Awka Districts. As acting DO, Awgu, he arranged for the transfer of a prisoner from Awgu to Awka. He gave the escorting warder sufficient funds for the two men's lorry fares and instructed him to report with his charge to the acting DO, Awka.

Three days later Dermott was sitting at the DO's desk in Awka dealing with arrears of paper work. In marched the prisoner, saluted smartly and said, "Prisoner No 1234, reporting from Awgu, sir."

"Where's the warder?" asked Dermott.

"He made me walk, sir. He's behind, seeing some friends."

"Sit down," said Dermott. "Make yourself comfortable."

Later that day the warder turned up. Dermott is reported to have ordered "change uniforms".

The war was far away from Nsukka at the end of 1939 and during the first two months of 1940. My short wave radio depended on batteries which soon became exhausted or it developed intermittent faults. I continued to see little of H and Mrs H who had a better radio than mine—and had to rely on back copies of the weekly *Times*, some many weeks out of date, and several-day-old copies of the Nigerian press for news. This situation contrasts vividly with the position almost throughout the world today when even the meanest household can receive by means of TV teletext or reliable radio up-to-the-minute reports. Inspiring war-time events, such as the rescue by HMS *Cossack* of 299 British merchant navy personnel from the *Altmark*, had receded into the distant past when I heard about them.

I had the telephone number of the officer in Military Headquarters, Lagos who dealt with mobilisation. Whenever I could persuade the telephone operator in Nsukka—and operators onwards down the line— to assist I would ask to be put through to him for a check of the position of my colleagues and myself on the mobilisation list. Sometimes I was assured that my group of cadets were to be called up "within a week or two". On other occasions the "week or two" became "five or six". It seemed that there was postponement after postponement, all at the behest of the government of Nigeria. The government were plainly resisting losing officers from the administration and the manpower situation was becoming increasingly grave as time went on.

I gathered that none of my colleagues had let up on preparations for the law and language exams and it was as well they hadn't for we were all still in post when the date for the examinations in March arrived.

The administrative service cadets posted to the Ogoja, Onitsha and Owerri Provinces, due to take the examinations, gathered in Onitsha on the previous day. We wrote the Ibo papers in premises belonging to the Church Missionary Society under the supervision of a good missionary canon. So transparent was his own honesty and so obviously did he believe in ours that he left us entirely unsupervised for long periods. In the Unseen Translation paper one of our number said, "...this is a damn long paper. Blunt, you do the first paragraph, Robin the second and third and Milne the fourth..." dividing it up amongst us.

Some weeks later, after we'd all heard that we'd passed, Angus Robin and I met the good canon at a function in Onitsha. Commenting on our performance in the exam he said, "You all did very well, really; except possibly for the unseen translation. There you all...I can't think why...made the same very odd mistake in the fourth paragraph."

The preparation of leave rosters and consequent inter-divisional postings was in peace-time a leisurely and well ordered process in spite of the considerable leave entitlement of a week's leave for each month served plus fourteen days each way travelling time. Officers knew many months in advance what Elder Dempster Lines ship they could expect to go on leave by and the more senior were made aware of their probable posting on return from leave. Those of us who had come out in July 1939 could, in normal circumstances, expect leave at the end of 1940. By March or April we would have had a fair idea of the ship and date of sailing. However, matters were very different in the early months of 1940. The war had already disrupted the normal pattern of events: ships were lost at sea, sailing dates were kept secret. Decisions to send X or Y on leave were sometimes made on as little as an hour's notice. Officers turned up in Lagos quite unexpectedly. Consequently postings became more and more unexpected and notice shorter and shorter.

I had no sooner returned to Nsukka after the law and language examinations, and my life there of inferior status under the unenthusiastic control of H, than I received orders from Dermott O'Connor to return to Onitsha and take over the District as acting DO until the return from leave of Peter Riley.

This was one in the eye for friend H—and indeed for Mrs H who gave me the impression that she shared her husband's poor opinion of my usefulness. They were on tour when the instructions arrived and as I left the next morning at dawn we were spared any sort of farewell. In fact, I never saw the Hs again as they retired shortly afterwards.

Peter Riley was a man of considerable reputation and it behoved me to leave the office in immaculate condition for his arrival. He was nineteen years my senior and at the time near the top of the list of senior district officers (he was to be promoted Resident, Ogoja Province twelve months later). He'd served through much of the 1914-1918 War in France with the Irish Guards and belonged to that special band of officers—of whom Dermott O'Connor was one—who had suffered the truly awful experience of trench warfare.

Very little memory remains of the month, two months, I had held the fort for Peter Riley. I had no illusions that I was anything more than a purely temporary *locum-tenens*. Jack, bless him, in a letter written on 22nd April commented, "Sorry to hear that your period in charge is not likely to be very long, but I hope it will turn out longer than you think. Congratulations in any case. They would not make anyone with so short a service acting DO unless your work and ability had impressed favourably."

Jack's words comforted but did not convince me. I felt that Dermott, who knew the Province backwards, was keeping a very close eye on my doings although he did not interfere. Rather than being a reward for work done, my posting was an expedient forced on him by the vagaries of the time.

Just about this time Peter Trevorrow, an ADO posted to the Onitsha Province, was sent at short notice on his first home leave since he had come out with the 1938 batch of administrative cadets. He was puzzled what to do with a very pleasing Ford two-seater which he possessed. Deciding that it would be better used than stored, possibly for an indefinite period, he asked me if I'd take it on. Of course I gladly accepted and took over his mongrel bitch at the same time. She was a wild and nervous but clever dog and I became quite fond of her.

I did my best to dispose of a rapidly mounting list of native court reviews and appeals. Thanks to the loan of Peter Trevorrow's car it was possible to make day trips to several of the outlying Onitsha District courts. I generally took Eronini, the senior interpreter in the

District Office, but occasionally J R Romaine, who was then number two, with me. Both were very good. They were expert at assessing the facts at issue, in separating largely frivolous or malicious causes from those of true complexity under native law and custom. Whenever I felt confident—with Eronini's or Romaine's support—to give a decision I did so. Any matters which I couldn't understand or which affected land I put back on one pretext or another: further evidence to be produced...the native court to rule on this or that side issue...I considered that Peter Riley with his far greater experience would bring the matter to an acceptable conclusion in a trice while I might only delay matters by a decision that might be appealed against. Criminal matters were simpler. It was often only a matter of checking that the native court had not exceeded their powers or given a judgement "repugnant to natural law and justice". Questions of fact could be left, in most instances, to the native court.

The other main task in preparation for Peter Riley's arrival was to go through previous handing-over notes and bring each item up to date.

When Peter R did arrive he was accompanied by his wife, Maureen. They were exactly the couple that the descriptions of other officers had led me to expect. He was in his mid-forties, dark, with a clipped moustache, incisive in speech and manner and near-perfect manners. Maureen was three or four years younger and a truly beautiful woman. I carry to this day a stolen glimpse of her at some bush rest house. It was already dark outside. She was sitting in a white silk dressing gown before a little travelling mirror putting on her makeup. An Aladdin lamp, placed near the mirror, produced a white circle against the white-washed walls. Her dark hair and serious expression enframed by the varied play of whites formed a Whistler composition all my own. I remember a little thrill of pride that she should beautify herself in defiance of the heat and insects and loneliness of life in the bush of Southern Nigeria.

It was important that we all dressed for dinner in those days, even in the far bush. It was an affirmation of our confidence in ourselves. The Nigerian, from house boy to established lawyer or politician, understood. I never once heard the custom derided.

Peter Riley was very much his own man. His was not a personality others lightly trespassed upon. Nor would he let the rest of us get away with inanities. Kat and I recollect a large dinner party at Government House, Enugu, just after the war. In spite of the numerous guests, conversation was at first politely general. Later some character proud of his hunting exploits began to bore one end of the table with a long-drawn-out account of how he had recently slaughtered a red forest buffalo: "...I got down wind of him...I crept to the mound...I reached the bush..." and then, heard by the whole table, he asked, "And do you know what I did next?"

"No. What?" said Peter Riley in sarcastic tones from the far end of the table. "Milked it?"

Riley hadn't been in Onitsha for thirty-six hours when he sent for me and said, "I hope you don't mind but I've had a word with Dermott O'Connor and we want you to go out to Nnewi and take the place over entirely. Normally you are supposed to correspond with the resident through me but please don't. Treat it as a separate District and deal direct with the resident. As you know in peace-time this place is supposed to have three ADOs but I've got nobody other than B G Smith as local authority and that's a full-time job on its own. So you'll just have to sink or swim in Nnewi. Of course, if there's a real difficulty and you feel you must have my help...OK...I'll leave it to you."

I was, of course, delighted: this was an enormous advance on H's attitude to me in Nsukka. Peter Riley agreed I could take Romaine as interpreter.

The conception of sub-districts, of which Nnewi was one, had arisen largely as an expedient in the 1930s. The establishment of the provincial administration (that is Residents, SDOs, DOs and ADOs) had been based on the 1931 census as modified by considerations of native authority efficiency, distances and travelling time involved and general workload. The workload, particularly in Iboland, had increased at a greater than anticipated rate and it was found convenient to post ADOs out to a number of sub-districts on a permanent basis rather than service the area by visits from District headquarters. ADOs posted to sub-districts in this way lived in houses built from the temporary buildings' vote and they were supported by a mixture of NA staff and such District HQ government staff as could be spared.

In the Onitsha Province there were three sub-districts: Agbani in Udi District, Nnewi in Onitsha District and one in Awka District. Peter Gunning's name was synonymous with Nnewi: he had spent seven of the preceding nine years there. He had large and easy-to-read handwriting and many of his judgements in native court land cases were masterly. Being accepted by both sides in long-standing disputes they undoubtedly saved several inter-village "wars"—fighting being the usual means of expressing dissatisfaction and frustration. Land was of fundamental importance to the Nnewi Ibo as indeed it was throughout the whole of the forest belt of Southern Nigeria. The provincial administration had come to recognise land policy and land legislation as basic to good administration in the "bush" districts.

There were, of course, many devices that the practised "bush" DO came to use when trying to unravel land disputes no matter whether they were small inter-family matters or large inter-clan disputes. Such included the age of boundary trees and the evidence of older members of the community who could remember their being planted; the location of the compounds of previous family and quarter heads; the position of family "ofor" sticks; the general pattern of expansion in virgin forest over the past fifty or one hundred years; the "ownership" of trees in the high forest...all these matters would prove of assistance to the experienced DO.

In several of my letters home in the early months of 1940 I mentioned staying in Enugu with Peter Gunning and unashamedly using his knowledge of Nnewi affairs. The custom of asking oneself to stay was firmly established in Nigeria. Even junior officers had plenty of servants who welcomed visitors both as a test of their mettle and, doubtless for the tips involved. Hosts were straightforward in saying..."Come but you won't see much of me. I'm doing...this or that...". Peter G, although eight years older than I, put up with my visits for two reasons: he liked to have first-hand news of Nnewi affairs, particularly of progress in land matters with which he'd been involved and because he welcomed a squash opponent. He found it difficult to find anybody willing to take him on in Enugu. Although he was a better player than I, I was determined to beat him and he relished the challenge. Squash courts, incidentally, marked the travels of Edward, Prince of Wales, round the pre-war Indian and colonial empire, many having been built in anticipation of his journeyings in the 1920s and early 1930s. Peter and I had one further matter in common: he had served four years in his university air squadron, held a reserve commission in the RAF and, like me, couldn't understand why he had not yet been called up. We swapped ideas for hurrying matters along.

It turned out that Peter's war wasn't quite as he had intended. Had it been, however, he might well have lost his life and the administration of Nigeria lost one of its most talented officers. He was a natural teacher and as soon as he was mobilised later in 1940 he found himself instructing at a Flying Training School. He was kept at this task for nearly four years of war in spite of pulling every string available to get himself transferred to combat flying. The more time that went by the more difficult he found it to secure the transfer he wanted.

The very first morning that I took charge of Nnewi there were a number of pressing problems. The previous night there had been a fierce tornado—a tropical circular storm—and a large tree which had been blown down from a *juju* bush alongside the main Onitsha-Owerri road was holding up a queue of twenty or so lorries. The local road gang, being inhabitants of the area, wouldn't cut it up. They were afraid to meddle with what the *juju* and spirits of the "bush" had done. So I sent for the NA lorry and instructed the driver to take the station gang to the site. Not being inhabitants of the quarter affected they were prepared to ignore the powers of the *juju*. But the driver, who did come from the affected area, begged me not to make him go. He was convinced, he affirmed, that the spirits of the "bush" would "get him for it". Romaine seemed to think his pleas were genuine so to save time, and cut the cackle, I said, "OK, OK. I'll drive the lorry."

It was a huge tree so I left the Nnewi gang to get on with it, telling them I'd return in the afternoon to pick them up. No sooner had I got back and called for the NA chief clerk to put me straight on a number of queries than Romaine came in. He said he hadn't wanted to bother me earlier but the tornado the previous evening had severely damaged his house. H O Nwosu, the chief clerk, Romaine and I inspected the damage. It would cost all of thirty pounds to repair. Nwosu pointed out that the temporary buildings' vote was only seventy pounds and this had to last another eleven months. Unlike common practice in United Kingdom government circles today, nobody ever overspent votes in Nigeria in those days. To do so would automatically result in the officer responsible being surcharged. However, Romaine was an essential member of the staff. He was a government, as opposed to an NA, officer; he and his family had to be properly housed. We'd find means of not overspending our allocation later. I arranged for him to occupy the senior service rest house for three nights while urgent repairs were carried out on his own house. Even to let a junior service officer occupy a senior service rest house was a risk in those days but I kept my fingers crossed that my superiors wouldn't find out.

I picked up the Nnewi gang as arranged and found them all in very jolly mood, laughing and singing happily. I learned later that they'd sold the timber from the fallen tree to the owner of a passing lorry who, being a stranger didn't set great store on the tree's magical origin. Plainly the proceeds of the sale had been converted into palm wine, fortuitously if not magically.

At this time I still possessed a small menagerie; the little Blue Duiker who'd spend the day in some near-by patch of forest but would show up around six p.m. most evenings and fill up her tummy until it was round and tight like a little blue drum with the milk that Isaac Mba always had ready for her; Trevorrow's bitch whose recent travels had calmed her down a little, and a grey parrot. The latter had a short but very pungent vocabulary. Sadly he could not be persuaded to speak on request and invariably reserved his foulest expressions for the wrong company.

The bitch would accompany me on land cases. I noticed that after a long walk in the hot sun one or other of the parties used to offer her a calabash of water. This, I fear, was recognised to be one way to the judge's heart. I wondered who'd put them up to it in the first instance.

The custom of buying *jujus* to assist or protect some activity was a common one amongst the Ibos. Crude phylacteries, intended to achieve a wide variety of effects beneficial to the purchaser, were available in the Onitsha market. I have a memory—it must have been post-war—of the host of Julian Huxley (who was on an UNESCO visit to Onitsha) telling us that his distinguished visitor had spent the whole of one morning amongst the *juju* stalls in the market using his extensive biological skills to identify the contents of a number of *jujus*...a shrew's skull wrapped in a lizard's skin, a snake's fangs penetrating the cast of a bird of prey, a mysterious collection of small bones wrapped up in a large leaf...all had come to light. Apparently Professor Sir Julian Huxley had been immensely intrigued and pleased that he had been able to identify the contents of most of the packages.

The Nnewis placed great credence in the power and effectiveness of such objects. My position naturally required me to show nothing but disdain but I can't say that I'm not superstitious—for instance, I hate—even to this day—seeing the new moon through glass.

An incident drawing together Trevorrow's bitch and phylacteries occurred soon after my arrival in Nnewi. An order arrived signed by Dermott O'Connor requiring me to destroy six houses. The circumstances were as follows: two adjacent villages, let us call them A and B, rightly foreseeing that as their populations increased they would require more "large" farm land went to court each claiming sole rights to a hefty area of "new" (previous unfarmed) land. "Large" farm land was farmed communally by the village as a whole; "small" farmland or "compound" farms were immediately adjacent to the scattered village houses and farmed by members of the natural family. The native court judgement, confirmed on appeal by Peter Gunning, and subsequently on further appeal by the resident, had demarcated areas of potential "large farm land" for each village. The demarcation was related to the size and probable future needs of each. It was logical and a fair assessment. But village A was greedy. The grass is always greener yonder than the grass at one's feet. They disliked being confined to the area earmarked for their future expansion. They devised what they hoped was a clever ploy: they persuaded one of their more adventurous family heads to leapfrog over virgin forest and establish a new settlement in the area reserved for village B's ultimate expansion. They built six new houses and planted yams round them in the manner usually reserved for compound farms. Representatives of village B complained. Dermott O'Connor ruled it was a defiance of his judgement and ordered the demolition of the houses. It fell to me to supervise the demolition.

The native administration court messengers of the area were reluctant to be involved, some claiming to be related to the family whose houses were to be destroyed. Both Romaine and Nwosu thought their attitude was understandable and advised me not to force them to come along. Consequently we were a small party as we walked into the area in the early morning...Romaine, two Nigerian police constables from the Nnewi contingent, and my orderly. And, of course, Trevorrow's bitch who led the way.

As we approached the site of the six new houses the path became narrower and less well-defined and we encountered a veritable swarm of *jujus*. Some were suspended from lianas across the path, others attached to overhanging branches, others again on the ground. At one turn of the path we found a row of pointed laths of wood. "Be careful," said Romaine; "they are not above poisoning the tips."

When we reached the site of the houses there was nobody to be seen; the two Nigerian policemen and my orderly were silent, not a little disturbed by the sea of phylacteries and *jujus* through which we had come.

I lit each roof—nine inches thick thatch grass—and soon all six houses were aflame. Nnewi Ibo dwellings were well constructed. They normally consisted of a single room provided with a door and a small shutter-covered window with thick mud-block walls rising to a massive sloping roof. The inner surfaces of the walls were plastered with a mixture of mud, a little palm oil and cow manure which dried into a hard glistening surface. The doors and windows of many houses were elaborately carved in the Awka manner. The single room contained day and night beds and had small areas set aside for the owners' *Chi*, and possibly other shrines.

The outer walls of Nnewi compounds, generally surrounding two or three huts, were only some four feet in height but they were rendered if not thief-proof at least thoroughly thief-deterrent by dead oil palm fronds. These fronds were laid loosely along the wall tops to a depth of two or three feet. They were prickly; any thief trying to climb the wall could count on pulling a mass of fronds after him with a resounding clatter as well as suffering considerable discomfort.

As soon as the last of the burning thatched roofs had fallen in we set off homewards. Maybe we'd gone a mile and a half when suddenly I had an alarming thought: suppose some old person had been left in one of the huts? I hadn't inspected the interiors of each before setting the thatch alight. There'd be a report to the resident and sure enough a blackened corpse would be found. I kept the thought to myself for another mile or so. How could I have been such a fool? The answer, I suppose, was that I wanted to get the job done and be off. The new houses were really very well built and it had seemed a shame to destroy them. The *jujus*, too, had been upsetting. I was the only person involved who didn't believe in the effectiveness of the damn things…or did I perhaps harbour in the depths of my mind a certain uncertainty?

I lagged behind with Romaine. Out of earshot of the other three I put my worry to him. He blanched (a blackman can surely blanche, believe me). "Ought I to go back?" I asked him.

Just then Trevorrow's bitch came up the path and rejoined us. Romaine paused for a moment and then smiled. "The dog showed nothing," he said. The bitch had, I remembered, cursorily inspected all the houses going through her usual smell-investigation routine and he was right. Had there been a person or even a corpse in any of those houses she'd have indicated the fact.

"You ought to be hunting a pack of foxhounds in the shires," said I to him. "You really know your houndwork."

Maybe he hadn't much idea what I was talking about but his mind was at ease and so was mine.

I realise with hindsight that in 1940 I didn't appreciate the importance to the war effort of Nigerian palm oil and groundnuts exports. The fact was that both were badly needed in the United Kingdom for foodstuffs and for the manufacture of explosives. Their assured supply turned not only on the avoidance of losses at sea but also on the continuation of a high level of administration in Nigeria. As our training progressed we were increasingly important to the latter.

There was a two-way pull on my age-grade. On the one hand we were becoming more committed to the administrative service. I see that as late as May 1940 I wrote to my father saying, "If only the climate didn't make one feel so enervated this would be an ideal job." On the other hand the reverses in Norway and the invasion by the Germans of Belgium, Holland and Luxembourg on 10th May—and, on the same day, the replacement of Chamberlain by Churchill—made us desperate to be in the forces. "Why won't they mobilise us?" we asked, time and again.

And in my own case there were two personal fears pulling in opposite directions. One was the element of loneliness and the other the horrors of trench warfare. I have said before—and I make no excuse for repeating it—that Jack's quiet and factual accounts of George's— and others'—sufferings in the trenches in 1914-18 absolutely appalled me as a child. Books that I'd read merely confirmed what he, certainly not designedly, had conveyed. On the other hand, since arriving in Nigeria I had been quite shocked by the loneliness in the life of a bush ADO To be deprived of the companionship of one's own kind, of one's contemporaries for days, even weeks at a time was a strain the otherwise excellent colonial administration service course at Cambridge had not prepared me for. Or if the warning had been there I'd missed it. Joining the forces would put an end to loneliness of this magnitude and I must confess that this thought did influence me.

May went and on 22nd June came the news of the armistice between Germany and France. This was too much. I wrote—and I know now that several of my contemporaries did the same—a formal letter of resignation from the service requesting the Nigerian government to release me and permit my return to the United Kingdom for war service.

Normal practice required me to address a letter for the chief secretary "through" the resident, Onitsha and this I did. Dermott O'Connor, as soon as he received my resignation letter, sent a messenger on a bicycle out to Nnewi summoning me to see him the following morning.

When I reported he was much gentler than usual. "I do know a little of this problem," he said. "They truly are going to release as many of the 1937-39 entrants into the service as can be spared. It's not an easy exercise to decide how many or when but I know you are on the list. The situation changes almost everyday. You won't know it but we have just lost at sea a number of administrative officers returning from leave. They were all experienced men and can ill be spared, poor chaps. We've got to keep this place going. Palm oil is badly needed in England. Government reckons it's counter-productive to keep officers out here for too lengthy tours. You'll be due for some leave towards the end of this year and if you haven't been called up before then you'll find yourself on leave in the UK. And you can always try your luck direct with the Colonial Office. I can't stop you then, can I? In the meantime I'm not going to forward your letter. OK?"

I didn't argue with Dermott O'Connor. Few did.

Peter Trevorrow returned safely from leave in the UK near the end of June. It was a wrench to give him back his car and dog. He was kind enough to say, however, that I seemed to have taken good care of both. Thereafter I was forced to use the Nnewi NA lorry for travelling on tour and a bicycle for other journeys. By the time my loads and two servants and orderly, Romaine and his camp kit and driver plus office boxes were all aboard the lorry was heavily loaded. However, the distances we had to travel seldom exceeded thirty miles and we managed.

August was taken up with the preparation of NA estimates. Sir Bernard Carr (we all referred to him, out of his hearing, needless to say, as "Boomer" Carr on account of his deep and resonant voice) was known to set great store on the whole range of financial control. Estimates, both NA and government, had to be realistic and accurate; expenditure and the accumulation of liabilities had to be rigorously controlled. He was said to be able to add columns of figures up at a glance—no mean achievement in those pre-calculator days. Woe betide the DO who did not take great care with the accuracy of his draft estimates or who failed to control expenditure throughout the financial year.

I was blessed at Nnewi by having H O Nwosu as NA chief clerk. He was a Nnewi man and knew the kind of tricks the various council clerks would get up to when drafting the estimates in the first instance. He must have been well into his forties when I knew him and like most Nnewis he didn't suffer fools gladly or waste words on idle compliments. I must have infuriated him earlier in our association by asking inane questions. There was one weekend in particular I remember.

I was suffering an attack of malaria half suppressed by the extra quinine I was taking. I insisted on continuing with the work of estimate preparation and must have made an absolute hash of it for once the fever had subsided I had to correct all my corrections and go back to the position originally reached by Nwosu himself. He didn't mince his words and I remember being impressed and not a little admiring when after the incident he gave vent to his feelings. All the Nnewis were blunt speakers and taught many an administrative officer to amend, if not mend, his ways. I guess Dermott O'Connor was well aware of this. I once overheard him say to a DO (I think it was Jim Smith), "We should send X to Nnewi. That'll test him."

About this time I first met L O Ojukwu. The credit for this meeting and for some twenty-seven years of truly "African" friendship that followed was Romaine's. It happened in this way.

There was a political problem concerning a proposed reorganisation of Nnewi Native Authority. I can't remember precisely what it was but it was causing us considerable difficulty.

"Why not talk to L O?" said Romaine "He's in town at the present."

I asked who LO was. Romaine was shocked. Everybody knew L O Ojukwu. He explained that he was a son of Nnewi who was already a millionaire. After leaving school in 1928 he'd joined the government Produce Inspection service. Then he joined John Holt Ltd as a clerk. He'd started his own transport service in 1934. By 1939 he'd built up a very large business linking Onitsha, Benin and Lagos. As soon as Romaine suggested it I sent a note by NA messenger to Ojukwu's house in Nnewi Nkalagu. I explained that we were faced with a problem and asked, if by any chance he was free at tea-time, could he be kind enough to come up to my house for tea and I'd seek his help. As far as I remember he came that same day. He treated me as a friend from that day on.

Years later, it could have been nearly fifty, I was talking to some old Nnewi acquaintances at an Anglo-Nigerian gathering in London and Ojukwu's name came up. One said, "Yours was the first European house LO was invited to." This is the sort of thing that Nigerians of that generation don't forget and it might have been true. Equally true was that from 1940 onwards Ojukwu was consulted by governors-general downwards. His business flourished; the transport company expanded into construction and other activities. He was knighted in 1960. He received honorary degrees from several universities. He was the father of Lieut Colonel Chukwumeka Odumegwu Ojukwu who was the General Odumegwu Ojukwu who led Biafra's secession attempt from Nigeria in 1967. LO died at the early age of fifty-seven in Nnewi Nkalagu.

I use the term "African friendship" advisedly. When an African talks about a "friend" and treats you as a friend he means a lot more than is conveyed by the same term in modern day Europe. Long experience in West and East Africa has shown me that much. It is more the relationship described by the mid-nineteenth century use of the term. There is no question of one friend seeking to gain advantage from the relationship. I was a very junior officer when I first met LO. He was already rich and powerful. The idea of his wanting assistance from me was laughable from the outset. The mores of the service prevented my seeking advantage from him on my own behalf. We both knew that. It was more a question of continuing kindly interest, one in the other; we met at odd moments throughout my service. Our conversation seemed always to continue from the point we'd reached at our last meeting. After I married Kat he took to her from the first moment he met her. There are several memories we have of him that we cherish as little jewels in our West African experience. Let me tell one here.

It was just after the war. Kat and I and the two kids, then aged about five and three, were going on leave by ship. We went aboard at Calabar but the ship docked for twenty-four hours in Lagos, presumably to pick up more passengers. We had entered Lagos harbour at dawn and by seven had made fast alongside the Apapa jetty. I was leaning over the rail idly watching the busy scene on the dock twenty-five feet below. A rose-coloured Rolls Royce drove up. Out sprang the driver immaculate in white uniform and black chauffeur's cap. As he climbed briskly up the gangway he spotted me leaning over the rail and seemed to recognise me. Sure enough. At the top he came straight up to me, saluted and said, "Mr Millin, Sar. Your car," pointing to the Rolls below. For a moment I hesitated wondering if all this was not some sophisticated confidence trick. "LO wait in the car just now."

I hurried down the gangway. LO was smoking a cigar in the cool of the rear compartment, an attaché case of papers on his knee. "I saw your names on the passenger list from Calabar and thought you'd like to do some shopping in Lagos. Just drop me at my office and you and Kat can use the car."

"A wonderful offer," I told him. "We do want all kinds of things but we can't leave the kids alone on board and they'd be hell's delight of a problem if we tried to take them round Lagos."

LO didn't waste time in making up our minds or in idle discussion. "That's all right," he said. "You stay back and look after the children— you're old enough, aren't you? I'll take Kat shopping. I'll bring her back at lunch-time."

Kat was ready in ten minutes and off they went.

She was brought back by the chauffeur at about ten to one, exhausted but highly successful. "He was so kind to me," she reported. "First thing he said was, "I know you haven't had any breakfast. So we stopped at that smart hotel on Iddo Island and he gave me a continental breakfast. He wouldn't touch a thing himself. And then he spent the morning going round the shops with me. He seemed to know the best places to go for everything and the right prices to pay. When we'd finished we left him at his office and the driver brought me back. I tried to give the driver a ten-shilling (nearer fifteen pounds in modern values) tip but he wouldn't take it."

August 1940 was a worrying and frustrating month. Air raid after air raid was thrown at the United Kingdom. All we could get on our radios were figures of our losses: we didn't know that the Battle of Britain was slowly being won. We lived in constant anticipation that the day would bring news that operation Sealion—the invasion of Great Britain—had been launched.

In the first week of September I was told that C T C Ennals was on his way back from leave and would be taking Nnewi over from me. He was ten years my senior and there was no question of my protesting on the grounds that I was just getting on terms with a reputedly difficult area. Had I done so I would, deservedly, have received short shrift. In any case I had been making a nuisance of myself pressing for mobilisation. Tom Ennals' arrival might provide the very means of securing what I wanted.

I got on the phone—I have a faint memory that it was Peter Riley's phone in Onitsha—to my military contact in Lagos. I told him I was about to be relieved by Tom Ennals. His immediate reaction was to say, "I've got you on our list for October release but there's just time to get you on this month's list. Your unit is number two Light Battery stationed in Zaria."

Everything seemed to be going my way. Dermott O'Connor was out of touch visiting a remote part of the Nsukka District. I had a sneaking feeling that had he been "on seat" he'd have ordered me to work in Onitsha itself until the military call up actually arrived. As it was when I told the story to Peter Riley all he said was: "You had better go, then." So in a couple of days' time I was in the train to Zaria.

CHAPTER FOUR

Service with the RWAFF

(i) Mobilisation at last and Zaria

I was on military duties from 1940 to 1943. There are arguments for leapfrogging those years and getting straight on with the civilian narrative. These pages are primarily concerned with the administrative service...how we as a service operated, where we succeeded, where we failed. But every day spent in West Africa was part of a learning process and influenced my later administrative work. I must, I feel, select from those years what I now judge with hindsight to have affected me later.

Jack, when he heard of my long-deferred mobilisation and move to Zaria, wrote a letter of rare prescience on 10th October 1940.

> "...well the very best of luck and good wishes and may it not be long before you are back at your own job again. You have been very unsettled these last few months and I quite understand your feelings at a time like this, but I hope you are now feeling happier and may have as good a time as possible. I hope you find some good chaps amongst your lot and also where you are is a healthier and more bracing climate. *I still think, after training, if circumstances permit, you may be recalled to your work, which after all is very important and must be kept going."*

In a little over two years he was to be proved right.

My battery commander was Dickie Beevor. He was nineteen years older than I and had seen service in the royal artillery in the 1914-18 war.

He had been released for military service by the Northern Regional Government where he was near the top of the "long grade" of district officers. Most of my fellow officers were in the same circumstances as Dickie and I...Nigerian civil list officers released for military duties. There was a very small number of "real soldiers"—regulars or long-serving territorials—amongst the four Light Batteries at the time in Zaria but these were few and far between.

The RSM showed me to my quarters—a two bedroomed "bush" house—advising me that I'd soon have to share with another officer. I'd been told that he would advise me of the time of the first parade on the morrow and warned that he'd probably offer me the services of a local lady. If I was minded to refuse, the answer I should give was, "Yes, Sergeant Major, I'd like a woman, but not the sort you might bring."

The RSM duly performed on both counts. "First parade 6.30, Sar. You like a woman, Sar?" He was a splendid chap who had seen service in German East Africa in the first war and I felt more than a little rude producing the standard reply regarding the local lady. But apparently it was expected of me.

When we were in barracks we worked reasonably hard from 6.30 in the morning to four in the afternoon but the hour and a half from five to 6.30 each evening was sacred to polo. This was exciting news; better still was the price of the ponies. Raw ponies could be bought straight from itinerant horse-coopers for three to four pounds. They were all neck trained and most could be put straight onto the polo field. If they were brave and not stick-shy you could keep them. If they were no good it was no great sacrifice to re-sell them at a loss of five or ten shillings...often back to the same chap you'd bought them from.

I bought three ponies on, I think, my second day in Zaria. One was a made polo pony, elderly, called Dan Bornu—Son of Bornu, not surprisingly since he was a typical Bornu pony: fourteen and a half hands, Roman nose, clean legged. He came, as they all did, with his *mai-doki* (syce). The latter's wages were minimal, about ten shillings a month. I never asked where Dan Bornu's *mai-doki* slept but was later told it was in the stable with his charge. He was an old man. As my Hausa improved, I discovered that he had an encyclopaedic knowledge of horses. Tack, too, was easily and cheaply bought in Zaria. Many peace-time regular officers, departing after secondment to the RWAFF, passed on their saddles and bridles to their ex-*doki*-boys and the latter were only too eager to turn them into cash.

Dan Bornu turned out to be the best and bravest polo pony in the station. He taught me, if not all I knew, at least a very great deal about the game. It was largely thanks to him that I had a handicap of three by Christmas. Amongst the *takarda* (papers) that his *mai-doki* preserved in an old OHMS envelope was a letter from Dan Bornu's previous owner—a government doctor posted to Zaria. Copying the address, which seemed to be an English retirement one, I wrote him an enthusiastic letter about the pony. Many months afterwards I got a postcard in reply. It merely said, "Glad you found the pony satisfactory." It was unworthy of both pony and syce.

Shortly after buying Dan Bornu I asked the syce to bring him along to the house on a non-polo evening so that I could exercise him. The old boy surprised me by saying bluntly, "No." After a struggle—for I had no Hausa at that time—I gathered that he judged that two chukkas three times a week was enough for the pony. He had tender legs and any more would put him out of the game altogether. The old boy added, "He won't exercise." Quite wrongly—I realised this soon enough—I insisted that he bring the pony along that evening.

They duly turned up. Dan Bornu seemed sound but he would hardly let the syce lead him to and fro for my inspection. I climbed on board and spent the next twenty minutes battling to get him to walk some half a mile down the cantonment track. At length I gave up. He was so wonderful on the polo field. This struggle was undignified and even cruel. We swung round heading for the stable lines. Unasked he broke into a fast clip of a canter and no matter what I did to slow him down kept it up until he'd gone straight into his box, nearly taking my head off on the lintel as he did so.

After that episode I gave in. The old syce, and the pony himself, knew what was good for him. Who was I to interfere? So long as he performed on the field...and perform he truly did.

He followed the ball like a terrier, turned quicker than I could turn him. Whenever he could—it was almost as though he'd read the rules—he would put the ball on my offside. And as for riding off...he had a knack of apparently giving way and then getting the opposition off-stride with the hell of a thump. He must have won me dozens of balls that the poor fellow I was marking thought were his.

As I write I hear a voice in the middle distance saying, "Enough. Enough. What's all this playing fields of Eton stuff? There is a war on. Pipe down, my friend, pipe down."

The fact was that everybody watched polo in Zaria in 1940: African soldiers off duty, the populace of the township, the native administration officials and their minions, the police, even the expatriates in government service. It was the only major entertainment. And the players were equally varied coming from all races and all ranks. Dan Bornu was well-known amongst the cognoscenti. I remember one four chukka match. By a well timed spurt Dan Bornu presented me with an open goal. All I had to do was tap the ball between the posts. But something in the spirit of the crowd infected me. Digging my heels into Dan B, I went at the ball at a gallop taking a full swing at it. Of course it popped up and I missed it clean. The crowd roared with laughter. Dan B was unable to contain his fury. He took hold, left the ball behind and shaking his head from side to side, galloped between the posts where the ball should have gone. There was a crowd of dan *gari* (citizens of the lower order) sitting on the ground, guffawing, some thirty yards behind the goal line. He galloped straight at them. They rose and scattered like chickens below a stooping hawk. It was the grace of God that he didn't hurt somebody. I wonder now if perhaps, even in his stimulated fury, he wasn't clever enough on his feet to be careful where he planted them. Those not threatened laughed immoderately. It doubled the entertainment to see their fellows flee.

Not only did all and sundry watch polo in Zaria but all races played. Several of the NA officials were good players. There was a syce, well worth a handicap of three, who played occasionally. (When I took over running the polo in November I made sure he played regularly.) Odd members of the Syrian and Lebanese community played as did expatriate members of John Holts, Unilever and "the French Company".

Polo in Zaria in 1940 did much for morale. I was later to become convinced of the inter-racial cementing effect of the game wherever it is played...Kano, Zaria, Jos, Kaduna, Katsina, Ibadan and Lagos in particular.

Nearly all the male ponies in Nigeria were left entire; geldings were seldom seen. However, one of the three I'd bought on arrival in Zaria was a gelding. He was a natural "good-doer" and always carried a bit more flesh than one would have wished. Whether it was related to his loss of goolies I cannot say but he was a clown of a pony, easily taught tricks. He'd roll on command and his *mai-doki* very soon taught him to mount the steps outside my quarters and take a lump of sugar off my shoulder as I sat at breakfast on the large veranda at the top. He lacked the meanness to be a good polo pony but I kept him on more for his sense of humour than anything else.

The RSM's warning that I should soon be required to share my quarters was borne out by the arrival after a few days of Peter Stallard. He was a Northern Region ADO, two years my senior, tall, thin and very committed. He was to have a distinguished war ending up as a lieut colonel with eighty-one Div in Burma. I met him again in 1956 in

Lagos where he was secretary to Abubakar Tafewa Balewa, the first premier of the Federation of Nigeria.

To revert to Zaria in 1940. Ba-Giwa, as I'd christened the gelding, hoping that the name was good Hausa for his condition (Bargery's immensely fat dictionary gives separate Hausa words for a gelded camel, donkey, goat, ram and cockerel, but, so far as I can discover, nothing for a horse), was the cause of a slight altercation between Peter and I. One morning when we were both having breakfast on the veranda Ba-Giwa performed his act of coming up the steps for a lump of sugar. Peter hadn't seen him do this before and was somewhat taken aback.

"I won't have that damned horse crapping on my steps," said he.

"Excuse me, it's my half of the steps," said I.

Peter shortly afterwards did move quarters. Whether it was to join a Northern ADO friend or whether it was to do with his disgust with me I don't know.

It was Peter Stallard in particular and other Northern administrative officers serving in the four light batteries in Zaria who first alerted me to the fundamental differences in the attitudes of Northern and Eastern Regional administrative officers to indirect rule. Kat's brother, Nigel Cooke, when I got to know him a year or two later, also did much to widen my perspective. There is no doubt we all became closely associated with the people with whom we worked. The Ibos were rough, rude, direct and, on the surface of our understanding, noisily quarrelsome people. Ibo NA council meetings often became a shouting match. But it wasn't necessarily the good DO who insisted on relative silence and ordered debate on European lines. Furious altercation was one form of discussion rooted in the remote past. Ibo ears became accustomed to picking up out of the general concatenation contributions of value and discarding the unacceptable. Sometimes, after several minutes of passionate shouting, there would be a sudden silence. A spokesman would stand up. "We are agreed," he'd say. "We'll build the maternity at Ihiala"—or whatever the decision was. How agreement had been reached only the old men knew. Admittedly, by the year 1940 the progress of local government in the south-east of Nigeria certainly had never pleased the officials in Lagos or in the colonial office.

After independence in Nigeria and the Cameroons—and indeed in much of ex-colonial Africa—the tendency has been slowly to denude local government of power and resources in favour of central government. The cynical would explain this by saying, "So that the senior men can get at the pickings first."

In 1940 many Northern expatriate officers prided themselves upon being the proponents of indirect rule. The relatively effective systems of Islamic government found in place in the early 1900s in such emirates as Kano, Katsina and Sokoto turned out on closer acquaintance to be thoroughly corrupt. The years from 1900 to the early twenties were spent in cleansing them. Indirect rule was introduced—and lauded as a workable system—as the process of reform proceeded. By the late 1930s, the functions of government in many areas of Northern Nigeria were carried out by the native chiefs and councils, with the assistance and advice of British administrative staff. Talking to my Northern colleagues at Zaria I was at first impressed by the degree to which indirect rule was functioning. Some of the larger Northern NAs were employing numerous expatriate technicians and running medical, transport, survey, works, printing, water and electrical supply services. But even then the more thinking Northerners were far from cock-a-hoop. There was a lot going on that shouldn't be. I began to wonder if the noisy chaos of the Eastern Region wasn't more democratic after all.

Obviously the atmosphere in which we'd worked for the past year had rubbed off on the 1939 in-take of administrative cadets. We'd all had the same background when we joined the service in 1938 and were very much of a muchness. But a year in Northern Nigeria and a year in the Eastern Region had already made different impressions on us. The Northerners, particularly those who had served in the bigger emirates, were more lordly. There was more point in the little anecdote concerning the staff list and the dinner table (page 44) in the north than the East.

By and large it would be fair to summarise the contrast between Northern and Eastern NAs in late 1940 as follows: there were in the north a number of large and effective NAs operating, by the values of the time, efficiently. In the Eastern Region, with a very few exceptions such as Onitsha Town, the NAs were chaotic and poorly operating. There was a belief amongst some Eastern officers that Eastern NAs might yet surprise by their sudden advance. In the north there were the first stirrings of unease that the apparently successful Emirate administrations might prove to have fatal weaknesses. Some officers rightly foresaw difficulties arising between the Emirate system and parliamentary democracy as well.

These thoughts were peripheral to our main task of training our batteries. It was, of course, just as much a job of training ourselves as training our rank and file. The Hausa peasant made a fine soldier: in keenness and smartness of bearing he lacked nothing. Mechanically he was a little numb. Our guns were 3.7 Howitzers which took to pieces for head porterage and became known as "screw guns". They were later to play an honourable role in the Burma campaign. There was one very heavy load of well over 300 lbs which was carried on a short stretcher by the two strongest men in the unit. Carrying only a rifle I remember marvelling at the dourness and guts of these two men: I found it hard to keep pace with them.

A strange experience occurred in December 1940. Letters from Jack, written in early September had warned me that my father was not at his best physically. He'd taken over, earlier in the year, as joint Master of the Otter Hounds and, in Jack's view, the effort and duties demanded of him were proving too much. He was losing weight and complained increasingly of lack of energy. Then followed a dearth of letters (possibly mail was lost at sea) and I had no news of him.

On the 13th December, I suddenly became convinced he was desperately in need of my prayers. The feeling increased in intensity throughout the day. It wasn't specific. It didn't allow me to speculate whether he was ill, or had met an accident, or some other catastrophe had come his way. I just knew that I must pray for him. This I did. All day…instructing a squad in the Bren gun…on formal parade…during rest periods…I prayed urgently and fervently, my mind as it were engaged on two tasks of which continuous and urgent prayer was one, my duties the other. When parades were finished for the day I walked slowly along the banks of the Kaduna river, praying more earnestly perhaps than ever before in my life. By dark I was exhausted and, tumbling into bed, fell into a troubled sleep.

The next day the feeling was there but less intense. I prayed at every moment I could but with slightly less intensity and urgency than the day before. It's hard to remember the precise details and sequence of events. The effort of prayer demanded of me the previous day had been almost if not entirely beyond my powers to meet. I was mentally, perhaps spiritually, deplete. I sent two cables home begging for news and details.

News came intermittently and not always in chronological order. By the 20th December 1940 I was aware that he'd been gravely ill but was now past the worst. It was well into January before Jack's letter of 21st December giving a fuller account reached me. And even then, by the standards of today, it was difficult to convey what precisely had ailed him. I gathered that he'd had severe intestinal trouble which had necessitated a major operation. A letter received later in January 1941 from my father himself confessed that he had little recollection of the acute stages other than a memory of the pain. So bad the latter, he confessed, that he'd cried aloud and begged for a pain-killing injection given in those days with great reluctance (possibly because of the side effects?). When at last they acceded to his request he said that the "taste" of the injection (I use his own expression) remained with him for days. For my father to cry aloud with pain was a dire thing. He had a very high pain threshold; he'd done no more than groan in the back of Bruce Rigg's car when he was taken from Bainsbank point-to-point to have his septic blind eye removed in Leeds; he'd broken many bones in his numerous steeplechasing falls. Stoicism was the unwritten creed of his class. For him to cry out the pain must have been very great indeed. I ached for him, ached for him, old now and so many thousand miles away.

He spent over six weeks in hospital before being allowed to return to his digs in Kirkoswald. As my life with Kat began in 1941 and reached the first of a long succession of peaks with our marriage on 11th August that year, my father's life began to fall away. He never recovered sufficiently to allow him once more to fish for trout on the Eden, and he never followed the Otter hounds again. He died on the 9th January 1942.

Round about Christmas 1940 I was transferred from Number Two to Number Four Battery. The rank and file of Number Four had been recruited from the eastern area of Northern Nigeria and spoke a different dialect of Hausa from their fellows in Number Two Light Battery who had all been recruited from the north-west. Although my Hausa teacher made light of the change in dialect I found it off-putting and my progress faltered. Nevertheless I plodded on; sometimes the little I'd learnt paid dividends.

On one occasion we were moving the four guns of the battery from one position to another. Each move entailed dismantling the guns prior to the rank and file carrying the various components forward. After one particularly arduous carry we were given a short rest period. Most of us, men and officers alike, flopped to the ground. I was lying on my back next to a little sage bush that was roughly face high. One of the men said something urgently in Hausa. I picked up the words "maciji" and "kwanta sosai"..."snake" and the order "lie very still".

The next instant the man who had called out, using the small carrying pad he had, swept a puff adder off the top of the sage bush, twelve inches from my face. It landed harmlessly six feet away and curled up into a small, defensive knot. He'd risked being bitten in the hand to save me being bitten in the face. I tried to thank him for what he'd done but my Hausa wasn't up to it.

To harden the men and exercise the officers we went on several long route marches at this time. Often we found our way across country but occasionally we trudged along the murram roads of the area. Approaching traffic would set up a huge cloud of dust which smothered and choked us as the vehicle passed. After a little experience I arrived at a conclusion which doubtless any physicist will tell you is a known fact—namely, the size of the dust cloud is proportionate to the vehicle's momentum. A light lorry moving slowly would stir up a minimal cloud; a very large vehicle travelling fast would leave an enormous cloud behind and, in the absence of a cross-wind, cause the marching gunners great discomfort for half a mile or more. I took to marching in the middle of the road behind my chaps attempting to slow overtaking traffic.

Peter Stallard's place in my quarters was soon filled by a very pleasant, easy-going character called Philip Dennis. He was short, strongly-built and invariably cheerful.

In December, a commander, Royal Artillery, was appointed to train and build up the gunners in Nigeria. We didn't then know, of course, of the imperial plan to send out no less than three British batteries of AA Artillery for the protection of the port of Lagos against possible air attack by the Vichy French. One supposes the appointment of a half-colonel as CRA Nigeria was timed to anticipate the arrival of the three batteries.

Lieut Colonel Graham de Burgh was the man appointed. He was a member of a well-known Anglo-Irish family who boasted a number of distinguished soldiers amongst their collaterals. Today, I suppose, the family are best known for Chris de Burgh the singer and song writer of world fame (who is, incidentally, the grandson of General Sir Eric de Burgh, about whom more on page 365).

Graham de Burgh's personal life, and indeed his professional life too, had been anything but tranquil prior to his arrival in Zaria. He bore the indelible stamp of those who had served in the trenches in the 1914-18 war. He had later distinguished himself and been decorated on the NW Frontier of India. Immediately before the outbreak of war in 1939 he had found peace-time soldiering lacking challenge and, according to stories which were told of him, had created situations to remedy the deficiency. He had, we learnt, an attractive

1 *Above,* Early days – Kitty's plateau transport in 1912; Nigel holds the pony.

2 *Below,* Jack Walton, the bachelor uncle, at Lynwood, c 1935.

3 *Above opposite*, Lynwood, near Penrith, a house built on the edge of the Beacon with fine views of the Lake hills to the west.

4 *Below opposite*, Kat with Jackie near Port Shepstone on the Natal coast, November 1942. It was this photo which prompted the crack about Winston Churchill, mentioned on page 136.

5 *Above*, The author's Hausa teacher and general mentor, Mallam Bello Dan Dago Kano; 1942, Accra.

6 *Above*, Dinga, a Bamenda Messenger, a splendid fellow, but usually drunk by sunset.

7 *Left*, Nsaw Ya (woman chief) visits the Milnes at Kikaikilaki. Naked by the dictates of custom, she was nevertheless a sagacious member of the native court bench

8 *Opposite above*, Babanki Daya; first reported ascent by Angus Robin and autho

9 *Opposite below*, Impromptu photo taken near tennis courts on first evening of visit by CCER to Bamenda, 1947. Freddy Kay stands behind Sir Bernard Carr, seated; Lady Carr, hands clasped, seated in the middle.

10 *Above*, Bamenda – "Some Mountains have come in the night". The sudden lifting of the harmattan haze caused the children to rush into the bedroom one morning with this exciti announcement.

11 *Below*, Foncha and a fellow member of the Cameroons House of Assembly meet two members of a visiting mission.

12 The jetty at Man O'War Bay.

13 Jackie and John at Nkambe, 1950. All their clothes were
handmade by Kat.

and intelligent wife and a number of riotous children but he was far from being subdued by the burdens of paternity.

Later in the war, following the German-Italian armistice of 8th September 1943, he twice distinguished himself by his actions. He had been senior British officer in an Italian-run POW camp having been initially taken prisoner by the Germans. He received orders that following the armistice of 8th September, allied prisoners-of-war should remain in their camps awaiting rescue by allied forces. He knew, however, that the Germans were likely to intervene and send POWs to camps in Germany. He decided therefore to ignore the questionable order and protect those for whom he was responsible by positive action. Consequently, ten minutes after the armistice, he marched all allied POWs out of the camp and released them in organised groups, each group properly led. There were six hundred prisoners involved. Thanks to Graham de Burgh's action, the majority of these men got safely back to British forces or to Switzerland.

Then, accompanied by his two staff officers, Colonel Dick Wheeler and Captain Reggie Phillips, he made a memorable journey northwards through Italy. Feeling that three persons was too conspicuous Wheeler left the other two. All three eventually successfully made crossings of the Alps into Switzerland, de Burgh and Phillips tackling the formidable Aosta-Zermatt route late in September.

But back to December, 1940...some little bird had told me that Graham de Burgh, although currently out of practice, had been a strong polo player with a handicap of four. I was running the Zaria polo by then and I begged him to play saying we'd do our best to mount him well. At first he was reluctant: "I'm out of practice. I'll let you down." Eventually we prevailed and for his first chukka took care to mount him exceptionally well. I even lent him my beloved Dan Bornu...an act far beyond the calls of sycophancy as all who have owned a really good polo pony will readily agree. I took care, too, to arrange the chukka tactfully—the opposing number two happened to be a weak player.

But all this wasn't necessary. Graham de Burgh was a perfectly good player, well worth his four handicap. If he was out of practice he was worth more.

I don't know if there was any connection with Dan Bornu or not but one evening, just as we were going into mess, de Burgh said to me, "You'd better read orders tomorrow for a change. I'm making you my Adjutant." And then *sotto voce*, so only I could hear, "You run the polo well. As good a reason as any."

New Year 1941 brought another change of course in my life—I met Kat whom I was to marry on the 11th August 1941.

Graham de Burgh, about two days after Christmas announced in the mess, "It's Jos Races next weekend. You've all been working hard so I'm taking a party. Who's coming? You…? You…?" and turning to me he said, "And you, young, Milne—get yourself a ride."

The Plateau Province was an area unique in the whole of Nigeria. The terrain was 4,000 feet above sea level and enjoyed a tolerable, even pleasant climate. The nights were cool, sometimes cold, and the days out of the hot sun quite bearable. Alluvial tin had been mined in the vicinity since the first decade of the century. The tin miners brought their families out, built themselves generous houses and developed gardens that grew a variety of semi-tropical and even temperate plants. It was a country within a country, remote from the rest of Nigeria.

Zaria to Jos was about 140 miles by road. The journey seemed to pass in minutes. I can't remember how large de Burgh's party was, perhaps about a dozen of us in three staff cars, but news of our invasion had apparently preceded us for we found ourselves allocated to different parties for a pre-race meeting dance at the Plateau Club on the evening of our arrival.

(ii) Zaria and Fortress Command

I found myself sitting next to a silver blond called Katherine Cooke who told me that until her mother had recently returned from the UK she'd been keeping house for her father. He was running the southern section of ATMN, the largest tin mining company on the Plateau. Previously she'd kept the family house running for her brothers and sisters in England as well as working herself. She was the easiest and most comforting person to be with that I had encountered in my twenty-four years of existence. Now, fifty-six years later, I feel very much the same…only more so.

It was a little surprising that her mother had managed, amidst all the regulations and counter-regulations of war-time England, being a woman, to secure a passage from the UK to Nigeria. When I put this to Kat she said, "Shush…we all say here she was deported."

Later I learnt that Kitty Cooke, her mama, had indeed found herself stuck in the UK, held there by regulations forbidding passages to females. But Kitty, being the personality she was, wasn't going to be deterred by a minor regulation. She promptly wrote to every Elder Dempster skipper she'd ever travelled with. As she had first come out in 1912 they were many. Her letters produced an immediate, telegraphed reply. "Can offer very uncomfortable passage. Be at Garstang Docks Liverpool Thursday. Confirm you are coming."

Her answer was, "Don't care if arse of swallow. Will be there."

It was she who came up to our table that evening and said to me, "We hear you are a jockey. Wally Nichols has a ride for you on Gana in the Plateau Cup. Come along, I'll introduce you to him." I started explaining that it was my father who'd been the jockey but she merely said, "Wally knows all that," and off we went.

Wally N was one of two brothers who ran a fleet of lorries out of Jos over all of Northern Nigeria. Kat's brother Nigel, a member of the Northern Administrative Service, later told me that, when he was an ADO in Maidugari just before the war, serving in desert country 300 miles NE of Jos, one of Wally Nichols' mail lorries would bring him a great hamper of green vegetables from his mother's garden at Barakin Ladi every week. Never once was a bill submitted. Wally N was a kind and generous man. When it came to racing however, he was more than a match for the Levantines who at the time dominated Nigerian racing...although I'm not sure the Jockey Club would always concur with some of his ploys.

He gave me a glance as Kitty Cooke introduced us. (To see if I could ride eleven stone, I guess.)

"Of course you're going to ride the old Gana," he said and added, "He's short of a gallop so I'm letting him go in a five furlong race tomorrow. He's too slow to win it so we'll let his *mai-doki* ride him. Just what he needs to stir him up before the Plateau Cup on Sunday."

After the first day's racing I visited Gana in his stable. He was big for a Bahr al Ghazal pony, a dark roan. But horror of horrors...he was standing on three legs, the weight off his bandaged off-fore. There was some heat there, not much, but he wouldn't put that foot to the ground.

I searched Wally Nichols out. "What's the matter with Gana?" I asked. He pulled a long face. "I'm awfully sorry but that five furlong gallop today set off that off-fore. He's always been vulnerable there. I think it's a tendon. He's got a wet bandage on it. He may be fit to go. We'll keep our fingers crossed."

I felt sick with disappointment. But there was nothing to do except wait until the morning. Wally N put the bad news about that evening in the club. The odds against Gana lengthened.

That evening, after Kat and her parents had gone back to Barakin Ladi, I found several members of the club who knew the Cookes well and were happy to talk about them. Kat's father, Nigel Cooke, had first come out to the tin mining area of the Jos Plateau in 1910. He had been stationed initially at Panshanu, some forty miles from Jos itself. His route had followed the pattern established during the earliest days of European penetration of the Western Sudan—sea-going ship to Lagos, small coastal vessel to Forcados and, a few miles on, to Burutu in the Niger delta. Thence up the River Niger by stern-wheeler to Lokoja. After that another four days by poling barge to Loko where there was a Royal Niger Company rest house. There he was met by the Company's agent who provided a horse for him and carriers for his loads on the long trek to Panshanu. Nigel took fourteen days over this last leg of the journey. Some of his carriers were slower than the main party and turned up two days later. However, not a single load was lost and there was absolutely no question of any pilfering on the journey. Apart for the substitution of steam for sail the route was as it had been for many centuries.

Kitty Cooke, Kat's Mama, first joined Nigel on the Plateau two years later, in 1912. History relates that three white women reached the Plateau that year, Kitty being the first of them. Anthony Kirk-Greene, in an article published in the *Nigerian Field* of 1961, quotes from Kitty's recollections:-

> The Plateau when I came here to live, had known the white man for only nine years...my appearance on the camp was such a novelty that one pagan woman walked one hundred miles to see me. To judge from the expression on her face as she studied me the expedition had proved unrewarding until I made the journey worthwhile for her by giving her a handful of salt.

I visited Gana's stable early on the following morning—the day of the Plateau Cup. Sadly, he was still tender on the affected leg. Wally Nichols joined me as I leant over the half door. He said, "We'll see how he is when we get the bandage off. But look here, old boy. Don't parade him in the ring. Don't even get up until the others leave for the start. I don't want the vet to spot him and make us withdraw."

I did precisely as instructed when the moment came. When I got up it was all I could do to make him leave the ring; he cantered very short down to the start and at first refused to line up under the starter's flag. But being an old war horse and seeing the others meant business he joined them. As the starter's flag dropped I felt a surge of relief—the vet, at least, hadn't interfered and he was galloping, it seemed to me, well enough. The only instructions Wally had given me—apart from keeping him away from the Vet's eye—was to say, "He's not fast. He'll stay but don't let the others get too far ahead in the early part of the race. Stay with 'em early on." There was a mile and a half to go. I did have to push him quite a bit early on but he had a lovely long stride. After a mile there were only three ahead of us and the old horse was quietly pulling them back.

He was the pilot, not me. I only had to stay there and the race was ours. I did nothing stupid, thank heavens, and we won by a length and a half.

Kat, sagaciously, had backed him only for a place. Kitty, bless her, had backed him to win. Wally N was delighted. He gave me a silver cocktail set that evening. Someone commented sourly, "He could damn well afford to; he'd sorted out most of the Plateau."

It was Graham de Burgh who opened my eyes some days later. "Wasn't that bandage a bit tight? Wouldn't he have been better without it?" he asked.

Graham de Burgh's convoy did not leave Jos until well after dinner on our last evening. It seemed a long journey back to Zaria. None of us could sleep in the vehicles, the lurches and the bumps were too much. We tumbled into bed around 3.30 a.m. and, of course, most of us were late for the next day's first parade at 6.30 a.m. The colonel wasn't, however. He greeted us fiercely as we made a somewhat shame-faced appearance.

The whole lot of us were for the orderly room that evening. We received a rocket for our lateness on parade. "If the colonel, twice our age, was there it was up to us to be punctual, too." Etc. etc....

It was only some days later that we discovered the colonel had spent the hours of 3.30 to 6.30 a.m. drinking in the mess with Dickie Beevor and that he'd gone to bed in comfort shortly after that first ill-attended parade. We, in contrast, had spent the day with our units battling against the soporific effects of minimal sleep and hot sun.

One or two of us, greatly daring, mentioned the unfairness of it all. "Rank has some privileges although you might not think it," said de Burgh, dismissively, a vulpine grin spreading over his face.

Kat told me in a letter written at the end of January that she'd accepted an offer of work in the Nigerian Secretariat commencing on 9th

February. She was proposing to take the train down to Lagos departing from Jos on the 6th Feb.

The colonel kindly gave me and Dennis three days off. We hired a car and, arriving in Jos, we asked Margaret Cothay, daughter of the Northern area manager of ATMN, to make up the party. We had a happy and relaxed two days. On the first evening the four of us dined in what was for war-time Nigeria considerable state at Hill Station and on the 4th February spent the day swimming and picnicking at Kurra Falls on the edge of the Plateau.

On the way to Kurra we passed a group of Plateau pagans. In the 1930s anthropologists working in the area had identified over twenty languages spoken by the non-Muslim peoples indigenous to the Plateau. The whole area had by then been brought under close administration and was relatively peaceful. Twenty years before, however, both Kat's and Margaret's parents had experienced very different circumstances. Then each village spoke a different language to its neighbour and travel through the area necessitated armed guards and extreme circumspection.

The women in the small party we passed were entirely naked. The men wore only grass-woven penis sheaths which swung to and fro in a most impressive manner as they walked. Both Dennis and I became concerned for the susceptibilities of the two young girls we had in our company. We felt that the "cock-boxes" in particular might prove an embarrassment to them. We needn't have worried. For all this was old hat to them...if "old hat" is the right form of words to use in this connection...As they told us at lunch they'd been concerned for the obvious disquiet shown by Dennis and me.

On return to Zaria I once again plunged into the military regime enlivened by three evenings a week of polo. I also increased the time set aside for Hausa lessons. Thinking back I find it hard to remember precisely what my attitude to Nigerian languages was at that time. One thing I was certain of and that was that I was hopelessly tone deaf and tonal languages were not for me. Few amongst my contemporaries-or even seniors-were linguists in the sense of being deeply versed in the structure and scientific study of an African language. The names of Eric Powell and Godfrey Allen only come to mind in this context. On the other hand Hausa was said to be relatively easy to learn and I felt compelled to acquire sufficient to be able to converse with the rank and file of the men I was going to war with. At the same time our brief association with Ida Ward at Umuahia had shown us that a knowledge of the life of the people was inextricably bound up with the language they spoke and proficiency in the latter was an open window on to the former. Again, the £25 bonus payable by government for a lower standard pass was not to be sniffed at-it was worth round about £750 in today's values. And a knowledge of Hausa might well be useful at some time in the future. Lastly, I had been impressed by the large body, in 1939/40, of literature on Hausa in English script. These factors, taken together, determined me to persist with Hausa.

Hausa is next only to Swahili as the most widespread of African languages. The latter is predominately a coastal language and has been spread inward from the East African coast, largely following the pattern of European invasion. Hausa, on the other hand, is a language of the West and Central African hinterland basically of Hamitic-mostly Berber—origin. It owes much, as does Swahili, to Islamic importations but it has, unlike Swahili, borrowed from surrounding African languages. Hausa, as a spoken language, underwent a high degree of expansion in the west and coastal Sudan, following the newly-opened roads built by the English, French and Portuguese invaders.

Written in Arabic characters by Mallams and Arabic scholars, Hausa is known by the generic name *Ajami*. So far as I was concerned I concentrated on spoken Hausa and did not undertake the task of learning the Arabic alphabet as a preliminary to *Ajami*. As in many languages colloquial everyday speech differs widely from the written form.

Not only is Hausa full of colloquial and idiomatic expressions but the language is rich in proverbs and statements bearing a hidden meaning. It is, in fact, primarily a spoken language. I remember being assured by Mallam Dan Dago Kano (of whom more later) that the ordinary Nigerian peasant is likely to have a vocabulary two and a half times the length of an educated Englishman's. This I can well believe.

The proverbs are often particularly graphic and afford one a rare insight into Hausa life. At the same time they frequently contrive to be a play on the words used. I could well accept that an educated European Hausa scholar might enjoy considerable intellectual amusement from swapping proverbs with members of the Mallam class. Certainly both my teachers, the Yoruba schoolmaster in Zaria and later Mallam Dan Dago Kano, had a lot of fun and amusement from this play with words.

The educated European is a little apt to mince his words rather than be crudely direct. The African sees nothing crude in being direct. The Hausa equivalent of the saying, "You can't do two things at once," is "Ba'a gama gudu da tsusan tsuli," (literally, "You can't combine running with scratching the anus.") but I'm told that the humour to Hausa ears is the play on tsusan and tsuli.

"Ya digo digo," meaning, "He dodged the raindrops," is beautifully explicit of a chap who is altogether too sharp for his own good.

"Giwa a wani gari Zomo," translated literally means, "Elephant in a different town hare"—a great man in a different town (where nobody knows him) is a nobody.

"One man's meat is another man's poison," is common to many languages. The Hausaman expresses it: "The place where one man spends the day another chooses for sleeping in." ("Inda wani ya ki da yini, nan wani yi ke nema da kwana.")

Some proverbs, simple enough in English conception, are found in Hausa in a much more complex form. For instance: "Gurbin ido ba ido bane," (the socket of the eye is not the eye itself) is best translated: "All is not gold that glitters." "Charity begins at home," is expressed in a manner that had to be explained to me at length before I could understand the meaning. The Hausa was "Inuwar giginiya na nisa ka sha ki," which directly interpreted means, "Shadows of a fan palm at a distance you drink it." "You drink it," is idiomatic for "you enjoy it." The hard-to-comprehend element refers to the fan palm. Because its fronds are near the top of the tree it throws its shadow some distance from its base. Thus an association with a man who gives generously outside his own home...that is a charitable man. But...and it is here that we come across a double-think, so to speak...it is still his own home that he gives to. Charity begins at home.

"Out of sight out of mind," is expressed as: "relationship is a matter of the feet." ("Zamunta a kafa ta ke.") If you don't make the necessary effort to go and see a person you don't form a relationship.

A proverb that I often used later on in the Bamenda District where the locals and nomadic Fulani were prone to disputing over cattle trespass was, "Kada kowa ya kuku da wani ya kuku da kansa"—"Let no man complain of another (for in doing so) he complains of himself."

And here's one for the protagonists of women's lib—"Mache da takobi abin tsoro." "A woman with a sword is a thing of fear." But the Hausaman, when he says it, has his tongue in cheek. It is a sneer rather than a statement of fact.

In April 1941 de Burgh's command was increased by the arrival in Lagos of three British batteries, one of 4.7 inch AA guns and two light AA batteries armed with Bofors. The sudden advent of so many British rank and file in Nigerian conditions of 1941 produced a multitude of problems. Colonel de Burgh was instructed to move to Lagos immediately. My post of adjutant was converted to Staff Officer RA and I was required to accompany him.

So far as my relationship with Kat was concerned this was an unbelievable bit of luck. De Burgh received his instructions in the morning. We both caught that evening's train to Lagos. I'd had a busy day: packed up the office documents, sold my ponies, sent a telegram to Kat, sorted out my own loads and was ready to go half an hour before the train arrived from Kano on its way down to Lagos. The journey from Zaria to Lagos took thirty-five hours so leaving at seven p.m. we had two full nights en route.

On arrival we found all three batteries operational but the men, quite unused to tropical conditions, were exposed to the insidious effects of the climate. Quinine was in process of being superseded by mepacrine as a prophylactic against malaria but the rules laid down for the latter's use were not being properly observed. There was already a very high incidence of malaria. This was exacerbated by the men's sleeping conditions: they were in tented camps but the measures to make the tents mosquito-proof were ineffective, merely increasing the temperature to energy-sapping levels and failing to keep out the hordes of mosquitoes, both anopheles and culicine which sought entry. The former were the malaria carriers but the latter were responsible for a wide spectrum of tropical diseases. The Nigerian medical and public health establishments at the time were depleted by the generalised effect of the war. The responsibilities imposed by the sudden advent of several hundred British gunners imposed a great burden on them.

In my old age I complain justifiably about the over-establishment and under-performance of government, local government and private enterprise employees charged with services to the public. In Lagos in 1941 attitudes were very different. Errors were made, it is true, but no complaint could be levied on account of absence of concern and immediate response. The colonial establishments, rudimentary as they were at that time, responded wholeheartedly and immediately to the needs of the British gunners in their midst. This was as true of local personnel as it was of expatriates.

A problem, which the civil government maintained from the outset was primarily the concern of the military authorities, was the sudden high incidence amongst the British troops of venereal disease. Nobody had warned the troops beforehand what they were likely to encounter in Lagos. As one gunner confessed in a letter which I censored at the time "...it's only too easy to f...yourself silly here." Professional ladies of the town gathered round the gunners camps each evening and as

111

their price in those days was only sixpence or ninepence they weren't short of custom. Local mores also allowed unmarried girls, by English standards, considerable freedom and there was no dearth of young ladies, presents given or not, willing to experiment in a new experience—sexual intercourse with an English soldier.

Venereal diseases were rife in Lagos and many gunners went sick. The military authorities, pressured by such civilian temporary-military personnel as myself, proposed the immediate formation of two or three brothels which would be carefully supervised and restricted to the military only. Counterparts at our own level in the Lagos medical and health departments and in the police and administration were ready to co-operate but the higher echelons of the colonial government said, "No." They sympathised with our predicament but did not wish to risk an adverse reaction from London. And so the problem dragged on; we did what one could with advice and the issue of prophylactics but we were no nearer a final solution when British AA support for Lagos was withdrawn in the latter part of 1942.

Graham de Burgh was also concerned by the absence of amenities for British troops. Inter-unit football was all right for the twenty-two players but hardly met the needs of the majority of the men. He pressed me to come up with other proposals. I looked first at an "adoption" scheme—each gunner to be "adopted" by an expatriate family. When I went into it I found such a scheme unworkable as most of the expatriate staff were busy for long hours and few were accompanied by their wives. Only a small percentage of our gunners could be looked after in this way. Sea bathing seemed to present the best prospect but even so the surf and undertow on Lighthouse and Victoria Beaches, open to the sea, already accounted for a number of drownings each year and it was considered unjustifiable to subject visiting troops to the risks. The only possibility was Tarquah Bay, which lay between the west and middle moles at the entrance of Lagos harbour. Here the bottom shelved gently down from the beach and the two moles protected the bay from the high surf and draw-back of the South Atlantic-facing beaches either side of the harbour entrance.

In co-operation with the commanding officers of each of the three batteries we organised regular "amenity" trips by the Marine Department launch, *Waafla*. I'm afraid that we ignored the absence of life-saving equipment for the full complement of the *Waafla* but required that an officer should always be in charge of each party.

I soon found myself hoist with my own petard for the scheme hadn't been running for more than a few days when my turn came to be in charge of a party. As we passed the yacht club, about a third of the way down the harbour, there was a series of four or five thudding explosions from the vicinity of the harbour entrance. The heavy, humid, air, the wind of our passage and the muted distant roar of the surf on Victoria Beach combined to dampen the sound of the explosions. "Not bombs," said one of the British NCOs. "No, nor shellfire," said another. Both knew what they were talking about.

The *Waafla* continued. As we rounded the mole into Tarquah Bay several of us simultaneously spotted a man swimming in laboured fashion midway between the central and eastern moles. The *Waafla* rolled dangerously as the passengers crowded to the port side. I ordered the men to take their heavy army boots off and to divide equally, half of their number on the starboard side, half on the port. The *Waafla* captain reluctantly altered course to bring the launch up to the man in the water but he suddenly disappeared from view and did not reappear. Without waiting for further instructions from me the captain turned again for Tarquah Bay. The captain was right: the *Waafla* bulging with thirty-five troops on board was unfitted for rescue work.

Reaching Tarquah Bay we gently ran our bows onto the sand and encouraged the men to wade ashore as quickly as possible.

A British sergeant and I and the *Waafla*'s captain and crew then headed once more for the harbour's entrance. We passed a fishing canoe the occupants of which told us that the Lagos dredger had been sunk just outside the harbour mouth. There had, they said, been explosions along each of the moles and the dredger's surviving crew were still somewhere in the water. The canoe's occupants were plainly too frightened to have stayed in the area or to have searched for survivors. The sergeant and I agreed that the explosions had almost certainly been caused by mines.

By now the flooding tide was flowing briskly and had reached a speed of three or four knots. We zigzagged across the harbour mouth searching for survivors. A shout came from the crew member in the bows—he had spotted a body six feet under water. Cleverly responding to the instructions of the look-out the *Waafla*'s captain kept station with the body. I went in over the side and reached him on my second dive. I seized him round the waist and kicked for the surface. Then the victim came to life enough to seize me with one arm round my neck. He was choking me. The *Waafla*'s sides were three feet above the waterline and it seemed an age before a line could be lowered and the drowning man pulled roughly into the launch. I followed. One of the poor chap's arms was broken in several places.

He was then quite dead. It seemed unbelievable that he'd seized me with his sound arm under the water.

We picked up two other bodies and two living survivors. One of the latter was treading water apparently unconcernedly. The other, I heard later, died in Lagos General Hospital from the effects of a penetrated lung.

There were suggestions that the mines had been laid either by a German U-boat or by Vichy agents using small vessels from French territories to the west. I don't believe that it was ever satisfactorily established which method had been used.

A few days after the loss of the Lagos dredger and most of her crew an incident occurred on Victoria Beach which left me deeply ashamed of myself. It was early on a Sunday morning. Kat and I visited the beach. There had been a fierce storm to the south during the night; it was nearly high tide and the surf on the steeply sloping beach was formidable. People were not nearly as adept in dealing with strong surf in 1941 as they are today. A few years back in Australia Kat and I watched the Australian young disporting themselves, with and without surf boards, in truly enormous surf near Sydney in a manner that very few experts anywhere could have emulated in 1941. That morning I don't think any of the few bathers on Victoria Beach were doing more than paddle as the great waves streamed in and drained rapidly back down the beach.

A small crowd had gathered a little way down the beach. Shouts and screams could be heard. A young Greek (as we afterwards discovered) was in trouble in the high surf. He was caught in the line of breaking waves and unable to free himself. One moment he'd be hurled under by a high breaking wave and the next washed back by the fast under-tow. Nobody would go in after him. I should have done so. I knew enough of the theory to have survived myself but the memory of the crewman's arm around my neck was too vivid and I feared he'd drown me along with himself.

I ran down the beach. There was, I'd remembered, a life buoy and a length of rope, in a glass fronted box somewhere in the vicinity. I found it and returned, perhaps four minutes later. The young Greek youth had been washed ashore by a luckily timed wave and was in the process of being thrashed with a large piece of handy driftwood, by a white man sporting a military moustache. I didn't intervene to stop the beating but the shame of not having gone to the youth's rescue has been with me now for fifty-six years.

The Governor and Commander-in-Chief Nigeria from 1935 to 1943 was Sir Bernard Bourdillon. I see that his pensionable emoluments when he was appointed were not far short of £350,000 p.a. in today's values—a measure of the importance of Nigeria in the imperial hierarchy. In 1941 he was aged fifty-eight but as I remember him he looked much younger. He had initially joined the Indian Civil Service in 1908 serving there until 1917 when he saw military service in Iraq rising, after the war, to the post of High Commissioner. Subsequently he served as Colonial Secretary, Ceylon and as Governor of Uganda before coming to Nigeria in 1935. He was heavy with experience of the British overseas interest.

In the ordinary course of events I wouldn't, of course, have come into contact with the governor being, as I was, a very junior officer with less than two years' experience of Nigeria at present on secondment (if that is the correct term) to the military. However, I was playing secretary of the polo club which we kept going as far as war-time exigencies permitted and Sir Bernard was a very keen polo player with two of the best ponies in the club. During the course of a chukka rank was forgotten. No matter whether the chap you were marking was an emir, or a general or the governor himself, you rode him off as hard as you could and the rules permitted.

After the last chukka one evening the governor got off his pony next to me and said: "Milne, would you like to play my ponies when I'm away. They'll need the exercise." I said immediately, "I would indeed, sir," and he added: "One thing though, I don't want their tails tied up. I hope you don't mind?"

I was honoured and flattered by his offer but I wondered where he had picked up his views about tails. Possibly India or the Middle East. The head Government House *mai-doki* could be trusted to pull the tails and keep them as showy as they presently were but trying to play serious polo with great bushy tails swishing about was a different matter. It would halve what handicap I might have. Any games I played on those ponies would have to be gentle ones, beginner's chukkas at best.

There might be a problem too, if I was to be posted away from Lagos during HE's absence but this could be dealt with when it emerged.

Kat was known to the Bourdillons. In fact she'd recently been rescued by Lady Bourdillon. On arrival in Lagos she had been posted to the secretariat as a secretary-typist. Sir Bernard worked in an office in Government House and was in the habit, whenever he required the services of a stenographer, of calling on the near-by secretariat to send someone along. Kat hadn't been more than a week in Lagos before her turn to take dictation from HE came round. Although it was only a few hundred yards to go the GH Daimler arrived for her and round she went in great style. She found Sir Bernard in a hurry. He rattled off the draft of a broadcast he was due to give on the local radio that evening. He wanted the transcript before he went off on some other engagement. The subject was an account of recent Nigerian troops' successes in Ethiopia. Kat had managed to keep up with the narrative but she was utterly foxed by the local names and didn't get one in ten of them. HE had found her a table and typewriter in an outer office and left her to get on with it.

She was sitting there wondering desperately what to do when Lady B came in. "My dear," she said, "you look very concerned. What is it?" Kat confessed. "We'll soon sort that out," Lady B said. "Bernard had a dispatch from Mogadishu this morning. Let's find it." She took Kat into the private secretary's office who rapidly produced the dispatch. Then all three got down to it and fitted the place names into the appropriate context. The private secretary ventured to improve the phraseology from time to time. Kat's relief, I'm sure, was palpable. Lady B had gained the reputation of being a kindly, no-nonsense person who performed her role as governor's wife with humour and quiet confidence. I could well understand why all thought so well of her. And he, too, was much liked in his own right. He possessed a rare common touch. He also did much before the war to expand higher education opportunities overseas for individual Nigerian scholars, a new policy which later paid dividends.

Just after the war the Bourdillons' son, B G Bourdillon, who had a colonial service appointment in Palestine, was killed in a Stern Gang-engineered explosion in the King David Hotel, Jerusalem. It seemed at the time to me a bitter wrong that a family who had done so much for pacification in the third world should be called upon to bear such a loss. Sir Bernard died two years later at the early age of sixty-four.

Marriage was planned more slowly and with greater deliberation by Kat's and my generation than it seems to have been since. Had either of us been seriously challenged from February to July 1941— "Are you Kat/Malcolm going to marry Malcolm/Kat..." the answer would have been "yes". Between ourselves, one to the other, we had not gone as far as that until about July. It was only then that the war seemed to have changed gear. There was a long road still to travel. We could see—or thought we could see—some way ahead for our own lives. Kat had been transferred from the secretariat to an MI6 Mission in Lagos. I was deeply involved as Staff officer RA in the fortress command of Lagos. We both believed we were putting out as much as we were capable of. We slept well at nights. Kat had her Force Road flat—a perquisite of her job. I occupied a room in the Ikoyi Club. There was no question in those days of our living together. The very suggestion was detrimental one to the other and to the establishments that employed us.

When I said to Kat, "I think we should get married soon," she asked for twenty-four hours to think the matter over. They were a bad twenty-four hours for me. Was there really doubt in her mind? I thought marriage between us was inevitable. Didn't she?

The next day Kat said, "Yes, of course we can get married," adding, partially in explanation; "You asked an important question and it's not my nature to rush into an answer without proper thought."

My father and the Aunts accepted all I told them of Kat and welcomed the prospect. Kat and Jack, in the months that followed were to establish a close understanding in their exchange of letters. My colonel readily gave his permission. Kat's parents did not demur and in fact Kitty at once plunged into arrangements for our marriage in Jos on 11th August 1941.

It was as well that Kitty didn't waste time for it transpired that the deeds of the Jos Anglican Church prescribed that only Bishops could perform marriage services there and the Bishop of Jos would be on tour far away until September. Kitty got round this apparent difficulty by arranging that we were married in the resident's office in a civil ceremony in the morning but went through a formal church marriage service (which could not be registered) for the benefit of the guests in the afternoon. She asked her old friend A A Cullen, then Resident, Bornu Province, to perform the civil ceremony in the resident's office. It says much for Cullen's loyalty to Kitty that he allowed himself to be made use of in this way and left his busy office in Bornu to undertake the 700 miles round trip in war-time.

I was at a loss to find a best man but this didn't deter Kitty one iota. She merely instructed Nigel, Kat's administrative service brother, then mobilised into a battalion of the RWAFF at Kaduna, to report for duty as best man at Jos on 11th August. The other day Nigel told me that he'd demurred to his father, "I don't even know this man Milne," but all he got was a crisp, "Don't you start making trouble. There's been enough already."

It was left to the elements to make a final gesture. The service in the Jos Church passed off well enough. Kat and I, followed by all the guests, then set off for a reception in the Cothay's house, twelve miles from Jos. A fierce tornado—tropical circular storm—raged across our route. We stuck twice and an easily crossable ford in normal flow rose two feet in as many minutes as Kat and I watched it. We got across but we gathered that numbers of the cars following had difficulty, several even finding that it was too much for them.

We had been lent a prospector's cottage, standing remote and lonely, in a little group of hills a few miles south of Kat's parents' house, for our twelve-hour honeymoon. We left the relative security of our chauffeur-driven car at Ladi and continued on my motorbike. Some old dear had warned Kat that marriage was a hazardous and unpredictable voyage. Kat commented that the good lady had been right from the word go.

During the night I was suddenly woken by a tremendous din on the corrugated roof of the cottage. "Lions!" I yelled. "Lions on the roof." Kat didn't say anything. She knew there were no lions within 300 miles of Jos. The din was much more likely to have been made by baboons disturbed from the rocks just above the cottage.

The following day we returned to Lagos and work.

Those who knew us both were unanimous in saying that I'd done a lot better than Kat in getting married. I now had a comfortable Ikoyi flat to live in in lieu of a small, dark Ikoyi Club bedroom. I enjoyed the services of Musa Biu, her excellent steward, and could share Kat's car. She, on the other hand, had merely acquired the multitudinous worries of a spouse in addition to her work which already kept her fully occupied.

The last four months of 1941 passed, for me, in a flash. I remember staff problem after staff problem arising, it seemed daily, and a continuous struggle to discover the correct "drill". I worked in the Commissioner of the colony's office block which had been given over to both the GOC Nigeria and the Lagos Fortress Command (I little knew then that I was to take over the same office block in 1956 when I inherited what had been the commissioner of the colony's role.)

The GSO1, Lieut Colonel C R A Swynnerton, was singularly helpful. Time after time, as problems arose, he would indicate in a few succinct words what course should be pursued. I would hunt up the regulations and produce action proposals. Doubtless he felt concerned that the interests of so many British gunners were involved not to mention the rapid expansion of the RWAFF batteries, lay on one staff officer's shoulders and he not a regular soldier to boot. He had the endearing habit—unlike many regular staff officers I served under during the war—of turning up in my office with problems or instructions rather than summoning me, the junior officer, to him. Whenever he appeared at my door with a paper in his hand I knew that something important was afoot. He would invariably leave the slip of paper behind. Often it bore a series of headings concerning the matter he'd come about and served me after he'd gone as a valuable aide memoir.

After the war Swynnerton was appointed a Major General and served as GOC Nigeria for a couple of years.

Kat was sworn to complete secrecy concerning her work. I never pressed her to reveal what went on knowing that it would have been waste of my time even to try. After the war I did learn the details of one operation her organisation had been involved in from one of the participants and a good story it made. Leonard Guise, earlier in the war an administrative officer of eight years service, had been seconded for King's messenger duties.

During the course of his travels he'd noted the position of an Italian cargo vessel tied up in Santa Isabella harbour, on the Spanish island of Fernando Po. Two German vessels of about 600 tons each were also tied up in the same harbour. All three vessels had elected to remain in Santa Isabella rather than run the risk of being sunk nearer home.

SOE planned to capture the three vessels and tow them back to Lagos. The personnel consisted of twenty-five government of Nigeria employees assisted by eight commandos and two SOE men expert in the use of explosives. This party on the outward trip were carried in two Nigerian tugs; the larger possessed relatively quiet turbine engines. The smaller of the tugs made so much noise that it was decided to use two canoes for the seizure of the two smaller enemy vessels.

All went well with the seizure, the Italian crew of the freighter offering no resistance and even the elderly Italian stewardess remaining silent. The reputedly ferocious German pair in charge of the two smaller vessels were entertained by an agent and when the raid actually took place were in no fit state to intervene.

There were, however, two moments when things became a little hairy. The commando charged with blowing up the anchor chains of the larger of the German vessels lit the fuse too early without issuing a warning to his mates who were caught by the resulting explosion. Guise, who was on the foredeck of the smaller German vessel, was flung on his back and a mills bomb that was blown out of his hand ended up at the feet of Bill Newington and the commandos where they were taking shelter behind a bulkhead. Fortunately the mills' bomb pin remained in place and the bomb did not explode.

It had been agreed that, once clear of the harbour of Santa Isabella, the larger tug with the Italian freighter in tow should proceed ahead. The smaller tug's engines seized up fifteen miles out of Fernando Po. The crew had no wish to be captured by any vessels the Spanish authorities might send in pursuit; not being in uniform they feared they might be treated as spies if caught. Repairs were effected with feverish haste and held up long enough to permit the party's safe return to Lagos.

SOE picked the Nigerian government members of the expedition with care. Of those I knew personally Deric Fountain went on to become a commissioner of police, Tony Abell to be Governor of Sarawak, Leonard Guise a high official in the Nigerian Federal Secretariat and Bill Newington made an enviable reputation as the atypical bush DO, fiercely loyal to his staff and the strongest of personalities. All four at the time were in their mid-thirties and were friends.

Bill Newington was DO Kumba when Kat and I were first posted to Bamenda in 1947. The Kumba-Mamfe link of the Buea-Bamenda road had not then been completed and it was necessary to motor through "the French side" via Nkongsamba and Dschang. The road from Kumba to the frontier was very bad as it was the middle of the rains. It wasn't long before we hit a rock with the sump. We made temporary repair on the roadside with soap and returned to Kumba, begging Bill Newington and Edmée for beds for us all. "You'd better warn Freddy Kay (then SDO Bamenda) that you'll be a day late," said Bill. I drafted a telegram and asked Bill to send it. I'd written: "Regret twenty-four hours delay stop Sump cock knocked off making repairs". "Hey," said Bill, "you mustn't waste words on a government telegram," and crossing off one word gave it to the messenger to dispatch.

About the time of the Fernando Po expedition I found myself suddenly catapulted into a situation where, in spite of not knowing the full facts, I still felt my superiors were teetering on the edge of catastrophe. Early one morning in the office I received an instruction to report immediately to the GOC Nigeria on Apapa Wharf. My motor bicycle was the only means of transport available and I covered the six and a half miles in twelve minutes. On the dock some 700 Nigerian troops were squatting being addressed by the GOC himself. Reporting to one of the general's staff I gathered the troops had just disembarked from one ship—having taken part in operations against the Italians in East Africa—and were refusing to re-embark on another ship for onward passage to the Middle East. They had been promised sufficient leave in Nigeria to visit their families before onward passage but this, owing to some last minute switch in convoy arrangements, was being denied to them.

The men were silent and sullen. The situation was on the verge of full scale mutiny. I felt sick with concern for the men. If ever there was a need for an experienced Hausa-speaking Northern Nigerian DO to talk gently to them this was it. Force…or the suggestion of force…was exactly what was not required.

A GSO II on the GOC's staff gave me instructions: I was to secure a firing party of British Troops from one of the three British AA Batteries in Lagos and return with them without delay.

I couldn't make out who was interpreting for the general, and so judge whether he was damaging or improving the situation. I knew absolutely that the suggestion of a firing party of *white* troops might result in untold damage to the Nigerian war effort. I had thoughts of refusing the order but this was discarded as soon as it entered my mind. I merely acknowledged the order and said, "I'll keep them out of sight."

The return journey into Lagos was as slow as I dared make it—twenty-five or thirty minutes. I was numb with the wrongness of what I was doing. The Gunner CO wouldn't believe me at first when I passed on the order to him. It took him thirty minutes to collect the men, check their equipment and dispatch them in a truck.

I left the firing party some 400 yards from the wharf well hidden behind a line of sheds. I then tried to report to the GSO II who had originally given me my instructions.

Miraculously the wharf was nearly clear of troops. A few men were climbing the gangway leading to the troopship's deck but most, it seemed, had already boarded.

The General had left. The GSO II, when I found him, told me that a Hausa RSM had sought permission to speak to the troops. The general, thank heavens, had agreed. Ten minutes of diatribe and some discussion later the men had, apparently of their own violation, started to embark.

The magic words, possible only to a Northerner long versed in the thinking and ways of Nigerian troops, had been said. A very dangerous situation, severely damaging to British and African relations, had been averted by the narrowest of margins.

The Japanese attack on Pearl Harbour on Sunday, 7th December 1941 altered the whole tenor of the war. The Americans lost five battleships, and thirteen other major warships were severely damaged, but within days the great industrial power and military potential of the United States was aligned not only against Japan but against Germany and Italy as well. It would take some time for the full effect of this major change in circumstance to bear fully upon the enemy but bear it surely would. Up to the 7th December 1941 it was hard to foresee the end of the war. After that date we felt it was never seriously in doubt, although, had we known it in December 1941 that we would be faced still with another three and a half years of war, we should have been dismayed and disappointed.

Each letter from home during the last months of 1941 bore worsening news of my father. He was seventy-three years old and the improvement following his severe illness in the early part of the year had not been sustained. His letters became shaky and infrequent. His spirit, which had brought him so stoutly through the crisis of the year before, slowly ebbed away. I was deeply sad to learn of his death on the 9th January 1942. A letter from Jack, written as he always did with realism, sympathy and understanding, helped. Kat's sympathy helped, too; she grieved truly for his death and was deeply sorry she would never know him.

There were no simple pregnancy tests in those days but about the time of my father's death we became sure Kat was pregnant. She was somewhat surprised to be asked by the doctor in Lagos whom she consulted "whether she wanted it". We presumed she was being offered an abortion, possibly in view of her war work. We consulted and the following day she told the doctor politely that she hoped to proceed to the full course. By February 1942 we had both been in Nigeria for over eighteen months and in the view of our respective superiors it was time we both had a break in a temperate climate.

I hesitated to expose ourselves unnecessarily to the dangers of the North Atlantic at the height of U-boat activity particularly now that Kat was pregnant. Our thoughts turned to South Africa from where Kat could probably get back to Nigeria. We discovered that if we could reach Matadi, eighty miles up the River Congo from its mouth at Pta da Pedroa, we could then travel by narrow gauge railway to Leopoldsville, thence by river boat up the Congo, thence by its tributary, the Kasai, to Port Franqui. There was a railway from Port Franqui to Ndola on the Southern border of what was then the Belgian Congo. Thence onwards we could travel by train via Lusaka, Livingston and Bulawayo to enter the Union of South Africa at Beit Bridge.

Kat's father's cousin, Colonel Owen Solomon, owned an orange farm-cum-cattle-ranch at Shooter's Hill, Otto's Bluff some fifteen miles out of Pietermaritzberg. Owen and his wife, Avis, had written to Kat's parents saying they would be able to put Kat and me up for our leave and invited Kat to stay on with them as a PG on very modest terms for as long as she wished. They were used to babies, having many grandchildren, and the arrival of ours would present no problem.

There was a maternity hospital in Pietermaritzberg, which was well regarded.

It seemed an ideal arrangement. I began to make covert inquiries. Ships connecting Lagos and Matardi were few and far between. At last, in late April 1942, we heard of one. She was a freighter of some 8,000 tons. Calling at Lagos she had a cargo to pick up at Matardi before returning to the United Kingdom. The agents in Lagos booked accommodation for us. The precise date of her arrival in Lagos was, of course, kept secret but we were advised to be ready from the end of April onwards.

Kat's Mama told us that Avis Solomon had been an Otto. The land had originally been acquired from the Natal government of the day by an Otto forebear in the middle of the nineteenth century by the practice of boundary riding. A man was entitled to purchase as much land as he could ride around in twenty-four hours. Owen's own family had farmed in Kent for many generations. He had first come out to the country when serving with a yeomanry regiment in the South African war. He stayed on although he served in France in the Great War ending up as battalion commander.

(Avis' and Owen's four sons all served in the 1939-45 war. Sadly the eldest and the youngest, Stanley and Tim, were killed during active service in North Africa. Cedric, having survived four years of war, died very suddenly of a heart attack in 1946 when playing polo on the family field at Otto's Bluff. Only Otto, the second son, was left to them.)

We packed up. Kat sold her car and I my motorbike. We sent Musa off to Angus Robin whom he served loyally for the next twenty years. We scribbled hurried letters, Kat to her parents, I to the Aunts. For some reason neither of us can give, we remember little of those last two or three weeks: what date we actually sailed, what the ship's name was, where she was registered. Kat does remember that all the deck officers spoke English and I remember she was fast enough to make membership of a convoy unnecessary. Her speed was also high enough to legalise her tackling the lower Congo in full flood. The current in this part of the river was truly formidable and ships unable to achieve the prescribed minimum speed were prohibited from entry.

We arrived at the mouth of the great river in the late afternoon—I remember taking on the pilot against a sun low on the horizon—and as night suddenly fell moving off upstream. We had some eighty miles to travel to the Port of Matardi, much of which we would undertake that night. One of the officers told us that about forty miles from the mouth we would pass close to a mid-stream island where the channel narrowed considerably. There, he said, we should understand the need for the minimum speed rule.

We dined as usual with the ship's officers. It was before the days of air-conditioning and ventilation depended on the speed of the ship's passage. Because of our slow movement against the adverse current, and following breeze, we found the air in the saloon and in our cabin unbearably hot and sticky. We decided to sleep on deck and took cushions to where we judged was the coolest spot.

About midnight we were awoken by the most active electrical storm either of us had ever witnessed. The sky over the north bank of the river was constantly riven by flashes of lightening, some horizontally from cloud mass to cloud mass, others vertically from cloud to ground. It was impossible to distinguish the sound of individual discharges one from the other. Just as the northern sky was aflame with a myriad flashes so were our ears assailed by a continuous roar of sound. We prepared for rain and were ready to take refuge in our cabin but no rain fell. We were slowly approaching the narrows and for a few minutes the ship appeared to be heading for the dark tree-clad slopes of an island ahead. A glance over the side and it was plain we were moving through the water at a high speed although our speed over the ground was minimal, judged by the slowness of the island's approach. We watched, at once anxious about the arrival of rain and the need to remove our bedding and yet fascinated by the electrical extravagance.

We brushed past the island, so close I wondered whether the pilot was in error, went back to our bedding and eventually slept.

We awoke at first light. The ship was at anchor riding a gentle three knot current. Matardi was in sight on the south bank three or four miles away. Going down to our cabin I picked up from the boat deck some fresh branches still bearing leaves. Had these, I wondered, been blown on board during the night or had our lifeboats, suspended well out from the boat deck, brushed them off the island.

(Kat, when I read the above passage to her the other day, fifty-five years after the event, said, "I seem to remember that we plucked those branches ourselves as we passed the Island." She may be right.)

As we went ashore a fundamental difference between the Belgian and British colonial systems was immediately apparent: Matardi was a little Belgian river port plonked down in central Africa. Nigerian towns, on the other hand, were just what the name suggested: African Nigerian towns which had accepted certain European innovations, such as railways, glass-fronted shops, tarmacadam roads. The engine driver and the guard on the train to Leopoldville, as we expected, were Europeans.

A revealing little scene occurred as we turned up at our Leopoldville hotel. We were met by a small coterie of porters, all immaculately uniformed, all—except one—strongly-built men of obviously Bantu descent. The single exception was a tiny, middle-aged man half the size of his fellows. He was plainly of pygmy origin, the first that Kat and I had seen. All moved forward when we had finished registering and I distributed the loads amongst them roughly on the basis of the biggest load to the biggest porter. The pygmy, handed some small bag of Kat's, turned puce with fury, flung it in the direction of the tallest of his fellows and seized the largest load of all, which was an ancient cabin trunk, once the property of my Aunt Kate, weighing about one hundred pounds. With an angry heave he got it on his head and marched off in the direction of our room.

No words passed between us. None were necessary. I wonder, now if he knew I'd learnt the lesson of his little demonstration well enough never to forget it.

If the difference between the Belgian Congo and the Colony and Protectorate of Nigeria required further emphasis it received it in full measure as darkness fell. The streets suddenly emptied of Africans. There was a nightly curfew. All Africans were required to leave the European town and spend the night in the "Reservation Indigène".

As we paid for our passages we were assured that the stern-wheeler that would take us up the Congo and Kasai was queen of the fleet and quite comfortable. An hour aboard brought home the reality. She was, by any measure, appalling. Our "cabin de luxe" was so small that one of us had to lie on the bunk while the other dressed; the bunk so narrow that Kat and I had difficulty in finding space enough to lie on our sides. There was insufficient width for both of us to lie at any time on our backs. Kat's burden presented a problem which we solved after a couple of nights by placing a gun case under the mattress between us.

The dining saloon was minuscule. It was necessary for all except the lucky pair of passengers who occupied the seats near the door to reach their places by clambering along the row of chairs.

The alleyway between the ship's rails and the cabins was so narrow that if one attempted to sit across it knees were drawn up to chins.

There was one latrine and one shower available for the twenty-eight first-class passengers. The former was near, but luckily downwind of, the "cabin de luxe." Even so we were often woken up in the night by the rattle of action from a few feet away.

The bridge and captain's accommodation occupied the deck above our heads. The captain, needless to say, was a white Belgian and—assuming that the individual we saw leaning over the rails from time to time was the captain—as scruffy as the rest of his command. He seemed to wear the same grubby singlet and pair of shorts throughout the voyage. We occasionally caught a glimpse of a stout, unkempt white woman whom we imagined was the captain's wife. She, too, never left the top deck.

There were two barges lashed onto the starboard side of the stern-wheeler. These were crammed with items of cargo and lower class passengers. There were no sanitary arrangements on the barges. When nature called, the more active suspended themselves over the stern; the less active and the old were supported by their friends.

We presumed that the captain had been given a fixed sum to feed the first-class passengers. He certainly showed no signs of overspending. Occasionally the stern-wheeler would come up on a fishing canoe paddling diagonally across the river and slow up enough to permit the occupants to seize hold of one of the barges lashed to our side. A fierce bargaining process would then commence, the captain shouting down to the fishermen, the latter conferring and then throwing their voices skywards. If agreement was reached a crew member would appear, take the fish and pay over a few coins. At least twice the captain grew irate, put the stern-wheeler into full speed ahead and did his best to capsize the canoe as the occupants continued to argue the price.

We tied up every night, generally at some small wharf backed by a few huts. On at least two nights we failed to reach a village and the captain was forced to make fast to a forest tree ashore. Whether it was a wharf or forest tree the procedure was the same: the stern-wheeler, and her unwieldy burden of barges would edge over towards the intended mooring spot. Twenty yards out a crew member would place the loop, spliced onto a stout mooring line round his neck, and slip into the dark waters of the river. The stern-wheeler, meanwhile, would maintain station against the slower bank side current with a trickle of power. For a few strokes we would see the white soles of the crewman's feet as he struck out underwater for the bank. Then, for what seemed an immensely long time even these would disappear and the only evidence of his continued progress towards the bank would be the line slowly being paid out from the coil on deck. Suddenly the crewman would reappear, brown-black against the blue-black of the muddy banks, and wade the last few yards ashore. The same three or four crew members specialised in carrying the mooring lines ashore in this way. They obviously took a pride in the time they could spend under water. They provided a daily spectacle and would often draw a round of clapping from the watching passengers.

Every night at supper the insects became intolerable. Perhaps the worst night of all was one of the two we were forced to moor off the forested bank. We had soup that night and it was necessary for each of us to make a little tent with napkin covering head and plate. Even so the soup plate became a trap for struggling, drowning insects which we had first to ladle on to the floor before attempting to win a spoonful of liquid for ourselves.

We may have had the cabin de luxe but it certainly wasn't de luxe travelling.

The stern-wheeler burnt a prodigious amount of wood. At each pre-arranged night stopping place cords of wood, each piece about six inches in diameter and three feet long would be loaded permitting a first light start the following morning. We relied upon trips ashore for exercise as it was quite impossible to walk the deck of the stern-wheeler so crowded was it with passengers and luggage.

I attempted to talk to the barge passengers but language was a difficulty and in any case most of them were singularly uncommunicative; life on the barges was so horrible it was best endured in silence. The only exception was a group of itinerant Hausa traders, most from Nigeria, all with cages of grey parrots which they were proposing to sell to European miners in the mining areas of Rhodesia. These chaps were an intrepid bunch and it was amazing what distances they were prepared to travel to make a small profit on their wares. The parrots they had purchased on the way down in the Cameroons and the Gabon. I talked with them in my limited Hausa.

Our evening ashore at the deserted town of Banningville, one hundred miles up the Kasai river, was an eerie experience. The roads in the residential area were sealed, bungalows were built on regularly spaced plots, but all was deserted. It was a dead town. There had been a devastating epidemic of yellow fever there the year before and the whole Belgian population had been evacuated.

We slowly walked the deserted streets, traversing another world. In the kitchen of one of the bungalows a small tree had grown up alongside the stove. In others, windows—and accompanying mosquito screens—were broken and lianas and young vegetation rooted inside thrust out through the holes.

I was wearing shorts and clapped my hand to the back of my bare knee. The palm came away covered in blood. I'd killed with that one smack some forty or fifty mosquitoes all feeding busily. Kat was wearing slacks and escaped the attention I received. We were glad that we recently had had anti-yellow fever injections in Lagos and hoped that they would be effective against the Banningville species of yellow fever should it differ from the Nigerian variety.

At length we came across other human beings. A small gathering of our fellow passengers were peering into the windows of a shop that was still, apparently, occupied. The occupants were Hindu; the owner a dealer in ivory, the members of his family carvers. They had decided to stay on but judging by the low prices they asked for their goods trade was poor. We had only a little money between us but Kat and I purchased cards of carved ivory buttons, salad servers, a letter knife and other items for a few pence in all. Each of the items we acquired would have been priced at well over ten pounds each in London 1942 prices. With many years of hindsight I realise we passed up that evening one of the very few opportunities that life will ever offer us for making a real bargain.

Night by then was near and Kat and I set off for the jetty where our stern-wheeler was made fast.

We were overtaken by a file of prisoners escorted by a warder bearing a rifle. They were—typical we felt of the Belgian Congo, unknown in Nigeria—chained together. We followed the file and watched them enter the arched gateway of the prison just as dusk turned into night. Here, were doomed men, it seemed, about to cross some lost Congolese Styx.

Our river journey came to an end at Port Franqui. We still had 800 miles to reach the frontier between the Belgian Congo and Northern Rhodesia at Ndola but this time our transport was to be by train and we were to travel in comparative comfort having a first-class compartment to ourselves. Wood was again the fuel and like the stern-wheeler on the Kasai the engine seemed to consume an enormous quantity. The train stopped at every small station and if wood was being taken on we were assured of at least half an hour's stop for exercise.

There was one occasion when the train restarted without warning. I managed to scramble aboard the last carriage but was confined there until the next stop. Kat, feeling unwell at the time with the dual effects of altitude and pregnancy, not having seen me get aboard, was most concerned. "It's all very well for you to laugh," she said when I rejoined her, "but I didn't see you getting on the train and you had all the money in your pocket."

The exciting element of our three day train journey to Ndola was the gradual increase in height—which meant a welcome drop in temperature—and the substitution of rain forest, of which we'd had our fill, with open savannah.

We read many hours a day and spent long periods gazing at the passing countryside. Wildlife was disappointing; we saw very little of note. The people, on the other hand, were a never ending source of interest. Their dress, appearance and behaviour patterns changed surprisingly rapidly and Kat, particularly, was quick to note changes in agricultural practices. We were being painlessly indoctrinated, without being aware of it at the time with the all-important relationship of the African with his land.

The rolling stock gradually improved—carriages were bigger, more modern, cleaner—as we progressed south. We left Livingstone in the early hours of darkness and although the train stopped for several minutes near the Livingstone Falls it was too dark to view them. We could hear the roar of the water and were forced to shut the carriage windows to keep the spray out.

We changed trains again at Bulawayo before joining the north-south line which entered the Union of South Africa at Beit Bridge en route for Jo'burg.

We were still wearing tropical clothes when we arrived at Jo'burg early in the morning. It was a great mistake. There had been a severe frost the night before and it was still freezing when we reached our hotel.

We spent two breathless days savouring the luxuries war-free civilised living could provide. Both of us remember particularly a coffee shop with limitless varieties of cream cakes and every brand of coffee that Africa can boast. The shops vied with pre-war London.

It was a day's train journey from Jo'burg to Pietermaritzburg. The Solomons met us and took us straight out to Shooters Hill.

Owen and Avis Solomon were precisely as Kat's parents had described them: both in their early sixties, he tall, thin, wiry and an English gentleman in every sense of that old-fashioned word; she, whiter haired than he, very active, a consummately good Zulu speaker with all that language's clicks and glottal stops. They hadn't suffered the loss of Tim and Stanley then and were quietly proud of their four fine sons serving with South African forces in the Middle East.

I hadn't been two days on the farm—spending much of the time accompanying Owen on his daily rounds—before I had to think again about race relations. We prided ourselves in Nigeria that there was no place for such a term. We treated our black colleagues and educated members of the public as we treated each other. True, we looked upon the peasant in the bush, the snotty-nosed children on the roadside, the great hoi-polloi, much as the educated middle class Englishman looked upon his less fortunate countrymen…people to be treated with politeness and courtesy but people, because of their inadequacies, basically different. The word "inferior" was never apt…we believed implicitly that no man was fundamentally inferior to another. The potentiality was always there. And I think the educated African of 1939 looked upon his bush cousins in the same way. But—and here I have to confess to my prejudice that the Union of South Africa was synonymous with bad race relations—this just wasn't so in the case of Shooters Hill. Owen talked to the farm labourers and squatters precisely as he would have talked to the labour on his father's farm in Kent. He knew everybody's name, what the young people who had left the farm were doing, how they were getting on, the family problems, even the feuds. And I did not see that Owen's practices should be so very different from those of his neighbours. All this, I felt, was far removed from the "reservations des indigènes" and the blatant separatism of the Belgian Congo. I should have a word or two to say on this subject when I got back to Nigeria.

The squatter system was basically "six on, six off". The farm in practice supported two labour forces; one force would work for six months in the year and then the other would take over. The girls were expected to work in the house or the dairy, men on the farm or in the orange orchards. During the "six-off" families would cultivate sufficient land shown to them by the farm owner to grow their annual food stuff needs. In addition each family was allowed a limited number of cattle. It seemed a workable and sensible system for the early days of farm development. Doubtless problems would arise as the second and subsequent generations of squatters took over.

One morning we spotted a light aircraft flying over the farm at about 4,000ft agl. Owen told us that aircraft were unknown in the area before the early 1930s. The owner of a neighbouring farm, seeing the first ever had said to his barely interested headman: "See that thing? It's an aeroplane. There's a man in it." The headman, slightly more interested now, asked, "Is there? How does he get his food?" At the same time an onlooker had asked, "Is there? How did he get there?" Two very logical responses.

Another morning Owen announced after breakfast, "There's too many damned dogs on this place. I've got to shoot some," and, looking at me, "Are you coming?"

He called for two ponies and handed me a shotgun fitted with a rudimentary sling. "Put that across your back," he ordered and, giving me a handful of cartridges, said, "These are loaded with SSG—they ought to be enough at short range."

I followed him out onto the farm. We hadn't gone half a mile before we came on a great brute of a dog, something that looked to me like a cross between a ridgeback and an English foxhound, hunting happily by himself. "There's one. Told you so," said Owen catching a brief glimpse of the dog. "No, leave him alone," he ordered, seeing him better (I hadn't even touched my gun, much less unslung it), "he's as game as hell. I know him. Only last year he treed a leopard."

Half an hour later very much the same thing happened. Two dogs, hunting hard, disappeared over the skyline. We galloped after them. "Oh, hell," said Owen, "leave that pair alone. They were sired by an old dog of Avis." She'll never forgive me if we shoot them." And so we let them be.

And so, indeed, it went on. At lunch-time, getting off our sweating ponies back at the house Owen thanked me for coming along. "Useful morning. Very useful," he said.

Needless to add, neither gun had been fired.

A dark and cloudy afternoon a little later on sticks in my mind. "I'm going up to the ford to meet the ox-wagon," he said. "Quite a sight with a full team." This time he persuaded Kat to come, too. "She can ride old brandy," he announced. "Just the quiet, steady sort for a pregnant girl."

(I noticed that poor Kat had to push Brandy at every stride in order to keep up. But that is by the way.)

The wagon was late. We eventually met it high up the valley side on "the short road" from Pietermaritzburg. It began to pour with rain. There were several near claps of thunder. We sheltered as best we could under a small clump of trees. It was truly quite something to watch the heavily laden wagon slithering and sliding down the rough track. The rain, the thunder and the struggling team of oxen put Owen in mind of a story he couldn't resist telling us.

"It was on old Oom Piet's farm, way over there," he said, pointing, "just like this: rain, a full team of oxen and lightening. Suddenly there was a great flash and poor old Piet dropped off his pony, struck. The pony miraculously survived. The headman picked old Pieter up and carried him, dead as he was, to the wagon where they laid him out. The rain came down worse than ever. The headman's son, who was an aware young chap, pointed out that they couldn't bring old Piet back to the farm wet as well as dead ("Huisvrou will kill you.") The headman agreed and they covered the corpse with sheets of corrugated iron to ward off the rain. Just at that moment the wagon itself was struck. In fact, the bolt of lightening flung the sheets of corrugated iron high into the air. Old Piet sat up, presumably revived by the second shock.

"Waar is my perd!" he cried.

"And that," said Owen, "is a true story."

But Kat and I by then were wet, and cold and disbelieving.

(iii) Gidan Shettima and GHQ West Africa

On the 13th June a telegram from Military HQ in Nigeria arrived instructing me to report to Imperial Movement Control, Cape Town for a return passage. We caught the night train from Pietermaritzburg on the 15th and reached Kimberley twenty-four hours later. There we caught a train to Cape Town arriving on 16th June. My diary records that we had tea that day at the Del Monica, the smartest and most frequented spot in town. Fifty years later Kat's nephew, a leading consultant in paediatrics in Cape Town, told me that the Del Monica had to some extent changed its spots; it had become the recognised meeting place where sailors met their tarts. We stayed at the Grand Hotel which in those days was very grand.

I reported daily to the IMC from 18th to 22nd June. They told me the convoy was still forming and there was no point in going aboard until the last moment. Kat bravely stayed on although the school holidays were about to begin and she was far from certain to be able to get a sleeper for the return journey to Pietermaritzburg. It was quite a shock when I reported to the IMC rather late on the morning of 22nd June to be told I'd better hurry as the convoy was due to sail in two hours' time.

Kat later told me she'd had a very uncomfortable train journey back. The train, as anticipated, was full of university and school children returning home for the winter holidays and all she could secure was a top bunk in a full second-class carriage. Bearable, perhaps, in her condition for a day but an ordeal for the four days the journey took.

I have no memories of the return to West Africa other than gales and calling at Walvis Bay. Being a gunner I was assigned to long hours of duty on one of the four inch guns mounted on the bows of the freighter. We weren't attacked, there was not even a major alert. I was missing Kat.

It must have been a particularly slow convoy following a long zigzag course far out into the South Atlantic for we took twenty-two days to reach Lagos. I found a regular soldier occupying my old post (which had been upgraded from captain to major) and myself ordered to report to Sharwood-Smith in the Gidan Shettima, Kano. Nobody would, or could, tell me what I was supposed to do there; it was all too secret. I did gather that the good Shettima had been a favourite concubine of a previous Emir and that he had built her a thoroughly secure house in the old city. Room entered upon room, room upon room; vast mud walls surrounded the compound; there was only one entrance door. It was an ideal place for a clandestine enterprise.

Sharwood-Smith was an enigmatic forty-three year old, a classical scholar with—as I judged upon meeting him—a love of adventure. He'd won an open scholarship to Emmanuel College, Cambridge in 1916 but had joined the RFC in 1917. He'd served on with the RAF (which absorbed the RFC in 1918) on the Rhine and the NW Frontier of India until 1920 when he joined the colonial administrative service. In 1942 his substantive civil rank was SDO. I can't remember his military rank, if any, at the time he was running the Gidan Shettima. It was the sort of quasi-military activity in which rank wasn't important. What mattered was that he was eighteen years older than I was and those eighteen years were heavy with the experience of West Africa that I lacked.

I have never really discovered what we were supposed to achieve in the Gidan Shettima. In mid-1942, of course, Nigeria was surrounded by pro-Vichy territories of indeterminate loyalty: French Equatorial Africa, Niger, Dahomey, the Ivory Coast, even the Cameroons but the situation was changing rapidly with allied progress in North Africa.

The Gidan Shettima was full of radio equipment manned by French speaking British signallers. One of their tasks was to monitor French radio traffic in West Africa. Information secured from this source was valuable in general moves against the Vichy regime, to persuade officers to "come across" (join the Free French forces of De Gaulle), or even to co-operate economically with the allies. We ran a number of agents, most of them Africans, employed by, or in close proximity to, "target" Frenchmen.

I remember Sharwood Smith asking an African visitor to the Gidan Shettima from Agades in Niger to bare his nether regions. This he was perfectly happy to do. There was nothing left. Everything...penis, testicles, the lot...had been cut off. But I gathered the chap was a consummately good agent and brought in the most useful and accurate information. If I remember rightly he was in his early thirties and of

Taureg descent. I believe that the practice of total castration still continues amongst the inhabitants of Agades in the Region of Air.

One of my early instructions was to organise, as a cover, a shooting trip along the 750 miles of the northern and north-western frontier of Nigeria from Lake Chad in the east to Birnin Kebbi in the west. The proposal was for me to make contact in person with various wobbly Vichy supporters who might be prevailed upon to escape into Nigeria and to change sides. The assumption was that my Hausa and schoolboy French would be good enough for the job (neither were). However, the general situation affecting Vichy's influence on the West African territories changed about this time and the idea of my trek was at first shelved and later abandoned.

Very shortly afterwards the whole Gidan Shettima unit was disbanded and Sharwood Smith himself returned to the Northern Region Provincial Administration as a resident. He was subsequently promoted Chief Commissioner, Northern Region and then, between 1953-1954 the post was successively upgraded, first to Lieutenant-governor and then to Governor, Northern Nigeria. As he received an advance in the Order of Knighthood in keeping with each upgrading of the post, Sharwood Smith received three knighthoods. He naturally became known in the service as "Three times a Knight Sharwood Smith". I didn't know his Hausa nickname at the time but my brother-in-law, Nigel Cooke, who was the last British officer to serve as Senior Resident Kano, told me it was "Mai wandon karfe" best translated as "Wearer of Iron Trousers". It was true that on many occasions when others might have elected to sit down Sharwood Smith preferred to stand...and stiffly, at that. The Hausaman said in effect, "He must have iron trousers. He *can't* sit down."

I was then posted to an intelligence staff job at GHQ West Africa in the Gold Coast. The headquarters occupied the whole of Achimota College, some six miles out of Accra. In many ways the large conglomeration of classrooms, residential quarters for the staff, dormitories for students and miscellaneous blocks of servants quarters were easily adapted to the needs of a large military headquarters. One snag was that the whole was spread over a considerable area. However, the time to walk the long distances between offices was reduced by the installation of a rudimentary telephone system.

The GOC-in-C was General Sir George Gifford, a fifty-six year old regular soldier with long experience of colonial troops. Later in the war he was to serve as Commander-in-Chief of the Eleventh Army Group in SE Asia. In the ten months I was to serve in GHQ I never once had a glimpse of General Gifford. He was reputed—whether rightly or wrongly I can't say—to be a pretty irascible character. There is one story about him, although probably apocryphal, nevertheless it illustrates the awe in which he was held. A subaltern, very busy compiling some tedious list, was finding the inter-office telephone of great help to him. He was in the middle of a call when a strange, alien voice came on the line. "Get off the bloody line," the subaltern cried in fury. There was a pause. "Do you know whom you are addressing?" the voice asked. "No," said the subaltern, still furious. "Who?"

"The GOC-in-C."

"Do you know who *you* are addressing?" asked the Subaltern. "No," came the voice, coldly. "Thank God," said the subaltern and hastily put the receiver down.

Needless to say I treated the telephone system with circumspection.

The junior members of the department for which I was working shared a large, dark, classroom of the college. One of my colleagues was an Australian poet called, if I remember rightly, John Manifold. He gave me much assistance with the job itself, but often our conversation, probably to the annoyance of the others, digressed into the theory and practice of verse writing. He was full of erudition and I often thought of him as being able to hold his own in the discussions of the Bloomsbury Group were that group to survive.

Our G1 was a tall, sarcastic regular soldier. Like Swynnerton he often came into our office but unlike Swynnerton he came only to complain or tear a strip off one of us.

It seemed he liked an audience for his rougher, more authoritative passages.

I had continued lessons in Hausa during my time in Kano and I searched far and wide to locate a teacher in Accra. At length a Hausa-speaking NCO on guard duties at GHQ itself suggested that I contact Mallam Bello Dan Dago Kano who, he averred, was living in Accra. I bought a bicycle and on one of my afternoons off visited the Mallam. I never discovered precisely why he had moved his immediate family—a wife and some young children—to Accra but believe it was to do with his family's trading activities. After an hour's discussion—he spoke impeccable English—on general matters I broached the subject of Hausa lessons. He hesitated; I could appreciate that he perhaps felt the role of mere teacher was below his dignity so I quickly said, "It's asking, I know, a lot but perhaps we could broaden our discussions to matters affecting my work as an administrative officer in Nigeria." The suggestion appealed to him.

Mallam Bello Dan Dago Kano was to become a member of the Northern House of Assembly and to establish for himself the reputation of a moderate of logical and constructive views. During our association in Accra I found his thoughts for the future and his philosophy of absorbing interest. Here was an intelligent and far-thinking Northerner, such as I'd not come across before, and I learnt a lot from him not to mention a fair whack of Hausa.

Our daughter, Jackie, was born in Pietermaritzburg hospital on the morning of 12th August 1942. She was a large baby—eight pounds ten ounces—but Kat's cable assured me that both she and the baby were fine. It was a fortuitous day for her to arrive for not only had grouse shooting played a large role in my life with the Aunts but I should be able to assure my friends and others in the future that Kat and I had been married on 11th August and Jackie had arrived on the 12th. It wasn't until October that a photograph of Jackie, taken with Kat looking a thousand dollars, arrived. By then Jackie weighed eleven pounds eight ounces and I showed the photograph round the office with some trepidation for nobody can say that babies of that age look particularly beautiful. Some wag spoke for them all when he declared: "Beautiful maybe not, but by hell you and Kat must be patriotic; it could be Winston Churchill himself."

It took me many years to appreciate that all healthy babies of that age look like Winston in his late sixties.

A letter dated 18th December 1942 from Kat brought news that Stanley Solomon had been killed in action in North Africa. Avis and Owen Solomon were very deeply upset; Kat said that Owen aged ten years on the day they received the telegram but they nevertheless went on with the arrangements for Jackie's christening which had been fixed for St Peter's Church in Pietermaritzburg on 22nd December.

Ever since Kat and I had parted in Cape Town at the end of June I had missed her with a sense of deprivation that was akin to physical pain. I knew that thousands of other men were in precisely the same situation; it was part of what war entailed. At the same time I remembered my chauvinistic attitude in Onitsha just before I'd been called up. Provincial administration work in Nigeria at a time when my country was grievously threatened seemed a matter of low priority. But in the two years between the war had changed. America had come in. Jack's prophecy, mentioned on page 94, was coming true. There were other priorities than serving in line regiments. Men were being directed increasingly to areas where they could make the optimum contribution. I'd had the minimum of training as a line soldier; the rest of the time I'd served in various staff jobs. So far as cold logic went I knew that my best contribution from about December 1942 could be made in colonial administration. At the same time I admitted to myself that above all else I wanted to be with Kat again. Return to the colonial service would probably mean that she could join me. I opted for the logical course for reasons which I have to confess were primarily selfish.

I had been told, off the record, that the Nigerian government had requested my release in October 1942 as they had a special job they wanted me to undertake. About Christmas 1942 I was told in great secrecy that serious discussions were being held in London, up to cabinet level, on the advisability of returning all colonial service personnel to their civilian duties.

Cabinet Paper WP (43) 25 of 14th January 1943 records the whole story. This paper is now available to the general public in the Public Records Office, Kew.

The secretary of state for the colonies, anticipating the outbreak of war, had asked colonial governments in February 1939 to be prepared to release officers with military qualifications for work directly connected with the war effort.

In the critical days beginning in June 1940 a further directive had been issued to colonial governments emphasising the earlier one and adding that deficiencies of local staff could be counteracted by curtailment of leave and longer hours of work.

These measures and others such as the posting to territories of colonial officers who had escaped from Malaya and Hong Kong helped but did not relieve the situation. Lord Swinton, then Resident Minister in West Africa, had given his view that the colonial administration in West Africa in particular was so over-taxed "that the machine may break down at some important point".

Cabinet (under Atlee's Chairmanship, Churchill was attending the Casablanca Conference at the time) accepted Oliver Stanley's—then S of S—recommendation that colonial service officers should be returned to civilian duties with minor provisos in the case of naval officers who wished to remain in the Royal Navy after the war and a few individuals who were urgently required on specialist military duties.

It was at the end of January 1943 before our proposed return to civilian duties became generally known, when Brigadier Thompson, the GOC-in-C's chief staff officer, surprised me by ringing me up on the inter-office phone saying, "Look here, Milne, if you really want it I can probably arrange for you to join a unit in Burma rather than go back to Nigeria."

I replied, "Thank you, sir, but no. I want to return to the work I've been trained for."

I wondered if I'd alienated him but apparently not, for he sent for me a day or two later and said, "We've got rather an urgent task and would be grateful if you could tackle it before you leave." He explained that the GOC-in-C was required to adhere to a very strict "white ceiling" of personnel. The return of colonial service expatriates to the four colonial governments of the command would leave vacancies in his ceiling but he had recently been instructed that all British Intelligence organisations in his command, even if reporting directly to London, were to count against it. It was necessary for an officer to contact the head of each "mission" in turn and come up with accurate figures. He would give me a letter of authority and transport would not be a problem.

I remember very little of that exercise save that the final figures were unexpectedly high and that a regular pattern rapidly emerged: the less significant the chap in charge was in terms of status and rank the more difficult it was to dig the figures out of him. The head of the major British intelligence unit operating on the West Coast was an elderly colonel. He'd had previous advice of my visit and had all the pertinent facts and numbers noted on a slip of paper. It took three minutes or so to make sure I understood the figures and I had the information I'd been sent to collect. Chaps in charge of little missions a tenth of the size were much more trouble. None queried my credentials—I can't think why not—and some were very hard to find in the first instance. At the time I attributed the reticence of the small man to psychological reasons—he didn't welcome an army captain prying into his so important organisation—but now, with the cynicism of old age, I wonder if some of those units didn't have more to hide.

It was almost an anti-climax to receive instructions to report to the secretariat in Lagos for return to civilian duties. Spending three days in Takoradi, waiting for a sea passage, I met Eric Shipton. He was on his way from the UK to pursue some undercover assignment in Persia having spent two years as HM's Consul General in remote Kasgar; he hoped to secure an onward air passage from Lagos. He was ten years older than me. Already his record as a mountaineer, and traveller in mountain areas was formidable; a dozen times my own modest climbs in the Alps and on British rock. But one of the nicest things about him was to treat all mountaineers, however humble their record, as his equal. We spent one of the three days tackling the walls of a ruined castle of Portuguese origin. One wall in particular he tried from one end, me from the other. Neither had any great difficulties and we met in the middle, each sitting astride the remnants of the wall and about seven feet apart. I suddenly spotted a large scorpion a couple of feet in front of him. He saw it at the same instant. A moment later we both realised it was either dead or the sloughed outer carapace of a scorpion. My relief was palpable, he merely grinned. It may be fanciful but from the outset I found him very much a loner. He would walk along looking up at the castle walls, at the little cliffs near Takoradi, at the distant views of sea and sky almost as though he himself were part of the scene. He seemed to merge with the natural world around him, to belong.

On the ship to Lagos he handed me some quite roughly typed pages comprising about 50,000 words in all, explaining that it was the draft of part of a book on mountaineering. Would I have a look at it and comment? The tougher the comments the more they would help him.

I did as he asked and handed the pages, together with some hastily scribbled comments, back to him just as the ship reached Lagos. It was not until some years later, well after the war, that I realised the draft he had shown me had been the opening half of *Upon that Mountain*—by any measure a classic of a mountain book. The devil of this recollection is I cannot remember how I commented.

A Government House car met Eric as the ship docked. Being a VIP he was to stay with HE. I thought it greatly daring of him to insist that I share the car with him and that he take me to the door of the Ikoyi Club, where I was to stay several miles out of his way, which he did.

An hour later he telephoned the club. Sir Bernard and Lady Bourdillon were going away that afternoon. They'd told him he was very welcome to ask a guest to dinner so he hoped I'd dine with him. He'd send a car to pick me up. Then he added, "Actually, I've something of interest to show you." He wouldn't say more.

I duly turned up and can remember that we dined in considerable state. After dinner he dismissed the servants for the evening and I asked him what it was he had to show me.

He replied by moving out into the spacious entrance hall and pointing at the inner wall of the large staircase which mounted, I think, three stories. "Quite a climb, there," he said. "I bet it is a first ascent."

We had a go at it. I took a different line to his and at one point, about twelve feet off the ground, got into difficulties. Trying to descend I fell off. I landed on my feet but bruised them quite severely. We were both climbing in our socks. I remember hobbling about Lagos the next day in pain.

Sadly, in later years, I was never to climb properly with Eric Shipton. In the late forties and early fifties, when I'd built up enough experience perhaps to suggest such a thing, we were in different continents. After that advancing arthritis of my hips wrote me off.

———————

I was posted to Nnewi in the Onitsha Province and on arrival in Onitsha in April 1943 found everybody—white officials, African staff, the commercial cadre—very subdued. The fact was they were all, young and not so young, very tired. Lord Swinton's warning to the war cabinet "...the machine is so stretched it may break at some important point" was no exaggeration. I was relatively fresh: I'd enjoyed some leave in South Africa less than a year before. Many of my colleagues in Onitsha had served two or even three years without a change and saw no immediate prospect of relief ahead.

In those days—without air-conditioned offices and houses, exposed to a wide range of tropical diseases, and the enervating effect of the humid heat of Southern Nigeria—a tour of eighteen months was an ordeal even to a young and active man. Longer tours took their toll. Add to this the additional work and responsibility burdens that war imposed and it will perhaps be appreciated that life was no sinecure. I was to go down from my natural weight of eleven and a half stone to nine and a half stones in the two years that lay ahead before we went on leave to the United Kingdom.

After the war the normal tour for senior expatriate officers was reduced to twelve months. I am sure that this considerably increased their output while on duty. Leave entitlements continued to be generous: one week's leave for each month served although of course leave entitlements which could not be enjoyed during the war had to be accumulated.

I found an exciting package of letters from Kat awaiting my arrival in Onitsha. Two or three days later a letter addressed to me personally was forwarded from the secretariat in Lagos. It was from Brigadier Thompson, BGS in GHQ Accra thanking me for the help I'd given the military, wishing me good fortune in the future and adding: "I've written to the Chief Secretary, Nigeria, telling him you have done a very good job of work during your time here."

We all of us receive "thank you" letters from time to time, some deserved some less so. Of those I have been fortunate enough to get none has given me more pleasure than that from Brigadier Thompson—how big of him to accept my wish to return to colonial service work.

(Looking up Geoffrey Thompson's military record after the war I was delighted to find that he had become a Lieutenant General and had received a knighthood before final retirement from his chosen profession. From 1961 to 1970 he became a director of Arthur Guinness and Son, Dublin—a company that in those days was reputed to appoint only true gentlemen to its board.)

CHAPTER FIVE

War-time Service in the Provincial Administration;
Oil Palm Production

There were three immediate priorities facing the provincial administration at that stage of the war. Perhaps the most important was to eliminate all arrears in the native court judicial system. Once this relatively effective system broke down people would begin to take the law into their own hands with dire consequences. Another urgent task facing DOs and ADOs in Eastern Nigeria, in particular, was to stimulate and increase the trade in oil palm products. These were wanted urgently in the United Kingdom for foodstuffs and explosives.

The third task was to recruit for the Nigerian military forces. There was no dearth of would-be recruits and it was possible to set very high physical and general standards. All three tasks necessitated wide and frequent travelling. It was important that the systems of judicial and local administration put in place pre-war by the colonial power should not only work but be seen to be working well throughout the years of war; consistent travelling in the districts showed the flag, as it were, but was also conductive to good administration.

By far the most important economic tree in the Eastern Region was Elaeis Guineensis—the oil palm. This tree grew wild in the rain forest areas and was also to be found in the damper deciduous and riverine forests immediately north of the true rain forest. Nigeria had produced oil palm products for the past four centuries. At the beginning of the twentieth century some 50,000 tons of palm oil and 100,000 tons of palm kernels were exported.

These quantities had increased to 125,000 tons of oil and 250,000 tons of kernels by 1924. The tonnage remained fairly constant until World War II.

An oil palm produced four or five clusters of nuts known as "bangers". A large banger would measure some twenty inches from

142

stem to conical bottom and would consist of seventy or so individual nuts. Each nut was wrapped in a few millimetres of oil-bearing pulp. The kernels were surrounded by a hard shell, the kernels themselves being about the size of an English hazelnut. The extraction of oil from the pulp surrounding the kernel, up to the outbreak of war, had not been an efficient process, less than sixty per cent by weight being won by the local method of boiling and skimming. Manually operated screw presses were introduced about 1930 and improved designs were produced just before the war. By 1939 there were still not many of these improved presses in the whole of the Eastern and Western areas of Nigeria—perhaps 150 in all. Most of these were owned by "big men" in the trade.

A system of produce inspection was introduced in 1928 which thenceforth ensured that palm oil and kernels exported from Nigeria met the requirements of European importers. Produce inspection did much, too, to popularise the extraction of palm oil by screw presses, the latter being able to produce much purer oil than the indigenous method of boiling and skimming.

Palm kernels were obtained by cracking the pericarps, left over by the oil presses, by hand. This, of course, was a highly labour-intensive process. There were small, mechanically driven cracking machines on the market but these were not in great demand in the early days of the war.

Extension work, from 1929 onwards, by the Department of Agriculture had attempted to encourage the use of improved oil palm seed to establish small plantations of higher yielding trees. For a variety of reasons—mostly concerning the time scale and expense involved—these methods were not met with an enthusiastic response. At a later stage in the war when every conceivable device was employed by the administration to expand the oil trade several of my colleagues and I found it productive positively to encourage the theft of high quality oil palm seedlings. We put the price up, established nurseries whenever feasible adjacent to a road and took away night guards. Seedlings disappeared in satisfactory numbers.

Shortly after Sir Bernard Carr became Chief Commissioner, Eastern Region in August 1943, a team of four oil palm production officers (OPPOs as they became known) was appointed under the overall guidance of J W Wallace, a regional deputy director of agriculture. The team consisted of L T Chubb, who was then an SDO of eighteen years' service, Bill Newington and Thomas Harding, DOs of thirteen years' standing, and Johnny McCall, the baby of the party, a DO of seven years service. All were energetic individualists and could be relied upon not only thoroughly to inform themselves of a complex African trade but also to make friends with its protagonists. Chubb was given responsibility for Onitsha Province, McCall Owerri, Harding for Calabar and Newington for Ogoja.

Lord Swinton, Resident Minister in West Africa, attended the meeting held to launch the team and kept close touch with its efforts thereafter. A note of cheerful optimism was struck from the outset. At the inaugural meeting the relatively minor point arose of a suitable telegraphic code name for the team, Bill Newington at once suggested "Crackers" and "Crackers" they became. It was, if one thinks about it, a pretty remote prospect that a team of four administrative officers could make in a few months a major impression on a trade which was some four hundred years old and which had resisted well intentioned governmental measures for the past forty years of colonial government. But they could and did…as I hope to demonstrate in the pages that follow.

One of the early tasks of the team of OPPOs was to enthuse and then mobilise the support of members of the provincial administration— the residents, the DOs and the ADOs; prior to this they had to educate themselves.

An oil palm, maybe thirty feet tall and swaying in the wind, takes some climbing. And climbed it must be because the bangers grow under the fronds protruding from the crown of the tree. The banger cutter used a sling often made of lianas which he placed round the bole of the tree and made fast round his waist with a toggle. He would move rapidly up the tree with a series of concerted movements: lean in, move the sling up with both hands, lean back against the sling and paddle the feet a short distance up the stem of the tree. It was a real athlete's work and I'm afraid there were frequent calamities. Sometimes the sling broke, on other occasions the cutter's feet slipped and he fell down the trunk of the tree. Other times the heavy bangers themselves caused damage, perhaps striking the cutter as they fell. It was truly a difficult job for the cutter to wield a machete and at the same time preserve his balance and security so far above the ground. Today, I am told, banger cutters can't be found in much of Iboland. They are simply not interested in facing the risks for the small wages involved. Things were very different in 1943, then there was no difficulty in finding young men.

Improvement of the evacuation routes for oil produce was another important element in procuring expansion of the trade.

Generally the bangers were head-loaded from the base of the tree to the nearest oil extraction point. As the war went on some improvement of the footpaths leading out of wild oil palm groves—that is clusters of wild oil palms in the high forest—to oil extraction points was undertaken by native authorities. Most native authorities, however, concentrated on improving what became known as "oil roads"—track or roads which permitted lorries to travel in all weathers between oil extraction points and a company's bulk buying station.

It is at this juncture that the Raleigh bicycle assumed an heroic role. Although slightly more expensive than other makes of bicycle on sale in the oil palm areas they were considered by the public to be much stronger and better value. A large group of bicycle carriers grew up. It was not unusual to see as many as ten four gallon ex-kerosene tins filled with palm oil or three large sacks of kernels carried on a single machine. The "driver" would mount and peddle away on the level or downhill but the merest incline forced him to dismount and push. The used kerosene tins were easily obtainable at about twopence each in the country markets.

Bicycle palm product carriers were a development of the "bicycle taxi" system which was a feature of much of the Eastern Region pre-war. You could hire either a first, second or third class bicycle. First class the passenger sat all the time on the heavy duty carrier, he would even be pushed up the hills; second-class required the passenger to walk whenever the driver dismounted. Third class passengers swapped propulsion duties with the driver...or so it was said.

After Kat's return to Nnewi in late 1943 she and I organised a Grand Oil Palm Sports Meeting, the object being to publicise the need for increased production. The local population scented blood and excitement—and turned up in their thousands. As the event took place in the rainy season—when storms were liable to occur at any time—a powerful rainmaker was engaged. Such gentlemen claim to be able both to bring and to hold up rain. This particular gentlemen, in return for a hefty fee, undertook to keep rain away until after the last event. This he successfully did. There were strong men competitions—who could lift the greatest number of tins of kernels—a rate of nut cracking competition and so forth. However, the event that raised the acme of excitement was the palm oil carriers' race. The winner was offered a voucher for three Raleigh bicycles, the second man two and the third one. Needless to say the prizes were donated by the large oil exporting firms and were very generous. A voucher for three Raleighs was worth a year's takings for a strong-limbed bicycle carrier.

In fact this race yielded all the blood and mayhem the crowd obviously longed for. The course was only 500 yards in length. The start was the wide drive outside the ADO's house. The twenty

145

competitors could be lined up abreast at this spot. Each bicycle was loaded with eight four-gallon debis filled with water in place of the usual palm oil—a load of about 320lbs for each competitor. The course then followed the drive for 150 yards to the rest house where it swung sharply left down the steep descent to the station proper. Thence it ran along the edge of the football field to the finishing line. There was a sharp bend at the bottom of the hill. The whole race could easily be seen by the crowd gathered on the football field or alongside the course.

We lacked a starter's pistol but I used my sixteen bore shot gun for the purpose.

The 150 yards straight to the rest house turn was the scene of much bumping and furiously shouted imprecations. Some four or five carriers turned the corner abreast closely followed by the rest of the field, all peddling fiercely and all quite oblivious of danger.

The bend at the bottom of the hill was too much for everybody. The leaders were going too fast to negotiate the bend had they been alone, much less tight-packed in line abreast across the road. A horrendous mêlée followed.

The crowd roared with delight. I retain a memory of bicycles rearing up, of shining black figures flying through the air and the most painful pile up. There followed a brief spell of relative calm as the contestants picked themselves up, sprang back onto their machines and headed for the finishing line.

Romaine, interpreter in Nnewi at the time and staunch friend in my errors, quickly came to my assistance. We gave the advertised prizes to the contestants in the order that they battled their way over the finishing line. Those who were injured in the pile up—some were—and others who had suffered damage to their machines were quickly compensated.

Inadvertently, Romaine himself became a prize winner in one event. Kat was supervising the weight lifting contest. Two competitors were vying for final place. Both complained bitterly that the last test, involving lifting ten debis of palm kernels attached to a pole, was far too much. They had struggled to lift the previous nine. Romaine brooked no argument. "It's very possible," he declared in Ibo and proceeded to demonstrate it was. Kat, to my mind perfectly logically, gave Romaine the first prize and adding the second and third prizes together divided the sum equally between the two remaining contestants. Fortunately for her they were cash prizes.

Growing knowledge of the trade in products of the oil palm in Nnewi and adjoining areas of Onitsha and Owerri Provinces emphasised the importance of waterways in the transport of oil and kernels. Many of the bulk buying stations manned by staff of the exporting companies such as John Holts and UAC had been established on waterways prior to the advent of organised government in the area. For instance, a map of Eastern Nigeria produced in 1901 by Philip & Son of 32 Fleet Street, London, now in my possession shows bulk buying stations at Abushi on the banks of the Niger some few miles south of Onitsha and at Ogutu on the Orashi River.

Another important link in the chain connecting the oil palm in the high forest to the finished product in the United Kingdom was the middle man. These gentlemen established themselves at strategic points on the flow routes of oil and kernels in increasing numbers as the war went on and the trade increased in importance. I used to think of them as serving much the same function as booster stations on a pipeline. Many established themselves on the banks of a waterway where they purchased oil and kernels from bicycle carriers. They then arranged onward transport to the exporting firm's bulk buying station generally by water. Others owned a lorry or, in some cases, a fleet of lorries and, having established themselves at some buying station, arranged onward transport by road. Sometimes the middleman was an individual operating on his own; Reuben's and Peter Nwanalude's names come to mind; their waterside buying points took on their names. At other spots a number of middlemen would operate in a loose partnership agreeing amongst themselves what prices they would offer.

Prices varied nicely with demand. Naturally, considering the heavy workload involved, bicycle carriers preferred a number of short hauls rather than a single long one. On the other hand put the lorry-owning middleman's vehicle out of commission or even absent with a load, and prices at his station would drop drastically, albeit temporarily.

Provided the waterways themselves remained clear, transport by canoe was a good deal cheaper than by lorry. Before the war the Marine Department had been responsible for "snagging" the major waterways of the whole of the south of Nigeria. A small department at the best of times, the marine department had allowed a higher proportion of their staff to serve on war duties than most others. By 1943 many of the waterways in Eastern Nigeria—and indeed in Western Nigeria also— had become choked with fallen trees following nearly four years of neglect. It was a matter of never-ending surprise to me how easily great forest giants could be overcome by a slight change in flow of the adjacent freeway. The next tornado, down they would come, often obstructing two-thirds of the waterway. Two such catastrophes in proximity might not entirely block the passage of canoes but could delay them considerably.

Some DOs had obtained the semi-official assistance of military engineering units very much on an old boy's basis but such help was not often forthcoming. There was nothing for it but for most DOs and ADOs to act themselves. Here OPPOs, and government behind them, were discreet. There could be no question of compelling untrained personnel to use explosives. On the other hand those of us who were willing to have a go were supplied from marine department stores with all the explosives, fuse, detonators and waterproof rubber tape that we required.

Dear Jack (who had been managing director of the Walton family group of small lead and coal mines from 1900 to 1924), hearing what we were up to, wrote me an excellent letter of safety instructions. I had developed the bad habit of pushing the detonator, rubber taped onto the end of the powder fuse, into a cartridge of ammon gelatine. He suggested that we should use a pencil-size pointed stick to make a hole in the cartridge rather than risk a premature explosion by my method. Nobody had warned us not to handle the ammon gelatine with bare hands. We had wondered where the severe headaches were coming from. Jack's letter solved that query. And he gave us an excellent tip for lighting the powder fuses. Often we had struck half a dozen matches, trying to light the small slow-burning gunpowder core. His tip was to cut the fuse at an angle thus exposing more of the powder core, place a match head onto the core and, holding it firmly in position, strike it by moving the match box smartly across it. By this method it was possible to light the fuse at the first attempt, even in a high wind.

Slightly earlier than Jack's helpful letter I had arranged for a British corporal, an explosives expert serving in a royal engineers' unit stationed in Enugu, to come out to Nnewi for the weekend and brief me on the use of "snagging" explosives. Unfortunately his visit wasn't a great success.

With hindsight I realise now that I was slow in appreciating his reactions—reprehensible, it could be said, in the light of my own fears on the tour in Anam and Nzam just after the outbreak of war. But by then I looked upon Nnewi virtually as home territory and I supposed assumed that my companion, trained for war, would take a visit to a Nigerian out-station merely as an interesting diversion. Anyhow, let me recount how the visit went.

I motored into Enugu to fetch him. It rained hard on our journey back and we became stuck in the mud two or three times. Darkness fell when we were still on the Enugu side of Awka. It was about this stage of the journey that I casually told him that as there was only one bedroom in my house I'd arranged for a bed to be put up in the rest house, 150 yards from mine, and he could bath there, too. Of course he'd dine and breakfast in my house. We could spend the morning experimenting with the explosives and I would motor him back to Enugu in the afternoon, myself returning late in the evening. He took all this in silence.

And then, pleasure for me, but, as I now realise, terror for him, we saw not one but two leopards on the road from Onitsha to Nnewi. The first was a quick glimpse but sufficient to silence him absolutely. The second was a magnificent viewing. He appeared huge as we followed him. He only turned off into the high bush after I'd blown the horn and switched the headlights on and off several times.

The following morning the corporal said he'd told me all that was necessary for the safe use of ammon gelignite and asked to be taken the eighty miles back to Enugu immediately. I had no choice but to do as he asked.

On the return journey he confessed that he'd never had such a terrifying night in his life. He'd kept the light (I'd lent him my only Tilley lamp) on all night. He'd neither undressed or slept a wink. The West African bush wasn't for him.

I'd no reason to think that this chap hadn't performed—and wouldn't continue to perform—perfectly adequately in his own unit. It was the suddenness of his introduction to an utterly strange environment that frightened him. Had I been quicker I should have appreciated that the high forest in the dark and rain—never mind the view of leopards—might terrify a young man who had spent the whole of his life in some Untied Kingdom conurbation. It would have been easy enough to have had a bed made up for him in my sitting room. I kicked myself for being so unthinking.

Snagging by administrative officers became a regular practice in the palm oil producing areas. No element of compulsion was involved. There was so much that had to be done in any District in the Region that priorities were left to the judgement of the man on the spot. Perhaps a quarter of the total cadre became competent at the work and built up teams of African assistants. District boundaries were not necessarily observed. I found myself invited to snag in the adjoining Owerri Province, and in other Districts of the Onitsha Province, and complied whenever possible.

Two Orifite men, Okpara and Awgu, became my regular snagging assistants. Neither could speak any language other than their native

Ibo and, although my Ibo lacked any ability to cope with the tonal complexities of the language, the vocabulary necessary to our work was a relatively small one and we seemed to get by. We always needed at least one other canoe in support and this Okpara and Awgu would arrange. They also arranged the hire of the canoe we would use ourselves in which we carried the explosives.

I collected supplies of explosives, fuse, detonators and rubber tape from the Marine Department stores in Port Harcourt, a round journey of about 200 miles. I remember one trip in particular after Kat's return which caused us both some amusement in retrospect. Visiting the Catholic Mission at Ihiala, near Nnewi Kat had told the good nuns of my periodic visits and the mother superior asked if she might go with me on the next to do some mission shopping. The nuns apparently rotated the office of mother superior and when my next trip was arranged the duties had fallen to a very pretty twenty-eight year old Irish girl. She, for propriety's sake and in accordance with mission rules, was accompanied by an older nun. The regular driver, poor chap, was banished to the box body astern and I drove, the two nuns occupying the bench front seat. On the return we carried 1,000lbs of ammon gelatine packed in five pound boxes, and coils of powder fuse together with the mission's and Milne family purchases of butter, cheese and bacon from the Port Harcourt Cold Store (rare delicacies, I may add, not obtainable elsewhere). Four boxes of fifty detonators each were carried in the glove compartment on the fascia panel. Accidents were common on the Onitsha-Harcourt road. Kat remarked afterwards that we had all been nicely poised for a powered flight to heaven should the worst have occurred on the journey back. Fortunately we did not come into collision with either a way-side tree or oncoming lorry.

The Ibo diet lacked protein. Fish killed or stunned by underwater explosions were eagerly sought. It did not take long for riverside communities to recognise the presence of a snagging party. Word would spread rapidly and in some areas fish-hungry onlookers became a great nuisance to us and a serious danger to themselves. On lengths of the Orashi River, for instance where the riverside population was dense and snags profuse, crowd control became a major part of the operation. So keen were the populace for the supply of stunned fish that daring young people of both sexes would creep through the jungle and lie near to the spot where we had lit the fuse for a major explosion. The moment the explosion took place they would plunge into the river and seize as many dead or stunned fish as possible.

I remember one particularly bad day in the Orlu Sub-District where my contemporary Eric Powell was ADO in charge at the time. Previously, on several occasions, we had snagged Orlu waterways at his request. On this occasion I was merely completing work on a section of river and had not troubled to get his specific permission.

The crowd of onlookers became more and more daring with each explosion. I asked Okpara and Awgu to go ashore to explain how dangerous the explosions could be and to warn the young people we would flog any person we caught within 200 paces of any explosion. To test whether they'd "heard talk" as the Ibo idiom had it, I lit a five-minute length of fuse connected to one cartridge of ammon gelatine, likely to result in a relatively harmless explosion. We stationed the upstream and downstream safety canoes only a short distance away from the spot where the powder fuse gave off its smoky bubbles. Of course the crowd crept nearer to the tell-tale fuse.

Almost simultaneously with the explosion we scrambled ashore and did our best to capture as many culprits as possible. I pursued one middle-aged gentleman, who bleated with simulated fear as he zigzagged over a yam field. After a little I was able to tackle him low and hold him, still hollering, on the ground. Okpara turned up and cut a formidable stick to beat him with. The stick was much too heavy and I forbade Okpara to do more than encourage the fellow's yells. There was complete silence in the surrounding forest but we were confident that all was heard. After a few minutes we released our captive and he ran off into the high forest.

The gentleman's cries had served a purpose, however, in warning his fellows and I recall that we were able to get on with unmolested snagging for the rest of the afternoon.

The next day I heard from Eric Powell that an agitated delegation had arrived at his house in Orlu the previous evening and reported that a mad European had severely beaten one of the Orlu sub-chiefs near the river that afternoon. They knew this as a fact because they had heard the chief crying out.

Snagging was physically demanding and a long day would leave one very tired but it provided a welcome break from the more normal routine of native court proceedings and council business. It wasn't long before word spread that the ADO Nnewi was prepared to snag waterways as was already happening in parts of the Calabar and Owerri Provinces. Requests to help with blocked waterways became common. I used to record them in a notebook kept for the purpose so that logical action programmes could be worked out. The smaller waterways were, of course, more subject to blockage by fallen forest trees than the larger rivers and it was on the former that the bulk of our work was concentrated.

Kat, after her return, would occasionally accompany me on snagging expeditions. On these outings she would leave Jackie and nursemaid with one of several Catholic missions in the District, often Ihiala. The nuns, both African and European, were delighted to have a European child in their care and doubtless spoiled her outrageously. Although only fifteen months old at the time, Jackie was able to recognise the spacious open surroundings and whitewashed two-storey buildings which were characteristic in Nnewi of medical or educational missions and put on her best behaviour whenever we approached one.

Kat's first expedition taught me more than one lesson. I was anxious to demonstrate the effectiveness of the open-sided cube principle which appeared to govern the direction in which the snags would be blown. Early on that day we came on an obstruction which I hoped would provide a spectacular verification of our theory. It was on a length of the Orashi River where the twenty-five yard broad stream traversed a section of high and dense forest. The river was very tortuous in that area and the snag was a ten-foot diameter tree which blocked almost the whole channel.

We carefully prepared a charge using five pound boxes of explosives and tied it onto the underwater side of the obstruction aiming at about twenty degrees from the vertical. We hoped that the greater part of the offending tree would be blown into the adjacent jungle ending up some thirty yards from the river.

After lighting the fuse we dispatched the accompanying warning canoe downstream and Awgu and Okpara started paddling our canoe upstream to perform the same function. Bend followed bend; we lost account of the sinuosities. But there was little current and we moved over the ground at a satisfactory pace.

At length Awgu and Okpara pulled into the bank. "We're far too near," said Kat with some trepidation. The two paddlers took her meaning and we moved on. They stopped again. "No, more...more," said Kat. Again they took her meaning and again we moved on.

Suddenly there was an almighty explosion, seemingly at our very elbows. Next, a huge log, the size of a grand piano, was climbing apparently quite slowly, end over end, into the air. It was black and glistening. It appeared to hang above the river about fifty yards downstream and then it fell with a tremendous smack into the middle of the waterway. For a perceptible time the river where the log fell was empty of water. We both distinctly remember the black mud shining in the sunlight and the contour of the river bed—there was a deeper channel near the middle. Fish were flung into the high branches of the forest trees near the bank and descended flopping their way from branch to branch for all the world like a swarm of drunken fruit bats.

Awgu and Okpara laughed; it could well have been the funniest thing they had ever witnessed. They lay in the bilge of our canoe rocking with laughter.

Kat and I took the incident more seriously: I, angry with myself for not having taken proper account of the river's many bends; she, not a little awed.

———————

As soon as I had received instructions, at the end of March 1943, to return to my civilian post in Nigeria I, had of course, cabled Kat and she responded immediately by spending three days in Durban during which she badgered Thomas Cooke to make the necessary train, river boat and air reservations to enable her to retrace our journey down. It was in fact four months before Kat and Jackie arrived in Nigeria and then only after a truly epic journey.

Several factors combined to prevent her. After a lapse of three days Thomas Cook reported that the bookings just could not be made. Kat thereafter dealt directly with South African Railways who early in May confirmed that bookings had been made on South African, Rhodesian and Belgian Congo railways and the river boat from Port Franqui to Leopoldsville. The onward air flight, Leopoldsville to Lagos, would have to be arranged by me from Nigeria. This was fine but in the middle of May Kat became ill.

Weaning Jackie had proved difficult. Kat developed breast abscesses which made her very unwell. She had two protracted spells in hospital in May and June. After an operation at the end of June she managed to secure fresh train and river boat reservations and finally departed on her return to West Africa with Jackie on 18th July. She was still far from fit and the journey from Pietermaritzburg to her parents' house near Jos in Northern Nigeria, which took three weeks in all, became a measure of the sort of person she was. Few women—particularly in her state of health at the time—would have begun such a journey much less completed it, as she did. The whole experience was brought to the very threshold of tragedy by the innocent action of a seven year old Flemish boy on the Belgian Congo Railway.

Kat was occupying a carriage between Elizabethville and Port Franqui with a Belgian mother and son who spoke only Walloon. She asked the pair, as best she could with no language in common, to keep an eye on Jackie while she visited the WC. On her return she found that the boy had given Jackie an unwashed mango bought from a vendor at a previous station. A couple of days later, as they boarded the river boat, Jackie developed severe dysentery and nearly died from the resulting dehydration. There was no doctor available. Kat had nobody with whom she could discuss Jackie's symptoms. There was no means of leaving either the train or the river boat. Kat was utterly frustrated and suffered anguish. Jackie's symptoms subsided after three days and she survived but Kat's instinct told her it had been a near thing.

At the time Sabena were running a Dakota on a fairly regular schedule between Leopoldsville and Lagos. Seats were reserved largely for government-sponsored passengers but I was able to get a reservation for Kat with the assistance of her old office. On the particular flight they came on they went up to 16,000 feet without oxygen and the only thing Kat remembered was that a packet of sandwiches she had placed under her seat on the floor of the aircraft froze solid.

The Bourdillons had left Nigeria earlier in 1943 on final retirement and the new Governor, Sir Arthur Richards, (later Lord Milverton) had taken office. He was visiting Onitsha and adjacent Districts in the first week of August, using the river craft reserved to the governor's use as residence and office and making day visits to outlying districts.

Although I didn't know about Jackie's illness en route or the full extent of Kat's breast troubles I had arranged for them to go on arrival straight up to Jos and Kat's parents' cool house in the hills where I could pick her up once the new governor had left Onitsha.

Dermott O'Connor, hearing that I was having difficulties meeting Kat, said, "Come on. It's an order. You can't leave her in the wilds of Plateau Province, Governor or not. Go and get her." So up to Jos I went by the next train.

I found Jackie in great fettle, fully recovered from her dysentery. Poor Kat was developing yet another breast abscess and was feeling far from well but she wanted to resume her old life with me and I wanted her presence in Nnewi more than anything in the world. Naturally Kitty thought it more sensible for them both to recover from the journey in the cool of Jos but back they came with me.

We had no sooner reached the Nnewi house late in the afternoon when a fierce tropical storm hit the area. Kat's abscess had worsened on the way down and she was feeling quite ill. She was also beginning to run a temperature.

Rain forced its way under doors and through leaks in the roof. We only kept our bed dry by spreading a large tarpaulin over it. It was a miserable welcome. To make matters worse the tornado had no sooner passed than I had to plough a way into Onitsha to attend a farewell function for the governor.

It was well after midnight when I got back. To be sure of dry bedding Kat had taken Jackie into our bed. Both had gone to sleep. Kat was awoken by a fierce blow on the affected breast, struck inadvertently by Jackie. It was sufficiently strong to burst the abscess. Kat was feeling some relief and already her temperature had moderated a little.

Early the following morning I took Kat, Jackie and the nursemaid into Onitsha where Kat was admitted into the small nursing home. The abscess was treated during the next few days and was not, happily, to reoccur.

Back again in Nnewi Kat, quietly resilient as always, soon established a regular routine for the nurse-girl and Jackie. Life returned to what passed for normal in the Eastern Nigerian bush of 1943.

Administrative officers in Eastern Nigeria used to say, half facetiously, that they were on duty twenty-four hours a day. Perhaps matters were more appropriately ordered in the Emirates of the North but in Iboland, certainly, there was an element of truth in the affirmation. The Ibos were a democratic people and expected access. Affrays and other resorts to violence welled up very quickly. If catastrophe struck the people reacted at once, day or night. The public were not afraid to travel in the dark. Good district officers, I learnt, always made a point of being available in response to serious complaints. True, certain unwritten rules had become generally accepted. Native court matters were restricted in the main to office hours as indeed were the bulk of personal complaints which did not involve dire urgency. The line between matters that demanded immediate reference to the DO or ADO and what could await normal office hours was firmly drawn by subordinate government and NA staff. During my own service I was to be woken up in the night perhaps a dozen times and cannot remember a single instance when I queried the junior officer's wisdom in doing so.

Kat and I were getting in a quick set of singles one evening just before dark when the Sergeant of police, wearing mufti, turned up. "We have two men, Albert Nwosu and Alfred Nwokedi, who want police protection. They say Nnewi Otolo villagers want to kill them. There are some villagers already outside the police station and others are said to be coming." I asked him what he wanted to do. "We want to get them into Onitsha straight away. I've only got six men in the station. The others are all out on enquiries. The Nnewi Otolo people could burn the police station here. They seem very angry."

The Nnewi police station, like the other buildings in the station, was roofed with palm mats and largely constructed of wooden materials. It would certainly burn well enough.

"OK," said I, wanting to get on with our game before dark, "use the NA lorry."

"That's the problem, sir. The driver can't be found."

I realised now why he had interrupted our game. "Have them ready with a constable escort and I'll pick them up in my car in five minutes," I said.

The villagers gathering outside the Nnewi police station were certainly in an aggressive mood. Nwosu and Nwokedi, both strongly built men in their middle thirties, were only too anxious to slip with their escort onto the relative safety of the back seat. I told them to crouch down on the floor out of sight until we had passed Nnewi Otolo.

On the journey into Onitsha I tried to find out what the trouble was all about. The story was a pretty garbled one.

Apparently the senior man in Nnewi Otolo, loosely called the Chief, had disappeared about two weeks ago and had not been seen since. The villagers were averring that Nwokedi and Nwosu were responsible and they were threatening their lives—hence the urgent request for police protection. Plainly this was the merest outline of the true situation. I would perhaps hear the full story later.

For the next several weeks I put the matter out of my mind. It was in the hands of the Nigerian police and if they wanted my intervention they would request it. There were a hundred more urgent and pressing matters demanding action from me.

It was Romaine who told me the full story two or three months later following the dismissal by a High Court judge of a charge of murder against Nwokedi and Nwosu. What had actually occurred went something like this: the Nnewi Otolo senior man had indeed disappeared. He had previously been involved with Nwosu and Nwokedi in a dispute concerning ownership of some palm trees. When he couldn't be found the villagers, possibly precipitately, blamed Nwosu and Nwokedi. A party of the missing man's kinsfolk consulted a powerful ju-ju. Having received a considerable fee (of the order of a goat, a basket of yams and ten shillings in cash) the ju-ju priest said he could describe exactly what had happened. The Otolo man had been killed by two Nnewi men—he then described Nwosu and Nwokedi very accurately—and the corpse still lay in the spot where they had hidden it.

Here I should explain that the West African habitually commands a more extensive vocabulary in his own language than the average educated European does in his. The former is capable—when speaking to a co-linguist—of conveying almost a photographic image of an area of bush so extensive is his knowledge of the names of vegetation and descriptions of terrain.

Having consulted the *Juju* priest, the kinsmen of the Nnewi Otolo chief returned to Nnewi and threatened Nwosu and Nwokedi and the latter pair sought police protection.

A search for the missing man was, however, fruitless. No corpse could be found. The kinsmen therefore returned to the priest, told him in so many words that he was a fraud and demanded their fee back. The Osu *Juju* priest wouldn't have any of it. He could see the exact spot where the body, now greatly decomposed, lay. If the Nnewi Otolo gentlemen would double his fee he'd be prepared, in person, to show them the spot. This offer was not to be resisted and after more haggling accepted, payment on results.

He led them straight to the corpse.

Members of the provincial administration were, if I remember rightly, ex-officio coroners under the powers conveyed by the Coroners' Ordinance. I know that I conducted a large number of inquests when serving at Nnewi. If the matter involved suspected foul play, a member of the Nigerian Medical Service was asked to give evidence as to cause of death and the file passed over to the Nigerian police for further action. Accidental deaths were sadly common in the area. A number of palm "banger" cutters fell to their deaths every year and, as our efforts to increase the production of palm products succeeded, their numbers increased. Many local communities were in the habit of snaring fruit bats as the latter hawked round patches of high forest at dusk. Snares were suspended from lines made fast to the upper branches of giant forest trees and the job of climbing the great trees and fixing the lines in place often fell to agile teenage boys. Although most were really excellent and fearless climbers, a number fell to their death. Female circumcision was practised throughout much of the Eastern Region, the operation being performed frequently by elderly women. Unfortunately sepsis was not uncommon and each year a number of young women died as a result of the operation. Although there were occasional pile-ups on the narrow roads generally by over-loaded and speeding lorries, such occurrences were relatively rare but nevertheless resulted in an inquest when they involved fatalities.

The traditional method of transporting dead persons was to tie the corpse to a light timber raft, cover it for decency's sake with a cotton cloth and place the raft across a bicycle carrier (generally a Raleigh). Two young men were required to trot along at head and feet of the corpse to prevent the raft unbalancing. A third man took control of the bicycle mounting for downhill passages.

I vaguely remember being told that a body in an advanced stage of decomposition had been brought into the station and that foul play was suspected. I hadn't, however, associated it at the time with what I knew of the Nwosu and Nwokedi matter. Presumably I had followed the usual procedure in being at Nnewi: as foul play was involved the body would be sent directly to the senior Medical officer at Onitsha who would conduct a post-mortem examination. I would find in accordance with his opinion and pass the file to the Nigerian police for such action as they deemed appropriate.

Anyway, to get on with Romaine's account of the Nwosu and Nwokedi saga: a Preliminary Inquiry had been held by the stipendiary magistrate serving in Onitsha (I was lucky in Nnewi, most PIs were held by district officers using their judicial powers). He had committed the pair for trial for murder.

Between the PI and the full hearing in the Nigerian High Court before a judge, the Otolo elders had conferred. They were quite sure that the two accused had indeed killed the chief during the dispute over the palm trees. "Let us," they said, "be certain that the judge makes no mistake at the trial." So they got together with the main witnesses and concocted new evidence making conviction doubly certain. It was, Romaine told me, neatly done. The witnesses' stories closely fitted together. It was a great improvement on the evidence presented at the PI.

During the high court trial the judge took careful note of the evidence of the first five witnesses for the prosecution and then threw his pen down. "Case dismissed," he ordered. The five witnesses had told very different stories to those they'd told at the preliminary hearing. Nwosu and Nwokedi were discharged.

Some weeks later Romaine and I happened to be in Nnewi Otolo discussing some native authority matter with the elders. I suddenly thought of Nwosu and Nwokedi and inquired, through Romaine, what news there was of them. Romaine hesitated in his interpretation, looking at me quizzically, but went on. "They are working in the coal mines in Enugu," somebody said. "They've gone away." "He means in Sierra Leone," some travelled wag in the crowd corrected.

There was laughter of a sinister kind.

———————

Increasingly we came to rely on letters written from home—particularly the thoughtful and detailed letters written by Jack—for news of the progress of the war and news of my friends. He was a sturdy and accurate student of events. Many of his prognoses, such as my own likely call up and later return to civilian duties, had proved singularly accurate. We couldn't rely on our short-wave radio which was always giving trouble and newspapers were often weeks, even months, out of date when we received them.

Jack told me of the death in North Africa of Joe Dawson, school and Cambridge friend—missing believed killed; of Scott, killed in action in the Middle East, member of "my" 1934 school rugger team and a redoubtable forward; of Hugh McCabe, in the Far East, member of Cambridge Lanjokúl and Vatnajokúl expeditions with Andrew Downes and me...news that caused me hopeless, frustrated resentment.

"Any man's death diminishes me...my friend's destroys."

My friends' deaths caused many feelings of guilt derived, I must suppose, from the fact that my life at that time was a happy, a very happy one. I had Kat and Jackie with me and jobwise I felt that I was achieving something worthwhile. True, I have never worked so hard before or since but as I tumbled into bed each night at around nine o'clock, exhausted, I felt a recurring conviction that I was being inducted into the work of the provincial administration at twice the normal speed and I was getting somewhere.

The months from Kat and Jackie's return in August 1943 to our departure on leave in the United Kingdom in April 1945 passed like light. Household servants were a great boon and without them my output would have been much reduced. Kat, bless her, took complete charge here. She not only looked after the nurse-girl and Jackie with kind and constant vigilance but ensured that I need never give a thought to any domestic matters.

There was, of course, a down side. The climate was appalling: temperatures constantly in the high eighties, humidity ninety-seven per cent or even worse. The human psyche seems able to discard memories of pain or physical discomfort relatively quickly and it takes an effort, now, to remember that we were living in dread of tropical disease and dark dangers of remoteness and the unknown all the time. Jackie was the first European child in the District and Dermott O'Connor left us in no doubt as to the responsibility he bore for having given us permission to have her in the Province.

He needn't have worried for we all kept Jackie under constant surveillance. Scorpions and snakes could easily get into the house— both had been found there although, of course, neither were common. At the first fall of night Jackie was put in her large mosquito-net-covered cot (an Ibo carpenter had made the lot from iroko wood to my instructions).

At the first onset of any disorder such as a temperature rise, a cough, a rash or diarrhoea, Kat and I would take Jackie straight to the Mission at Ihiala where the Irish nuns specialised in child complaints. We felt that the first essential in treating many tropical diseases was speed in diagnosis and the Ihiala nuns had accumulated a vast experience.

We all took daily a prophylactic against malaria. At the time the prescribed dosage for Jackie was a third of a tablet of mepacrine. Mepacrine was superseded shortly afterwards partly because of its side effects. It produced loss of scalp hair amongst some women takers and in time turned all who took it regularly yellow. It also had a foul taste if chewed. It was hell's delight tricking Jackie each morning into swallowing her third of a tablet. Kat would secrete it in a small portion of cake, in a teaspoonful of jam, in a spoonful of thick soup… all of which Jackie would normally wolf on sight…and hope for the best. After John's arrival, however, Jackie's attitude became much more responsible and she set the tone for regular taking of prophylactics.

As always amongst the litigious Ibo, judicial appeals and requests for review of native court proceedings placed considerable pressure upon the administrative cadre. During the war these pressures were increased to an appreciable degree by the high rate of recruitment that had taken place in Iboland and the litigation bearing upon serving soldiers' allotments home. Recruitment, particularly to the Pioneer Corps and to transport units of eighty-one and eighty-two West African Divisions had continued at a fast pace during the years 1940-43. Considerable sums of money were sent home by way of allotments during this period. Many of these payments were the subject of litigation; a wife named on the allotment had returned to her parents or married another man and was no longer entitled to the payment…and so forth.

E R Chadwick, at the time a forty-year old district officer with sixteen years' experience, told an interesting story concerning allotments and what he termed "a myth with a purpose". In his District (I believe it was Udi) the native authority decided to tax allotment payments as income received by the allottee. The rate of tax was small but the whole conception of income tax was relatively new and produced considerable resistance in many parts of Iboland. The question of allotments came up at a council meeting: a middle-aged lady asked if she could make a statement on behalf of the allottees. This was permitted and she said, "Yes, it was quite true that many wives in the area had received allotments by post. These were allotments of salary sent by their husbands serving in the pioneer corps. All the husbands had recently been shipped home and the ship carrying them had been torpedoed and all the men had been drowned. The issue of taxing allotments thus need not be raised again as allotments would cease."

There was a long, pregnant silence following her statement.

The meeting was suddenly startled by the sound of nailed boots. A smartly dressed pioneer corps soldier, uniform newly starched, marched briskly up to the DO's chair, saluted and said, "Yes, sir. It's very true. I was one of them."

Chadwick quickly said, "I've heard nothing and I can assure you that I would be the first to be told if such a tragedy occurred." But nobody would listen to him. He was convinced that the whole meeting implicitly believed what the soldier had said.

The "purpose" of the myth outweighed the logic of the soldier's statement.

L T Chubb in his capacity of OPPO visited Nnewi at frequent intervals. We were in the midst of the oil palm production belt and were beginning to show a satisfactory increase in the volume of the trade.

As the trade gradually became more lucrative the OPPOs played an important part in the discussions with government, and the purchasing companies, on the level of price best calculated to produce an optimum flow of produce. Too high a price and equally too low a price could produce a detrimental effect.

Imported goods such as Raleigh bicycles, gunpowder (important for funeral ceremonies), salt, cloth, stockfish, bicycle tyres and hubs were all in short supply and consequently in heavy demand. Their importation and distribution was controlled by government in consultation with the major importing firms. Efforts were made to ensure that the oil palm middlemen received generous supplies on two grounds: items such as bicycle and bicycle spares were vitally necessary to the expanding oil palm trade and secondly, all these items could be sold at a good profit by the oil middlemen thus increasing their buying capacity.

In 1943 most of the large firm's buying points were controlled by Europeans. A notable exception was a grand character called Fred Cann. He was short and fat with a shiny black pate. His most notable characteristic was a pair of brilliant red braces with which he used to keep his baggy trousers aloft; invariably the braces were twisted and a supporting button or two missing. But he was wise and witty and trusted by all the middlemen at his buying point. Sadly he was getting on in years and retired at the end of the 1944 season.

Beach visits always paid off. It was even possible, once, to help Fred Cann. I visited his station in the midst of a very busy morning's buying. One of the two weighing machines had just broken down. Both machines were required to cope with the volume of produce coming in. Produce once lost was never recovered. Fred was furious. He had nobody available to mend the machine. I offered to take it into Onitsha for him and have it sent back that evening. He eagerly accepted and in fact received the machine dully mended, in time for two hours' buying that same evening. I remember the incident because a day or two later he recognised my car approaching the vehicle he was in on the main road and got out in order to stop me and say thank-you.

A white child had never been seen in the Nnewi Sub-District before Jackie's arrival. If seriously questioned quite a few market mammies would tell you "…yes, we know European woman but children…we haven't thought about that." It would be too much to say that they supposed Europeans emerged from some kind of chrysalis already grown up but it was nevertheless true that a European child in Nnewi in 1943 was an object of extreme interest.

Occasionally, when I had an afternoon meeting to attend, or some short inspection to carry out, I would take Kat, and Jackie and the nursemaid in the car. While I got on with whatever the job of the moment was the car would be surrounded by an enormous silent crowd of wondering people, staring at Jackie. Sometimes they questioned Kat and the nurse-girl interpreted. One such visit was to see Eric Powell, then in charge of the neighbouring Orlu Sub-District. Just after we left him the car developed engine trouble. We came to a halt and I discovered that the mechanical petrol pump had partially failed and petrol was being thrown over the interior of the bonnet—the diaphragm was almost gone.

Darkness—and mosquito time—was near and I felt we had to get back to Nnewi before Jackie was exposed to mosquito bites so I made a dangerous temporary repair by tying my shirt round the petrol pump to block the spray of raw fuel and we got going again. There was enough diaphragm left to keep the engine at about 2,000 rpm.

All went well until we skirted an evening roadside market where we were forced by the crowd virtually to halt. The engine stalled and at the same time the spilling fuel ignited. The nurse-girl in the back with Jackie, locked, instead of releasing the door and the engine under the bonnet was in flames. I opened the bonnet and tried to quench the flames with a brand new riding mac, ruining it in the process and failing to put out the fire. Kat in the meantime got the back door open and Jackie and the nursemaid safely onto the road. The crowd came to our rescue scooping up great handfuls of sand which they flung into the engine compartment. Very soon they had put out the fire.

We were only some seven or eight miles from Nnewi. I was determined to get back before dark. So we cleaned up what sand we could from the engine compartment, repositioned what was left of the shirt to limit the spray of leaking petrol, figuratively crossed our fingers and asked the crowd to give us a push start which they did with a will. To our surprise the engine restarted at once. On arrival at Nnewi we turned off the fuel as we tackled the last hill to our house and stopped outside the door—this time without fire breaking out.

Romaine's father—a spry little man half Romaine's size—was an excellent mechanic and ran a successful repair organisation in Onitsha. It was he who cleaned up the engine and fitted a new petrol pump diaphragm which he cut to size from a piece of galvanised rubber—the car having first been towed into Onitsha by the NA lorry.

This little adventure must have been recounted to Jack in one of Kat's letters for I still have a letter from him in which he commented, "How fortunate Romaine Senior is such a good mechanic and was able to make a diaphragm when no spares were available. Your car sounds rather a liability, though."

A day's snagging left me exhausted. I still found the physical effort in the heat of midday of placing the charges, sometimes working against a swiftish current, and climbing in and out of the canoe, very wearisome. There was one evening on the Orashi River itself just above a confluence with a side stream where after lighting the powder fuse I sent the safety canoe up the side stream to stop any traffic while I swam down the Orashi to a sandbank about 100 yards distant from which I could stop any up-river traffic that might come. I'd left a ten-minute fuse burning, considering it more than adequate for my 100 yards' swim but the current downstream was negligible and I found myself travelling more and more slowly through the water and becoming more and more tired. I became so tired, in fact, that I didn't really care if the charge went off before I had climbed out of the water onto the sandbank. I guessed hazily that the shock waves through the water might be damaging. It was only when I did eventually scramble out onto the sandbank that I realised that I'd been swimming with my gym shoes full of silt.

It was impossible to work in a relatively small service such as the colonial administrative service without forming close ties with a number of other officers. In my case I realise now that respect played an essential part—I sought the closer acquaintance of those I felt had the most to contribute. Consequently they tended to be my seniors in age and experience. Jim Smith was one. I mentioned his relationship with Dermott O'Connor briefly on page 51. I remember once in Onitsha about that time Dermott being particularly rude to him. Among other things he said, out of the blue, "You have far too many ADOs. Whatever can you be doing with them?"

Jim Smith resented being spoken to like that, particularly in front of one of the ADOs in question...me. "Teaching them manners," he replied briefly.

Dermott, I may add, only grinned. He always appreciated a touch of spirit, no matter who showed it.

Kat and I became very fond of J S Smith. He was always his own man in Nigeria: confident, humorous, firm and kindly. We wanted him to become a godfather to John when the latter arrived in 1944 and he demurred for several weeks. In the end he wrote a gentle letter explaining that much as he would like to accept on reflection he had decided that he could not on the grounds that we were Anglicans and he was a Roman Catholic. Such was his faith that he would find it incumbent on him to emphasise to John in years to come the superior aspects of Roman Catholicism.

He had a sense of humour very much his own. Just about the end of the 1939-45 War I met him casually in the Enugu Secretariat. At the time he was Resident of the Owerri Province stationed at Owerri. He told me that the previous evening he'd taken his dog for a walk on the Owerri Golf Course. He had been surprised to see hordes of young men on bicycles, followed by others trotting on foot, pass in the direction of the railway station where the daily passenger train halted for about thirty minutes. A short while later the same hordes appeared travelling in the reverse direction, this time heading back to the Owerri Township. Intrigued, Jim Smith stopped one of them. "What are you all doing?" he asked. "Well," said the young chap he'd stopped, "we heard there was a giant on the train so we went down to look at him. Now we are going home again."

Perhaps Jim Smith's most important contribution to the Eastern Region was the "Outsiders" cricket team which he made into an institution. On major public holidays—Christmas, Easter, Whitsun and the like—he would raise a team of cricketers who would come into Enugu to play the best that Enugu could muster. The cricket was taken very seriously but the benefit extended to wives and supporters who were given a reason to visit Enugu, wear their best clothes, meet their fellows and generally unwind and relax in the relatively westernised surroundings of Enugu after many months in the Provinces. Wives, husbands and supporters all benefited. There was never any suggestion of a colour bar as such at any time during my service in Nigeria. African members of the government services were invited to Enugu for Outsider matches on precisely the same terms as expatriates although naturally some took advantage of the holiday to visit their own homes elsewhere in Nigeria.

A good many Africans were redoubtable cricketers. In my time I think particularly of the fast bowling of Nuha of the Prison Service and the batsmanship of Albert Osakwe of the administration.

J S Smith used to select his team many weeks—months even—in advance of the matches. It was always a delight to get one of his postcards: "Dear Malcolm, We are counting on you to field in the covers…" or whatever.

Writing of J S Smith and postcards reminds me of his wartime chess game. During the war he used to play long distance chess with a friend in Scotland. They would record each move as it was made on a postcard sending the postcard back and forth. Jim was amused but also somewhat concerned to receive a separate letter from his chess opponent in which the latter stated that the chess postcard had been the subject of an investigation. His Scottish opponent had received a visit by an MI5 security representative bearing the chess match postcard apparently removed from the postal services. The latter had said, "Yes, he appreciated the postcard was supposed to record chess moves 'KP to QP three' or whatever but the quality of play was so bad that MI5 wondered if there wasn't a code involved. Hence the inquiry."

Revonons à nos moutons…Llyn Chubb was one of the Outsiders' regular bowlers, offspin and medium fast. He took a lot out of himself physically in his OPPO work and just after the war certainly lacked the fire he had shown in the early days of the war. His place was taken after about 1946 by Stan King, mentioned on page 78.

The name Outsiders was particularly felicitous for there was always a slight suggestion that those who served in the Provinces—as opposed to the secretariat in Enugu—were rougher, tougher, real "outsiders" in fact.

But by far the most important aspect, to my mind, of the Outsiders' matches was the contribution they made to race relations in the Region. Pre-war African members of the senior service and their families had been reluctant to join "the club" or to accept invitations to expatriate gatherings. The change over was only slowly coming and it was understandable in many ways that this should be so. But cricket matches and polo in Ibadan and Lagos in particular did provide occasions when families could mix without strain. Liberal opinion in England used to have it that European expatriates were snobbish and reluctant to mix but this was far from the true situation in Nigeria in my experience.

Sir Bernard Carr had been appointed Chief Commissioner, Eastern Region in August 1943. There was an Outsiders' match over Christmas that year and I was invited to play. Not only that but Kat, me and Jackie were invited to stay at Government House by the Carrs. It was of course a great honour for us and, as I realise now, a neat stroke by them for it saved them having to make a difficult choice amongst the senior officers. After all, at that time, Kat and I were the only members of the administrative service with a baby in the country.

I still possess a letter from Jack commenting on our 1943 Christmas in Enugu. It was written in January 1944, at a time when he was far from well with the heart disease that brought his own death in November 1944, at the relatively early age of sixty-six. It would have been understandable if his thoughts had turned entirely to his own condition but no; he devoted the bulk of what he had to say to the affairs of Eastern Nigeria. After this length of time I marvel at the pertinence of his assessment.

Let me quote him:-

"Sir Bernard and Lady Carr seem to have made a very sound start. You all need a rest and a complete change of environment. The idea of having as many of you as possible into Enugu over Christmas was an excellent one. It is useful too, for the high-ups in Enugu to be able to meet their juniors socially and to assess them away from their work.

From what you have told me in the past four years I have built a most favourable impression of discipline and morale in the Colonial Service. Seniority seems to be properly respected. So it should be for there is no substitute for the experience which can only come with time. On the other hand there is a tradition of open discussion between juniors and seniors which is good in your circumstances. I feel that you are all enthusiasts—you would not be there if you weren't—and I sense a readiness of the seniors to be persuaded by logical argument even if it comes from below. In the result you all appear to speak with the same voice and I am sure this is very important in dealing with alien races."

To my mind Jack puts across in those two paragraphs much of what I am struggling to explain in the whole of this book.

———————

After the little break over Christmas 1943 we were all once again engulfed in work. There was no time, so far as I was concerned, even to keep a diary. Numerous opportunities for acting in charge of Districts arose and for most of the year I found myself combining at least two peace-time appointments. There was a short period, at the end of 1944, when I held down three appointments, one of which was acting for Llyn Chubb as OPPO for the Onitsha Province while he went on leave.

1944, my fifth year in West Africa, was in one way a mounting crescendo; the long hours of work were beginning to pay off. Oil palm production was increasing satisfactorily; it was possible just, to keep pace with the all-important list of native court reviews and appeals; and at the same time I felt I was accruing experience at an accelerated rate.

Kat was expecting our second child in June. Although she would have been game enough to have had the child in Enugu, her mother and father were virtually certain to remain in the Jos area for the rest of the war. Nigel Cooke was then in his mid-sixties but his knowledge and experience of tin mining in the area meant that his services would continue to be in demand for as long as his health permitted. There had been several European children born in the Plateau hospital at Jos and the MO currently in charge was expert in gynaecological medicine. Kitty, bless her, was enthusiastic about having Kat and Jackie and the nurse-girl, to stay as long as necessary. Everything, as it were, fell into place.

Dr R C A Savage, senior specialist in Enugu, agreed to keep an eye on Kat during the months of her pregnancy and make sure all was well. In May he had doubts as to the position of John (we were already confident it would be a boy and we had already decided upon a name) and thought there was a danger of a breach presentation. He promptly referred her to the MO in Jos. She went up there by train accompanied by Jackie and the nurse-girl. The turning manipulation was a partial success. Kat is confident her father successfully completed the process by taking her, a day or two later, down a very rough track to inspect a new mine.

Kat briefly returned to the Eastern Region but returned to Jos about three weeks before the baby was due. We all felt that the cool air of the Plateau Province in May/June would set her up for John's arrival.

In spite of the great press of work I had determined to brave Dermott O'Connor's possible wrath and seek permission to be in Jos for John's arrival. But Dermott got there first. As I entered his office he greeted me quite fiercely with the words: "I've an order for you, young man. You are to go up to Jos for your child's arrival. When is it due?"

I said, "The middle of June."

"Right," he replied. "You are to be up there from the tenth to seventeenth as near as the trains allow. No argument."

During those fraught days the staff at Nnewi and, indeed, Onitsha Post Offices did me some real kindnesses. For instance Kat sent me a telegram addressed to Nnewi after the manipulation saying all was well. The Nnewi Postmaster knew at the time the telegram arrived that I wasn't in Nnewi but was staying the night at Ihiala some seventeen miles away. He sent his son on a bicycle to deliver the telegram to me the same day at Ihiala. Normal routine merely required him to put the telegram with the next day's mail for collection by the Nnewi Messenger.

On another occasion Kat had sent a telegram addressed to me at the District Office, Onitsha, thinking I was working there. Immediately following its arrival the Post Master in Onitsha telephoned the contents to the district clerk, Onitsha. The latter, knowing I'd been called unexpectedly into the secretariat, Enugu, rang me there and relayed the contents.

I have cherished little acts such as these down the years.

John's actual arrival was characteristic of Kat's unflappable nature.

I duly took Dermott O'Connor's instructions and arrived on the Plateau on 12th June. I was met off the train in a rainstorm by a heavily pregnant Kat who said, "I think we'd better stay in Jos in this weather. I'm sure John's arrival is near." So that afternoon Kat's parents took us into the comfortable Hill Station Hotel a mile and a half away from the hospital. I made arrangements with a local taxi owner/driver who promised faithfully to respond to a telephoned call any hour of the day or night.

At luncheon on the 13th, Kat ordered a second helping of pudding and said, "I hope you don't mind. The pains have just started but this pudding is too good to miss."

I sprang up, rushed to the telephone and got only the taxi driver's wife. She said, "He's just gone on a call but will be with you just now." Twenty minutes later, no taxi having shown up, I rang again. "He may have gone to Pankshin," said the wife casually, although it was over sixty miles away.

There was no time for further delay. I went the rounds of Hill Station but no car, either guest or hotel owned, was available. The last had just left. To make matters worse a low, black sky to the west betokened the imminent arrival of a tornado. The Ibo receptionist said, "You can have my bicycle, sir."

By now even Kat was anxious to get to the hospital.

She got on the bicycle and pedalled away. I trotted alongside, trying to keep up on the level, pushing up the hills. By then the tornado had hit us full belt and we became soaked to the skin, literally in seconds. Kat laughed and said, "This'll cool you down."

We were met at the main entrance to the hospital by the English matron who said to Kat, "First things first—a hot bath for you my girl," and turning to me she said, "You go off and get dry. Come back, if you wish. We'll look after her."

I bicycled to Hill Station, had a hot bath and changed. By then the Hill Station car had returned.

Rather less than an hour and a half after leaving the hospital I was back. "You've got a very fine son," said the Matron, "and they are both OK."

Kitty drove herself into Jos from Barakin Ladi on the evening of John's arrival and repeated the journey for each of the three or four days that Kat was in the hospital. On one of her visits she brought along the Yorkshire wife of one of Nigel's assistant managers. She told me with a smile that this good lady, on first seeing John, had exclaimed, "Oh, ain't he like his father," adding, by way of damage limitation, "but never mind, he's healthy."

Kitty had not learnt to drive a car until she was into her sixties. Her mentor had been one of Nigel's mine drivers...an Ibo, in fact. According to Kitty his favourite admonition to her while she was learning was, "Take your foot from the fire, Madam." After one or two short journeys with Kitty driving I could well understand why.

On the first occasion Kitty gave me a lift from the hospital to Hill Station we had two excitements. She had a pre-war Vauxhall with, I think, four forward gears. One of her driving foibles was to ignore gears two and three; she would use only one and four. There was a slope from the hospital entrance to the main gates where there was a right-angle turn onto the main road. Possibly influenced by the slope, Kitty chose gear four to start with. After a few jerks and bucks we arrived at the gates at a fair clip. She grappled with the turn onto the main road bravely, working on the steering wheel with great verve. She made it...just but ran a front wheel onto the far grass verge in the process. A European Military dispatch rider motorcycling down the main road at the time was gravely threatened; but he was too good for her. He went further onto the grass verge and escaped. "My God, Malcolm," said Kitty, "how was that?"

I could only reply, "Bloody marvellous, you scared the daylights out of him."

But our excitements on that mile and a half drive were not over. Hill Station, as the name implies, stood on the top of one of the several hills that made up Jos Township. The normal route from the hospital to the hotel entrance entailed a sharp ninety-degree turn to the left near the top of the hill. This didn't suit Kitty's preference for gears one and four, however, so she took a detour through the township where she could have a clear run at the hill. "If I go fast enough," she confided to me, "I can just trickle over the top without having to change gear." The only snag to this otherwise excellent approach were two roads, bearing a fair amount of traffic, which crossed Kitty's preferred route at right angles. As we stormed at the hill I had to endure a kind of double-barrelled Russian roulette. Fortunately nothing got us but for a little while I'd almost (but to be truthful, not quite) have changed places with the agony Kat had so recently endured.

The main traffic in the vicinity of Barakin Ladi were familiar with Kitty's style of driving and would pull onto the verge on their side of the road whenever they spotted her approaching. Nigel, short of banning her entirely, which he was much too wise to essay, simply put the whole thing out of his mind. Possibly the turning point for him was the day she arrived back at the house for luncheon with a fresh cow horn stuck in the radiator...and had been quite unable to explain how it had got there.

The post office officials at Barakin Ladi were used to Europeans as there were a number employed in the tin mines and took a great interest in their affairs. Kitty, as the Number One white woman in the area, generally received the attention of the postmaster himself—an elderly Ibo (Ibos were to be found all over the North of Nigeria at that time). She took along a number of telegrams and a couple of cables to tell friends and relations of the arrival of John. The postmaster carefully checked them and then went through them again. "But what of the husband?" he asked Kitty.

I was combining the jobs of ADO Nnewi with acting DO Onitsha and acting OPPO Onitsha Province in June 1944 so had to get back a couple of days after John's arrival. The Onitsha District I was keeping warm for Jim Smith who was due back from a much needed leave in September. I knew that he worked to very high standards which I did not have the experience or knowledge to approach. On a number of files I left him a minute saying that I did not know how he would wish to proceed so that I had left the matter in abeyance pending his arrival. So far as OPPO matters were concerned Llyn Chubb had made himself a veritable walking encyclopaedia of the palm oil trade throughout the Region while I had only some knowledge of the Nnewi, Onitsha and Orlu areas. Acting for him I felt that any time such as I had was best occupied in keeping the correspondence up to date and visiting district officers throughout the Province who were an important link in the production chain. I had to be careful because of my own junior status. Chaps with double or treble my experience wouldn't want to be told what to do even if they were not as active as they should be.

Kat stayed with her parents for ten days after John's birth and then came down by train bringing only John with her. Jackie and the nurse-girl stayed on at Barakin Ladi as guests of Kitty and Nigel. Kitty was genuinely delighted to have her grandchild on the premises and Jackie certainly developed a lot during the months she was there. Kat and I guessed she had a great fuss made of her.

During this period we lived in considerable style in the DO's house in Onitsha—a T2 which Jim Smith would occupy when he returned from his leave. I remember it particularly because the upstairs consisted of two complete suites: bathroom, WC, dressing room, bedroom, thus, on nights when young John was suffering from indigestion or otherwise wanted to exercise his lungs, it was possible to put five doors between his cot and my bed. In consequence I seldom lost any sleep although I fear Kat did. However, she soon accustomed John to having his last feed at night at ten p.m. and his first in the morning at six a.m. This meant that he was seldom taken from the protection of his mosquito net when the Onitsha mosquitoes, reputedly as big as hornets and very numerous, were out.

One evening I returned from hearing native court appeals just after dark. Kat was complaining strongly of the cold. The rains were about, it's true...cool, yes but cold—definitely no. However, as the evening went on, she put on more and more warm clothes and piled poor John's bed, even putting a woollen jersey over his night-shirt. It took us until midnight to realise she was ill...John was more than warm enough. It was a quite severe bout of malaria but fortunately there was an experienced MO in the station and she recovered in a few days.

At the end of September 1944 Kat and young John went up to stay with Kat's parents. She found Jackie very happy and much grown up although she was only two years and two months old at the time. When they were away I took the opportunity of doing some of the rougher travelling in remote parts of the Province.

Kat, Jackie and John and the nurse-girl were due to return on a train arriving at Enugu at six a.m. on a Thursday morning. I had established a temporary home in a rest house at 1,100ft (which was cooler than most of the Onitsha Province) near Nine Miles Corner (which surprisingly, was nine miles out of Enugu). It was a relatively cool spot from which I planned to do several days' OPPO work after their arrival. I visited the Enugu Secretariat on the Wednesday morning, completing the work I had to do unexpectedly quickly. A whim made me visit the station master about lunch-time—he was a Nnewi man and had recently been very helpful, when he was on leave in Nnewi, in a long standing land dispute affecting his village. In his office was an Ibo engine driver. The latter told me he was driving a north-bound train to Makurdi in thirty minutes time. Talking about my family coming on the south bound train he said, "Come up with me on the engine. You can surprise your family in Makurdi."

I immediately agreed, re-parked my car outside the stationmaster's office and gave him some money to send a messenger out to the Nine Mile Corner Rest House saying I plus family would be back for breakfast the following morning. I'd never travelled on the footplate before and this seemed a great opportunity to try a new experience.

There was one immediate oddity: the great frame of the engine, from the junction with the tender to the front buffers, didn't bend. The impression was that the front of the engine was always heading off into the bush to left or right of the track as the direction of the bend dictated. And there were many bends. It was a weird impression and took some time to become used to. We were burning Enugu coal—a soft, quick—burning bituminous coal—and I was surprised how hard the fireman had to work, not only to keep up a full head of steam but also to move coal forward from the tender.

We reached Makurdi just after dark at about seven p.m. The train bearing Kat and the family arrived punctually a few minutes later. Our greetings were barely over when a shining saloon, smartly uniformed police orderly beside the driver, drove up. Out emerged the short, stout figure of Cullen, the senior resident who'd married us at Jos. He was now Senior Resident, Benue Province with his headquarters at Makurdi. Kitty had warned him that Kat was on the train and knowing that the train stopped for two hours at Makurdi he'd come down to ask her to dinner. Eyeing my somewhat grubby state with disapproval he said, "You'd better come, too."

Jackie had had her evening meal and was ready for bed. Kat had fed John at six and wasn't due to give him his last feed until ten. So we left the young in Kat's compartment in charge of the nurse-girl and went off in style to dinner at the residency.

Cullen was a kind and amusing host. Dinner was a leisurely meal and time slipped by. The train was due to leave at 10.15 p.m. Just time for the pudding, I remember thinking.

In came the pudding. Cullen's face turned puce. "How many times have I told Ali I won't have it overcooked like this," he demanded and, laying hold of the pudding dish, pushed it violently towards the "small boy" who was helping to wait on us. (I laughed to myself at this point. He's chosen the "small boy" to be rough to rather than the steward himself who was a venerable old boy who plainly had been with Cullen for many years). Kat was as aware as I was of time fleeting past and what it would mean to John if the train left without us.

Suddenly the pleasant little dinner party became an ordeal, then a nightmare. Twice I plucked up courage enough to say, "We mustn't miss the train. Perhaps we should leave the pudding." But he pooh-poohed the suggestion. "Plenty of time. Plenty of time."

As it was, whistles were blowing and the guard was waving his flag for the last time as we scrambled aboard. "Told you there was plenty of time," said Cullen by way of farewell.

Trouble met us as we arrived at Nine-Mile Corner Rest House. I'd replaced Trevorrow's bitch with another mongrel bitch who had seemed right enough when I'd left her the previous day. When we arrived Isaac Mba met us with a long face and said she'd been hiding in a dark corner since early the previous day. She wouldn't come out or eat. I looked at her and thought her very sick. I moved her to a spot where Jackie couldn't get near her and consulted Kat. Because of the possibility of rabies—her behaviour was suggestive of "dumb rabies"—we decided to consult a doctor at once. We all therefore motored straight into Enugu. The MO pointed out that the dangerous, infectious, time of rabies was approximately three days before the sufferer's death. He suggested that I, because I'd handled the bitch, should commence the uncomfortable series of rabies injections straight away together with Isaac and others who'd in any way been in contact with her. If she recovered, the injections could be stopped; if she died within the next forty-eight hours the injections must, of course, be completed. In the meantime Kat and the kids should keep well clear of the bitch and not on any account handle her.

We returned to the rest house and spent a concerned night. The bitch had been alive at ten p.m. when Kat and I went to bed. Isaac reported early the following morning that she'd died during the night.

Anti-rabies injections caused considerable muscular soreness. The usual technique was to administer them subcutaneously in the front of the stomach on one side on days one, three, five, etc. and on the other on days two, four, six, and so on. I have had to suffer this series of injections on three or four occasions during my time in the tropics and in general have discovered that the more qualified and refined the administrator the more painful the injection. I formed this opinion in the Cameroons some years later following the attentions of a newly qualified medical assistant. He treated the syringe rather like a dart. He aimed at the injection site and flung the syringe at the stomach. The resultant sharp prick as the needle penetrated was a good deal less painful than having the stomach skin and muscles held in the manipulator's hand while he fumbled with the needle.

Although Jackie and John were pioneers so far as government families were concerned—they were in fact the first government European children in the Region—the Garretts had had their children with them for a number of years at Oji River Leper Settlement. Both Garretts were doctors and, rabies apart, would help if either of our two developed alarming symptoms. So far as we know now neither Jackie nor John suffered any long-term harm from their years in the tropics. Both kids soon became good about taking regular doses of malarial prophylactics and we kept a very close eye on them for symptoms of tropical diseases. We were all careful not to drink unboiled and unfiltered water and to ensure that fruit was well washed with clean water before we ate it. We endeavoured to treat the young in such matters as sensible mature beings, each of whom owed it to the others to ensure that we all observed the rules of tropical hygiene.

1944 was a brighter year for all of us. The war in the west was moving on apace. On 15th August the Allied Seventh Army landed in the South of France; Falaise was captured by the British and Canadian Forces on 17th August and the Dunbarton Oaks Conference—when the allies discussed the United Nations Organisation—was held in Washington DC on 21st August.

We, in Eastern Nigeria, caught something of this resurgence of spirit and, as it were, quickened our pace. Previously we had slaved to survive. Now there was an element of construction in all we did. We were travelling hopefully.

Christmas 1944 came on us almost unexpectedly. There was, once again, an Outsiders' match in Enugu and I was asked to play. The big event of our visit to Enugu, however, was son John's Christmas Day Baptism. C J Patterson, then Anglican Bishop on the Niger christened John in the little All Saints Church in Enugu. John Brayne-Baker, Lady Carr and Bryan Smith stood in as proxies for the three godparents, one of whom was in Maidugari and the other two in the UK. The baptism certificate was marked No 1 and I suppose that John's christening was the first that had ever been conducted in the little church. I remember that B-B, as he was always known, gave us all luncheon after the service. He was a dear fellow, small and gentle but far from a push-over. He was dark-haired and wore large dark-rimmed tortoise shell glasses through which he used to observe the modern world with more than an occasional glint of pained comprehension in his grey eyes.

B-B was a compulsive talker. He had a lot to say and he said it thoroughly. I've forgotten what the subject was but he held to it resolutely as we were all helped to the first course—a kind of fish mousse. The trouble was that the fish was bad...very bad. B-B was served last; even then he went on with his discourse. We all sat in front of our plates horrified with what had been placed on them but none of us with the courage to say it was bad. At last B-B paused in his monologue and took a forkful. "Umoji," he called to the steward "take it away. It's uneatable."

I'd occasionally bicycled into Onitsha during my first spell in Nnewi to play tennis at the CMS mission where Pat was then working in education. Once or twice on wet evenings he and I, for exercise, put on boxing gloves and had a few rounds. Later, Pat became the Right Reverend Cecil John Patterson, CMG, CBE, DD, Archbishop of West Africa. For a number of years I used to dine out on the remark "...the only Archbishop I've hit on the nose was..."

Although Pat was a relatively small man he had a great natural ability at many forms of athleticism. Perhaps cricket was his best game. He was no mean batsman—possibly he could have found a place in an English county side as a batsman alone had he wished to. But his true forte was as a wicket keeper. Even after he became Bishop on the

Niger he could sometimes be persuaded to play for the Outsiders. On the few occasions that Jim Smith did persuade him there would be an extra bounce in Jim's stride so cockily certain was he of winning. It was almost as though he felt that not only had he got the best wicket keeper in Nigeria on his side but possibly the Almighty also.

Incongruous in a Bishop was the state of Pat's hands—his fingers had suffered cruelly as a result of his wicket keeping.

I still carry a memory of a Vermeer-like scene just before luncheon on the day of John's christening. We were gathered in B-B's dark panelled sitting room. The room was cool and shady in contrast to the brilliant sun outside. Pat's canonicals presented a touch of rich purple against the subdued tones of the rest of the room. He was holding a glass of some drink and talking quietly of ordinary things. Both Kat and I observed the state of his fingers and remarked about it to each other afterwards.

The first two months of 1945 passed like light.

Jack's long illness throughout 1944 and his death on 11th December had been a slow sadness. When he went, very peacefully as Alice in a simple most moving letter, received in January 1945, said to me, it had seemed inevitable he would not survive the war. It is now, as I write, fifty-three years since he died. I regret his going more heavily now than I did all those years ago. The young are galloping so fast through life that they take the death of those they love in their long stride. The old stumble and totter and wonder if they, too, might not fall.

As we entered 1945 the last heavy blows of war were falling. Japan had had recourse to the desperate device of kamikaze pilots. The air war in Europe was inflicting great damage on German cities, the harm that ours had suffered three years before largely forgotten. On 19th January the Red Army reached the Eastern borders of Germany. There was a massive 1,000-bomber raid on Berlin on 3rd February. On the 4th February Stalin succeeded in extracting a number of concessions from the sick Roosevelt at the Yalta Conference—concessions which, for good or evil, provided many of the grounds for the Cold War that was to follow.

Early in March I received instructions to proceed on leave to the UK. I had a total of seventy-two weeks of leave due to me, having enjoyed none, save for four weeks in South Africa, since first appointment in 1939. There was no question of the Nigerian government, in the short-staffed situation of 1945, allowing me to take more than half my due, nor did I want to. Once I had recouped my vigour and weight (I was then under nine and a half stones) I was anxious to get back into the fray. The balance of leave due to me could be accumulated. Sir Bernard Carr, in an encouraging conversation, mentioned twenty weeks of leave subject "to the exigencies of the service" and we planned round this figure.

Instructions followed that we were to take passage in a "civilian troop ship" due to leave Lagos about 20th March. I gathered that we could have our full entitlement of baggage, which in fact was a good deal more than the 660 lbs made up into twenty loads that we planned.

Two loads were heavier than most of the others. These made up the "Lion's Play-pen". Kat, before rejoining me from Pietermaritzburg had suggested that a play-pen would be useful for Jackie. The Awka Carvers' Guild seemed just the people to oblige. They worked in Iroko and produced a variety of articles from this fine wood such as chests, tables, trays, even shutters, decorated with hand carving based on the traditional patterns for carvings on compound doors. When I talked to the Awka headman, he confessed to some difficulty in understanding what I meant. I did my best to explain with the aid of pencil and paper. A week or two later I called to collect the finished article. It was beautifully made: the hand carvings were delightful, some based on the cicatrizations that young girls suffered in the cause of beautification. (The headman said he thought this appropriate as the play-pen was required for a female child.) It took to pieces for travelling but the only trouble was that it was massive. The servants when they saw it couldn't believe it was required for a toddler and seeing that I insisted it was a play-pen called it "The Lion's Play-pen" and that name remained.

We were instructed to take a coastal vessel from Calabar to Lagos and there await the departure of the "Civilian trooper" to the United Kingdom. Our loads went ahead on board a Milikain lorry (Milikain was a young Armenian who had run a small transport business based on Onitsha throughout the war) and the company hired us a saloon car for the transport of ourselves and our motley collection of "wanted en route" loads. There wasn't room for the driver and he, poor chap, had to find his own way down to Calabar.

The day of departure came at last. Our coastal vessel was already loading at Calabar. We were going on leave at last. There was a festive feel in the air and Kat, who was driving, responded and drove briskly. Our borrowed car was loaded almost to the roof. Kat, Jackie and I were in front. John occupied a large cardboard box which later served him excellently as a travelling cot all the way to England. He was placed on top of the loads filling the rear of the car with about a foot to spare between the box and the roof of the car.

There may have been plantain leaves strewn across the road as a warning sign but if there were we missed them. We rounded a corner at a fair speed for the conditions—maybe fifty miles per hour and there, immediately ahead, were faced with two labourers digging a ditch. They were busy about three-quarters of the way across the road. There were trees on the verge, the two labourers scrambling out of the ditch on the left; the ditch was about eighteen inches or two feet wide. "Keep going," I shouted. "Keep going." Kat bravely accelerated and we banged over the ditch still going, I guess, thirty or forty miles per hour.

We pulled up fifty yards beyond. The labourers had fled. Jackie, seated on the bench front seat between Kat and me was unharmed. In the back where there had been a foot of space between John's cardboard box and the roof was now a jumble of boxes. John's box was jammed hard against the underside of the roof. We quickly dug him out and to our enormous relief he was laughing. It had been to him some new kind of bouncy game, vastly pleasing.

Kat to her credit continued to drive. I egged her to go faster but she wasn't having any.

We stayed that night with Cuthbert Mayne then Resident, Calabar. He was a splendid chap, probably the only one of the administrative officers serving in the Eastern Region of whom I'd never heard—and in the future never was to hear—a hard word spoken. We arrived at the residency around five p.m. There was a note of welcome from him saying he wouldn't be back until about seven p.m. but his steward would look after us—show us our rooms and fix supper for the kids.

We only knew Cuthbert Mayne by reputation at that time. His welcoming note was precisely the sort of thoughtful touch that we'd been led to expect. Having regard to my junior status we were honoured to be asked to the residency in any case rather than use the rest house.

About two years into the war Cuthbert Mayne, along with a number of other senior administrative officers, had been ordered, at very short notice, to take leave. The UK-bound convoy they joined experienced U-boat trouble off the bulge of Africa and they eventually entered port at New York. There Cuthbert and his colleagues were stranded for about a fortnight. They were all short of dollars just when a little ready money would have been so useful. "Don't worry," said Cuthbert. "We'll go racing."

This was no idle remedy. For those who knew Cuthbert was a great racing man. He spent his leaves at race meetings both on the flat and steeplechasing. He had an encyclopaedic knowledge of breeding and must obviously have been a natural judge of a horse. Both these attainments paid off for the story goes that those who went racing with him and followed his advice won bet after bet.

There is another, rather later, story about Cuthbert Mayne told me by Peter Gunning. It concerned Sir Clem Pleass's time as Governor of the Eastern Region. Cuthbert was then Deputy Governor and Peter Gunning was Secretary, EP, the third post in seniority in the Region. Clem Pleass proceeded on leave; his post was taken over by Cuthbert Mayne, and Peter Gunning moved up to occupy the post of Deputy Governor. No sooner had Sir Clem and Lady Pleass flown off after a little farewell ceremony than Cuthbert Mayne said to Peter Gunning, "Look here, Deputy Governor, there's no time for any useful work before luncheon. I think we ought to have a gin." They were duly served in the governor's large office adjacent to Government House.

After the second gin Peter was idly looking at a locked glass-fronted book case containing a number of confidential files.

"I know, I know," said Cuthbert, "you want to look at the Confidential Report Files."

Peter replied, "The idea had entered my head, certainly."

I must explain that officers of the government service were never shown their annual confidential reports unless they were adverse and the officer was judged to be able to remedy matters by a knowledge of the criticism.

"Well," said Cuthbert "I'm now the senior man. We'll look at mine first."

Peter fished and duly produced a very thin file entitled "Mayne, C J". There was only one page in the file. It read simply, "For Mayne C J, see Gunning, O P."

They quickly found the file "Gunning, O P". It, too, was miserably thin. In fact there was only one page in it. It bore the scrawl of Clem Pleass's unmistakable hand. "Thought you two would."

Kat, when I first told her this little story many years ago commented, "But I thought Clem Pleass hadn't a sense of humour."

Cuthbert Mayne's authority the morning after we stayed with him in Calabar produced a warder and a gang of prisoners to carry our loads onto the MV *Pathfinder* that was to take us to Lagos. I carefully counted the loads going aboard as the prisoners mounted the gangway in single file each bearing his burden.

At sea during the afternoon I checked our baggage and found Jackie's high chair missing. It, too, had been made by the Awka Guild and was a very successful piece of work. It took to pieces for travelling. I could only guess that the prisoner carrying it had walked down the departure gangway—which I hadn't checked—still carrying his burden. Doubtless there was a quick sale on the dockside but I doubt if it made more than a penny or two as high chairs of that description were quite unknown in African society in 1945. Anyhow, it was a quietly humorous theft. I almost felt "good luck" to the thief.

We boarded the *Almanzora* for the journey from Lagos to the United Kingdom. So far as we could ascertain the designation "Civilian Trooper"' simply meant that the ship carried civilians as well as troops but both, we gathered, were required to conform to military discipline for the duration of the voyage. Kat and I hoped John, aged nine months and Jackie, aged two years, would oblige. We were allocated a four-berth cabin to ourselves which helped, but poor Jackie's bunk had a public address loud speaker on the other side of the thin cabin wall and the intermittent roars from this must have caused her lasting harm—although fifty plus years after the event I am unable to say precisely what harm.

I was made a member of one of the crews required to man the naval four-inch guns mounted on the bows. This entailed a number of gun drills and four hours' duty every twenty-four. The whole thing was organised in a very gentlemanly manner including my being allowed to check on Kat and the kids in the bath in the midst of a St George's Channel midget submarine attack.

The children ate separately from the adults. Kat told me they were given some extraordinary menus on occasion, John once being offered a large steak and chips. (Perhaps on that day the adult and children's menus had been transposed.) There was a complicated and varied system of "sittings" for the adult meals. We had to keep on our toes to make sure we attended at the right time. The trouble was that Kat and I were supposed to eat together so we were forced to shut the young in our cabin at our meal times. They didn't take kindly to this and the consequence was we had to take turns to slip down to the cabin.

It was comforting to be sailing in convoy. The presence of great grey shapes ploughing along each side of the *Almanzora* was always reassuring. Although heaven knows what problems such close proximity posed for the helmsman on a dark night.

The convoy's exact position was kept a deep secret but it was possible for the amateur navigator, aided by the nearness of the vernal equinox, to calculate a rough daily position. One morning, about 200 miles (we guessed) short of abeam the Straight of Gibraltar we altered course by ninety degrees to the East and made for the North African coast. That afternoon we all entered Casablanca Harbour. Crossing the bar each ship had to turn broadside onto the great swell coming in from the Atlantic and how they rolled. Not being a sailor I had no idea how drastically a loaded freighter could roll but time after time I expected to see one ship or another turn turtle. It was no better when our turn came. The motion was horrific. We'd tied John's pram to the railings but at one stage we were frightened he would be thrown from the pram. As soon as we could we ran down to the cabin. There poor Jackie sat on the floor where she'd been flung from her bunk. She was surrounded by broken glass and other items we'd thought were securely fixed.

The harbour, by contrast, was a millpond. The whole convoy anchored a mile or so offshore in calm water. Almost at once we were visited by a small fleet of "bum boats." The occupants, strangely, wanted clothes—trousers, shirts, jerseys, shorts—anything wearable. The condition didn't seem to matter so long as the garment, whatever it was, was recognisable. I felt a positive rogue in accepting money for worn out shirts and shorts that I was only bringing home to tear up and use for car cloths.

One or two other passengers warned that the UK banks would refuse to change Moroccan money but I took the chance and later found that the Manager of the Penrith branch of Lloyds succeeded where so many had, apparently, failed.

The word was that the convoy was to remain in Casablanca Harbour for at least two full days. The ship's first officer, whom I'd noticed was a great admirer of the opposite sex, issued an invitation to harassed mothers of children that he had a company agent's boat due at ten a.m. and would be delighted to fill it with these ladies if they were able to make arrangement for their children's' supervision. Kat had given John his morning feed and she duly joined the party. Off they all went, our ship's first officer, resplendent in his best uniform, surrounded by his accompanying harem, surely the envy of Casablanca.

At about noon we learned that the convoy's plans had been changed and we were due to sail at 12.30. There was every sign about the ship of our impending departure and I became very concerned that the first officer wouldn't get his party back in time. I was tied to the children and couldn't make the moves that the situation demanded. However, at the very last moment, the agent's launch was spotted approaching and a few minutes later up the gangway climbed the absentees.

But did we sail? Not a bit of it. The whole convoy stayed at anchor. Later that afternoon we learned that this staying put was just as well for the third officer for he, too, had apparently gone ashore in the same party as Kat. When the ladies had been safely rounded up and embarked on the launch it had been forced to leave without him. Now he was nowhere to be seen and, as we gathered, the convoy was likely to sail at any moment.

As it was we enjoyed a peaceful night, gently swinging to our anchor in Casablanca Harbour.

Just after daybreak the following morning, Kat and I were leaning over the rails watching the North African town of Casablanca emerge from the night. The colours changed as we gazed and in the distance we spotted the bow-wave of an approaching launch. It paused briefly at the gangway almost immediately below us and a single, male figure clambered out and mounted, a little unsteadily. It was the third officer, looking more than somewhat tattered. Still dressed in uniform of a sort, he'd lost his cap and his jacket hung open. As he neared, Kat laughingly whispered, "Look, he's lost all his buttons." Sure enough he had; cuff and front were all bare of the bright brass buttons he'd sported the day before.

Although we made discreet inquiries later on no one would tell us what he'd been up to. But he'd timed his return to the ship very well for the convoy sailed about eight a.m.

The rollers over the bar were just as horrific as on our arrival; this time we had the children well secured.

We sailed into rough weather. As we neared the south-western approaches the convoy changed course every few minutes. Visibility in the fierce rain storms fell to two or three hundred yards. I wondered how so many ships safely kept station. Spells of duty on our four-inch gun became an ordeal rather than a light diversion as previously. Life took on a grimmer aspect but summer in England was coming, the war was ending, we were homing after nearly six years' absence and we were young. The Ibo had kept us on our toes. We had boundless enthusiasm for our life in Nigeria but we were thin and tired. The rain forests of Southern Nigeria were enervating in the extreme. As the cooler airs of Mediterranean latitudes reinvigorated us Kat and I realised that, more than anything, it was change we wanted.

As we entered St George's Channel we learned that the war at sea was far from over: the convoy ahead of us had been attacked by a pack of midget submarines and several ships sunk.

Watches were doubled. My gun crew practised assiduously. We were all advised that night to sleep in our clothes, life gear at the ready.

The amateur navigators amongst us had spotted, in the far distance, the hills of Wales and we were forecasting a ninety-degree turn right for the safety of the Mersey when our turn came. It was eleven a.m. in the morning; one moment it was all slow plough and roll, the next merry hell was loose. Destroyers tore through the convoy seemingly from nowhere, dropping long lines of depth charges. Great thudding explosions were heard which seemed ominously like torpedo strikes. We searched the sea ahead from our gun emplacements but saw no targets.

Then the *Almanzora* lifted two...three feet out of the water (such was the impression) and the wind of an explosion threw us to the deck. The certainty was that we'd been torpedoed.

I remember that before going on watch that morning Kat had told me that she and the kids would have a bath around mid-morning. I must have told the gun commander this for the first thing he said to me as we picked ourselves up was, "Go down and check your family."

I rushed below and found Kat and the two kids all together in a half-full bath, all laughing. "The ship came right out of the water," said Kat "but we all stayed in the bath."

"Quick," I said. "We've been hit. Get dressed."

Kat wouldn't agree. "No, another ship," she said but by then was busy dressing the kids.

She was right. "The ship alongside us in the convoy," said one of the gun crew as I got back "At one moment she was there. The next she'd gone."

We never learned how many ships the convoy lost. Rumour talked of three and added that the attack had been by the same pack of midget submarines that had been responsible for the losses in the convoy ahead.

We tied up in Liverpool that same evening. Warned that the customs men were coming down to the ship we gathered the majority of our loads and had them ready for inspection in our cabin. But nobody came. At about eight p.m. we were advised by the ship's staff that the customs were delayed until the morning. We could put the young to bed. This we duly did. At ten p.m. we received a counter instruction: the customs were not going to inspect at all and we were all expected to leave the ship by midnight and get what accommodation we could ashore. This seemed harsh on the passengers but I learned that the order was given in consideration of the crew—they had been away from home for many months and deserved their freedom that night if possible.

CHAPTER SIX

First Post-war Tour: Enugu Secretariat

Kat and Jack had corresponded right up to a month or so before his death at the end of 1944 and had established a close understanding. Kat's detailed, no-nonsense but kindly accounts of our doings had appealed to him from the outset. Kate and Alice had accepted his favourable impression of her. From the moment we all met at Penrith Station it was as though they'd known her as long as they'd known me. There were no areas of constraint between them, no hesitations on either side. The kids, from time to time, infuriated the Aunts as all young children can annoy the late middle-aged. But as they put on years the two youngsters captivated the Aunts entirely.

I remember one occasion on a subsequent leave, perhaps John was five or six years old at the time, when Kate said to me quite seriously, "You don't discipline that child sufficiently."

"Right," said I, "I'll whale the daylights out of him the next time he puts a foot wrong."

John, of course, obliged in the course of the next half hour or so. "Go to your room," I ordered.

There I said to him, "Kate thinks I don't discipline you enough. Put that cushion over your seat and yell every time I clout you."

This he did and after about three smacks and three realistic cries from John came a tap at the door. "Malky, Malky, that's enough. Oh that's enough." Kate's voice.

"No, you silly old fool…you said discipline the child and that's what I'm doing." John raised another yell or two of simulated anguish. But the lesson (on both sides?) was learned and honour on both sides had been satisfied.

A joke that Kat and I shared was that Jackie and John, right from the first moment they could speak, called the Aunts by their bare names: Kate and Alice. No Aunt Kate and Alice or, more accurately Great Aunt Kate and Great Aunt Alice.

If ever there were two typical Victorians, in dress and speech and manner, it was my two dear Aunts but they never blanched or flinched at this mode of address. They even secretly liked it.

Somewhere here there is a rule to be deduced but precisely what rule I'm at a loss to formulate.

The Fadhli Sultan, when I was serving in the Aden Protectorate some five years later, one day became very angry with me and the British in general. I was pressing some point of view, and citing the British precedent, which he was reluctant to accept. "You British...you British..." he spluttered, momentarily at a loss to find a typically national sin heinous enough to fling at me..."you British..." at last he had it: "You people who beat your children."

Guy Rowley, old friend of my father and Jack, prominent member of the Shikari Club, had given me a day's fishing on his Eden water west of Glassonby on 8th May. Then, with a day to go, 8th May was declared VE Day. I persisted in my plan to fish that day for frankly selfish, mundane reasons. The high sky and the gentle south wind— the first warm wind of summer—transformed, however, what had started as a purely selfish outing into a day of remembrance for my school and Cambridge friends who had not survived the war. A long day wading in the Eden bustling its way down to the Solway has a mesmeric effect. As that day wore on I found my thoughts returning, more and more, to Big and Little Joe Dawson, John Forest, Andrew Downes, Hugh McCabe, Scott, Chapple and Hartley Graham...friends who had given their lives. Life seemed to me then—and still does— so intensely valuable that to give it away is a gift beyond comprehension. I prayed that day that they slept easy and I pray so still.

I was ordered to return by air in September having by then enjoyed six of the seventeen months due to me. The balance could be accumulated—a nice little cushion of leave to have for the future. Kat and the kids were promised a sea passage "shortly after" mine.

The schedule service was operated by Imperial Airways using DC3s. We flew only during the hours of daylight with the same crew each day, night stopping at Lisbon, Villa Cisneros and Freetown and landing at Lagos on the fourth day. Kat and I were later on to do that same trip flying ourselves in our venerable C182 in quicker time...but all that is another story.

My appointment was the last one I would have chosen for myself— Assistant Secretary (Finance) in the Eastern Provinces Secretariat in Enugu. One or two old hands whispered, "Don't you worry. You've got a wonderful clerical service assistant. The Boomer thinks

185

the world of him. And the Secretary, Eastern Provinces hates native administration finances so much he'll never do more than initial your minutes and pass them straight on to the Boomer."

The assistant was J M Onyechi MBE a slow spoken, rather portly, Onitsha Ibo some eleven years older than me. He should have been in my place; I wasn't, if the truth be told, up to doing his work. Justice, however, was on its way and less than two years later Onyechi was promoted to the senior service.

Sir Bernard Carr, the Boomer, I should add quite rightly set great store by the degree of competence native authorities exhibited in the management of their finances. He always said that their ability in this area was an important pointer to their overall performance.

In the six months that I had been away the tempo of work in the Eastern Region had slowed virtually to normal peace-time levels. There was no longer any question of combining two or even three jobs; staff were once again becoming available; we no longer felt driven. This, of course, was a great physical as well as psychological improvement.

In the United Kingdom, however, the months immediately following the cessation of hostilities in Europe and the Far East, so far as government agencies were concerned, were marked by tiredness and muddle. Kat and the Kids had been assured of a sea passage shortly after my departure. Although Kat regularly rang the Crown Agents she heard nothing further. In November a British dockers' strike threatened not only further delays but a possible loss altogether of her passage entitlement. She wrote a number of despairing letters to me, bewailing her enforced stay in the United Kingdom. The Aunts, as one would expect, were happy to continue to give Kat and the children and nursemaid (we had engaged Lilian in Penrith and she was proving an excellent acquisition) a home for as long as they wanted one. But Kat and I were anxious to continue our life together and Enugu in many ways was as good a place as any in the Eastern Region for us to be. I had been allocated a T3 house in Abakaliki Road near the edge of the Golf Course. We should be very comfortable there.

Kat kept up her pressure on the Crown Agents and the colonial office requesting a passage for herself and the kids to Lagos. She even went so far as to instruct Thomas Cook's to seek passages from England to Cape Town and Cape Town to Lagos, direct passages from the UK to Lagos apparently being unavailable. I applied what pressure I could from the Nigerian end. At last, on the 11th December, she received a telegram from the Crown Agents saying a passage was likely to be available on SS *Thysville* departing about 17th December.

Three days later she received an unsigned telegram saying the *Thysville* sailing was postponed until 21st December and then another merely stating that *Thysville* would not now sail until "after Christmas". On 28th December she received yet another telegram instructing her to arrange for her heavy baggage to be placed on the London-Southampton boat train at Paddington before seven p.m. on 31st December and she herself and the children should travel on the boat train departing Paddington at 7.05 a.m. on 1st January 1946.

31st December was in the midst of a cold spell and post-war travelling in England was not only very cold but chaotic and crowded. Kat's journey from Carlisle to London took ten hours and she only secured a seat for herself and the children by standing in an ill-formed queue from six a.m. to 7.30 a.m. on Carlisle Station. There was, of course, no restaurant car on the train but the Aunts had anticipated this by giving Kat their precious Fortnum and Masons hamper which they had filled with food they could ill spare. The hamper, they said, she could return "next leave".

Thanks to the assistance in London of an Aunt of Kat's who took over the care of the young, Kat herself was able to load all her heavy items on the boat train at Paddington as instructed.

New Year's Day 1946 was a day that tested even Kat's equanimity. Although they were on board the boat train well before the departure time of 7.05 a.m. the train didn't actually leave the station until nearly mid-morning. They duly pulled up alongside the *Thysville* shortly before dark. It was by then bitterly cold. For some reason they were ordered to remain on board the boat train.

At last, at about eight p.m., they were permitted to mount the icy and perilous gangway and go on board. Her cabin was tiny but there were seven berths. She found she was meant to share with two separate mother-and-child combinations. She soon discovered that neither of her adult cabin mates had any experience of the West Coast of Africa. One was dressed in thick Scottish tweeds and confessed that it was so cold in England that she couldn't bring herself to pack any summer clothes. Kat wondered how she would fare from the Gambia onwards.

Jackie and John had had their supper in the boat train from the remains of the generous hamper that the Aunts had given to Kat the previous day but the two other young in the cabin had to go to bed hungry.

Quite late, about nine p.m., orders were given that all passengers should collect their heavy baggage from the wharf where they had been unloaded from the boat train.

In those days anybody planning a normal tour of duty in West Africa was forced to take with them a great number of items not readily obtainable in their country of destination. English companies such as Humphreys and Crook Ltd or Griffiths McAlister specialised in supplying the items required in West Africa. In 1946 it was accepted that even for a bachelor twenty loads averaging fifty pounds each was a normal requirement.

Kat had with her eighteen loads including some half a dozen metal trunks...nearly a thousand pounds in all. The three women in Kat's cabin only managed what was by any measure a herculean task by careful co-operation: one stayed on board attempting to pacify the four naturally unsettled children and the other two helped each other lug the items up the treacherous, freezing gangway.

The SS *Thysville* was due to sail at dawn on 2nd January. In fact, she didn't actually depart until 3rd January. The delay produced a small stroke of fortune. The lady with the tweeds decided that the conditions on board were not for her and her offspring and she left the ship. Her place was not filled. As a result Kat and her adult companion found that there was just enough space for both of them to dress or undress simultaneously and they had two spare bunks on which they could place unwanted items.

This, however, was a very fleeting ray of sun in an otherwise dismal voyage. To begin with the passengers were regimented in a manner that wouldn't be tolerated for two minutes today: "Do this...do that..." "First children's sitting at 5.45 p.m....second at 6.15 p.m...." Woe betide the child that didn't put enough away in half an hour to satisfy its hunger and indeed, for that matter, woe betide the child that objected to vinegary hors d'oeuvres for supper since that on many evenings was all that they were offered.

To make matters worse the weather was appalling. Gales lasted until they were five days out with seas to match. Kat, never a good sailor, was dreadfully seasick but she kept on her feet. With two young children she had to. John, aged eighteen months wouldn't be separated from his mother for a moment. Kat had only to turn her back and he would exercise his lungs in stentorian fashion. There was nobody on board the *Thysville* he would allow to pick him up. He maintained this firm prohibition throughout the voyage.

Kat later recalled an occasion during the second week out when at last they were steaming through gentler seas. There was an egg and spoon race for adults. She had to collect four eggs, one at a time, from the far end of the deck and deposit them in a basket at her end. John, struggling in the arms of Kat's cabin companion, bellowed continuously but his cries rose to a roaring crescendo as Kat departed sinking to diminuendo as she returned. After a couple of laps the spectators caught on to what was happening and applauded John in the same rhythm.

Jackie, too, had her moment. She had made great friends with a group of British other ranks on board. There was a baby show for under threes. Jackie at the time was three and quarter years old and unable to compete. The other ranks wouldn't tolerate this and demanded that the rules be changed to "Three Years and Below". The judges were so intimidated that not only did they agree but also awarded the prize to Jackie.

Kat had no means of telling me the precise date and time of the *Thysville's* arrival in Lagos and was wondering what onward arrangements she would have to make as the ship at last docked at Apapa. However I solved the problem for her by being the first to climb the gangway. John recognised me and held out his arms to be carried.

I had arranged two rooms at the Ikoyi Club. Kat slept all the remainder of the day of arrival and all the following night...about eighteen hours straight off. She confessed later it was the first proper sleep she'd had for fifteen days.

I'd engaged a new nursemaid for the children and had brought her down with me from Enugu to meet the family. Both Jackie and John took to her immediately. They obviously instinctively felt at home with an African girl even after their ten months' absence from Nigeria. Olive Olisa—for that was her given name—was an orphan brought up by the nuns of the Catholic Mission at Ihiala. She was a quiet, straightforward girl and we all missed her when she left us at the end of the coming tour to get married.

We stayed one more night at Ikoyi having decided that we would attempt the road journey, Lagos-Enugu, in one long day rather than have the hassle of a night stop en route. As it was we were lucky in catching a ferry over the Niger without delay at Asaba and averaged just over thirty-five miles per hour for the 400-mile journey.

In an attempt to keep up the Hausa I'd learnt in Accra I'd engaged a Hausa-speaking steward, Dilla Biu, and Hausa-speaking second steward, Ali. Both were to remain with us for a number of years and both were to become close allies of the young. The African—and here I generalise about the East and West African, diverse as they are in so many ways—are naturally very good with young people. They are prepared to listen to what is said and to answer seriously. They are, above all, prepared to treat the young as equals. If you bring me today

189

fifty persons, ten of whom have been brought up as children with Africans, I will show you those ten.

John and Jackie were to have three tours as children in Enugu and John, largely because he wandered round the township more freely than Jackie, became well-known. Some years later Kat revisited Enugu and was pulled up by a policeman for some minor infringement. He was questioning her almost with hostility. She said something to the effect "...when I was here before this wasn't so..." and he said, "When were you here?" Kat said, "When John was little..." "Oh," he said, "you are the mother of John Milne?" "Of course," said Kat. "Ah, John Milne," said he. "Pass on pass on," and he saluted smartly.

I had to wait fifty years before John himself told us one or two stories of his adventures in the township of Enugu in his pre-prep school and prep school days—times when Kat and I thought he was engaged in harmless bicycle rides—and only then did we begin to understand why he was long remembered.

But I'm writing now of 1946, the year in which John had his second birthday and Jackie her fourth. And although by then both kids were self-possessed little personalities, well able to regulate their own affairs, we had to wait another five years, during which they went with us to Bamenda and Aden, before they returned to Enugu and John made many local friends and became a much talked of personality in the township.

Our days began early in Enugu. Kat and I breakfasted at 7.15 a.m. and I left for the office on the dot of 7.45 a.m. The children had a habit of disappearing about this time. I didn't give the matter any thought until one day Kat said, "I've discovered the little devils are having two breakfasts regularly."

It came about in this way. The Africans are great talkers. They take pride in language. The children sensed this but they were only in the earliest learning stage themselves and did not readily distinguish between Ibo, Hausa and English all of which they heard used around them. *Abinci* was an important Hausa word meaning "food" which they often heard. Dilla and Ali would always announce, "Abinci ya yi," when a meal was ready.

Our next door neighbours were a childless, very friendly couple called Brenchley who made a great fuss of our children, welcoming them whenever they cared to call. Our two Hausa-speaking stewards found it difficult to pronounce the "r" in Brenchley and made do with calling them "the Abincis".

The children made a regular habit of visiting the Brenchleys in the early morning and after a little while the Brenchley staff set places for them at the breakfast table. It was but a short step for our two to consider themselves asked to breakfast every morning. "What can you expect, Madam?" said Dilla to Kat. "How should the *ya-ya* think differently with a name such as Abinci?"

Workwise, the whole of that tour was a monotonous grind and I made no secret of the degree to which I depended upon the knowledge and experience of Onyechi. But we were a disciplined service and it was my duty to put the emphasis upon native administration finances that Sir Bernard Carr himself did.

As Jack had deduced in 1944 policy in colonial territories such as Nigeria might originate at any level—the top or even the lowest rungs of the service. But it always took time to refine and to receive the concordance of the secretary of state himself. I was amused to receive in 1947 a circular from the Secretary of State in which the following occurs:

"An efficient and democratic system of local government is the foundation on which the political development of the African territories must be built".

Sir Bernard Carr's own words of a year before.

Enugu, in the years immediately following the war, was infected by bats. Our T3 and the secretariat itself—to mention but two buildings—stank with their droppings particularly after heavy rain. The bats managed to penetrate between the tiles of the roof and hung suspended from the underside strewing the ceilings of the room below with their droppings. Although vaguely aware that there were over one hundred species of bat in West Africa I knew no more than two broad species: the large fruit bats which hawked on the wing round groups of trees in the high forest and the smaller, insectivorous bats that infested buildings. I was afraid to handle either species because they were reported to be carriers of rabies—a disease no one flirted with.

Every three years there was an organised blitz on bats affecting the secretariat; the tiles were removed and great heaps of dead creatures were removed. Staff quarters, on the other hand, although government-owned, were the responsibility of the occupants.

The onset of the rains in 1946 made us aware of the degree to which our T3 was infested. I had heard that carbide gas was an effective deterrent although I believe its use was prohibited under some local

191

regulation. Ignoring the latter I purchased several tins of carbide (readily available in Enugu for use in bicycle lamps) and made three gas generators each consisting of two tins; the lower holding the carbide and the top tin containing a small hole which allowed a steady drip of water onto the carbide. We positioned the tins one Sunday just after lunch. That evening at the club Kat's tennis opponent commented. "You know, an extraordinary thing happened this afternoon. About 2.30 a huge swarm of bats flew round and round our house and then settled in the roof.

Kat kept very quiet. "I couldn't be sure they were ours she said to me afterwards. "We live at least two miles from the Xs."

But our bats had left our T3 and we weren't bothered again that tour.

Kat's arrival with Jackie at Nnewi in 1943 had pioneered the advent of European children in Eastern Nigeria so far as government families were concerned. Although only three years had gone by since then Enugu in 1946 boasted at least a dozen children and their numbers increased rapidly in the years following. The war had wrought a number of changes not least to the attitude to life in the tropics. The health risks persisted, of course, but tropical medicine was steadily growing in effectiveness. Mepacrine, for instance, as I've mentioned, had taken the place of quinine as a prophylactic against malaria.

As with so many drugs, side effects emerged as experience of the use of mepacrine grew. One of the hazards was loss of hair. I remember a particularly attractive young bride who shortly after her arrival in Enugu entirely lost a beautiful display of curly brown hair. Happily her hair grew again but it was twelve months before she could dispense with a wig.

John thoroughly alarmed Kat and me one Sunday afternoon. We were all resting after a leisurely luncheon and after about an hour Kat noticed that John was singularly silent. She checked his bedroom and found him comatose with a large bottle of mepacrine tablets in his bed. His mouth and the front of his shirt was stained a bright yellow. It was impossible to be sure how many tablets he had actually consumed.

I suppose that etiquette required me to ring the little senior service hospital, find out which MO was on duty, ring him and then bring John along for examination. But all this would take time. R G A Savage lived only a few hundred yards from us. He was the senior specialist in the Region. He had helped Kat when the breach presentation threatened. He, I knew, would help us now.

It took two minutes to motor to his house. In response to my knock on his open front door he lent over the railings at the top of the staircase. He had a wrapper round his waist and wore a singlet. "John has eaten an unknown number of mepacrine tablets. Will you please look at him?" I said.

"Of course," he replied briefly and, pausing only to select one of three medical cases placed against the hall wall, climbed into my car, dressed as he was. That is the sort of chap—Scots father, Ibo mother—Rici Savage was.

John perked up a little as the examination progressed. "I don't think he has eaten enough tablets seriously to harm him," said Savage, at length. "Let me know at once if there's any change."

I took Savage home again and then Kat and I did our best to clean John up and make up our minds how many tablets he'd actually swallowed. Working forwards from the probable total contents of the bottle to the probable total number of tablets which should still be in the bottle we found a discrepancy of about twenty. Maybe he had had this number in his mouth but he'd spat out a good many and possibly even vomited others. It wasn't possible to be certain. It's a nothing story really, as he soon recovered, but it worried us considerably at the time. Savage was a hero and it was worth all the fuss to know how much we could rely on him.

In later years, when discussing the ages of other colleagues' children, Kat and one or two of her friends began to remark an odd coincidence in dates. Just after the change from quinine to atebrine (the proprietary name of mepacrine methane sulphonate) some married couples who'd previously had no children began suddenly to produce. This was before the days of the contraceptive pill. The thought was that quinine in the doses we took as a malarial prophylactic had also served a role as a contraceptive. I haven't heard of any work done by a colonial Kinsey on this point but if any researcher is so minded he or she would be well advised to make inquires now whilst the relatively few couples who might provide information are still alive.

Throughout 1946 there had been an increasing volume of complaints by members of the public against two categories of Nigerian government official; sergeants of police and guards on the Nigerian Railways. It was alleged that the former were making excessive demands for money at every turn of their normal duties on pain of "humbugging" those who didn't pay up. And, of course, the opportunities for humbug were myriad.

Railway guards had posed a problem to the management for some time. In 1946 it was more of a question of an old abuse rising to unacceptable proportions. They were allegedly in cahoots with the drivers of stopping passenger trains, halting them a mile before and a mile or so after mainline stations. There they would take on or put off as the case might be "Guards' passengers". These persons paid the guard about half the normal fare but in return had to be prepared to walk a couple of miles at a number of stations. Of course the management carried out checks from time to time but word of the check generally seemed, in some miraculous way, to reach the guard and engine driver prior to their arrival at the checkpoint.

There were opportunities for petty corruption over the whole area of government. The colonial government—that is to say the senior British expatriate officials at the time serving in the Nigerian government—were well aware of the problem. There was constant pressure by these officials at best to eliminate, at worst to contain, what went on. In the Eastern Region of Nigeria the public at large were prepared to tolerate a reasonable degree of extortion largely because of its historical association with the Kola system but beyond a certain point would cry, "Halt. Enough is enough."

The Kola system was endemic throughout much of West Africa. It can be briefly described as "payment for local services rendered".

Land disputes before the native courts often involved inspection by the bench of the disputed area. In many courts the custom grew up of one or the other of the parties involved in the case paying the cost of feeding the inspecting panel. District officers knew about this practice but in the absence of complaint did not interfere.

Another factor affecting petty corruption by government officials was the pressures bearing upon any holder of a salaried post. The change from tribal systems to western practices was taking place in Eastern Nigeria in the years immediately following the First World War but the change was slow and ancient customs in many instances were still valid. For instance, in the kinship system, if a member has a stroke of good fortune and secures as a result some wealth, he does not keep it to himself but shares it with members of his family or other dependents. For many years—right up to independence in fact—paid employment was regarded in some areas as a shareable stroke of good fortune. Paid employees would be subject to considerable pressures to pass on a portion of their salaries. As wages were paid on the basis of the wage earner supporting only his immediate family there was considerable pressure upon the individual to increase his earnings by methods Western society might consider corrupt.

The third factor affecting the attitude in Southern Nigeria to petty corruption by government officials must be placed at the feet of the British Medical Association itself. In the earliest days the establishment of medical personnel was fixed at a level to deal with expatriate employees and their wives only. As wealth grew expatriate doctors found that there was a growing demand for their services from the public. They successfully prevailed upon the BMA to force colonial governments to allow private practice as a condition of recruitment. The position was reached in the late twenties and early thirties when the medical service was expected to be available to expatriate and local officials alike but many doctors, in exercising their rights to private practice, were neglecting their duties to the latter. In 1934 the BMA were persuaded to surrender their enforcement of the rights of their members to private practice, although when I reached Eastern Nigeria as late as 1939 doctors recruited before 1934, for complex technical reasons, still retained the right.

By charging for yaws injections, for example, some expatriate doctors were able to make very considerable incomes in addition to their government salaries. Locally recruited medical personnel were aware of this and understandably themselves arranged sources of additional income. One such was to charge patients in government hospitals for all services; there very soon became regular tariffs for medicines, bedpans, dressings and the like. (Food was provided by the patients' relatives). Nothing the medical department could do to abolish these charges was effective. And of course the junior employees of other departments said to themselves, "If the medicals can do this, we can do the same."

When first drafting these observations I omitted to make any mention of expatriate members of the senior service...the administration, the veterinary services, the agriculture, the police, the legal and so on. The reason simply was that these were incorruptible. ('Rubbish," cries a deafening chorus fifty years later; "Vide Sir Robert Walpole: all those men have their price." Maybe. But then I was never tested nor were any of my colleagues.) And another thought for the cynical. "Spin-doctoring" (in the modern sense of the word)—we never blurred the truth save from stupidity or ignorance. The colonial empire would have lasted weeks not decades, had we tried to be clever with the actuality.

To revert to 1946-47 and to the complaints by members of the public against railway guards and sergeants of police in particular: here it was largely a matter of the public saying, "Enough is enough."

One day early in January 1947 the Secretary, Eastern Provinces called me to his office. "I've a job for you," he said. "HH has a Parliamentary Delegation staying at GH and wants them taking care of all day tomorrow. Take them where you like and show what you will. Just keep them on the go until seven p.m. There's seven of them and they travel in two cars. You'd better drive one of the cars."

He mentioned their names which meant nothing to me other than the leader—Lord Llewellin—who had held important office in Churchill's war-time government.

"The leader is a very good chap," SEP continued. "Get out a programme as soon as you can and check it with him."

DOs and others I planned to visit on the morrow were hard to contact and it wasn't until the afternoon that I got a programme together. I had to wait until after dinner before I was able to speak to Lord Llewellin on the phone and read the programme over to him. "It sounds fine," he said, briefly.

The following day Lord Llewellin and a Conservative MP sat in the back of the car I was driving and a tall, gangling MP joined me in the front. My companion was very talkative and indeed seemed well informed on Nigerian questions.

The first scheduled stop was to be Onitsha. As we approached Awka, about two-thirds of the journey Enugu-Onitsha, the conversation turned to petty corruption and my companion trotted out all the anti-British comments that the Zik press had recently made in connection with the railway guards and police sergeant matters. To the obvious amusement of the pair in the back I got involved in a quite heated debate with him trying to point out that so-called petty corruption had its roots in indigenous customs which couldn't be changed overnight. But he was a much livelier debater than me and rapidly got the best of it. Anyway, I was trying to drive as well as discuss. I lapsed into silence, angry with my own inadequacy and with him.

By this time we were approaching the village of Awka. Compound after compound lined the roadside, most containing an Ibo-style house of high pitched thatched roof surmounting mud walls. One compound, however, possessed a smart wrought-iron entrance gate and a modern, concrete block built, two-storey house behind.

"Ah," said our talkative young MP, "the chief's house."

"There aren't any chiefs as such in this area," I explained. "The local government body consists of a council of equals."

But he wouldn't have it. "No, surely only the chief could build a house like that."

Sarcastically I said, "Only a railway guard or sergeant of police could afford to build a house like that."

By this time Llewellin and his companion in the rear seat were laughing outright. "Hi, stop," the former said. "I bet you the boy is right. We'll go back and see."

So back we reversed; the second car in our small party catching up as we halted by the iron gates. There didn't seem to be anybody about. We climbed the imposing steps to the entrance, pushing open the twin doors. Many "modern" Ibo houses possessed a reception chamber near the entrance. This house was no exception. There, facing us as we entered, was a huge photograph, at least two feet by two feet, mounted on an easel. It portrayed a railway guard, in full uniform, seated on a stool, two crossed flags between his legs...plainly the owner of the house.

"Told you the boy was right," said Lord L.

I later learnt that the young MP's name was James Callaghan. Maybe, fifty years ago he wasn't always right but he was certainly, even then, a master of polemics.

Working day in day out with J M Onyechi I got to know him pretty well. For what it was worth I had done my best for him by recommending on at least two occasions his promotion to the senior service. At last, on 11th May 1947, he got it.

It might be thought that Onyechi and I, working as closely together as we did, each would come to have a detailed knowledge of the other's family affairs. But no. This was 1947 and, had I pried into his private life, it would have smacked, almost, of anthropological inquiry and been bad manners. He never asked Kat or me to his house nor had he ever told me how many wives and children he had. He preferred it that way. He would have come to our house had we invited him but would have felt the visit an ordeal, perhaps a nuisance, so we never suggested it.

In Kenya, twenty-five years later, we found that attitudes and relationships had changed dramatically. There one's African friends dropped in and were entirely at their ease. It would have been bad manners, in fact, not to show interest in their domestic affairs.

In Nigeria in the late 1940s only Ojukwu and Mbanefo visited us unprompted but they were exceptional men already confident of their place in both Western and African society.

A year or two after Independence I heard Onyechi had been dismissed from the service on grounds of some financial irregularity. It certainly would not have been a crude fraud and if subtle would not have been easily discovered. Since by then fraud was endemic in Nigeria, I feel that Onyechi's dismissal was much more likely as a result of some successful vendetta against him, almost certainly rooted in a matter far remote from his official duties. I was sad to hear that he'd left the service for in the years I'd known him he'd made himself a true master of his subject and had done a very good job indeed on behalf of the Eastern Nigerian government.

Working in the Enugu Secretariat gave me an opportunity of getting to know several of the wartime and post-war entrants to the administrative service. They brought with them all the changes in attitude that six years of war had wrought. I particularly, and Kat in her less demanding way, found it hard to get on terms with them.

Their formative years had been spent in the crucible of war; ours in peace-time England (uneasy peace that it was). We had looked to a full life-time service ahead; they were in doubt and were unsympathetic to much of our way of thinking. I found it harder to work with them than I did with my own peers and earlier entrants to the service. They were, however, men of high calibre prepared to work hard and many, deservedly rose rapidly in the service. When it came to accelerating arrangements for Independence, which was one of my main tasks in the Cameroons in 1959-61, I found that I encountered more difficulty with the post-war expatriate segment of the service than with any other. Lacking in pre-war experience, they were not aware how fast the African had, and could, evolve. Paradoxically they wanted to put the brakes on.

Early in 1947 I had trouble with several re-occurring attacks of amebiasis—amoebic dysentery. The bouts of diarrhoea were fairly easily brought under control temporarily but would come again. I found that I was feeling vaguely unwell most of the time. I was to go on being troubled for nearly five years. Nobody could be certain where the causative organisation—the amoeba cysts—lay: the liver and the walls of the gut were both suspect.

We went on leave on 12th May 1947. I remember that we took Olive Olisa with us as far as Takoradi which greatly helped us to settle down on a crowded but jolly ship.

Playing deck cricket one day in the sunny, cool mid-latitudes I was taught not to field too close to the batsman when the bat flew out of his hands and broke my nose. Kat noticed the ship's doctor—a very young newly qualified character—deeply immersed in one of his medical tomes just after the incident. "I wonder what he had to look up about a broken nose?" she asked.

We berthed in Southampton early in the morning. The boat train to London was waiting. We found ourselves on a very crowded platform at Waterloo just before midday. It seemed that London had not yet come to terms with the rigors of peace. The Aunts were expecting us and there was a train to Carlisle at two p.m. Winning a taxi in the mêlée outside Waterloo was a matter of bribery. At Euston we counted our bags...sixteen, seventeen...eighteen...one missing. Kat at once identified it as a kit bag, tied round the neck with a cord. The taxi driver, grumbling, took me back to Waterloo. I begged him to wait and ran onto our arrival platform. There by a pillar, safe and sound, was the missing bag. I seized it. Simultaneously a large hand came down on my shoulder from behind. "Is that your bag, sir?" it was a railway policeman. "I've been watching that bag for half an hour, sir," he added.

"It's ours," said I. "If you want proof, open it. You'll find the top article is a child's chamber pot, inverted, and immediately under it is a cured ham."

"My God," he said, "it's yours all right," and turned away.

The Aunts were still at Mealsgate and were as welcoming as ever. The kids by then were three and five years old. They were really very grown up, a fact I attribute as much to the Africans with whom they'd been in close contact as to ourselves. Peoples of Negro or Bantu origin are good with children—make no mistake about it. They treat the young, and very young, as full members of the group; they give them proximity and confidence; above all they do not badger or force them into particular behavioural patterns. The days when the English upper classes saw their children for half an hour in the evenings were surely as damaging as the modern parents (or parent) allowing their young to run wild with their peer groups. Our own constant struggles against the climate and tropical diseases, and our frequent travelling as a family group of four, had all been factors influencing Jackie and John.

The Aunts remarked approvingly upon the changes in both children. This was, of course, a matter of degree. I'm not suggesting that the young were paragons, merely that they'd had certain advantages in terms of advancing to an early maturity over their fellows left in a purely English environment.

We took the Aunts—or rather it was the other way round for we travelled in their Morris—for a holiday in Ireland. It says a lot for the plainness of their lives at other times, and for their innate gentleness, that we all got on so well together. The only slightly critical note that Kat remembers is of Alice commenting on the frequency with which John demanded that the car be stopped so that he could have a pee. Kate would have been sixty-seven and Alice sixty at this time and memories of the behaviour of the very young had faded.

So far as I was concerned the highlight of that leave was to be a climbing trip to the Alps commencing with a meet of the Fell and

Rock Climbing Club at Arolla in Switzerland. I remember training for the Alps by tackling the long, easy ridge climbs on Ben Nevis with Eric Arnison over the weekends. We got in four routes in one day on our last effort by dint of moving together whenever possible. For the time being my amebiasis was quiescent.

I had known of Eric ever since I had first lived at Lynwood as a boy of twelve. But he was fifteen years older than me and it was 1947 before I came to know him well. He'd been to St Bees, leaving ten years before I arrived at the school. He belonged to a Penrith family firm of solicitors which has now seen service from five generations of Arnisons. The senior partner as I write these lines is one of Eric's sons. Eric was an all-round sportsman, being a good shot and an excellent fisherman, but his forte was mountaineering. Having, like me, read fairly widely on the history of climbing both of us found our greatest pleasure in essaying the famous routes of the past—the Brenva route on Mount Blanc...the Zmutt...

It was at Arolla that I gave up thirty years of teetotalism. We tackled the long Les Douves Blanches ridge—four ropes of three each if I remember rightly. Those who knew the route said, "Don't bother to carry any water. There are lots of snow patches in the gullies."

The climb went on and on. Four ropes slowed us down. 1947 was an exceptionally dry year in the Alps and my friends were wrong. There weren't any snow patches that year. Reaching the summit after about fifteen hours of effort we had all developed a truly magnificent thirst. But it was an easy descent to the Col Bertol followed by an hour and a half trot down to the Arolla Hotel, built at the end of a mule track some eight kilometres distant from the nearest motor road at Haudères. The others were unanimous: "We are not spoiling a thirst such as this by drinking from mountain streams on the way down." Misguidedly I fell into line.

We reached the long Arolla bar absolutely gasping. The good lady in charge had anticipated our arrival and the bar counter supported a row of metre-high glass vessels filled to the rims with either "bière brun" or "bière jaune". My friends each seized a vessel of their choice. I meekly ordered lemon.

Most of the others had already disposed of their first meter of bière and were ready for the second. The dear lady serving at the bar was still fiddling about looking for a lemon for me. At last she found a desiccated fruit...one. It was too much. I seized the nearest metre of bière and downed it without pause. Since then, I'm afraid, I have never looked back. I have cheerfully spent the last fifty-two years searching for the happy mean…between drinking too much and not enough.

———————

Early on during our leave I'd had a note from Sir Bernard Carr thanking me for what he termed "a lot of tedious and unrewarding work on native administration finances" and saying it was his wish to post me to Bamenda District our next tour with the intention that I should take over from Freddy Kay, the SDO, when the latter went on leave in the autumn. This, of course was tremendous news. It was one thing to act for a few weeks—or even months—in charge of a District as a result of the exigencies of war; it was quite another to be promised in peace-time conditions what without doubt was the best and most exciting District in Eastern Nigeria. An ADO formally becomes a DO after passing the promotion bar reached after nine years of service. I still had to serve another two years before I could expect a District of any description much less the best available.

This news had confirmed Kat's and my intention to order an Austin 16 and have it delivered as soon as possible during our leave.

British cars had a high reputation before the war. We understood the Austin 16 was built to pre-war design and was constructed to the highest standards. It turned out to be an excellent car—just the vehicle for the rough Bamenda conditions—but there was one design fault which was nearly fatal for us: the front doors were hinged on the trailing edge and opened, as it were, the wrong way.

We had, in fact, collected the car the day before I went on the Arolla trip. Kat and the two young used it to visit Kat's sister and her husband in Ipswich and met me there on the day of my return from Switzerland.

I drove back to Kat's sister's house. Kat and John were in front; Jackie in single state in the back. John was fiddling with everything in sight. Suddenly, at thirty or forty miles per hour in a built-up area, John opened the front door latch and before Kat could grab him he was gone, pulled out of the car by the wind-opened door.

We stopped and ran back. He lay by the kerb very still, blood oozing from his forehead where I feared he had hit the edge of the kerb.

A woman, most concerned, took us into her house. John came to in Kat's arms, whimpering quietly. I phoned the hospital. They said, "Bring him here."

They kept him for two hours. A doctor and nurse appeared and said, "He's obviously had a bad tumble and he's concussed. But we can't find anything broken or any internal damage. Keep him as quiet as you can in a darkened room and ring us at once if he deteriorates in any way. He'll be much happier at home with his own family round him than he would be here."

They were right about John wanting the reassurance of his own family. Twice, at least, during the ensuing night he climbed out of his small bed and came across to Kat and me. "Where's Mummy, where's Daddy...where's Jackie?" he kept asking.

A week later, such is the resilience of the very young he was virtually normal again.

Not so, I must add, for Kat and me. Fifty-two years after the incident we both remember it with sick trepidation. How the young can tear you apart.

My work with native administrations during the past tour had pointed to a greater reliance being placed in the future on using the two-tier United Kingdom local government system as a model for future developments in Eastern Nigeria. I sought the help of the colonial office in arranging attachments to Cumberland local government bodies. Swift, the Clerk of Carlisle City Council, went to a lot of trouble in organising the sort of short attachments to both the county council and the city council that I felt would be most useful. The thought of grafting modern local government concepts onto ancient tribal customs, some of them in his eyes pretty outlandish, appealed to him.

Petrol was still rationed. I was given a generous allowance for the local government work. The surplus came in very handy for climbing and fishing trips in the Lake District. Eric Arnison, whose own sources were drying up at this time, was I remember most appreciative.

Our leave came to an end in October 1947. It was very sad to say "goodbye" to the Aunts. The fitful, watery sunshine was in keeping with their smiles. "Eighteen months and we'll be back again," we said.

Jackie and John, expert travellers, although unable to boast more than eight years between them, settled back and prepared to tolerate the long run from Cumberland to Southampton. Kat ran her eye over the essentials in the cubby hole in front of her: water for the kids, sweets to bribe them during their bored moments; money, papers and a tin of keys.

I was secretly glad that there was a morning cover of mist on Blencathra and that the clouds over the Borrowdale valley were weeping freely. It would have been too much to have left the Lake District bathed in autumn sunshine on a perfect climbing day. I bustled up Dunmail Raise at fifty-five...Ambleside... Windermere...Kendal...Lancaster passed swiftly by...all chockfull of youthful memories. We lunched near Knutsford, tea'd at Oxford, had a night at Winchester where we got two excellent double rooms in a good hotel. The next day was devoted entirely to boarding ship— such things were done in more leisurely fashion in 1947. We had to burrow beneath a pile of heavy luggage fifteen feet high on the dockside to extract our own loads sent ahead by rail. I supervised the loading of our new car which was soon expertly stowed without a scratch on its pristine paint. Our ship—whose name I forget—was a civilian trooper and presented a sad contrast with Elder Dempster Mail boats. Had the war not intervened she would have been scrapped in 1940.

Better that we should draw a veil over much of that voyage... regimentation, queuing for a dirty, saucerless cup of tea, the incessant blare of the broadcasting system, waiting for other people's children to topple off the rails into the rolling equatorial sea...

Las Palmas was an interlude...intense last minute bargaining with the earnest vendors on the long stone pier...their prices reaching rock bottom as the gangway was swung aboard. We had no time there to visit a beach and swim away the mental and physical grime of our incarceration on board as the ship sailed quite soon after first coming alongside.

Freetown and Lumley Beach was a different story. We were first ashore and after the essential preliminary wrangle with the owner of an ancient, probably verminous and certainly near-decayed taxi— fifteen shillings to Lumley Beach and back with nothing for an hour's wait—we were on our way.

The beach, after our crowded, hot existence aboard, was for a little while a world apart: the palm-fringed club house, the sun slanting along the silver sand and the warm blue sea—deep blue as it can sometimes be early in the tropic day. We rolled and swam, lazed and ran, free at last after the sorely regimented days. Soon, however, the sun became uncomfortably hot, the glare from the sand hurt our eyes and we were glad to get back into the taxi.

Three more days hugging the coast and we sailed into the modern harbour of Takoradi. There was an anxious half-hour as two cars were extracted from the forward hold. I stood by in an attempt to protect the paint of our Austin but all was well.

Another day at sea and we entered Lagos harbour. The white walled, red roofed houses, shuttered against the morning sea breeze, half hidden by the giant casuarinas on Magazine Point, looked deserted. However the usual urchin was sitting behind his home-made fishing rod on Government House jetty and the usual loafers idled on the grass verge at the water's edge. The European style architecture of the commercial buildings on the front suggested coolth.

Chapter Seven

Bamenda

By an unlucky chance our sea-bourne connection to the Southern Cameroons had sailed an hour or so before our arrival in Lagos. We were faced with the choice between a three week wait in Lagos followed by an eight day sea passage to Victoria or a journey of some ten days by train, lorry and launch. Our car, in any case, would have to wait direct sea transport to Victoria.

We elected for the wait in Lagos. Kat spent a lot of the time shopping. I was given a temporary job in the secretariat. The young attended a small private school. This they greatly enjoyed for the first two or three hours each day. Later the heat made them peevish and lethargic and their enthusiasm for kindergarten waned.

We were all relieved when the 300 ton MV *Pathfinder*—which was to carry us and our car to Victoria—arrived. The tiny seven foot by seven foot four berth cabin offered to us was the best of the three available and as the saloon was occupied as an auxiliary cabin there was nowhere we could spend the days at sea.

However, the captain was a sportsman and we spent most of our time on the bridge. Both children became great hooter-pullers. We proceeded up river to Calabar—our stop on the way to Victoria—to a series of cheerful but irregular toots. Kat, poor thing, was overcome by the inshore swell and had spent much of the time on her bunk.

At last we tied up alongside the small jetty in Victoria.

Kat and the kids disembarked down the gangway in a civilised manner. For some reason our precious Austin 16 had to be put over the side onto a very small barge before it could be landed. I have a memory of seeing the car suspended above the tiny barge which was bobbing up and down alarmingly on the swell. However, the Cameroons' gang in charge were highly skilled and all was well.

We arranged for our heavy loads to be taken up to Bamenda by kit car. The owner insisted on allowing three days for the journey. The rains were at their heaviest, the roads were bad—and when a

Cameroonian transporter said "bad" he meant "virtually impassable" as I was to learn—and much of the route lay up the "French side" as the road from Kumba to Mamfe had not then been completed. However, optimistic as always, I decided that we should attempt the journey in one day in our Austin 16.

We reached Kumba without incident, paying Bill Newington, the DO a brief visit in his office en passant. The "French side" was a different matter. Very soon after crossing the frontier the road to Nkongsamba deteriorated almost beyond belief. An extra heavy rainstorm developed. We came to a junction of what had by then become two streams; left or right? We stopped in doubt. The windows misted up. The young became fractious. It was midday and we had made miserable progress. Now, in fact, we were halted. At length a farm worker came past. He was using a huge plantain leaf as a shield from the worst of the rain. His hoe was held under one arm. He didn't welcome my attempt in my best French, to ask him the way to Nkongsamba. "Na tak wo'man hand," he said shortly in pidgin, trudging on.

Kat interpreted; "He means left," she said. We took the left fork and promptly hit the sump on a rock and had to return to Kumba in the manner described on page 120.

There was no doubt that Bamenda was the delectable spot that we had been led to expect. The Government Station, comprising the brick-built ex-German fort established in 1902 (and rebuilt in 1907/8), hospital, prison and housing for the District staff including about ten senior service quarters and houses for forty-five police, twenty prison staff, and twenty hospital junior staff, was built on a gently sloping shelf terminating in a trachite cliff at an altitude of about 4,500 feet asl. The Government Station overlooked the *Abakpa*, the mixed township of about ten thousand souls, 500 feet lower down.

The senior service houses, occupied then entirely by expatriate personnel, boasted large gardens. They were separated from the junior service housing—as in all stations in British West Africa—largely on medical grounds.

There was a piped water system which served both senior and junior quarters with a regular supply of excellent water. Several of the senior service quarters possessed a simple but ingenious system of hot water supply: this consisted of the ubiquitous forty-four gallon steel drum (originally used for carriage of petrol) placed in a small brick-built tower above a fireplace. This construction was always built outside the main house at a sufficient distance not to threaten the thatch with fire and was connected to the bathroom by a single hot water pipe. An hour's preparation each evening before bath-time was not a problem in a land where there was no shortage of labour.

The station had been extensively planted up with blue gums. The Forestry Department had a regular programme for coppicing and were able to ensure that all the staff enjoyed a supply of firewood adequate for all purposes.

Freddy Kay was very much in charge of the Bamenda District, large as it was. In talking of it to our friends in England we used to say "it was the size of Wales and twice as mountainous". Freddy was thirteen years older than me and well up the list of senior district officers in the Nigeria staff list—our *vade mecum* of precedence. He'd been up to Trinity Hall, Cambridge where he'd taken two degrees: a BA in an arts subject and a law degree. Five foot ten or eleven in height he was sparse in build—very much the build of a first-class tennis player of the time, which in fact he'd been. I had an inkling that Sir Bernard Carr had marked him out for accelerated promotion. I now think, with hindsight, that this was correct. With hindsight again, there was one warning: Freddy wasn't quite as physically active as his build and appearance suggested. He was only forty-three but I noticed he was often too tired to play tennis and quite frequently he was bad tempered to boot. His work came first and he was a very good district officer indeed, concise in the legal aspects of his work, pains-taking and constructive in his dealings with the native authorities. We weren't to know it, of course, but only four years later he was to return to Bamenda as a resident and there suddenly die of a heart condition at the early age of forty-seven.

But to return to 1947: Bamenda was remote, cut off from Provincial Headquarters by the then absence of a road link between Mamfe and Kumba. The District "team" consisted of half a dozen expatriate officers, all great individualists; and a strong, slightly aloof SDO at the head was desirable. Freddy Kay filled this role with distinction.

Nobody seemed to know anything of Sir Bernard Carr's promise that I should have the District on Freddy's departure on leave so I kept quiet about it.

We were allocated the ADO1 house which had previously been occupied by J H D Stapleton and his wife. He was a good Hausa speaker and had recently passed an examination in Fulani. These two languages helped him in his main task of dealing with grazier-farmer disputes which were a perennial problem in the District. Freddy Kay hoped that I would be able to carry on Stapleton's work. Although I only had rudimentary Hausa I was to spend the first three months

207

in the District concentrating on this problem. Stapleton had left a draft set of Grazing Rules which were to become the model for the future.

The ceiling of the sitting room in the house we had inherited from the Stapleton's boasted a set of wires strung below it. We were told that Mrs Stapleton, an ex-opera singer, wished to keep her voice in usage and had had the wires put in place to improve the acoustics. Only the other day, as I write these pages, I put this to Stapleton himself. He assured me it was nothing to do with his wife's singing voice—the wires merely improved the acoustics; full stop. So do stories grow.

The house, built of stone, was sited twenty yards from the edge of the Bamenda escarpment. Here the escarpment took the form of a 300-foot high trachyte cliff. By many measures it was a horrifying place for children but ours had spent their short lives beset with objective dangers—tropical diseases, poisonous insects, rabies, roads that held cars deep in the mud, snakes…even the hot sun. They took it for granted that they should treat these dangers just as the rest of the "team" (Kat and I) did. As a special treat, I let them over the cliff on my climbing rope and they had a good look down and saw why it was unwise to go anywhere near the edge unless they were roped up.

The trachyte was too friable a rock to yield good rock climbs by European standards but nevertheless I was able, with considerable "gardening", to make one climb of about 200 feet, ending on our lawn. We christened it "the Garden Slabs".

We had a full household for Christmas Day 1947. Kat had arranged a drinks party on the lawn at midday as a preliminary to a leisurely Christmas luncheon. Staying in the house was Hilda Gregory, Education officer (Women) for the Province. She was sparse and thin; workwise she knew her mind and quietly got on with a very effective job. She often stayed with us when visiting Bamenda and was a great favourite with the children. They found the name Hilda Gregory rather difficult to grasp and christened her, for expedience sake, Gravy. The Staff List, plainly compiled by gentlemen for gentlemen, didn't give ladies' ages but I guess Hilda G was some ten years older than me. One of the nicest things about her was her willingness to tackle anything in the way of adventure suggested to her: "I've a pony that hasn't been backed yet. Like to have a go?" "How about a rock climb this morning. Like a try at Garden Slabs?" and of course her answer was always, "Of course I would." The other couple breakfasting with us had done some climbing in Wales and were eager to try the route. "OK," I said, "ten it is."

There was an easy path down to the bottom of the climb. We duly met at ten and started the descent. Hilda G was still in her room when we left and the kids said they would root her out.

She caught us up at the bottom of the climb. The other two were sensibly dressed...thick shirts, long trousers; trachyte can be quite prickly. But Hilda, bless her, was wearing her hot weather gear: the slimmest of tops, not much more than a bra, bare midriff, the briefest of shorts. "Hi," I said, "you'll be very uncomfortable like that especially if you need a tight rope."

"Oh Malcolm, don't make me go all the way back to change. I'll be OK."

The first two-thirds of Garden Slabs were easy enough, little more than Moderate in the Fell and Rock Classification. The last thirty feet, however, ending up on our lawn itself, was a good deal more demanding; it would have been classified as Very Difficult or possibly Mild Severe.

Kat was presiding over the little drinks party as I led the final slab and took a firm anchorage on the grass. I'd done it so many times in the past few months that I didn't find it particularly difficult. The other two climbers managed the slab with the help of a tight rope. Hilda was the last to essay it. For some reason she found it a good deal harder than the others had and needed a very tight rope. In fact I almost lugged her up the last dozen feet. Over the edge she came. The rope round her slim waist had slipped upwards and the top half of her outfit was no longer where it should have been but somewhere under her chin and askew at that.

"Oh dear," she said, as she adjusted her clothes. "I don't think I'm going to be a very good rock climber."

The incident obviously made an impression on John. During a pause in the conversation at luncheon he suddenly said: "Poor Gravy, you know that rock scraped her front."

John, still under four, didn't waste words. He reserved what he had to say to Kat and me to things that in his mind really mattered. For instance, one morning at breakfast he announced matter-of-factly, "I killed a snake this morning."

We knew that one of his Bamenda Messenger friends had given him a miniature Bamenda staff—which all Bamenda men affected in lieu of a spear—but hardly credited that he'd used it to kill a snake. I'm afraid that I thought that he'd allowed his imagination to run ahead of the facts. I merely said, "Where is it?"

"In the big bed," he replied shortly.

On my way to the office I paused for a word with the warder in charge of the gang of prisoners whose duty it was to keep the gardens of the senior service personnel in the station neat and tidy. Quite extraneously he said, "John did a fine thing to kill that puff adder."

By then some of the prisoners had gathered round. One of them said in pidgin, "E dey fit too much. We fear for him."

I suppose he meant, "He was very confident. We were worried."

I got the story from them. John had been talking to one of the prisoners when they spotted the puff adder moving very slowly into a clump of plants. John was the only one amongst them with a stick— he had his miniature Bamenda staff—he calmly hooked the puff adder out and then killed it with a couple of blows. To prove it they showed me the dead snake still in the large flowerbed. It was only about one and a half feet in length but was as thick as a man's wrist; plainly quite large enough to have inflicted a fatal bite.

I went back to the house and had a discussion with Kat. If John had been an African child the warder and the prisoners would not, I was sure, have allowed him to tackle the snake. The trouble was that white men were often thought to be masters of a superior kind of magic to any that might be possessed by the African. John, aged three and a half, had confidently killed the snake and they quite understandably assumed he knew he was safe.

It would be wrong for us to tick John off but he must be weaned from the notion that his Bamenda staff was designed solely for snake bashing.

It was decided that I should have a man-to-man talk with him on the subject of snakes. Try and get across that snakes in general were even more frightened of us than we of them and that they were very unlikely to attack unless they were threatened or cornered. It was better to leave them alone rather than try to kill them on sight. Of the two main families—the cobras and the vipers—the former reared up and could strike as far only as the height of their head above the ground; the latter, on the other hand, were more unpredictable and could strike as far as they might lunge forward. Some of the cobras could spit venom which was not only very painful in the eyes but might damage one's sight. Better, much, that he should treat his Bamenda staff as a weapon for emergency use only.

John and I duly had the discussion and I think that as a result he thought again about snakes. But the staff was to feature in at least two other incidents before we left Bamenda.

Farmer-grazier disputes were a constant source of trouble in 1947 in the Bamenda District. They were of relatively recent origin, being a product of the settlement of the Bamenda Highlands as a whole. Four hundred years earlier—so word-of-mouth history had it—the whole area was relatively sparsely settled supporting only small pockets of resident peoples. In the succeeding four hundred years the Bamenda Highlands proved to be the end-point of a number of migrations from the NW, N and NE. Each successive wave had not only pushed the sparsely scattered earlier peoples off the highlands but had itself come to a halt. The migrants were largely subsistence farmers. From about the turn of the century Fulani cattle keepers with their herds began to arrive in increasing numbers in the highlands of Bamenda, Mambila, and Obudu. At first there was plenty of land for all: ample space near the established villages for the type of shifting cultivation practised by the agriculturists; wide open grasslands for cattle grazing. Bamenda District had been brought under close administration in the 1920s and 1930s. By the time we got there in 1947 there were only a few fringe areas that hadn't seen a touring administration officer and even these areas retained some memory of German patrols in the years 1900-1915.

As the degree of administration became more marked, disputes between villagers and nomadic cattle keepers increased in numbers. More land was required for farming purposes. The women—who by custom did the farming—preferred the sites of disused cattle kraals which were well manured. This upset the graziers who intended to use the kraal site again as they had carefully sited it in the first instance well away from villages and with easy access to water.

On the other hand a Fulani owning a large herd of cattle was a rich man. Some such decided to graze were they willed and settle any disputes that might arise by bribing local officials. This naturally upset the women whose hard work was destroyed.

By native law and custom outright ownership of land was not recognised. Rights, such as they existed, were based on the conception of usage. The expansion of population and the introduction of closer administration demanded changes in the land usage practices. It was in this field that Stapleton had made a valuable contribution with Cattle Control Regulations tailored to the particular needs of the area where they applied.

During the early part of my service in Bamenda I concentrated my touring on areas where grazing disputes were frequent. Nearly always there had been previous native court proceedings and I was involved in an appellate jurisdiction more often than not.

The Fulani cattle owners, feeling themselves protected by the Pax Britannica, had grown somewhat arrogant. Many lived with their families in the *Abakpas*—the stranger settlements that had grown up as satellites of the larger grassfields villages such as Bamenda, Bali, Kumbo, Wum and Nkambe—leaving the management of their herds to poorly paid locals. The Grazing Rules, however, placed civil liability for cattle trespass upon the herd owners so it was no defence, when trespass was alleged, for the herd owners to plead their servants had deliberately flouted their instructions.

It was occasionally alleged that the women had plotted from time to time to "punish" a herd owner by deliberately digging and planting a "bait" farm in a cattle area. The Grazing Rules laid down, however, that farms erected in such areas reserved for grazing, were dug at the farmers risk and had to be adequately protected by fences.

Whenever judicial proceedings were involved it was advisable to visit the disrupted area. Often an inspection made matters plainer. I normally arranged to have a pony waiting at the nearest point on the motor road.

The fines and compensation awarded against herd owners were often pretty stiff but nearly always they were paid on the spot. This, I think, was an act of cattle-owner arrogance. "See how rich I am. This petty fine barely touches me."

On quite a few occasions we ended our last farm inspection about half an hour before sunset. I started the practice—and the cattle-owning parties in the cases that followed kept me up to it—of taking out of my pocket a one pound note and announcing: "We race to the motor road for this." One pound in those days was all of twenty-five pounds today so to most of us it was well worth racing for. But far nearer to the cattle-owners' hearts was the prospect of a race over rough ground probably ending in darkness. Ndonga, or whoever was the Bamenda Messenger on duty that day, would line us up and off we'd go. Unlike the point-to-points of Jorrock's day there were no obstacles to jump but falls were frequent...ant-bear holes, even cattle trails (cattle seem in soft soil to cut very narrow two feet deep tracks) were both able to bring a pony down...sudden dips near water holes were also a hazard. Some ponies seemed to spend more time on their knees than galloping.

The court clerk and his messengers, Ndonga and the farmer participants in the case, and the hangers-on, being unmounted, would trudge back to the motor vehicles. There I would hand my own pony over to the *doki*-boy who would set off on his journey either back to

Bamenda or wherever our night stop was to be. I generally had the NA lorry in attendance for Ndonga and the other staff.

What pleased me most about all this was the sporting instincts of the Fulani cattle owners. Here was a relatively rich Fulani cattle owner, maybe fined fifty pounds or more for damage to some local farm, willing to risk his neck in a cross-country race with a mere one pound as prize. I often used to reflect how this spirit would have delighted my father. It seemed, for the moment, that I was moving not in the far away grassfields of Bamenda but in nineteenth century rural England...talk of brothers under the skin.

(So much for the situation that we were led to accept up to about 1949. The presence of Dr Phyllis Kaberry and later Sally Chilver-not to mention some of the earlier work of Jeffreys-sparked off a surge of later research which suggested a much longer period of human habitation of the whole of the Bamenda District.

However, one of the main objectives of this book is to illustrate the attitudes of the colonial power to problems on the ground as perceived at the time of occurence and I must be careful not to anticipate.)

The Bamenda Corps of Messengers have been mentioned in a dozen books touching on the years 1916-1961 when the area was British Mandated or trusteeship territory.

I make no apology for mentioning them here for they were a splendid body of men and I was twice able to improve their lot a little; once in 1948 and again when I was Deputy Commissioner of the Cameroons in 1960.

When we arrived in Bamenda in 1947 there were eleven men in the Corps of whom no less than seven had already had more than twenty-four years of service. One, Abanda, had had three years service with the Germans before being taken over by the British administration in 1916. Three others including Old Chinda had been first employed in 1916. There were only two who had been recently taken on: S N Ngandi and Mallam Abubakar and both of these men were splendid individuals well up to the high calibre of the Corps as a whole. Abubakar, as his name suggests, had Hausa as his first language. But he was fluent in Fulani. He, naturally, had an important role in cattle trespass matters. He taught me a considerable amount of Hausa (so far as my lack of ability at any languages permitted) on our many treks together. In the station Jackie taught Abubakar English, using her PNEU books as an aid.

213

Let me quote from the submission I made on the messengers' behalf:

"Elsewhere in the Eastern Provinces messengers perform the relatively menial tasks associated with the name but the circumstances in Bamenda are different: the one or two Government Interpreters appointed to the District from time to time have understandably been unable to acquire all of the twenty-four main languages spoken and the Corps of Provincial Administrations Messengers have had to fill in. They have acted as guides and interpreters through the years. They carry in their heads and pass on the information truthfully and accurately to each officer in turn as occasion arises the details of many miles of administrative boundaries and particulars of innumerable arbitrary settlements of local disputes. Their knowledge of native law and custom in the twenty-four tribes of the District is immense. They interpret the people and their customs to the Administration and— what is even more important—interpret the Administration to the people.

Anyhow, as a result of the submission the Bamenda Corps of Messengers were upgraded, in spite of the additional cost involved, to the status of unqualified interpreters.

Whether it was to celebrate the upgrading of the Corps of Messengers, or for some other reason I cannot remember, but one wet evening Kat and I had the eleven of them to our house. The invitation mentioned drinks, six p.m. to eight p.m. and they arrived precisely on time each bringing his drinking horn. These vessels were made from the horn of a cow forest buffalo and couldn't be put down save on their sides. Our guests sat on lines of chairs placed against the sitting room wall, each drinking horn held at the ready.

There was no polite conversation or even remarks by individual guests as I'd half expected. The invitation asked them to a drinking party and a drinking party it was going to be.

I went round the room with bottles of beer. They went down almost as quickly as I could pour. No sooner had I done one round that it was time to start again. Only some twenty minutes had gone by and all the beer in the house was finished.

Kat and I headed for her store. "What the devil do we do?" I asked her.

"I've only got this," she said, pointing to a shelf of miscellaneous bottles.

There were four or five bottles of French brandy passed onto us by a holy Catholic Father who lived on the frontier and had a number of smugglers amongst his parishioners; there were several bottles of wine I'd bought in Douala on a recent visit and there were one or two oddities such as ginger wine and even cider.

"There's nothing for it," said Kat, "but to mix the lot." The bath seemed the obvious receptacle. Dilla, who as a Moslem we believed to be TT, was put in charge. His job was gently to stir the brew and to ladle out the contents into one of our water jugs while I did the round of the ever-poised row of horns with the other jug.

I tried to slow the process by making a few words of conversation each time I filled a horn but I precious soon ran out of remarks. Chit-chat of any sort was plainly off the menu.

At length even the bath was dry. "Dilla," I said, "go tell the gentlemen that the drinks are finished." This he did for very soon old Abanda, the senior amongst our guests, got to his feet and made a little speech of thanks. They all filed out still steady on their pins.

The dry season was advancing and there was virtually no limit to the travelling that was required. Much was off the motor roads but it was often possible by leaving Bamenda early in the morning to arrange to meet carriers and ponies at the last motorable point and still get in a full days' trek to our destination for that night.

Kat and the kids were happy to come along. The Baptist Missionary in Bamenda, Paul Gebauer, and his wife was always ready to lend one of their two large ponies together with a Western Cowboy's saddle for the use of the young. This saddle with its high cantle and rising pummel was just the thing for two kids of their size to share. In extremes one could hold onto the cantle and the other the pummel. We have in fact a memory of their being led across a partially dried bog. The pony was buckjumping from hassock to hassock and both young were yelling with fear and fury at each jump. The Western style cantle and high pummel came into their own.

My mind was always directed towards my next climbing season in the Alps—or, as I half hoped, even higher mountain area—and I preferred walking to riding.

Kat could have Shagi or other pony if she wished.

Footpaths between villages cleverly contoured the terrain wherever possible. If a climb was inevitable—and many were in that country— we endeavoured to get it over as soon as possible, i.e. choose a short but steep path rather than a fairly steep and long one. My father had travelled with ponies in Ladharki, and later in Tibet in the 1890s, and I remember his telling me that a handful of ponies' tail was a great

215

help uphill. I passed this tip onto Kat and although the hills in Bamenda were a good deal less extensive than those my father had encountered she nevertheless adopted the practice and found it an effective energy saver.

On one trek we planned to camp on the rock bar at the down-valley end of Lake Nyos. The lake was high, cool and very beautiful, the waters free of bilharzia, ideal for us to bathe in. There was a village about two miles distant to the north of the lake where the carriers could stay and another village high up on the opposite side of the lake where I would have at least two days' arrears of native court reviews and appeals to deal with.

Kat, the kids and the carriers reached the rock bar about midday and established the camp. There was a spare tent Dilla and the two horse boys could share so Kat kept them with her. I got on with a land dispute en route intending to rejoin the family just before dark.

About five p.m. there were still several witnesses to hear so I adjourned proceedings until the following day and being unencumbered left at a trot to join the family.

As I breasted the high ground overlooking the lake there was a pervasive smell of burning. The whole of the hillside opposite was black with little wisps of smoke still rising from the burnt grass. I couldn't see the campsite itself; apparently it was obscured by a small mound. Alarmed I broke into a run.

I was greeted by Kat. "Quite an afternoon," she said. "No sooner had we made camp and the carriers gone than some hunters turned up on that side of the valley. They set fire to the grass. It was so dry that it appeared to explode. I was terrified for the kids and the ponies and Dilla and the *doki* boys for the grass on the whole of that side of the valley was burning so fiercely I thought it must spread all round us. In fact," she added, "we all went into the lake, ponies as well. Luckily the fire didn't burn back across the bar but it could have done."

We had supper as darkness fell. The kids had a lot to say about the reflection in the lake of the rising full moon. "It's going the wrong way," said Jackie, referring to the reflection.

The next afternoon I got back in time for tea. Kat hadn't minded spending the day at the camp. "Even if they light up the grass on the other side of the valley we can move onto the burnt side and be safe," she said.

After tea she and I climbed slowly up the unburnt side of the valley. I had a shotgun in case there was a chance of a francolin partridge. We'd left the kids talking to the horse boys but we now spotted them climbing up through the burnt grass. John, as always, was armed with his Bamenda staff. We called a greeting but the young wouldn't, or couldn't hear us. "I'll fire a shot," said I. "That'll stir them."

As the sound of the shot echoed from side to side of the valley the ground all round the kids came alive with a large pack of baboons. We saw John move to Jackie's side using his staff as a spear at the ready, pointing at first one baboon then another. The baboons had obviously been picking up partially fire consumed insects and small mammals and, on the seeing the kids had clapped flat to the ground as baboons sometimes will. I'd heard of baboons mobbing dogs and for a few moments watched intently. The baboons contoured away along the hillside using their silly-angled gait and John and Jackie resumed their climb. We kept a very close eye on them after that but all was well.

Thirty-nine years after our visit to Lake Nyos in 1947 the area was the scene of a major volcanic disaster which resulted in the deaths of some 2,000 persons and countless head of livestock.

Prominent vulcanologists are still divided over the precise causes of what occurred but agree the main sequence of events.

The geology of the whole of the Bamenda District, they explained, could be described as "recent volcanic". In these areas the magna core rises close to the surface. Gases such as carbon dioxide, sulphur oxide, hydrogen sulphide and carbon monoxide—and perhaps cyanide— are formed in the cooling process and rise up into chambers and fissures in the earth's under-surface. Crater lakes such as are found at Nyos, Essumbi, Wum, Oku and Kumba all provide conditions where gases can build up over many years. An earth tremor, or other triggering mechanism, can result in an explosive emission of poisonous gases with disastrous consequences for all living things downwind of the site.

During the 1986 catastrophe several western nations, including Israel whose Prime Minister happened to be visiting the Cameroons a few days after the incident, provided medical assistance and aid. We still await a truly legitimate explanation of what actually occurred. Bearing in mind that the same sort of thing happened at a crater lake near Djindoum in 1984 killing thirty-six people with toxic fumes, an authoritative forecast for the next likely site for a similar occurrence should have been on the agenda.

After the Nyos 1947 trek we met the lorry on the ring road about fifteen miles north of Bafut. First, however, we had to cross the Menchem River. There had been several heavy thunderstorms during the previous three or four days higher up the Menchem. In consequence the river was quite high; well above its lowest dry season level. In theory this made no difference for the Menchem tie-tie bridge—by which all the party other than the ponies would cross the river—was a good fifty feet above water level. Psychologically, however, it made a considerable difference: at the bridge site the turbulent, coloured waters of the Menchem had grown hostile and menacing; it was now no place to fall in.

The bridge was built entirely of lianas. The narrow footway was an elongated bundle of creepers encircled at intervals by twisted bands of creeper. Two great suspension cables, again made of twisted lianas, were anchored each side of the river at a point where the channel was narrow and the banks high...at a point where the flow increased in menace. It was a work of art—forest art—but it frightened me and I'm sure it frightened Kat and the kids.

The carriers essayed the crossing first. One hand grasping their staff steadying the load on shoulder or head the other seizing the vertical suspension cables in turn. They moved slowly, often pausing for the swaying oscillations of the bridge to cease.

Ndonga picked up John and put him on his shoulders. I noticed that he had a firm grip of the back of John's trousers' top—Ndonga's other hand being free to grasp the vertical cables. I noticed, too, that John had seized two fistfuls of Ndonga's short and curly hair and was holding on white knuckled. The head carrier took up Jackie in like fashion and then went back for his own load. Kat crossed under her own steam; she took her time but managed very adequately.

Kat and the kids safely over the tie-tie, I went up river to the spot that the *doki* boys had selected to swim the horses across. One of the horse boys, it seemed could not swim so, hot and sweaty as I was, I cheerfully took his place.

The technique for swimming the ponies was to shorten the reins by knotting them on the ponies' necks, pull up the irons as high as they'd go and grasp the pummel of the saddle. The pony could be steered by a switch on his nose, if necessary.

Ndonga had said that there were crocs in the Menchem at that point but they were few and far between and in any case the kafuffel of getting the ponies across would drive them off. As nobody seemed very concerned I took Ndonga at his word. The *doki*-boys had selected a one hundred yards long pool and we needed it, the current being swift enough to take us diagonally downstream a good eighty yards.

I dried off in the hot sun on the climb up to the waiting lorry. We were back in Bamenda in time for a very late lunch.

Shortly after that trek Freddie and Constance Kay went on leave and on instructions emanating from Enugu I took over the District.

It was without doubt a plum posting and we were very pleased to be there. Everything seemed to be going our way. So much so that we were hardly surprised to receive a letter from Swynnerton, now a Major General and the then GOC Nigeria. He remembered his wartime association with me and felt emboldened by it to ask a great favour (there he was "coming into my office" as though any Nigerian DO in his senses couldn't strive to do a favour for the GOC). Would we, he went on, organise carriers for a fourteen days' trek in the highlands of Bamenda. He would have his wife and ADC with him. They wouldn't mind doing a "DO's length of trek" but not every day. They wanted a couple of weeks away from the humidity and hectic social life of Lagos. Photographing and bird watching were their main objectives but they'd bring a gun and hope to shoot a few francolin or guinea fowl for the pot.

Mail between Bamenda and Lagos could take ten days so we telegraphed a reply. We had in mind exactly the trek they described along the line of hills between Banso and Wum: a motor road at each end and three rest houses en route. We hoped they would stay the nights of arrival and departure in Bamenda with us. We'd guarantee them plenty of hot baths and, if necessary, which we hoped it wouldn't be, any pedicure required by the rigors of their trek.

They arrived almost to the minute of the time they had promised and we had a splendid evening. The following day I escorted them the fifty miles to Banso and saw them off on the first leg of their trek. Their vehicle followed us back to Bamenda.

We received intermittent reports of their progress and all went well until three days from the end. A very bedraggled messenger turned up in Bamenda just after first light. He was a Kom man and said he'd been travelling all night; he'd been lucky enough to get a lift on a produce lorry for the last fifteen miles into the station. He bore a hastily written note from the general. He'd burnt down "my" rest house on the edge of the Kom escarpment. The fault was, he said, entirely his: they'd enjoyed too large a fire. It was more than the fireplace could cope with. Unfortunately they'd lost most of their possessions including a pair of Purdey guns. However, they weren't going to cut their trek short. The Fon of Kom's people had been very kind and they had enough necessities to keep them going. He hoped I'd relent sufficiently to pick them up on the Bafut-Wum road as arranged. They'd spend the last three nights in a rest house about fifteen miles from the road.

Kat and I really grieved for them. They'd seemed to be enjoying their trek until the fire. The rest house could be re-roofed for about fifty pounds but God knows what the Purdeys were worth. I only prayed that they were insured. It was still early in the day and we could mount if not a rescue operation at least a relief exercise.

I got Kat to put together and weigh the sort of necessities she thought they might need most.

I then had words with Sergeant Bafutmai who was in charge of the Nigeria police in the station. Could he give me a very strong policeman who would volunteer to carry about fifty pounds of groceries the fifteen miles up to the rest house the General's party hoped to reach that evening?

Indeed he could. We were ready to leave in twenty minutes. Kat's "necessities" weighed fifty-five pounds in all but packed neatly into a canvas bag. They included two bottles of gin, a roll of Bromo, bread, self-raising flour, a little oatmeal, salt, pepper, butter, cheese, marmalade, jam, coffee and sugar. Kat felt that milk, eggs, some meat, chickens and some vegetables could be purchased locally. We didn't know if they'd lost any clothes in the fire but it could be cold at 6,500 feet and we included about four jerseys. I'm afraid that I carried only a small rucksack but I slipped a bottle of whiskey in, and a torch.

John Ntumbe, the police constable-turned-porter was a cheerful character. He glanced at the canvas bag and said it would be "a small ting to carry".

We kept going steadily, reaching the rest house where Swynnerton's party was due about 4.15 p.m. It was well met for only a few minutes after our arrival Swynnerton himself arrived. It was a joy to watch his delight as he and John Ntumbe unpacked the bag. He flung an arm round the grinning constable's shoulders and I noticed he gave him a twenty-shilling tip—no mean award worth twenty-five pounds in today's money. I guessed that the locals would provide locally brewed corn beer and the carriers and constable would have a merry evening.

It would be dark in less than two hours and I wanted to be sure of finding the narrow path that zigzagged for some three miles down the heavily forested side of the Menchem Valley. Once on the path, although it was only a foot or so wide in many places, I reckoned it would be easy enough to follow it even without the torch. The latter ought to be kept in reserve.

With promises to meet in three days' time I left. It was, of course, largely downhill and I kept up a brisk trot for much of the next two hours, only slowing into a walk for the short inclines out of stream beds and such like that crossed my way. I found the entry into the high forest just before darkness fell and had time to cut a six-foot switch with which I could feel the edges of the path as darkness became absolute. There was one short but steep section over a rocky bluff where we'd had to use our hands on the way up and I didn't want to go blundering down it in the dark.

The moon wasn't due to rise until after ten at least—I wasn't sure of the precise time—and it soon became very dark indeed. Occasionally I could estimate the direction the path took by a slight lightening in the canopy overhead but the best progression was made by feeling the path edges with the switch—very much as a blind man feels his way in urban surroundings.

I was tired by then having walked and trotted some twenty-five miles since morning. Wearing gym shoes—it was long before the days of "trainers"—I made very little noise. I almost wanted to become absorbed in the soft blackness of the night, to give way, as it were, to the warm embrace of the darkness. But the day was nearly over and I plodded on.

Suddenly there was a shuffle, not part of my own pattern of movement, somewhere on the path just ahead. I yelled with fear. The other object, too, called out sharply. I hurriedly took the torch out of my rucksack and shone it on my face. A laugh came out of the night ahead and swinging the torch onto it there was an old hunter with a handful of throwing spears laughing with relief. We exchanged a few words in Cameroons pidgin and passed, he upwards, I know not where, and me down towards the tie-tie bridge over the Menchem and my waiting car.

The Swynnertons gave us as a "thank-you" present a brand new tent that they had bought especially for their trek. It served us well for Jackie and John made it their own tent on all subsequent treks and Kat and I used it in Kenya before passing it on to a second generation of Milnes.

———————

Bamenda was also the scene of an encounter with the GOC-in-C, West Africa, which was as unfortunate as the contact with the Swynnertons had been delightful.

It must have occurred in the early part of the 1948 rains for the roads, I remember, at the time were dreadful. One evening I received a telegram from Military HQ, Accra which read: "GOC-in-C General Irwin and wife returning private visit Kenya arrive yours evening fifth stop Request provision rest house and all facilities."

221

It was the seventh when the telegram arrived and so far as anybody in the station knew no general had passed through in the past two days. He would probably arrive that very evening.

To make matters worse Bamenda in those days only had a bare rest house. Visitors were expected to bring their own tables and chairs, cooking utensils and beds which they always did when they had reserved the rest house.

However, the 7th was a miserably wet evening and Kat and I decided to make our august visitors as comfortable as we could. We felt they would prefer sleeping in the rest house although they would have to dine and breakfast with us. We therefore furnished the rest house bedroom with our own things: rugs, beds, dressing tables and so forth. We also provided our best lamp—a Tilley. We had some hurricane lanterns which we could make do with in our house.

I didn't think an officer travelling privately, however august, was entitled to a Quarter Guard but I decided to provide one in any case. The senior service policeman in the station was away; the excellent Sgt Major Chop Bafutmai, who was next in command, provided a guard in twenty minutes flat.

But, of course, no general turned up that night. At breakfast a weary quarter guard commander asked if he could dismiss his men.

The same thing happened the next night—no general. The rains had been intense and we guessed the road through the "French side" into Equatorial Africa, eventually Uganda, was well nigh impassable. We wondered what vehicle the general had elected to use.

On the third evening after we'd received the telegram Sgt Major Chop came across to our house about eight p.m.

"I think the Big Man cannot come tonight," he said. "Dismiss the Quarter Guard, sir?"

"Yes, of course."

Five minutes later one of his men brought over our precious Tilley lamp. "Sgt Major Chop think you want to use this, sir." How right he was. It was the only light fit to read by.

Ten minutes after that a very breathless constable appeared at our door. "General done come, sir," he said.

I called Dilla and drove across to the rest house, Dilla holding the Tilley lamp.

The general was sitting on the edge of one of the camp beds slowly rocking back and forth. His lady was somewhere in the shadows. Sgt Major Chop was holding a hurricane lantern whose light was insufficient to do more than illuminate his bright buttons.

The general was nearly speechless with fury. "Are you responsible for this," he spluttered, addressing me. "I've never been received so badly in my life. By God, the Big Guns are on my side and you'll get the thick end of the stick for this."

"Don't you dare address me like that in front of my police," I said. "If you want to complain come outside," and I marched out into the night. The rain had started again. Inexplicably he followed me.

"Look here, sir," I said, "all I'm required to provide is a bare rest house. All these things—" and I waved towards the bedroom, "—are ours. We've been expecting you for a week and tonight giving you up, I had just let the Quarter Guard dismiss and recovered our only good lamp."

But he wouldn't listen; he merely swung back into the rest house repeating the thick end of the stick threat.

His lady, on the other hand, was perfectly reasonable. I said, "If you don't mind awfully, we've arranged for you to sleep here rather than in our small guest room but we hope you'll come straight across now, have a hot bath and dine with us. We can talk about plans for tomorrow after dinner. I see that Sgt Major Chop is looking after your driver and orderly"—the two latter were African privates.

I never got a single word out of the general either that night or the next morning. He used his wife as an interpreter: I made suggestions about the route for the morrow to him: she passed them onto him, he replied to her. She addressed Kat and me. It really was a silly sort of game. We played it for fourteen hours. It seems at this length of time unbelievable but I was thirty and he was fifty-five—a difference in our ages which weighed heavy in the late 1940s.

They were travelling in a barely recognisable Humber staff car so battered and mud covered was it.

It had rained for most of the night and there wasn't a chance of his getting through to Mamfe in his vehicle. I could use the NA four-wheel drive truck and give him a lead as far as the tarred strip of road twelve miles north of Mamfe. He didn't reply as I suggested this and I took his silence as acquiescence.

Of course the Humber staff car got thoroughly bogged down at least twice on the way to Mamfe. We towed them out each time, the general and his lady staying put in their seats.

I halted at the start of the tarred strip into Mamfe. "Sir," I said, "may I have a word?" The general got out and walked a few yards down the road with me. "I'm so sorry about last night," I said, "but we had been expecting you each evening for nearly a week and we did think that we'd made the best arrangements for you that we could." But once again he wouldn't listen and merely repeated his threat: "The Big Guns are on my side and you'll get the thick end of the stick for this."

I returned to Bamenda a very worried chap. District officers didn't quarrel crudely with anybody. Differences of opinion...yes, but slanging matches...no. I had let the administrative service down and I blamed myself for the whole incident. That same afternoon I wrote what I hoped was a factual account of what had occurred to Sir Bernard Carr, the chief commissioner in Enugu. This explanation should have been addressed, by government usage, *Through the Resident Buea*, but I felt it essential that Sir Bernard should have my explanation at least simultaneously with the general's complaints. So I sent the resident a copy explaining why the original had gone direct to the chief commissioner.

SC Ngandi, the youngest of the Bamenda Messengers, was fiercely loyal and if anybody could get through to Enugu that night in spite of rain, mud and scarcity of traffic, it was he. I motored him down to Batibo where he found a lorry bound for Mamfe and Ikom.

Two days later I received an open telegram from Sir Bernard Carr. It read: "If general honours me designation Big Gun regret not on his side."

I slept better that night and today, fifty years after the incident, feel as warm a glow of appreciation to Sir Bernard as I felt in Bamenda so long ago.

A single anecdote about any individual seldom does justice to the whole man. When Kat and I went to Kenya in 1968 Noel Irwin and his wife had recently left the country for final retirement in Somerset but many Kenya settlers remembered them well. Quite a number had served under him during the war and spoke well of his considerable talent as a soldier. His obituary opined that his misfortune was to be associated twice with failure, the most notable example being the Dakar expedition which he commanded. Here, however, the fault lay with General de Gaulle who wrongly estimated his support within Dakar.

The same obituary does add: "Irwin was not always easy to serve. He had a rough tongue on occasions, and his standards were high."

I experienced the high standards and the rough tongue...the latter, I still feel, unnecessarily.

G B McCaffrey, by virtue of his posting as senior police officer in the District, was ex-officio Deputy Sheriff, one of whose duties was to take overall charge of executions. His absence during General Irwin's ill-fated visit must have been prolonged by a week or more for just after that visit I was appalled to receive a letter, addressed to me by name from the Resident Buea appointing me Deputy Sheriff for the purpose of an execution due to take place in a few days' time. I was, of course, aware that the tradition of the administrative service required AOs to stand in for departmental officers whenever the particular role could not be performed by a junior official of the department involved. I was aware, too, that in remote stations in Northern Nigeria and perhaps in other Regions, too, AOs had officiated at executions. But the subject had neither been mentioned on the administrative services course that I'd attended at Cambridge nor in any of the literature bearing on my appointment to the service.

I was a strong abolitionist, holding that judicial executions were unacceptable because of the long period of mental anguish inflicted on the condemned man.

I promptly sent the execution warrant back to Bridges with a letter saying I should be obliged to resign my appointment in the colonial service rather than supervise an execution.

Fortunately for me Bridges was a kind man and instead of making an issue of my refusal—which he might well have done—he merely redirected the warrant to Paddy England, a police officer of fifteen years' experience then serving in Victoria. Paddy, I was soon to learn, had officiated at a number of executions and was able to close his mind to the horror.

Willie Serle, the government doctor, was also required to attend. Kat and I asked him to dinner the night before the grim event. We were putting up Paddy England and the conversation turned to the following day.

"Can't you," I said to Willie, "can't you give the poor chap an injection tonight and make him oblivious to the whole event tomorrow?"

"If you don't object," said Willie, turning to Paddy.

Paddy merely said shortly, "Go ahead."

So they left our house straight after dinner to pick up Willie's bag and go on to the prison.

They were away a long time. Eventually they returned. "Heavens!" said Kat. "What *has* happened?"

Both had been wearing for dinner white shirts and light coloured slacks. They were now almost unrecognisable—their slacks and shirts stained with red ochre, blood on Paddy's chest, their hair wildly dishevelled.

Apparently when the two white men, accompanied by Nwokedi, the chief warder, had gone into the condemned man's cell he had thought "this is it" and had fought bravely for his life. It had taken the combined efforts of the three to pin him down and administer the injection.

Worse was to follow. When Paddy England was dropped by Willie Serle back at our house the following morning he was deeply angry and wouldn't eat any breakfast. Willie Serle disappeared in the direction of the hospital without saying a word. I got the story, later in the day, from Nwokedi.

The injection had made the victim so comatose that he couldn't stand on the trap. He had therefore to be strapped to a board kept for like eventualities. The board had to be held upright prior to the trap lever being pulled. There had been an error of timing and the victim's face had hit the edge of the trap as he went through with sufficient force to make him come to and scream with agony.

Freddy Kay, before his departure on leave, had drawn up proposals for the reorganisation of the native authorities in the District other than those in the north-east. Eight remained which I determined to tackle. The physical difficulties were considerable. The total area was some 2,000 square miles but the population was sparse and scattered averaging about thirty to the square mile. It was rather as though a giant hand lay on the country. The back of the hand was the plateau running from Nsaw to Nkambe, 6,000 feel asl. The highest point was Ntum Binka 7,200 feet asl. To the north and east and west the ground fell away beyond Nkambe and the fingers of our hand were the gradually descending wooded ridges which made travelling in the north and east so difficult.

The Valley of the River Donga, which formed the Northern boundary of the Southern Cameroons, was approximately 800 feet asl. The high ridge was grassland, but as the terrain descended the forest cover increased.

By then the Bamenda Ring road was motorable to mile 120 but, apart from this road, travelling was by inter-village footpath. Largely because of international pressure, compulsory communal work for path clearing, long sanctioned by native law and custom, had been precluded. Where in the days of path clearing travel along the inter-village paths had been feasible it had now become difficult. In some areas the administrative officer's party (no other government departments regularly visited the area) had to force a way through a tangled mass of vegetation over broken and rugged country. Journeys were measured in hours rather than by approximate distance.

As late as 1948-mostly based on the work of Jeffreys-we took it for granted that there had been a series of Tikari, Mambilla, Jukun, Tiv and Fulani migrations into the NE area. Up to 1949 1 found old men in the villages passed on the way down into Mfume (precisely as Jeffreys himself had found) who would swear they could trace the various migration paths backwards and identify the graves of their "big men" ancestors at various points on the route.

The peoples living in the high grasslands villages lacked palm oil for cooking. Supplies were carried up from Mbem and Mbaw the sellers often returning with meat. This trade provided the main, if not the only, incentive for intercommunication between the eight groups.

No generally accepted lingua franca had become established. This, we thought, reflected both the recency and the diversity of the migration waves. There were signs that even Fulani might become an inter-group means of communication but I think that this was because many young men had served at one time or another as cattle herd boys for the Fulani herd owners and were familiar with the language.

Freddy Kay's proposals for the SE Federation of Native Authorities embodied several novel and progressive features including the representation of women on both the reorganised native courts and the native authority council. Here, he was wisely giving effect to the findings of Dr Phyllis Kaberry, a distinguished anthropologist working at the time amongst the women of the Bamenda District.

Further advances in Kay's recommendations—which were all accepted in 1949—included the substitution of numerous small disparate native authorities by a single, financially viable body, the formation of standing committees for day-to-day business in the clan areas, the reduction of all native court benches and the separation of the judicial and executive.

Normally a district officer in working up a large NA reorganisation proposal, such as that affecting the eight north-eastern NAs, would wish to consult each NA at least once but desirably several times during the exercise. This was going to be quite impossible. One NA, Mfumte, appeared to have been visited once only since it was created. Because of the time and difficulties involved in travelling in any of the areas it was not feasible, at the best, to visit each more frequently than once every eighteen months.

Another major difficulty was that the funds of the eight NAs were held in the strong room in the Bamenda Treasury nearly 150 miles from the remoter parts of the Misaje and Mbembe areas.

Freddy Kay had already proposed the regrading of the Bamenda District into a Province comprising three Districts: Bamenda, Wum and Nkambe. A decision on this larger proposal, involving as it did changes in the provincial administration establishment and the cost of creating two more District headquarters at Nkambe and Wum, (Bamenda itself would become both Provincial and District HQ), could be expected soon.

Dr M D W Jeffreys, who had served as SDO Bamenda for several years, had recorded copious notes on the peoples who had migrated into the Bamenda District. I had arranged a trek into Mfumte and on the way down spent the evenings reading Jeffreys' notes. There were several of interest.

The Rom Chief, for instance, could recite the names of his eight predecessors and describe exactly where each was buried. He also ascribed the multiplicity of languages in the area to the depredations of the Fulani. He had told Dr Jeffreys: "We all originally were one people living at Bakimbi. Then the Fulani raided us several times and we were forced to scatter. First the Wimbu left—that is the present Wiya— then the Ntems and lastly the Tans. Bakimbi became deserted. When we were all together we spoke Tikari. Now we speak Rom and the others who have left us speak Leiuga and Ndimbu." He went on: "Both these words, Leiuga and Ndimbu, originally meant, "What do you say?"

The Rom Chief also remembered the Germans. "When they were building their road," he said, "they shot seven men because they were not strong enough to do the work. My people who were also working on the road saw the shooting and left in a body and hid themselves in the forests of the Old Rom. I, Nyanganji, myself saw three of the men shot by the Germans. Two on one day and one on another. Thus if a man deserted from the road work his brother would be caught, tied to a tree and shot. This shooting was done by native German soldiers on their own accord. These soldiers came from Bamum, Yaunde or Tikari. No white man was present when the shooting took place. Flogging of workmen in public was very common and these native soldiers also used to rape our women. Nkot, who are our neighbours, occasionally fought with us but it was a friendly matter and only done with sticks."

Jeffreys recorded another singularly interesting fact about the area of Rom. I quote his exact words:-

"There are signs of ancient dwellings on the mountain tops. Stone monoliths: stone foundations: grindstones: but the Rom people know nothing about them.

(Here we have possibly the first inkling in Jeffreys' work that there had been habitation of the NE area of Bamenda District long before the eighteenth century. I'm told by scholars interested in the area today that the research by hagiographers, paleobotonists and archaeologists, sparse as it was in the years 1950 to the 1990s, does nevertheless suggest that there was truly very long human occupation.

However, I say it again: the length of the pre-eighteenth century human occupation of the area was not of great importance in 1949 to people like myself who were engaged in revising the Native Authority system.)

On this particular trek, during which I studied Jeffreys' notes about the Rom people, I'd left Kat and the Kids in the comparatively pleasant surroundings of the Ndu Rest House, a stone built cottage just off the motor road. They told me afterwards they'd had a fire in the sitting room all day and they'd had to wear jerseys even at midday when they were outside, so pleasantly cool was the weather.

It seemed preferable, on arrival at Mfumte, to dispose of outstanding native court appeals and reviews before talking to the council about the main purpose of the visit—namely the NA reorganisation. By four o'clock on the first day only two court cases remained: a civil claim in which a woman sought three years of salt money from her husband and a criminal case concerning a serious assault by a woman upon her husband. The court clerk pointed out that the same couple featured in both cases.

The combined court and council chamber was a large circular building built entirely of local materials in the manner of traditional Mfumte meeting houses: thirty feet in diameter, three feet high circular mud walls and a high thatched roof. There was an open space between the eaves of the thatched roof and the mud walls broken only by upright posts at seven or eight feet intervals. It was a large building having its own impressiveness.

It suddenly dawned on me that the two remaining cases were attracting very considerable interest. During the earlier part of the day the court had been fairly full and that was that. But now a vast, silent and obviously very interested crowd had collected: the court was tightly packed and a number of onlookers were even seated on the ground outside. The chairman of the bench that had heard the criminal case spoke up: "This woman did a very bad thing. We want her sent to prison for a long time," he said.

Ndonga was interpreting. Although he was fluent in Mfumte, his English was very rudimentary and I had difficulty in understanding what he was trying to say. My own grasp of Cameroon pidgin—a language on its own—was poor and when Ndonga descended into pidgin I probably misunderstood a lot. Ndonga, however, had a fair knowledge of Hausa and when I got the same drift from his so-called English, his pidgin and his Hausa, I reckoned I wasn't far from getting his meaning.

Ndonga and the court clerk between them gave me the facts of the assault charge and the civil claim. Apparently the husband had been a professional smuggler carrying goods backwards and forwards across the Anglo-French border. His most recent absence from home had been three years. By native law and custom the wives were responsible for the subsistence farming necessary to feed the husband when he was there and to feed themselves and the children. The husbands were expected only to take part in the heavy initial bush clearing necessary for the establishment of new farms and for giving the wives regular increments of salt money—salt being a rare and expensive commodity in continuous demand.

Returning after his long absence the husband had demanded instant resumption of conjugal rights. The wife refused, I gathered in somewhat forceful terms, saying something in the vernacular to the effect of "...give me three years of salt money and you can f— yourself silly..."

At this point in the recital—which even the pidgin speakers could follow—great paroxysms of laughter swept through the spectators. There was, if seemed, considerable sympathy for the wife's attitude, especially from the women present.

The narrative continued. The husband, I was told, pressed his demand. But he was only a little man, relatively puny in contrast to the sturdy wife who had grown strong with her farm work and care of the children. Wishing to deter his importunities she seized a delicate portion of his anatomy—which happened to be particularly available at that moment—and dragged him out into the street, eventually releasing him with the words, "Cool down and go find my salt money."

The laughter among the spectators became continuous. Men and women lay on the ground, weak with laughing; members of the bench sitting behind the litigant slapped their thighs with mirth; the husband smiled weakly, even the wife's surly face broke into a grin.

It took five...ten...minutes for the laughter and the cries of appreciation to quieten. At length there was complete silence. Everybody was now waiting on the DO. What would he say? How could he add to this hilarious situation?

I disappointed the spectators: "We'll take the civil claim first," I said "It's the simplest matter to resolve. The custom is for husbands

14 *Above,* The Aden Crater Rim, at the spot where the author changed his mind about descending it with his family on Christmas Eve 1950; without a rope it was too difficult.

15 *Right,* Rocks outside the author's temporary quarters at Al Qara.

6 *Below,* The Milnes' home in Khormaksar, a suburb of Aden.

17 *Above*, RWAFF engineers prepare
assemble and launch a Bailey Bridge
in 1954.

18 *Left*, Bailey Bridge nose about to
touch on self-help constructed
abutments.

19 *Above opposite*, The Hon Dr Esen,
Minister of Welfare, listens as
Malcolm Milne explains something.

20 *Below opposite*, The "nose" has just
reached the far abutment, permanent
panelling in foreground.

21 *Left*, Self-help road (of a sort); typical young oil palms.

22 *Below*, Government House Lagos; photo taken around 1912. The lawns in the foreground were improved 1938.

23 *Opposite*, Cameroons mountain eruption site, 1959 This picture shows one of the main craters just after it had ceased to exude lava.

Opposite above, Malcolm Milne and
Muna stand on cooling lava. Eight
inches below the surface it was still
ed hot and Mr Muna set the bottom
of his walking stick on fire by
thrusting it in.

Opposite below, The lava enters the
forest and burns a path a mile wide
and four or five miles in length.

6 *Above*, It was possible to see three
distinct craters, one below the other.

27 *Below*, A view of one of the small
subsidiary craters.

28 Mr Muna shares the hard work of cutting a path through the thick growth near the unmanned P & T station.

to give their wives salt money. It is a reasonable custom. Not repugnant to natural justice. There is no reason why this man should not comply. Let the husband pay the wife thirty pounds which I understand is the customary amount for three years of salt money. And," I added, "the costs of this case."

There were a few remarks from the crowd but silence soon resumed. They wanted to hear what I had to say about the assault. I thought hard. In a way I was on trial as much as the woman in the dock.

"We can't have our wives assaulting us in this manner," I said to the old men on the bench; "it threatens the very institution of marriage." The crowd broke out into renewed laughter as soon as Ndonga spoke in Mfumte. "An example must be made of this woman..." Here there were yells of encouragement from the male members of the crowd. "Let her pay ten pounds' compensation to her husband for the indignity and pain occasioned by the assault and let her be fined ten pounds for the assault itself."

Again addressing the old men on the bench I said, "It's no good sending the good lady to prison. That would merely deprive the husband of the satisfaction he originally sought."

Ndonga never later mentioned the case to me. I have no means of knowing whether he approved of the judgement or not.

An incident of a more tragic kind occurred in a remote part of the District shortly after our return to Bamenda. McCaffrey was involved in a trek along the SE borders of the District and once again I was temporarily overseeing Nigeria police matters on his behalf. Sgt Major Chop reported that the native court clerk's wife in Essumbi—a remote under-administrated portion of the District averaging about 2,000 feet asl to the west of Bamenda—had been innocently working in her compound with large pestle and mortar when a man had appeared armed with a Dane gun and shot her dead. There seemed absolutely no motive for the killing. A witness had recognised the aggressor as an Essumbi man living in the remote forested country astride the Bamenda-Obudu (Sub-District of Ogoja Province) border.

Sgt Major Chop had sent a police constable down into Essumbi to arrest the accused and bring him into Bamenda for questioning. The constable returned saying he had been unable to find him. Chop had immediately sent two fresh constables to the area instructing them to secure the assistance of members of the NA and not to return without the accused.

Early on the day that Chop referred the matter to me the constables had returned to Bamenda. It seems that they had indeed found the man's house and as they approached he had climbed onto the roof threatening the constables that if they came a step nearer he would shoot them. "Fearing" they had returned to Bamenda to "report".

This was too much. With Chop's agreement I ordered the constables to be ready in an hour's time to return to Essumbi with me.

Kat quickly put together a night's requirements and together with Ali (who would have to try his hand at cooking supper for me that night) and the two constables we left in the NA lorry at midday. From the road end to Essumbi was a five-hour trek which we completed just before dark. I sent out word that evening that I wanted to see all the members of the native authority council one hour after sun-up the following morning.

Essumbi itself had been reached by a reasonably good footpath. Beyond, I was told, the inter-village paths were indifferent, even non-existent in some places.

This was the area Sharwood Smith[3] had travelled in the 1920s and at that time he had needed an armed escort who had had to repel attempted ambushes by the locals on more than one occasion. Matters had greatly improved, of course, in the intervening twenty-five years but there was still large reservoirs of belief in magic and darkness.

Most of the NA council members turned up the following morning within an hour of being "invited". I enquired if they knew the man we were after. "Oh yes," they said. "We know him very well. He has a very powerful *juju*."

"Before the sun reaches..." and I pointed to about an hour ahead, "I want you to call one hundred young men and bring them to me here. I'm going to send them down with the police constables to bring in the man I want."

There was a long silence. At last one of their number spoke. "That we don't want to do," he told me.

I asked the court clerk who was also clerk to the NA how many pairs of handcuffs he could put his hands on. "Six," he replied.

The police constables had a pair each. That made eight in all. I'd observed that the meeting house had a long pole which connected the upright pillars supporting the high roof. It was about eight feet above the ground. There were several benches in the building. "Place the benches beneath the pole," I ordered and then, turning to the

---

3   See Sharwood-Smith's excellent reminiscences, *But Always as Friends*, George Allen and Unwin, 1969.

assembled councillors, I said: "I'm sorry but my request to you gentlemen to assist in the maintenance of law and order by arresting the accused is a legal order. You have refused to obey it. I am therefore forced to arrest sixteen of your number.

The sixteen men were then stood on the two lines of benches, eight each side. The wrist of one councillor was handcuffed to the wrist of his companion on the other bench over the pole. "I require some time to consider the matter before taking you all into Bamenda."

I then left for the hut where I had spent the night and where Ali stood guard over my travelling gear.

Half an hour later—it might have been forty minutes—a messenger appeared from the meeting house. "The councillors all say that they will send their young men to bring in the accused. They want to talk to you, sir."

Apparently they decided that government (personified by me) had stronger magic than the wanted man was said to possess. I unlocked all the handcuffs. The councillors sat in a more comfortable group. "We'll have him brought in today," they said.

"Thank you, gentlemen. You can hand him over to the two police constables whom I'll leave here. They'll bring him into Bamenda. I must go now as there is work at home."

Two days later the PCs duly turned up in Bamenda with the accused.

Sgt Major Chop interrogated the accused. He told me later the full story.

"The man," he said, "had just married a wife. He had paid a big dowry and waited a long time for her to come to his house. The wife fell very sick. He consulted a *Juju* priest. The latter said that it was a very bad spirit that was troubling his wife. A very bad spirit. She would surely die unless he could do a very bad thing himself. It would have to be bad enough to neutralise, as it were, the badness of the spirit troubling the wife. He took his gun and looked for a really bad thing to do. He saw the court clerk's wife pounding corn. So he shot her dead. But his wife died in spite of what he'd done. He went back to the *Juju* man who said that the bad thing he'd done was not bad enough."

Sgt Major Chop went on: "He lost his wife; he lost his money to the *Juju* man and now he will lose his own life to the government who will hang him."

After the trial and conviction the DO was required to write notes on the accused's background and motivation. This I did as factually as possible.

But he was not hanged. The sentence of death on him was commuted to one of life imprisonment. Eleven years later, when I had to exercise the Queen's Prerogative of Mercy myself, and had read the guidance instructions, I understood why: a genuine belief in magic or *juju* did not constitute the element of *mens rea* required by Nigerian law for a murder conviction.

Was it possible that the law we administered in such distant parts of the Empire so many years ago was more liberal and humane than the law administered at the same time in the United Kingdom itself?

———

In the years 1947-50 the colonial office, anxious to afford the post-war Development Plan every assistance, recruited a cadre of development officers on short-term contracts. Many of these men had served with distinction in the services during the war. Once on the ground in Nigeria a number turned out to be of exceptional merit. Although their qualifications had on paper been less than required of recruits into the regular post-war colonial services it seemed manifestly unfair to hold the best of them on their short-term contracts. Consequently a fair number were promoted in Nigeria to the senior service on permanent terms. These promotions blocked, to some extent, promotions from the Nigerian junior to senior service. In 1950 to 1951—when independence became suddenly much nearer—the need was to accelerate the promotion of Nigerians of all grades. The promoted development officers, as it were, got in the way. But the country needed their services and would have been poorer without them. It was a catch-as-catch-can situation.

We had a splendid Australian development officer called Mick Walters in Bamenda. He was later promoted into the administrative service.

One morning Kat came into my office in the Bamenda Fort and said, "Go and look at Mick's kitchen." His house was only a few yards from the fort so I obediently peered into the kitchen. There lay a very naked lion. Mick had skinned it on the brick kitchen floor for want of a better surface. I was surprised, to say the least, for lions were very seldom seen in the Bamenda Highlands. Apparently a Fulani cattle owner had complained to Mick that a single male lion was following his herd of cattle down from the north and Mick had duly shot the animal. It was the first I'd heard of it.

Molly, Mick's wife, was a Tasmanian, her father having been the premier Anglican bishop on the island. Molly had never been nearer Europe than the Cameroons and confessed she hadn't given a great deal of thought to the great world north of the antipodes. She wanted her daughter to join her in Bamenda and afterwards to go to school at Cheltenham. She was talking of her plans one day to Kat and said she thought the daughter was old enough to travel on her own. Could she, she asked Kat, get from London to Cheltenham by train. "Oh yes," said Kat. "Easily."

"But how many days is it?" asked Molly.

Molly had been quite unperturbed by the lion in her kitchen. She'd taken it for granted that prides of lions would be two a penny anywhere in Africa.

Mick Walters quite possibly saved me from getting badly hurt in an incident I misjudged. Bamenda in those early days had been untouched by organised trade unionism. Untouched that is until about Christmas 1949 when a Bakweri trade unionist whose name I'm afraid I forget, was posted to the District. This chap was a natural demagogue possessing the ability to inflame his audience with a stream of abuse directed against the colonial power, against white officials, against the iniquities of their own lot. He employed the age old device of attributing all the hardships and ills his audience suffered to those whom he wished to deride and damage. There was no logic in what he had to say but it was the sort of stuff the Bamendas had not heard before and they loved it. It had taken him only a week to organise a strike of road labourers. What the issue was never was very clear but his wild oratory was treated as magical and 400 road labourers had gathered on the day I'm describing in the Bamenda Fort outer part, which served the PW department as yard and stores, in response to his call. Unfortunately the district engineer was out of the station and as usual on such occasions the DO was expected to act.

I had been told nothing of the trouble brewing amongst the road labourers and was taken aback to find the PWD part of the fort full of excited and indignant men.

The union official took the opportunity to harangue me in his most aggressive manner.

I asked him to send the labourers back to their respective work areas and to bring along to my office a list of all the complaints he wished to make. I promised to go through it with him item by item. Having said this I turned round and walked towards the gateway in the wall separating the divisions of the fort and leading to my office.

Sgt Major Chop had joined me by this time.

At that moment a PWD lorry, parked near the entrance of the yard, started up and moved slowly towards the entrance gates.

"Stop 'im, stop 'im," shouted our good demagogue and twenty or thirty labourers near the vehicle, laughing and cheering themselves on, heaved the vehicle onto its side.

"Right," I said to Sgt Chop. "Arrest that lot." Chop obediently seized a couple of labourers and holding each by the collar marched them towards the door in the wall and the police office beyond. I took a man by the arm and followed him.

Seeing this, our demagogue, egging on the labourers near him to do likewise, picked up a piece of scrap iron from a pile against the wall and advanced against us screaming out, "See the white man hates us, I told you so". They kept on coming, their dangerous makeshift weapons held aloft. Suddenly the situation itself was dangerous.

At this moment Mick Walters, grinning broadly but knowing nothing of what was going on, as he told me later, strolled through the door from the inner fort. But he took in the situation very quickly.

I should explain that he was the strongest chap for his height that I'd ever come across. About five foot nine he gave the impression of being very nearly five feet across the shoulders. His biceps were the size of an ordinary fellow's thighs; his hands were quite small but immensely powerful. He had already a reputation among expatriates for after-dinner feats of strength and I am pretty confident most of the labourers present that day had knowledge of him—he probably had an appropriate pidgin nickname although I didn't know it.

He went up to the largest labourer and said, "Hi, you don't want to carry such a big thing [it was quite a small weapon, in fact] 'e be too power for you," and amidst the ensuing laughter he took it out of the man's hands and threw it back on the pile. He then went down the line and disarmed the lot, including the Bakwerri trade unionist, each time with a joke. The situation had changed once again. This time the magic ingredient was a combination of Mick's reputation for strength and his good humour.

As previously mentioned the Southern Cameroons then was administered as a Province by the Eastern Region of Nigeria. But a number of departments were not then fully regionalised and the staff were consequently controlled from departmental headquarters in Lagos. An example was prisons. Nwokedi, our excellent chief warder, was directly answerable to the director of prisons. The latter was a man of vast experience—he had served in the home prison service and in the services of a number of colonial dependencies—but had not until then inspected the prison at Bamenda. He turned up without warning one Thursday. Kat and I offered to put him up and he accepted gladly. He was very keen; after quickly swallowing a cup of tea he was up in the prison checking on Nwokedi half an hour after his arrival.

He returned just before dinner. "Wretched fellow, Nwokedi, seems useless," he said.

"We'd always thought him pretty good," said I. "What was the matter?"

Apparently he'd infuriated the new D of P by losing the key of the gallows. "He'd damn well better find it by morning," said the director threateningly.

Kat went very silent but the atmosphere soon changed and we chatted of other matters.

The next morning the director of prisons was up shortly after first light and walked in the cool Bamenda air to the prison. He returned for a late breakfast obviously in a much better mood than the night before. "How was Nwokedi this morning?" I asked.

"Oh better. Much better. In fact I agree with you. He's very good value," said the D of P.

"Did he find the key of the gallows?" I asked.

"Oh, yes. Everything as it should be."

Kat intervened. "I think I'd better confess," she said. "You see Thursday is the day we slaughter a cow. On Fridays I parcel it out to all junior and senior staff, who put an order in. We do it at cost so all the folk here get their meat very cheaply. I'm afraid that I prevailed on Nwokedi to hang the beast overnight and he uses the gallows. If he'd produced the key when you unexpectedly asked for it last night you'd have seen a corpse hanging in the gallows. He was only protecting me. Mind you, he misjudged you, too. He didn't think you'd inspect so soon after your arrival. Most of our visitors require the whole evening to recover from the journey up".

The D of P in his letter of thanks to Kat for putting him up wrote: "I see it's another Thursday today. I hope it's tender as always."

Writing of Nigerian government departments puts me in mind of the Geological Survey. We used to laugh about the small size of the department saying that the total staff consisted of the director, R R E Jacobson and the deputy director, E H Jaques. In fact the department was slightly larger than that but not much. In 1948 (when Freddy Kay and Constance were still in Bamenda) Jaques and Jacobson were both engaged in an exploratory survey on the Mambilla Plateau which they reached through the Bamenda District. The DO Bamenda at a distance of 140 miles from their headquarters, was the nearest, or at least the most easily reached administrative officer and they arranged for him to supply their monthly whiskey ration—imported drink still being rationed at that time. Regularly, once a month, a messenger appeared from them bearing a grubby note (we said it was the same piece of paper used each time) "Whiskey ration, please." Apart from this we never heard from them. They were, we understood, searching for extra thick deposits of mica required for some western world electrical purpose and I believe they worked all hours. Eventually, the task completed, they passed through Bamuda on their way back to Lagos. We arranged a party for them. At first they were a little hesitant in accepting. Jacques said, "I'm not very sociable, I'm afraid, I've only seen one white face in the past six months and that, God help me, was Jacobson's." Jacobson was said to have made exactly the same remark about Jacques.

The party went on and went very well. Far into the evening someone (and I put my money on Constance Kay, for it exactly reflected her surrealistic sense of humour) asked them separately the same question "If you only had Jacques/Jacobson for company surely you must have quarrelled a lot?"

She apparently got the same answer from both of them. "Oh yes, we quarrelled regularly once a month when the whiskey ration arrived. Jacques/Jacobson wanted to drink it at one go. I wanted to make it last the month."

The African—East or West—is a great talker. Conversation plays an important part in social intercourse. We used to encourage the kids, whenever the opportunity offered, to chat with groups of locals, and the messengers, always ourselves expressing great interest in what they had to retail afterwards.

While Jackie got on with her lessons John would spend hours sitting with the Corps of Bamenda Messengers in the shade of a group of trees just outside the fort.

Working in my office I quite often heard laughter as John made some comment which particularly appealed to the messengers' sardonic sense of humour. One day I heard laughter mingled with applause and went out to investigate. I was immediately concerned to see a cyclist sitting on the ground near his overturned machine bleeding profusely from a great tear in his calf. I bound it as best I could with dressings from the office first aid box and sent for the NA lorry to take him up to the hospital for proper treatment.

John, armed with his miniature Bamenda staff, watched but appeared a little crestfallen. Old Chinda recounted what had happened.

The cyclist, glorying in his new machine, had gone up the hill a little way and, turning, had ridden past the assembled messengers and onlookers at great speed. He'd repeated the pass, this time making several onlookers leap to safety out of his path. John, apparently, was ready for him, for he thrust his Bamenda staff into the front wheel spokes, bringing the cyclist down in spectacular fashion and causing the injury to his calf.

Old Chinda seemed to think John had done exactly the right thing and was full of amused approval, as were the other onlookers. Unfortunately I didn't agree; clouting John, I sent him home bellowing tears of mortification and fury.

Some years later he told me he reckoned I'd treated him unfairly because the messengers had egged him on to bring the cyclist down but I still didn't agree.

Jackie at about the same time had a different encounter. She was helping the *doki* boys groom the ponies one morning when a self-announced magician came to the yard for a chat. He told her his name, his parents' names and listed the miraculous cures of which he was capable. Jackie being proud of her recently acquired ability to write, said, "If I had a pencil and paper I would write down all those things."

His reply was, "I can write very well and I will do it for you."

He kept his word and the same day appeared at the front door of the house with the list reproduced below:-

Makat-Nkot
My mother's name = Sakabi
My father's name = Gabken

Kinds of medicines which I have 1947

1 I have something to remove anything which can be in a mans body
2 I have another to cure a woman who is sick of a woman disease

239

3 I have another to cure a man who is sick of a falling
   sickness
4 I have two eyes of leopard and a star if any which
   man hide some thing I will take it
5 I have some medicine if a person poison another I will
   give some medicine to vomit it out
6 I have some medicine for (Yos) and Gorilia
7 If a woman can not conceive I will wash her with some
   medicine and she will conceive
8 If any witch man wants to kill any child when I reach
   there I will wash the child and he will be well again
9 I have some medicine if a dog bites a man I will put
   the medicine in the wound and it will be well
10 All people are glad with me because I have different
   kinds of medicine to help them with

   Name Njinguying

I imagine by "Yos" and "Gorilia" he was referring to Yaws and
Gonorrhoea.

Kat and the kids planned to come with me on a trek from Ndu to Bum
and on to Wum where we would be met by the NA lorry. Dinga, one
of the Corps of Bamenda messengers I had not seen a great deal of in
the past spoke Bum and was to accompany us. He'd had twenty-nine
years service at the time and his reputation was as high as the other
members of the corps. I didn't know about a little weakness that my
other colleagues had considered too trivial previously to mention. It
was in fact a tendency to get very drunk once he'd considered the
day's work was over. He always recovered by morning and was always
then on a par with the best of them.

Carrier work was keenly sought after by the locals largely because
they appreciated the ready cash in an area where paid employment
was non-existent. The normal procedure, when touring in the area,
was to ask the Chief of Ndu to produce the requisite number of carriers
which he was glad to do.

We travelled as far as Nkambe in the NA lorry. On the evening
before our departure from Ndu, I realised I'd forgotten to ask for the
carriers. As ill-luck would have it I sent a message to Dinga about
4.30 p.m. asking him to alert the Ndu Chief. Why I didn't send the

message to Ndonga, who was also with us, I can't think. A number of pretty free talking little birds later told me what had transpired.

Dinga, when he got my message, was too drunk even to walk the few yards to the Ndu Chief's house so he deputed the task to a friend. The latter promptly treated it as a birthday present; he sold the news that thirty carriers were required on the following day to a bunch of about thirty-five strangers in the market.

In the meantime, Ndonga, alert as always, realised I'd forgotten to order the carriers for the following day and took it upon himself to have a word with the Ndu Chief.

As a result some sixty-five chaps turned up at the rest house the following morning for the thirty loads that there were on offer. And, of course, a tremendous kerfuffle broke out. The bunch of strangers had paid good money for the information and none of them were going to give up lightly. The Ndu Chief's men thought the job as of right was theirs.

Not knowing any of this at the time I kept aloof. It was the sort of dispute one always left to the Bamenda messengers to sort out. But, the row if anything growing in intensity, curiosity got the better of me and I slipped out of the rest house to see what was going on.

As I rounded the kitchen, where the worst of the battle raged, I was impressed by one particularly fierce combat between a tough old Ndu man dressed in a ragged shirt and a string jock strap and a trousered youth, whom Peter Awgu, our cook, said was from Misaje. Peter, himself, sat head in hands guarding his cook box. I later learnt that he had slipped a sack of gari in it intending to sell the gari at a profit to a compatriot in distant Bum.

However, it was Ndonga, ever the strong man, who restored order and got the cavalcade on the move. He seized Dinga's staff and rapped the yaw-scarred shins of the warriors, growling out appropriate insults in three or four of the Bamenda languages. Turning towards the horse boys he switched to Hausa and asked them whether they wished to spend the rest of the day adding to the scars of laziness on their backsides or whether they proposed to saddle the horses.

We had hardly got moving, when Kat, who was riding Shagi, said, "You take him. He won't go an inch." Shagi—the Bastard—was living up to his name. Ears back, toes dug in, he'd gone more and more slowly, finally coming to a halt in a field of maize. The carriers, their unwieldy loads bobbing above the long grass quarter of a mile ahead, were almost out of sight. The kids, sharing uncomfortably the western cow saddle borrowed from the Rev Gebauer in Bamenda were out of hearing if not out of sight.

241

I quickly looked Shagi over...bridle, girths, saddle, feet. There didn't seem to be anything wrong. I vaulted aboard, determined to teach him the lesson he obviously needed.

Hardly had I given him the one-two which he so richly deserved when he began to rear. My father had always said, "If a horse rears get off and don't get on again." But Shagi in spite of his bad character was too beautiful a pony to discard and anyhow he presented a challenge.

My father had also said, a little non-sequitur, "You can of course pull him over backwards, that'll sometimes cure 'em of rearing."

I slipped off, threw the reins over his head, determined to try the prescribed treatment. Unfortunately the combination of the gym shoes I was wearing and the damp mud path polished smooth by Ndu bare feet was not conductive to such behaviour. I got him half over when I slipped and ended on my back. Shagi swivelled and down he came planting one foot on my outstretched right hand.

For the rest of that trek all the native court judgements I should have written were in fact written by the court clerks to my dictation.

I'd bought Shagi for his looks. He was a bright chestnut and had good conformation. Bargery, that compendious Hausa Dictionary, had a word for chestnut...Shari. But the horse-boys wouldn't have it. They insisted on calling him Shagi...the Bastard...on account of his contrary nature. He'd been initially trained—as so many Fulani ponies had— to answer to a thong and spear; the thong tight round his nose and held in the rider's left hand and the spear away out to the right borne in the rider's right hand.

Later on we got him to go with a bit and snaffle bridle but he always remained thong-trained as well. Whenever I wanted to show off before visitors I would do figures of eight at the canter with the aid of a thong and stick.

Another problem with Shagi was that he could gallop, really gallop, if he wanted to. But most of the time he just wouldn't.

However, a day did come when in spite of himself he really went at a vengeance. It was the occasion of the first visit to Bamenda of Sir John and Lady Macpherson just after Sir John's appointment as governor-general of Nigeria. We planned to mark the day of the Macphersons' arrival in Bamenda with the first ever Bamenda Races. We spread word amongst the Fulani who promised us that we should have a full card for every race. One or two of the leading Fulani also suggested that the Macphersons' car should be accompanied by a mounted escort of Fulani from the point where it arrived at the race course round the course to the governor-general's pavilion. And would

DO Millin lead the escort? It seemed a feasible suggestion and we went ahead with it.

When I first saw the escort on the day of the races I was glad we had, for the thirty mounted men looked thoroughly impressive with their long robes and magnificently caparisoned saddlery. All had raw hide thongs round their ponies' noses and carried formidable spears in their right hands.

We trotted sedately ahead of the governor-general's car coming to a halt in a long line facing the pavilion. We waited while the VIP party took their places.

I'd told the mounted escort that we would return to the point where we had met Sir John's car and there disperse. They lined up, knee to knee across the track, behind Shagi and me. We trotted a few yards. At that point...spontaneously...they broke into a gallop, a furious line of charging horsemen, spear points lowered. Shagi sensed, and I guessed saw, what was happening. He didn't wait for those spears to come any nearer. He broke, unurged, into a splendid gallop, right fore leading round the right hand bend, belly to the ground. By Jove, now he had to, he could gallop. Kat told me he'd gained a couple of lengths round that bend alone. I scuttled off down the road up which Sir John's car had arrived. By now we were heading away from the delighted crowd who'd seen the DO hunted like a hare, and the Fulani were prepared to slow up.

It would be good to record that the rest of the meeting went very well but in fact we did make (or rather I made...for it was me who'd done the arithmetic) one rather drastic error. I'd calculated the odds on the tote so as to leave a small profit towards the costs of the day. The tote was being operated by the NA Treasurer assisted by a number of expatriate wives in rotation. After about the fourth race Kat discovered that I'd given erroneous instructions—we were making twice the profit on the tote we'd meant to. But the unlucky punters who'd lost money made no complaint so we kept quiet and deposited quite a tidy little sum in the treasury for the use of any of our successors who might venture to organise another race meeting in Bamenda.

Just after Christmas 1949 I received a severe blow in the form of a hand-written letter from Bridges, the senior resident in charge of the Cameroons Province. He said that Freddy Goodliffe, twelve years my senior in age and eleven years my senior in the list of administrative officers had complained that he, Goodliffe, had the worst District in

243

the Cameroons, namely Mamfe, while I had the best. He asked if this situation was just. There was no argument about the relative merits of the two Districts from the amenity point of view.

Bridges had replied that he did not consider it just and had posted Freddy Goodliffe to take over the Bamenda District and was now writing to give me two options: I could do a straight swap with Freddy Goodliffe and take over the Mamfe District or, as I was scheduled to go on leave in early May 1949, I could stay on at Bamenda as number two to Freddy Goodliffe and he would find another officer to take over Mamfe.

There was no mention whatsoever of Sir Bernard Carr's letter to me saying it was his intention that I should take over Bamenda from Freddy Kay.

Postings within a Province were primarily the concern of the resident but as officers were fed to him from the HQ of the Region a reasonable amount of consultation was called for.

I gave the matter a couple of days' thought. I was no more than a name to Bridges. I didn't think he had ever spoken to me since he took over the Province. On the other hand he had served with Freddy Goodliffe and knew him well. They were old friends.

Perhaps he considered that Sir Bernard Carr's undertaking to me to have the Bamenda District after Freddy Kay was exhausted.

Again he might never have heard of Sir Bernard's wishes. If I was to bring them up now I could easily precipitate a row between Bridges and Sir Bernard. I judged Bridges to be a slightly obstinate but straightforward man who would stick to his guns. Neither would thank me for causing unnecessary contention.

There was no question of moving Kat and the kids to the heat and potential disease of Mamfe which climatically really was a most unpleasant station.

I had no choice but to accept Bridges' offer and revert, much as it hurt my pride, to the position of number two at Bamenda.

Freddy Goodliffe turned out to be basically a very nice chap. He was a little like Groucho Marks in looks and style—wild black moustache, long loping stride and pretty outlandish in many of his remarks; but at bottom a kind and friendly person. I settled easily enough into a routine with him. One of the first things he asked me to do was finish the proposals for the north-eastern Reorganisation. When they were ready they were issued—as indeed was right and proper—under his signature and I can't remember feeling resentful that I'd done all the work...a fact that bore witness to his basic niceness.

Although I didn't know it then Freddy G had been a choral scholar at Cambridge and was related on his mother's side to the distinguished director of music at the university. He had, for those who appreciated it, a deeply cultured element in his makeup. But his usual mode of address, particularly to strangers, was often highly unexpected. He would come out with the most startling remarks.

Just after his arrival, a German Lutheran missionary, called Angst, a giant of a man, came into the office. I was still acting as the DO and introduced Freddy to him. Previously, in telling Freddy about the Angsts, I'd mentioned that the wife was equally large, a veritable giantess. She was so vast, in fact, that she was pregnant and had suddenly surprised us all by producing an infant. On my introduction he came out with, "Hello, Hello; how's the old Milch Cow?"

I was horrified but Angst only laughed heartily taking it as an excellent quip. It was amazing how Freddy got away with it.

A F P Bridges retired in 1949 and enjoyed a long retirement in the west country only just failing to make his century. He had been the principal founder of the Nigerian Field Society when he invoked the assistance of D R Rosevear and Edwin Haig in 1929. After his retirement he was duly honoured by being made Life President of the Society. Not content, and worried by the vicissitudes the Society was passing through in the 1960s, he took on the role of secretary in addition to life president. For very many years he continued to support the society in this way, taking on the secretaryship from time to time, as the circumstances demanded.

In time to come, when Nigeria settles down, naturalists, archivists and scholars will surely honour Bridges' contribution to the *Nigerian Field*, freely given without question of return or reward.

Gerald Durrell was occupying the Fon of Bafut's Rest House during April and May 1949 collecting animals (His obituary in *The Times* of 31st January 1995 contains an error—it recorded his first collecting trip to the Southern Cameroons as having occurred in 1947-48. In fact the trip lasted some six months in all and extended well into 1949. The letter from the Fon's office agreeing to Durrell spending two months at Bafut quoted by Durrell on page ten of *The Bafut Beagles* was dated 5th March 1949. This more nearly coincides with Kat's and my memories of him.)

There was really very little about Durrell's first expedition to the Southern Cameroons that concerned the government. District

245

officers—or at least those whose assistance he sought—gave him what help they could. The Forestry Department, who were responsible for game licences and wild animal conservation, issued permits for the collection and exportation of numerous protected animals. Other administration officers knew of his activities very much as we knew of the activities of practically every other expatriate in the Province. Expatriates were, after all, not very thick on the ground. He was only twenty-four at the time but early on opinion hardened that he drank by our standards far more than was good for him. We gathered that he did virtually no collecting himself but relied on local hunters. This we could understand for the welfare of captured animals must be paramount and doubtless it was a full-time job looking after those already brought in.

The Forestry Department began to complain that local hunters were apt to kill many females with young at heel in order to produce one specimen for exportation. This, if true, was a serious matter but as far as I remember no body of evidence was built up sufficient to support cancellation of export permits. The question wasn't raised during the period I was in charge of the Bamenda District nor, as far as I knew, after Freddy Goodliffe came in early 1949.

All who had met Durrell—invited him to meals in their houses or come across him officially—spoke well of him. They described him as young, ebullient, amusing and very cheerful. He had rapidly acquired a sound grasp of Cameroons pidgin.

They were unanimous in saying that he had a rare gift of getting on with the locals. His sense of humour appealed to the latter and they felt at ease with him even when he was scornful or rude.

He didn't begin to write his best-selling books until 1953-54 when the *Overloaded Ark* and *The Bafut Beagles* were first published. These were an immediate success and went into many impressions. Over the years he wrote some thirty books including two novels and seven specifically for children. Many of his books dealt in light, lucid and amusing vein with animal collection and conservation. His stature as a naturalist increased with time.

Of course he embellished many of his anecdotes—and good luck to him—but there is one statement in *The Bafut Beagles* that caused me to scribble angrily "Balls" in the margin of my copy. He describes amusingly teaching the Fon and his entourage to dance the conga. He then comments: "...few Europeans in West Africa spend their spare time teaching the conga to native chieftains and their courts. I have no doubt that if they had seen me doing that dance they would have informed me that I had done more damage to the White man's prestige in half an hour than anyone else had done in the whole history of the West Coast."

Nobody would have told him any such thing. When he wrote those lines I suppose he was about twenty-eight years old and had had some nine months' experience of West Africa. He was too wrapped up in his own youthful ego to appreciate that the "White man's prestige" was at that time indeed a factor but was a fluid, mobile and highly subtle concept not likely to be influenced one way or the other by his antics. We knew all about his ready aptitude to mix with the locals and considered that it probably assisted him in his object of collecting animals.

One impression that Durrell left with us all was that he was running that first collecting expedition of his on a shoestring. He appeared perennially short of cash. Having now read David Hughes' recent autobiography of him I suspect that this was due to an over-expenditure on animals and alcohol and generally poor financial management. I don't believe he was ever realy in dire financial peril for there was a rich mother in the background whose darling he was...but it made a good story.

———————

Just before Christmas 1948 I had to make a rapid visit to Victoria, primarily to deposit tax money in the bank there. The road Bamenda-Mamfe-Kumba-Victoria was open then although the section Mamfe-Batibo was one-way: up one day, down the next. All being well it was possible to do the trip in six or seven hours each way. The Bamenda custom was to ask a colleague visiting Victoria to make purchases and I had quite a list. I took Dilla along to help. Philip Barton, who'd recently joined the colonial service after eight years' service in Burma, asked me to drive back an International Van which he'd purchased and which he believed would be well suited for touring in the Bamenda District.

We travelled down to Victoria in the NA vehicle; I took along a spare driver in case he might be helpful on the return journey.

We picked up Philip Barton's new van. The driver's manual suggested that it would do the return journey up to Bamenda...just...on a tank of petrol but to be sure I took along a full eight-gallon drum. Three of us travelled in the van—the NA spare driver, Dilla and myself.

There was a lot of low-gear climbing on the twisty forest road between Mamfe and Batibo. Sure enough the van ran out of petrol on a steep incline well after dark on the return journey.

247

Dilla was always a quick moving chap and we'd no sooner stopped than he had opened the doors of the van, removed the eight gallon drum of petrol and a bush lamp. He lit the latter and placed it on the road nearby. The petrol filler point was about halfway down the van's body and about waist high. The neck was flush with the body and a funnel was required. A search of the van yielded nothing and I guessed that it had either been forgotten or was on board the other vehicle, probably some distance behind. There was nothing for it but to juxtapose the neck of the eight-gallon drum to the van's filler point and hope not to spill too much petrol in the process. I picked up the hurricane lamp and carried it a good twenty yards down the road. We were then high enough to be cool and it was a dry night. I remember thinking that the tunnel of vegetation down the road, seemingly meeting overhead, was beautiful in the half-light afforded by the hurricane lamp. I even remember individual leaves standing out, very black and fifteen feet or so above our heads.

The NA driver, helped by Dilla, picked up the eight-gallon drum and gingerly tried to decant the petrol into the van's filler. They spilled more than they poured. With an exclamation of disgust Dilla himself seized the drum in both arms (it must have weighed a good eighty pounds) and standing opposite the filler point seemed to be making a better job of transferring the petrol.

Suddenly the whole scene was brilliantly lit. A great broad ribbon of fire flashed up the road from the lamp to the vehicle. Flames roared out of the van's filler, three feet in the air. Dilla flung the drum into the ditch and I thought, "It must explode." We were about to lose Philip's brand new vehicle.

I jammed my handkerchief into the filler point apparently quenching the flames and springing into the driver's seat tried to start the engine. After what seemed a very long time it started and I drove the van up the road, about twenty yards. Getting out I saw poor Dilla thrashing about in the ditch, both legs seemingly on fire.

There seemed no way to help Dilla other than to spring on him and try to put out the flames burning the legs of his slacks. By dint of rolling on him and pushing his legs into the damp vegetation in the bottom of the ditch I managed to stop the active burning and pull him to his feet.

The van, so far as we could see was little the worse although we couldn't find the petrol cap. We reckoned that we'd probably got about three gallons into the tank. The road below us was still ablaze. Dilla was groaning with pain; his slacks from the thighs down were merely charred rags. He'd burnt his hands and forearms in addition to his legs. I couldn't get him to Bamenda hospital and have him properly treated quickly enough. We decided to risk that we had petrol sufficient for the thirty-five or forty miles left.

We piled into the van, sacrificing the eight-gallon drum and the lantern. I sat in the middle of the bench seat supporting Dilla as best I could. The NA driver drove and off we set.

Dilla told us that in throwing away the eight-gallon drum he'd soaked his legs with petrol and it was this that had caused the worst of the burns. He kept putting one arm, then the other, then his legs out of the window into the cool night air. Had I known more of the treatment of burns at the time I'd have tried to stop him for he was merely making the burns worse by thrusting them into the slipstream.

Our lights must have alerted the charge nurse for he met us at the door of the little hospital. One look at Dilla and he said, "We have no proper lights here. The doctor can't treat him until morning."

I replied, "Please send for the doctor. I'll bring the Tilley light from my house."

He agreed and I motored as quickly as I could to the house to find Kat still reading in bed by the light of our one and only Tilley. I was able to get back to the hospital almost as soon as the doctor. He made Dilla as comfortable as he could that night.

Kat said afterwards, "You know some instinct told me to stay awake until you returned. That's why I was still reading."

Kat also recalls that Dilla was in hospital for three weeks; he made a good recovery although he was left with prominent scars on both shins and thighs of his naturally thin legs.

We had been booked to go on leave on 3rd May 1949 travelling by an Elders and Fyffes' banana boat from Tiko to Liverpool. Those boats didn't waste a minute in turning round in the Cameroons, partly because the cargo was very touchy. The bananas had to be cut and loaded on the same day.

They had a small passenger capacity—twelve, if I remember rightly, the maximum number permitted without a doctor on board. They hammered along at eighteen knots non-stop to Liverpool. The captain was required to inspect every refrigerated hold daily, examining the cargo in each. One single ripe banana, apparently, might set off premature ripening throughout the ship.

We had been instructed very firmly to board our ship within an hour of her arrival in Tiko since a delay in taking on passengers might put the cargo at risk.

This was all very well and I planned to comply but on the other hand I wished to keep the family in the cool of Bamenda as long as possible. I accordingly arranged for Elders and Fyffes to send us a telegram giving the estimated time of arrival of our ship. We would allow ten hours for the journey down...a margin of thirty per cent for "eventualities". It nearly wasn't enough.

We were four hours ahead of schedule when we passed Mamfe on the way down and all appeared well until, about halfway between Mamfe and Kumba, we came upon a long queue of vehicles. It seemed a fifteen-foot bearer of a two-bearer culvert had collapsed preventing the passage of vehicles in either direction. The local road gang of four chaps were trying to make a repair but having worked most of the day in the hot sun had become very tired. It looked as though repairs wouldn't be completed before dark. We would miss our ship unless we got across in the next four hours or so. The lorries' occupants were naturally anxious to continue but in the fatalistic African manner were equally prepared to wait.

Kat took the two young for a walk. They later complained of having been well bitten by "sweat bees", small bee-like flies that alighted on sweaty limbs and stung annoyingly.

I walked down the line of vehicles—most were "Mammy Wagons"—telling the occupants that the road gang were too tired to finish the repair before dark and if we wanted to pass it was a case of "harambee"—self-help. I asked for—and got—three or four strong men from each vehicle, as many as possible bearing machetes. We cut a forest tree down near the damaged culvert, trimmed it and laid it across the gap. It was amazing how easily thirty of so men could move a twenty-foot sap-wet tree length. We then cut cross-timbers and tied them in place with lianas. Packed with earth we had a reasonable makeshift bridge. I suggested that the Bamenda NA kit car, in which we were travelling, was the lightest vehicle to test our work, and they agreed. I drove across and we inspected the culvert. It seemed that lorries should be able to get across and we left them to it.

We were on the high seas a few hours later and we never heard whether they'd all safely crossed. I hope they did.

I see from my record of service that the leave lasted from 3rd May to 3rd October 1949. A summer in England. The Aunts were still at Mealsgate and we made Croft House our headquarters.

I told a local GP that I was still suffering from intermittent amebiasis and couldn't get rid of it. He looked the disease up in one of his manuals and offered me a course of emetine. He didn't say anything about bed rest so I accepted. After about four days of treatment in the Aunts' house I happened to be talking on the phone to a colonial doctor friend and I mentioned the treatment. He asked what dosage the GP had prescribed and, when I told him, said, "Good God, that's a horse's dose. He'll ruin your heart. I'll talk to the colonial office medical adviser and have you properly treated."

Two days later I found myself in the Tropical Diseases Wing of the Edinburgh Eastern General Hospital under a one time director of the Indian Medical Services called Sir Alexander Biggin. I was in a ward with a number of ex-POWs from the Far East, one or two of whom were really ill with tropical diseases (including amebiasis) they'd acquired while prisoners of the Japanese.

(Amebiasis ceased to be a problem in the 1970s, and later when a drug called flagyl came on the market but all this was 1949.)

Edinburgh promptly found I'd picked up an intestinal worm and expelled it in a couple of days but they were unable to find any amoebic cysts in my stools. However, Sir Alexander rather grudgingly accepted my story of constantly feeling below par coupled with reoccurrence of active amebiasis and agreed to a course of emetine. They administered the course in conjunction with doses of a sleeping draught— to reduce the risk of vomiting the drug—and insisted on bed rest.

I'd arranged to instruct voluntarily in rock climbing at the Glenmore Lodge Outdoor Training Centre for a fortnight at the end of June and after that to accompany A B Hargreaves and Eric Arnison on a climbing expedition in the Alps. Kat, the kids and the Aunts were booked to stay in an Aviemore hotel so that I could join them on my days off from Glenmore.

Although kept in bed or occasionally allowed a few hours in a bedside chair for the emetine course, I was aching to be up and moving freely on the hills again. Kat nobly visited me by train from Carlisle leaving the young with the Aunts. On one of her visits she ran into Sir Alexander Biggin in the corridor and he said to her, "You know we simply can't find any amoebic cysts and I wonder if really your husband isn't a little neurotic about this condition?"

Kat instantly replied with the polite equivalent of "balls". "He's the last person to be neurotic," she said and told him of my arrangements for Glenmore and the Alps. Whether he was convinced or not I never discovered.

Most of us in the dysentery ward felt that some of the "high-ups" as dear Jack would have called them—who made a daily round of patients—were just a shade too grand so we mounted a charade for their edification.

One poor chap, who had been reduced to half his normal weight while in Japanese hands, had been prescribed emetine retention enemas. He had to endure this dreadful experience daily and hold the dosage of emetine for an hour lying on his back with his knees raised. Shortly before the daily round of the great we rigged him up. There happened to be a massive brass fire hose nozzle, about three feet in length, in the corridor outside our ward. This we connected to a giant fire hose and placed it between his raised knees in the "retention" position, modestly covering the business end with his bedclothes.

When the party of the great arrived we chorused, "We anticipated his treatment for today."

Some were amused. Others, including Biggin, weren't.

Feeling somewhat weakened by my stay in the Eastern General I returned to the Aunts in the middle of June just in time to get reasonably fit again for the Glenmore Course. To my surprise and Kat's annoyance the pupils on the course were the third year of Anstey Physical Training College for young ladies...all girls, all in their early twenties and several singularly attractive. As there were sixty on the course and on days when everybody was rock climbing, we had to increase the cadre of volunteer instructors—none of us wanted more than three learners on our rope. Ideally two pupils to an instructor—particularly for the more demanding climbs—was an optimum number. Luckily there was a large force of young forestry department cadets operating in the vicinity of Glenmore Lodge and as several were excellent climbers it wasn't too difficult for Charles Cromar, the principal, to find extra instructors at short notice.

The instructors who'd volunteered for the whole fortnight of the course had a daily, early morning meeting with Charles when the day's work was arranged. Two ropes on any particular climb was generally considered enough...more became a crowd...and I often found myself paired off with the wife of a well known Scottish mountaineer, a doctor. She was nine or ten years older than me which seemed a lot to my thirty-two years—but I remember her lithe physique and steady ability to lead up to mild severe standard.

She was determined to show me a new climb on the cliffs above Loch Einich which had recently been "made" by her husband.

It is an accepted mountaineering canon that new routes often bear the characteristic imprint of their originator. This is certainly true of the many rock climbs in the Lake District such as the New West on Pillar and other routes first pioneered by the Abraham brothers of Keswick.

The opportunity to try the Loch Einich climb came on one of our days off—the pupils were sailing that day on Loch Morlich near the Lodge and we rock-climbing instructors were free.

It was a thoroughly interesting route, well worth our eight-mile walk up Glen Einich on what turned out to be a very hot day. It consisted of a series of quite difficult problems connected with easy climbing in between. Exposure wasn't really a factor. The New West was classified only as "very difficult" but the situations and directness of the route suggested a far higher classification. I struggled with the problems on the Loch Einich route but we got up in the end. The climb certainly had character.

It was a long and very hot trudge back down the Glen. I'd told Kat of our plans and she'd said she might walk the young up the glen in the afternoon to meet us. Halfway back my companion followed my example and stripped off to her waist. I was slightly surprised but assumed it was good Scottish practice...she could certainly afford to do it figurewise.

A mile or so from the road she said, "Your wife mightn't like me like this; oughtn't I to put my shirt on?"

I said, "Hell, no. You've been like that halfway down the glen, why should you dress now?"

Just after that we met Kat and the two young, both rather fractious in the heat. Kat and my companion, it emerged, knew each other. They'd met just before the war.

That evening Kat, who had never turned a hair at cock boxes and nakedness in Nigeria, tanned me fiercely. "That woman...how dared she? Who the hell did she think she was?"

Now, down the perspective of fifty years on, I marvel at how dumb I was. Dear Heaven...one's sins of commission and omission. Which are worse? Kat, of course, had had enough. I never gave it a thought at the time but I realise it clearly now. She wasn't really attacking "that woman". It was the whole situation. Here was I, as she thought, lording it over a lot of doting girls all day and obviously loving it while she was left with the Aunts, who, much as she really liked them, were not her age grade. The heat and the topless female were the last straw.

I have to confess that there is an inconsistency here. When I first read *The Bafut Beagles* which I suppose must have been round 1954-55 I understood that Durrell's "youthful ego" had blinded him to the true nature of the "White man's prestige" but only a year or two before I couldn't see that my own not quite so youthful ego had blinded me to Kat's feelings. Know yourself is an admirable precept not always easy to follow.

It was important to "know yourself" to get your own reactions right when talking to native authorities. Often one of them, or maybe some bright spark in the audience, would say, "Here you are, DO, advising us to follow this or that course or build up this or that institution, and yet in your country that particular idea is a failure." And out they would come with chapter and verse often culled from the Zik press in support of what they were saying. In the early days of my service I found myself angrily refuting their contention..."Anything is better than the barbarous animism found here." Later I learned to treat their criticisms seriously but if possible to belittle their magnitude. "No system is perfect." Later still, when independence was just round the corner, one asked, "What do you suggest instead?" The situation became difficult when it was pointed out that European (or more likely British) vested interests were responsible for the defects. They often were.

On the other hand, especially in the early days or in the more bucolic areas, the council members might want to close the meeting. Perhaps they had a long way to walk home or they wanted to attend a session of the local drinking club. They would say, "Let the DO decide. What the DO says is good for we." Whenever this was said to me I used to feign anger. "What do you think the government pay you people salaries for? You have to live with what you decide...you and your children. Make up your own minds what you want."

The situation changed again during the last four or five years of my service when I was operating at permanent secretary level or above. Then I was dealing with individual ministers, with cabinet committees or in the case of the Southern Cameroons with a small government. Almost without exception they were people of high intelligence who knew exactly what they wanted.

Throughout this work I have done my best to portray as faithfully as possible what my own attitudes were at each particular moment in my service. They changed because I was getting older, they changed because the whole objective of my work changed: I joined a service with what I believed was a job for life eventually to find that that same service was being used to disband the empire, no longer to continue to maintain it.

To return to 1949; the Aunts, together with Kat and the kids had as their companions in the Coylumbridge Hotel—I remember now it was the Coylumbridge where they stayed—a very pleasant colonial governor and his wife. Kat used to laugh to see letters on the hall table addressed to Lady Champion "...as though she was a lady tennis player..."

I don't believe we inquired what territory Sir Reginald Champion was governor of. Partly this was because the mores of the service forbade me to make up to a high-ranking officer in the service in the hope of securing some possible advantage at a later time. It was partly too because I didn't really care. He was not governor of my own territory and the colonial empire in 1949 was still large and widespread.

Kat told me that the Aunts and the Champions had got on well enough and she, too, had found them a singularly pleasant and unpretentious couple. I squirm, in retrospect as it were, for it was simply bad manners on my part not to have informed myself where he was stationed.

The trip to the Alps, long arranged by A B Hargreaves and Eric Arnison, went off as planned. Eric eventually had to return to his solicitor's duties in Penrith and Maud, AB's wife, joined AB and me. We climbed in the Zermatt and Saas Fe areas and developed a regular routine: day one: valley-hut; day two: hut peak-hut; day three: hut-peak-valley where we joined Maud—who didn't climb—in an hotel. She didn't seem to mind the days she spent on her own and for a fortnight or so the arrangement worked very well.

Even from my earliest youth I had been obsessed with mountains; they called me with a strange allure. Aged five or six I used to tackle the Helm above Newlands on afternoon-long solo expeditions. It was only a pimple and the path to the top didn't involve a scramble, never mind a climb, but to me then it was a veritable Everest. I recall once on the way up coming across an elderly couple and regaling them with my powers as a mountaineer. And then, at Ellery Wood Cottage, there were the sun-warmed morainal boulders in the fields near by. They instilled in me a love for rock per se.

At St Bees a few boys had Bell's—and their parents' permission to climb with Stanley Watson who I believe was the first professional guide in the Lake District. I asked Jack if I could join them and got a very crisp negative in reply: "Rock climbing is a silly, dangerous game pursued only by a few cranks…" This caused Joe Dawson and me to have one or two attempts on our own using a doubtful rope. Much better if we had been taught under knowledgeable supervision and learnt *ab initio* to use a rope properly…and a safe rope, too. However, I eventually wore Jack's and my father's objections down and in my Cambridge days quite often had climbing friends to stay at Lynwood.

There was a touching story told about Stanley Watson at about this time. He'd been promised several times his ordinary fee to stand in for the hero in a film involving a climbing sequence. After some delay the weather became suitable for out-of-doors filming. The cameramen found a fearsome crag rigged up their cameras with great ingenuity and then said to Stanley, "Climb that." Stanley was forced to reply, "I can't."

I owe a tremendous debt, accrued over many years, to A B Hargreaves and Eric Arnison for their companionship on the hills. Both were in their forties when I got to know them well. AB was a well-regarded, one could say famous, climber. He'd pioneered his share of new rock climbs, become a master of using "nail techniques" when rock climbers were turning more and more to the use of rubber soles for the hardest routes and possessed an indomitable spirit. He was only a short man and Eric used to describe him as "five foot five of sheer angry determination". In ordinary life he was an accountant turned company managing director. Eric was a lawyer and, had he been a Hausaman would have been known as "mai-son mutane" which could be interpreted variously as "a lover of mankind" or "a student of people". There wasn't a family in Cumberland that he did not know and about whom he could not speak with humour and affection. Both Eric and AB had had snow and ice experience on British hills in winter and the Alps in summer and were both all round mountaineers.

If you are going to spend two or three weeks with a chap in the high hills you must have plenty to talk about. There are long approaches when interesting conversation reduces the effort and there are hours spent in the huts. I found everything Eric and AB had to say of interest. Both, in their different environments, worked to high technical standards. My banishment to West Africa meant I was often ten years out of date in quite ordinary topics. They, on the other hand, were intrigued by what we were trying to achieve in Nigeria. They plied me with questions.

And yet…and yet…I can't say that I totally enjoyed climbing. In summer, on sun-warmed rocks, up a route I knew…yes, maybe. It was that element of fear, fear of exposure[4], that was almost always present. Even on a long climb in the Alps, when we reached our summit, the descent could always present problems and fear was always there. It used to take me several days to work myself up mentally for a demanding route. There was often the abasing knowledge that I was planning below my highest level. I was, I felt, capable of something more demanding if only I could bring myself to face it. This constant battle with cowardice was demeaning.

In later years I was to put in a fair number of instrument hours ferrying light single-engined aircraft long distances. One planned as meticulously as possible (I used to advocate twice the anticipated air time to be spent in planning) and one came up with simple, arithmetical answers. It was possible to approach nearer to the parameters and the same niggling sense of cowardice was absent.

But of course there were other boons to be won from mountaineering: you became exhilaratingly fit; difficult routes sweetly climbed left a great sense of exultation and friends made on the mountains were friends for life. The climbing rope was more than a symbolic tie; his life, your life had been in the other's hands.

Prior to leaving the Cameroons I'd been giving thought to my career. I was coming up to ten years' service in the tropics. I counted myself as more competent than a number of administrative officers in the long grade of longer service but I had to admit that some of my contemporaries, such as Angus Robin, Eric Powell and Philip Barton, for example, were probably my superior in many of the facets of the administrative officers' function. I was not a clear case, such as Ralph Grey, (later Lord Grey of Naunton) for accelerated promotion. The appointment as Acting DO, Bamenda had been a minor achievement but Bridges' and Freddy Goodliffe's (justified) intervention had, to put it bluntly, both annoyed and shaken me.

One answer seemed to be offered by a circular letter, which I had received in March 1949, inquiring if any long grade officer was interested in a direct swap with an officer of about ten years' service from the Aden government service who wished to broaden his experience of an administrative officer's work. My copy had been accompanied by a note which read: "Would Milne be interested?"

I replied affirmatively but had heard no more during our 1949 leave and had put the possibility to the back of my mind.

---

4 Exposure is a semi-technical mountaineering word, and refers to the fearsome drops.

We travelled back to the Cameroons again by banana boat arriving on 3rd October 1949. We were greeted by two items of information: the proposals converting the Bamenda District into a Province had at last been approved and I was to take over the new Nkambe District. The second was that there had been an error of communication and we weren't supposed to be in the Cameroons at all. My application to go to Aden on secondment had been approved. We were expected there.

Correspondence between remote territories was pretty slow in 1949. Most letters travelled by sea mail and I believe the average time to write a letter in a major secretariat was nearer three than two weeks.

John Gibbons had recently taken over the Southern Cameroons as the first commissioner. He laughed when he heard of the nonsense about our posting and said, "It'll take a few weeks to sort out. Go up to Nkambe and enjoy yourselves."

A site had been chosen for the new District headquarters at Nkambe itself but the plans had not yet been approved and we were forced to make a temporary HQ at Ndu, using the stone-built rest house there as combined dwelling and office. The young both slept in the tent that the Swynnertons had given us and became very proud of it. John had been more than usually fussy when it was first pitched, insisting on the exact spot he wanted.

Jackie kept Kat up to the mark with her lessons. Kat was using the PNEU system and Jackie was determined that she didn't fall behind her contemporaries in England; it was she, rather than Kat, who laid down when lessons should be.

John, to put it gently, was always more interested in people than in books. He lacked Jackie's staying power with lessons. However, he earned his keep. Although he was only rising six at the time, his Cameroons pidgin was better than mine—he certainly understood more. I didn't hesitate to use him as an interpreter whenever I was stuck. Odd complainants often came along to the rest house out of office hours and pidgin was the accepted language. He really was most useful.

Our thoughts were naturally directed towards Aden but there was nowhere in the Cameroons that I could get the information we wanted. It was not until January 1950 that we finally departed from Ndu for England en route to Aden.

CHAPTER EIGHT

Aden Interlude

The Aunts, as always, gave us a home in Mealsgate while we waited for an onward sea passage to Aden. The weather in January and February 1950 in the north of England was bitterly cold. The Lake District hills were covered with snow and I was determined not to pass through England without one or two climbs so I rang round all my climbing friends.

Eric Arnison was away on a client's business in Australia; AB was too involved in Barrow-in-Furness to get away even for a day. I found, however, that Colonel Rusty Westmorland and a friend of his, Dr Lythe, were prepared to do a gully climb with me on Great End before they descended by footpath to attend a meeting of the Keswick Mountain Rescue organisation which Rusty Westmorland had formed. Lythe was the Honorary Doctor of the branch so he, too, felt obliged to go to the meeting. Rusty W said, "We'll leave the rope with you and you can rope yourself down Cust's Gully which will give you a lot of interest in these splendid snow and ice conditions."

It was more than kind of them to do this for me and I accepted gladly. There is, however, a little story attached to the aftermath of the climb.

Rusty Westmorland in 1950 was twice my age. He'd been born in Penrith and had served throughout the 1914-1918 War in local forces. Following the war he had joined the Canadian Army and had honed his mountaineering skills as a climber member of the peak party of the Survey of the boundary between Alberta and British Columbia. Still in the Canadian Army during the Second World War he was charged with raising and training Canadian Mountain Warfare troops. After the war he'd retired to his native Cumberland and at once had made an outstanding contribution to the organisation of mountain rescue in the United Kingdom. Right up to his late sixties and beyond into his seventies, he used to delight his Cumberland friends with his skill on difficult rock. He flowed up routes—I can't describe his style

259

otherwise. I used to say that although he was twice my age he could lead routes of twice the difficulty of those I could safely lead. I'd been taken up "very severe" category climbs by him and he'd never hesitated.

Our climb on that early February day I remember very well. We attacked the gully next to Cust's. Because I was so keen he insisted on my leading. It was really cold. Fine snow was falling all the time. Visibility was only a few yards.

All went well until I was halted by a ten-foot problem—a steep step of ice in the gully we were climbing. I had no crampons which would have brought it within my powers. Nor for that matter had Rusty—we were both shod with vibrams which can best be described as simulated nailed soles made from hard rubber. Not ideal for ice climbing.

I had a couple of goes at the ten-foot pitch but failed, miserably. At length Rusty said, "Let me have a go." Despite his vibrams he climbed it smoothly. His icework and ice-axe control was, I must admit, far better than mine.

I led the rest of the climb which came out on the summit plateau of Great End. "I'm afraid we've got to hurry down or we'll be late," said Rusty, giving me the rope. "Cust's Gully is only about twenty yards over there," he added, pointing into the murk. "You can't miss it."

I cut steps down the first twenty feet of Cust's Gully and came to a steep pitch bulging with ice which I did not dare to essay without the protection of a doubled rope. There was a huge flake ideally suited to a doubled rope and I cut down nearly the length of the available rope—some sixty or seventy feet. Cust's Gully seemed damn hard but I was committed now and on I went. Two more pitches and nearly the full length of the rope available in use each time and the going was as difficult as ever; there was precious little "gully" about the route, such as I could see in the minimal visibility. Then, damn it, there was no rock available to put the doubled rope over and pull it down after me. I had a sling in my pocket and managed to jam it over a protuberance. This would mean sacrificing the sling as I recovered the rope—if it held in the first place. It was getting dark by now and the thinly falling snow was as persistent as ever. Anything for quicker movement on the crag and speedy progress on the path to my waiting car at Seathwaite. And then I got a glimpse to my right (I was face in to the crag) of screes. "Thank heavens," I thought, "I'm nearly down."

I couldn't see more than about twenty yards in any direction but there was a steepish slope of snow below me and I could glissade. Slinging the coil of climbing rope over head and one shoulder I started to glissade. Suddenly the snow changed to ice and I was out of control, feet first, virtually falling. Obeying the rule I rolled over onto my ice-axe, slowly forcing the pick into the ice to brake, using both hands. There was a bang as the point hit a stone and I saw the ice-axe describe a neat parabola, apparently upwards. There was a stab of pain as my left arm straightened. I was now seriously out of control. There were some two-foot high flakes of rock protruding out of the ice down to my right; I swam and fought towards them as I fell…I hit them with a sickening crack. "Shit," I thought, "I've broken my femur." I lay quite still for a minute or two, almost comfortable and then the thought came quite slowly and from far away, "If you don't move you'll die in minutes in these temperatures." At that moment, almost as though somebody looking after me had placed it there, my hand touched a partially buried fence post. I discovered later it had fallen from a fence some shepherd had erected at the top of the crag to stop sheep falling over…a common practice in the Lake hills.

Using the post I got to my feet. The leg wasn't broken for I could put my weight on it although I couldn't move it. My left collar bone did appear broken for I couldn't lift the left arm upwards. I could see the line of the Seatoller Beck in the dim light that was left…the way to the car.

It took me until about nine p.m. to manage the two miles from the foot of the crag to the farm house and outbuildings at Seathwaite where I'd left the car. As behoved a Lakeland farm in winter at that time of night all was silent and in pitch darkness. Even the dogs were silenced. It seemed far less trouble to clamber into the car and get myself to the doctor in Keswick (whose house I knew) rather than wake the good folk at Seathwaite.

The joint memories of John and Kat remind me that the car was a Standard. I only recall that it had a bench front seat and that the gears were on the steering column. Abandoning the fence post—without which I wouldn't have got down—I dragged myself across the front seat and got the car going. I did the whole journey in second gear—shades of Kat's Mama in Nigeria.

It was after ten when I halted outside the doctor's house-cum-surgery. Keswick had far from gone to bed. I guess the last house of the cinema had just finished; there were a number of people in the streets. I asked one or two passers-by to help but they pretended not to hear. Maybe they thought I was drunk. At last the doctor himself emerged. I'd stiffened up and couldn't move without the aid of something such as the fence post but he and his wife helped me into their warm sitting room. He telephoned Kat in Mealsgate and by good luck she was just able to catch the last bus Mealsgate to Keswick. She was with us in less than an hour. I don't recall the rest of the evening but I gathered Kat motored me to Carlisle Infirmary where I was made comfortable for the night. She, poor thing, still had to drive back to Mealsgate in spite of the snow on the roads.

By five p.m. the following day I'd been sorted out. My right leg was encased in plaster from hip to foot, the fall against the flakes having done no more damage than to tear the muscles in my right thigh—the ligaments, they hoped, were OK. My left collar bone was rather messily broken and my arm was strapped uncomfortably across my chest. But I was allowed home and that was the main thing.

Thinking it over I'd obviously missed Cust's Gully and descended the face—or part of it—in the poor visibility. I determined that as soon as I was fit enough I'd go back to Great End and try to retrace the line...and if possible find the ice-axe.

Rusty W's comment when he heard the story was, "H'm, you learn by experience, don't you?"

About ten days before I was allowed finally to discard the plaster the hospital staff had cut it neatly into two halves which I was told to wear fixed together by bandages. On the last day Kat, the kids and I had quite a little ceremony taking the plaster to the Mealsgate rubbish pit where we left it looking like a rather grubby human leg.

It must have acquired some kind of totemistic importance for the young for the day after we left it they made a secret journey to the rubbish pit and recovered it. They set it up as a scarecrow in the Aunts' vegetable garden. Kat wouldn't take a bet it would be the first object the long suffering Aunts would dispose of on our departure.

Shortly after I'd got rid of the plaster on my leg I went up to London to see Sir Bernard Reilly in the colonial office. Sir Bernard was recognised as the colonial office expert on the affairs of Arabia Felix. He had some official CO status at the time but the title in no way did justice to his knowledge or influence. He'd been, amongst other roles, the last Governor and Commander-in-Chief of Aden when it was administered by the Indian government.

I told him that I'd accepted the transfer to Aden for two reasons: to broaden my administrative experience and to enable Kat and me to have the children with us for a little while longer before we were forced to send them to prep schools in the United Kingdom. I thought I'd learn a lot from the government of Aden which by repute was a tight and very well administered little colony. He immediately said, "You aren't going to Aden Colony; you are expected to serve anywhere in the Eastern or Western Aden Protectorates."

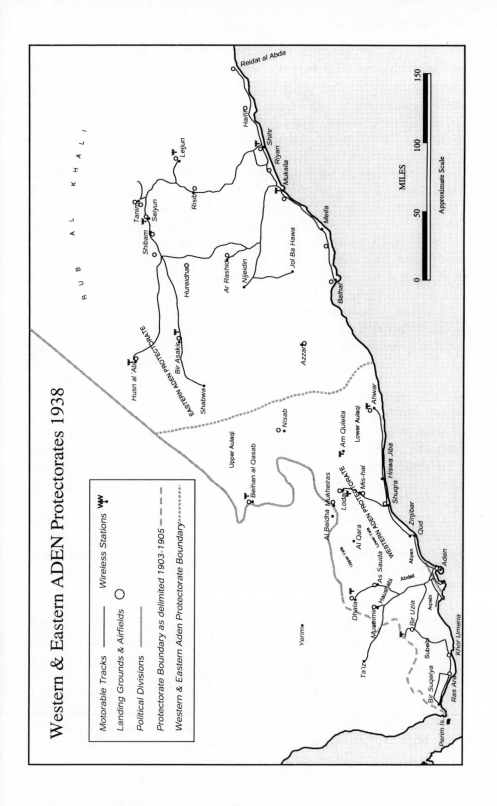

Western & Eastern ADEN Protectorates 1938

Motorable Tracks ———
Landing Grounds & Airfields ◯
Political Divisions ⋯⋯⋯
Protectorate Boundary as delimited 1903-1905 —— ⸺ ——
Western & Eastern Aden Protectorate Boundary∘∘∘∘∘∘∘∘∘

Wireless Stations Ⓦ

Reidat al Abda

R U B   A L   K H A L I

Hairir
Shihr
Lejjun
Riyan
Mukalla
Taniff
Seiyun
Risihr
Melfa
Shibam
Ar Rashid
Njieidin
Jol Ba Hawa
Hureidha
Balhaf

EASTERN ADEN PROTECTORATE
Husn al 'Ab
Bir Asakir
Shabwa
Azzan
Nisab
Ahwar
Upper Aulaqi
Am Quleita
Lower Aulaqi
Beihan al Qasab
Shuqra
Hiswa Jiba
Zinjibar
Al Beidha
Mukheiras
Loda
Mis-hal
Qud
Al Qara
WESTERN ADEN PROTECTORATE
As Sauda
Abyan
Aden
Abdali
Yerim
Dhala
Hausjabi
Muselmim
Bir Uzia
Aqrabi
Subeih
Taiz
Bir Suqeiya
Ras Ara
Khor Umeria
Perim Is.

MILES
0   50   100   150
Approximate Scale

263

This was a major shock. Beyond telling him I'd misunderstood the original offer I did not pursue the matter. My immediate thought was that we'd come so far and I had caused HMG trouble enough with my accident that it was no good my trying to right the posting in London. After talking it over with Kat we agreed there was nothing we could do but carry on to Aden and hope service in the Protectorate wouldn't be as bad as the prospects led me to anticipate.

We sailed at last for Aden during the first week of April 1950, in one of the East India Line ships - the Caledonia. She was a fine ship. If "posh" derives from port-out-starboard-home, we had a "posh" cabin. The only slightly discordant note of the voyage was to be warned, quite seriously by the first officer, of the risk of child stealing in the Suez Canal and the Red Sea. Apparently young girls particularly—African, Asian or even European—were much valued as slaves and sold readily in the markets of Saudi Arabia.

Kat and I made friends on board with an Indian couple, Group Captain Lal and his wife. He'd been in England for a year's course with the prestigious Imperial Defence College. His wife and two young children had joined him in London. He was a little older than me, highly ambitious and a transparent idealist. I found much in common with his thinking on the problems of government in under-developed areas and his idealism also struck a familiar note for it was a characteristic common in my own service. To say so is probably a criticism of us both but we were perhaps too imperialistically minded - we should have seen by then which way the wind of change was blowing. Our thoughts should have turned more to small countries in a world too big for them.

On arrival in Aden we stayed—and swam in their gubernatorial swimming pool—with the Governor of Aden Colony and Protectorate and his lady. We'd known for some time that they were the same Champions that Kat, the Aunts and kids had stayed with in Aviemore the year before.

Sir Reginald Champion himself was on the last tour of a conscientious career in the colonial administrative service. He'd served throughout the 1914-18 War with the East Surrey Regiment and still in the army had served with the Occupied Enemy Territory Administration of Palestine during the years 1917-20.

In 1920 he transferred to the colonial administrative service and worked for the next eight years as a DO in Palestine. He was later promoted to the post of Political Secretary, Aden, where he served from 1928-34. After various appointments in the Middle East he was promoted to Chief Secretary, Aden, and worked there from 1942 to

1944. He was Governor and Commander-in-Chief of the Colony and Protectorate of Aden from 1944 to 1951. He retired from the colonial service in 1951 but promptly began a new career taking holy orders. He finally retired as Vicar of Chilham, Kent and died in 1982.

I can't say that I knew Champion, even cursorily, for he left the affairs of the two Aden Protectorates very much to the two officials charged with direct responsibility—Basil Seager and Hugh Boustead. At the time I put this down to good governorship—why keep a dog and bark? After he'd gone on retirement his taking of holy orders in the Church of England seemed to me to be some sort of repudiation of the Shaf'ai Sect of Sunnis, the Sharia code of law and 'Urf'—a rejection almost of that part of the Arab world.

Some of the misunderstanding about my own posting had arisen because I had been promised a house in Khormaksar, a suburb of Aden. This promise was honoured on our arrival—however, I was posted as Senior Political Officer, Fadhli State, and told that Kat and the kids could live in the Khormaksar house whereas I was expected to camp out in Zinzibar (the tiny capital of the Fadhli State) during the week.

The so-called Western Aden Protectorate consisted of seventeen tribal chieftainships, some in treaty relationship with the British, some not. Doreen Ingrams' description of the degree of government in each in her book, *A Survey of the Social and Economic Conditions in the Aden Protectorates*, printed in 1949 by The Goverment Printer, British Administration, Eritrea, is pretty frank. I quote:

"Government" is a misnomer for the type of misrule which prevails throughout most of the Western Aden Protectorate and a good deal of the Eastern. In the former, with the exception of Laheg and the few areas in which adviser agreements have recently been concluded, there can be said to be no real government in any of the tribal territories but different degrees of authority. In some cases chiefs may have a loose control over several thousands of tribesmen and subjects, in others they may have control over a few dozen, and the extent of a chief's authority depends on his personality.

Except in certain areas which have recently come into closer relationship with the Government of Aden, there has been no attempt on the part of these chiefs to improve the conditions of their followers and subjects. They are almost all self-seeking, obstructive, suspicious and only interested in enriching themselves, which they do by taxation and oppression. Taxation is often exorbitant and unjust and the revenue from it is spent by the chiefs and their relatives on purely selfish objects. It may well be wondered why the oppressed have put up with the system for so many centuries, but in the Western Aden Protectorate there is no wealthy and cultured section of the community as is to be found in the Qu'aiti and Kathiri States in the Eastern Aden Protectorate. In the Western Protectorate there are no mercantile centres of importance and no cultural centres at all.

The Fadhli State was said to have come under closer British supervision than the remaining WAP states but the degree to which British influence, even then, was manifest was pretty minimal. This was brought home to me by an incident which took place very early in my appointment.

The young Sultan was officiating in a grazing dispute between two extended Bedu families. One side's case was being argued by the elderly father of two sons and he was making a poor showing. So much so that the elder son said words to the effect of—"You foolish old man. Let me put the case." The elder son then, very rudely, pushed his father in the chest. To lay hands on another person was a great breach of etiquette inviting the direst of penalties. To lay hands on your own father in the presence of the Sultan was a double insult.

The Fadhli Sultan, angry at the younger man's behaviour, chided him and roughly pushed him away from his father.

At that moment the younger son joined the group. He wasn't aware of what had gone before; all he saw was the Sultan manhandling his brother. Honour—sharrif—allowed him only one course of action. It was abominable that his brother should be—as he saw it—assaulted. He pulled out his jambia and thrust it deeply into the Sultan's body. He had no other course open to him. He was, as it were, the captive of honour.

By this time the Sultan's four-man bodyguard had fiddled with their Lee Enfields and succeeded, each, in getting a bullet into the breach. A fusillade of shots rang out. The younger brother was hit in the arm and thigh and fell to the ground beside the Sultan. The latter exhibiting great bravery and compassion, in spite of his wound, took his fountain pen out of his breast pocket and placed it on the man's chest as a sign that the shooting should stop.

The Sultan, severely wounded in the liver, spent the ensuing three weeks in Aden hospital where he made a good recovery.

The young Bedu, near to death by starvation, was still languishing in the Fadhli "prison" eighteen months later while the holy men argued whether he should live or be executed, the 'Urf being unclear on this point where the aggressor on a Sultan's life survived the attack as well as the Sultan.

The house we were allocated in Khormaksar was brand new, one of a small housing estate. There was no garden; sand lapped the doorstep like the waves of some Martian sea.

There was an airfield and RAF establishment a few hundred yards to our north. The RAF was present in strength, partly for the larger, strategic reasons of empire and partly to transport officers of both protectorates. There were permanent airfields at Riyan, about twenty miles east of Mukulla and at Ras Karma on Socotra Island. There were landing grounds in the WAP which could be used by the RAF Avro Ansons (the aircraft they used primarily for transporting political officers) at Dhala, Mukeiras, Lodar, Beihan al Qasab, Ahwar, Ras al Ara and Jau al Milah.

Just after we arrived we learned that there was an RAF flight lieutenant, his wife and two small children who were temporarily without RAF married quarters and we offered them a home for a few weeks. Considering the heat, the dust and the vicissitudes in general of living in Aden we got along surprisingly well with our companions. It no doubt helped that I was away most of each week. The Duttons, for such was their name, occupied the larger of the three bedrooms. Both families shared the upstairs bathroom; fortunately there was also a WC and washing arrangements at the foot of the stairs. We shared the kitchen and we all had access to the large living room although I seldom remember the Dutton family using it.

All the Milne family remember a violent Sunday afternoon when we gave a children's' party in the Khormaksar house. A ferocious dust storm was raging and it was necessary to shut all the doors and windows. The temperature in the house soon became abominable. I got out my climbing gear including a three-strand nylon rope. All the guests were in the six to ten age bracket and all without exception, demanded to be taught to abseil. Most, I guess, wanted to sample the rigors of the sandstorm but the wind was so strong I feared the flimsier kids might be blown away. So Kat and I organised a game involving abseiling and exposure to the sandstorm, keeping them on a safety rope.

Sweaty kids emerged, one by one, onto the open balcony where, secured by a safety rope they abseilled the seventeen or so feet to the ground over the balcony rail in the full blast of the sandstorm. Reaching the ground, still on the safety rope, they banged loudly on the front door; Kat admitted them, undid the safety rope and pushed them into the downstairs washroom where they sponged off the dust and sand that the sandstorm had liberally plastered them with.

Apparently it was voted a wow of a party.

Two further memories remain from that little party: Kat fed the young in the Arab manner; they sat crossed-legged round a cloth spread on the floor. So thirsty were they in the heat that Kat had to make continuous circuits with a large jug of lemon drink. We exhausted our supply of cold, boiled and filtered water and the cook had to visit neighbouring houses to "borrow" supplies from them. (We learned later that "borrowing" between servants in this way was common Aden practice—friends told us they'd dined out on their own dinner service.)

I had several "Beihan chairs" in the house. These were circular bands of embroidered material which, placed round crossed knees and backs, greatly eased the posture of sitting cross-legged. Several of the larger young were accustomed to using them.

I suppose roughly half our guests were English; the rest comprised the sons of Arab colleagues and Indian children whose parents had remained in Aden after the transfer from the Indian government. As the afternoon wore on the children divided themselves up—as children will—into groups. Both Kat and I remarked afterwards that race was very definitely not a basis for division. The criterion seemed to be brightness...interesting.

When I arrived in the Western Aden Protectorate the establishment of political officers was ten, nine were in post but the vacancy caused by the murder of DC Davey in Audhalli in 1947 had not been filled. The establishment of Arab assistant political officers was seven and I found these men of impressive calibre. They were paid local rates which, although no doubt generous by Aden standards, were a mere pittance compared to the salaried paid to expatriate political officers. I felt that in my case particularly—and indeed in the cases of other less experienced expatriates who nevertheless were Arab speakers—this was wrong.

Sa'id Abdullah was the assistant political officer posted to the Fadhli State and he was always by my side. Not speaking Arabic I had to use him as an interpreter and I was very much in his hands. He was a more intellectual character than the Fadhli Sultan and about four years the latter's junior but he lacked the strength of character the Sultan undoubtedly possessed. Rank alone would, of course have given the Sultan a degree of moral ascendancy but I always felt Sa'id Abdullah was not a man to press a view strongly.

Just before the end of my tour in Aden I had recommended Sa'id Abdullah for an educational visit to the United Kingdom. We had no sooner got home than I heard his application had been successful and he was due very shortly. We arranged to meet him at Carlisle Airport the day he was to fly into Heathrow from Aden—fortuitously there was an air connection Heathrow-Carlisle which he caught.

It was the first visit he had made out of Southern Arabia. He stared enthralled at the Eden Valley countryside as we motored him from the airport to Temple Sowerby. It was an unpleasant autumn day; the Pennine and Lake hills were covered with low cloud but the fields of the Eden Valley itself still had their late summer green lushness. At length he commented: "God surely has blessed these people but where are the irrigation canals?"

He politely studied all he was shown in England and impressed most of the officials and others that he met by his intelligence. Whether a view of life so alien to Southern Arabia was of any lasting use to him I shall never know. It a letter he wrote later he told me how impressed he had been by the exteriors of several cinemas that he'd visited...many picture houses in those days were very grand; Plazas, Palaces or Emporiums.

To return to the WAP...some eight years before our arrival in Aden, Sultan Abdullah bin Uthman had been thrown out of the Fadhli State by the British and forced to live in exile at Shuqra, fifty miles down the coast from Aden. The Sultan's and my Land Rovers crossed one day on the beach and we pulled up for the occupants to exchange news. The sultan was on his way back from a visit to Aden.

Sa'id Abdullah effected the introductions. I had been given loose instructions by Seager—the British Agent in the Eastern Aden Protectorate—to call on Sultan Abdullah in Shuqra from time to time...to keep an eye on him...and the present occasion gave me an opportunity to arrange a meeting.

The "shamal" was blowing half a gale and we had to shout our greetings. The sultan had purchased in Aden a small .22 repeater rifle; he demonstrated his prowess with it by firing at a shell on the sea's edge. He hit a portion of the shell with each shot until he'd reduced his target to the size of a small coin—wonderful shooting in the high wind. I was truly impressed.

Ex-Sultan bin Uthman (as I suppose one should refer to him) was then about thirty-five and a small lively man. I found it hard to think of him as a tyrannical fellow forced in 1941 by British decree to abdicate his power. We made an arrangement for me to meet him at dawn on the beach some ten miles SW of Shuqra in ten days' time.

"I'll show you some sport you won't forget," he said on parting.

Sa'id Abdullah warned me that the shamal wind blowing steadily from the south was causing an upwelling of cold water on the shores of the Gulf of Aden and this brought shoals of fish inshore. The sharks followed them and were to be seen frequently in the surf cruising close inshore. The "sport I wouldn't forget" was harpooning the sharks.

And so it proved to be. We met the sultan at first light, as arranged. He had two Land Rovers with him, each bearing three or four Nubian slaves in the open backs, carrying harpoons the size of a large broomstick and hundreds of feet of hemp line coiled on pieces of driftwood. The harpoons were armed with detachable heads tied to the line.

"Mr Milne, you use this Land Rover and follow mine until we find a shark," said the Sultan.

Down the beach we cruised, all eyes on the surf. Suddenly we spotted fins that the first Land Rover had apparently missed. Willed on by all in the vehicle I seized a harpoon and plunged into the sea. A small swell suddenly disclosed a great grey body coming at me from the side, larger than I'd anticipated from the size of the fins. I leapt towards the shore. The splash and movement turned him. Three yards away he swung across my front and, as he passed, I hurled the harpoon as hard as I could, aiming just below the central fin. The harpoon head hit the bone-hard base of the fin and fell back harmlessly into the sea. There was a yell of derision from the occupants of my Land Rover which changed to cries of triumph as Sultan Abdullah, who had come back to us, flung his harpoon home.

It took us twenty minutes to drag the sultan's fish above the high water mark and another five to dispatch him with repeated blows to the head with a piece of driftwood. As he died, two parasitic sucker fish, the size of herrings, fell off onto the sand.

The Sultan's victim was fourteen feet long but was soft mouthed. Sa'id Abdullah explained that he was a ray—rays and sharks being closely related. It took our combined effort, and much vocal instruction, to get him onto the tail board of the Sultan's vehicle and to make him fast head and tail to the front bumpers.

The soft sand at the mouth of the Wadi Hassan delayed our vehicles for some time. All sank to the axles and had to be manhandled to safety. The tide was on the turn, threatening total loss unless we moved quickly. At last we were free again and a little way along the beach we approached an old man, his arms full of nets, wading stiffly ashore from a huri, anchored twenty yards out. As soon as the old man reached dry land he flung his burden down and ran to kiss the sultan's hand and knee. "Eat with me," he commanded and as we were all hungry by then we moved to his shelter.

Pieces of driftwood supported a few torn mats. Two sheets of corrugated iron kept the drifting sand at bay. Our host waded back to his canoe. He returned with a number of small fish which he fried for us with a little oil using a prop from his shelter for fuel. In the same oil he cooked some khobz. I noticed that he used his entire supply of meal. We sat in a circle, eating with our right hands...Sultan and slave, European and servant, host and our driver, braking the same bread and sharing the fish.

"The camels will not lack food this year," said our Arabian host and went on to explain the signs portending a good sardine year.

"I must not omit to tell you," wrote Marco Polo of the Arabian coast, "that all cattle live upon small fish and nought besides."

Omitting the Land Rovers, the scene of eating men, the cooking pot, the long beach and the salt-caked huri riding the incoming waves might well have belonged to the time of that hardy traveller. The conversation had little changed.

I cherished with delight the prospect of telling some of our horsy friends in Cumberland that I'd visited the Gulf of Aden where the ponies—the little true Arabs of Arabia Felix—ate dried sardines. I'd seen photographs of ponies nosing into mounds of dried fish in proof of what I'd been told.

The sun, our friend of the early morning, was now the enemy. But the food had given us new energy and we drove on, eyes shielded against the glare. Ahead the masts of several small dhows took substance from the constantly changing mirages down the beach. We stopped where a little gathering of Bedu gazed in awe at a veritable monster of the deep, harpooned that morning from a sambuk. It was a saw fish, nearly twenty feet long, and so massive that I had to take a short run to climb its back. The enormous saw—a bone-like structure five feet long and about twelve inches broad, armed with pointed teeth along the edges and the forward end—had been cut off and lay on the sand nearby. After a few moments of polite exchange of conversation with the sultan the senior fisherman casually mentioned that one of his crew had fallen overboard while the great fish, by then nearly dead, was being secured alongside. A sideways swing of the saw had "caused his friend to suffer some injury".

Abdullah bin Uthman hurried to the wounded man's hut, murmuring pious expressions of sympathy. It was one of a number of small compounds, walled with brushwood, enclosing brushwood huts, some having door posts built up with mud. The sand, always blowing in the wind, kept clean and sweet what in wet West Africa would have been a sorry quagmire.

The wounded man, face averted, lay on a bamboo bed silently enduring the Will of God. I removed a little of the dirty cloth covering his affected arm and saw that the flesh, from shoulder to forearm, was terribly lacerated. It was better not to disturb the covering, dirty as it was. Two women, who had been crouching unseen in a corner, sidled out, weeping loudly, faces hidden in their veils.

Abdullah bin Uthman picked the wounded fisherman up tenderly and carried him, light as a child, to the Land Rover bearing the ray. A brother gathered up a cloth and a little money and the party left for Aden hospital. The sultan told them to try and sell the ray and to use the proceeds.

"Such is God's will," said Sultan bin Uthman as we returned to our hunt.

It was Sa'id Abdullah who again spotted the next fin. The sultan and I were travelling in the same Land Rover and he raced me down the beach and hurled his harpoon while still running. He missed giving me a chance to redeem my "sharrif" which I duly did.

Instead of running out to sea the shark yawed about in the shallow water. We followed his movements from the beach hanging grimly onto the line. Just as one tries to keep abreast with a salmon hooked on rod and line in some Scottish river we tried to keep abreast of our fish. Sultan bin Uthman, whose "sharrif" balance was then in the red, followed the fish with grim purpose, determined to avenge his miss. The shark turned towards him; he sprang aside falling headlong but recovered sufficiently to thrust at the shark from a sitting posture. This thrust, and hearty pulling from the slaves on shore, caused the shark to swing away again. Just as well, for the royal person would have been little improved by coming into violent contact with the rough skin of our quarry, much less the cruel teeth.

It took five rifle shots through the head to quieten our victim when at last he was dragged up onto the dry sand. He was a tiger shark, some thirteen feet in length, with one-inch teeth. We took him into

Aden to show Kat and the kids before the Sultan's men went off with him to the market.

———————

Journeys by Land Rover from Aden up and down the beach to Abyan, and beyond to Shuqra, were governed by the state of the tide. At high water, vehicles were forced up the beach into the soft sand above the high water mark and the going was very slow and hard on the engines. The ideal time for passage was between one and two hours after high water. Any longer than about two hours after being washed the sand again became soft. Needless to say the Arab drivers made themselves expert at judging the optimum conditions. Expatriate political and agricultural officers, on the other hand, preferred to study the tide tables.

One oddity about the juxtaposition of the Gulf of Aden and the Red Sea was that at certain times of the year high tide on the shores of the Gulf was lower than the ensuing low tide at the same spot.

Used as I was to the employment of Land Rovers in Nigeria, I was appalled by the short life of the same vehicles in Aden. Many engines were completely burnt out after as little as 3,000 miles.

Christmas 1950 brought near calamity for the Seagers. Basil and Heather decided to spend the three days of holiday in the cool heights of Dhala, eighty-eight miles from Aden up the old Turkish road.

On Christmas Eve I took Kat and the young, then aged six and eight, round the rim of the Aden crater. I hadn't properly reconnoitred the route and assumed wrongly that we could walk the whole of it. After five hours (quite enough for the young, considering their age and the high temperature) we found ourselves above the crater area of the township and unable to descend without the aid of a rope which I didn't have. There was nothing for it but to scramble back up to the rim of the crater and descend from there. I tried to make amends by going back ahead of Kat and the two young and returning with bottles of cold water which we drank before finally descending to sea level. We were all tired and more than ready for a late luncheon when we eventually reached our Khormaksar house about four p.m.

Alas, we found a messenger on the doorstep bearing a very garbled wireless signal from Dhala to the effect of "the tribes have risen. Seager was badly wounded. Escort member(s) killed and Mr and Mrs Seager want immediate evacuation by air to Aden. Seager also requires doctor."

For some reason I cannot remember I was acting as Seager's deputy at the time. Perhaps Allen, the substantive deputy agent, WAP was on leave. Anyhow, I had to act and obviously act quickly.

There remained two and a half-hours before darkness. There were night landing facilities at Khormaksar. Provided we could get an aircraft up to Dhala before dark we could evacuate Seager and his wife that evening.

But reference to the RAF was a waste of time. I couldn't even raise the duty officer for twenty minutes. When I did get on to him he was unable to contact any senior officer. He told me that all airmen had stood down, the hangers and aircraft were locked up and it would not be possible to get a single aircraft into the air that evening. If a doctor was needed urgently at Dhala he would have to go up there by road, such as it was.

I said that I would take up a road party that evening. He promised faithfully to arrange for an aircraft to evacuate the Seagers the following morning. I had to leave matters there.

The only expatriate of initiative I was able to contact was a young medical officer. He was ready to use any means available of reaching Dhala.

He and I decided to travel up to Dhala in a Land Rover taking in the back an escort of five Protectorate Levies which the Arab duty officer had offered. We felt that the message reference to "the tribes have risen" was likely to be either a transmission error or a gross exaggeration of the true position. We accordingly departed just before dark. I told Kat that I would come back with the Seagers in the morning. There was no time to secure arms for either the doctor or myself.

We found the first forty miles or so of road, built by the Turks in 1915, in reasonable condition and averaged eighteen miles per hour. Later, as we began to wend our way up the escarpment to the high Dhala Plateau, our speed dropped to below ten miles in the hour.

As we climbed, the night air grew cool then cold. So much so that on reaching 4,000 feet asl we'd closed all the windows and the escort in the back had tightly laced the canvas cover. There was no longer any question of them springing out of the vehicle should an emergency arise.

As we breasted the last steep rise preceding the Dhala Plateau half a dozen figures rose from the side of the road and halted us. I remember thinking, more or less, "What the hell!" It didn't seem greatly to matter whether the figures were hostile, bent on our destruction, or not. We were tired with the continuous bumping and cold. The driver opened his door and began a long conversation with one of them. They were members of a sub-tribe, allegedly loyal to the British, and were "keeping the pass open". We thanked them and passed on.

Basil and Heather Seager were staying in a small, fortified building to which Seager had been taken after the incident. He was lying, semi-conscious, in the small bedroom. The doctor, carrying his case of instruments, entered and closed the door. I had time for a horrifying glimpse of blood on the low, whitewashed ceiling. Arteries must have been severed.

Heather Seager, angry and distressed that the RAF had failed to evacuate Seager that day, told me what had happened.

After lunch she and Seager had decided to go for a walk. He arranged for his escort of four riflemen to travel in their Land Rover which followed them at about 300 yards distance. Some two miles from the fortified building they had met a Holy Seiyid riding a donkey, accompanied by his own escort of four tribesmen armed with rifles. Seager had greeted the Holy Seiyid, "Greetings of God."

"Greetings of God" came in reply.

"Min ain?" asked Seager—"From where?"

The Holy Seiyid replied, giving a name in the Dhala Confederacy.

"No," said Seager, "your accent is that of a man of Qu'taba in the Yemen."

"Yes, you are correct," said the Seiyid. "I am Seiyid Abu D'aim."

At this point Heather realised that the Seiyid was under the influence of the narcotic drug *qat* and a premonition of evil seized her.

She was right, for, some years before, Seager had had a long passage of disagreement with the Seiyid and had procured his imprisonment for a while. Unfortunately, before she could intervene, Seager replied, "I am Seager," emphasising his name.

The name "Seager" penetrated the *qat*-befuddled mind of the mounted Seiyid. He sprang off his donkey and attacked Seager with his jambia. Seager defended himself as best he could with his hands and arms but received a number of wounds in both forearms, to one side of his face and on his chest.

Heather threw stones but found she hadn't the strength to check the Seiyid. As the Seagers' Land Rover drove up, the Holy Seiyid's escort took up positions behind rocks and low bushes and brought their rifles to bear on Seager's men.

A battle began between the two escorts. Two of the combatants—one on each side—were killed instantly. A further two of Seager's men were wounded. Seager's driver bravely drove the vehicle into the midst of battle, sprang out and bundled Seager, Heather and the remaining sound escort into the back. He drove off at speed for the fort where Heather did her best to stem the blood flowing from

Seager's many wounds. At last the bleeding moderated and Heather felt she could keep Seager alive at least until an aircraft arrived that evening. He had lost an unknown but very considerable amount of blood.

As Heather finished her account of what happened the doctor's ministrations were punctuated from time to time by low cries from poor Basil Seager; it was plain that the task of sewing up the jambia wounds was causing him, weak as he was, considerable pain. After a little Heather could bear it no longer and went into the bedroom. I sat miserably alone, numb with the horror of it all.

Heather didn't sleep. During the night Basil called her weakly three or four times. The doctor and I dozed uncomfortably in our chairs. Dawn was a relief and at first light I took the Levies down to the airfield, posting them on the perimeter with the task of preventing any hostile interference. I sat with my back to the wall of the small building near the runway, awaiting the arrival of the aircraft. Every speck in the southern sky was the aircraft approaching until it turned into hawk or vulture. The sun had climbed high and grown hot when, at 10.30 a.m., the aircraft did arrive.

Two or three high-ranking RAF officers descended the steps. I fleetingly wondered what their function was. Surely not sightseers.

Seager was carried aboard on a stretcher. Heather and the young doctor followed. There was a short debate amongst the RAF officers; they all boarded and I was told there was no seat for me but they would send another aircraft to pick me up later that Christmas morning.

Kat met the aircraft on its return to Aden. She was appalled by Seager's appearance: the robust, sunburnt fifty-two year old she had recently known was reduced to a wrinkled, very white, old man of half his former size. Nobody said anything to her about plans for my evacuation.

I waited on that Dhala airfield from the time they took off—about eleven a.m.—until five p.m. in the evening. No aircraft came. No W/T message was sent. The Levi Land Rover carrying my escort waited too. They had wanted to see me into an aircraft before they left, they said. The driver now suggested that we all return by road to Aden. He'd like to be off the Dhala Plateau before dark in case...in case...

They dropped me off at the Khormaksar house at 11.30 p.m. Kat had kept a large plate of food in the oven.

Seager recovered in some weeks, aided by a strong constitution and massive blood transfusions. His facial wound would disfigure him for the rest of his life. Heather became more silent than before and her deep blue eyes harder than I'd known them.

As for being left uninformed on the Dhala airfield all Christmas Day I put in a note of complaint to the RAF but merely received a cursory note in reply saying that it had not been possible to send an aircraft specially for me as it had been found that all available aircraft were out of hours. As it only needed an engineer's signature to extend the check life of an engine or aircraft this, to say the least was an empty excuse.

A lot was heard in colonial circles round about 1950 of the Abyan Scheme in the Western Aden Protectorate. It took up much of my time as I was an ex-officio director. I strived to learn what I could of the history and basic organisation so that I could compare the project with similar large-scale efforts in Nigeria of which I had some knowledge. I was supposed to be the political representative on the board but the two main agriculturists involved, Brian Hartley and Congdon, the general manager were far better equipped than me in this area.

The Abyan Scheme wouldn't have got off the ground, much less seen the rapid development it did, had it not been for the two of them.

Brian Hartley's father and grandfather were both Yorkshire civil servants of farming stock. Brian won a colonial service scholarship to Oxford and later to the Imperial College of Agriculture in Trinidad. He served in Tanganyika with distinction from 1929 to 1938 when he was appointed to the Aden Protectorate. When Kat and I arrived in Aden in 1950 he was Director of Agriculture of the Protectorate and had been appointed OBE and CMG. He was by then one of the leading "arid lands" agriculturists in the world.

Major J L Congdon, having acquired an agricultural training before the war, was on military service from 1939-41. He served then with the British Military Administration of Eritrea from 1941-47. In 1950 he was appointed Manager of the Abyan Scheme. He stood in Hartley when the latter was on leave and Hartley reciprocated when Congdon was on leave. Both officers were under very considerable pressure for several years.

Brian Hartley was a great character by anybody's measure. One of the pleasantest things about him was his invariable cheerfulness. He always wore a smile and was able to see the lighter side of any problem...the smile, to be truthful, had an enigmatic quality for he was an unorthodox character and often produced highly original—and at first hearing—definitely unusual solutions to problems.

In later years I heard that he had spent a lot of time in his prep school days with his cousin Vivian Hartley who later as Vivian Leigh, the actress, was married to Lawrence Olivier. Those who knew them both said there was a lot in common between Vivian's and Brian Hartley's characters.

The Abyan Scheme was inspected by Sir Herbert Stewert CI in March 1950 and he wrote a valuable report which formed the basis of our work on the scheme throughout the remainder of 1950.

The Lower Yafa Mountains ended abruptly some twenty miles from the sea in the Abyan area. They were deeply cut by two wadis—valleys of the rivers Bana and Hassan. The coastal plain had virtually no rainfall, the average being under one and a half inches a year. The highlands of Lower and Upper Yafa, and of the Kingdom of Yemen to the north, enjoyed a rainfall of twenty to twenty-five inches, restricted to short periods. The courses of the rivers Bana and Hassan were dry for most of the year but occasionally flooded. It was calculated that there was enough floodwater, even in a dry year, to irrigate 30,000 acres annually. In the 1951 flood there was sufficient flow to have cultivated 50,000 acres in the Abyan area.

There were signs of many very ancient irrigation works both on the sides of the two wadis and on the Abyan plain. Centuries of insecurity, prior to the arrival of HM Government, had left the area derelict. The partial peace following the interest in the Aden Protectorate by the British after the transfer of responsibility from the India government to the colonial office in 1937 had prepared the ground for an organised project. The Abyan Board was formed in 1947.

Once the board was formally established, development was possible on a partnership basis between the landowners which included the states and individuals, the tenant farmers or owner occupiers who provided the ploughs and oxen and the labour, and the board itself. The latter was established as the development authority, and the constructor and operator of irrigation works, as well as water controller. Cotton had been proved as an extremely promising crop in 1947-50 and the board was vested with special powers for its control and marketing.

The revenue of the scheme in 1950 was divided twenty-five per cent to the board, fifty per cent to the tenants and twenty-five per cent to the states and landlords.

The first spate was expected in March-April annually and later flows were expected between July and September. Each flow carried enormous quantities of silt so that land where water was applied was continually rising.

The foot of the mountains where the wadis Bana and Hassan debouched formed the boundaries of the lands of the Beni Qasid. These people were individualistic tribesmen bearing little allegiance to anybody. Partly driven by poverty (aren't we all?) but, I believe, more driven by ancient custom, the Beni Qasid spent moonless nights raiding the rich Abyan Scheme. The Abyan Tribal Guards, and on occasion Aden Protectorate Levies had counterattacked and over recent years a number of Beni Qasid had been killed. The tribesmen demanded "blood money" for each loss and the demands added up to a formidable total. The Beni Qasid cited the claims as justification for further raids and so the situation gradually assumed heavier import and became more complicated.

Aqil Ahl Qat, the Lower Yafa Sultan, whose home was the remote and mysterious Al Qara in the midst of the Lower Yafa mountains some one hundred miles from the coast, was said to exercise a degree of influence over the Beni Qasid. It dated from pre-Islamic days; his remote forebears then exercising some influence by virtue of their lineage as priest kings. Memories were long in the dry clear air of the Yafa mountains and Seager, ever the scholar of Bedu affairs who could think like a Bedu, together with Abdullah Hassan Jaffer, the most senior of the Aden corps of Arab political officers, talked to me about this situation in connection with complaints about the Beni Qasid raids on the Abyan Scheme.

Seager put it rather like this: the Lower Yafa Sultan may not be more than *primus inter pares* amongst the Lower Yafa chieftains but his line does still hold the priest-king thread. A visit by a British political officer to Al Qara would do something to lift his prestige. The payment of blood money on Beni Qasid killed on Abyan raids would not only enhance the sultan's prestige but might even stop the raids on the Abyan Scheme for a year or two. "You," he said to me, "can be the British officer. I'll give you Abdullah Hassan Jaffer to help. You can take an Aden Protectorate Levi escort and a box of Maria Theresa dollars to pay 'em off."

Secret emissaries moved between Aden and Al Qara averaging a month for each journey. At length the details of the expedition were agreed. The Sultan would receive the party "suitably" in Al Qara. The matter of blood money could be "discussed". An escort of tribesmen would be provided for the journey to Al Qara and back to the mouth of the Wadi Hassan.

In spite of my lack of Arabic—for which I would have to rely on Abdullah Hassan Jaffer—I was ordered to take charge of the party. In fact I knew, and Seager knew, that the man really in command would be Abdullah Hassan Jaffer who was a consummately good negotiator and who had met the Lower Yafa Sultan some years before. I was merely there as the European figurehead.

There was an RAF officer in Aden at the time who had taken a large number of aerial photographs of "no-go" territory including a very full set of the Lower Yafa mountains. He produced one of Al Qara and others of the route there from the mouth of the Wadi Hassan which to my untutored eye appeared to present serious physical difficulties—there was one pass which seemed impossible for animal transport.

We departed Aden during a bad spell of monsoon weather. Sand drove to a height of twenty feet like powder snow in a blizzard; visibility was reduced to a few yards. As we left the beach for the north-east, the following wind caused our Land Rovers to boil and frequent pauses were necessary, radiators towards the wind, our heads and eyes covered against the driving sand.

Sultan Hussain pressed us all to spend the night in Abyan. It was a relief to wash from a tall earthenware jar, throwing tepid water over a dust-caked body with an aluminium mug.

We ate at sundown—mutton and rice, chicken roasted with liver and a variety of fruits from Australian tins. The Sultan tried, without success, to persuade us to abandon the journey: the unreliable and angry tribes of Bana Qasid would fail to honour their safe conduct; there would be an incident in which we would suffer. If, the Sultan went on, we persisted in going, it would at least be wise to take with us one Hassan Moksin, a trader from the coast. He would be a travelling weather-cock, a man who would crow loudly if he felt there was trouble ahead.

We spent several hours the following morning searching for Hassan Moksin. At last he was found and consented to come...at a price. He would bring his pony for whose hire we would pay.

Towards evening we gathered at Fort Hatat where the Wadi Hassan emerged from the mountains onto the coastal plain. The air had cleared and fifty miles away to the south-west the lowering sun touched with red the long ridge of Jabel Shamsham above Aden.

The off-white fort, perched almost jauntily on the lower slopes of the hills where the Wadi Hassan had torn a narrow opening into the plain, was a lonely outpost of government. As the light began to go I talked in my stilted and inadequate Arabic with the Naib of the garrison on the roof of the fort.

We made camp below the walls of the fort. The following morning, just before sun-up, two Bedu youth, singing, wandered our way followed by their browsing goats. One put his hand into a sacking bag from which he pulled a puff adder. Placing it on the ground he handled it in much the same way a rabbit catcher at home handles his ferrets…and with as much fear. Thanking him for his offer to sell we politely declined, buying instead two young goats.

Shots were heard from far up the Wadi and a sentry answered the salute. We all moved down to level ground below the fort where we sat with "Beihan-chairs" round our backs and knees as we awaited the tribal escort who would take us to Al Qara.

There was a long pause, some coming and going. At length fifteen Beni Qasid tribesmen, their turbans and shirts stained blue with indigo, moved slowly towards us. They sat in a silent, grim circle a little distance away.

Hassan Moksin whispered that they objected to our *firka* of government guards. If we are to travel "on their face", he explained, we must take no escort of our own.

But it was pointed out that the escort was there out of compliment to our host in Al Qara, Sultan Aqil Ahl Qat. This explanation was accepted and the two protesting goats were led off to be slaughtered under a thorn tree. The tribal escort would eat with us before we all set off.

I'd been offered a side-arm but refused it, more out of laziness than political acumen. I knew that I'd walk much better without it. Abdullah Hassan Jaffer told me later my refusal had made a profound impression—"here's a fearless European"—but I must confess that was pure lucky inadvertence. What I did do deliberately was say to the escort, "I was born in the mountains of Cumberland and I can walk step for step with you people." From then on I was committed to go ahead of the main party with the tribal escort. Before dark that evening it had developed into a marathon, neither side wishing to be the first to give up. But they, armed to the teeth, had had me all day at their mercy, and we had developed some kind of rapport as the day wore on.

At dusk I began to regret having issued the challenge for we went on into the night. Darkness slowed us down somewhat. At length the going underfoot eased and we were walking on short-grazed turf. There was a smell of water in the air. It was a *gheil*—a spot where an underground stream emerged for a few yards. By mutual consent we lay down where we stood. The little men of the escort wrapped their robes around their shoulders and slept. I found an easy little mound as a pillow and slept, too.

The main party caught us up around midnight. I was awoken by my servant who produced a hurricane lantern and asked if I wanted him to erect the small camp bed we had with us. Requesting only a piece of cloth to cover the "pillow" (which had turned out to be a little heap of sun-dried camel droppings) and taking a blanket, I slept on.

Much of the following day was spent in getting our animals over the difficult Maokaba Pass. On the steep rocky pitches near the summit many of the camels—especially the heavier draught animals—had to be unloaded and hauled up. Hassan Moksin's pony cut his knees. The donkeys alone were sure footed and some climbed fully laden.

The tribal escort resumed the challenge of the day before but now our relations had improved somewhat and we arrived on the summit with a burst of laughter, exclaiming at the beauty of the scene that lay stretched out before us to the north. We turned our backs on the struggles of the animals still tackling the steep ascent and looked across at the many peaked mountains of Sarrar before us. Between lay a relatively populated area, the valleys a rich green with growing crops. But there were no villages, as one would expect, in the valley bottoms. What houses there were—each a fortified stone *dar*—were perched astride the high ridges, the range of a rifle shot between. I did not envy the womenfolk of this mutually distrustful area their daily chores; to descend two thousand feet for wood and water seemed unduly wasteful of human labour.

Extra care was needed during our descent of the Wadi Sarrar because several tribesmen had lost their lives in "incidents" in the Abyan area and their fellows were said to be eager for revenge. Every now and then we saw groups of armed men watching us from high on the valley sides but no wrong-head shouted an insult and no fool fired the first shot.

Towards evening, from the summit of a subsidiary pass above Bir Al Wadien, we had our first view of Al Qara. Storm clouds were massing to the north, frequent flashes of lightening promised the long awaited advent of rain. The cool, damp air was invigorating after the great summer heat of the plains. We were feeling full of well-being and some of us perhaps a little intoxicated that we had got this far so easily.

A member of the tribal escort pointed and off to the north, silhouetted against the dark sky, I could just make out on the summit of a high conical hill the outline of a slender minaret—the mosque of Al Qara.

We camped that evening in a bowl of the hills at the junction of the Wadis Am Hada and Munqa. The friendly turf was gay with a lovely little red flower. One of the secrets of Arabia Felix—and she has many—is simply this: the contrast of harsh, hot desert with the green pleasances of the highlands.

The messengers of Sultan Aqil Ahl Qat arrived before dawn with instructions for our approach. We were not to move until requested to do so. On arrival in Al Qara we would find our reception prepared.

Parties of tribesmen passed our camp, singing on the march. Although none would approach us all fired salutes to which we would reply with an equal number of shots. In spite of this reserve we felt that the tension had lifted. We were, by then, within the grazing lands of the Sultan's own family—the Ahl Afifi. The possibility of any sort of incident had now become remote.

The orders to advance arrived and we trod our way amid the bunded fields in the Wadi Munqa toward Al Qara. Coffee and *qat* bushes were plentiful and near the occasional houses—no longer built on the high ridges—grapevines clung closely to the branches of wild fig trees.

Rounding a low hill we saw the citadel of Al Qara 1,500 feet above us, the fortified *dars* white against the sky beyond. The twisting, mile-long path to the citadel was black with tribesmen. Hassan Moksin estimated that three thousand armed men awaited us. His guess was a good one for the sultan, later in our visit, told us that he'd fed three thousand men that first day.

The sultan himself, surrounded by a party of retainers brandishing swords, came slowly down the path to greet us. Tribesmen, bare chests rubbed with indigo and oil of sesame, pressed forward. As the parties met the saluting began: a cannon from the heights above fired twelve times, every tribesman lining the route pressed near, discharging their rifles from the hip as they approached. A servant of the sultan stationed himself in front of us, doing his best to make an opening in the press ahead.

Clothes stained from contact with the oil and indigo, dizzy from the noise and throng, at last we won our way to the sultan's house. Bars were placed across the narrow door and only the elite was admitted.

We climbed up to a white-walled room near the roof, the floor soft with rugs from Beihan, Yafai, India and Persia, piled so high that they lapped, wave-like, against the walls. Numerous cups of sweet tea and glasses of coffee-coloured water were pressed on us. I feared the latter had been collected from the rain pits we could see in the courtyard below which held heavens knows what filth besides...I drank only the tea.

Rested, we stood ceremoniously on the flat roof, looking across to the minaret proudly standing against the Upper Yafa Mountains beyond, a seething crowd of tribesmen below. Our appearance was the signal for a fresh burst of saluting. I was punctilious in pressing the sultan to take the place of honour...well to the edge of the parapet and nearer to the hail of shots.

That night the skies opened and the rain fell amid crash after crash of thunder. Intermingled with the magic of the line of Sultan Aqil Ahl Qat was a belief that he possessed a drum which would beat of itself in a storm telling him all things. I listened carefully during those hours of electrical disturbance but heard no drum.

I was given a *dar* to myself on the very edge of the little settlement of Al Qara. From the door, which faced north, bare rocks extended for twenty or thirty feet and then descended in a ridge which seemed, after a cursory examination, to offer interesting problems as a rock climb. I was also provided with two guards who never let me move, even ten yards outside the *dar*, without following me. On the second day in Al Qara, while the Arab members of my party slept off the effect of the *qat* session they'd enjoyed the night of arrival, I started to explore the descending ridge. One of the guards followed me down keeping always about twenty feet above me. I suggested in my poor Arabic that he should let me continue alone but he wouldn't hear of the suggestion. After a hundred feet of descent or so I came to a pitch that was going to prove hard for me unencumbered as I was with rifle. I felt it might be too much for the guard with his sandals and rifle and returned to the *dar*.

Doubtless he thought only that the rocks had beaten me.

We stayed in Al Qara for three nights, the first night and most of the following day being taken up with the *qat* session to which I was mercifully not invited. The third day was given over to negotiations with the Sultan and his tribal heads for the settlement of blood money claimed by the Beni Qasid. The box of freshly minted Maria Theresa dollars was opened and the contents distributed. Needless to say Abdullah Hassan Jaffer was the chief negotiator on our side. Oddly enough, years later, my widowed sister Marie married a widower John Challen whose family firm had been associated with the minting of the Maria Theresa dollars for Arabia Felix. I believe he even remembered our special order in 1950. It only shows how small the world is.

The Sultan, greeting me before the blood money discussion began said, "We haven't seen a European here for some time."

I had it in mind that Brian Hartley might have visited Al Qara before the war so I replied, "Oh, you mean a visit by Mr Hartley before the war?"

The Sultan said, almost testily, "No, No. In your calendar the fifteenth century."

I hope he was right.

Our journey back to Fort Hatat and Aden passed without incident.

Passengers on ships which took on fresh drinking water when calling at Aden used to complain that the water had an unpleasant taste and being rich in salts had a diarrhoeic effect. Luckily Kat and the young were not adversely affected by the Aden water but I was. I expect, too, that my life up country exposed me to fresh attacks of amoebic dysentery. I know that I suffered a lot and spent much of the time feeling below par. As each attack cleared I felt energetic again and life assumed a brighter colour.

The work of political officers in Aden demanded a high degree of physical fitness just as did the work of administrative officers up to the rank of resident elsewhere in the colonial empire. Very few officers failed to take an hour's brisk exercise daily. It was the custom and we all enjoyed it. I had an added incentive because, like Angus Robin and one or two other colleagues, I wanted to be in good fettle for mountaineering during my leaves.

By October 1950 I began seriously to assess the benefits and drawbacks of my secondment to Aden.

I could have enjoyed and benefited from service in the small efficient Colony of Aden but this was not a possibility as Sir Bernard Reilly had explained to me in London.

Service in the WAP, although great fun—experiences such as shark fishing with Sultan Bin Uthman and the Al Qara journey were not to be missed—had taught me nothing of administration and my contribution to the WAP had been minimal.

There was virtually no government as we understood the term in Nigeria in any of the multiplicity of states forming the two protectorates. The future of these states was anybody's guess but it was already clear that a confederacy of states within the British Commonwealth was not a possibility. We were toying, as it were, with occasional devices for improved standards of living—female education, health measures, an odd agricultural scheme of the Abyan model—but none of these measures were taking place in areas which saw their future in an independent Arab state within the

Commonwealth. We were not building up a single country out of the states with whom we had treaty relations—the last thing the rulers wanted was any kind of union. We were merely travelling along with them in a temporary and tentative manner (somebody one said we were "playing about on the perimeters of time"). Our relationship, such as it was, could be broken overnight.

The task in Nigeria, in comparison, was clear. There we were working with a realistic objective in view. Also the peoples by and large were responding to our efforts. We were getting results.

Even relations with the Abyan Board were politically unsatisfactory. Kat has kept a number of notes that I wrote her from Zinzibar in which I mentioned that the States' Representatives on the board loudly complained that they did not know what the board was up to. They wanted more meetings of the full board and they wanted a comprehensive break-down of the plans already being put into operation. Much as Hartley and Congdon were to be admired as operators I feel now that they would have laid stronger and more enduring foundations had they gone a little more slowly and less authoritatively.

I think I had some success putting these views to Bill Goode who was Chief Secretary to the Aden government at the time but I had none at all with Brian Hartley and Congdon. Naturally they wanted to get on with it and who is to say they weren't right in the then circumstances of the scheme. I didn't press the matter with them because I was not sure enough of my own views.

I'd been trained in the problems of nation-building in West Africa, Nigeria, and hankered to be back. It seemed to me that one tour in Aden would be enough. To stay longer would mean that I would be falling behind my contemporaries. I was ambitious to climb in the Nigerian service; my experience in Aden wasn't helping me; in fact it was probably handicapping me.

A diversion in the cool weather of January 1951 was a polo tournament in Addis Ababa. This was great fun and teams from a number of East African Territories took part. The AOC Aden generously put his DC3 at the disposal of the Aden contingent and there were more than enough seats in the aircraft for the Aden team and reserves, together with supporters and all our saddlery. On arrival we were handed over to our hosts; I was to stay with the Deputy Police Adviser to the Emperor—a short, crisp and plainly very efficient character called Bill

Wright. Previously he had served for many years in the India police, reaching high rank; he was about fourteen years my senior. Unfortunately he had to go off on some important police business during the tournament and he only had time to say, "Use the place and servants as your own. Here's the key to the whiskey decanter. The cook has money to buy all the food you'll need. Have a good time," before he was off.

I wasn't to meet Bill again until a dozen years later in England when daughter Jackie married John Wright, Bill's younger son. Bill was then working in police affairs in the Home Office, little changed.

Addis in the fifties was very much the capital of the Kingdom of the Horse. Haile Selassie, the Emperor, was escorted on ceremonial occasions by a bodyguard mounted on Australian Walers. The Ethiopian Armed Forces relied for transport to a considerable extent upon the famous Ethiopian mules—bred out of Ethiopian mares by Kentucky Jack donkeys, the latter were often sixteen hands in height, really wicked beasts, requiring a posse of half a dozen men to prevent them killing the mares after service.

The last polo event was a match between the Ethiopian side and a team picked from the European visitors. The Ethiopians mounted us visitors, as they had throughout the tournament; as was to be expected, we suffered quite a handicap ponywise. However, one of the ponies allocated to me was a cracker; she was a little mare and I'm afraid I played her in three chukkas in that last match. Tired as she was in the third chukka she was better than any of the other ponies on offer.

One incident which firmly stays in my memory was the arrival of His Imperial Majesty on the field of play. There was a huge crowd. The two teams were lined up ready to be presented to the emperor. The Royal Pavilion was to shelter his Royal Highness. Custom apparently forbade the hoi polloi from gazing upon the seat that HM would eventually occupy—this was surrounded by screens.

We stood waiting for at least ten minutes, putting our weight first upon one leg, then the other. At last there was a great roaring of engines at the main gate and members of Haile Selassie's government arrived, each in a huge American car, the drivers impressively revving the engines. Round the polo field the magnificent cavalcade drove and, pulling up near the Royal Pavilion, each Minister took his seat.

Then, at the far side of the field, appeared a little, old, rather dilapidated 1938 or 1939 Austin which came straight across the polo ground to the spot where the teams were lined up. The Adviser on Police Affairs—another ex-India policeman and a very polished character—introduced the teams, taking care never to use the same

Royal Title twice running. "...Mr Hartley, O Lion of Juda..." "Mr Milne, Your Imperial Highness..." "Sire, Mr Gillon..." The small figure then hurried to the screens surrounding his seat; they were whipped away and down plopped the royal bottom, giving no time at all for the gaze of the multitude to pollute the Royal Chair.

That evening there was a very fine reception at the royal palace although I can't remember the Emperor himself appearing. All who had been associated in any way with the week's tournament were invited together with a great number of Ethiopian notables.

The guests, all of whom seemed to arrive in chauffeur driven cars, entered by the great palace doors at the top of a flight of steps. At the bottom of the steps, one on either side, sat rather miserably two somewhat tatty lions. They were moored to rings set in the steps by the thinnest of chains—the sort of chain one would have hesitated to use on a headstrong labrador, never mind a lion.

One of our team, Mike Gillon, spoke fluent Italian and was a great success with many of the Amharic guests, most of whom spoke Italian in addition to their native Amharic. Evening dress had been decreed for the reception and nearly all the guests conformed. Mike joined a group of Amharics who were drinking, as he was himself, the Ethiopian drink, Tedj, made from honey. All the group, save one, were immaculately dressed. The single exception rather spoiled the effect of his evening dress by wearing no shoes: his large bare feet protruding very obviously from below his evening trousers. For a moment Mike was nonplussed. Should he address him in Italian or what? His judgement temporarily deserted him and he tried pidgin:

"'Ee be fine stuff, this Tedj, huh?"

The Ethiopian gentleman lifted his glass to the light, studied it for a moment and then said in an incontrovertible Oxford accent: "Yes, indeed. Slightly akin to the Anglo-Saxon mead, I think."

Sadly I did not hear this exchange but Mike told the story and it went the rounds of Aden.

Our return journey in the good AOC's DC3 was marred by a somewhat dicey take-off. The two chaps flying the machine hadn't, I feel, done their arithmetic, for they opted to start their take off run from a turn-off well down the runway. It was a very hot afternoon. The density altitude of the 9,000 feet asl airfield must have been nearer 12,000 feet than 9,000 feet. The aircraft was full; it was plain we weren't going to become airborne in the distance available. They wisely abandoned the take-off but needed all the remaining runway to pull up. Using the full runway they got into the air all right at the second attempt although not surprisingly our climb performance wasn't particularly impressive.

———————

The Abyan Scheme was visited by a strong Secretary-of-State-appointed mission between 23rd January and the first fortnight in February 1951. The party consisted of G F Clay, Agricultural Adviser to the S of S, J F Cummins formerly Deputy Financial Secretary in the Sudan, Dr H Greene, Adviser to the S of S on Tropical Soils and G Lacey, Adviser to the colonial office on Drainage and Irrigation.

The Mission's terms of reference were wide. They were asked to examine the technical and agricultural problems that had arisen and to make recommendations for modifications in the existing organisation of the scheme, for the future development of areas brought under irrigation, for the establishment of appropriate research, and to advise on the future financing of the scheme in both the short and long-term.

Kat, who had acquired quite a reputation in Aden for her stenography, was made secretary of the mission. She later confessed that she had never worked so hard in her life. She'd spent the greater part of the last night before the Mission returned to England typing nine copies of the final version of the report. There were no photocopying devices in those days. She'd been helped throughout that night by an Arab messenger whose role had been to prepare each set of nine pages of typing paper with inter-leaved carbons. The heat had been so great that everything stuck to hands and arms—air-conditioning was still several years away.

On technical and agricultural matters the Mission relied heavily on the experience of Hartley and Congdon. I was involved as SPO in the area.

I learned a lot in terms of experience from the Mission, not least how a mission of that kind can be conducted. They eventually came up with no less than fifty-four recommendations for the future improvement of the project. I was mildly pleased to find that the majority of my own reservations regarding the conduct of the scheme were covered—without my having raised the matters specifically.

Had one possessed at that time an Olympian knowledge of the future of Aden and the Aden Protectorates, one's further comment might have been "Why put so much money and effort into what in a few years' time will be reduced to dust?"

(When writing the above passage in early 1998 I rang up the London Embassy of the Republic of Yemen and had an enlightening conversation with an officer who assured me he was a native of Aden town itself. He described recent developments in Aden, referring frequently to the sites of new cinemas, but told me he had never heard of an Agricultural Scheme in Abyan.)

The amoebic dysentery caught up with me again in the hot weather of 1951 after I'd done some thirteen months in Aden. Another full course of emetine was prescribed and I went into hospital in July. This time the curative drug had a marked effect and I remember little of the course of treatment other than watching a goat eating a discarded bandage out of the window of my room.

I was discharged from hospital at the end of July but ordered to take things very easily in my house for a fortnight. Kat reminds me that she had the downstairs telephone taken off the hook to prevent me going up and down stairs to answer calls on the published number.

In the first week of August a Caledonian line ship, on passage from India to the UK called into Aden. By chance there was an empty four-berth cabin previously booked from India to England for a family identical to ours who had been forced to cancel at the last moment. The Aden government decided to take it up and we were given rather less than twelve hours to pack up and get on board. Kat remembers she received the news in her office at 12.30 p.m. I was informed in the house a few minutes later. Kat, of course, was the heroine of the next few hours. She not only did most of the packing, bought English shoes and clothes for the young (they had grown rapidly in Aden) but she also arranged for an Indian tailor to copy a suit of mine using some light tweed that he hadn't been able to sell in Aden for the past dozen years. He finished the suit at eleven p.m. and brought it down to the ship himself just before we sailed. Kat also secured an offer from another Asian shop (a grocer's) to take back for what we'd originally paid all our unused tins of fruit and so forth. This was most accommodating of them and leaves a warm memory of unsolicited kindness, which we remember to this day.

As always the Aunts took us in; this time at the Cedars, Temple Sowerby, where they were safely—and I hoped finally—installed. The Cedars was a pleasant village house dating from the eighteenth century which had been owned previously by a well-known dog artist. The Aunts, having no use for his studio, turned it into a box room and thereby acquired a spacious spot that was not only easy of access but also well lit.

The leave before we'd made close friends with Mary and Robin Nicholson who owned Sleastonhow, near Kirkby Thore, the next village to the Aunts'. During the war Robin and his father had been tied to a family-owned engineering firm which had been fully turned over to Ministry of Munitions work. Mary had run a family farm nearby with conspicuous success. When we first knew them Robin's father had retired, the engineering firm had been sold and Robin was running the farm on Sleastonhow where he was building up a herd of pedigree shorthorns.

The Nicholsons were also old friends of Rosemary and John Milward. John was senior consultant in general surgery at a hospital in Derbyshire where he was highly respected for his wide interest in medical problems. Mary and Robin told him of my attacks of recurring amoebic dysentery and he was at once intrigued. I hesitate to try and convey anybody's views on such a multi-faceted subject as tropical medicine but I gathered that John had said something to the effect that if I'd been in the hands of tropical diseases experts for five years without alleviation it was time some less esoteric branch of medicine had a look at me.

He offered to do just that. Mary took him up on his word at once. The following weekend the Milwards stayed at Sleastonhow and we were asked to lunch. After lunch Mary said to John, "Take him upstairs and tell us what's wrong with him."

John examined me as well as the absence of medical aids permitted and asked a lot of questions concerning my medical history. "Shall I tell them what I think?" he asked. "Of course," said I. "Go ahead."

We returned to the drawing room and John said, "Well, there's one thing. He's got an appendix that must come out in the next week at the latest." He then described the trouble in technical terms. "When we remove the appendix," he went on, "we can make a proper examination of the intestines and see if the amebiasis has left any scars which may need repair."

The upshot was John got on the phone that afternoon and I was committed to an appendectomy in four days' time.

Because of the extensive gut examination during the operation the few days following in hospital were not very comfortable. Back in Cumberland I soon began to feel better. The colour of life changed and I never suffered from recurring amebiasis again. In later years flagyl came on the scene and the threat of long-term amebiasis was removed forever.

John Milward reported that the appendix was very much in the condition he'd anticipated. He'd had it thoroughly examined by his pathologist and found it "full of amoebic cysts". It was plainly the source of my reinfection. The gut, he added, showed signs of having been ulcerated but not sufficiently to require remedial attention.

His report alone made me feel better. I blessed the day Mary Nicholson had sought his help.

Kat and the young were none the worse physically for their sojourn in Aden. We found places for both young at Brackenbrough Towers School near Penrith which they attended as day pupils. The headmistress was a Mrs Johnson, a lady of considerable charm and character well known to Eric Arnison and other of my climbing friends in the District. She pointed out that John would soon pass from kindergarten to prep school age and she helped us to find a place for him the following year at Rickerby House Prep School near Ecclefechan just over the Cumberland border. We determined to have him with us for one more tour overseas but Jackie so fell for Brackenbrough that we arranged for her to become a boarder as soon as our next tour commenced.

Much of that leave was taken up with determining *where* my next tour was to be. Kat and I had firmly come to the conclusion that the Aden Protectorate was a waste of time. I immediately applied to revert to Nigeria and followed the application up with a number of visits to London: one was to meet Bill Goode, Chief Secretary of Aden; another to contact Ralph Grey who'd long been a colleague in Eastern Nigeria and was at that time acting as chief secretary of Nigeria; others to officials in the colonial office. Aden were short of staff and wanted my services for a second tour. Nigeria, particularly the Eastern Region I'm glad to say, wanted me back as soon as possible. I mentioned in the colonial office the initial misunderstanding regarding the wording of the secondment offer (PO Aden) but this was dismissed with the remark, "You mustn't hold a pistol to the head of the Aden government or everybody will be doing it"—a rather non-sequitur comment in my view.

At length, in January 1952, a firm decision was made that we should return to the Eastern Region of Nigeria. Sir James Pyke-Nott, who'd taken over from Sir Bernard Carr as Lieutenant-governor of the Eastern Region, wrote saying that he proposed posting me as Assistant Secretary (Intelligence) in his secretariat. This appeared an ideal posting: it would prove deeply interesting and I had no doubt it would give me a good opportunity to catch up on the two years of Eastern Regional affairs I'd missed.

Our actual return was delayed for another month by the chief medical officer in the colonial office who wanted to be assured that I was fit enough to resume work.

CHAPTER NINE

Regional Intelligence

John, Kat and I reached Nigeria on 12th March 1952 and I lost no time in getting to grips with the job. Kat, not having seen Kitty and Nigel for nearly two years, took John up to Jos for a visit.

Events elsewhere in the colonial empire, and particularly in East Africa, had demonstrated that the political intelligence and security systems which were then in place were inadequate. Colonial governments were being caught out. Remedial action in Nigeria involved the appointment of officers in each Region specifically charged with responsibility for intelligence matters. Their principal duties consisted of the preparation of political intelligence reports using material supplied by residents (fed in turn by DOs). Later, Joint Intelligence Committees, comprising representatives of the provincial administration, uniformed police, CID, and other sources of intelligence gathering, were to meet and report as a single body. The AS (I) would compile the resulting reports. The title of the post changed at least twice. It varied from AS (Intelligence) to AS (Political Liaision) but, being new, became what the individual incumbent made it.

A letter I wrote to the Aunts—which they kept amongst other papers in their newly acquired box room—gives an outline of the job, as I saw it. They, of course, knew Jim Smith, being unlikely to forget a wartime salmon he'd given them.

The Secretariat
Eastern Region, Enugu

5th April 1952

My Dear Kate and Alice,

I have just come back from a visit to Jim Smith—on business. My job here requires me to go and see all the Residents, every month if possible.

Jim Smith is Resident, Owerri Province and has a very attractive house in Owerri itself. Quite the Country Gent when I arrived at 7.30 p.m.; sitting in a bow window reading the airmail copy of *The Times* with a decanter in front of him.

Have been terribly busy—eight a.m. to seven p.m. daily—but should be easier shortly. And anyhow, the job's a pleasure and I don't mind the long hours. I carry rather a burden. Although the title is Assistant Secretary (Political Liaison) I am the *de facto* Chief Intelligence Officer and am expected, amongst other duties, to forecast disturbances before they occur and persuade the authorities to have the forces of law and order teed up ready to deal with them.

Just before we got back to Nigeria a real inter-tribal war broke out in Bamenda. 20,000 Widekums attacked 10,000 Balis, attempting to drive them from lands the former claimed and the latter occupied. Freddie Goodliffe, with a handful of police, managed to prevail on the attackers to parley for two days until troops and police could be rushed up. Even so some 2,500 houses have been burnt and many hundreds of acres of crops destroyed. Fortunately casualties were light—only sixty or seventy with about ten per cent fatal.

Freddy G did very well without having to fire himself. As you know the object always is to restore order without using firearms and to avoid bloodshed. It's a fine tradition and we are very anxious to preserve it.

It's more than kind and generous of you both to say that you'll lend us money to pay for a new car, but don't forget I'm entitled to a loan from government and in any case will receive a generous allowance on the car which will cover the cost of the loan.

Kat and John are expected down here tomorrow morning. It will be wonderful to have them back. They should be in the train at this moment…if all is well.

The new constitution—under which we have government by a cabinet of African Ministers—has resulted in a much improved atmosphere in the country. Racial antagonism—

which was stirred up by the Zik Press—is no longer so marked.

This constitution is supposed to last for five years but I fear it may not. Nationalistic agitation will start up again sooner rather than later. We seem to have entered a phase of accelerating demand for independence. I'd go so far as to say that in five years we may find Nigeria has Dominion Status. All this is a far cry from the feeling when we first came home in 1945; then the accepted thought was that Nigeria could look for another fifty or sixty years before independence.

But don't worry: I shall be eligible for a pension in five years' time and won't be too old for other employment.

Tonight I dine with Sir James and Lady Pyke-Nott. Bad luck Kat missing it but they didn't know she was coming back so soon.

Our heavy loads from Aden are said to be in England. I wonder when we'll see them? Have not yet decided whether to have a flat or a house here, both of which are on offer. Am waiting until Kat can see what's going.

Very much love,

Malcolm

Kat and John were in favour of our taking the top flat in a block of three. It was airy and cool and gave us splendid views over the station. There was ample accommodation for our servants at ground level and a lock-up garage for our car. The only snag was the sound-proofing; we heard rather more than surely we were meant to hear of the occupants of the flat immediately below us.

Late one night—it must have been after eleven p.m.—John, then aged seven, came into our bedroom and said, "I heard Mrs. X cry for help just now (the Xs occupied the flat below). Oughtn't we to do something?"

I'd heard the same cry and I didn't judge that it had been a cry for help but the moment didn't seem appropriate to explain the matter fully to John so I merely said, "She'll be all right," and we left it at that.

John attended a small "ad hoc" school in Enugu and we received good reports of his performance, particularly of his "leadership qualities." "Hmm," said Kat, "I think they mean he's compensating for not having Jackie to boss around."

Coincidentally, Jackie did christen him FAB when she came out for the next holidays. Asked what FAB meant, she explained, "Fussy AND bossy."

It was about this time that John acquired a bicycle with which he explored Enugu much more thoroughly than we guessed. Stories he later told us made us realise quite how much he'd learned of the Ibo way of life in the 1950s.

I even wonder now if he hadn't been pulling our legs about the cry for help in the night.

Kat was taken on as a temporary secretary-typist—which made a nice little addition to the family income—and to my delight posted to my office. Peter Gunning was acting as Secretary, Eastern Region at the time and was responsible for the posting. He obviously didn't give a toss for the element of nepotism involved; he rightly guessed that I'd get far more work out of her than I would have with some other temporary employee.

I was required to produce monthly Political Intelligence Notes (Regpins) which generally ran to about 7,000 words and Periodical Assessments (Regsums) at intervals of about three months. These latter normally were about 9,000 words.

We used to receive National Political Intelligence Notes (Pins) at fortnightly intervals from Lagos for the information of lieutenant governors. These could be shown to residents and officers i/c Districts visiting Enugu but copies were not to be entrusted to the postal services.

I also had to produce a monthly summary of the Eastern Region Press which generally ran to about 6,000 words. Here I had to invent a code word which was to be telegraphed confirming receipt of the document. I see that I used the names of mountains; Dom, Great Gable, Dru, Matterhorn…

In the years 1952-53 the following newspapers were published in the Eastern Region:

Eastern States Express	published daily by Dr Udoma in Aba. Circulation about 2,000.

The Nigerian Daily Standard	Published daily by the Old Calabar Press, Calabar. Edited by proprietors, particularly Barrister Okon. Circulation about 1,500.
Eastern Nigerian Guardian	Published daily by Zik's Press Ltd. Port Harcourt. Editor F O Ebuwa. Circulation about 2,000
Nigerian Spokesman	Published daily by Zik's Press Ltd Onitsha. Editor P C Agba. Circulation about 1,200.
New Africa	Published daily by Renascent Press Onitsha. Principal owner P C Chukwurah. Editor Nelson Ottah. Circulation about 1,000.
The Nigerian Observer	Published twice weekly by Eniton Education Stores, Port Harcourt. Editor Nana Dymonds. Circulation about 750. Somewhat ineffective.
The People	Published daily by People's Press, Port Harcourt. Editor Nwagwu. Circulation about 750.
The West African Pilot	The largest paper published by Zik's Press, Lagos, daily. During the political crisis in the E Region Azikiwe arrange for an air mail edition to be available in Enugu. 3,000 to 4,000 copies sold daily in the ER.
The Lagos Daily Times	Although published in Lagos the paper had a circulation of about 4,000 copies in ER. Best paper in Nigeria in terms of impartial and factual reporting. (Not Zik-owned.)

The population of Eastern Nigeria, including about three quarters of a million persons in the Southern Cameroons, was just over eight million in 1952. The total number of dailies sold, including those produced in Lagos, was about 7,000 papers of the Zik Press and 10,000 papers of other proprietors. On our return from Aden in 1952 I noticed changes in the Eastern Regional press, particularly in the Zik group. Prior to 1950 misrepresentations, attacks on individuals, bitter diatribes against the "Colonial" government were common. But these attacks lacked coherence. In the two years that we'd been away the Zik group of papers had shown a considerable improvement in presentation and effectiveness. They had outstripped the independently owned papers. They had always been anti-British, anti-imperialist and nationalist in tone. From about 1950 they had developed a new set of ideas which they pursued relentlessly. The first was freedom. The only possible aim for a Nigerian patriot was independence, immediate self-government. Nothing could be done, nothing achieved, until the day dawned..No thought was given to betterment of individuals or to training for the responsibilities that would follow self-government. A subtle corollary was the suggestion that Nigerians had no responsibility for what was being done in the interval. This was a damaging suggestion and did less than justice to successive constitutions from the Richards constitution onwards. I suppose it was originally conceived by Azikiwe himself...it certainly four years later provided a potent argument in the African Continental Bank matter.

Flowing from the suggestion that anything done prior to independence was not the fault in any degree of Nigerians was the conviction that everything that was patently wrong in Nigeria had been imposed on the country by the "Imperialists". Africans were an exploited race at the mercy of foreign vested interests. Self-pity has long been characteristic of West African disparate psychology (it has been said that the vein of melancholy running through Negro spirituals springs from the same source). The West African inferiority complex shared with other subject peoples was shamelessly played upon. A distinguished observer wrote in this connection: "...we must learn the technique of how to deal with the inferiority complexes of our colonial peoples—and chiefly by cultivating the quality of personal relationships with them which makes this kind of sensitiveness out of the question..."

A wrong-headed attitude to government civil service posts was deliberately inculcated. It was represented that the struggle for self-government was the struggle for posts. Every time a vacancy was filled by a European and not an African it was a step away from the ultimate goal. Merit and the dire need to educate African members of the service was lost sight of.

All who did not support the views expressed in the Zik group of papers were enemies of the true Nigeria. Members of the regional Houses of Assembly, and members of the national House of Representatives, were branded "government flunkies" whenever they advocated a less extreme line than that of the nationalist press.

Suspicion of government was constantly fostered. Nigerians must not trust the pronouncements of high-ranking officials however progressive the substance of their pronouncements might be. Communist Russia, and, for a short time in 1952, the USA were the only two powers whose colonial policies, so far as the Zik Press were concerned, were above suspicion.

The 7,000 daily circulation of the Zik Group papers made considerably more impact upon the Region than the 10,000 independents. The extreme nationalism that the former purveyed was heady stuff and much more exciting reading than the moderate and down-to-earth line pursued by the latter. In the month to 15th May 1952 a comparative study of the regional press clearly portrayed the moderation and realistic nature of the independent press. For instance foreign news items were selected with discretion and no effort was made to distort or magnify any particular item for propaganda purposes. Local news was factual and comment was generally moderate, although there were some sharp criticisms of government actions in one or two instances. Most editorials showed a sense of responsibility some being noteworthy in this respect. The new *Nigerian Daily Standard* wrote: "...Self-government must be preceded by development of the hands and minds of the people..." and added, "...we must be amenable to discipline and shake off the dust of cowardice and abstain from every form of deception, theft and corruption..." *New Africa* pursued the same thesis: "Self-government begins at home, if we cannot administer our village or town effectively, it is pretty certain that we will make a mess of administering the whole country." The proprietor of the same paper wrote: "...self-government must be earned by ability, efficiency and responsibility and not by noise and fury alone." An editorial in the more influential *Eastern States Express* stated "...to our minds what will ultimately determine the position of our country is not how soon or how late we begin to govern ourselves but how well and honestly we do so."

At about the same time emphasis was laid on the need for an increased tempo in rural, as opposed to urban, development and the need for women to become more active in politics.

The non-Zik Press occasionally was hostile to the colonial power. The Macpherson Constitution was said to be a device for muzzling nationalists by paying them high ministerial salaries. An editorial in the *Eastern States Express* in the middle of May 1952 pointed out that the imperialists' notion of self-government was self-government within the Commonwealth. This, the editorial went on, was not true freedom because the Dominions still remained subservient to the all-powerful "vested interests".

About this time Elspeth Huxley published a highly critical article in the UK *Sunday Times* entitled "Experiment in Nigeria". One moderate and well-informed Eastern Nigeria editor wrote: "...Mrs. Huxley's comments in this article are so acid, so cynical, so unfriendly that we are at a loss to understand what object she hoped to achieve by writing it." Several of my expatriate colleagues felt that, had she determined to do the maximum harm of which she was capable to the goodwill built up in the past two years, she could not have made a better job of it nor timed her efforts to better effect.

With hindsight we realise, of course, that she was right insofar as the succeeding fifty years were concerned. But did she not see beyond?

A factor which be-devilled politics in the 1950s in the Eastern Region—if not in other parts of Nigeria—was the inability of the populace at large to understand the difference between delegates and representatives as understood in Western Europe. They were able to comprehend the former. Delegation is wedded to the traditional African manner of conducting affairs. The NCNC Delegation to the UK in 1947 was at pains to point out that it had a mandate from the people of Nigeria. In Port Harcourt Mr Nwapa became popular because he was in the habit of asking members of the Ward where he was elected what line he should pursue on each motion before the council. In the Budget Session of the House of Assembly members spoke as though their function was to be the spokesman of their own constituency in spite of the fact that all had signed an NCNC party declaration and agreed to support NCNC policy at all times.

A quick reading of the preceding few pages might suggest that the life of the expatriate official in 1953 in Southern Nigeria had become intolerable...he was continuously subjected to vilification and misguided abuse. This was far from the case. In the years 1939 to 1961 I can only remember two occasions when I felt the other fellow was going too far. There was the incident with the road gangs in Bamenda recounted on page 235; there was a young firebrand in the early days in Nnewi before I was mobilised. Once or twice I'd had passages with him in Nnewi council meetings when I reckon he got the better of our exchanges. Ibo council meetings always tended to be quite fierce as the Ibo were renowned for their directness of speech. Doubtless what was said was toned down a bit by the interpreter but in any case discussions were on purely council business and the members were entitled to their opinions. Beyond these two incidents recounted above I really can't recall anything untoward.

All societies are in flux; Nigerian society in the 1950s, our own today. But there is little comparison between the rate of change. Today in Western Europe the media are all-pervasive—radio, television, the press, internet—persuade the mysterious X per cent to support your case and the chances are you're there. The pendulum swings too far and too fast. We veer from extreme to extreme.

The media in Nigeria of the 1950s consisted of the press alone. About one in a thousand persons came into possession of a newspaper sympathetic to their cause. Word-of-mouth—political "lectures", political meetings, general gossip and rumour—was far more important. It says much for the energy and acumen of politicians of the time that political parties were built up so quickly and effectively.

Nor must the disparate nature of Nigerian society be overlooked. There was a great time gap between a remote bush village and the relatively sophisticated groups in the fast growing townships of Nigeria. Most inhabitants of the remoter areas did not know how Nigeria was governed and had little idea of what independence entailed. But they voted, as some authorities have said, as they were told. I feel it more accurate to say "they voted as the masses voted, in the consensus direction".

There were other factors that prevented the life of the expatriate official—particularly members of the administrative service—from becoming intolerable. The Nigerian possessed in generous measure the readiness of the West African to laugh. One could often bring the most heated discussion to an end with a timely joke; the value of the joke was deemed more important in the general scheme of things than the original point at issue—and, who is to say that this is not a truism in many fields?

Again, the Nigerian, in keeping with many African peoples, has good manners. Understandably the precise usages differ from tribe to tribe and the sort of thing that we might demand of good manners in this country. But there is much in common between all systems and the crux of the whole matter is the attitude that holds that manners are important. The attitude of Nigerians I came in contact with was such that I used to advocate from my earliest days in Nigeria, quite seriously, that a mission in manners should be mounted by Nigerians to London.

As to promotions within the service; it was wrong to suggest that the struggle for independence was one with the struggle to Africanise the service. Although in 1953 a precise date had not been set for independence it was coming sooner rather than later; it was inevitable. The need was to leave Nigeria with the best possible service. It could be assumed that an independent Nigeria would wish to have a wholly Nigerian service. Regional public service commissions with a preponderance of African members were set up in the early 1950s. Later, when the federal nature of the central government was decided upon, a federal public service commission was also set up. The problem facing these commissions was to hasten the degree of Africanisation of the service and at the same time maintain standards. Merit remained the basic criterion of promotion. Promotions on such a basis could not be gainsaid by Africans or expatriates. Where two applicants of equal merit were vying for the same post, the African was selected. As time went on and independence approached, numerous devices to persuade expatriate personnel to stay on at least until independence were introduced. By and large the United Kingdom and Nigerian governments made a successful job of building a post-independence civil service.

It was about 1953 that officers of my length of service (fifteen years) were brought seriously to realise that we could no longer think in terms of a job for a West African working life but rather that we were engaged in a process of dissolution of the colonial empire.

Dr Nnamdi Azikiwe already played a major role in Nigerian politics in the early 1950s. In March 1953 I attempted to analyse his character as it was known to my colleagues and to myself.

Comparing what we thought of him then with his lengthy obituaries in The Times and Telegraph of 14th May 1996 there is little I would amend. Even the portrait photographs which accompany the obituaries are revealing. The Times' picture shows him aged somewhere in the middle sixties; a riven, driven and angry man about the time he abandoned the Biafrans—his own people. The Daily Telegraph photograph is of a much younger man, probably taken in his early fifties when he became the first premier of Eastern Nigeria. There is no doubt there of his intellectual ability or of his forcefulness and there is much to be learnt from those cold, far-seeing eyes.

I always believed (although I never could publish this belief as others didn't share it) that Zik's relationship with the West and with Britain in particular was affected to a large degree by his father's experiences in Zungeru where he worked as a clerk on Lugard's staff. Most men, black or white, could not fail to know Lugard well without acquiring an admiration (not necessarily affection) for him. I wonder if the effect of Lugard upon Zik's father didn't trigger a profound reaction in the youthful Zik. "We Africans are as good as that. I'll show them."

Azikiwe gave many expatriate officials the impression in 1953-54 that he simply hated the British. But I never could quite accept such a view. I felt then as I feel now that, although we British were in the forefront of his tirades against expatriates, his opposition to the British was a much broader and more complex matter. Perhaps he foresaw an enlarged (British) Commonwealth of nations as a possible rival to his own idea of the eventual emergence of a powerful Confederation of African nations.

He was always a vain man but in many areas he had much to be vain about. In his days in America he'd exhibited a considerable athleticism, boxing professionally at one time to help raise his university fees and he'd taken part in track athletics at a high enough level to justify an application to take part in the 1934 Empire Games—an application that had been refused on representations from the South African Team. On his return to West Africa he showed great skill first as a journalist, then as a newspaper proprietor and later as a many-faceted businessman. True, the financial stability of many of his enterprises in the Nigeria of the 1950s was dubious (so much so that it was not unfair for one observer at the time to comment: "He and his associates have little to learn from Hatry."). The financial relationship between the African Continental Bank (owned by Zik) and the Eastern Regional Government, led by Zik, was the subject in 1956 of a Commission of Inquiry which reported in terms critical of Zik (see Chapter Eleven).

The Commission of Inquiry mentioned above reported three years after my attempt to assess Zik's personality but there was no doubt in 1953 of his brilliance and intellectual power. In 1965 Dame Margery Perham described him in a broadcast as "a strange, brilliant, protean character from the Ibo forests". In 1953 we would all have agreed with her that "strange" and "protean" were apt but "from the Ibo forests" in his case was inaccurate. Zik was of Onitsha Ibo stock. The Ibos hail from Eastern Nigeria nearly all of which is high rain forest. But Zik himself spent his first eight years in Zungeru—far from the Ibo forests. He was educated in Onitsha, Calabar and Lagos—large townships remote from a village of the high forest. He worked as a young man in Lagos. At the age of twenty-one he went to the United States. He returned from the USA in 1934, at the age of thirty. He then worked in the Gold Coast and later in Lagos—again far from "the Ibo Forests".

Zik's personality was free of the influences of life in the high rain forest; he lacked the deep animism, the darkness, that a youth spent in the high forest nearly always left. This broadened him to a great extent, allowed his natural brilliance greater scope. He was often unpredictable, even to his Ibo associates.

He was without peer as a lecturer and orator and was able in the 1950s and indeed through his life to command in the ER, and indeed throughout Nigeria, a high degree of public support by his charismatic oratory supported by the outpourings of his press.

In the early 1950s Zik made large investments in property in Lagos, Onitsha and in Nsukka, probably as a form of insurance against the possible later failure of his commercial or political ventures. He built a house with a swimming pool—later founded a university—in Nsukka. He was to spend much of his life in the latter town. Nsukka enjoyed a slightly better climate than Lagos or Onitsha, being 1200 feet higher than either, but what other factors predisposed him to make his main place of residence there are not clear to me.

Following independence he succeeded Sir James Robertson as governor-general of Nigerian 1960 and later became first President of Nigeria from 1963 to 1966 when the country was declared a republic in 1963. He was always in favour of one Nigeria. As President he faced a major political crisis following the general election in 1964. The NCNC had boycotted the polling booths claiming that the census returns of that year were false. Although Azikiwe's sympathies lay with his own NCNC he nevertheless invited Sir Abubakar to form the government. He was deposed in the 1966 coup being wisely out of the country at the time.

In 1989 the *Daily Telegraph* published in error his obituary. Zik's comment was: "I feel ashamed to belong to a profession that could make that kind of blunder." *The Times* was able to remark, in his real obituary of 14th May 1996 "…it was a proof perhaps that even in old age he had not lost his capacity to sting."

Sting he always could.

Another task that came my way as Assistant Secretary (Political Liaison) was an attempt to measure the volume and effect of hostile propaganda circulating in the region.

Mao Tse-Tung had proclaimed the inauguration of the Chinese Peoples' Republic on 1st October 1949. From 1950 onwards Nigeria was subjected to a steady flow of Chinese propaganda communist in nature, most of it hostile to what Britain was seeking to achieve.

There was also a constant stream of communist propaganda from the USSR largely transmitted through Czechoslovakia which was damaging to British interests.

More surprising to officials at my level in government was the mass of material of American origin. This material was subtle but was damaging and indeed critical of British intentions in Nigeria. It seemed to be largely university generated: the universities of Columbia, Pittsburgh, Princetown and Massachusetts together with the University Commonwealth Studies Centre were variously involved. In general the tone of the propaganda suggested an overall jealousy of Britain's colonial record which we felt was hardly compatible with the ostensible relationship Great Britain and the USA in 1952. We had learned that there was a general understanding between our two governments that the USA would not seek to intervene in territories which had a colonial relationship with Great Britain.

We complained through intelligence channels about the American actions. Other territories must have done the same for an intelligence officers' seminar was organised at short notice in London to which all colonial IOs were invited. We were told that the seminar had two purposes: to assess the degree of US intervention throughout the colonial territories and to examine possible remedial action.

Reaching London I was annoyed to find that George Mallaby, then an under-secretary in the cabinet office, was chairman of the seminar. I had no right to be annoyed by Mallaby's involvement as I had never met him. However, I knew of him and had developed a profound hostility to him. Pure prejudice, maybe, but my school, St Bees, was involved.

Mallaby had been appointed headmaster of St Bees in succession to E A Bell in 1935. St Bees, in common with many other minor public schools at the time was going through a difficult period. I assumed, in common with many of my friends, that the new headmaster would serve a reasonable period, at least sufficient to put the school back on an even keel. But not so, Mallaby. He had accepted what must have been the first more promising job to come his way—that of district commissioner for the recently declared Special Area of West Cumberland—less than three years after taking up his appointment at St Bees. I know the school found Mallaby's early departure damaging and difficult.

During the war he'd served in the secretariat of the Cabinet running at one time the Prime Minister's Map Room. He seemed highly successful in placing himself in the way of the main chance and he was plainly a man of marked ability. Both these characteristics added to my prejudice against him; he should, in my view, have used that ability primarily in building up St Bees; headmastership, I considered then as I still do today, being a role for men of true vocation. Unfairly, unreasonably possibly, I harboured a hearty dislike of the man.

I'm afraid that some of us treated that 1953 seminar rather lightly. A visit in high summer to London for three or four days provided an enjoyable break from our normal duties and there was a festive air amongst us. The final session took place on a very hot afternoon after, so far as a few of my friends and I were concerned, a very good luncheon.

Mallaby opened the final session by reviewing all that had gone before. He outlined accurately enough the degree of American intervention. He then propounded the United States' views; on the one hand this, on the other hand that. It seemed to many of us that he was warning us that the United Kingdom government would take the view that we had no choice but to accept the antipathetic propaganda.

The meeting went again into general discussion. I was awakened by a roar of laughter. Apparently I'd gone to sleep and Mallaby had spotted it. "Mr Milne, you don't seem to be very interested in your colleague's remarks..." he was saying.

Without thought, as one seems to react on such occasions, I replied, "You covered it all very comprehensively, if I may say so, in your opening remarks. I can only, perhaps, add the warning contained in the Hausa proverb, "she ya sa kafa a grigi biu parta karia", which can be best translated, "he who puts foot in two canoes splits arse". (The words "parta karia" can be quite explosively spat out.)

The laughter was with me.

Although our life in West Africa was often illuminated by flashes of wit, the occasions when I can claim to have been the author of the witticism are few indeed. In fact I can think of only one other incident where I can claim some credit.

One of the steps taken to strengthen the security systems in colonial territories was to send Major General Dunlop, in 1953 Adviser to the Secretary of State on Security, on a tour of inspection of African territories. Dunlop was a crisp, hardworking man whose mind was full of the various devices for improving the systems we had and in particular for increasing the security of key documents.

For security—rather than prestige—reasons the office in which Kat and I worked was adjacent to Peter Gunning's (Secretary, Eastern Provinces) office. There was, in fact, a connecting door that Peter generally kept locked.

My office possessed two pretty secure safes in which we held documents of high security rating. There was one document, which by special instruction was kept in Peter's safe and this was the master copy of the Regional Defence Plan. Dunlop had duly inspected all the documents held by me and had expressed himself as satisfied. He put great store, however, in inspecting the master copy of the Defence Plan. He wanted to go through its contents and check the security of the safe in which it was held. He'd been badgering me to make an appointment with Peter since his arrival.

Peter, who used to make light of the ordinary pressures of work, was really pressed at the time. Every occasion I suggested an appointment with Dunlop he merely groaned. Finally on Dunlop's last day in Enugu I arranged for them to meet at ten a.m.

Dunlop duly turned up in my office at 9.55 a.m., looking at his watch. Seeing that ten a.m. had arrived he said, "He promised ten o'clock and ten o'clock it shall be." Striding to the communicating door, he knocked briefly and, finding it unlocked, marched through.

There was no sign of Peter. But the master safe was wide open and a bunch of keys on a bright chain were hanging from the lock. Needless to say the precious Defence Plan lay prominently in the safe.

"My God, my God," said Dunlop, "I'm going to dine out on this for the rest of time."

"No, no," said I, "it's only Peter's sense of humour."

Kat, who'd joined us through the communication door, obediently laughed, lending veracity to my lie.

Dunlop spent an hour with the Defence Plan sitting at a table in Peter's office. At length he expressed himself satisfied and I locked up in his presence as ostentatiously as possible. There was still no sign of Peter.

Later that morning Peter told me that he really had been tied up with HE and a minister and it truly had not been possible to let Dunlop know...even if he had remembered Dunlop's appointment.

Labour problems in the Enugu Coalfield had troubled government ever since the first colliery had been opened in 1915. The coal (a sub-bituminous, non-coking variety) had nevertheless played an important role in both world wars, a railway connecting Enugu and Port Harcourt having been built primarily for the coal in 1915-16.

In 1952-53 three collieries were in operation in the Enugu coalfield: fifty per cent of the production was absorbed by the Nigerian Railways.

Coal had been exported to other parts of West Africa—and occasionally to places outside West Africa—but demand had fallen off since World War II largely because of the high production costs and irregular deliveries due to strikes. In 1953 the pit-head cost had risen to £1-17-5d—a high figure.

When I took over as AS (Political Liaison) in 1952, total coal production in 1951 had been 548,000 tons—a figure increased to 700,000 tons in 1953.

The Enugu coalfield was a particularly sensitive area in those years largely because of an incident in 1949 when the Nigeria police in dealing with a violent strike had been forced to fire and had killed twenty-one striking miners and wounded another fifty-one. Many high officials criticised the authorities on the spot of having over-reacted to the perceived threat. The Nigerian Coal Corporation—a statutory corporation—was formed in 1950 to take over the assets and liabilities of the government department previously involved. One of the most forceful and realistic members of the new corporation was L O Ojukwu. Naturally, there were strains between the Coal Corporation—whose primary duty was to operate the collieries at an economic level and to increase coal production—and the Government of the Eastern Region, then in the process of transferring power in a steadily increasing degree from expatriate to Nigerian. Again there were strains amongst the miners themselves, the interests of the underground workers often differing from the interests of the surface men. As both groups were represented by the same union—the Coal Miners Union—understandably disputes between them added to the difficulties.

Presidency of the Coal Miners Union was a much sought after office, for experience had shown that the incumbent could do pretty well for himself provided he stuck to a basic rule for keeping his members happy. And that was, of course, to show them from time to time that he had procured an improvement in their conditions of employment. They would even tolerate some temporary diminution in take-home pay provided he could prove that at the end of the day there was an overall improvement. The favourite weapon was a "go-slow" and Diewait—the President in 1952—became skilled in using it.

I don't know the derivation of the name Diewait. It certainly isn't an Ibo name, probably "manufactured", bearing as it does connotations of death and destruction. Nor was Diewait himself a nice man; during the war he had been implicated in the murder of a British officer in India; he had later incited and taken part in a mutiny in Burma; later still he had served a prison sentence for assault in

Bende and had been dismissed from the Faith Tabernacle in Umuahia for embezzling the funds. But he was a dynamic speaker, a successful demagogue. His weakness was that he was something of a moral and physical coward; he was inclined to hesitate or even flee at the critical moment. Nevertheless he exercised considerable influence in Eastern Nigeria particularly during the time I served as AS (PL). I see that he was mentioned in every PIN I wrote during that period.

About May 1952, Diewait and the union executive had employed a local barrister called Nwosu to advise them. Nwosu had nearly died of consumption after qualification in the United Kingdom and had spent some months in an iron lung in a South London hospital. He was believed to have harboured feelings of gratitude to the British for the kindnesses bestowed on him during his treatment and this may well have been so for there was a change in the union's tactics for the better at this time. The general objective of securing the maximum benefit for the men at the risk of a "go-slow" was maintained, but the tactics pursued by the union adhered much more closely to those employed in the UK and were more easily understood by the expatriates employed in the Enugu coalfield. Nwosu's appointment was welcomed by government and a significant improvement in colliery management/miner relations followed.

The differences between the two factions within the union suddenly came to a head round about the first week in March 1953. In the last PIN I wrote before going on leave on the 17th April 1953, I was able to report that Diewait's faction had lost ground and recognition had been withdrawn from him and his friends. He had, in fact, been offered fresh employment as Time Keeper in the Public Works Department in Onitsha, a hundred miles from his cronies in the coal fields.

At the same time as the Coalminers Union was splitting, the governor himself was faced with two really major political—more correctly—constitutional problems. Following political manoeuvres in both the Nigerian House of Representatives and the Eastern House of Assembly both Eastern and National governments were paralysed.

Sir John Macpherson was visiting Enugu at the end of March 1953 to discuss both matters with Clem Pleass. The latter had given him a number of background papers to read prior to their discussion. Amongst these papers was a political appreciation I'd just written on the Eastern Regional matter. I got it back from Sir John marginally annotated. It was revealing to note what points had caught his attention at that hectic moment in Nigerian affairs.

In the Nigerian House of Representatives, Anthony Enahoro (AG) had tabled a motion seeking the attainment of self-government for

Nigeria by 1956. The Sardauna of Sokoto proposed an amendment changing the wording to "as soon as practicable". The Council of Ministers, by a majority decision, decided to support the Sardauna's amendment. The four action group members of the Council of Ministers resigned their portfolios on 31st March so that they would be free as ordinary members to support Enahoro's original motion. The NCNC members in the House of Representatives split over the issue. The party's four central ministers decided loyally to support the Council of Ministers' decision (to accept the Sardauna's amendment). In the event a dilatory motion was proposed by an NCNC floor member "that this debate be now adjourned". This was carried.

The NCNC and AG ordinary members then walked out of the chamber and the constitution affecting the central government was paralysed.

In the Eastern House of Assembly Dr Azikiwe had regained by March 1953 much of the political ascendancy he had lost since the inauguration of the 1951 Constitution. On 21st February 1953 the ER Appropriation Bill was put back by forty-four to twenty-five votes, the twenty-five including the six special or official members. The ER Ministers were called upon by their party, the NCNC, to resign, but refused to do so. While this situation continued, the ER Government was also paralysed. The constitution did not provide for the dissolution of a regional legislature except on a dissolution of the centre. However, the constitution was very soon amended and on 6th May the Eastern Legislature was dissolved.

Nevertheless, the "high ups", as dear Jack would have called them, were a jump ahead and on the 21st May Mr Lyttelton, S of S, announced that a conference of the three regions would be held in London to provide for faster regional autonomy and to discuss the constitution.

The conference was held from 30th July to 22nd August and recommended that a number of subjects should be allocated to a central federal government and that there should be a small number of concurrent subjects. All other subjects should be vested in the regional governments whose legislation should no longer be submitted to the central executive.

We were on leave throughout the summer and had to rely on the national press in the UK to keep abreast of Nigeria affairs.

The Aunts once again took it for granted that we would spend our leave—or the greater part of it—with them. They had settled down well into Temple Sowerby. It was a friendly little village and, although the A66 passed through it, the Cedars stood well back from the road and the traffic noise wasn't oppressive. The Ainscows, father and son, ran the small medical practice based in the village—Daddy Ainscow the Aunts had known as a tennis player from the pre-war years when they were at Lynwood. His son, Donald, had married the sister of Mary Nicholson so we had a tight little nucleus of friends and Temple Sowerby was very much home to us.

On our first morning John was late for breakfast. It transpired that he'd spent the two previous hours doing the round of his friends in the village. The Aunts were a little put out, at first, having had to wait for him, but he made amends by his recital of village news. In those two hours he'd learned more of village doings, scandalous and not so scandalous, than the Aunts had learned in the past two years. They pretended at first to be shocked by what he had to relate but Kat and I were amused to see how very interested they really were in all that he'd unearthed.

Jackie loved her school and couldn't wait for the commencement of the summer term. It was suggested to her that she should revert to being a day girl while Kat and I were on leave but she wouldn't hear of it.

John on the other hand, was a different proposition. He saw nothing but the darkest of clouds ahead. With Jackie's headmistress' help we'd secured a place for him at Rickerby House prep school that summer term. Kat and I felt that he'd take to prep school life more readily if he spent his first term with us in the country. But no. Although not yet nine he had very firm ideas about his personal freedom. In Nigeria, and earlier in the Cameroons—ever since he could remember—he'd been free to wander where he would and talk to whom he pleased. He found great interest in people—a characteristic of the Victorians, and possessed by both Jack and my father—and he valued his independence highly. The thought of a closely supervised life at a prep school appalled him and he made no secret of the fact.

The last week, as he felt, of freedom with us all at the Cedars was no fun at all. So much so that when the first day of school at Rickerby came, I funked taking him there and, full of cowardice, left it to Kat. While I went climbing with Eric Arnison Kat borrowed the Nicholson's Ford Estate and took John to Rickerby House.

Poor John; we were told later by the headmaster and his wife that he'd been inconsolable for the best part of a week. As Kat drove away down the drive John followed her at full gallop, Mrs. Richardson (the HM's wife) bringing up the rear. At length she cut John off and suggested he go and see the boys' guinea pigs.

"I don't like bloody guinea pigs," said John.

"Well, the garden," suggested Mrs R.

"I don't want to see your f-ing garden," replied John.

Later, when I quite gently took him to task for using the f-word he said, "Well, you use it and I know it's a strong word."

John became head boy of his prep school before he left. Right from the age of eleven or twelve he knew what he wanted to do in life and that was to become an expert on the land—on everything connected with it. Right through his prep and public school days, and beyond, he concentrated his learning in this direction. For example, there was a master at Rickerby House who was an accomplished ornithologist; knowledge of birds and all appertaining to them was more than just an interest to him. John early on spotted this and assiduously cultivated this chap. Doing so he built up a sound grounding in a subject ·that , although perhaps related to the land, is nevertheless seldom mastered by agronomists.

I am not surprised today-forty-odd years on-that he is recognised as an agronomist of rare breadth of vision and considerable depth of knowledge.

CHAPTER TEN

First Superscale Post: Acting CDS

Towards the end of our leave I had a letter from Peter Gunning, then still acting as Secretary, Eastern Provinces, telling me that E R Chadwick, the Community Development Secretary, had been very ill with trypanosomiasis (sleeping sickness) and although he was recovering, would not be able to resume duty for some months. There was even a possibility that he might be retired on medical grounds. Although the Community Development Training Centre at Awgu had continued in the hands of I C Jackson, the headquarters post had been left vacant while Chad was sick.

Community development in the region had continued to be encouraged in the hands of district officers and residents. Chadwick's post as CD Secretary had been graded two steps above a normal head of department to accommodate his rank at the time...he was a staff grade officer. The suggestion was that I should take over but I wouldn't act in his exalted personal rank: I would act in Grade II on a par with other acting heads of department in the Region; fair enough in the circumstances.

I was substantively in the Long Grade which carried annual increments of salary and was designed to accommodate an officer for nineteen years. I had served fourteen years but in common with other of my colleagues of like service was beginning to hope for an acting appointment in the superscale—which Grade II was.

I had considerable reservations about succeeding E R Chadwick who was recognised as one of, if not the leading practising expert, on CD in the colonial empire. I also harboured doubts about the philosophy of the CD movement itself. But I was loath to miss this opportunity of acting in (and probably substantive promotion to) a superscale post. I was a professional administrative officer supposed to be able to turn my hand to anything that was established as an administrative function. I was determined to see what I could do.

Peter Gunning had also warned me that the headquarters organisation, partly because of Chad's personal methods of working and partly because of his absence sick, was in a pretty confused and chaotic state. He gave me Chad's London hospital address and suggested that I should arrange a take-over in London before I returned to Enugu.

Chad—as everybody called him—was thirteen years my senior in age and had joined the service in 1927. He had gone through the administrative service mill, working in many Districts in Southern Nigeria, securing promotion to SDO after nineteen years' service. He'd subsequently been promoted Resident and then Senior Resident (Staff Grade). Many administrative officers found a particular area of their vast miscellany of duties at which they excelled and which particularly interested them. Chad's, needless to say, was the self-help movement. Bernard Fagg, a same-year colleague of mine, became immersed in antiquities; and Colin Hill in NA finance—there were many examples.

Chad had devoted much of his time as CD Secretary to travelling and to work on the ground with communities involved in CD projects. When he had time to commit his findings to paper his writings were pure gold. The organisational, the administrative side of his work, had languished somewhat.

Thinking about the job ahead, I saw my role as probably being twofold. I would collect and try to write up as much of Chad's philosophy as could be recovered. Secondly, I would seek to bring the promotion of CD into the ministerial orbit. There shouldn't be great difficulty about this as Chad in the past had worked in consonance with African opinion and the self-help movement, community development…call it what you will…was held in high regard by all political parties. I didn't know it at the time, of course, but I was soon to work under Dr Esen as the Minister responsible, after 1st October 1953, for Community Development. More about our relationship later but it was to be a thoroughly enjoyable one.

As to my doubts about the Nigerian self-help movement in general…we are touching here on a vast area of community behaviour, the problems of which have been with us in Europe for over a thousand years. Many of the fine parish churches, for instance, which so enhance the British countryside, were really the product of community development of the time. The whole field of charity activity, in fact, comes within the same ambit. In my own time in Nigeria the self-help method of securing infrastructural development was always greatly uneven, although attitudes could also change rapidly in the same spot. The Nnewi Improvement Union in the early days of the war was unremitting in its demands for contributions from "sons abroad" who were wage earners. It was not unusual for young Nnewi workers to be "required" by the Improvement Union to contribute as much as one third of their salaries. Understandably poll tax and later income tax diminished somewhat the readiness of all citizens to contribute voluntarily to local development.

By 1953 it had become widely accepted in many parts of Nigeria that the activities of government alone would not provide in the foreseeable future the infrastructural needs of the area. Many communities felt the need for, say, roads and bridges, schools and water supplies to be so pressing that they would rather provide these perceived essentials by local effort than wait for government to fill the need at some problematic time in the future. In such cases as these, the self-help movement was obviously valuable and I felt duty bound to assist. But in areas where doubt existed, where life was basically hard enough without further demands on the time and energy of the inhabitants, I felt that it was unjustifiable to try to persuade the communities to undertake more than they already were forced to tackle. After taking over from Chad I visited Nkambe District in Bamenda Province. There I came on a road project three days on foot away from the nearest motorable road. The remote communities were determined to build a road into their area. But a gang of women working on the project told me that they'd been three days walking to the place of work from their village. They would work for three days and then walk back home. Nine days for three days' work done. It seemed far too much. My heart bled for them.

Returning to 1953: I arranged a brief take-over from Chad at the end of our leave, late in the year. He was still very unwell. Possibly the powerful drugs that he'd been taking had affected him and he complained more than once about his deafness. He'd always been slightly deaf and had discovered that a continuous background noise helped his hearing. For this reason he insisted that we meet on Euston Station; we talked with the noise of steam trains in the background. It may have benefited him but it made things difficult for me; I hardly heard a word he said.

I remember Chad regaling a group of us in the secretariat before he became ill with a story that he told against himself. One of his objects in the community development field was to build up communities' pride and satisfaction in their self-help achievements. He hit on an idea of invoking the aid of the Regional Information Service cinema unit. This unit was under the control of A G Ridley, Director of Information and a splendid officer, always ready to turn his hand to any proposal, however unorthodox, which might strengthen the cause of government. Chad suggested to him—and he immediately accepted the idea—that rural communities should have film records made of any unusual and worthwhile community project.

A village in the Udi District, badly in need of a village school, health centre and new market planned to construct these projects by self-help labour. Chad and Ridley arranged to have the whole thing filmed: the first clearance of the site, the construction of the one and a half miles of road into the area, the construction of the buildings and so forth. The final ceremony, when a VIP opened all four projects, was also filmed. The last few feet of the final reel recorded a party of chiefs escorting the VIP up the new road.

The object was to enable the village to hold a magnificent cinema show; to see themselves on the screen and to ask their friends from nearby villages to savour their achievements. The nearest commercial cinema was in Enugu, twenty-five miles distant. Few of the participants in the CD project had ever been to the cinema, much less seen themselves and their neighbours on the screen.

Chad, of course, attended the showing. It was a perfect night. The whole village, more than 8,000 souls, turned up. Their numbers were increased by about two thousand from neighbouring villages. There were so many present that viewing had to be arranged on both sides of the screen. Chad was congratulating himself that he'd come up with a really effective aid to the spirit of self-help. The final shot was of the body of organising chiefs slowly coming up the new road. They appeared nearer and nearer on the screen. The elderly senior chief of Udi Akebe could be recognised limping slowly along. The audience one moment grew silent, the next they disappeared; melted silently into the warm darkness and were gone.

The last few feet of film passed through the projector, only Chad and a few sophisticates from the Department of Information remaining.

"What the hell was that?" asked Chad. "What happened?" Someone told him. The Chief of Akegbe had died the previous week and nobody in the audience was going to let him approach any nearer.

Kat and I flew back to Nigeria in January 1954. Kat spent the first few days with her parents on the Plateau and then joined me in Enugu. We were waiting for the allocation of a permanent house and in the meantime took up quarters in number thirty-seven—one of the chalets attached to Enugu Catering Rest House. The accommodation consisted only of a double bedroom, a tiny dressing room and a sitting-cum-dining room but we felt that without the children (who were of course, at school in England) this would be ample for the time being.

There were so many outstanding matters to deal with in CD HQ that I hardly knew where to begin. There had been a gap of over ten months without a senior CD officer and papers had continued to flow during this time. Heads of registries had done their best to keep the departmental files but each needed careful scrutinising to spot important papers "languishing" as it were in the files and requiring urgent action. A filing system to meet the requirements of the new ministerial set-up was also needed.

An equally important task was the tracing and dating of Chad's important contributions to the subject. He had relied a lot upon word-of-mouth exhortation; his written papers were few but all his notes and other writings were of long-term value and I was anxious they should not be lost.

So far as work on the ground went, residents and district officers had continued to encourage the self-help movement during Chad's absence; some, obviously, with greater success and enthusiasm than others. All this activity needed recording.

One of the problems facing officers in the field was to keep pace with constitutional change. The degree of ministerial responsibility had increased during the past year; further changes were shortly due. It would be necessary—as I'd foreseen when first warned about taking on the job—to involve my minister as commitedly as possible and to devise in consultation with him arguments for securing the backing of the Regional Government.

Records that I was able to trace showed that in the four years 1949-52 the following total of self-help projects had been achieved:-

983 miles of motorable roads
211 water points either constructed or improved
130 markets reconstructed
115 village primary schools
58 maternity units
54 village halls
43 home craft training centres
64 villages to segregate leper patients

The Onitsha District considered itself an "average" CD District and an assessment had been made of the position there on 1st April 1953.

This amounted to eighty CD projects in progress to a total value of sixty thousand pounds (nearly one million in today's values). The schemes included water supplies, roads and bridges, maternity units, postal buildings, soil erosion projects, and water tanks. Village primary schools—the need for which was so generally accepted at the time that there was hardly a village without a school completed or in hand—have been excluded from the figure of sixty thousand pounds.

Measured by the standard of Onitsha as an "average" CD District Ahoada was without a doubt a "good" one. Stan King had been Acting District Officer, Ahoada for upwards of four years.

Lieut Colonel W A S King MBE had at one time during the war been the youngest Lieutenant Colonel in the British forces. He was then commanding a battery of heavy AA guns in Hyde Park. This battery was one of the first to possess women officers and I remember Stan telling me that Mary Churchill had been on his strength. Sir Winston had apparently used Stan's command post to view two or three of the German raids on the City of London. Appointed to the colonial service in 1947 Stan King brought the same energy and leadership qualities to his work in Eastern Nigeria as he had exhibited in the army. Feeling in Ahoada was strongly in favour of the self-help movement but unfocussed. The local populace felt the need for many kinds of project but were uncertain where to start and on what projects to concentrate. Stan King provided the leadership they lacked, helped them to clarify their objectives and to plan ahead. He had a broad streak of Rabelaisian humour in his makeup which appealed to their own sense of humour; they developed a deep dependence upon him and wouldn't hear of his transfer out of the District.

Some of Stan's contemporaries and even his superiors felt he was overdoing the CD component of his duties and neglecting other important aspects such as the improvement of NA procedures, native court matters and so forth. But with so much to do—and so much left to the initiative of district officers themselves—I believed that a certain unevenness was inevitable. There were DOs and even residents who didn't set any store by the self-help movement and there was little I could do to remedy the situation. So I asked myself why carp about the antithesis?

Kat and I travelled pretty extensively in the months of March and April of 1954 visiting Awgu, Onitsha, Nnewi, Awka, Udi, Aba, Ikot Ekpene, Owerri and Okigwi. At each place I called on the DO or resident, discussed CD problems and saw as many projects in operation as time permitted.

It wasn't all that easy. I was very sensitive to the fact that Chad had performed the same task from the height of his personal rank…he would have been senior to everybody he talked to. Many of the SDOs I met probably knew more about the self-help movement than I did. I tried to measure each officer's personal knowledge of the subject and his commitment, and took notes of any schemes or devices he had which might be of interest to officers elsewhere.

Not all government funds available for expenditure up to 30th September 1954 had been spent. It behoved us not to "go to bed" with these monies for if we did the next year's allocation might be reduced. They hadn't been spent, of course, because there had been nobody available to make the necessary judgements which normally would have fallen to Chad. We didn't want to make any quick decisions. It took some time to assess a list of projects and select those truly worthy of help. On the other hand we didn't want to lose the funds in aid which played a valuable role so, with the Lieut-governor's knowledge, I distributed sixty per cent of the funds amongst the best CD Districts with instructions to the DOs to keep them on deposit until we had prepared a list for assistance. In modern values we accumulated a fund of about half a million pounds in this way.

Chad's HQ in the Enugu Secretariat had been provided with a government vehicle and driver. The driver was a short, strongly built Owerri Ibo called Mark Eze, then about thirty years old. He'd come up the hard way, having started as a "driver's mate" on a "mammy wagon" plying the Onitsha-Lagos route. There was little about the mammy wagon business that he didn't know and as we drove about the Eastern Region he constantly regaled Kat and me with snippet after snippet of information.

There was a huge trade in Nigeria in the years immediately following the war—and even earlier—conducted largely by three-ton lorries. The chassis and engine were imported but the bodies were locally constructed. Naturally the bodies differed from area to area but they had one thing in common: nearly all were capable of carrying twice the normal legal burden. These vehicles were a constant hazard on the road. Many of the main traffic routes such as those connecting Enugu to Onitsha, Aba, Owerri and Port Harcourt, and equally in the other two Regions of Nigeria, exhibited at least one lorry skeleton per mile.

Kat and I, on a journey from Lagos to Ibadan on the tarmacadam road as it was then, came on an accident which almost unbelievably had left five mammy wagons jammed abreast across the carriageway entirely blocking it. The accident had occurred on a hilly tortuous stretch of road and we could only imagine two vehicles racing abreast in each direction had suddenly come upon a fifth lorry.

Nearly every mammy-wagon carried a slogan painted in large lettering on the headboard above the driver's cab. Often this was repeated above the tailboard. Mark explained that in most cases the slogans were exhortations from the lorry-owner to the driver. Less frequently the slogan was by a driver of some renown to his master, the lorry-owner. Examples in the second category were: "WE-WE; SENIOR WE-WE; NO PROFIT IN RASCALITY; BETTER BE LATE THAN THE LATE". Exhortations from the lorry-owner to the driver included: "NO SWEAT, NO SWEET; REMEMBER SIX FEET; NO TELEPHONE TO HEAVEN;" and many others.[5]

We used to encourage Mark Eze to explain the precise meaning of the signs. "WE-WE" apparently referred to the many Ibos serving during the war as drivers in the West African Pioneer Corps. These men found it easy to get jobs as drivers after the war and used to gather in the same drinking places at towns on the lorry routes where they used to night-stop. They always referred to themselves as "We, we ex-service men." "Senior We-We" was a well-known character. He'd been a sergeant in the Pioneer Corps and was greatly respected. The charisma of his army rank stuck to him.

"No telephone to heaven" was a prime example of an owner's advice to a driver. "It's all very well you driving recklessly, going over the Khud and then telephoning me for my help," would say the owner to the driver, "but wait until you have a serious accident and kill yourself. You'll find there is no telephone to heaven."

(I venture to use it as the title of this book. The words carry a secondary meaning. The colonial service was always very much on its own. District officers in particular, often far away from their headquarters, were sometimes forced to make quite big decisions with reference to no one…just to get on with it.)

I can't remember the make of the vehicle Chad had bequeathed but I suspect it was American. It was a kind of minibus from which he had removed all seats except the first two, bench type. The space behind enabled us to carry ordinary rest house loads and office equipment.

Mark Eze seemed to have friends everywhere we night-stopped and was never at a loss for accommodation.

Catering rest houses, as opposed to bare rest houses where you had to see to your own meals and travelling equipment, were

---

5   M C Atkinson, author of the excellent *An African Life* has published a full list of lorry slogans.

gradually being introduced especially in the main centres. Kat and I used them increasingly as time went on. Travelling as much as we did in 1954-55 we hesitated to ask DOs and others to put us up. There was provision for passing "guest of government" allowance over to one's host but the vote was limited and in any case there was a marked financial advantage in drawing travelling allowance for oneself which of course one could not do if "guest of government" allowance was also drawn.

One morning Eze reported for duty just after first light. We must have been setting off on a day's travelling. I noticed he was silent and looking grey and drawn as, indeed, Ibos can look. I said facetiously to him, "What's the matter with you? You look like death warmed up."

I saw him stiffen at my asinine reference to death (never a subject for humour amongst Ibos) but he came straight out with it: "Senior We We has had it. He went over the khud last night and died."

"Poor chap," I said contritely.

He saw my sympathy was genuine and later told Kat the ill news, unprompted.

We had an accident while Mark Eze was driving which was singularly akin to the incident described on page 45. Whether it was caused by a genuine mechanical failure or whether Mark Eze himself was in some way responsible (perhaps I'd unknowingly angered him by something I'd said) I shall never know. It happened a few miles north of Owerri on the main road from Onitsha. There was, for those days, a fair amount of traffic—we met another vehicle at least every mile. We were moving at forty miles per hour or so down a section of road bordered by thick subsidiary jungle with roadside shade trees planted at roughly five metre intervals. Mark Eze was driving, me beside him and Kat on the bench seat behind us. Seat belts, of course, were not used in those days. We met and crossed a lorry coming from the opposite direction. Suddenly our vehicle plunged across the road to the right and came gently to a rest ten yards or so into the jungle. We had passed neatly between two shade trees. Had we hit either we would have suffered major damage. As it was our sudden deceleration did bring Kat over into the front compartment and left Mark and me plastered against the fascia panel. But, as I've said, none of us were hurt.

Once again (I remembered the Awka incident) the fault was a failure of a steering link. I recollected Mark Eze unavailingly turning the steering wheel to the left as we plunged across the road.

Maybe it was a genuine accident...maybe...maybe. We all know that Pliny, many thousand years ago, commented, *"ex-Africa semper aliquid novi,*" but some observer of equal sagacity might well say, "Much that comes out of Africa we shall never truly understand."

There were always far too many mammy-wagon accidents. Most were caused, it's true, by the attitude of the drivers and drivers' mates. Give them a little palm wine and the power and the speed intoxicated them entirely. We have more than once seen the driver's mate standing on the right hand step of the vehicle fighting with the steering wheel while his master, the driver, sits slumped in the driver's seat, seemingly drunk with a heavy foot pressed down on the accelerator pedal. (The agonised cry of Kitty Cooke's mentor—"take your foot from fire, Madam"—assumes a new urgency as I write this.)

A major cause of accidents on self-help roads was related to bridging. The Eastern Region was well provided with streams. The builders of self-help roads could manage spans up to twenty to twenty-five feet but for wider bridging points they resorted to piles. This type of bridge was beyond them and there were resulting accidents, some involving fatalities. The solution of the problem of dangerously insecure bridges had to come from within the CD movement itself. It was not possible or desirable to legislate against insecure bridges. We couldn't have the public claiming that the colonial government was prohibiting development.

I realised early in 1954 that the answer almost certainly lay with a United Kingdom firm named Engineering and Industrial Export Ltd which had offices in Grosvenor Square, London. This firm had bought up great quantities of military equipment immediately after the war including the whole available supply of ex-RE Bailey Bridging. The sale and supply of the bridging had been entrusted to a subsidiary firm, Thos Storey Ltd, whose sales office was in Victoria, London. It was they with whom we dealt using the good offices of the Crown Agents for the Colonies.

Major S C Riggs, a newly-appointed development officer, who was at that time in charge of the Awgu Community Development Training Centre, had served in the REs during the war and was an expert in the use of Bailey bridging. Give him the span and the maximum load for the bridge and he would prepare, with the Crown Agents, a detailed order for all the items required, from basic panels down to such minor details as swaybraces and button stringers.

We had, in fact, everything to hand to fulfil a long-felt need to improve bridging on CD roads: local populations desperately keen to open up their areas to lorry traffic who themselves possessed a local capability of building properly designed masonry abutments, a ready means of ordering and shipping the necessary bridging equipment, and central funds to pay for the material ordered in the United Kingdom. And, almost to paint the lily, the West African Engineers were prepared, as part of their training, to camp in the area of a new bridge and actually assemble and launch it.

Riggs was capable of designing the abutments. It soon became almost routine for the locals to provide either the labour for, or the cost of the abutments. The Bailey bridge system thus developed, was handed to Hon Minister on a plate when he took office in October 1954 and he accepted it without question.

Shortly before the formation of the 1954 government, when I'd already placed several orders for Bailey Bridges and was generally deeply committed, I discovered to my horror that a cousin by marriage, a chap called Hempsal whom I'd never met, was principal shareholder of Engineering and Industrial Exports Ltd. I was dealing with a relative, surely quite unacceptable in the colonial service of 1954. I asked for an interview with Clem Pleass and said, "I'm afraid I've made a fool of myself dealing without knowing it with a cousin." He heard my story and then chuckled. "Forget it," he said.

In August 1954 a conference on social development was held at Ashridge between 3rd and 12th August. The vast buildings and gardens, dating from the sixteenth century, had been donated to the nation by the trustees of Urban Broughton in 1928 as a college of citizenship in memory of Broughton's great friend, Bonor Law. The surroundings were superb, the conference well organised and the paperwork was kept to a minimum but even so I felt that I was attending on false pretences. Social development is a wide term embracing a myriad of approaches to social problems, much of it well wrapped in esoteric language. I'd come from Eastern Nigeria where only thirty years before there had been tribal social systems in place developed over the previous 1,000 years or more. Naturally the introduction of economic systems based on western European lines were creating pressures for change but what kind of change? We simply did not know. We needed to learn more of the systems we already had before advocating change.

I'm afraid I felt that my time at Ashridge would have been better employed in promoting one water point in Eastern Nigeria than in listening to a large number of professional and semi-professional sociologists propounding sociological theories, some with a colonial tinge maybe but all with precious little pertinence to what we were trying to achieve on the ground.

Long before Ashridge, Chad had agreed a definition of community development as it applied to Eastern Nigeria: "a movement designed to promote better living for the whole community with the active participation and on the initiative of the community."

In the same paper first issued in 1951 by Chad, he had emphasised that the initiative should come from the people themselves but if it is not forthcoming spontaneously it could be stimulated by a number of techniques. He had also pointed out that the movement knows no boundaries of department and embraces all forms of betterment. He added "the modern conception of CD revolves around the three pillars of local initiative, community effort and co-operation."

Chad's directive had assigned responsibility for CD to the provincial administration and provided for the training of government staff at the Awgu CD Training Centre.

When Chad first became ill he was concerned by the problem of local leadership within the CD movement. He had left notes on the subject pointing towards possible policies for the Man O'War Bay Training Centre in the Cameroons. Awgu, of course, was designed to provide training in techniques required within the movement—matters such as the design of Bailey Bridge abutments, design of water points, building techniques and so forth but leadership per se was a different matter and here Chad's thoughts were turning more and more towards Man O'War Bay.

Soon after taking up the appointment of CD Secretary in the Eastern Region I wrote to the Outward Bound Trust in the UK seeking advice on leadership within the self-help movement. Spencer Summers MP replied and suggested that I make contact with T G Bedwell who, he knew, was interested in exporting the Outward Bound idea to the Commonwealth and colonial territories. Contact with Tom Bedwell was a lucky move for Nigeria at large and for me personally, for his help and advice were of immeasurable assistance to us.

Kurt Hahn, later the headmaster of Gourdonstoun School, Moray and Tom Bedwell had set up a naval wartime pre-entry school at Aberdovey. In 1941 Lawrence Holt of the Blue Funnel Line invented the name Outward Bound Sea School and secured the financial support of his company for the venture at Aberdovey. Character training through seamanship was the principal objective of the new school.

The Aberdovey Outward Bound Training School had proved so successful during the war years that Tom Bedwell, Julian Holt (brother of Lawrence Holt) and Kurt Hahn expanded the work of the Outward

Bound Trust after the war. By 1950 some five OBT establishments were functioning in the United Kingdom.

Man O'War Bay in the Cameroons under United Kingdom trusteeship was the first Outward Bound type training establishment to be set up in West Africa. It was situated three miles from Victoria and reached by a rough track. The jungle came down to the rocky and highly indented coast. Man O'War Bay itself had taken its name from the days of anti-slave-running patrols. British naval vessels would anchor there, hidden from the open sea, in readiness to pursue British, French, Spanish or Portuguese slavers operating in the vicinity. There were disused buildings ashore which were gradually adapted to the school's use. The 13,500-foot high Cameroon Mountain, the summit of which could be easily seen from Man O'War Bay on a clear day, was only a few miles inland and lent an air of dignity and serenity to the scene.

The sea provided a ready means of training. It was a novel adventure for many Nigerians who had spent their entire lives 500 miles from the sea to acquire minimum seamanship skills—equally it was no mean experience for all Nigerians, no matter from where they hailed, to explore the upper slopes of the Cameroons mountain and to be subjected to temperatures below freezing and to the effects of rarefied atmosphere.

Eric Shipton, the mountaineer and writer whom I had met en route from Achimota to Nigeria, had taken over the Easkdale Outward Bound School, and Eric Arnison was on the committee of management. Because of my interest in mountains and my contacts with the Outward Bound School in the Lake District I had been associated with Man O'War Bay from the outset and was a member of the Nigerian Controlling Committee. The CD Secretary was an ex-officio member of the committee so in a sense I had a double responsibility to the organisation.

As to Tom Bedwell himself: it was only after he'd stayed with us for some time in Eastern Nigeria that we were able to learn something of the power and influence that he exerted in the UK. For instance he was a close friend of George VI, whom he had first met when Prince Albert (as he was then) and he were fellow cadets at Osborne. Later he'd helped run the Duke of York's camps. Keeping up the friendship, he'd known the present Queen and her sister Princess Margaret since they were children.

A measles epidemic at Dartmouth had affected Tom Bedwell's eyes and he'd had to leave the Royal Navy. At the outbreak of the First World War he'd served in Churchill's Naval Brigade and after the defence of Antwerp had been captured and interned in Holland.

Paroled he'd become British Vice Consul in Rotterdam. Between the wars he'd formed with Claude Bell the firm of Bestobell which he was later to control. At the outset of the Second World War he'd rejoined the navy and was immediately involved with pre-entry training. He'd had close contact with the Aberdovey Sea School from its start and had become a founder trustee of the Outward Bound Trust. He kept up his interest in the Outward Bound Trust, became a governor of Gourdonstoun School and was on the founding committee of the Duke of Edinburgh's Award Scheme.

Characteristically he had constantly refused honours and awards throughout his life.

The help he so generously gave me lasted the whole of the time I was CD Secretary and included, amongst many other matters, drafting the Man O'War Bay School pamphlet. Even by today's standards *Outward Bound to the New Nigeria*, the ten page pamphlet aimed at a purely Nigerian audience, and describing the activities of Man O'War Bay, is a small classic.

What's more Tom Bedwell's efforts on behalf of Man O'War Bay and social development in the Eastern Region were all performed at his own expense. This amounted to a considerable gift in itself. He stayed with us twice and his airfares alone were no small sum.

I learnt a lot from Tom Bedwell. We travelled widely in the Eastern Region. Alone with him I found he was a person of very firm opinion which he didn't hesitate to propound. He was, however, a great respecter of chains of command and in public was most punctilious not to appear opinionated. He had the gift of so presenting a problem that in the end the recipient, rather than he, came up with a solution. The better I got to know him the more inclined was he to talk strongly about matters on which he felt deeply. With hindsight I wonder now if in 1954 he was not already beginning to show signs of the asbestos-induced illness of which he was later to die. He was twenty years older than me and being physically an energetic person I must have proved a stressful companion for him. I noticed that he had to ration his energy very carefully.

The morale of expatriate members of the public service was low at this time particularly amongst officers of about my seniority. A number of us had been working hard in superscale posts, most Grade II—head of regional department level—for a year or more without securing substantive promotion to the post. Independence was approaching at an accelerating speed; many of us now thought of half a dozen years at the most. Acting appointments did not affect our pensions, substantive rank did.

In my own case I began acting as CD Secretary on 22nd January 1954. It was not until 1st July 1955 that I received a formal offer of promotion to the post. There was a further delay while it was confirmed that the substantive promotion would be effective from 1st October 1954. Although the uncertainty and delays affected several of us equally, and were brought about by the rapid changes in constitution rather than by any decision of the governor of the region and his immediate staff, we nevertheless found them upsetting. The longer the delay the greater the chance that one might make some error to block the promotion. I say this because I did make a mistake which I felt at the time could perhaps be used against me by a public service commission obviously wishing to promote Africans rather than expatriates.

I've mentioned (page 317) that when I took over in January 1954 I found the CD records in pretty chaotic condition. One of the missing items was a stores ledger. Amongst other quite valuable items handed over but not recorded were two cameras worth then about eighty pounds each. I duly entered these cameras and the other items in a new stores ledger but not very long afterwards one of the cameras was stolen when we'd been using Mark Eze's vehicle. It had been on top of our luggage in the rear of the vehicle and was probably stolen through the open window when we stopped at a roadside market. I considered myself responsible for the loss. Rather than report it and establish a board of inquiry (which would doubtless have judged me part responsible) I simply replaced the camera with an identical one purchased in the United Kingdom. The replacement with postage and customs, cost me over ninety pounds (at today's values about £1,500). Perhaps this was a cowardly action but I felt that nothing should be allowed to affect my substantive promotion (worth in today's values about £8,500 p.a.).

From October 1954 until I went to Lagos in December 1955 I worked as CD Secretary within the ER Ministry of Welfare to Dr E A Esen, Minister of Welfare. One's formal relationship with the Minister was modelled upon the procedure which had been built up in the UK over the years for the cabinet system of government. Approaches to the government by means of cabinet (Exco) papers, and overall policy matters were the responsibility of the permanent secretary to the ministry. Within settled policy and in the formation of new policy heads of departments were encouraged to work very closely with their ministers.

The publicity opportunities and the bulk of the work falling to the minister were mostly in the field of community development so that

I saw a lot of him-a good deal, in fact, more than did the permanent secretary. Later in Lagos I was to act as the Permanent Secretary of the Federal Ministry of Health. There I found that the head of the principal department falling within the ministers' province-the Director of Medical Services-a strong-willed, very experienced and effective African named Dr Manuwa, who never even bothered to discuss cabinet papers with me before putting a final version prepared by him on my table for my signature before submission to cabinet. I must confess that I acted in rather the same way in the Eastern Region with the PS of the Ministry of Welfare.

Dr Esen, my minister, was a dear chap. After qualifying in Edinburgh he'd gone into private practice there. Someone—I can't remember who—told me that his practice had been in the poorer section of the city. I gathered that he was a good medical man by any measure but my interlocutor told me that he had a double appeal in the slums of Edinburgh. Many of his patients thought that being black he must be a master of occult practices in addition to understanding European medicine. They perhaps felt they were hedging their bets in going to him. Whatever the truth Esen harboured a genuine affection for the European and he was quite unmoved by the hostile excesses of the Zik Press although he must have been equally adroit when dealing with Zik's party for he was recognised as a loyal member of the NCNC.

Immediately after his appointment as a member of Zik's government he disappeared for several weeks. The party office said he was on a political tour; his African staff told me his recent appointment as a Minister had boosted his status as a medical man and he was busy dealing with a number of well-paid consultations that had unexpectedly accrued. Perhaps it was a matter of

The Truth as usual lies between
For truth herself is seldom seen.

When he did turn up in his office in Enugu I'd accrued about fifty files, on all of which I badly needed his instructions. "I'm awfully sorry, Minister, but..." and I warned him there would be two or three days' work involved.

He eventually made an appointment from me to bring the files along to his office on a Friday afternoon. Just before we were due to meet he rang up and said, "I've got a delegation of constituents here and I guess I won't finish until late." So I proposed the following day, at midday. "May I suggest you come along to my house where we won't be disturbed and we can have a Star while we grapple with the files." Star beer was a quite excellent locally brewed beer, a product of a Nigerian subsidiary of Heineken's, and of interest to both of us.

We duly met. The formidable pile of files was on a table Kat had got ready for him.

We plied through files 1 to 4 in about an hour and to the accompaniment of two ice cold Stars. Esen then threw file number 5 onto the floor. "Malcolm," he said, "you know my mind now. You deal with these," and he pointed to the rest of the pile.

I mustn't give a wrong impression of Esen. He was no fool at all and he was blessed with a deep race-embracing sense of humour; I'm sure the Efiks—his own people—were just as amused by his sayings as were the people of the waterside at Leith or wherever it was that he had practised. He travelled a lot and remembered what people had said to him. He also had a great facility for mastering and carrying in his head the essentials of a situation.

Launching Bailey Bridges provided wonderful opportunities for publicising community development and the minister's part in the movement. It had become increasingly the practice for the local community to build by community effort the approaches to and the abutments for bridges. The steelwork for the bridge would be paid for by government in lieu of grant-in-aid and the bridge itself could be launched either under Major Riggs' supervision or by a unit of the RWAFF engineers. We held a spare "launching nose" at the Awgu Training Centre which was available for each launch.

It was no small matter to ensure that the timing was right: that all these elements were in place on the launching day. This task fell to me.

The steelwork could be assembled in three to four hours by a trained team of engineers. Attached to one end was the launching nose—a lighter projection of the bridge itself the far end portion of which was cocked up at an angle sufficient to compensate for the sag as the nose was pushed across the gap to be bridged. The weight of the bridge was sufficient to compensate for the turning movement of the nose. Once the nose, followed by the bridge, was pushed across the gap the nose was dismantled and used again.

Esen, on his public appearances, invariably wore Efik robes but he affected two European additions—a blackthorn walking stick and a white straw hat. These two objects became closely associated with him. The hat was always immaculate and I guess that at one time he must have bought half a dozen.

On one formal opening of a bridge—I can't remember where—all had gone well to the point where the launching nose was about to ride up over the far-side abutments. Esen then said to me, "I hope, Malcolm, the locals have carried out their share? Paid for both abutments and approach roads?"

As a matter of fact they hadn't. About three weeks before the opening ceremony had been arranged they had said to the DO, "We are very tired and want a rest before we collect the money for the second abutment."

I'd got everything in place and rather than postpone the ceremony I'd told the DO to pay on condition the village promised to reimburse him the cost involved. This he'd arranged.

So I was forced to confess to Esen that there was still £1,500 in cash owing.`

"Stop," he ordered. "Stop. Pull the nose back." He then said to the councillors: "We won't launch this bridge until the £1,500 is paid."

There were cries of lamentation. At length the elders asked if they could discuss. They gathered in a group. There was the usual furious verbal set-to common amongst the Ibo. It seemed no decision could possibly be arrived at. Suddenly there was silence. The spokesman said, "Give us until three o'clock and we will have the money."

Dr Esen said we would return at precisely three o'clock. This we did and they had the money albeit in small coins. It took the DO and Major Riggs quite a time to count but it was there all right.

We left the bridge across the gap before dark.

Jackie and John flew out for the school holidays while Kat and I were still occupying Chalet number thirty-seven. Jackie had the tiny dressing room; John used Swynnerton's tent pitched in the compound.

The Corona Society played a helpful role in assisting the young through London on their way to join their parents in the various colonial territories. By a lucky chance holidays for both of our two coincided and it was possible for them to travel on the same aircraft.

So excited were we at the prospect of having both kids with us again that we slept very little during the week preceding their arrival. The aircraft from Heathrow to Kano in Northern Nigeria carried so many holiday-bound young that it became known as the "Lollipop Special". The name stuck throughout the fifties. John spent most of the journey out—we were told—with a gang of his male contemporaries, some bound for Kano others for Lagos. Jackie, more sophisticated, had asked to be shown the flight deck and had formed a close relationship with the flight crew. Perhaps she'd been recommended as an amusing companion by one air crew to the next for she spent most of the journey, Kano to Enugu, in the company of the captain of the local Kano-Enugu aircraft. At Enugu she devoted her first moments on the ground to paying a suitable farewell to the crew of the aircraft—only then did she greet Kat and me.

The school holidays passed appallingly quickly and it seemed no time at all before they were due to return to Kano by local aircraft and thence onwards to London. On the day before their departure we asked them to choose the menu for luncheon and both opted for palm oil stew, a thoroughly satisfying West African delicacy. It was a Sunday; during the morning John and I joined a group of climbers on Juju Rock. He tied on as number three on my rope and between us we had a very attractive, newly arrived bride. Like dear Gravy in Bamenda some years back this good lady wasn't really properly dressed for rock climbing...she was wearing the briefest of shorts. We climbed steadily all morning each party completing four or five of the short routes. John climbed well but, I noticed, was very silent, apparently absorbed in the climbing. On the way home in the car he said, "You know, it was very interesting watching X climb in those shorts. I learned a lot."

We'd acquired a massive thirst with our efforts. John went straight to the fridge but complained he couldn't find a cold squash. "Have a Star, old boy," I invited. He didn't wait to be asked twice and taking out an ice-cold Star downed it at one go. "Boy, that was good," said he and seized another, most of which he swigged.

Lunch arrived and Dilla, knowing John's liking for palm oil chop, served him first. He took an enormous helping, piling his plate high. Suddenly he rose to his feet, placed one hand each side of his heaped plate and said to Kat, "Keep this damned table still," adding, as he staggered off to his bed in the Swynnerton tent, "And keep the palm oil chop for me later."

Elsa Hughes-Jones stirred up one little luncheon party at Chalet thirty-seven without, I feel sure, really meaning to. Kat and I were giving a staid and very proper luncheon to Major and Mrs Riggs and their ten-year old daughter. Both Kat and I knew that he, and doubtless his wife and daughter, were highly religious and of an austere way of life. He was a great help to me and we took pains not to damage their susceptibilities.

The Hughes-Joneses were old friends of ours. We'd first come to know them in Bamenda where he had launched, and subsequently run, a government ranch at Jakiri. He was a Veterinary Department Development Officer appointed just after the war. Elsa, in her unmarried days during the war had enjoyed a walk out with a cousin of mine, a little escapade not known to some of my family.

In the early 1950s the H-Js did another fine pioneering job about seventy miles NW of Bamenda just on the Nigeria side of the Cameroons-Nigeria boundary. Here there was a 4,500' to 5,000' uninhabited plateau about 200 square miles in extent. During the rainy season a few nomadic Fulani herds of cattle reached the area but there was grass to spare. Government decided to establish a ranch on the plateau as an incentive to settle some of the Fulani; and who better qualified to set it up than Viv and Elsa H-J?

Development funds were made available to extend the motor road from Obudu twenty-five miles to the foot of the plateau and eventually up the escarpment to the site chosen for the ranch itself. Funds were also provided for a ranch manager's house and to establish the kraals, dips and fencing for the ranch itself. Viv supervised the road, house and ranch construction and Elsa played a full role on the ranch. At first they lived in a tent; after a few months they graduated to a small timber house which Viv constructed. Later Viv built a very pleasant stone ranch house and converted their erstwhile timber residence into a hen house. I'd kept the area in mind because Chubb, who knew the Obudu Plateau well, had once told me that the tongues of forest, creeping up the valleys towards the plateau level, were the homes of extended families of mountain gorillas, probably the last left in Nigeria.

Elsa occasionally descended on Enugu from Obudu. She could do the journey in a day once the road up the escarpment had been built. She was always welcome, no matter which of her many friends she descended upon. Life on the Obudu Plateau bore little resemblance to the drawing rooms of Mayfair or even to the slightly stilted dinner parties of Enugu. We all had come to take Elsa's racy manner and colourful vocabulary for granted.

She breezed into our small luncheon party for the Riggs' with a cheerful, "I'm bursting Kat, where can I go?"

I said quickly, "Straight thorough the bedroom. I'll show you."

Elsa hearty as ever said, "I'm not going into the bedroom with you, Malcolm. You'll rape me."

It was a bit of light hearted bandinage to her, and to us, but oh dear...the Riggs' responded with frozen faces. Only the young daughter showed any interest. I could imagine her asking her parents later, "What did that funny lady mean by rape?"

John was always fascinated with Elsa and paid several visits up to the plateau to stay with Viv and her, long before my CD days. Because she rode everywhere, he took to riding, too, although he never became enamoured with horses as Jackie did. I remember John on a pony called Kali (the Hot One), aptly named, whom he rode on a very tight rein developing hefty biceps in the process.

We recall too, John describing how Elsa almost certainly saved a herdsman's life. Leopards were always a pest on the Plateau, breeding in the patches of forest on the edge of the high ground and taking young calves. So much so that Viv was forced to kraal breeding heifers and their calves separately, putting the young calves into a specially secure kraal with a man on guard all night.

To enable the calves to be separated from their mothers the herdsmen left a four feet length of rope attached to a hind leg. They used to get hold of the rope and drag the calves off to their kraal each evening.

In one herd there was a singularly dangerous heifer. She would attack anything that came near her calf. On that particular evening Elsa and John were sitting on their ponies watching the process of separation. The evil heifer was some way from her calf. Taking a chance a herdsman got hold of the rope and dragged the calf towards the kraal. The mother spotted what was happening and charged. The herdsman let the calf go and it tried to rejoin the mother but she ignored· it and continued her charge. The herdsman ran; feeling the heifer was overtaking him, he stopped and faced her, brandishing his heavy staff. She took absolutely no notice and came straight at him. At a range of six feet he flung his staff hitting her accurately on the nose. On she came. He tried to side-step her, slipped and sprawled on the ground. She was on him in a trice, jumping on him with all four feet and trying to horn him on the ground. Elsa, digging her heels into her pony and whacking him fiercely with her stick, rode straight at the heifer, hitting her a real thump amidships. For a brief moment the heifer staggered back and the herdsman scrambled to his feet taking refuge behind Elsa's pony. For the next thirty seconds or so Elsa and pony pivoted while the heifer pursued the herdsman. Then several of the nearby herdsmen gathered and drove the heifer off. She started to graze as though nothing had happened.

John was convinced that, had Elsa not been there, the herdsman would have been killed.

Elsa and Viv retired from Nigeria after a few short years, both, we believed, having been left tidy sums, and bought a farm near Ledbury. Elsa became a stalwart figure with the Ledbury Foxhounds running their pony club for many years; but foolish girl, she chain-smoked and was often laughed at for her croaky voice. Dying of a heart condition in her early sixties—her thoughts as it were running ahead a little—she suddenly said to Viv, "Don't you dare bury me on a hunting day."

"Part in friendship—and bid goodnight."

What else? Dear friends...

———————

Zik wrote to all the ministers of his government in July 1955, asking for a full account of each Ministry's activities. Of course, permanent secretaries were told to draft the replies and the PS Ministry of Welfare and I put our heads together and produced a reply for Esen. Rather to my surprise he considered the draft very carefully and made one of two alterations all of which were highly pertinent and each an improvement. The CD policy that had been built up over the past four or five years in such close association with the community leaders was acceptable to Zik's government. All of this was very much the foundation that Chad had laid. He'd also made a further contribution which emanated almost entirely from his own thinking: he'd analysed the movement carefully and correctly and had lit on a number of factors which acted rather like booster pumps on a long pipeline; he'd identified a list of these incentives. They were of general application throughout the Region. Examples were such things as regular mentions in the local press, passing references in ministers' speeches dealing with other subjects, opening and completion ceremonies for projects, cinema shows (the Udi incident on page 316 excepted), simultaneous celebration ceremonies amongst sons abroad and at home.

Bailey bridges were accepted as a spectacular means of replacing dangerous timber constructions and consequently were as popular with ministers in Enugu as they were with the beneficiaries.

It was noted that a works pool of such equipment as saw benches, block making machines and tipper trucks was being built up at Awgu where operators were being trained by Riggs. Machines from this pool could be loaned to deserving projects.

The importance of co-operation, exemplified by the activities on combined CD and training missions of the Royal West African Engineers could also easily be publicised.

In October 1955 I was offered transfer to the Federal Public Service. The intention was that I should take over as Acting Chief Administration officer, Lagos a post currently held by "TX"—let us call him—who was about to go on leave preparatory to retirement. I was wanted as soon as possible in view of "TX's" imminent departure and the impending arrangements for the Queen's visit to Nigeria in January and February 1956.

Cuthbert Mayne and Peter Gunning were acting as Governor and Deputy Governor respectively of the Eastern Region at the time. They said they wouldn't stand in the way of my transfer because of Sir Clem Pleass' oral agreement to let me go if offered an opportunity, but they were adamant—quite understandably from their point of view—that I couldn't be spared until 19th November at the earliest. A relief for me wouldn't be in Enugu until 12th November and Chinn, the S of S's Advisor on Social Welfare was coming to Enugu about 15th November and had asked for me to bring him up to date on ER community development matters. Further, CD grants moneys were ready for distribution and it wouldn't be fair to ask my relief—who wouldn't know the history of the projects involved—to make recommendations for the distribution of grants.

"TX" in the meantime had decided that he wanted to be involved in HM's visit and had used the delay in my arrival to get his own tour extended. He was five years older than me and traditions of the service forbade my making a fuss. His decision to stay on meant, however, that I would have to serve for longer than anticipated as his deputy.

PART TWO

CHAPTER ELEVEN

The African Continental Bank Ltd

At this point in the narrative I must stray from my own part, such as it was, in the scramble for Nigerian Independence—and the doings of the Milne family—and try to sketch one of the major problems that afflicted my superiors. I was too junior at the time to be directly involved but all of us at Regional head of department level knew roughly what was going on. The fuller story of the African Continental Bank Scandal has come into my possession bit by bit over the years but I am particularly indebted to Michael Pleass—Sir Clem Pleass' son—for letting me have a copy of the African Continental Bank chapter from his father's at present unpublished memoirs.

The starting point is a visit to Nigeria by a mission from the World Bank in 1954 which pointed out, in the Banking Section of the Report, that European banks were playing virtually no part in developing local, African entrepreneurship.

One solution was to strengthen African-owned banks but the mission argued against this on two grounds: many African-owned banks in Nigeria were inadequately financed at the time. If they advanced large loans to individuals on the strength of deposits of government moneys a dangerous contraction of credit would become necessary when government began to spend its reserves. Secondly, transfers to African-owned banks would not be free of political motives. This second comment was already justified.

Dr Azikiwe, the premier of the Eastern Region, was principal shareholder in the African Continental Bank. The Eastern Regional Government had no sooner taken office than it became very persistent—and on occasions deceitful—in transferring government funds to the ACB.

An additional complication was present. A federal form of government had been introduced for Nigeria, operative from 1st October 1954. Banking had become a federal subject. Banks were required to hold a license and the ACB was not licensed.

The Licensing Authority was the Financial Secretary of the Federal Government. He was reluctant to license the ACB on grounds of its unsatisfactory financial state. Government funds could not be transferred to the ACB in any event until it was properly licensed. Undertakings by the ACB staff were made, however, and, on the understanding that the ACB would receive a substantial injection of overseas funds by the end of January 1955, a license was promised by the financial secretary.

Because banking was a federal subject the future of the ACB was not solely a matter between the Governor ER and Premier ER It involved also the Governor-General and his staff and behind them the Secretary of State himself.

On 17th May 1956 Mr E O Eyo, previously chief NCNC whip in the Eastern House of Assembly, who had seemingly fallen out with Dr Azikiwe, tabled a motion in the EH of A, recommending that an independent commission of inquiry be set up to inquire into the circumstances in which government funds had been invested in the ACB in which the premier had an interest.

The Eyo motion in the House of Assembly, set for 26th June 1956, was blocked when it was shown that Dr Azikiwe had filed a writ of libel against Mr Eyo and the matter, being *sub judice*, could not be debated.

However, the Secretary of State (the Right Hon Alan Lennox-Boyd) himself intervened and set up a tribunal of inquiry to inquire into the whole matter on the 4th August 1956.

The S of S's tribunal reported its findings on 20th December 1956.

So far as I know nobody—Nigerian, British or even American—criticised at the time any of the tribunal's findings as being prejudiced. The tribunal certainly reported unanimously and within its terms of reference. But a moot point, deriving from differing attitudes concerning standards in Nigeria and the UK, did arise.

It became plain as the tribunal progressed that the findings and subsequent action by the Government of Nigeria against Dr Azikiwe would have to be determined by new thinking on the matter of standards.

The S of S had laid down in a dispatch dated 1st December 1951 the standards that he expected ministers in colonial territories to observe. Observance of these standards was cited as a condition precedent to further political advance. Every minister was made familiar with them at the time he was appointed.

The Foster-Sutton tribunal in arriving at Finding No 4 stated that they were guided by what they conceived to be " the standards of right-thinking citizens unbiased by their political opinions".

Legislation made in the United Kingdom but bearing upon Nigeria in the latter's colonial status used the same term.

Sir Clem pointed out that Dr Azikiwe could maintain that a general election would provide an adequate test of what was and what was not an acceptable standard. At the same time he was confident that Azikiwe would win any election held to determine the validity of any matter concerning the ACB.

It followed that any action—so far as it was not criminal—concerning the ACB would be judged acceptable by the " right-thinking" citizens of the ER.

Put another way the ACB matter was weighted on Azikiwe's behalf and a potentially insoluble problem lay ahead.

Knowing that the S of S was contemplating himself setting up a commission of inquiry the ER Exco advised Sir Clem Pleass to appoint Mr A V Savage, an acting Puisne Judge, as sole commissioner. Sir Clem acted as advised but was informed by the S of S that his action was *ultra vires* because the inquiry would relate, at least in one part, to banking and banking was a federal subject.

ER Exco disagreed with the advice that had been tendered to the S of S and then advised Sir Clem to set up a three-man commission consisting of Mr Savage as chairman and with two prominent NCNC lawyers, Messrs Balonwu and Kane, as members. Sir Clem declined to accept this advice.

R F A Grey was acting as governor-general of the Federation in the absence of Sir James Robertson on leave. Sir Clem was of the view that unless the libel action could be quickly heard the best way to bring the matter to conclusion was for him to use his reserve powers to set up a commission of inquiry if Exco did not itself agree to such a course, as he thought was likely to happen. Grey persuaded him that what he proposed was not appropriate since the legislation concerning the use of reserve powers made it mandatory that prior to the use of reserve powers there had to have been "governmental misconduct which local public opinion would recognise as such...and a substantial loss of public confidence...in the government". Neither of these requirements could be satisfied.

However, as I have already said, the S of S brought the discussion to an end by himself setting up a tribunal of inquiry on 4th August 1956.

He appointed Sir Stafford Foster-Sutton Kt, CMG, OBE, Chief Justice of the Federation of Nigeria as Chairman and Sir Joseph de Comarond, Kt, Chief Justice of the High Court of Lagos and Chief Justice of the High Court of the Southern Cameroons, and Mr Vincent

Akinfemi Savage, Chief Magistrate in the Eastern Region and presently acting as a Judge of the High Court of the Eastern Region and G F Saunders Esq, FICA in England and Wales and a JP as members.

The report of the tribunal is published in paper Cmnd 51 of January 1957.

Critical findings of the tribunal are briefly summarised below. The numbers in brackets are the paragraph numbers of the Tribunal Report Chapter XVI—Conclusions.

1   (191): Dr Azikiwe and Mr Blankson[6] both understood Dr Azikiwe's letter of 30th January 1954 merely created an agency with Dr Azikiwe as principal.

2   (192): It was accepted that Dr Azikiwe's primary motive was to provide an African Bank with the means of liberalising credit but he was attracted by the financial power his interest in ACB gave him.

3   (193): The control of the Zik Group of newspapers gave Dr Azikiwe considerable political power which he wanted to retain. The ACB was an important factor in financing the Zik Group of Companies.

4   (194): The conduct of Dr Azikiwe fell short of what could be expected.

5   (195): The deposit of £30,000 by ERPDB in ACB came at a very appropriate time and made Azikiwe's investments in ACB and the Zik Group of Companies more secure.

6   (196): It is not true that Dr Azikiwe severed entirely his connection with ACB in January 1954.

7   (197): Azikiwe was guilty as a minister in not fully severing his contact with ACB when it was proposed to invest public moneys in ACB.

8   (198): Dr Azikiwe in the opinion of the Tribunal still considered that he could speak for the bank as late as 3rd July 1956.

9   (199): There was suspect haste but no impropriety attached to the transfer of the proceeds of securities of ER Marketing Board to ACB.

---

6 A K Blankson Governing Director, Chairman and General Manager, ACB Ltd.

10   (201): Mr Ojike[7] died before the Tribunal reported. He erred, however, in not fully observing the directive of Exco at its meeting of 11th December 1954.

11   (202): Dr Mbanugu's[8] conduct and that of his deputy chairman of the Finance Corporation was also open to question.

Now let us turn once again to Sir Clem Pleass' part in all this, the knowledge of which I cull largely from the ACB chapter of his so far unpublished memoirs.

Sir Clem Pleass was born on 19th November 1901. He was appointed Lieutenant-governor of the ER in 1952, an appointment that was upgraded to that of Governor on 1st October 1954. He retired in 1956 having devoted the whole of his working life—thirty-two years—to the service of Nigeria. He died on 27th October 1988. His obituary mentions that he was soured by the campaign that was waged against him by the Zik Press in the last years of his governorship.

I feel that this is a misjudgement: "saddened" perhaps but "soured" no. Sir Clem has stated how he tried orally to make it clear to ER ministers shortly after they took office in 1954, that he was in sympathy with their wish to use an African-owned bank to hold government funds and for that bank to assist the African entrepreneur. But at the same time he made it clear that he was bound by the federal regulation requiring the bank selected to be properly licensed which, in turn, would be governed by the bank's financial health.

Sir Clem was on leave in December 1954. On 13th December Exco were shown a recommendation by the ER Produce Development Board that they should place £30,000 of their funds on deposit and current account with the ACB. Mayne who was acting as governor refused to accept the recommendation until he had first obtained the Licensing Authority's assurance that the ACB's finances had been restored to put it on an acceptable footing.

After some correspondence the F/S accepted the assurance that the ACB would be put on a sound financial footing by the injection of UK cash consequent on amalgamation with a UK banking house. This transaction would be completed by January 1955. On this understanding Mr Mayne accepted the advice of Exco in a meeting held on the 30th December 1954.

---

7   Dr Ojike, member EH of A, former Minister of Finance from October 1954 to January 1956.
8   Dr Mbanugu, Chairman of ERFC.

Sir Clem on his return from leave early in 1955 reminded members of Exco that it was because of the over-caution of European banks that the old development board and later the ERDB had been established. One of Sir Clem's aims at this juncture was to ensure that a clear statement of the financial position of the ACB was put in front of Exco for its information.

In an Exco meeting of 24th August 1955 Sir Clem informed members that Exco was entitled to know the views of the Finance Corporation and, in particular, they had the right to know where a sum of £850,000 belonging to the corporation had been invested. (One presumes that all the NCNC ministers did know but the President, Sir Clem, had been kept in the dark so as to prevent his possible interference.) The reply was: "At least the ACB and NEMCO have benefited." This was the first notification to Exco that there had been an investment of government moneys in ACB.

In July 1955 the F/S sent Sir Clem a copy of an agreement between the financial corporation and the ACB in which ACB shareholders were, *inter alia*, allowed to retain their shares. (These shares, previously valueless, had acquired value by reason of investment by FC. in ACB.) The agreement was unduly favourable to shareholders. It allowed Dr Azikiwe to be chairman of the bank for life and to have the right to appoint four directors.

It was plain that Dr Azikiwe was in all circumstances master of the ACB.

Sir Clem had not pressed Dr Azikiwe to sell his shares in the ACB when the latter assumed office in October 1954 because he, Sir Clem, knew it was very difficult to sell shares in Nigeria since there was no stock market or stock exchange.

In fact, Sir Clem had discussed this very point when visiting the colonial office in October 1945. It had then been agreed that the S of S himself—the Right Hon Alan Lennox-Boyd—should have a "Minister to Minister" talk with Azikiwe. This he did on 10th November 1955.

Dr Azikiwe maintained that he was not connected with the ACB at all during his premiership. However, he agreed to drop the provisions of the agreement in regard to his own position as chairman and the right to nominate directors. Later in November 1955 he published a statement to this effect.

Mr E O Eyo[9] quarrelled with the premier and was dismissed from all his appointments in April 1956. He put down a motion seeking an

---

9   Member EHA, Deputy Speaker, October 1954 to December 1955. Government Chief Whip, January 1954 to June 1956. Chairman ERDC, February 1955 to April 1956.

independent inquiry into the ACB's relationship with the government. The motion was slightly amended on 17th May 1956.

Exco discussed the motion on 5th June 1956. The premier announced in this meeting that he had instructed that civil proceedings be instituted against Mr Eyo for libel.

A draft white paper on the matter was presented to Exco on the 20th June 1956. Sir Clem took the opportunity provided by the discussion on the paper to ask for a copy of the agreement between the ACB and the Finance Corporation. This was reluctantly produced and showed that Dr Azikiwe had retained an active interest in the affairs of the ACB in spite of his (Dr Azikiwe's) assertions to Sir Clem and to the S of S to the contrary.

When discussing the white paper in Exco on 20th June, Sir Clem attempted to persuade ministers that the white paper showed quite clearly that Dr Azikiwe had retained control over the ACB and this was contrary to what would have been expected of a minister in the United Kingdom. Dr Azikiwe immediately challenged Sir Clem on this point, pointing out that Lord Chandos (previously Mr Oliver Lyttelton) had been chairman of AEI before he became a minister and had resumed the chairmanship on ceasing to be a minister.

The case of Lord Chandos differed since the directors of AEI made the request for Lord Chandos' return as chairman. Lord Chandos himself had retained no caveat in the matter. But Dr Azikiwe and members of ER Exco did not accept this point...or so they maintained.

Sir Clem has stated that throughout the whole of the matter of investment of money in the ACB he had two main objects in view: One was to discuss the matter in Exco and show members that as the shares in ACB were initially valueless the subsequent investment should not have benefited Azikiwe and the other shareholders. Secondly, he was anxious that there should be no possibility of blaming British officials at the autumn 1956 constitutional conference if by then there was any question of attributing blame.

On 22nd June 1956 the *Eastern Sentinel* (one of the Zik Group of papers) published an article saying that (British) officials were now seeing to it that Britain may judge that the ER of Nigeria is not yet ready to manage its own affairs and some ER legislators are not aware of the fact. The following day an article appeared in the same paper headed "ER Governor must Go". The article maintained that the governor was not being co-operative with African ministers.

When Mr Eyo's motion came to be debated in the Easter House of Assembly on 26th June 1956, a backbencher drew the speaker's attention to S Order 25 (3) which read:-

Reference shall not be made to any matter on which judicial
decision is pending in such a way as might, in Mr Speaker's
opinion, prejudice the interests of the parties thereto.

He went on to point out that the premier had instituted a libel
action against Mr Eyo. The speaker held that the matter should not be
debated.

On 27th June 1956 the opposition in the EH of A asked the governor
in writing to appoint a commission of inquiry into the matter. On the
same morning the opposition boycotted the House of Assembly and
sent a telegram to the S of S saying that they were not prepared to
take any further part in the proceedings of the House, or to attend the
London conference on the revision of the constitution until the premier
had cleared himself.

The S of S, having received the telegram from the opposition asked
for a full report on the matter. A report was prepared and after
agreement with the premier (Azikiwe) was sent.

In his reply the S of S stated that proposals for the further advance
of Nigeria towards independence would be discussed at the
constitutional conference. But he thought it essential that before the
conference was held the allegations that had been made against the
ER government should be fully investigated. He thought the best way
of doing this was himself to set up a commission of inquiry under the
Commission of Inquiry Ordinance.

The ER Exco in reply to the S of S's suggestion advised that a
commission of inquiry be set up by the ER government and should
consist of one commissioner, Mr N A Savage, Acting Puisne Judge. Sir
Clem accepted this recommendation which was transmitted to the S
of S. The latter, in a further telegram, stated that he was advised that
the Governor ER could not, either with or without the advice of Exco,
appoint such a commission since the inquiry must relate in part to
banking and banking was a federal matter. The S of S expressed
willingness to appoint Mr Savage and requested that the premier
should formally ask him to set up such an inquiry.

Exco discussed the latest telegram and disagreed with the advice
tended to S of S by his legal advisers. They advised Sir Clem that
he should appoint a committee of three—Savage as chairman, and
two prominent NCNC lawyers as members. Sir Clem did not
consider this advice was in the interests of public faith and refused
it.

However, as has been said, the S of S himself brought the discussion
to a close by appointing a tribunal of inquiry himself.

Sir Clem Pleass asked that Mr Stephen Chapman QC be briefed by the crown agents to represent him at the inquiry. The tribunal granted Mr Chapman permission to appear. A Labour member of parliament, Mr E L Mallalieu QC represented the ACB throughout the inquiry; Sir Frank Soskice QC represented Dr Azikiwe. The tribunal itself was assisted by Mr Brian MacKenna QC and Mr W A B Forbes, a barrister and by a solicitor, a Mr Cyril Russell. Most of the members of the public who gave evidence were represented by counsel.

Sir Clem, however, was nearing retirement (he would reach the retiring age of fifty-five on 19th November 1956) and he suddenly realised that he would not be able to afford counsel's fees so near to the end of his service. The colonial service came to his rescue. Ralph Grey, as Acting governor-general, sent a very strong plea to the colonial office that HM Treasury should pay. The treasury, true to form, refused, whereupon the S of S himself, Alan Lennox-Boyd, said that he thought Sir Clem should have counsel and if the treasury would not pay, he, Lennox-Boyd, would pay out of his own pocket. This finally shamed the treasury into paying. Ever since the Aba riots of 1929 it had been implicit that senior officials in Nigeria would be represented by counsel at inquiries should circumstances demand it. When I first heard of Lennox-Boyd's action, I experienced a thrill of pride—what a S of S to have behind us.

A small storm occurred just before commencement of the tribunal proceedings. ER Exco received a subpoena to produce all relevant Exco papers. Exco, of course, advised against. There is much to support maintaining the tradition that cabinet papers are secret to cabinet. But Sir Clem Pleass had the S of S's express instructions to use his reserve powers to ensure that all relevant cabinet documents were made available to the tribunal and this he did. He confessed afterwards it was a difficult order to obey.

In July 1956 Sir Clem expressed the view that, no matter how the tribunal of inquiry found, the people of Eastern Nigeria and members of the NCNC would still support Azikiwe. The probable action of the premier, he thought, in the event of an adverse finding, would be to ask for a dissolution of the ERH of A and to hold a general election. It would probably be suggested that the tribunal and its findings had been a trick on the part of the British imperialists to show the people of the ER were unfitted to govern themselves. Sir Clem was certain Dr Azikiwe would win a majority on such an issue.

As the tribunal progressed and it became clear that the report must be adverse to Dr Azikiwe, emissaries were sent round the E Region warning the populace what was happening.

Sir Clem Pleass went home on retirement in November 1956 and the report of the tribunal was not formally published until January 1957.

Sir Clem Pleass recorded that he went home on the same aircraft as his own counsel, Stephen Chapman, together with E L Mallalieu MP, QC who had represented the ACB. At Rome airport the three discussed the inquiry and Mallalieu expressed the view, "quite forcefully", as Sir Clem described the scene, that McKenna had been too tough in his examination of Azikiwe. He threatened to make that point if ever the report of the tribunal was discussed in the House of Commons. Sir Clem asked how otherwise the truth could have been forced out. Mallalieu refused to modify his attitude.

L O Ojukwu later said that the inquiry had been worse than many observers appreciated with fabrication of documents and so forth.

`The last paragraph of Sir Clem Pleass' obituary in the London *Times* of 26th November 1988 reads:

> This conflict with Nigerian Ministers dimmed his accomplishments and the satisfaction he might otherwise have had in his final appointment. But today Sir Clem's qualities and the service that he gave are well appreciated by official Nigeria.

From the end of June 1956 Sir Clem had been the object of attack by NCNC Ministers and the Zik-owned press. Zik had sent a long telegram to HM the Queen, copied to the S of S, demanding Sir Clem's immediate recall. The NCNC also boycotted invitations to Government House but most ministers were pleased enough to meet Sir Clem and Lady Pleass at parties given by somebody else including the Speaker of the EH of Assembly.

At the time we construed this as an attempt on Zik's part to make the issue "Azikiwe versus Pleass". We felt the whole matter was becoming remote from reality, a distortion of the truth.

An English climbing friend with whom I'd discussed the Zik matter in the middle of 1956—and who could be described as a responsible middle-aged large company MD of good repute—sent me extracts concerning the Foster-Sutton tribunal from the *Financial Times* with the message: "Poisonous man...I hope he gets his deserts." His judgement, by the standards he represented, were fair enough. But the governor-general of Nigeria and his staff and Sir Clem Pleass and his staff, could not act by the same standards. They had to recognise that public opinion in ER would support Azikiwe; they had to accept the numerous undertakings Azikiwe had given that he would take steps to amend the agreement of ACB with the ERFC, that he would drop the provisions of his agreement with the ACB to make him chairman for life and give him the right to nominate four directors, and he should make a public statement to this effect.

It was from 1954 onwards probably impossible, certainly unwise, to remove Azikiwe from the scene for anything short of blatant criminality. He was a consummately clever politician, head and shoulders above the majority of his contemporaries. He successfully engaged in moves to enrich himself and his family and to strengthen his political hold on the masses from 1950 onwards but he took care never blatantly to infringe the criminal code of Nigeria. He lied to the secretary of state and frequently to Sir Clem Pleass but in general he ensued that his most heinous lies were told for him by his henchmen. His numerous undertakings to be a better boy provided the excuses the British senior officers in Lagos and London required to treat him lightly.

The findings of the Foster-Sutton Tribunal were critical of Dr Azikiwe, true, but not so critical that criminal action had to be taken against him. A gentle slap on the wrist he was prepared to accept— but perhaps not to forgive. His campaign against Sir Clem personally was an added insurance; it enhanced his image with the people of Eastern Nigeria that he should be at daggers drawn with the "Imperialist Governor"; if he could turn the issue into a simple matter of personal antagonism between Azikiwe and Pleass so much the better. It was characteristic of him that he elected to fight on more than one front at a time.

Let me return to the "high ups"...the British colonial officials from the secretary of state down...of the time. Presumptuous as it is for me to make a judgement I submit that they were nearly always right if not always right in the way they carried out the ultimate policy of the government of the day. At my level, and I believe at levels way above, we all had a duty to point out the drawbacks of any policy decision. There was no doubt that colonies such as Nigeria, Ghana, Sierra Leone, to mention West Africa alone, were not ready for independence; they simply did not have the requisite machinery in place. The past forty years have demonstrated the correctness of this view. The final decision—the decision to disband the colonial empire many years prematurely—was taken by the British governments of the day in response to pressures from the West African politicians, the United States and the Afro-Asian Group in the United Nations and the near certainty that it would not be possible to ensure peaceful regimes in these territories in the face of world opinion.

Officials at my level, and indeed at the level of a colonial governor, had no option but to carry out the policies laid down by Her Majesty's Government or resign. A few officers did resign but for many of us the financial penalties of early resignation were too great to accept. And, too, many of us felt our loyalty to Great Britain exceeded our loyalty to our immediate charges.

As I have already observed on page 343 I do not consider Sir Clem Pleass was "soured" by the attack on him during the last two to three years of his service. Perhaps it can be suggested that he was partially at fault in allowing the situation with Zik and the regional NCNC ministers to build up at all. Even if he was, there was two and a half years for those above him to have become accessories and he was always removable if he had been judged to be at fault. I believe that he saw more clearly than most of us quite how black the days ahead were likely to be and was saddened for the people for whom, and amongst whom, he had worked for thirty-two years.

Azikiwe responded to the report of the tribunal by continuing his policy of promising changes when finally forced to do so. His promises were sufficient, coupled with his virtually unassailable political power, to enable him to become governor-general of Nigeria on Independence and subsequently to become the first president of independent Nigeria in 1963. Perhaps the apex of Zik's career came shortly after the Nigerian elections of December 1964.

The NCNC boycotted the polling booths claiming that a recent census had unduly inflated the Northern figures. Dr Azikiwe's sympathies plainly lay with the NCNC but he correctly invited Sir Abubakr Tafewa Balewa of the NPC once again to form a government which he duly did.

Azikiwe was finally unseated by the military coup of January 15 1966. Wisely, he was out of the country at the time, a fact that probably saved his life. He never lacked good timing in any of his moves.

CHAPTER TWELVE

Chief Administrative Officer, Lagos, and Acting Permanent Secretary

The ACB matter dragged on from 1954 to 1957. I must now return to our arrival in Lagos on 19th November 1955 which was something of an anti-climax. "TX's" decision to stay on for the Queen's visit meant that I was committed to serve as his No 2 in my substantive rank of SDO until he elected to go on retirement leave. I would lose the equivalent of £220 p.m. acting pay as well as the kudos of acting in a Class 1 post and he, rather than I, would be involved in the arrangements for the Queen's visit. But he was an easy enough chap to work with and the change of scene and job was indeed a tonic.

The CAO Lagos was the heir to Commissioner of the Colony. The change in constitutional arrangements by January 1956 had resulted in the mainland Districts of the colony—Badagary, Epe and Ikega—being transferred to the Western Region. The senior post was consequently no longer on a par with the commissionership of the Southern Cameroons and in my view was rightly graded as Class 1 (Resident). I don't think "TX" really appreciated this. He continued to occupy the commissioner of the colony's old and very beautiful 1905 wooden house on the marina next to Government House. This was tactless to say the least for he must have known the site was required for a new house that was about to be built for the prime minister of the federation. I thought him misguided that he did not make the site available rather than wait to be pushed out of it.

I felt, too, that "TX" was slow in initiating the transfer of administrative functions still performed by the CAO's office to the ministries where the new constitutional arrangements pointed they should be. The governor-general's staff were very over-pressed chasing the changes in arrangements required by constitutional advances and suggestions from the incumbents were always welcome. "TX" should have shown the initiative, not waited to be pressed.

As to the CAO's remaining roles: there were statutory duties, some quite onerous, under no less than thirty-seven Nigerian laws. In addition the CAO, or members of his staff, were chairmen or members of fifteen non-statutory committees. His general executive duties included boards of survey, law and language examination for senior officials, visitors to Nigeria, arrangements for ceremonial parades and so forth. Probably the most time-consuming of the CAO's tasks lay in connection with his chairmanship of the Lagos Executive Development Board. The board's staff in my time were headed by a very competent British chief executive officer who was a master of United Kingdom practices in town planning and urban development.

The LEDB was a statutory body charged with the duties of town planning control and the general planning and development of Lagos Township. It also was engaged in major slum clearance and redevelopment schemes and by 1956 had succeeded in clearing and redeveloping some fifty per cent of what was then called Lagos Island (the area of central Lagos bounded by Five Cowerie Creek, the Lagos Lagoon and the harbour fairway). In spite of the board's activities Central Lagos in 1956 still contained some of the most horrific slums in the world.

Living conditions in Lagos got out of hand in the first fifty years of the twentieth century. Prior to the development of the town as the main port and capital of Nigeria, the housing pattern had been one of huts round the roughly quadrangular compounds of deceased founders of families. I am indebted to the 1936 *Nigeria Handbook* for the following description of later development.

> The local system of inheritance caused the pattern of compounds to be split up into smaller units, the open spaces being filled with new houses. The increasing economic and administrative importance of Lagos attracted a great influx of persons from the interior. These persons attached themselves to a local chief and in return for small services were given land on which to build within the compounds. It became manifest that the "dependent squatters" would eventually claim ownership of the land so the original compound families imposed a rent, the huts erected by the immigrants being regarded as compound property. Thus a system of landlord and tenant gradually came into being. The landowners, finding the new arrangements highly profitable, let the open spaces of their compounds increasingly to new

immigrants until the compounds, once fairly sanitary, became slums of the most overcrowded type.

Kat and I were temporarily housed in the top flat of a block of flats built just behind the controversial house occupied by "TX". It gave us an excellent view over the harbour fairway and we could recognise the faces of our friends on board passing liners which at that point came within fifty yards of the shore.

The funds available to the LEDB from a variety of sources had increased considerably over the years and it was proposed to spend over fifty-six million pounds (in today's values) on major slum clearance projects on Iddo Island.

One of our first visitors to the flat was L O Ojukwu. He breezed in one Sunday afternoon and announced that he was about to visit the UK on business. Kat, thinking he was looking tired and somewhat overstressed said spontaneously, "Oh that's splendid. You'll be able to have a good rest on the ship."

He replied, "Good God, you don't think I can afford doing nothing for fourteen days on a ship, do you? I'm flying, of course."

He then said, "Come and see my new house in Ikoyi. The Queen is going to visit it and it's not ready yet."

We obediently followed his car down to Ikoyi. The house was quite splendid: large, airy and well-designed. There was an enormous ornamental staircase; the lower steps were marble, above was wood. "The silly fellows," he said, referring to the Italian firm building the house, "ran out of marble halfway up my stairs. Now they've got to fly a new lot out from Italy. It'll be ready for the Queen's visit, don't you doubt it."

He showed us into a palatial bathroom on the first floor. Just then a house telephone rang and LO, with an apology, disappeared to take the call. Kat and I examined the bathroom. On the floor was a huge bath mat, very white save for a naked footprint, giant sized in black. On the back of the door hung two bathrobes, white as can be but each with a large black hand printed across the shoulders. We were laughing at the black additions when LO returned. He guessed what had amused us. "Just my sense of humour," he said.

Down the corridor was a wide picture window overlooking a high wall behind which was an Ibo compound in exact similitude—tall Ibo dwelling hut with round mud walls capped by a high pointed thatched roof; one or two full-sized oil palm trees, a large pestle and mortar and an old lady, cloth knotted round her waist, bare from the waist up, busy pestling what looked like yam pulp in the mortar.

"That's my mother," said LO quite matter-of-factly. "She doesn't feel at home in a modern house such as this so I've built her an Ibo compound where she can live as she's always lived."

"Because he can do things like that that's why he is the man he is," said Kat later to me, equally matter-of-factly.

The Queen and Duke of Edinburgh were in Nigeria from 28th January to 15th February 1956. I found myself filling in for "TX" on routine duties but had little to do with the arrangements for HM's visit.

Practically all that Kat and I were required to contribute was to put up HM's Nigerian ADC—Major J T U A Ironsi. He was an Ibo, born in 1924 at Umuahia in Owerri Province. He had joined the Nigerian Army as a private in 1942 and by 1955 had risen to major. He was to spend 1963 at the Imperial Defence College, London and he became head of the Nigerian Army in 1965. Following the Nigerian military coup of 1966 he took over as head of government. He was assassinated in the counter-coup of 29th July 1966.

All we can remember about him, poor man, was that he was a tall, heavily built Ibo, extremely punctilious about the shine on his boots and the perfection of the iron crease in his trousers. Writing of boots...he apparently used the WC next to his bedroom in the local manner—that is to say that he stood rather than sat on the seat. The polished mahogany became quite severely scratched by the nails in his boots and when he left the flat we had to pay for a replacement.

During the several days he was with us we did our best to look after him and help him to adhere to the very tight timetable laid down for HM's entourage.

I shed a tear on his behalf the day ten years on when we heard he'd been cruelly and coldly killed in Ibadan; but by then violence was sadly endemic in Nigeria.

There were many tales told of the royal visit, some doubtless apocryphal. At one reception in Government House, Lagos, the Bamenda Fons had been invited. Sir James Robertson waited on Her Majesty at the top of the first flight of stairs and escorted her down to the group of VIPs gathered below.

Sir James towered over HM but the pair made a truly regal impression as they descended the last few steps. Somebody heard the Queen say, "Sir James, quick, remind me how to pronounce the names of the Bamenda Fons." He obediently went through the list: "The Fon of Nsaw, Ma'am; the Fon of Bikom, the Fon of Bali, the Fon of Wum and the Fon of Bum." He pronounced the last in the correct manner—"Boom". The Queen was heard to say, "You know, Sir James, I was always brought up to pronounce that last one very differently."

R F A Grey, the then Deputy Governor-general of Nigeria, was knighted by HM on the last morning of the visit. Apparently it was an entirely unexpected little ceremony: Ralph Grey was suddenly informed "HM awaited him in the small drawing room." He hurried to obey the summons and found HM alone there, save for the sword bearer. "Kneel down, Mr Grey," said the Queen, and knighted him.

Ralph Grey, delighted, rang up Esmé, his wife. Ralph was good at imitating folk and he said in an assumed voice, as Esmé answered the phone, "Is Lady Grey in the house?"

Esmé replied, quite crisply, "There's no Lady Grey here."

"Oh yes there is," said Ralph in his ordinary voice.

Shortly after Ralph Grey had been knighted, the Queen and the Duke of Edinburgh gave a little drinks party in Government House for the officials who had been primarily responsible for the arrangements. The visit had been a great success. Unexpectedly the Queen was heard to say to Peter Stallard, "Mr Stallard, I have a complaint about you."

There was sudden silence. How could HM have a complaint about Peter Stallard, the secretary to the Prime Minister, who had done so much to ensure the visit was the success it was? The guests listened aghast.

The Queen continued, this time her voice was kindly and full of concern: "...Mr Stallard, you are much too thin. You must really do something about it."

Ralph Grey, quick as could be, interjected, "All lost in your service, Ma'am."

Kat and I were very amused to listen to a small African gentleman in canonicals being presented to HRH the Duke of Edinburgh at one of the GH Garden Parties.

"How do you do. And what are you?" said the Duke.

"A Reverend...sir."

"Yes, yes; I know," said the Duke. "But what *sort* of reverend?"

"Just a reverend Reverend, sir," humbly replied our little friend.

That day we noticed that the Queen had been escorted round the garden party in a clockwise direction and the Duke, in a separate little party, in the opposite direction. The Queen finished her walk first and waited for the Duke at the previously arranged rendezvous point. The Queen, ever conscious of time and precise adhesion to the timetable, stamped her foot with annoyance at the Duke's dalliance.

But he was enjoying meeting local characters and wasn't to be hurried.

The story goes that Sam Morfor, a floor member of the Southern Cameroons House of Assembly and a great humorist, although certainly not a Fon or a chief of any description, insinuated himself uninvited amongst the party of Bamenda chiefs. He had his ceremonial umbrella carrier and draped over his shoulder in imitation of the chiefly robes worn by the Bamenda Fons was a finely woven bath mat. (Kat assured me it really was a bath mat.)

It was Sam Morfor, too, who some four years later when the Southern Cameroons elected in a plebiscite to join the Republic of Cameroons grew tired with a debate in the House of Assembly concerning the arrangement for changing traffic from travelling on the left of the road to the right. "It would be much preferable for car traffic to change on the first day and lorry traffic to change on the second," he said. Nobody at first saw the joke until a character in the public gallery did and guffawed.

I recall, too, that when I was posted to the Cameroons in 1958 Sam Morfor came along to our house and pretending to be a Hausa trader tried to sell us a rug, bargaining enthusiastically. We went along with him for a little while and then asked him in for a cup of tea. He didn't know it at the time but both Kat and I recognised him from his prank on the occasion of HM's visit to Lagos.

Outrageous character that he was, the old Cameroons Hansard shows that he could, when the mood took him, make really valid contributions to serious debates in the House. Some of his speeches are not only witty but full of good sound sense.

There is one more story about Sam Morfor that sticks in my mind. It may have been just before the Southern Cameroons amalgamated with the Republic of Cameroons, round about 1961...I can't remember...but poor Sam had gone too far and was up before the judge of the high court on a charge of sedition. Things, in fact, were going badly for him. At about 12.30 on the second day of the trial he'd been handed a bunch of letters allegedly written by Sam himself. One was likely to do him serious damage if proven.

The judge took the opportunity to say, "I think we'll adjourn for luncheon now."

And Sam from the dock quickly said, "Your Honour, this is the first time these letters have been shown to me. May I please study them during the adjournment?" The judge, perhaps unthinkingly, agreed.

After luncheon Sam handed back the letters to the prosecuting counsel and thanked him for the opportunity to study them.

It later transpired one (the incriminating one, no less) was missing. Sam had had it for lunch. The case collapsed.

"TX" wanted to retire but it now emerged that he had three or four months of service to put in, in order to draw his maximum pension. Although older than I, he was on the same substantive grade and I began to find his ditherings and changes of plan quite tiresome. It was eventually arranged that he should go on leave from 11th March 1956 until 27th June 1956; he'd return on that last date and allow me to go on leave. I'd return and take over from him. His final retirement could take place in November 1956.

The three months he was absent were, I felt, rather a waste of time. The Federal Minister of Power was now also Minister of Lagos Affairs. There was much to do to bring the office of CAO Lagos in line with the new federal ministerial arrangements. Many of the tasks still performed by the CAO should, in fact, be transferred to the new ministry. Probably the establishment of the CAO's office could also be reduced. Only acting for "TX" I felt that I couldn't very well tackle any of these tasks in his absence.

About this time Nagogo, Emir of Katsina, brought his redoubtable polo team to Lagos to play several matches in the south. The emir was a high handicap number three and three of his "Brothers" (same father, probably different mother) made up the side. A very good side it was.

In one match I remember at least two "under the belly" goals being scored at a fast pace by their number two.

Sir Ralph Grey was acting governor-general "Granddad"—as Sir James Robertson was known—being on leave. Ralph was guest of honour for the match Katsina-Lagos. I was marking the emir. As bad luck would have it he fouled me blatantly and then did it again in front of the VIPs' stand. It was too much and I yelled at him, "If you do that again I'll knock your bloody head off," in English which he understood very well. I thought I heard him say "*uwarka*" in reply which is quite rude in Hausa.

I hoped Ralph Grey hadn't heard but early next morning in the office, the red telephone rang and the ADC's voice said, "HE would like a word with you."

Ralph's voice came on the line. "I don't understand this game of polo. Here you are saying the most dreadful things to the emir bang in front of my seat and yet at dinner last night he said you are a good chap and he wouldn't mind having you in the north."

"Did you hear what he said to me yesterday?" I asked quickly.

"No."

"Uwarka," said I.

Sir Ralph laughed.

Bless the emir for putting things right at dinner and bless Sir Ralph for laughing.

———————

Both the children came our for the Easter holidays and promptly got involved with what Kat and I felt were a very fast set of holidaying young. Although ours were only thirteen and fourteen at the time they were large and advanced for their years. Among their friends was a seventeen-year-old who had a driving licence and made free of his parents' Jaguar.

I remember one lunch-time putting my foot down. "You've been going out far too much and having too many late nights," I said, heavily. "From now on it's every other night at the most, starting tonight."

"We can't do that," they said. "We've promised to go to a party at Ikoyi Club tonight."

Of course I weakened. "…if you've promised…but you've got to be home at ten p.m. OK?" Reluctantly they agreed.

Kat and I dined alone, missing them. At ten I wanted to go to bed. "The little devils, they aren't back yet…"

I left the mosquito-proofed house, got the car out and motored to a point on the opposite side of the golf course to the Ikoyi Club.

I strode across the fairway towards the bright lights of the club. There they were, sitting in a neat circle round a table on the lawn—a dozen or more of the gang. One, obviously younger than the others, was slowly raising a huge tankard, presumably of beer. As he did so, he spotted me emerging from the darkness of the golf course into the bright circle of light. His eyes, alarmed, met mine over the rim of the tankard. It was John, all right.

He carefully placed the tankard on the ground under his chair and slipped off into the darkness behind it. I swung round and retraced my steps.

When I got home, ten minutes later, both kids, if you please, were sitting at their ease chatting to Kat. I never asked them how they managed to get home before me but I guess it must have been their seventeen-year-old pal with the Jag.

———————

29 *Above*, The Commissioner's Lodge, Buea – the Milnes with soldiers of The King's Own Border Regiment, all of whom hailed from the Penrith area of what was then the county of Cumberland.

30 *Below*, Far right is Lieut Colonel W A Robinson who commanded British troops in the Southern Cameroons for eight months.

31 *Above*, 1960 – Sir Louis Mbanefo, then Chief Justice, Nigeria, visits the Southern Cameroons.

32 *Opposite above*, Malcolm Milne with Mr Jua, a minister of the Southern Cameroons.

33 *Opposite below*, The Hon Sir Abubakar Tafewa Balewa, first prime minister of the Federation of Nigeria, receives a gift of silver from the British government on Independenc 1960. It was presented by Viscount Head, High Commissioner for the United Kingdom ii Nigeria.

34. Ahidjo, President of the Republic of Cameroon, speaks on his arrival on 31st September 1961, to take control of the Southern Cameroons.

35 *Above*, Sir James Robertson with John Foncha and his wife.

Below, S T Muna, Acting President of the Republic of Cameroon, and Mrs Muna, with old friends, 1980.

37. Michigan, Oct. 4, 1984, with Ferdinand Nwogu and Akin.

38 Reading a message of farewell at hand-over. C E King, British Ambassador to the Republic of Cameroons, between Ahidjo and Mrs Foncha.

39 Sam Morfor, Government Chief Whip and wit – he once grew tired with a debate in the House of Assembly concerning the arrangement for changing traffic from travelling on the left of the road to the right. "It would be much preferable for car traffic to change on the first day and lorry traffic to change on the second," he said.

About this time Geoffrey Gardner-Brown came to Lagos as Deputy Chief Secretary having served for the previous four years as Colonial Secretary, Bahamas. He was physically only a small man but he was to make a considerable impression in Nigeria, ending up as Deputy Governor-general in 1959.

Leonard Guise, who'd had a distinguished career in the Nigeria service and was in fact some six years older than Geoffrey G-B, was thoroughly cross when Gardner-Brown was brought in over his head. He'd confidently expected to be promoted to the post of Deputy CS. When Geoffrey arrived Leonard Guise, in a fury, was heard to exclaim: "Bloody little man, I don't know why they gave him the job. You can't hear what he says, you can't read what he writes and when he's halfway down the corridor you can't even see him."

Leonard Guise had neatly encapsulated all three of Geoffrey's handicaps: it was true he was quite small; he did speak in a low voice and his handwriting was truly atrocious.

Kat and I nearly ended Geoffrey G-B's career for keeps. I write "Kat and I...." but I suppose the fault was entirely mine. We took him sailing one Saturday afternoon. A tornado had been threatening for some two hours but, partly to add a little excitement, I'd dallied on the return trip from the mouth of the harbour. The tornado hit us when we were nearly back—between the Motorboat Club and the Yacht Club. We were crossing the mouth of a little bay. The water wasn't very deep and the bottom yielded a good anchorage. We were only three or four hundred yards from shore. "Let's ride it out here," I said. "It's a good spot." The other two were somewhat hesitant but didn't argue with the skipper.

We dropped sail and made everything as fast as we could in the few minutes available. I paid out a couple of hundred feet of anchor cable as we bounced about head on to the rapidly increasing wind.

The anchor did drag but relatively slowly and even at the height of the tornado—winds gusting seventy to eighty miles per hour—we still were a safe distance from the lee shore with, I may add, several cars on the shore road watching what they doubtless thought was our plight. At one moment I believed we might even blow over backwards in the worst of the gusts so I made the other two join me in the bows.

After about thirty minutes the worst was over but G-B had become horribly cold and was shivering violently. We were all pretty chilled but he was the worst affected.

The next day we learnt he'd acquired a chest infection and pleurisy was suspected. Poor chap he really was quite ill for the ensuing ten days or so. But he was a sportsman and didn't, we gathered, hold it against us.

"TX" returned from his shortened leave at the end of June 1956. Kat and I went on leave ourselves. We stayed as usual with the Aunts. It was strange, having John and Jackie at their respective boarding schools relatively near by, and not to take them out for weekends. Nowadays, forty-two years on, our grandchildren come home at the drop of a hat but in those days boarding school meant boarding school and most children spent the whole term incarcerated. Out two chide us to this day for not being more alive to the opportunities and I don't blame them although it shouldn't be forgotten that my attitudes were those of the 1930s and the Aunts themselves were true Victorians—the boys were banished away to boarding school and the girls were "brought up" at home. As I write it's over 110 years since Alice and Kate were "schooled".

Sir Owen and Lady Butler were neighbours of the Aunts in their Penrith days and by a coincidence used to stay in the next door house to the Cedars in Temple Sowerby. It belonged to a relation of Madge's. Tightening the coincidence all round, Owen Butler had served from 1921 to 1951 in the colonial service, Gold Coast. He'd been knighted in 1951 ending his service as Chief Commissioner, Ashanti. He was a keen trout fisherman and gave me many days on the Eden and Esk in the 1950s. The Eden in those days had an excellent summer run of herling and sea trout. By the river it was always "Malcolm" and "Owen" but in public and even with our relations, it was "Sir Owen" and "Milne", as it more behoved our colonial relationship.

One August morning that leave, the Butlers, staying next door, were idly chatting with the Aunts over the fence, so as speak, when a messenger on a bicycle delivered a cable addressed to me. It was from Gardner-Brown in Lagos offering me promotion to Class I with effect from the day we'd left Enugu for Lagos, right back to 17th November 1955. It meant recovery of the not inconsiderable acting pay "TX's" peccadilloes had cost me but it also meant a significant rise in the service, definitely one that I'd not expected. I was more than chuffed and certainly showed it. Not so, Sir Owen. He was furious. "Great God," said he, "I had to wait twenty-one years for that promotion and you've got it after…what is it?…seventeen years."

"Seventeen is my lucky number," said I, facetiously but Owen Butler wasn't at all amused. He was, in fact, so angry he avoided us for the rest of the time they were in Temple Sowerby and I can't remember being asked to fish again that leave. Of course, hindsight tells me that I should have explained in front of the Aunts how the approach of Independence was hastening promotions all round...but was too full of myself to think of it at the time.

A few days later I received a letter confirming the cable and adding that "TX" was off on retirement on 15th October 1956 and it was Sir Ralph Grey's intention that I should take over that day. Could I shorten my leave and be back in time?

I certainly could.

At last I was Chief Administrative Officer, Lagos on my own, acting for nobody. As soon as we returned I got down to administrative changes—the transfer to ministerial responsibility of matters until then dealt with to finality by the CAO. The approval of the chief secretary was required in each case before gazettement as the responsibility of an appropriate minister. What was left of the CAO's duties and staff would be transferred to the responsibility of the Ministry of Power and Lagos Affairs.

The slum clearance and general town planning activities of the Lagos Executive Department Board were, of course, of high importance to Lagos. As a temporary measure I was charged with keeping an eye on these matters for the immediate future. Surpassing the LEDB on the eve of the May/June 1957 Constitutional Conference in London, however, was the matter of the future political status of Lagos as federal capital. There is available to public scrutiny at page 55 of PRO file CO 554/911, a Secret and Personal letter from Sir Ralph Grey dated 13th December 1956 to T B Williamson, a head of department in the colonial office. This letter provides a very clear impression of the depth of thought that was given to one item only in the great set of briefs that were being prepared for the secretary of state at the forthcoming constitutional conference. The briefs consisted, so far as could be foreseen, of arguments the various delegations at the conference might produce together with the answers that the governor-general considered most suitable in reply.

The letter in question contains an observation by Sir Ralph typical of his humour...and humanity. He was writing of a ministerial committee consisting of Ribadu and two NCNC Ministers. "We had relied upon Ribadu[10] to give us backing against the political machinations of the two NCNC members but he proved a man of straw, at first preoccupied with the Pilgrimage and subsequently drunk with its effect."

---

10 who was a member of the NPC and a Moslem.

As soon as the Lyttelton Constitution had been introduced all the new federal ministers with any pretensions at all to Islam had done that year's Holy Pilgrimage including, of course, Ribadu himself. They had, as Grey so correctly observed returned "drunk with the effects".

We then had in Lagos a dining club, consisting of fifty per cent African members and fifty per cent expatriate members. I wasn't a member but dined fairly frequently as a guest. One evening, just after the Holy Haj in question, I was dining in the club and sitting at the long table opposite Archbishop Leo Taylor.

The Archbishop was a small, thin man nearing retirement age. He was known in Catholic circles as a very good churchman. Non-Catholics such as myself, knew him best as a wit. He had a reputation for dry and very direct comments on current affairs. I may add that one of his pleasures in life was fine wine. Woe betide the host who did not provide it. Kat also told me that he had surprised a small coterie in Lagos of persons with artistic interests by his ability as a portrait painter. Oddly enough I have since put this to several Catholic priests who knew him but none has borne it out. Kat assures me, however, that there were people in Lagos well qualified to judge who had expressed admiration for his abilities. They all felt, she said, that he had a vivid gift of penetrating his subject's superficial appearance and laying bare the essential man below.

Anyhow, on the dining night I'm talking about there happened to be three federal ministers as guests, all Moslems and all wearing the green veils in token of their recent pilgrimage.

"Look at them, look at them," said Leo Taylor in his crackly voice, loud enough to be heard by most of the table. "Look at them…like the Brides of Christ. But don't tell me they are virgins."

Lagos stewards, most of them members of the well regarded Guild of Domestic Servants, had of course noted which of the new ministers had celebrated the Haj and which hadn't. At drinks parties they would proffer a tray of drinks, seemingly all alike, containing Coca-Cola. "Ya Minister," they would ask, "Coca-Cola ou Coke Islami?"

"Coke Islami," most Ministers would reply. Needless to add, Coke Islami was half brown rum, identical in appearance to pure Coca-Cola.

I'd taken over the old CAO's office—a spacious building in Broad Street. However, the new Ministry of Power and Lagos Affairs needed housing and I was ordered by the chief secretary's office to house them. I set about accommodating both organisations in Broad Street. The CAO's was the first office to be provided in Lagos with air conditioning (I vaguely remember on experimental grounds) and I certainly hadn't objected. To have cool office accommodation and to have the town noises of Lagos blocked out were great luxuries. We converted a large committee room into a palatial office for the minister and I gave my office over to the permanent secretary. I was to be back in it as acting permanent secretary very soon but first had a foolish, some could argue self-inflicted, accident which my superiors, short-staffed as they were, nevertheless treated with kindly tolerance.

It was a Sunday at the end of April 1957. The young were out for the school holidays. I had the use of an unoccupied house at the end of the East Mole. A little party of us sailed to the spot, anchored off the base of the Mole and had a picnic luncheon in the house. After lunch I challenged the party at large: "Come on...there's a traverse round the walls of this room. Not to touch the floor." I can only suppose there were sufficient bits of decoration and so forth available to make a traverse possible. Anyhow, crossing a window opening I fell out of the window ending up with my feet twelve inches above the ground level outside impaled by my right arm-pit on the one and a half inches high window catch. John, not yet fourteen years old, was out of the house in a twinkling and showing surprising strength lifted me off the catch.

My armpit had suffered considerable damage. I spent the night in the Creek Hospital and the following day underwent surgical repair of the damage. A couple of days to get over the effects of the anaesthetic and I was told to keep the wound dressed and gradually increase the use of the arm aiming at normality in a month. Office work was feasible because I could prop up the arm sufficiently to write. Kat's diary records that I umpired several polo games one-handedly—the affected arm strapped tightly to my chest. Nine days after the accident the governor-general inspected various LEDB projects and, apart from being one-armed, I had no inconvenience accompanying him.

On the seventeenth afternoon Kat happened to meet Sir Ralph Grey in the corridor of the Secretariat. "How's Malcolm's arm?" he asked casually. Kat said, "I'm very worried; they told him to use it increasingly but he can't use it at all now and it's gone septic."

Sir Ralph replied quietly, without hesitation, "We can't let him become septic in this climate. Have him ready for this evening's aircraft and get him up there in time. I'll fix things on the phone now."

Early the next morning I found myself in the Royal National Orthopaedic Hospital at Stanmore. Later the same morning they told me that they would sort out the sepsis with antibiotics—then regularly used in the UK but relatively unknown in Lagos—after which the damage could be re-repaired surgically (we were right in thinking—as we had—there had been errors in the original "repair").

I was back in Nigeria exactly a month after I'd fallen through the window, my right arm functioning as it ought. Nobody in authority mentioned the matter to me. I was never chided, as I might well have been. What a service to take such care of its own.

And the ward I was in at Stanmore was an experience that I wouldn't have missed: I appreciated it at the time but now with the perspective of years I value it more. Most of the patients were motor bike casualties, young and all determined to get back to the joys of normal movement as soon as possible. I remember two in particular. Both had been involved in horrific accidents and both had broken more bones that they could count on their fingers. They were committed to wheelchairs for most of the day. I suppose they had about twenty-five per cent movement control between them.

The hospital was very forbearing in encouraging activity of any kind. One day these two chaps, co-operating cleverly, managed to get into the hospital grounds. On their return they were greeted as achievers. Their ambitions soared. They knew that Stanmore hospital was built on a hill and about five hundred yards down the hill was a pub. This they determined to patronise. Combining again and with the help of the kerb as a brake, they got down the hill. There was no lack of volunteers outside the pub to push them into the public bar. At lunch-time they telephoned the hospital porter. They hadn't the combined power to get up the hill. Could he please help?

Amongst the miscellaneous duties attaching to the CAO Lagos which I hadn't yet been able to transfer to ministerial responsibility were such matters as telephone priorities, Boards of survey, arrangements for state ceremonies, claims for ex gratia gratuities, law and language examinations, petitions and, lastly, visitors to Lagos. This latter duty was a major burden and ministers didn't hesitate to pass on all guests of government who didn't qualify in importance for Government House invitations.

Kat and I had been assigned No 2 Osborne Road when the CAO's house on the Marina had been demolished to allow construction of a house for the federal premier. No 2 was quite large enough to permit regular entertainment; we found ourselves being required to put people up and to arrange a number of "do's". One of the latter was a dinner party for a bunch of doctors most of whom were staying at

Government House. Perhaps Lady Robertson and Granddad were out that night or perhaps they thought their guests would appreciate a change...I can't remember. Heaven knows why the medical convention the doctors were attending was being held in Lagos at all. There must have been dozens of more salubrious spots in the colonial empire but we were foist with the duty and that was that.

For once we determined that we'd liven the dinner party up with a pair of our friends so we asked Charles and Maeve Davidson to come along, warning them that they were to meet a gathering of tired conventionites who'd probably much prefer to be writing home to their lonely wives rather than dining with us.

Charles was an Anglo-Argentinean, a few years older than Maeve. He'd first met her in India during the war when a brother officer, serving in the same special unit, had asked Charles to look after her while he was off on some assignment. Maeve was a daughter of General Sir Eric de Burgh who had been Chief of Staff in India from 1939-41 and was related to Graham de Burgh, my CRA at one time during the war. She's better known today as the mother of Chris de Burgh, the popular singer, who uses his mother's family name.

Maeve has never been anybody other than her true self. She is the most natural, unaffected person it is possible to meet. She is also considered by most people who know her to be something of a wit. Like the principal of one of Somerset Maughan's short stories, her form of wit consists of being able to comment on those about her, and the great world around her, in kindly and simple terms, the essence of which is truth.

To go back to our party for the doctors...as ill luck would have it, Maeve and Charles were late, thirty or forty minutes late. No 2 Osborne Road had a long, very wide passage, almost an entrance hall, leading down to an open area where we normally sat with our pre-dinner drinks. That evening none of the doctors seemed very keen on drinking and conversation became stilted and difficult. We did our best but it looked as if the party would be a catastrophe.

At length a car drove up, followed a moment or two later by another. Maeve came steaming down the passage. I rose to meet her.

She, bless her, had obviously taken our invitation quite seriously and searched long and hard for a suitable dress for the occasion. She'd come up with a dark blue, low cut velvet obviously from her grand days in India a dozen years before. It must have looked stunning on her then when she was an Irish nymph, the toast of Simla. But Maeve had grown a little in the intervening years; she was now almost chubby. She was also very well provided for upstairs. The velvet, to put it gently was under a certain amount of strain particularly in the area of the bumpers.

She said, as she advanced. "I'm so sorry Malcolm we're late. I had a puncture."

"Do tell me," said I without thinking, "which one?"

Charles, who for some reason had come in another car, had by then joined us. Possibly because he was really sensitive about the few years difference in age, he was in the habit, facetiously, of introducing Maeve as "my daughter". He duly did this with the doctors. There was no reason why they should doubt him.

"I hope you've met my daughter?" said he to one or two of them.

They looked round, puzzled, for the mother.

But thanks to Maeve and Charles the atmosphere had suddenly changed and the rest of the dinner party went very well.

Kat and I were almost sorry to hear the GH car drive up, followed by two others, to take our guests home. The GH car, as behoved its status, parked first, blocking the exit and holding up the others. After cheerful good nights—several goodnights in fact—we got our guests aboard and waved our farewells. But would the GH car start? It seemed not. The starter whirred, then whirred again. Our farewell waves grew embarrassing. Suddenly there was an almighty crack, rather like a single Bofors shot, and the GH car started.

Charles had got his own back because we'd laughed at Maeve's tight dress—he'd stuffed a potato up the GH car's exhaust.

Maeve's father died in 1973. About that time she and Charles acquired Bargy Castle in County Wexford, then a rather dilapidated castle-cum-farmhouse which had been in the de Burgh family for generations. Maeve farmed the farm and bred blood horses while Charles set to and converted the castle into a thoroughly unusual B and B. He worked with the masons and carpenters and he bought large amounts of old Irish furniture, mostly oak, some of it almost medieval in age; lastly he saw to it that, in the modern fashion, every bedroom had its bathroom. The castle walls were so thick that for some rooms he was able to hollow out the walls to make bathrooms. Later in the 80s and 90s money came in from other sources and they allowed the B and B venture to lapse.

Staying with them long after our Nigerian days had ended, Kat offhandedly asked Charles how many bathrooms they had at Bargy. Charles came up with one figure, Maeve with another. To settle the matter Kat and Maeve did a count. The correct number was twenty-nine.

That may have been the visit when we turned up quite early in the morning. Two guests, whom we knew well from the Cameroons days, were just departing...a retired colonial judge and his recently acquired and reputedly very rich wife. They were just getting into their car...not, admittedly a brand new Rolls but a very smart one all the same. The only thing was the Rolls was heaving from side to side. I got down on hands and knees trying to discover the cause. Nobody else seemed to give a toss. There, far under the car, was a silver chafing dish presumably holding the remains of the breakfast kedgeree. An old pig had pushed it out of reach and was seeking by means of a series of shoves to recover it.

Nobody but me thought it funny. I suppose not. It was, after all, County Wexford.

But back to Lagos in 1956. Just after the dinner party for the visiting doctors Gardner-Brown sent for me and among a number of other matters said, "Oh, by the way...We've nominated you for the next course at the Imperial Defence College. You'll be in London for roughly a year so keep it in mind if you are making any future plans."

I'd heard it said that attendance on an IDC course was tantamount to joining the most select club in the empire which I suppose in those days wasn't far from the truth. Senior officers in the forces, generally of brigadier or major general rank, formed the bulk of the course. They were joined by the odd civil servant from the UK service and by a few individuals from the empire overseas. (Group Captain Lal whom I met on the ship to Aden, had just come from an IDC course.) The course, as I understood it, broke up into syndicates and each syndicate studied real problems facing HMG at the time.

It was a great honour to be nominated. I wondered if G-B, having only been in the country since February 1956, had over-estimated my abilities. But he had said. '...we...we have nominated you,' and I felt reassured that he must have consulted Ralph Grey and possibly Granddad himself.

However, the course he was referring to was many months ahead and I was kept so busy in Lagos that after a few weeks I put thoughts of the nomination to the back of, if not right out of my mind.

As was, sadly, to be expected ministers appointed under the Lyttelton Constitution soon found themselves under pressure from members of the business community, and various sections of the Nigerian population, soliciting favours. The pressures went far beyond the limits of permissible lobbying.

It was the following year before burgeoning corruption of this sort caused me a problem. I was acting then as the Permanent Secretary of the Ministry of Lagos Affairs, Mines and Power. The minister was Alhaji the Hon Muhammadu Ribadu, MBE, MHA, no less; the villain a gentleman called Mr Yassim. (There is no point using his real name...he was one of many at the same game.) Mr Yassim was an astute businessman of Middle Eastern origin, highly successful in acquiring wealth rapidly. One of his companies possessed the agency for a make of car popular with rich Nigerians, he owned a number of grocery shops and more than one hotel.

His technique was simple enough. He would allow the minister, or other vulnerable Nigerian VIP, to acquire goods from one of his enterprises—groceries or even on occasion, a car—and not bill them. Should he later make a request to the Nigerian gentleman concerned which was not promptly gratified, in would go a bill.

I was discussing a number of problems with the minister one morning when he said, quite out of the blue and not in connection with anything we'd been discussing, "Mr Yassim must have his planning permission."

I knew that Yassim was seeking planning permission for a petrol station but had gathered the police traffic department were opposing and so were the town planning authority. Although town planning was within the minister's portfolio the police were still a reserved subject and nobody in the governor-general's office would thank me if I allowed a conflict to arise on such a relatively small matter possibly involving the use of reserve powers. So I said to the Minister: "Town planning is always a difficult matter because there are so many ministries involved in each application. But I'll get the facts of Yassim's application and see what can be done." Ribadu, as I remember, merely grunted which I took for acquiescence.

I did nothing for a couple of weeks and then Yassim phoned me and asked outright: "What about my planning application? Why hasn't it been granted?"

I responded by offering to set up a meeting with the head of the traffic unit, the chief planning officer for Lagos and the federal lands officer, all of whom would be involved in a planning application of the sort he mentioned. We could find out what the difficulties, if any, were all about. He reluctantly agreed to come; I asked him to bring connected papers.

Unfortunately all three officers were expatriates. Nigeria had been promised independence by 1960 and, had they been Nigerians, I felt that their persuasive powers might have had more effect on Mr

Yassim...he would have to live with Nigerian officials for as long as he was in the country...expatriates would probably leave on independence.

Maybe it was ingenuous of me but I really did think that if we explained the whole matter to Yassim we could persuade him not to pursue the planning application. Confidentially we all realised there were other requests he could put to the minister but, of course it was not for us even to hint that we were aware of his relationship with Ribadu.

But no; we did our best. We were very polite, even obsequious. We explained the technical objections, we explained the divisions of responsibility between ministries, we explained the difficulties that might arise were the matter to be discussed in cabinet (Exco). But he hardly listened. After an hour and a half he got to his feet and made for the door. "Look here," he said, "this is just wasting my time. The minister said I was to have the permission and that's that."

I accompanied him to the door and opened it for him. Putting an arm across his shoulders I said, "Oh dear; but you know what the real trouble is, don't you?"

"No. What?"

"You're up against a secret society," and I pointed to my tie which happened to bear the red and black pennant of the Lagos Yacht Club. The other three, by a chance in a hundred, were all wearing the same tie. He spluttered with fury and marched out.

Bad—and no doubt rude—as the joke was it did embody a truth: we, the colonial power, that is, were trying to leave in Nigeria something of the standards we believed to be current in contemporary Europe.

After independence in Nigeria and in many of the ex-colonial countries grand corruption became widespread. At first a trickle, then a flood; British traders were just as involved as traders from every other trading nation.

(Those who wish to pursue this subject should contact Transparency International (UK), St Nicholas House, St Nicholas Road, Sutton, Surrey or read George Moody-Stuart's *Grand Corruption* available from the publisher—Worldview Publications, Oxford.)

Relations between Ribadu and Yassim hadn't by any means been altogether easy for some time. Ribadu's private secretary told me an amusing little story dating from the previous Christmas. The minister had said to him, "Yassim has given me some presents. Ought I to give him something in return?"

The PS had said, "Yes, you should, Minister. About the same value."

The PS had been pretty sure the minister had had gifts totalling several hundred pounds from Yassim in the previous year (quite apart from purchases from Yassim's companies). He was a little concerned to be ordered to take two rather scruffy turkeys and a debi (an old four-gallon petrol tin) of honey to the minister as a return gift. However, he did as ordered.

Yassim lived in a penthouse flat in one of the buildings he owned. Nobody answered the PS's ring for several minutes…time enough for the turkeys to leave a mess on the floor and cast a feather or two. The debi of honey had become even more revolting than when he'd set out. At length Yassim himself appeared at the door.

"I've brought some presents from the Minister," said the PS.

"Filthy stuff. Take it away," said Yassim.

"Oh no," replied the PS. "I can't possibly take them back telling the Minister you'd refused them. He'd be most offended."

Out of Africa. Witness to a Giant's Toils by J L Brandler and published by the Radcliffe Press in 1993 is a very well written and objective point of view of a gentleman deeply engaged in the commercial life of the city. It describes the colonial administrative service in the following terms:

> The Administrative Officers, starting as Assistant District Officer and rising to Governor, were all men educated at University, mainly Oxbridge graduates carefully selected and highly motivated. They were firm, fair, efficient, intelligent and incorruptible. They could also be very arrogant. Their task was to rule on behalf of the British Government and to make sure that the interests of that Government were paramount. To retain that paramountcy they had to ensure that the country was run smoothly and its inhabitants were happy. One must admire the fact that a few hundred of these men could run a country of thirty million people and run it well.

Although complimentary, Brandler's description of the administrative service was deserved. The incorruptibility of the service was easy for us. We were well paid. We were recruited from a section of society where corruption, whatever profession we had followed, was unthinkable. A colleague of mine committed suicide after an auditor had discovered a small error in the travel allowance he had claimed. The poor chap was unwell and in a very weak state at the time. The thought that he might be judged to have made the claim corruptly was too much for him. Had he been well, of course, he would not have acted so drastically. During my twenty-three years in Nigeria

370

and eighteen in Kenya I was never offered any kind of bribe, nor, I'm sure, were any of my colleagues.

It was a different matter for the Nigerian for the reasons mentioned previously in this book. But the worst service—and I don't mind saying it again—done to the cause of incorruptibility was the insistence pre-war of the British BMA that doctors serving in the colonial medical services must be allowed private practice.

I well remember Dermott O'Connor's sympathetic smile when in the early days, full of ignorance, I first tried to bring the matter up.

The cold fact was simply that the BMA in the late twenties and early thirties were too strong for the colonial office. The moral must be when in a position of power use that power sparingly and with great circumspection. Those who controlled the BMA of the time had never read Edmund Burke upon the Americas or, if they had, they'd ignored it.

After amalgamating the CAO's office with the Ministry of Lagos Affairs, Mines and Power, I found myself acting almost continuously as a permanent secretary, looking after one or other federal ministry while the permanent incumbent was on leave or otherwise engaged out of the country. Between April 1958 and September of the same year I was working continuously to Ribadu. The permanent incumbent was A C C Armstrong who was ten years older than me and had had considerable experience in the colonial empire, having served in the Gilbert and Ellice Islands and Fiji before transferring to Northern Nigeria. He was of permanent secretary rank and well able to hold his own, not only with the Yassims of this world but with the formidable negotiation team placed in the field by Shell and BP. The exploratory stage of oil development in Nigeria had at that time come to an end and the large oil companies were seeking to negotiate a "fifty-fifty" oil development agreement with the Nigerians.

In fact I was still acting as PS when the leader of the negotiating team arrived in Lagos. On his second day there Kat and I went to considerable trouble to arrange a drinks party for him where he could have an opportunity of meeting all those officials in the government with whom he was likely to deal.

I was standing with him halfway through the evening pointing out the various personalities. "Who is that rather lost-looking blond over there?" he asked. He'd already been introduced to her. "My wife and your hostess," I replied.

Instead of making some apology he grew angry and hardly said a civil word to me for the rest of the time he was in Lagos.

Extraordinary. We had gone to much bother to make that a particular party a success.

I suppose it was about this time that Ribadu had ordered me to get Yassim his planning permission. I never heard how Armstrong dealt with the matter. Perhaps he prevailed upon Ribadu to submit a paper to Exco in which he stated he was about to act contrary to official advice and leave it to his fellow ministers to take the blame. I'm sure it was not a matter for the governor-general's veto.

Nigeria in the years 1955 to 1960 owed a lot to Foley Newns (later Sir Foley Newns). The Council of Ministers asked him, when he was on leave in 1957, to seek the advice of the British government on the wider question of the integration of departments with ministries.

He reported to the four Nigerian governments (the federal government and the three regional governments) on his return. As a result it became clear that they wished to absorb the best of the British practice but—to use his own words—"not necessarily all of it all at once".

Foley was made chairman of a committee consisting of the secretary to the prime minister, the senior of the permanent secretaries (then Armstrong) and three heads of department—Dr Manuwa about to be knighted, W Macmillan, Head of Establishment and I Wynn Pugh CBE, Director of Federal Public Works.

Some of the administrative officers, available to Nigeria in 1958 for posting as permanent secretaries were junior in terms of length of service and experience to a number of technical heads of department. The latter had always been somewhat touchy—understandably—on their relative position in the hierarchy. If Foley Newns' reports tend to over-emphasise the roles of heads of department I am sure it was done deliberately (probably with Sir James Robertson's concurrence) to meet the susceptibilities of men such as Sam Manuwa.

Foley Newns knew how pressed all ministry staff were and did not run to excessive paper. Although the successive reports that he produced were models of brevity, they were classical documents and those of us concerned with the details of the change over from the "colonial system" of government to the ministerial systems introduced by successive constitutional changes consulted them at every turn.

In one of his reports on the Northern Regional Government Sir Foley bravely touched upon the problems caused by the incompatibility between the basically Moslem and basically Christian attitudes. The very same difficulties bedevil political settlement in Nigeria today forty years later.

Sir Foley's career didn't end with Nigerian independence in 1960. He was appointed Deputy Governor of Sierra Leone after leaving Nigeria in 1959 and had periods of administering the government of that country. Between 1961 and 1963, after the independence of Sierra Leone, he was made Advisor to the Government—an appointment that demonstrates the high regard that ex-British colonies had at least for some of their erstwhile administrators.

Between 1963 and 1971 he served the Government of the Bahamas and subsequently was consultant for a relatively short period to a number of territories on the verge of independence. Many of his writings on government procedures and cabinet government were circulated widely through the (new) Commonwealth. I don't think he ever fully retired: a week before his death at the age of eighty-nine I was entering into correspondence with him on a point concerning Northern Nigeria in 1959.

Armstrong having returned, I was due leave. Kat and I went straight to Austria where we arranged for Jackie and John to join us for the Christmas school holidays. We had a wonderful family holiday, mostly in St Anton in the Arlberg. The skiing of both children developed fast.

We had felt that we were becoming rather a burden for the Aunts: Kate in 1958 was seventy-eight and Alice seventy-one, so we planned to be in Temple Sowerby for only the minimum of time. The Ski Club of Great Britain welcomed me as a long-term representative at one or other of the Arlberg Centres. I applied. The Centre paid for my accommodation and skiing in return for my looking after ski club members—a benefit that reduced our total expenses by at least thirty per cent.

Our leave was cut short because I was required to act once again as Permanent Secretary of the Ministry of Lagos Affairs, Mines and Power, Armstrong being required for special duties. Fortunately for me he had brought the "fifty-fifty" oil agreement up to signing point, the final miscellaneous "matters of detail" to be agreed in Paris. This latter move was more a device at the instigation of the oil companies than necessity. The Nigerian members of the team, including the minister, were, of course, delighted at the prospect of a week in Paris at somebody else's expense. The result was that the deal was completed in double quick time; perhaps Nigeria hadn't got as much as she might have but neither Armstrong nor I were involved and the basic "fifty-fifty" agreement was sound enough.

Gardner-Brown phoned me one morning and asked if I'd call in to see him when next in the Lagos Secretariat. As the secretariat was only a few minutes' walk from Broad Street I went straight round.

"Now, look here Malcolm," he greeted me, "the place is yours if you want it. Understand that. We promised it to you and we'll still send you. No hard feelings. But we plan to make Stanley Wey Permanent Secretary for Defence and we want him to go first to the Imperial Defence College course—the place, in fact, we were reserving for you. They won't give us another place."

At first I must confess I didn't appreciate what he was talking about but before he'd finished I'd had time to collect my thoughts.

At that distance from independence—it was just over two years away—it was plainly much more important to be a good government man, "good company man" so to speak, that to pursue one's rights, imagined or real. Had S O Wey been an expatriate (which he wasn't, he was a Lagosian) and had it been five years earlier I might well have reacted differently but, as it was, there was only one way I could respond.

"Of course he must go," I said, "it's far more important in the long run," and so it seemed in the relatively optimistic view that the majority of my colleagues and I held at the time.

"Right," said G-B "we won't forget it." That promise, if promise it was, I also put out of my mind. There was so much else to think about.

Soon after this little passage with Gardner-Brown I was required to take over the Ministry of Health as acting PS. Dr Sir Samuel Manuwa CMG, OBE, LLD (plus several medical qualifications) was still very much the elderly autocratic head of department. Having sat on Foley Newns' committee dealing with the integration of departments he considered himself (and he almost certainly was) an expert on the subject. He was prone to hold long conversations with the Federal Minister of Health (the Hon Ayo Rosiji MHR), covering points of policy which he never mentioned to me. He was also in the habit of submitting Exco papers to me for my signature, faired and in final form, without having first discussed them with me. He also didn't deign to tell me his thinking on the single most important activity the ministry was engaged on at that time—namely the design and construction of the large training hospital being set up in conjunction with the University of Ibadan. I guess he only submitted the Exco papers to me for my signature knowing that the Secretary of Exco wouldn't accept them otherwise.

CHAPTER THIRTEEN

Southern Cameroons, 1958-59

On the 8th August 1958 I received instructions in writing from Gardner-Brown which were to adumbrate my last three years in the colonial administrative service. I was to go to the Cameroons under UK trusteeship in my substantive rank of Class I. During October, November and December I would be on special duties supervising the Visiting United Nations Mission and the Victoria Centenary Celebrations and would act as Electoral Officer for the general election to be held in January 1959. John Dudding, the Acting Deputy Commissioner of the Cameroons (in non-trusteeship territories the equivalent post was deputy governor) was due for leave at the end of December 1958. Dudding would be employed in Lagos after his leave and I would continue as Acting Deputy Commissioner. As such I would administer the country on Field's absences on leave or attending meetings of the trusteeship committee. (His absences, particularly to New York and London became more frequent as independence for the Cameroons grew nearer). Finally, I was to continue as Acting PS of the Ministry of Health until our departure for Buea in the Cameroons about the 21st September 1958.

This posting would give me several opportunities of administering the Southern Cameroons on my own. To be solely responsible for the government of a colonial territory, even a small one such as the Southern Cameroons, relatively unknown, was after all the zenith of our careers. I would reach that point at the age of forty-two...satisfactory going I congratulated myself.

In the event it didn't prove easy to get to Buea (the capital of the Southern Cameroons) by 21st September. We had Jackie and John staying with us for their summer holidays and they had to be back in England in time for the start of the Christmas term, in those days round about the 15th September. We had all our heavy loads in Lagos including a sixteen-foot half-decked sailing boat which we planned to fish from and to explore the exciting coastal waters of the Southern

Cameroons. We could have done the journey by road via Ikom and Mamfe but the rains were still on and the boat would have presented major difficulties particularly on the ferries between Ikom and Mamfe and on the very muddy roads between.

To cap the difficulties, no coastal vessels were scheduled to sail from Lagos to Victoria in the Cameroons after the departure of the *Swedru* on 1st September. I therefore sought the permission of the federal government, and of John Field to travel on the *Swedru*.

However, as was often the way in Nigeria, plans were changed again at the last minute. I was required to remain on at the Ministry of Health for another month. By then the *Mendi Palm* had been scheduled to sail from Lagos to Victoria departing Lagos on the 10th and arriving on the 17th October. I therefore booked for Kat and our loads on the *Mendi Palm* and arranged to fly Lagos to Tiko in the Cameroons on 15th October.

I had some Ministry of Health business to see to in Kano and managed to combine that task and seeing our two young safely on board the "Lollipop Special" from Kano to the UK on 16th September. BOAC operated a daily flight from Lagos via Kano to the United Kingdom principally using Argonauts and Constellations although they had some Hermes and Stratocruisers. English schools then were prone to start and finish term on roughly the same dates. Consequently at least one aircraft each way at the beginning and end of each school holidays was packed with young and naturally known as the "lollipop special".

There had been one gravely serious accident northbound when an aircraft taking off from Kano had experienced fatal wind-sheer flying into a tornado; there had been another incident involving a south bound aircraft which was quite extraordinary.

Although passengers and air crew grew very hot and thirsty in this latter incident before they were rescued, nobody, by the grace of God, was injured. In those days, before GPS and other magical aids to navigation became standard, aircraft flying the vast empty reaches of the Sahara by night were forced to rely on astral navigation. The navigator would from time to time carry out a star fix and give the pilot a true course to fly by means of entering and resetting as necessary a display instrument—the Variation Setting Corrector. Unfortunately the navigator of this particular flight, faced with an unfamiliar display on the VSC, had misread five on the instrument to mean five degrees when in fact it represented fifty degrees. They had been flying fifty degree right of course for the past several hours and were lost. Night gave way to daylight. The fuel situation made a landing essential.

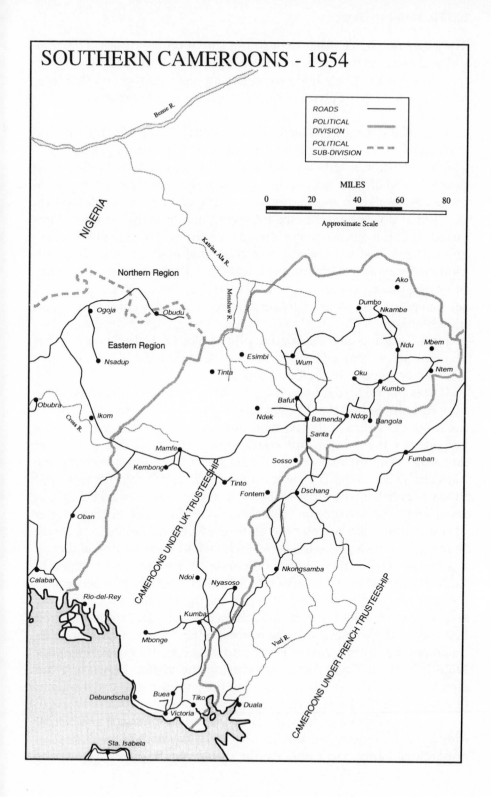

SOUTHERN CAMEROONS - 1954

ROADS

POLITICAL
DIVISION

POLITICAL
SUB-DIVISION

MILES

0   20   40   60   80

Approximate Scale

Benue R.

NIGERIA

Katsina Aia R.

Menshaw R.

Northern Region

Ogoja   Obudu

Eastern Region

Nsadup

Esimbi   Wum

Tinta

Ako

Dumbo   Nkambe

Ndu   Mbem

Oku   Ntem

Kumbo

Bafut

Obubra

Cross R.

Ikom

Ndek

Bamenda   Ndop   Bangola

Santa

Mamfe

Kembong

Sosso

Fumban

Tinto

Fontem   Dschang

Oban

Calabar

Rio-del-Rey

Ndoi   Nyasoso

Nkongsamba

CAMEROONS UNDER UK TRUSTEESHIP

CAMEROONS UNDER FRENCH TRUSTEESHIP

Kumba

Mbonge

Vuri R.

Debundscha   Buea   Tiko

Victoria   Duala

Sta. Isabela

377

They had no choice other than to put down on the desert. This they did and came to no harm. It was truly a miraculous landing.

Whatever the precedents were, seeing one's own off on that long leg over the empty Sahara at night was a traumatic experience and I hated it.

I saw Kat depart from Lagos on the *Mendi Palm* for Victoria on the 10th October. We met for a few minutes on the morning of the 15th. The *Mendi Palm* night-stopped at Calabar and Kat was able to get down to the airfield for a quick chat as my plane landed there, en route Lagos-Tiko in the Cameroons. Kat duly arrived at Victoria on the 17th and we spent the two following nights as the guests of John Dudding at the commissioner's residence, the Schloss, the Fields being away. We moved temporarily to a chalet belonging to the Mountain Hotel where we were cool and comfortable after the heat and humidity of Lagos. Buea, even in the rains, was an ideal climate, temperatures seldom exceeding seventy degrees Fahrenheit and nights cool enough for a blanket.

John Dudding gave me a great pile of files to study. Knowing that I'd come across Durrell ten years before he included a file on Durrell's 1957 collecting trip to the Cameroons.

It was plain Durrell had changed very considerably during those ten years. It seemed that his success as a writer-collector had gone to his head. As before, officials who met Durrell and his wife socially considered them both, but particularly the wife, charming and amusing. Without exception all commented on him adversely the moment he did not get his own way. As soon as officialdom appeared in any way to balk him he went berserk and resorted to wild behaviour and deceit. For instance on 9th February 1957 he had written a letter of complaint to the Secretary of State, the Rt Hon Alan Lennox-Boyd. Referring to the reply to this letter (which had been written in fact by a junior official in the colonial office) he later wrote, "I am given to understand that the secretary of state himself sent out instructions..." He was told in the plainest of terms by the colonial office that the secretary of state had issued no such instructions and all that Durrell had received was a copy of the normal letter usually issued in such instances, i.e. in this case a letter addressed to the governments of Nigeria and the Cameroons introducing the visitor, explaining the circumstances of the visit and inviting the governments concerned to offer any help they might consider appropriate.

Durrell also threatened to use his connections with *Life* and *Nature Magazine* whenever he felt in any way thwarted, the sanction apparently being bad publicity for the trusteeship territory of the

Cameroons. Many observers in the Cameroons concluded that these diatribes against authority were connected with his heavy drinking and slight mental imbalance.

This view is supported by a recent biography, *Gerald Durrell: Himself and Other Animals,* by David Hughes and published by Hutchinson in 1997.

Reading the Durrell file given me by John Dudding I got a picture of a spoilt child behaving badly.

Although John Dudding and I were the same substantive grade he was Acting Deputy Commissioner and thus senior to me at that moment. Gardner-Brown in his letter concerning my posting had written of Dudding going on leave "at the end of December or in early January". But John Dudding was true to the Nigerian form: when the senior man has a good posting he sticks on to it as long as he can. John D also probably got an inkling that he wasn't returning to the Cameroons. Anyhow, it was 21st January before he finally left. At the time this was irritating to me, taking over. I'd read the files and wanted to get on with the outstanding problems in my own way. Now, of course, at the long distance of writing, it appears all very small stuff. Perhaps I should have been more patient. As it was, I fretted. Maybe Fields spotted this for early in January he sent me up to Bamenda, again on special duties. The object was to study the "Kom troubles" and devise measures to ensure the maintenance of law and order throughout the coming election and to preserve free speech.

Dating from July 1958 there had been demonstrations by women in the Kom area in large numbers, some acts of lawlessness by the women's society (*Anlu*) in particular and many reports of high intensity of feeling. Amongst the Ibo the women rather than the men indulged in violent demonstrations and the same thing was true to a large extent amongst the peoples of the Bamenda District. In Mid-December the *Anlu* were well on the way to taking the law into their own hands. These women looked upon themselves as the long-stop of society...they were the last element to stand firm against what they viewed as the ultimate harm.

The whole of the Bamenda Province appeared to be KNDP in sympathy, with political feelings running very high, particularly on the succession issue exacerbated by the success (from the KNDP point of view) of the "sell to the Ibos" rumours. (The KNDP supporters had put it about that the KNC party encouraged the sale of land to Ibo foreigners.)

There was also a slight whiff of anti-European feeling, strange to Bamenda, in the air. In December 1958 the government of Dr Endeley was still in power. Officials were looked upon, correctly enough, as the servants of the government. The public at large were apt to confuse a due observance of orders with political sympathy. They were, in fact, beginning to believe that officials were tarred with the KNC brush. Since many government officials, in 1958 in the Bamenda Province, were Europeans there was thus the beginnings of hostility to Europeans as such. The Fon of Kom and his immediate entourage were widely recognised as KNC supporters. An outbreak of lawlessness anywhere is infectious; I felt that an outbreak of lawlessness in Kom might spread to other areas.

Ken Shaddock, the DO Bamenda, was coping very well. All along he had acted with restraint and sympathy tempered with firmness. I felt, however, it was too much of a risk to hope that the situation could be mended sufficiently by the middle of January with the limited resources at Ken's command. He needed top level assistance.

So far as basic grievances were concerned the absence of a truly representative local government body was important. What native administration there was had its headquarters four days walk from Njinikom, it had only ten Kom members none of whom were women and generally was out of touch with the needs and aspirations of the Kom area. The method of application of the Soil Conservation Regulations (later suspended) had done harm and provided the KNDP and the *Anlu* with good opportunities to resist. The Grazing Regulations, of great importance to the women who did most of the farm work, had been haphazardly enforced and many genuine grievances had arisen.

The Fon of Bikom was himself a problem. He drank too much, was loath to tour his area, was over-demanding regarding presents and was notoriously ungenerous when entertaining visitors.

Lastly, as has already been said, he and his supporters were supporting a political party against the wishes of most of his subjects.

Ken Shaddock had tried to prop him up from time to time. For example, Ken arranged for a meeting between *Anlu* representatives and the Fon. Tempers rose during the discussions and the Fon's *Chindas* (unofficial police) began to beat the women. Instead of stopping the beating the Fon merely turned away. The Fon also behaved badly in the native court. So much so that had he been an ordinary member, the DO would have sought the premier's approval for his removal. (Native Courts came within the premier's schedule.)

As for political machinations: I found that the KNDP supporters had quite gratuitously done damage in a number of areas. Members of the KNC weren't the only bad boys by any means.

The women's society—the *Anlu*—had not been formally active for the past thirty years but recently their "half and half" interventions hadn't helped the situation. So much so that a number of KNDP supporters harboured serious doubts whether *Anlu* had a place at all in the structure of modern Bamenda society.

I suspected that in the past co-operation between the police and the provincial administration had not been as close in Bamenda as was desirable. I held talks with Shaddock and with Jones (the then Superintendent of Police, Bamenda) and was left in no doubt that the two of them would co-operate far more effectively that their respective predecessors had in the past.

The Anlu Society had instigated a boycott against the RCM schools. The women assured me that this was done for political reasons. Many men affirmed that on the contrary the women wanted their children at home to draw water, hew wood and baby sit. There was talk of bribe-taking by the cattle assistants in connection with the contour regulations. I asked the Provincial Education Officer, Emerson, to support me in a talk to the women but I got nowhere. The women listened politely to what we had to say and that was as far as it went. All these were problems and dissatisfactions that I was confident Ken Shaddock would sought out in time.

I merely recommended that a 9/6 education rate due to be collected in December be postponed until after the coming election.

Having reported the situation to Field very much on the lines above, I reiterated the view that no single remedy existed. The remedial action should be very much on the lines Shaddock had already thought of; namely, sympathetic attention to and removal of real basic difficulties; local government and native court reform; attention to the position of the Fon including further action designed to improve relations between him and his people, and lastly—but by no means least—a firm steady enforcement of law and order (past offences by *Anlu* being dealt with neither vindictively nor with undue leniency).

Several ministers of the Cameroons government were officially concerned and of course the whole matter—and remedial action—had to be discussed with them before action was taken.

I recommended that the police post at Njinikom itself should be increased to at least ten men in all and that Bamenda should be made up to approved strength, that a three-way W/T communication linking Bamenda-Wum-Njinikom should be installed and the Njinikom police detachment should be provided with a Land Rover. The police recommendations were drawn up in consultation and with the support of Jones, the DSP at Bamenda.

Lastly, I suggested that the premier's office should look at the early introduction of a Kom Clan native authority.

I was back in Buea after approximately a week on the Kom problem. This had entailed several public meetings where members of the adjacent local authorities, the police, local politicians, members of the *Anlu*, representatives of the Fon, a European missionary who had lived in the area for many years, a Catholic priest living in Bamenda, and others, all spoke their minds. I had private talks later with most of those who had spoken publicly and found that they had little to add to what they'd already said. It was an encouraging experience to have a problem, or rather series of problems, discussed so openly.

I remember thinking then that here was a lesson that we, the mentors, might well learn from such openness of discussion.

During the past two or three years I've had the privilege of talks on Cameroonian affairs, particularly as they were in the late 1950s, with Sally Chilver of Oxford. Her name needs little introduction: she is justly famous in British, European and American academic circles. In her long and very active life she has served as Principal of Lady Margaret Hall, Oxford and had been briefly Director of Oxford University Institute of Commonwealth Studies, after service in the CO Research Department. She insists that she is a social-historian but the truth is that she emerges always at the summit of whatever discipline she approaches. Her love affair with the Cameroons (and if true love be compounded of long, deep knowledge, great affection and no small measure from time to time of irritation, love affair it was) dates from the late fifties when she stayed with Dr Phyllis Kaberry in Nsaw and then in Bali. Sally Chilver collaborated with Dr Karberry on several occasions and naturally acquired a comprehensive knowledge of her findings.

Dr Kaberry was a social anthropologist who carried out a classical study of the women of the grassfields. Freddy Kay very wisely included a number of her recommendations in his reorganisation proposals for the SE Federation referred to on page 227. He also noted—and corrected—an error in the Nsaw Intelligence Report which she had pointed out to him.

Phyllis Kaberry has been dead now for many years but a couple of years back I put doubts which had arisen in my own mind in 1958-59 before Sally Chilver somewhat as follows: the work of anthropologists such as Meek among the Ibo and Phyllis Kaberry and Edwin and Shirley Ardener in the Cameroons had made my contemporaries and I feel how little we really knew of the true life of the people. We had a technique for extracting the legal implications of native law and custom when dealing with native court appeals but by and large we left it to the benches of the native courts to find the facts in such matters. Was, perhaps, the whole thrust of government policy misdirected in 1959? Had we departed too far from the indigenous system?

Sally Chilver's reply was comforting. She pointed out that in 1949 we had been thinking in terms of perhaps sixty years before total independence. Freddy Kay had been right in pausing sufficiently to embody some of Phyllis Kaberry's findings. In 1959 on the other hand we were operating under a number of constraints. Independence for Nigeria had been agreed for 1960. The instructions of the British government were to close down the colonial empire; American pressure to abandon our colonies was no longer to be resisted. The Cameroons was UN trusteeship territory and the policies of the Afro-Asian Group were all-important; they commanded the majority vote in the Trusteeship Council and they were strongly opposed to colonialism in general and the British colonial empire in particular. Perhaps the greatest constraint of all was the question of timing. In 1949 we had, as we thought, time in hand to move thoroughly and relatively slowly. With independence round the corner we had no time at all. The general objective was to leave the trusteeship countries and the colonial territories in as good shape as possible to take their place in the community of nations. This, in our view, included parliamentary democracy supported by modern methods of local government, police control, finance and jurisprudence. When we had taken over these countries half a century before we had found indigenous systems in place, many of which were well adjusted to the way of life at the time. I believe that had we—the colonial power—had longer, not only would we have slowed down the change over from the indigenous to the new but we would have embodied more of the old in the new...we would have studied more deeply the findings of the Kaberrys and the Ardeners.

For many years now I have thought Robert Graves to be the greatest of the Georgian poets. I have carried about with me a copy of his poem, *Dedication to the Poetic Muse*, which I have read and re-read many times always glorying in the strength of his powerful natural metaphors (Sister of the mirage and echo/ Volcano's head...the Mountain Mother). It's a veritable talisman to me.

Well, Sally Chilver is the daughter of Robert Graves' brother, Philip Perceval Graves. He was *The Times* Correspondent at Constantinople from 1908 to 1914. He served in the army in Egypt, Palestine, Arabia and Turkey from 1915 to 1919 and after that was correspondent of *The Times* until his retirement in 1946. He was justly held in great respect for his numerous writings on the Middle East, including a life of Sir Percy Cox. He edited the memoirs of King Abdullah of Transjordan in 1950.

Sally Chilver in becoming a scholar and expert in African affairs worthily follows two such lions amongst men.

Shirley & Edwin Ardener, then working for a research institute of University College, Ibadan, published a comprehensive study of the labour employed in the SC plantations in 1960, entitled *Plantation & Village in the Southern Cameroons* (OUP). I remember this volume as being particularly helpful to John Field and me in writing reports to London, and the Trusteeship Council.

After Edwin's early death, Shirley continued much of their joint work and is now recognised in her own right as almost certainly the greatest living authority on the ex-Southern British Cameroons in the years 1959 to date. Her work on the establishment of the Buea archives alone has been particularly valuable to scholars.

Dear Alice had suffered a severe stroke and died after three days at the beginning of November 1958. Kate then aged seventy-eight, was left in a very dithery state. Mary and Robin Nicholson, our Cumberland friends, came to the rescue and took untold trouble on our behalf. They protected our belongings at the Cedars against the depradations of a relative and spent much time and trouble making future arrangements for Kate. I don't know what we should have done without them; I was very busy in the Cameroons and absence from my post then would have prejudiced my future there.

Jackie joined us in Buea on 15th January 1959. She was then seventeen and had one more GSE subject to pass before she started the long haul to qualification as a physiotherapist. One of Muna's sons—Daniel—was also in need of special coaching and he and Jackie used to visit daily a Catholic father who lived halfway down the hill from Bua. As Muna was a minister in Foncha's newly elected government, he and I had transport available. It was not a difficult matter for one or other of us to ensure that the young had a vehicle to take them to their tutor.

The general election was held as scheduled on 24th January 1959. Foncha's KNDP won fourteen of the twenty-six seats against the twelve seats taken by Dr Endeley's KNC party. The KNDP also won a majority of the popular vote.

John Dudding at last handed over on 21st January 1959 as deputy commissioner and went on leave. A few weeks later I was offered substantive promotion to the post of Deputy Commissioner of the Cameroons (in Group five—one group above class I) to be effective from 21st January 1959. This seemed to shut the door firmly against any other contestant for the post unless I was sacked or otherwise pushed out of it.

Mary Nicholson came out to stay with us in February 1959. She was even then, I veritably believe, beginning the obscure form of leukaemia which caused her death in 1967. She suffered three days of what appeared to be very severe flu just before she flew back. A doctor in Douala, having taken blood tests assured us it was not malaria. During the early part of her visit she was bothered by prickly heat. So much so that she allowed a "magician" to treat her. We met this character one afternoon when Mary and I tackled the two hours' trudge up to Hut One on the Cameroons Mountain. We found him in occupation of the hut. It was clear that he was paying no fees but the place was neat and clean and I didn't think he was doing anybody any harm so I made no comment. He announced that he was a magician. Mary at once said, "If you are a magician can you cure this prickly heat for me?"

He replied immediately, "Surely," and dabbed Mary's wrists with the liquid from one of several phials that he produced.

In ten minutes the weals had gone. Mary took the cure for granted. Her father's family came from the Highlands of Scotland where fairies flocked. She herself was close to the mysteries of the occult; she treated the incident as part of the Cameroonian scene.

John Field left for a duty visit to London early in February 1959. On the 6th February the mountain began to show signs of erupting. I informed the Governor-general of Nigeria in his capacity of High Commissioner for the trusteeship territory:-

6th February 1959

Priority Govgen Lagos
COD

M...22. Series of earth tremors being experienced today of moderate intensity x Geologist advises that pattern of increasing frequency may presage major earthquake or alternatively they may die away in which case we can breathe again x Am taking advice as to which public buildings must be evacuated and at what stage necessary x Am preparing plan in consultation works police medic etc. for emergency action in event major earthquake x In Geologists' opinion this may be false alarm but we must obviously take all precautions x Public not excessively disturbed x Milne.

The following day was a Saturday. Jackie volunteered to help one of the government secretary-typists (I think her name was Muriel Parker) to shred a number of secret files in the deputy commissioner's office which were due for destruction. I had agreed to play in a cricket match and saw no good reason to cancel either the game or my place in the team. About three p.m. there was a quite severe earth tremor. Jackie reported later that the filing cabinets had chased the two girls round the office. I was taking guard at the time and remember very well the pitch appearing to roll at me.

Muna's ministry was primarily concerned. During the next few days he and I made several trips up the mountain to see for ourselves what was happening. There was an unmanned Posts and Telegraph's Transmitting station at 10,000 feet on the north-eastern slopes, reached by a very rudimentary road barely passable by Land Rover. Initial eruptions took place along a half-mile line of weakness some three miles from the transmitting station. By driving the commissioner's official Land Rover to the station, and then walking, Muna and I could watch the lava emerging from the depths between lunch and tea.

On our trips we kept the Land Rover as light as possible taking only a photographer with us. Muna certainly did his share of cutting a path through the thick vegetation near the P & T station. I have one very Mau-mau photograph of him at work with a machete. There was no nonsense about his dignity as a minister preventing him doing labourers' work. We formed a bond at that time which has lasted for forty years.

It was singularly interesting to observe at close quarters the formation of the vent holes. The line of weakness I have mentioned was well marked on the ground. Neither of us had any hesitation in standing quite near it—within thirty yards. At each earth tremor—and there were several on the first occasion we were in the area—the earth heaved upwards quite visibly along the line of weakness. Odd spots heaved more than others and some turned, before our eyes, into miniature craters: one moment an upwards heave of soil and surface vegetation the next a rupture and an issuing stream of lava.

The main lava flow, plainly visible from Buea at night, threatened to cut our only south-north road near Lower Ekona village. This flow became quite formidable in size; lava rolling down the slope at a perceptible speed...about five hundred yards a day. Red hot lava on the leading edge soon changed into great grey masses of lava boulders fed always by fresh red lava in the centre.

Seen from Buea at night there were periodic flashes of light. It took us a while to discover what these were. What was happening was this: the red-hot lava would reach and surround a great forest tree, perhaps piling to a height of eight feet up the trunk. All would appear well for a moment or two. Then suddenly, the whole tree would disappear in a flash of spontaneous combustion; it was there one moment...gone the next, in less time than it takes to record.

Kat and I spent several evenings sitting in the Buea garden as night fell, watching the progress of the lava flow threatening Ekona. The red ribbon, showing clearly the changes of slope was of never ending interest.

Both local people, except for the directly threatened at Ekona, and expatriates grew to take the eruption much as a matter of course. There was no exceptional concern.

We made emergency plans for action, should the south-north road be cut at Ekona or should the village of Ekona itself be in imminent danger. And, of course, I continued to report regularly to the governor-general and to decline as gracefully as possible offers of help by the Federal Nigerian Government.

There were murmurings amongst the peoples living near Ekona to the effect that the sacrifice of white cockerels having proved ineffective in stopping the flow of lava threatening Ekona, the next stage was to sacrifice white dogs. Kat asked, when she heard this, "You don't think matters will progress to a white child do you?"

In fact the lava flow, which had reached a depth of over fifteen feet, came to a halt 8,000 feet WNW of Ekona by the second week in March.

I visited Lagos between 23rd and 25th March and was able to report that all was well and the eruption appeared over.

Kitty, Kat's Mama, came to stay on 25th April. I see from the diaries that Kat kept that I was very occupied with work during Kitty's visit; writing nearly fifty years later I much regret not spending a great deal more time with her.

She had a long experience of Nigeria dating back to 1912, and she possessed a great fund of stories about people and events in days past.

The Duke of Gloucester and Princess Alice representing the Queen were to visit Nigeria and the Southern Cameroons, in May 1959.

The Fields were due back in the middle of April. Before they arrived Major Michael Hawkins, the Duke's private secretary came out with the task of finalising all the details of TRH's visit. He was an Australian by birth and had had a distinguished war in a British cavalry regiment. Life was not entirely easy for him as he had lost an arm during the war and later became a diabetic. When travelling on his own he was forced to find somebody competent to administer daily the regular injections of insulin he required.

On the Sunday of his visit to us we took the day off and did "a West Coast Trip". It was brilliant weather and the scenery along the rough road westwards from Victoria was at its most attractive: patches of jungle interspersed with the long-abandoned ex-German plantations, rocky bluffs standing above the blue sea and chances of seeing an elephant. Round about midday we drove down to Isongo, a deserted German mini-harbour which had once served the plantations. The jetties were still in place and the deep water of the harbour quite clear. It had been used only by smugglers' canoes during the past forty years, the latter on their way back from the Spanish Island of Fernando Po. They had left no signs of their visits.

We decided to swim in the clear waters of the harbour before we had a picnic luncheon.

I was exploring amongst the old jetties when I noticed Kat swimming as fast as she could towards the middle of the little harbour, perhaps forty yards travel. There, in the centre, was Michael Hawkins obviously in difficulties. Kat reached him and brought him safely ashore. It emerged that he was entering a diabetic coma and rapidly losing all strength. He'd forgotten to have his insulin injection earlier that morning. Kat told me that once ashore he'd gasped out the word "sugar". As she had some in the picnic basket she was able to provide it for him quickly.

Michael Hawkins was the last chap to make a fuss, particularly about himself; he seemed to perk up after taking the sugar; it was evening before we left the West Coast road.

He was extremely easy to deal with officially, largely because he knew precisely what TRH would want and how far the duke was prepared to go. There was one matter only on which we differed. This was the venue for the garden party.

I don't blame him for he lacked any knowledge of the regularity and the certainty of the Buea climate. When he was with us in April the weather was ideal for an outdoors garden party in the cool of

Buea. The sun shone for nearly twelve hours each day, there was hardly a cloud in the sky. The garden party, however, was to be held on the 26th May and by that date many people who had lived their lives in the area assured me the rains would have started. Even if it was not pouring down all day in Buea it was, in their forecast, certain to be drizzling and unpleasant.

Naturally Michael thought the Schloss garden to be ideal for the garden party and he absolutely insisted on the arrangements being made to hold it there. The best I could do, after long argument, was to persuade him to let me have an indoor venue prepared, just in case.

It was quite true that the onset of the rains in Buea was predictable to within two or three days and, sure enough, the 26th May turned out to be a typical Buea wet season day. There was steady rain all day and the whole area was shrouded in thick mist—we needed car lights to go up and down safely the long and twisty Schloss drive.

However, in the interval following Michael Hawkins' visit I'd had the reception hall in the Mountain Hotel enlarged and we were able to have the party originally planned for the Schloss garden there instead.

The Gloucesters' visit went off even better than we hoped, amply repaying the meticulous planning of Michael Hawkins. Kat and I were delighted to see that seven years after his visit to the Cameroons on the eve of his retirement he was knighted.

The Fields went off on leave as soon as the Gloucesters' visit was over. As they were to be away until the end of October Kat and I (and, of course, Jackie) moved into the Schloss. There were a number of VIPs expected in the territory and it was appropriate that we should be able to entertain them in better style than would have been possible in our house.

Margaret Field had produced a carefully researched thirty-page pamphlet called *The Commissioner's Lodge and Gardens, Buea*. She was a keen gardener herself and wrote with knowledge and real enthusiasm about the many terraced gardens lying below the Schloss. She would have liked to have returned them to their pristine 1905 condition and replanted them with their original plants. Unfortunately funds were not available.

The deputy commissioner's house also possessed a fine garden. John Dudding was a good gardener and had spent freely from his own pocket. He left the four-acre garden in very good shape for Kat. He had made a speciality of collecting epiphytes and tree orchids and told Kat that he'd left over forty different species scattered about the four acres. Kat never counted them but from time to time we certainly remarked orchid blooms of extraordinary variety and delicacy.

The Schloss and its gardens had been built by Jesko Von Puttkamer. He was the third German governor of the territory since it had become a German protectorate in 1884. The protectorate originally comprised what was later to become the Northern Cameroons, Southern Cameroons and the Cameroon Republic, but was far from being "pacified" let alone explored that year. In fact the area around Buea was not bought under German control until 1904. That year Puttkamer decided to remove his headquarters, until then at Douala, to Buea. The latter place would be much healthier for his European staff.

In 1905 the Commissioner's Lodge—the Schloss—was finally completed and Puttkamer moved in. Early in 1906 he was recalled to Germany—to answer questions concerning the cost of the Schloss— and in 1907 dismissed, so never again visited the Cameroons, although he published his memoirs in 1912.

There are two stories about the Schloss. Neither are substantiated by Margaret Field's researches but both one would like to believe.

The house was plainly very expensive to build. Puttkamer is said to have grossly overspent the vote and to have used the money allocated to the roads' vote to make good the difference. I find this believable enough. I agree that in my days in the colonial service I would have almost certainly been personally surcharged for a like situation but we were particularly fierce on financial errors. However, virement from one vote to another has frequently been done on a governor's authority and I find it hard to credit that Puttkamer, in 1905 Germany, was brought to book.

I've heard it alleged that the real reasons for Puttkamer's dismissal involved a little more than the mere overspending of the vote.

A clue is to be found in the form of the two intermingled "P"s which decorate the wrought iron gates leading from the first to second level of gardens at the Schloss. These gates were still intact in 1961. The "P"s, of course, are said to stand for Paulina and Puttkamer and the degree of intermingling to represent Puttkamer's intentions if not his past achievements. In order to secure the lady's passage to the Kamerun he indicated to the authorities that she was his cousin—a statement which in all the circumstances was not credited.

An element of tragedy enters the story because Paulina, who was a beautiful German singer, did secure a passage and come out to join Puttkamer but found the embraces of the captain of the ship more attractive to her than the past or imagined future attentions of the colonialist Puttkamer and returned by the same vessel. Or so it is said.

I don't really know if the second story substantiates or decries the earlier one. There was a German piano on the large balcony outside the main bedrooms at the Schloss. A visitor in the 1920s claimed to have heard—and seen—a ghostly figure playing an air from Listz on this piano He—it was a male visitor—said there was a great feeling of sadness about. Was this Paulina on her one night ashore?

The long twisty drive to the Schloss and the gardens themselves were planted with a wide variety of roses popular in Europe around the turn of the century. Margaret Field identified a number of these and made a sketch plan of their distribution which used to be kept with the Schloss documents. Possibly this note has found its way into the Buea archives, renovated in 1997 by Shirley Ardener of Oxford.

There is strong evidence that some of the original German furniture in the Schloss was removed by Lord Ludgard when he was Sir F J D Ludgard, Governor of the Colony and Protectorate of Nigeria and is possibly still to be found in Lagos.

A remarkable feature of the deputy commissioner's house in our time—apart from the collection of orchids—was the huge circular bed of multi-coloured petunias in the front. The bed was about fifteen feet in diameter and rose to a height of some five or six feet in the middle.

An amusing reflection on the ability of *homo sapiens* to use his (her) eyes was provided on the night in August 1960 that Kat and I gave a birthday party for Jackie in the deputy commissioner's house. The front was brilliantly lit, the petunia bed looking quite splendid. That afternoon the head gardener had killed an eleven-foot cobra stealing the eggs under a sitting hen. We placed the body of the cobra near the petunia bed, equally well lit. Thirty or more cars drove up to deposit the guests. Nobody, absolutely nobody, commented on either the petunias or the snake.

Once the wet season, which lasted from May until September, had set in, the cloud base on the coastal plain was reduced to about 1,500 feet and Buea itself was cloud-bound. I remember closing the bedroom windows to prevent the all-enveloping mist drifting into the room. Window seat cushions in such weather became damp and clothes had to be kept in heated cupboards.

Elders and Fyffes had hired an aerial crop-spraying organisation whose work became very hazardous in conditions of broken ground-level cloud. One young and conscientious pilot, Jerry Fretz, pushed his task too hard and was killed slipping out of a cloud in a steep turn. The same company possessed a twin Apache which government and commercial bodies hired for journeys to Lagos. Instrument departures from the airfield at Tiko were made hazardous by the unreliability of the small non-directional beacon at Tiko which was also subject to "coastal effect". Add to this the 13,500 feet Cameroons Mountain to the NW and one can form some idea of the dangers of an instrument departure from Tiko in bad weather. An accident, I' afraid, was waiting to happen and happen it did.

On 2nd July 1959, the Apache, with only the pilot aboard, took off from Tiko and promptly disappeared. A labourer in Buea said he'd heard an aircraft flying in cloud at approximately the crucial time but the noise had suddenly stopped. We mounted a search party to search the lower slopes of the mountain between 6,000 feet and 9,000 feet NW of Buea. By early afternoon the wreck had been found. The aircraft in climbing configuration had flown straight into the mountain. I could only grieve. It was a matter for the Civil Aviation Department of Nigeria to determine the cause. It would be several months before they reported. I feared, though, that the pilot had been misled by the unreliable Tiko NDB. No pilot in the world could make so drastic an error inadvertently.

As far back as 23rd February 1959, Muna, in Foncha's absence, when talking of future staffing problems following Nigeria's independence promised for 1960, had told me that it was the policy of Foncha's government to rely on Ghanaians or expatriates rather than on the continued services of Nigerians. He also said that he and his colleagues had agreed with Foncha before the latter's departure that they really needed an expert to advise on the implications of secession. He asked me if I could help by suggesting the sort of background the advisor should ideally have and by suggesting names.

It seemed plain to me that the Cameroonians were wide open to the wrong sort of influence and advice unless a suitable secessionist expert was found as soon as possible.

I passed these fears onto Gardner-Brown who in turn enlisted the help of Granddad himself in his capacity of High-Commissioner for the Cameroons. Sir James Robertson wrote to Eastwood in the colonial office echoing our fears of the wrong appointee. (We all had a recent visit by Nkrumah to the Cameroons in mind. Sir James feared that George Padmore might be appointed.)

As a result of all this Sir Sydney Phillipson KBE, CMG, was appointed to report upon the financial, economic and administrative consequences to the Southern Cameroons of separation from the Federation of Nigeria.

Somewhat unfortunately the 14th Session of the United Nations Assembly overtook the preparation of Sir Sydney's report and the document, when it did emerge, had to bear the following note:

The Government of the Southern Cameroons wish to emphasise that the attached report by Sir Sydney Phillipson was written before the UN General Assembly at its 14th Session decided that the Southern Cameroons should be separated from the Federation of Nigeria by the 1st October 1960 and that a plebiscite should be held between that date and March 1961 to decide whether the Southern Cameroons should achieve independence by joining an independent Nigeria or by joining an independent Republic of the Cameroons. The period of separation will therefore be very short and a considerable number of conclusions and recommendations in the Report are consequently no longer apposite as they were based on a general assumption that the territory would remain separated for a substantially longer period than that which is now contemplated. The circulation of this Report will accordingly be restricted and it will not be for sale to the general public.

Ralph Grey with his near-genius for giving personalities appropriate and kindly nicknames used to refer to Sir Sydney as "Rosebud". He was small and delicate, always immaculately dressed. If he didn't affect a silver-headed cane in later years he ought to have done. His manner and reports were in keeping: the latter beautifully set out, concise and nicely rounded. He had been in the Ceylon service in his early days and had subsequently served as Financial Secretary, Uganda and, from 1945 to 1948, as Financial Secretary, Nigeria. He was twenty-five years my senior and Kat, and, in a formal, slightly distant way, we became very fond of him. The last memory we have of him dates from three years before his death. He gave us a very good dinner in London and then took us to the last performance at the (old) Old Vic of Ibsen's *Peer Gynt* with Leo McKern as Peer Gynt. It was a rip roaring fantasy and so beautiful and spirit-stirring that I shed tears today at the memory. Leo McKern was in those days young, well-covered and ugly but his performance reached the heights. I have a recollection of reading a passage in McKern's autobiography in which he implied that sometimes an actor in his career plays a part which is made for him and he for it. He remembers as such his role at the Old Vic. I remember it too, for his performance, backed by the magic music of Grieg, was quite simply the theatrical experience of my life.

There was a battalion of the Nigeria Regiment stationed in the Southern Cameroons, primarily with the role of protecting the territory against possible incursions by the dissidents from the neighbouring Republic of Cameroon. There was, in fact, very little risk that the latter would be active on the British side and the battalion was really there to see and be seen. They were almost entirely officered by Nigerians other than one or two of the company commanders and the battalion commander who were British military personnel on secondment.

The GOC Nigeria was an old friend from our time in Lagos. He arrived in the Cameroons in mid-July and Kat and I enjoyed entertaining him at the Schloss. No sooner had he left than Granddad himself, Sir James Robertson and entourage, arrived for a three-day visit. He had a very full programme but the second evening I was able to take him for a walk to see the then quiescent lava flow above Ekona.

It was on this walk that he suddenly startled me by saying, "Look here, how would you like to be left alone in Buea? We have other work for Field."

To my surprise I found myself answering at once. It was almost as though somebody else was speaking for me. I must confess that I never gave a thought about Field. I assumed that "the other work" mentioned for him would be a promotion and he would accept it. My thoughts were directed solely to the prospect of upsetting the present arrangement concerning the two of us.

I found myself trying to make a number of points: Field had been in Buea for three years and had got to know the personalities involved in determining the future of the country. He had also got to know the officials in the colonial office dealing with Cameroonian affairs and was on terms of easy d/o correspondence with them. Apart from this he had many contacts in the Trusteeship Council itself. It would always be easier for him than for me to deal with visiting missions and to assist British officials in their work in Lake Success. I felt fairly confident in looking after the country when he was away and in any case we kept up a very comprehensive correspondence. I had at least one long letter from him each week, luckily I could read his handwriting without strain. (Granddad laughed at this although he made no other comment on what I was saying.)

I added—and it makes me squirm to remember this; I only hope Granddad did not consider it too unctuous—that I considered myself Field's deputy. When he was away I would try to forward his policies rather than introduce my own variations.

I later consulted son John, then aged sixteen, about this conversation. His immediate reaction was to say, "I think you are wrong." He may have been correct but what he didn't know at the time—and I had not come to terms with the conviction myself—was that we were doing the Cameroonians a wrong. We should have struggled harder to continue our trusteeship for several years longer. But the forces against us were too strong and I judge now that had I, as Commissioner of the Cameroons taken this line in 1959-61, I should merely have made a great nuisance of myself and achieved nothing.

As it was my conversation with Granddad above Ekona that evening—and his tacit acceptance of what I said—meant that I had firmly committed myself to the role of loyal deputy to John Field for the next two and a half years...until independence, in fact when Kat and I left Buea and the colonial service for the last time.

On the 14th August the Earl and Countess of Perth visited Buea. He was the Seventeenth Earl and from 1957 until 1962 was Minister of State for Colonial Affairs. Although he was only ten years my senior I quickly received the impression that he was heavy with experience of affairs of state. He had served in the War Cabinet Office and the Ministry of Production during the war. The Countess was the easiest of guests and got on well with Kat and daughter Jackie, also with the daughter of a French doctor in Douala, Anne Blaché, who was a friend of Jackie's and was staying with us at the time.

The Earl was familiar with the United Kingdom business world and knew exactly what contacts he wished to make in the Cameroons. We spent an hour discussing his programme. I felt that he was likely to hear more from the heads of Elders and Fyffes and the CDC if he saw them alone than if I were there to inhibit what they said. I would do the honours, introduce them and so forth and then leave him alone with them. He made a point of giving me a résumé of what they'd said after each meeting. Only the other day I discovered that he'd written a long letter to Lennox-Boyd giving a full account of his Cameroons visit. It is to be found at the Public Records Office, Kew reference CO554/1744. He didn't copy it to me for the rather strange reason that he mentioned me in complimentary terms in a short paragraph at the end. However his account tallies precisely with my memory of what he told me orally at the time.

In August 1959 the future of the Southern Cameroons was on the agenda of the Trusteeship Council. They did not know what they would later recommend nor, of course, did Granddad.

The immediate problem in the Cameroons was staff. Many of the junior posts—clerks, P & T workers, teachers and so forth—were held by members of the Nigerian service on secondment. In the main these people were not popular with the Cameroonians and in any case they disliked working so far from home. Should the Southern Cameroons decide in the forthcoming plebiscite for separation from Nigeria, there would be a danger of an exodus, even if Nigeria was still prepared to assist the country with trained staff. Perth knew that Sir James Robertson and his expatriate staff were well aware of the problem but felt that the dangers and difficulties were pressing enough for intervention by HMG. He therefore recommended an early review of the whole problem in conjunction with the Federal Government.

Perth's initiative here was to result in two lines of action: the recruitment in the UK of a number of ex-colonial personnel on retirement for service in the S Cameroons on temporary terms with the principal duty of instructing Cameroonian staff and, secondly, the payment of a special Cameroons allowance (payable to all non-Cameroonian staff, Nigerian and expatriate, serving in the Southern Cameroons). This allowance became known as SCRIP and was fixed at ten per cent of salary.

Perth held two long discussions with Paterson, Financial Secretary, Balmain, my deputy and me on the subject of financing the territory in the period prior to a final decision as to its future.

The Federal Government of Nigeria was really being very long-suffering in continuing to spend money on federal public works and federal services within the Southern Cameroons, without a firm promise of reimbursement should the Southern Cameroons ultimately opt for separation from Nigeria. The problem was made more pressing by a report from Foncha that the federal government shortly intended to cease work on the all-important trunk road from Kumba to Mamfe and onwards to Bamenda and the ring road encircling the Bamenda Province. It was understood that the road-making equipment currently being used on these roads was urgently required elsewhere in the Federation of Nigeria.

Perth told us that he could not foresee HMG letting the Cameroons down but he repeated the warning originally given by Lennox-Boyd that this did not mean that the Southern Cameroons could expect the golden key to the Bank of England. He also thought it likely that Sir Sydney Phillipson's report would probably conclude that the SC could get by on its own resources so far as recurrent expenditure was concerned but would require HMG assistance for capital works and for services previously supplied by the federal government to the magnitude of one million a year (a sum of thirteen million per annum in today's values).

Both Sir Sidney and Lord Perth were enthusiastic on the subject of the future economic prospects of the Southern Cameroons.

Perth of course had full talks with Foncha, the premier, and separately with Dr Endeley, the leader of the opposition. Foncha was inclined to live in what one might describe as "the desirable future". He was apt to construe an expression of agreement for an idea into a promise to assist. At that time he was convinced Nkrumah would support his proposal that the SC should continue for a period under trusteeship before determining its future.

Regarding the views then current in the colonial and foreign offices and the treasury, Perth said that they could best be summarised as a balance against further trusteeship; the cost and defence considerations weighed heavily against as did the relatively small size of the territory—about one million people in all. However, Perth emphasised that the matter was still open.

Field's leave had not gone well for him. Visiting the United Kingdom, principally to hold talks in the colonial office, he'd had to go into hospital to have a kidney stone removed surgically. This had kept him bedridden for fourteen days. He then went to his home in South Africa to recuperate and enjoy the balance of his leave. Sir James Robertson wrote to him in the middle of August suggesting that he should go direct to London and New York from his leave without spending a short spell en route in the Cameroons as he had planned, adding that he would arrange for me to meet him in London and update him on Cameroonian affairs before he, John Field that is, went on to Lake Success for the council meeting dealing with the future of the Cameroons. This latter date was expected to be about 23rd September.

I accordingly flew to London on 12th September. We all felt that Foncha ought to be supported in New York so with Andrew Cohen's assistance (Sir Andrew Cohen was British Representative on the Trusteeship Council of the UN) it was agreed Muna should visit New York with Foncha.

Lennox-Boyd very kindly gave a splendid luncheon party in Foncha's honour in the penthouse of the Dorchester Hotel overlooking Hyde Park. It was a glorious September day and Foncha turned up wearing Bamenda robes topped by a small, highly decorated, Bamenda cap. The effect was spoiled somewhat by a T-shirt he was wearing below the Bamenda robes, the armholes of which were distinctly grubby. Lennox-Boyd, even sitting at table, towered above Foncha. I recall Foncha, in his confident manner, looking up at him and saying, "You know something, Secretary of State?"

"No, what do I know?" said Lennox-Boyd, politely, looking down at his guest.

"We have pigeons in our country, too," said Foncha sawing away at his half-partridge. Muna scowled; nobody laughed.

There had been a conference in Mamfe presided over by Sir Sydney Phillipson in early August. Representatives of the KNC and the KNDP both attended and it was hoped that the meeting would agree the questions to be put at the forthcoming plebiscite on the future of the territory. It was typical of the Cameroons that although agreement was very near it was not possible to reach it. This same characteristic...this shying away from agreement the moment it comes close and seems logical is as strong today—in 1998—as it was in 1959. It is a sad weakness of the body politic.

At the UN's General Assembly's 82-Nation Trusteeship Council in September-October 1959, Foncha (KNDP) and Endeley (KNC) agreed that one of the alternate questions for the plebiscite should be *association* with Nigeria. Foncha wanted the second alternative to be "separation from Nigeria and continued trusteeship until the SC was in a position to decide its future". Endeley, on the other hand, wanted the second alternative to be "reunification with the French Cameroons after the territory becomes independent on 1st January 1960".

As neither party would move from these positions, the African delegation at the UN was asked to find common ground between the KNC and KNDP.

Liberia finally submitted a draft resolution to the Trusteeship Council which proposed that a plebiscite should be held not later than March 1961 and that the questions should be:-

1   Do you wish to achieve independence by joining an independent Federation of Nigeria?

or

2   Do you wish to achieve independence by joining the independent Republic of Cameroon?

The Administering Authority (the UK) in consultation with the Government of the Southern Cameroons was asked to take steps to separate the administration of the SC from that of the Federation of Nigeria not later than October 1960.

This resolution was adopted by the Fourth Trusteeship Council of the General Assembly by a vote of seventy-four with Afghanistan and Iraq abstaining. Foncha, Muna and Endeley returned to Buea with one proposed question which nobody in the Cameroons wanted.

I returned to Buea on 18th September. On the 19th October a bit of good luck came our way. For the past two years we'd had a personal saloon car which none of us liked. There was nothing specifically wrong with it but we all wanted to be rid of it. On the evening of the 19th we lent it to the driver of the commissioner's official car to take his family down to Victoria. On the way back he'd left the road on one of the many bends and ended up jammed on a large boulder, the chassis distorted and the engine damaged beyond repair. The driver, luckily, hadn't been hurt. The insurance company in Lagos where the car was insured, offered me the precise sum in compensation for the total write off as I happened to owe government for the unpaid balance of the purchase loan. We were about to go on leave and planned to spend the greater part of the leave skiing in Austria. I was able to order a front-wheel drive ID 19 Citroen for delivery at the beginning of our leave. It served us loyally in the Alps; we did not need to use chains even after two and a half feet of new snow. It proved to be equally efficient in the mud of the Cameroons' wet season.

Foncha himself genuinely believed that he had a role to "educate the masses". He was apt, however, to pursue this deviously. Immediately prior to independence in 1961 Ahidjo, President of the Republic of Cameroon, added to his package of persuasive undertakings, a number of secret promises regarding Foncha's and Muna's future. Foncha was regarded by his own supporters with suspicion. But this was two years into the future. Let me return to 1959.

Foncha's acceptance of the second plebiscite question in New York in 1959 infuriated Jua and others within the KNDP leadership. Consideration was said to have been given to Foncha's removal as party leader but Foncha was nothing if not a fighter and he talked his way out of this threat on his return. He reminded his critics that when he had met Ahidjo in Buea in July 1959, before going to New York, he had made it quite plain to him that he was thinking in terms of a loose confederation. What he did not confess was that Ahidjo himself had made it equally clear that he was talking of a federation. Nor did he point out that in any case Ahidjo held the stronger cards.

He and Ahidjo had further meetings in January, May, July, October and November 1960, where virtually the same things were said. At each meeting Ahidjo remained quite firm and consistent regarding the basic federal relationship possibly to come. Foncha apparently refused to accept that he had made little impression on him. Observers began to wonder if this was blind obstinacy or something less admirable.

To be fair to Foncha, I believe he manifested, more than many, the propensity to dichotomy of thought I first remarked amongst the Ibo twenty years before (page 45). He contradicted himself, in the sense of Western logic, many times in the United Nations debates. He did the same thing in his talks with Field and myself. He calmly ignored frequent changes of attitude which any Western European would be ashamed of making.

Throughout 1960 there was widespread opposition in the Southern Cameroons to the questions proposed for the plebiscite, neither of which the majority of the people wanted. This was demonstrated to the plebiscite officials who undertook in September 1960 a campaign to inform the peoples about the alternatives.

Victor Julius Njoh, in his work, *Constitutional Development on the Southern Cameroons 1946-61*, summarised the reaction to the alternative questions as follows:-

KNDP: – When Foncha had left for the UN in September 1959 he had promised to secure a two to three year extension of the trusteeship period. He had accepted the second plebiscite question thus breaking his promise to his party at home.

KNC-KPP Alliance: – applauded the "compromise".

The majority of individuals in the Southern Cameroons including most of the Chiefs: – strongly condemned the "compromise" and demanded succession. However it was pointed out that at this point the chiefs began to act individually and separately rather than present a single unified front. Each wanted to protect his own personal interests.

The KUP:– resolved at a meeting in Buea on 24th January 1960 that the "compromise" was "a departure from the fundamental principal upon which the UN was promulgated with regard to trust territories."

The CCC (Cameroons Commoners Conference of Mamfe):
– also opposed "the compromise" as did the **CIP** of Chief Manga Williams.

Towards the end of 1960 the disquiet in the Southern Cameroons concerning the two plebiscite questions reached serious proportions. A conference of the major political parties was arranged in London in November 1960. The Rt Hon Iain Macleod had taken over from the Rt Hon Lennox-Boyd as Secretary of State in October 1959 and the former therefore took the chair at the conference. It was attended by Field, Foncha, Muna, Endeley, Motomby-Woleta, Kangsen, Ncha, Effiom, Fon Galega II, Chief Oben and Kale. At one stage Field and the secretary of state were favourably inclined to seeking an amendment to the UN resolution concerning the plebiscite alternatives but they were advised by the British staff in the UNO that there was no chance of an amendment being made and they accordingly abandoned the suggestion.

Following the September 1959 resolution of the UN the KNC-KPP Alliance, led by Endeley, wasted no time in pursuing its desire to join Nigeria; they secured firm proposals for action in the event of the plebiscite going their way. In May 1960 British and Nigerian officials met and worked out details. It was proposed that the Federation of Nigeria would comprise the Eastern, Western and Northern Regions (the latter including the Northern Cameroons if the NC plebiscite resulted in a pro-Nigerian vote) together with the Federal Territory of Lagos and the Region of the Southern Cameroons. The latter would be a full, self-governing Region. The SC would be given a Governor, a House of Assembly, a House of Chiefs, a High Court, an Executive Council and a separate public service.

The KNDP under Foncha immediately published in response a pamphlet entitled *United Cameroons Federal Constitution*. This pamphlet did not bear the firm agreement of Ahidjo or the government of the Cameroon State and it included a number of provisions which were most unlikely ever to be agreed. These latter included the creation of no less than three heads of state and a clause permitting the Southern Cameroons "Region" to have its own military force.

The pamphlet in fact reflected merely what was Foncha's conception of a loose confederation. It differed very considerably from the type of constitution that Ahidjo had already described to KNDP leaders.

Meanwhile the Northern Cameroons plebiscite held on the 7th November 1959, provided something of a shock for all concerned with

401

the future of the Cameroons under United Kingdom trusteeship. Approximately eighty-eight per cent of the all-male electorate voted. 113,859 votes were cast. Of these 70,546 votes chose the second alternative, namely:

> "(b) Are you in favour of deciding the future of the Northern Cameroons at a later date."

42,788 favoured the first alternative, namely:

> "(a) Do you wish the Northern Cameroons to become part of the Northern Region of Nigeria when the Federation of Nigeria becomes independent?"

525 votes were rejected.

The reaction in Northern Nigeria to the result was sharp. As Sir Andrew Cohen pointed out in UN circles, it did not necessarily mean that the N Cameroons were refusing affiliation with Nigeria for all time. This argument did not carry great weight with such as the Sardauna of Sokoto, the Premier of Northern Nigeria nor with the government of the Northern Region. The informed view was that the populace as a whole did not fully understand the implications of either question. People voted largely on the strength of local issues. For instance, the Dikwa people of Chamba origin did not want to be ruled in future by Yola. According to VP Punyong of Jesus College, Cambridge (see his PhD thesis entitled *The United Nations in the Political Evolution of Cameroon*), it was the prospect of this plebiscite that was responsible for the formation of a political party—the Northern Kamerun Democratic Party (the NKDP) as far back as April 1959. The party advocated secession of the NC from Nigeria and its development towards independence either as a separate state or in unity with the SC. Punyong quotes Foncha as claiming, as late as 1997, that his party—the KNDP—helped form the NKDP.

I see no reason to dissent from this view.

The Plebiscite Administrator was Lt Col Sir John Dring who had previously served in the Indian political service. The United Nations Plebiscite Commissioner was Dr Djahal Abdoh. The former was charged with arranging the plebiscite; the commissioner on the other hand was charged with ensuring that the plebiscite was actually operated in accordance with UN requirements.

The imminence of independence in Nigeria had caused a number of problems affecting the status and future employment of expatriate members of the overseas service (as the colonial service was now called). A steady stream of documents was issued to officers from 1956 onwards. The study of these documents and action upon them put a considerable strain on men and women already labouring under an unusually heavy workload. It was difficult to switch from local problems to those affecting our own future. Many of my contemporaries will confirm that we almost resented having to deal with documents affecting ourselves…difficult to believe as it may sound.

By 1959, after twenty years of service, I found myself working with confidence in the higher ranks of a unified and closely knit service. At the same time, in keeping with my friends, I saw that the service itself was coming to an end. I had taken on a job for my working life. Halfway through, the ground below had been cut away; it was no longer a job for life. A continually reducing service would be required for a few years but even that would bear little resemblance to the service I'd joined. Great Britain had decided, rightly or wrongly, to abandon the colonial role. A disciplined, close-knit service built up to administer the colonial empire world-wide was being used to push the territories under our auspices, willy-nilly, into independence and subsequently to disband itself.

Put in the simplest terms I was faced in December 1959 with applying to join one of the Special Lists, A or B. List A involved an undertaking by HMG to find me employment anywhere in what remained of the empire at a value not less than the value of the post held when joining the list. (The "value" of a post varied with the emoluments, climate and distance from the UK, but in practical terms was the highest figure HMG would accept.) At the end of the five-year period, or on reaching retirement age, an officer could be forced to retire. He would receive the pension and associated benefits that he would have received in HM Overseas Service had he continued in that service.

Officers on Special List B, on the other hand, would continue to seve in Nigeria and were required to give one year's notice of retirement and on retirement receive earned pension plus a sum of compensation calculated according to age—the maximum being payable at the age of forty and falling away on both sides of this figure.

In my own case, taking into account my recent promotions (I had received a further personnel promotion to Federal Permanent Secretary grade on the 23rd December 1959), it was to my financial advantage to retire on the 1st October 1961 on Special List B terms.

Special List A was a gamble. Take it and receive continuous promotions, one might be better off on a retirement pension alone. At worst one could earn one's final salary for five years and be forced to retire at the end of the five year period, in which case one would lose the capital "lumpers" (worth in my case about £120,000 in 1998 values).

Plainly, the final decision as to which list to apply for was a personal one depending upon the circumstances, foresight and family commitment of each officer. The financial aspect was only one of several factors.

The views and intentions of post-war recruits to the service differed fundamentally from those recruited pre-war. The former had joined a post-war service at the time when independence was fast becoming a probability for many colonial territories. (1947 was a peak year for post-war recruitment). Recruits were taking on a long-term pensionable job even then, but not as a job for life. Independence for India and Pakistan was just around the corner; Ceylon (Sri Lanka) was to follow. Admittedly independence for the Gold Coast (Ghana) and many other territories was ten years away but attitudes had changed considerably from attitudes in 1939. There was, in 1947, a world-wide growing hostility to colonialism; in America, particularly, this attitude was hardening.

With the hindsight of sixty years I believe that when we joined the unified colonial service it was at its zenith. The interruption of the war years, and our return to colonial duties following a decision of the war cabinet, if anything, strengthened our conception of a family relationship: the service was not only eminently fair to us, it took care of us. We, in return, obeyed the accepted usages of the service: we were encouraged, at whatever level we served, to say what we thought but we did what we were told. Many matters arose where there was no service precedent and no time to seek one; here we strove to act on lines we believed to be the most acceptable to the service. We tried to be, in later parlance, "good company men".

If Jack Walton represented the opinions and attitudes of the informed British observer between the wars when I first gave him details of the mores of the lower levels of the service (which I believe I did) then his letters of reply are of historical value today.

It is difficult now to remember precisely what was in my mind in 1959. The best I can do is to sum up as follows; the unified service that I had joined in 1938 was on its way out. At the present rate of the gallop to independence the service I knew would be virtually superfluous by, say, 1964. I was confidant (I believe now, over-confidant) in my own abilities. I believed I could secure employment in a number of spheres. This proved true up to a point for the next twenty-five years but I realise now what I did not admit to myself in

1959 was that I was more interested in the variety and quality of life than in the building up of a reputation or in accumulating wealth. Very near the surface was a conviction that the next twenty or thirty years must be spent in the pursuit of objectives which I judged to be true substitutes for the rapidly disintegrating colonial service.

Probably I was at one with most of my contemporaries—and many of my seniors, too—who considered privately that the sudden acceleration towards independence of colonial territories was doing both the countries themselves and us as a colonial power, a disservice. The direction was right enough but the speed was wrong. Most of us appreciated the pressures that were being put upon the colonial powers, particularly the British, by the Americans and by the Afro-Asian Group in the United Nations, the latter so ably orchestrated by Krishna Menon. The Afro-Asian Group, as I have already pointed out, commanded the majority in the Trusteeship Council so that as far as the trusteeship territory of the Southern Cameroons was concerned there was continued trusteeship, whatever the wishes of the local population, would involve a major dispute.

True to the tradition of the service, nearly every British officer, having voiced his misgivings within the confines of the service, accepted the instructions that flowed down from higher authority (in the end the British cabinet) and worked conscientiously to achieve them. Few resigned at this point.

In the Southern Cameroons the test upon the loyalty of expatriate staff became increasingly severe. As I will try to explain in the pages that follow, the gap between the over-confident forecasts of the members of the KNDP government and the likely flow of events widened. So much so that a conflict arose between the role of expatriate staff as loyal servants of the Cameroons government and their duty as representatives of the trusteeship authority.

Much research has been undertaken in the past forty years by Cameroons' scholars and others into the dozen years spanning the reunification of the Southern Cameroons in 1961. A number of researchers have asked, "What was the true intention of HM Government at any one time?"

My answer from my knowledge of discussions that took place at the time, reinforced by documents that have subsequently been released under the thirty years' rule for examination at the Public Records Office, Kew must be "precisely as was publicly stated at the time". There was no secret agenda and no secret agreements that I was aware of. Various possibilities were examined but not pursued.

As late as 17th June 1961, Sir Roger Stevens, who accompanied C G Eastwood to a meeting in Buea of the Southern Cameroons Chamber of Commerce, said that, in the event of Foncha and Ahidjo not being able to agree the arrangements for the federation by the 1st October 1961, then the United Kingdom would be bound to continue as trustee until the matter had been resolved by the United Nations. This statement hardly suggests some hidden intention.

Chapter Fourteen

Southern Cameroons, 1960

The Republic of Cameroon became independent from France and the UNO on the 1st January 1960. The English press, *The Times* in particular, was gloomy in its comment. Violence organised by the banned UPC had originally been directed at France and the UNO. Ahidjo and his government had demonstrated in the three years or so preceding independence that nationalistic advance could be secured by democratic means. The violence however, still continued. The UPC was forced to re-direct its campaign against Ahidjo and his democratically elected government. It came to entangle its actions with traditional tribal rivalries and personal jealousies. It even tried to maintain that Ahidjo was a mere puppet of the French. The terrorist movement within the republic lost a measure of its validity by this switch.

John Field, Mike Cartlidge (the Commissioner of Police) and I all felt that Ahidjo was considerably under-estimated as a leader. He himself was quietly confident that the French would come to the assistance of his country if need be. He did not treat the terrorist threat as more than a potential nuisance. There were too many metropolitan French enterprises in the country to sacrifice to the forces of disorder. Subsequent events proved him to be right.

Kat and I were due for leave during the first three months of 1960. Robin and Mary Nicholson had proved the most wonderful of friends and since Alice's death had taken over the role previously played by the Aunts; they not only acted in loco parentis for Jackie and John in our absence abroad but were also very hospitable to Kat and me.

We spent the Christmas holidays of 1959-60 with the two young skiing in Austria. The new Citroen ID 19 served us right royally both on the snow and in the United Kingdom. It became as important to us as a shell to a snail.

Kate, eighty on the 2nd April 1960, was in a nursing home in Malvern. After Alice's death in 1958, their nephew Miles Bellville and

his wife Nan had given Kate a flat at the Bellville family home—
Tedstone Court. Kate had managed adequately there on her own—
relying of course on the nearby presence of Nan and Miles—until the
end of 1959. Then her condition worsened quite suddenly: her memory
grew confused and unreliable and she became bedridden for much of
the time. Miles found her a place in a nursing home some twelve
miles away at Malvern. I made several trips during our 1959-60
leave, some with Mary Nicholson, down from Cumberland to see
her.

Shortly after our return to Buea in 1960 I received encouraging
reports about Kate's condition from the medical officer in charge of
the nursing home. So much so that with Kat's ready help I began to
make arrangements for Kate to join us in Buea. She would have to be
accompanied on the flight out but first she would have to undergo
prophylactic injections for cholera, yellow fever and typhoid, any one
of which might prove an ordeal to an old lady in her state of health.

Only a couple of weeks later the medical officer wrote again; he
advised that we abandon plans to have her in Buea—her condition
had once again deteriorated and in his opinion she wasn't fit to
undergo the injections, much less travel.

Kat and I had pioneered with children in the bush of Eastern Nigeria
in the 1940s. We felt that there was no reason why we shouldn't take
on the care of the old especially as there were many good African
servants available in the 1960s. However, thinking the matter over at
leisure, I realised that her presence would have placed a grievous
burden on Kat, and it certainly would not have commended itself to
my superiors; nor would I have encouraged any of my subordinates
to do the same thing.

Nevertheless, I still have a guilty feeling towards Kate of duty not
done.

We returned to the Cameroons by banana boat, MV *Manistee*,
arriving at Tiko on 13th April 1960.

Immediately we landed I was involved in discussions concerning
military and police operations in the Southern Cameroons in the period
March to October 1960. Nigeria was to become independent on 1st
October 1960. Before this date the Nigerian military forces in the
Southern Cameroons would have to be replaced by British forces.
Police services were currently made available to the Southern
Cameroons by Nigeria as one of the "agency services". It had been
proposed—but not at that point agreed—that, in the interval between
1st October 1960 and the final settlement by UNO of the future of the
Southern Cameroons, police and other agency services would continue

to be provided on a repayment basis by Nigeria in extension of the current agency arrangement.

Sir James Robertson, in his High Commissioner of the Cameroons capacity, was very sensitive that Nigerian personnel serving either the police or military in the Southern Cameroons should in no way be the cause of embarrassment to Nigeria. He therefore laid down stringent rules for their employment.

He drew attention to the delicate political situation in both the Southern Cameroons and the Republic of Cameroon. At the same time he emphasised the general touchiness in the world at large concerning independence and colonialism. Liaison between the two territories was to be reduced and in future, so far as the employment of the police was concerned, restricted to senior administrative and police officers. The primary role of the military was to discourage terrorism by their presence. Nigeria's strategy in permitting a military presence in the Southern Cameroons was not to assist the government of the republic to eliminate terrorism but rather to safeguard the security of Nigeria. The troops should consequently be used sparingly in assistance to the police. Their main role was to be passive except for frontier patrolling. Liaison by the military with their opposite numbers across the frontier was to be restricted to officers and conducted with the utmost discretion.

Before going on leave I had asked E D Quan, who was Assistant Secretary (Establishments) if he would kindly do some research for me while I was away. It wasn't an urgent matter and Balmain, who would be acting for me in my absence, wouldn't be interested but I would.

I asked him to trace the later careers of the Bamenda Corps of Messengers, after I'd worked with them in the Bamenda District ten years before. Since then Bamenda had become a province and it was possible several of the corps had gone to Districts other than Bamenda.

Quan produced the results of his work the day after we got back having written about fifty words on each. Only A Dinga had retired, the others were scattered but all serving still.

I slipped a copy of Quan's report into the folder of documents I always carried on tour and made a point of chatting to each of the Corps before finally leaving the Cameroons at the end of 1961. I felt vaguely then, and know for certain now, that working with these men had greatly enriched my time in the colonial service. There was something very special about that corps; service was their watchword.

Foncha had been forced to rationalise his position regarding the plebiscite questions laid down in the UNO to the extent of saying that it was now (as at April 1960) his wish that the questions should remain as suggested and if the plebiscite vote went in favour of the Republic of Cameroon then sovereignty should first be transferred to the Southern Cameroons. Only after a joint SC/R of C body had determined the shape of a United Cameroon Republic should sovereignty be transferred to it at a date to be agreed.

President Ahidjo had signified little more than interest in Foncha's proposals. He took care to say nothing that was binding on himself or the Republic of Cameroon. He was particularly non-committal in his remarks regarding timing. There was a strong feeling in the Republic of Cameroon that unification should be effected immediately following a plebiscite vote in favour. Johnson (the British Ambassador to the R of C. appointed on independence) and others close to Ahidjo thought that he would be unlikely to frustrate this desire for early unification. It seemed to us in the SC that Foncha had placed himself in a difficult position: it was extremely unlikely that the UNO would transfer power in the first instance to a SC government in the absence of agreement by HMG, by R of C and by all the parties in the SC.

Foncha's difficulties were intensified on 11th March 1960 when J M Boja, originally a KNDP member of the House of Assembly for Wum, crossed the floor of the House and joined the KNC. This left the numbers of elected members as thirteen KNDP and thirteen KNC-KPP Alliance. However, the KNDP party could count on the vote of a nominated member (Mrs Muna) which gave them a working majority of one. The official members were required to vote with the government on matters previously agreed in Exco. The KNDP government naturally ignored requests for fresh elections so long as this situation continued.

Foncha and his ministers, with their wafer-thin majority, understandably became very sensitive to threats that other members of their own party might cross the floor either in response to genuine political conviction or as a result of bribery by the KNC-KPP Alliance.

In the middle of the year Foncha was shown a document signed by D N Frambo, KNDP Member for Mamfe (South,) stating that he had transferred his political loyalty to the KNC-KPP Alliance. He was alleged to have been given £2,000 as an inducement by Dr Endeley and Mr Mbile, the leader and deputy leader of the opposition. Mr Frambo, when questioned, accused Dr Endeley and Mr Mbile of having forced him to sign the letter of resignation from the KNDP at gunpoint. He made no mention of the £2,000.

Dr Endeley and Mr Mbile told a different story. They said that Mr Frambo was genuinely anxious to cross the floor but he felt constrained by the fact that he owed the sum of £2,000 by way of repayment of a loan to the KNDP party. He agreed to sign a letter stating his intention of changing parties—provided the £2,000 was first made available to him.

The H of A was in recess at the time. Mr Frambo's true intention would have only become manifest on his actual record in the House of Assembly.

Foncha's government promptly set up a commission of inquiry under J E Burke. The commission, among other things, was expected to find out if on any occasion during 1959-60 money or other inducement was given, promised or offered to influence the words or conduct of members of the House of Assembly. In his terms of reference the inquiry commissioner was also asked to advise, in the light of his findings, whether amendments should be made to the law of the Southern Cameroons to render the corruption of a legislator in his capacity as such a criminal matter.

Mr Burke made an interim report of his findings on 18th September 1960 which was published. He found the allegations that Frambo had been forced at gunpoint to sign the letter of resignation to be false. He found that £2,000 had changed hands and that the money had come from a Mr H L Leman, an expatriate businessman resident in the SC. Mr Burke also accepted that the letter of resignation had been drafted by Mr Mbile.

As to possible amendments to the law regarding the corruption of H of A members, Mr Burke promised to convey his recommendations to the commissioner of the Cameroons at a later date. He also found that Mr Frambo never had any genuine intention of turning his political coat. He had, in Mr Burke's view, attempted to bring off a "conjuring trick" and had succeeded to the extent of making the £2,000 disappear.

Mr Frambo continued to support the KNDP. Neither Mr Leman nor Dr Endeley and Mr Mbile saw the £2,000 again.

Mr Frambo himself died on 27th September 1983. The Frambo affair was a "bubble" in the sense that it burst and disappeared into thin air but it did indicate the sort of problems that the wretched Foncha had to contend with.

On 17th May 1960 Southern Cameroons police, ably assisted by Nigerian military units, arrested twenty-seven people and secured large amounts of arms, military clothing and money in a terrorist camp situated just on the Southern Cameroons side of the SC/R of C frontier in a remote part of the country. Twenty-six of the captured persons stood trial on a charge of being a member of a proscribed organisation. All were convicted and sentenced each to six months' imprisonment. The operation was judged to come within the terms of Sir James Robertson's directive.

I visited London between 26th June and 3rd July 1960 largely in connection with the recruitment of ex-colonial service personnel for temporary service in the Southern Cameroons. There were a number of quite excellent officers applying. Most had found retirement in the UK hard to adjust to and welcomed the prospect of some months' further service in an interesting situation. One luncheon interval I was free of appointments from twelve noon to 2.30 p.m. and walked across St James's Park to an open-air restaurant near the Serpentine in Hyde Park (which I believe was closed a year or two later.) All the tables were occupied but I asked the head waiter if he minded me inquiring of the occupant of a sizeable table if I might share with him. "Go ahead, sir," said the waiter. The occupant was obliging and we soon were chatting. He told me he was a doctor at St George's Hospital, in those days just across the way. "H'm, colonial service in West Africa?" he said in reply to my telling him why I was in London. "You send a lot of chaps to my department. Batty as bless you, all of them, when they come in. but do you know what? We send them upstairs to the tropical disease department. They de-tick them, and what have you, and we never see them again."

I laughed but remembered sadly Kendal Robinson. He had won, over the first dozen years of his service, a reputation as a very good "bush DO". His primary concern was for the peasant. He found it harder to summon sympathy for the educated and more sophisticated. I had served under him briefly as a cadet at Nsukka. Since then Kat and I had met him in Eastern Nigeria from time to time. Although he was a Cumbrian and related to Lady Butler our leaves had never coincided. He was promoted to Resident, Class I, in 1952 and found his way to the Western Region. There, unfortunately, he came up against one of the new Western leaders—I think Awolowo himself.

Most members of the administrative service, including Kendal Robinson, had taken the improved terms of service following the Harragin Review. Salaries had been increased roughly in keeping with rises in the cost of living but on the down side officers had been required to accept the right of government to demand compulsory retirement after reaching the age of forty-five. In the middle nineteen-fifties, the period of which I'm writing, this provision—which became known as "Harragin-ing" was a necessary and useful one. It enabled governments to get rid of dead wood and at the same time could be used to expedite Africanisation. The Nigerian Federal, Northern and Eastern governments used the process sparingly and with discretion. Not so the Western Regional Government which was understood to "Harragin" officers far too readily. Doubtless as a solution to the clash of personalities with Awolowo, Kendal Robinson was "Harragina-ed." Kendal Robinson was, when told, appalled. He was killed shortly after in an accident involving a bus. Most of us thought it was suicide.

Just after this tragedy, which I must emphasise happened way back in 1953, Kat and I were passing through Lagos on leave. The ADC to the governor-general (Sir John Macpherson) contacted us and asked us to drinks that night at Government House.

When we got there we found to my consternation that we were the only guests. We sat out on the extensive GH lawn as darkness fell a little before seven, Kat and Lady M chatting easily, Sir John asking me about Eastern Nigerian affairs. Suddenly apropos of nothing that had gone before, he said, "Did I do wrong in "Harragin-ing" Kendal Robinson?"

I said, "Yes," and tried to explain why I thought so.

Surely, I asked, there were posts in Eastern Nigeria, even the Northern Region, to which he could be transferred? He was a bush DO, a resident for a remote province; he should never have been allowed near Awolowo or any other sophisticated politician. He was, I added nastily, much too honest.

The responsibility for retiring Kendal R lay primarily with the establishment secretary and governor of the Western Region. Plainly the latter had consulted Sir John. What I'd said seemed to sadden him. He grew silent; our conversation—between the Big Man and the junior officer—died away. I begged permission to take Kat home.

I shall never know whether he agreed with me or not. It was a pity that I hadn't then met the St George's psychiatrist for what he told me half in joke was a profound truth, which I might have passed on to Sir John Macpherson.

I digress into the past...we must return to 1960. On page 401 I tried to explain that Endeley and members of the KNC-KPP Alliance had wasted no time in procuring the agreement of the United Kingdom and Nigeria governments to the steps that would be taken should the plebiscite on 11th February 1961 go in favour of Nigeria. The Southern Cameroons would become a separate Region of independent Nigeria with all that entailed.

413

Foncha and his ministers hadn't reached agreement with Ahidjo, the British or, indeed, anybody, of the action necessary if the plebiscite went the other way. They did, however, put the cat amongst the pigeons when they told John Field on 20th July 1960 that Ahidjo had made it clear to them in their recent talks that the Republic of Cameroun would not be able to assume responsibility for the security of the Southern Cameroons if the plebiscite went that way. Ahidjo apparently said that the internal and external security of the Cameroons in such an eventuality would have to be a matter for local provision.

The general assembly, when it had resolved on 16th October 1959 that the Southern Cameroons should be given the option of joining either of two independent and sovereign states—Nigeria or the Republic of Cameroun, naturally supposed that either state would be able to provide internal and external security for all who dwelt within its borders. This was the first time that any mention to the contrary had been made.

Sir James Robertson had two weighty responsibilities that might conflict: as Governor-general of Nigeria it was his duty to leave Nigeria, about to achieve independence on 1st October 1960, as free as possible from outside risk. At the same time he was High Commissioner of the Southern Cameroon and had duties, under UK and UNO fiat, to that territory.

Foncha and his ministers went even further. They told John Field that Ahidjo, in the course of their immediately recent talks, had shown them he shared their views about the timetable for reunification. It was the business of the two territories, the Republic and the Southern Cameroons, to decide for themselves exactly how the federation would be achieved and when. There would be a lengthy period of engagement followed by eventual marriage, not unification as soon as possible after the plebiscite as the United Nations seemed to think.

Sir James and his close advisors in Lagos feared that propaganda based on such conceptions might produce, if unchecked, a plebiscite result that would prove unwelcome or dangerous to Nigeria. Many Cameroonians, in favour of a "third choice", might vote for unification with the R of C in the belief that the period of engagement might be indefinitely postponed and unification never happen at all. The Southern Cameroons could be subject to a terrorist take-over from the east or alternatively Foncha might seek assistance which, in the event of Britain being unwilling to provide it, might well be from a country inimical to Nigeria, such as China.

I merely outline the salient details of this development here in order to illustrate the kind of problems that were prone suddenly to emerge in the hectic days prior to independence. John Field had returned in July and it fell to him, rather than me as his deputy, to bring the matter to conclusion. Fortunately the problem is covered in two quite lucid dispatches now available to the general public in the Public Records Office, Kew (Reference CO 554/2412).

Towards the end of 1960 I had a long discussion with Mike Cartlidge about the character of Foncha. Field was away for a relatively short time so Kat and I remained in the deputy commissioner's house while I acted as commissioner. We'd had a dinner party: Foncha had been a guest, some two other ministers with their wives and Mike was also there. Foncha was the last of the Cameroonians to leave. I saw him out to his car—chauffeur driven with a police orderly—and reaching the door before the orderly—opened it for him. Going back into the house, Mike said, "You are the Queen's representative. You shouldn't have opened that door." He was a friend and knew very well that I welcomed his private views on such matters.

I said, "I try to adhere to the English system of manners. I'd have opened it for any guest." Mike stuck to his point.

The agency services for the period 1st October 1960 to 3rd March 1961, which included Civil Aviation, Customs, Geological Survey, Meteorology, Police, Posts and Telegraphs, Labour and Prisons, were estimated to cost £393,650 (approximately five million pounds in 1996 values). Nigeria, in a decision I suspect owed much to the esteem in which ministers held Sir James Robertson, agreed to continue to provide these services at bare cost until the results of the plebiscite were finally implemented.

John Field had continuously pressed Foncha and his ministers to come out with a clear statement agreed by Ahidjo of the effect of a plebiscite decision in favour of unification with R of C.

Foncha, accompanied by Muna, Jua and Effiom, then visited Ahidjo in Yaounde between the 10th and the 14th November 1960 and had long discussions with him. They came back with three, very unsatisfactory documents.

The first was addressed to the administering authority and the United Nations saying the Southern Cameroons must have its own military force for which training should start immediately. A speeding up of the rate of Cameroonisation was requested together with financial assistance by the British for both the military forces and agency services.

The second document was headed "Outline Proposals for a Draft Constitution for a Federal United Kameroun Republic". It was a dubious and non-committal paper.

415

The third document was a resolution by both sides to implement the proposals in the other two documents and contained the significant clause: "...the implementation of reunification cannot be automatic but gradual."

In conversation with me after their return from Yaounde (Field was on tour in the Bamenda area) the ministers said they felt they had returned to the position they had taken up after the election of the KNDP government in 1959. (Namely, immediate unification is impossible and a period of separate existence must intervene.) They also said they felt strengthened by Ahidjo's statement that the Southern Cameroons must have a military force of its own. Jua spoke of a period of separate existence of "at least five years". (Foncha and Muna did not comment on this.) They all agreed the period of separate existence must be dependent on:-

a)   The internal situation in the Cameroons.
b)   The speed with which a military force could be built up.
c)   the rate of economic development in the country.

They all said, too, that in the event of a communist coup in the R of C, they would abandon reunification entirely. They also told me they understood the military assistance treaty between the Republic of Cameroon and France had been extended for another year.

There were a number of queries concerning the documents produced by Foncha. Whatever Foncha's wishes may have been at the time, or have since become, the fact remained that in 1959 he had accepted the United Nations' proposal that sovereignty should be transferred to either Nigeria or the Republic of Cameroon. The United Nations were unlikely, without agreement of all parties, to vary their previous resolution.

Field was in London in November 1960 and on the 4th December he went on leave. I was left with the task of explaining the weakness of Foncha's position to him and to his ministers, early in December 1960. I tried to do this.

On 8th December I received a letter from Foncha which he requested I should forward to the United Nations and to the HMG. This letter demanded my immediate removal from office on the grounds that my attitude and my criticism of the documents they had jointly produced with Ahidjo were non-constitutional on my part and a major source of opposition to him and his ministers. This was becoming typical of his tactics. Anything he construed as opposition to his designs he would attempt to swat out of the way. He and his ministers

416

had to be persuaded that it was my duty to put to him squarely anything I considered as a weakness in his or, for that matter, Ahidjo's position. It would be a dereliction of my duty were I not to do so.

I had a further meeting with Foncha and leading members of his government on the 8th December. We covered the ground once again. I emphasised the following points:-

a) President Ahidjo had made several public pronouncements welcoming immediate reunification following a favourable plebiscite result. There was a strong feeling in the Republic of Cameroon in favour. Let them ask themselves whether it was likely that President Ahidjo in the face of this feeling would publicly support transfer of sovereignty to the Southern Cameroons, even for a short time.

b) If Foncha's proposal was to be put into effect the public support of Ahidjo together with the concurrence of the opposition in the SC and the support of UNO and of HMG would all be necessary. Was this support likely to be forthcoming?

c) Was it not more realistic to suppose that the R of C would accept sovereignty over the SC, rich or poor, and that the UNO would draw up a unified constitution and, if necessary, implement it? HMG surely could be expected to do no more than impartially enforce the peaceful conduct of the plebiscite? Finally, if SC joined the R of C, could HMG continue to have separate financial, military or any other sort of relations with what would then be part of an independent state?

d) I also understood that Ahidjo had had the assistance during the Yaunde talks of French advisors. Were Mr Foncha and his ministers wise always to go it alone?

This time I made an impression on Foncha and his ministers. The premier informed me that he proposed to withdraw the letter dated 8/12/1960 and asked me not to forward a copy to the secretary of state. He also said that copies endorsed to the Colonial Secretary, London, the Secretary-general, United Nations, New York, the UN Plebiscite Commissioner, Buea and the press had not been distributed.

All this took place as though the Conference in London, at which this matter had been discussed, had never taken place. Foncha was certainly a dogged character who wouldn't take "no" for an answer. This characteristic of his was picked upon by visiting journalists and mentioned more than once in reports in *The Times* and *Telegraph*.

As the Fields were to be on leave for January and February and there was a constant flow of visitors, Kat and I moved into the Schloss. To tuck in some sort of exercise each day I took parties for an hour's jogging each evening. Daughter Jackie and her French friend, Anne Blaché, were always game to come along as were a surprising number of our guests.

There were two roads down to Victoria from Buea: the tarred road which joined the main Kumba-Victoria route and a rough stone macadam track direct to Victoria via Soppo. Normally we trotted down one or other of these routes and arranged for a vehicle to pick us up and take us home, the prospect of jogging uphill being too much of an ordeal.

One particular evening, time was short because we were giving a dinner party. We trotted down the Soppo road for an hour. Anticipating the vehicle would soon pick us up, I increased the pace. Another half-hour went by. No vehicle. Everybody had had enough. We started to walk, all becoming thoroughly bad-tempered. Another half-hour went by. Darkness fell. At last the lights of an overtaking car approached us. It was Kat, in our car. "Gosh, I'm glad to find you. I sent the Schloss car down the tarred road nearly two hours ago." All my fault as I'd taken it for granted, for some reason, that she knew which road we'd chosen.

On Christmas Day we gave a dinner party for twenty-five expatriates at the Schloss, Muna having very thoughtfully said sometime before, "I guess you will be asking people to the Schloss on Christmas Day. Don't ask any Cameroons people. We all have duties to be with our families on such a day." We didn't want to overspend the entertainment vote, leaving it depleted for the Fields, so we paid for this party from our pockets. Nobody knew this and I'm afraid we gave offence to those residents of Buea who weren't asked and thought they should have been. Official entertaining is always an invidious matter…almost an open licence for hurting people's feelings.

The practice of the junior man giving up his house to the visiting senior man when the latter is visiting on official duties, on the other hand, is vested in early colonial custom and Kat and I never resented observing it for one moment.

(Jackie aged five at the time, did though. Saying goodbye to Sir John Macpherson and Lady Macpherson after their 1948 visit to Bamenda, she said boldly, "Goodbye, I'm glad you're going."

"Why are you glad?" asked the governor-general kindly.

"We can go back into our nice clean house now—instead of the dirty, horrid house where we've been."

The Macphersons laughed and he said, "I'm so sorry, Jackie. You should have mentioned it earlier."

As in the case of much in West Africa at that time we were betwixt and between many policies and usages. Circumstances were changing rapidly although behavioural customs often lagged behind. An example was the personal relationship between permanent secretaries and their ministers. Jua once hinted to me that one or two of the former were still treating the latter as district officer and village schoolmaster when in fact the country was within a year of independence. London doubtless envisaged that administrative officers could change their attitudes overnight but of course people aren't like that...these things take time. I got hold of the worst offender amongst the permanent secretaries: he was intelligent and tough. In fact, after retirement from the colonial service, he had a distinguished second career in British government. But could he sympathise or even understand the predicament of his minister...he could not. In a year the latter would be on his own. If still in power, he'd be administering African affairs in an African government; his very life might be in his own hands. The British permanent secretary's job was at that stage not to attempt to teach the minister anything, however right and proper he might think it. It was to strengthen the minister in his own decision-making; to try and understand his thinking. We spent three of four hours discussing this. The PS's views remained "what's right is right" and he would advocate it to the end.

I blamed my lack of persuasive powers. It certainly wasn't a matter to make an issue of so late in our relationship with the Southern Cameroons. A pity, though, as a more sympathetic understanding would have helped.

Put it down to my intrinsically puerile nature, or what you will, but I always believed Sundays during our time in the Cameroons should be a *dies-non* so far as work was concerned. Religious observance apart, they should be as far as possible playdays, pure and simple. And, of course what better playground than the Cameroon's coast in the 1950s and 1960s? We had our good Sprite, half-decked and a fine sailor in the partially sheltered waters of Victoria Bay. We had, too, an outboard engine which was a real boon when the stiff day-time sea breezes fell away in the evenings. I had bought in Spain a really powerful under-water gun which fired a two and a half foot steel harpoon as thick as a pencil. Snorkelling was in its early days as a sport although the young Spaniards in the Island of Fernando Po—twenty-five miles off the Cameroons coast—used to go after sharks in groups of five or more. A few French expatriates from Douala drove their high-speed motorcraft through the waterways intersecting the mangrove-covered islands of the Republic of Cameroons coast to the rocky, fish-bearing waters of the Southern Cameroons coast.

Our servants counted on the fish we caught for them and would wake us bright and early on Sunday mornings generally with the words, "All your fishing things are ready in the hall, sir."

Mike Cartlidge became a regular companion on our jaunts. We remember one Sunday towards the end of 1960 when Ted Sainsbury, then Chief Justice of the SC, came too. The idea, that Sunday, was to sail out to Mondole Island in the *Snipe*, anchor twenty yards off the rocks and, using the boat as a base, spend the day snorkelling. As we approached the island we spotted at first one then two bodies seemingly drowning cheerfully in the surf beating up against the rocks. I write "cheerfully" deliberately, for every now and again one or the other of the drowning men made a cheerful but half-sleepy gesture.

Neither Kat nor I can remember whether we all acted automatically or whether we agreed a plan of action. I found myself managing the *Snipe*: getting sails down and anchoring in fifteen feet of water some thirty yards off the rocks. Kat and Mike both had a drowning man in tow heading for the boat. Ted was hauling a capsized dugout, which he'd spotted in the surf, out towards the *Snipe*.

With some difficulty we lugged the two locals aboard the *Snipe* and Mike and Ted righted the canoe which they baled out and made fast alongside. Both local gentlemen smelt overwhelmingly of palm wine; all they wanted to do was lie on the floorboards of the *Snipe* and groan. We made them as comfortable as we could and fished the rapidly shelving water off the rocks for the next four or five hours. Kat, who was not armed with snorkel and gun, made periodic visits back to the *Snipe*, on one of which she reported that our friends were then sleeping peacefully.

As evening approached, the breeze died away so we started the outboard and motored slowly back to the mainland, towing the canoe. The two locals seemed recovered. They did not thank Mike and Kat for undoubtedly saving them from drowning but did vouchsafe the information that they'd visited the island to make a sacrifice. The sacrifice, if such it was, had obviously involved liberal intakes of alcohol. At one point one said, "And who are you, anyway?"

Mike replied, pointing to me, "That's His Honour, the Acting Commissioner; that's the Chief Justice and I'm Chief of Police." We all were, admittedly, pretty scruffy.

"And who are you two?" asked Kat.

One answered, "I'm Jesus Christ," obviously not believing a word of what Mike had said.

I've heard a similar crack told a half dozen times amongst half a dozen races. I wondered then, and still do, whether our Cameroonian friend said what he said spontaneously or whether he'd made use of some like riposte heard amongst his own people. Perhaps the rule should be: "Beware; every joke has been made before."

We parted with great amicability. "Come to our village and we will give you some drink," said one. We thanked them but said that we wanted to be back in Buea before dark. I noticed that they wrung Mike's hand with particular warmth. I couldn't put it into pidgin but I could imagine them saying of him later, "Quite a card, what?"

Another little incident, bearing on the Cameroons coast, also features Mike Cartlidge. This time we were some twenty miles down the West Coast road. The party consisted of Mike, Jackie, Kat's very lame sister, Nat, crippled with rheumatoid arthritis who was staying with us at the time, and Kat and me. Mike, Jackie and I had our underwater gear. Kat and Nat were shore bound. Every now and then we'd passed some exciting headland, black rocks descending into deep fish-full sea and the three of us had plunged into the warm water, excitedly exploring all we saw. We fished round one such headland and came upon a black sand beach, piled high by wind and incoming waves. Nat and Kat somehow had reached the same beach and were gesturing to us, one arm beckoning, the other with fingers to mouth, commanding silence. We waded out of the sea to join them. There was a very strong sea breeze and the noise of wind and waves was loud, almost a constant roar. Kat pointed up the beach; we peered over the top. Immediately inland was a lagoon. Less than forty yards away three elephants were wallowing in the water.

The same thoughts entered my head and—as she told me later— Kat's. "If they charge or come our way we must scatter into the sea. But what about Nat, who can only move with slow difficulty?"

Fortunately, the elephants either saw us, bad as their eyesight is said to be, or got our wind. They lumbered to their feet and in single file climbed up the steep bank at the side of the lagoon, disappearing into the jungle above.

We returned to the car all a little subdued. We hadn't moved more than twenty yards down the road when we came on the spot the elephants had obviously crossed: there was their track for us all to see, the tall grass still rising where it had been trampled. We stopped and examined the spoor.

Some devil took possession of Jackie and me; we began to follow the track into the tall grass where the elephants had obviously gone. Thirty, forty yards in, we came without warning on a cow elephant lying down. We froze where we stood. The elephant, plainly alarmed by the sudden cessation of movement rose to her feet. She was pointing our way. We didn't wait to see if she was charging us or retreating. We turned and belted back to the road.

There Mike, Kat and Nat were laughing heartily. "Get in the car, get in the car," I ordered furiously. But they only laughed. Apparently, as I learnt a few minutes later, Mike had been throwing stones to one side of where he imagined Jackie and I were, to frighten us. Our precipitate exit from the elephant grass merely confirmed, so they thought, the success of their ploy.

These things happen in split seconds. Imagining the cow was coming our way I had no time to argue. Maybe I knew instinctively that Mike was too big to hit and that Kat was the easiest target; as she was still not getting into the car, I struck her a fierce blow on the arm. Jackie's example, and this drastic action on my part, persuaded them, at last, to move and they all climbed into the safety of the car while I tried to explain what had made us run out of the elephant grass.

CHAPTER FIFTEEN

Southern Cameroons 1961

The Fields returned to Buea on 18th January 1961. I was due some leave but plainly had to defer it until the plebiscite, to be held on 11th February 1961, was safely over.

Field once again pressed Foncha to agree with President Ahidjo the terms of a statement which would satisfy Resolution 2013 (xxvi) of the UN Trusteeship Council of 1960—namely, a statement that fully informed the people of the SC of the constitutional arrangements that would have to be made in the event of a plebiscite decision in favour of the R of C.

The document they eventually produced was little more than a rehash of the paper summarising the meeting between Ahidjo, Foncha and Assale which had taken place on 13th October 1960. A diversion contained in the document—nothing if not time wasting—was a formal expression of regret that Northern Cameroons Representatives had not been present at the conference in May 1960.

In January 1961 an official pamphlet was produced by the SC government entitled: "Southern Cameroons Plebiscite, 1961. The Two Alternatives." This set out in full detail the steps that would be taken if the plebiscite result was in favour of the SC joining Nigeria as a Region. In the preamble it was stated "…a plebiscite vote in favour of joining the R of C would mean that the governments of the R of C and the SC would unite in a Federal United Cameroon Republic. The arrangements would be worked out after the plebiscite by a conference consisting of delegations of equal status from the Republic and the Southern Cameroons. The UK and the UNO would also be associated with the conference. During the short period while the arrangements were being made the UK would be ready to continue the trusteeship."

With the benefit of hindsight it was clear that this statement suited the machinations, and partially formed plans, of both Ahidjo and Foncha.

Ahidjo's own position in January 1961 was not as strong as it was to become in later years, particularly after 1972 when the federal system was to give way to a unitary state. True, he was president of an independent state but every man's hand was against him—or seemed to be. Most West African politicians had realised by then that power was synonymous with wealth and wealth was desperately sought. His priorities in June 1961 included building up the power of his own position, the need to maintain good relations with France and his desire to satisfy the popular demand in the Republic for "reunification". He might be forced to treat the Southern Cameroons on equal terms in order to woo them but I never believed that he intended treating them in this way for a moment longer than necessary; the SC was less than a quarter the size of the Republic. His immediate plans might involve promises of office for Foncha, Muna and possibly Jua, but again I didn't believe that he intended to honour these promises for very long.

I was aware (I didn't think either Field or I had received specific instructions on the matter) that from about 1960 onwards there existed an understanding between France and Britain that neither country would dabble in the affairs of ex-colonial territories previously in the possession of the other. Ahidjo in 1961 was convinced that the future relationship of France with the independent Republic of Cameroun would prove to be an important asset to his own position and to the future of his country. In public pronouncements, of course, he might be bound for political reasons to deny any such dependence.

Foncha, as the past thirty-seven years has demonstrated, was batting on a much more difficult wicket. He himself was prejudiced against the Ibos and I am sure he was right in alleging the majority in his small country felt the same. The Ibos were quite simply better traders, better politicians and more tightly organised than his own disparate peoples, charming as the latter could be. A major objection to joining Nigeria, even as a full Region, was the danger of being dominated by the Ibo. Reunification was a romantic, almost poetic concept. It was a useful flag to wave but not a plebiscite-winning conception.

Even Foncha's most fervent supporters did not relish the possibility of the Southern Cameroons becoming—as was indeed to happen in ten years' time—absorbed into a Cameroun State. Equally, the possibility that sovereignty might well be transferred willy-nilly to the Republic of Cameroun after the plebiscite was as frightening to him and his Ministers as it was to the man in the bush.

Foncha and his Ministers at this time, just before the plebiscite, subtly changed the main thrust of their exhortations to the public.

They let drop the suggestion that a vote for the republic might well be a means of securing an independent Southern Cameroons. There were obviously difficulties, they hinted, in the way of agreeing the arrangements for a United Federal Republic. In fact, agreement with Ahidjo might not be obtained for a very long time in which case they could enjoy the best of all worlds—they would not be tied to the Republic of Cameroun and the vote for the R of C might well prove to have been a vote for a free and independent Southern Cameroons. The public are quick to believe what they want to believe but slow to face the logical reality of a developing situation. Feeling against domination by the Republic of Cameroun was second only to fear of domination by the Ibos. I felt it quite likely that Foncha's last minute switch in propaganda secured a large number of votes that he might not otherwise have won.

An incident occurred on 1st February 1961 which put the plebiscite temporarily out of our minds. That morning a middle-aged lady was sitting on the steps of my office when I arrived. She said without preamble that the British troops stationed in Buea had lost her son Domonic the day before high on the Cameroons Mountain. The facts were not disputed. The previous day a party of the King's Own Border Regiment had wished to climb up to Hut Two at around 10,800 feet and explore the area near the hut before returning to Buea that evening. They had hired Domonic, who was a hunter familiar with the paths from Buea to Hut One, and on to Hut Two, as their guide. At about three p.m., some two miles west of Hut Two they had suddenly missed him. They had searched fruitlessly until about five p.m. before descending as darkness fell to the point where the path entered the forest belt and so on to Buea. They had hoped that perhaps Domonic, for some strange reason of his own, had wanted to go ahead of them.

As soon as the lady told her story, I phoned Robinson, the OC Troops. He immediately agreed we must do all we could to find Domonic. He ended by saying, "Tell me how I can help." Field was equally concerned. He was happy that I should spend the day organising a search. The Buea telephone exchange offered their help by giving me priority on all telephone calls for the next hour. Robinson promised to have a search party of twenty men divided into four units with a man in charge of each unit, all with a day's rations of food and water, plus one party bearing a stretcher, ready at Upper Farm (where

425

the path to Huts One and Two commenced) by 9.30 a.m. Kat, quick as always in such circumstances, soon had a rucksack packed for me and also said, "Bella wants a walk. She would like to go, too."

Bella was our family dog, a not very well-bred pointer.

We did the climb from Upper Farm to Hut Two in three and a half-hours. Early in the ascent one of the soldiers said, "We can go faster than this."

I replied, "Maybe, but we aren't having any hourly breaks so you'd best learn a steady rhythm you can keep up all day."

Robinson had included half a dozen or so of the previous day's group in the search party. "That'll larn 'em," he'd said on the phone. "In any case they must have some idea where they lost the poor chap."

We searched in a series of two to three miles of countoured beats to the west of Hut Two. Each time that we decided to search back to the east we moved up about 1,300 yards. This width of swathe allowed approximately fifty yards between each searcher.

Sadly we came on absolutely no trace of poor Domonic.

Our return to the tree-line was well timed. Darkness fell as we reached the first of the trees. We sat and ate our rations. I told those who didn't know it the tip about using a long thin stick to trace the edges of the path in the darkness. We set off downhill, and homewards, all very tired and depressed at our failure.

Bella led the way keeping a few feet in front of me. I could just distinguish her white shape against the darkness of the forest; soon we began to outpace the main group. "Bloody fellow," I heard one soldier say, "he must have eyes like bloody radar."

As it was one of yesterday's party speaking—who'd originally lost Domonic—I didn't slow up.

Robinson was waiting for us at Upper Farm. He was upset by our failure and quite splendidly sent up further search parties during each of the next four or five days.

Domonic was never found. Even his mother disappeared. It was, for me, one more African story without explanation or end.

––––––––––

Registration of voters in the plebiscite had taken place between 26th October and the 22nd November 1960. The United Kingdom plebiscite staff numbered thirty-three in all and operated the usual electoral safeguards where those who did not find their names on the electoral roll—and thought they should be on it—had the opportunity to appeal.

Voting in the plebiscite took place on the 11th February 1961, as arranged. The result was not unexpected: 97,741 in favour of joining Nigeria and 233,571 for union with the Republic of Cameroon.

On 6th February Kat and I received a telegram telling us of Kate's death. My mind was full of last minute difficulties concerning the plebiscite. Kate's health had been deteriorating rapidly and her demise was not unexpected. Then, I let her go, largely unmourned, but, later thro' the years, I shed many a tear for Kate, Alice and Jack.

Whenever it was convenient, government staff had put up plebiscite officers working in same area as themselves. Kat and I had G E Adeane, the serious-minded and thoroughly nice son of Lieut Colonel Sir Michael Adeane who was the Queen's private secretary at the time. We did our best to make him comfortable in the strange environment of the Southern Cameroons and to protect him against tropical diseases.

We went on leave at the end of February. Jackie had been invited to stay for some weeks with an elderly married couple in Lille who thoroughly spoilt her in addition to teaching her quite a lot of French. John, nearly seventeen, had gone back to Rossall for the Easter term. Kat and I went out to Austria hoping to get some high-level skiing before the season closed.

I was longing for the fitness that would surely come with a fortnight or more on the snow but somehow, as the days went by, I felt slacker and slacker. After six days of this Kat persuaded me I was ill so I consulted the resort doctor. He quickly said, "Look at yourself…you've got jaundice," and sure enough I was as yellow as one used to become in the days when mepacrine was the recommended prophylactic for malaria. He advised Kat to take me home to the United Kingdom where I could be hospitalised. Effort of any sort, even getting out of bed, became more and more of an ordeal. Kat said she had to prop me up as I tried to walk from the taxi to the London Tropical Diseases hospital.

They kept me there for three weeks. After the first week I felt much more normal so long as I was in bed or sitting in an easy chair. Any sort of activity and the aches, pains and nausea returned.

Kat spent the first week in digs near the hospital after which she went to stay with Mary and Robin Nicholson, then she, poor girl, started the same trouble. Mary and Robin insisted on her remaining in bed at Sleastonhow, treated by Mary's brother-in-law (the local GP).

It was the end of May before we were back in the Southern Cameroons, both still feeling weak and wobbly.

A lot had gone on during my absence. I did my best to catch up during the course of long conversations with John Field and Jim Balmain (who had acted as deputy to John Field when I was on leave).

At the end of April John Field had taken Foncha and Muna to London primarily to see the secretary of state. On the 27th April there was a preparatory meeting in Eastwood's office, which E B Boothby of the Foreign Office attended. The main subject discussed was, of course, the steps that would be necessary to procure the federation of the SC and the R of C in accordance with the plebiscite vote. Foncha said that as soon as he returned to the Cameroons he would seek to discuss with President Ahidjo the draft constitution that he'd given to the president in December 1960. Subjects which they had provisionally agreed should be federal would be included. The next move was to agree the substantive constitution of the federated states. The last step, Foncha envisaged, was to establish some joint body which could deal with matters of detail that might arise as a result of the establishment of a federation and the transition to it.

Foncha contemplated that the work of the joint body might continue for a year or even more. (Very much the period which he and his ministers had mentioned to the SC public before the plebiscite.)

Foncha said that the parties to the federation would have to strike some bargain as to the finances of the federation and the Regions. Eastwood quickly replied that he could not make any statement about the provision of UK assistance after 1st October 1961, nor could he make any promise about the SC's wish to have their own security forces. This was a matter which should be raised by joint request of Ahidjo and Foncha. He did, however, agree with Foncha that security might prove to be a difficult matter. He added that he had to make it clear that the British battalion would be withdrawn before the end of trusteeship.

John Field told me that the meeting with the secretary of state (then the Rt Hon Iain Macleod) the following day went very much the same way. Foncha mentioned that he would like a general election as soon as possible and certainly before the 1st October. The S of S said that he was not in favour of spending £50,000 or more on a general election in the present circumstances. He preferred amending the constitutional instruments so that Foncha could bring two or perhaps three more ministers onto his team. He would have the opportunity of broadening his government by taking on members of the opposition.

Regarding security: Foncha expressed his thanks for the presence of British troops in the SC. The S of S repeated Eastwood's warning of the previous day. No promise could be given that these troops would remain in the SC after trusteeship ended. At one stage in the discussions both SC ministers made it clear that they did not want R of C police in the SC—it was apparent that they were well aware of the methods of policing the latter employed and they wanted none of it in the SC.

There was a third meeting between Field, Muna and Foncha with Boothby and Eastwood on 2nd May. Eastwood confirmed that the constitutional instruments were being amended so that the number of Foncha's ministries could be increased. Foncha emphasised that a force of at least 500 police should be in a position to take over from the British battalion on the latter's departure. Eastwood pointed out that the Nigerian government must first be asked if they were prepared to release Cameroonians from their force. At one stage Boothby said that the relationship of the new federal state to the United Kingdom would have to be centralised at the capital and through the British ambassador and his staff. There would be a British consul at Buea if the capital was Yaounde but relations with HMG would be through the ambassador's office. R of C was after all an independent state.

An important conference—from which much was expected—was held in Buea from 15th to 17th May 1961. It was presided over by John Field. The governments of the Republic of Cameroun and the Southern Cameroons were represented by Ahidjo and Foncha, supported by ministers and officials. The United Kingdom government was represented by Sir Roger Stevens of the Foreign Office and the British ambassador and ambassador-designate from Yaounde. The deputy commissioner (Balmain acting for me,) the attorney-general and the financial secretary, Southern Cameroons, were also present.

The report of the conference, with appendices, runs to fifty pages; it reads more like a dossier of differences than an agreed solution of outstanding difficulties.

Ahidjo firmly pointed out that, in the absence of an operating Federal Republic of Cameroun, sovereignty would have to be transferred on 1st October 1961 to the existing Republic of Cameroun. The constitution of the Republic of Cameroun would have to be revised so as to accommodate the Southern Cameroons and this would be done in the next few weeks. Ahidjo reiterated, significantly, that from the 1st October until creation of a federal set-up, sovereignty would lie concurrently with himself and a Southern Cameroons representative.

It was felt that the Southern Cameroons would need UK assistance with personnel. Ahidjo welcomed the possibility of aid here, not only for the Southern Cameroons but for the federation as a whole. He hoped the UK would maintain budgetary assistance until "economic equilibrium" was reached. He also welcomed the UK proposal to continue after 1st October the preferential tariff system the Southern Cameroons already enjoyed. He hoped this would be for some time. He hoped, finally, that the UK government would assist in stamping out rebel activity in the Republic of Cameroun. But he changed the subject when told the military advice was that a combined SC/R of C operation was necessary. The suggestion of a *combined* operation put him off.

Ahidjo had produced a very clear statement of the relationship between the two territories as he hoped it would develop. Foncha, as I deduced from the minutes of the meeting, had a number of reservations the most cogent of which concerned the arrangements for security in the federal republic.

Sir Roger Stevens expressed HMG's agreement that the constitution of the federal republic was a matter solely for the two Cameroons to decide. HMG's assistance regarding the preference tariff could only be extended for a short time; it was agreed the agency services must come to an end as soon as the post-plebiscite arrangements were put into place. HMG was concerned about security arrangements. It felt that training up to 1st October 1961 could best be undertaken by the Republic of Cameroun although HMG might be able to help with recruitment up to that date.

The conference broke up after four sessions without being able to agree a statement to the press.

Just before Kat and I returned to the Cameroons at the end of May 1961 I was required to join the Anglo-French talks on Africa scheduled to take place in the Quai d' Orsay between 24th and 26th May. I gathered that these talks were held on a regular basis between members of the French and British foreign and colonial offices. I was included because I happened to be in London and because the Cameroons was to be on the agenda.

The custom was for each side to speak in its own language. My French served me well enough in mountain huts but in the rarefied atmosphere of the Quai d' Orsay I was sure that I should not be able to pick up fine nuances of meaning or even hold onto the gist of what was being said. I knew from experience that once I'd lost the drift I might as well not have been listening at all. P MJohnson, the British ambassador in Yaounde and R M Hadow of the Foreign Office both promised to help me and we sat together.

The talks started in the early evening of the 24th May. The first two items on the agenda concerned labour organisations in Africa and the ECA. The third covered a draft note which the British proposed to present to the government of the Republic of Cameroun concerning the meeting held in Buea between 15th and 17th May. The French were asked to comment which they promptly did: they had never envisaged the possibility of involving UNO forces in security arrangements for the Federated Republic of the Cameroons. The proposed training of 120 police for the SC component of the security forces was insufficient. It would be unwise to keep the secretary-general of UNO formally aware of British and French plans for the security of the Federal Republic of the Cameroons.

The meeting resumed on the morning of 25th May. French and British officials both agreed many of the conclusions that a recent meeting of heads of British missions in Africa had arrived at—in particular the features which had tended to bring African thinking into line with communist purposes. They agreed, too, the divisiveness of many current Portuguese policies. Discussions continued for the whole of the lengthy morning meeting on similar lines—the general changing scene in Africa. It wasn't until the last session, that of the morning of the 26th May, that talk once again settled upon specific Cameroons' problems. Lord Perth had taken over the leadership of the British contingent during the morning. The French were apprehensive about a possible recrudescence of terrorism in Cameroon and anticipated that the government of the Republic of Cameroun might ask for assistance which itself could create a problem.

The French had provided four battalions with air support to the Republic of Cameroun in 1960. Order had been restored then and there were now two Republic of Cameroun battalions with a third in process of formation. There was a gendarmerie of 3,000 men and another 3,000 *Guardes Civiques*. One French battalion was left. In all the security forces totalled some 10,000 men.

The Cameroun Republic would not be able to recruit, train and finance any more security forces once the third battalion was completed. 120 men in the Southern Cameroons, if trained between May and October 1961, would help the situation.

Sir Roger Stevens recognised there would still be a security gap in the SC on 1st October. The possibility of delaying the departure of the British battalion would once again be looked at and referred to ministers (whose view so far had been that it must go on 1st October).

At the close of the session Lord Perth reiterated what the British might do on the economic side. The statement did not evoke any response from the French delegation.

So ended the Anglo-French talks of May 1961.

The London *Times* on Monday 19th June carried a long article bearing the title: "Storm Clouds over the Cameroons", which summed up with impartiality the difficulties then facing Foncha. It paid respect to his "dogged persistence" and added "...but it would be more reassuring if the two parties could come together again, for the Southern Cameroons cannot afford the luxury of an opposition." When acting as Commissioner I had made the suggestion of a coalition government to Foncha in the latter part of 1960 but he had merely cited it as one of my "sins" inimical to his efforts in his threat at the end of that year to procure my dismissal. The innate inability of the Southern Cameroonian to compromise on even the simplest of issues was a great handicap to Foncha and his friends although they didn't realise it. A single unified request would have been hard to resist at any stage...at the appropriate time it could have been crucial.

Foncha's government asked Attorney-general Smith (who was acting for Harvey Robson) to produce a legally argued document giving their views on the transfer of sovereignty to an independent Southern Cameroons. This he duly did on 19th June 1961 (PRO reference OF/371/154699). Even at that late date the request would have carried much more weight had it been made by all the political parties in the SC acting together.

Eastwood and Gardner-Brown, accompanied by Hunt (Deputy HC Lagos) and John Field, representing the United Kingdom, and officials of the Nigerian ministries of foreign affairs, establishments, defence and the police met on Tuesday 21st 1961 in the cabinet office, Lagos, to discuss outstanding matters concerning the separation of Nigeria and the Cameroons. The meeting was marked by the readiness of the Nigerian side to facilitate in every way possible to them the easy disengagement of Nigeria's responsibilities in the Southern Cameroons. Regarding currency: it was agreed that Nigerian ministerial approval would be sought for the continuation of Nigerian currency in SC for at least six months after 1st October. Agreement was also obtained for the extension of the agency services to 1st October 1961; the extension of existing secondments to the Southern Cameroons to the same date, and the future possibility that non-

Cameroonian staff serving in the SC might remain on in the country.

Observing from the sidelines, as I did, the whole process touching Nigeria proceeded with dispatch and goodwill.

Sir Roger Stevens, Mr Gardner-Brown and Mr Eastwood had held discussions of an entirely different complexion with representatives of the SC Chamber of Commerce in Buea on 17th June 1961. They met an influential group consisting of Hugh McCartney of UAC, Phil Taylor of Elder and Fyffes, Belsham of CDC, Halwood of Kamerun Ltd and Lamb of the Coast Timber Company. (See PRO Kew reference 554/2468.)

Sir Roger Stevens described to the meeting the inconclusive discussions that had been held with the governments of the SC and the R of C between the 15th and the 17th May and the extensive consideration that had been given to the security situation. He added that he had been instructed by HMG that he should proceed in the current meeting on the assumption that the UK battalion would be withdrawn after 30th September 1961.

The reaction of the members of the chamber of commerce was unanimous. All anticipated that they would lose up to eighty per cent of their expatriate staff if news spread that the territory was to be left without adequate security protection. The loss of staff would result in a breakdown of their economic contribution to the country. They looked to HMG to provide arrangements for the orderly departure for staff who would not wish to remain after 1st October and for their military protection.

Sir Roger Stevens promised to report the views of the Chamber of Commerce back to ministers in the UK, adding, "We should all hope for the best but prepare for the worst."

I cannot remember discussing specifically with John Field this reaction of the chamber of commerce although of course the meeting must have featured prominently in our many talks. I know that at the time I did not treat the security situation with the same concern that those at a greater distance did. I believe that Field's thinking veered in the same direction as my own. It was important that we did not gratuitously provoke the terrorist leaders; their quarrel was with the R of C, let it remain so.

Lord Perth, in London on 12th June, had had a meeting with representatives of Cameroons' commercial interests which we were told covered very much the same ground as Sir Roger Stevens' meeting did. The high level commercial representatives reacted to the news that it was intended to withdraw the British battalion on 1st October as strongly as those in Buea.

On 23rd June 1961 the UK Foreign Office sent a joint telegram to Foncha and Ahidjo conveying HMG's final views to both gentlemen regarding the matters raised between 15th and 17th May. HMG considered that the UNO resolution required the termination of UK trusteeship on 1st October 1961 and consequently after that date HMG would cease to have any responsibility for the affairs of the SC. HMG— the telegram continued—regards this as a final decision by the UNO and would not be able to support any proposal for the extension of UK trusteeship or any other arrangement other than SC joining the R of C on 1st October. In these circumstances HMG saw no alternative but to re-affirm its decision to withdraw the British battalion on 1st October 1961. HMG would not, therefore, oppose any arrangements that might be made for ensuring the security of the territory by CR forces. HMG hoped that the necessary arrangements would be made amicably between the two sides in the time remaining before the inevitable termination of trusteeship on 1st October. HMG recognised that the decision regarding the withdrawal of the British battalion after 1st October might result in the departure of a number of expatriates. It would not be practical for HMG to supply a technical and aid mission after 1st October but HMG would be prepared, as soon as federation was instituted, to make a free grant of half a million pounds to enable SC to meet its immediate financial obligations. HMG would also extend for a limited period the existing preferences on Cameroons' products entering the UK markets.

These firm decisions by HMG cleared the air for John Field; the presence of parameters made it easier in future for him to confine the discussions with Foncha and others to reality...to suggestions and possibilities that had a real chance of implementation.

On the other hand they made Foncha's task more difficult. He was, in effect, being driven into a tunnel with steadily converging sides rather in the same manner as the hunters of Nkambe tackled groups of the red forest hog. What he seemed oblivious of was fact that at the convergence of the sides a pit had been dug from which there was no escape.

As far back as December 1959, Sir James Robertson had sent Foley Newns for five days to the Southern Cameroons to see if he could help the ministers and officials to improve the operation of their new ministerial system. Newns returned appalled at the situation and at the prospects for further disintegration which threatened to occur after 1st October 1960. He had quite a lot to say on the subject of Foncha himself. Much of his judgement in December 1959 was borne out by Foncha's actions and thinking in the intervening period—up to June

1961. It is helpful to our understanding of the complicated final phase of Southern Cameroons' affairs to have Foley's opinion of Foncha's role. Let me briefly paraphrase Foley's 1959 report. [11]

Foley considered that it was attempting the impossible to expect a top-heavy complicated ministerial system with a rapidly changing constitution to work with ministers lacking formal education and who were mostly served by officers who had little experience outside the Districts. He judged Foncha to be " a nice little man in his own lights quite sincere". He understood that Foncha and his ministers were much more honest than many of the more sophisticated ministers in West Africa but he feared most of them were "incapable of appreciating the complications of the present situation". "They are living in a dream world," he wrote; "all their thoughts and activities are governed by a few barely-valid prejudices." Among the latter he cited their pathological dislike of the Ibo, their emotional belief in "reunification", their susceptibility to false flattery, their misjudgement of the large number of offers of "help" they had received. Most surprising and alarming of all to Foley Newns was Foncha's apparent belief that unification would proceed much as he envisaged (the retention of many British features including the English system of jurisprudence and the English language...). Their intense antipathy to Endeley and his party and their reaction to the recent development of political activities in the native authorities presented further examples of their naiveté.

At one point Foley wrote: "...HMG as administrating authority has responsibility not to allow these nice little people to commit suicide. This they will do if they join the Republic of Cameroun. The people on that side are more sophisticated and will swallow these people up."

Newns also pointed out in his report, "It is quite contrary to all British ideas of organising constitutional development in colonial territories to leave the future of a country entirely to the representatives of one political party which had only a bare majority and whose leaders are incompetent to appreciate the issues involved."

The FO telegram of 23rd June 1961 marked a new phase in Foncha's dealings with all round him—with Ahidjo, with HMG, with his own party, with the Southern Cameroons' public. His price—in the sense that every man has a price—dropped. He became more cheaply persuadable by Ahidjo. As this became increasingly obvious I admired his good qualities (and these he had in fair measure) the less and I feared for his people the more.

---

11 CO 554/1661/55200

Field, on 12th July 1961 informed the secretary of state by telegram (CO 554/2259) that his ministers had more than once asked him what HMG's attitude would be if they failed to agree with Ahidjo on the terms of the federal constitution the latter offered. (They anticipated that Ahidjo's offer might not conform with para five of the General Assembly resolution.) Field told the S of S that his reply to date had been that the question so far was an academic one but he had drawn ministers' attention to the portion of the FO telegram which stated that HMG would support no proposal other than that the SC joins the R of C on 1st October.

On the 14th July Boothby of the Foreign Office wrote to Sir Pierson Dixon, British ambassador in Paris, conveying the legal advice that HMG had received to the effect that the Southern Cameroons' ministers had a strong case (CO 554/2259)—namely, that the transfer of sovereignty should be to a newly created organisation representing the future federation rather that to Ahidjo and Foncha acting together.

We are beginning here to see Foncha and Muna—at Ahidjo's behest—flying a different track to the remainder of the ministerial flock. Later the other ministers—Jua, Kemcha, Effion and Bokwe—followed largely because they feared that otherwise they might lose the offices they currently held.

We can go back a little further in tracing this shift. On 26th June Field was able to report that Foncha and his ministers had studied the constitutional proposals left behind by Ahidjo. At first Foncha and Muna argued strongly in favour of accepting them but then had been forced to give way. Field had had good information that Foncha had already accepted Ahidjo's offer to amend the constitution of the R of C leaving a place for him as vice-president. It was said, on less good authority, that Muna could expect office and that Jua, on Foncha's elevation to vice-president, could be assured of the premiership of the SC. The news of Foncha's acceptance of the promise of the vice-presidency was leaked in Yaounde giving strength to the rumours affecting Muna and Jua.

The outcome seemed dependent upon the degree to which those in the Southern Cameroons, who were opposed to any close association with the R of C, were prepared to oppose Foncha's double-dealing and to mobilise the support of the opposition and the non-party representatives against him. But there wasn't anybody willing to take the risk and in the end the SC Ministers reluctantly followed Foncha.

I was required to preside over an official level meeting on 24th July to agree the process of hand-over of security arrangements following the cessation of British responsibility at midnight on 30th September 1961. (The 1st Bn of the Grenadier Guards had taken over from the 1st Bn of the King's Own Scottish Borderers at the end of May 1961.) The meeting took note that the British battalion would remain fully operational until midnight on 30th September. Lt Col Fraser, the Force Commander, F Mullin, the then Acting Commissioner of Police, Jack Kisob the Secretary to the Premier, W Oliver the British Security Adviser and J D Sowerby of the Special Branch represented the Southern Cameroons' delegation. The whole process was governed by the agreements that had been arrived at during the Foumban talks the previous week. No political diversions were allowed to intrude and an agreed plan of action was obtained on every point that arose.

We had been sure that Foncha had received a copy of Ahidjo's proposals for a federal form of constitution before the Bamenda all-party conference held earlier in June, but Foncha hadn't distributed them to most of the delegates on the grounds that members of the opposition, taking exception to them, might sabotage the conference. The delegates at the Bamenda conference were thus invited to make and adopt proposals many of which were contrary to what Ahidjo had already decided with Foncha's agreement.

Consequently, when they arrived in Foumban, the Southern Cameroons' delegates, other than a few KNDP members, were dismayed to be given copies of Ahidjo's proposals and to discover that they differed very considerably from the suggestions they themselves had made at the Bamenda conference.

They couldn't be expected to debate Ahidjo's latest proposals unless they were given time first to study and discuss them amongst themselves. They asked for—and were granted—the 17th, 18th and 19th July to do this. Dr Endeley had pointed out at the introductory meeting on the 17th July that it was not the exclusive right of the SC government to pronounce on the proposals. The opposition in the SC, he said, was prepared to work for the success of the conference but first required time. Too much haste in arriving at conclusions could prejudice the future of the SC.

Before the Foumban Conference proper got under way Foncha explained that his initial proposals particularly sought to preserve the cultures of the R of C and the SC. The difference would be preserved in the Regions but could be blended at the centre. He also said that he aimed at a very loose form of federation, almost a confederation.

Ahidjo, on the other hand, explained that, a confederation being plainly unsuitable, it was intended to build a federation. (Later study revealed that he had a strong, centralised federation in mind.)

He also added that in discussions between what was an independent sovereign state and a territory under trusteeship (such as the SC in fact was) the former must be the final arbiter of what could be included, although he would be prepared to consider suggestions for changes to his own proposals. This latter statement was at variance with an undertaking he had earlier given at Victoria when he had said that both parties would negotiate reunification as equals.

The SC had proposed a bi-cameral legislature to protect the regional interest. This was not accepted by the R of C. Similarly, Foncha's request that the SC should manage its own affairs was not accepted by the R of C. A clause, however, prohibiting secession was inserted in the constitution.

Dr Victor Ngoh, a senior lecturer in history at the University of Yaounde, had the last word to say on the Foumban Conference. On p 213 of his excellent 1990 book, *Constitutional Developments Southern Cameroons 1946-1961*, he commented "...the biggest winner from the Foumban Conference was Ahidjo. He was able to take home a strongly centralised federal system and he changed the system in the Republic of Cameroon to a presidential regime which was to his political advantage."

The question of the Southern Cameroons was raised in the UK House of Commons on 1st August 1961 by G M Thompson MP. (Later Lord Thompson of Monifieth.) He explained that he was moved by three concerns: regard for the physical safety of British nationals serving in the country; regard for the Cameroonians themselves and lastly concern for the good name of British government and the British people who would be blamed if things went wrong. He criticised the government on a number of points most of which (although he was not to know this) were scheduled to be dealt with at the Yaounde Conference due to be held in four day's time. The Parliamentary Under-Secretary for State for the Colonies (the Hon Hugh Fraser MP) replied in crisp terms but vouchsafed very little. For instance no reason was given for government's failure to fight harder in the Trusteeship Council for a third choice being offered to the peoples of the Southern Cameroons when the plebiscite took place.

A tripartite meeting was held in Yaounde from 5th to 8th August 1961. Delegations attended from HMG, from the R of C and from the Southern Cameroons, the two latter led by Ahidjo and Foncha respectively. From time to time, as necessary, Foncha and Ahidjo broke off to hold bipartite meetings to deal with matters that hadn't up to that point been settled between them.

Eastwood reported in a 2,000-word minute to the S of S the principal points of agreement which can be summarised as follows: a federation will come into force on 1st October 1961. Ahidjo will be president and Foncha vice-president. There will be a federal legislature of fifty, forty of whom will come from the National Assembly of the Republic and ten from the House of Assembly of the SC. An indeterminate number of ministers will be allowed to remain in their legislatures.

The provisional constitution will remain in force until 1st April 1963, before which time there will be a general election and the constitution established on a permanent basis.

The arrangement proposed at the official-level meeting concerning the hand-over of security arrangements, referred to on page 437 were accepted. The British battalion would move out on 1st and 2nd October and sail on the 3rd October 1961. They would be replaced by approximately 900 republic armed men. There would be no security "vacuum". The British-built camps were to be handed over free of charge.

Agreement with Nigeria had been obtained for the continued use for three months of Nigerian currency; thereafter it would be replaced by a CFA franc currency. The two issuing authorities would work out the details.

The argument about transfer of sovereignty, which was at one time threatening to become dangerously controversial, suddenly dissolved. Some bright fellow—the record does not state who—pointed out that all that was necessary was an exchange of notes between HMG and the Republic of Cameroun saying that, suitable arrangements having been agreed between the two parties, the SC would join the Republic on 1st October. HMG would state that British authority would cease at midnight on 30th September.

On 8th August 1961 there occurred an incident which might have been used, so heinous was it, to bring the whole process of reunification to a standstill were the authorities so minded. Round about twelve noon a party of approximately thirty armed and uniformed Africans under the command of a European entered the area of Ebudu CDC Camp near Tombel—about one and a half miles on the Southern Cameroons side of the frontier—and murdered twelve men, all of whom turned out to be CDC labourers. New cartridge cases of French origin were found on the scene. The Nkongsamba military command at first declared that terrorists were responsible but later admitted there had been a CRSF operation in the area south of the border. Inquiries by the SC police and military the same afternoon and written up by a senior police officer in great detail established beyond doubt that the perpetrators were CRSF personnel, probably members of the dangerous and ill-disciplined *Gardes Civiques*.

On the afternoon of the 15th August a delegation of two from the Republic arrived unexpectedly in Buea. They had, they said, been sent on "a fact-finding mission" by President Ahidjo. Field being out of Buea that day I saw them in my office. The force commander and the commissioner of police joined me.

We gave them a résumé of the evidence that had satisfied Field that the culprits were members of the CRSF. They stated that they were not impressed by the evidence—they considered it equally compatible with an attack by terrorists. However, they became very perturbed when I informed them that there almost certainly would have to be an inquest.

I told them we could not anticipate any action HMG might take but speaking for ourselves we were gravely concerned at the great damage that had been done to the reputation of the CR security forces which might prejudice the hand-over of responsibility. As officials our main object was to get things back on the rails again. In view of the general knowledge in the SC of who the culprits were and in order to restore confidence it would be, I suggested, wisest to accept blame, apologise and pay compensation. They appeared to be willing to offer ex-gratia compensation when Goillandeau (French liaison officer with SC forces who was interpreting) butted in and said that would be an admission of guilt. The meeting therefore ended with their undertaking to continue with their investigations and inform us of the result.

The R of C delegation, without telling us, later that afternoon had a private meeting with Foncha and persuaded him to issue a statement (which he did not mention to Field—although security being a reserved matter, he should have done.) part of which read:-

> Although there are various versions of the people responsible for this atrocity it is true to say that, at the moment, the facts have not been known. Top level Government investigations are being carried out at the spot. The Representatives of the Government of Cameroun have undertaken to conduct full investigations and make the facts known. We both agree that whoever is guilty of this cruel murder will be severely punished.

The R of C government did not move again in the matter until Foncha next visited Yaounde which he did about 23rd August. They then proposed to him that there should be a joint SC/R of C inquiry with the task of establishing, if possible, those responsible and reporting their finding to both governments.

It was difficult to believe that this proposal was more than a device to delay matters until after the 1st October. But the offer could hardly be refused and that was the way we had to proceed—a polite acceptance of a joint inquiry by us and nothing achieved by the 1st October 1961.

Terrorism in its various manifestations was a trigger word within the British establishment in 1961. There had been experience in Cyprus and Malaya; there was the horrific example of Zaire almost on our doorstep. Mention the word in a dispatch to the United Kingdom and one would produce an almost instantaneous reaction. However by the middle of 1961 I'd had seven years experience of the territory in posts varying from ADO to acting commissioner. I was aware of the high regard with which the British were held by the public on both sides of the SC/RC border and was of course aware of the ALNK policy of establishing camps astride the frontier and their instructions to desist from terrorist acts on the British side. Active terrorism must have a true grievance on which to thrive. There was no grievance of that sort on the British side. Right up to our last night in the country…30th September 1961…neither Kat nor I had ever locked an outside door at night.

———

It will be recalled that two battalions of the Nigerian army had been stationed in the Southern Cameroons under stringent instructions up to the date Nigeria became independent (1st October 1960). Thereafter, until the plebiscite results were finally implemented, the Southern Cameroons were protected by British troops. The first unit to be sent was the 1st Battalion of the King's Own Border Regiment plus supporting troops. They served in the territory from 1st October until the end of May 1961—some eight months in total.

From the date of their arrival in the Southern Cameroons, in late September 1960, until John Field's return on 18th January 1961, I had been acting as commissioner and Jim Balmain as deputy commissioner. He, as the official member of Exco responsible for security, and I in my overall responsibility, found the War Office instructions issued to the battalion group commander perfectly adequate. In short, the role of the United Kingdom troops in the Southern Cameroons was to assist

441

the civil authorities in the maintenance of law and order and public morale, and to act as a deterrent against terrorism and other subversive activities. Although there were a number of terrorist camps astride the SC/R of C frontier there had been no terrorist acts in the SC.

Balmain was invited to deliver a paper to the King's Own Border Group on the role of British troops in the SC by the CO of the group as part of a staff exercise on 9th January 1961. He summed up the instructions to British troops in the following words: "It is hoped that the very presence here of British troops will have the necessary prophylactic action and that because they are here it will never be necessary to use them."

The commissioner took advice on security matters from the Joint Intelligence Committee—a body consisting of the heads of all intelligence-gathering organisations in the SC chaired by the deputy commissioner.

The plebiscite result on the 11th February in favour of the Republic of the Camerouns did not produce any immediate re-think by the JIC. The policy of using British troops in a purely prophylactic role continued until the change over from the King's Own to the Grenadier Guards 1st Battalion occurred at the end of May 1961 (and my return from leave). On 26th June Field received a telegram from the secretary of state for the colonies[12] which reads as follows:

> Ministers agree that operation should be mounted against ALNK camp of 200 referred to in Force Commander's Note given to UK delegation and recommended by them. Operation must of course be completed by 1st October and if it is not a complete success British forces should not thereby become committed to further anti-terrorist operations. Any persons captured during operation should be transferred to civil custody.
>
> I understand that it will be necessary to declare a state of emergency in certain restricted areas and I agree this should be done."

Presumably the British delegation referred to consisted of Sir Roger Stevens and Messrs Gardner-Brown and Eastwood. I cannot remember being involved in any discussion between these gentlemen and the force commander but it obviously took place as the telegram from the S of S subsequently confirmed.

---

12 CO 554/2571

An operation against the ALNK Camp at Sasso; code-named "Direction", went ahead on 10th July 1961 but was handicapped by bad weather and could not be claimed as a success. The prime minister (the Rt Hon Harold Macmillan) directed that no further such operations should be carried out without reference to him. In particular no second attack was to be made on the Sasso ALNK Camp.[13]

In June/July 1961 a new problem began to emerge. The several organisations covering the security situation in the Southern Cameroons and the Republic of Cameroun, were unanimous in reporting a build-up of trained terrorists in the camps astride the SC/R of C frontier. The JIC, which consisted entirely of service members (other than myself as chairman,) proposed on security grounds that British forces available to the Southern Cameroons should take action at once to eliminate the terrorists or at least slow down the build-up. On political grounds, and in the light of HMG's known wishes, such action was not on the cards. After discussions between Field and the members of the JIC and me which continued far into the night of the 16th July, Field wrote a dispatch to the S of S for the colonies *strengthening* the arguments for British intervention and asking whether HMG, in the light of the JIC recommendations, wished to vary their previous instructions to him for the employment of British troops.

The reply was, "No." The four ministers principally concerned concurred. The prime minister (Harold Macmillan) minuted, "I agree." (CO 554/2574)

No terrorist aggression against British property or nationals occurred during the remaining two and a half months of trusteeship.

Although the R of C had had the status of an independent sovereign country from 1st January 1960 Ahidjo still had a number of French officers on loan or secondment to his staff well into 1961. Several of these officers were men of the highest calibre and were recognised as such by British officers serving in Nigeria or the Southern Cameroons with whom they liaised from time to time.

In 1961, particularly, French officers complained strongly to their British opposite numbers that the SC administration was prejudiced against the RC armed forces and that there was an undue degree of pro-terrorist sympathy on the SC side of the frontier. They said in so many words "...here are these two territories about to unify politically and you British are allowing theses dangerously wrong beliefs to persist and damage the prospects of Union."

---

13 CO 554/2571

Expatriate officials who had been in the country some time, and of course the bulk of the Cameroonians themselves, saw the matter otherwise. The French colonial system had differed considerably from the British, especially in the use of armed force. I am not arguing that the British system was better or worse or less effective than the French, but I do aver that it was liked better by the inhabitants of the Republic and Southern Cameroons than the French system. Hence the greater popularity of the British commented upon by English-speaking and French-speaking members of the public in SC and R of C alike. To maintain that the British administration owed a duty to the future unified Cameroons to seek to modify attitudes that had been formed over many years was vain. It was to urge the impossible. Had we attempted it we should have been vulnerable to all sorts of queries as to why we were interfering. Foncha and his ministers had long pressed Ahidjo to allow them control of security matters in the Western part of the future unified republic but it was a battle they had lost.

Some thought must be given to Ahidjo's personal standing in August 1961. The Foumban Conference had, it is true, strengthened his position a little by inclining towards a presidential regime (see page 458). Nevertheless, he still needed to keep very much on his toes. He counted on France as a friend should he be in deep need but he had to avoid giving the impression that he was merely a stooge of the French. The terrorist movement almost helped him in a way. It had passed through the stages of being directed against him and his government as creatures of France. It had become more tribal in nature, directed mainly against old scores and tribal jealousies within the Bamileke. There was evidence in the middle of 1961 that he was using the "carrot and stick" technique: taking drastic action against the terrorist groups one moment and offering amnesty the next.

As to the aid personnel working in the R of C mentioned above: I don't believe Ahidjo treated these gentlemen any differently to any other African leader in a similar position—predominantly he *used* them. Splendid personalities that many of them were, it was a mistake to listen too readily to what they said. They seldom were fully in the president's confidence.

At the end of August 1961 the Republic of Cameroun sent an economic mission to the SC with the object of studying the structure of the economy and placing in relief the main difference with that of the R of C. Alastair Paterson, the financial secretary, summarised the main findings in a report dated 15th September 1961.

On the 8th September 1961 John Field issued a proclamation establishing a police force for the Southern Cameroons. The proclamation contained a section empowering adaptation to the successor authority to Her Majesty.

Field wrote a final dispatch to Eastwood of the colonial office on 14th September 1961. In it he made the following points:

Civilian Morale: greatly improved in recent weeks. Although difficulties are anticipated, most people are now resigned and coming round to the view that they are likely to be at less at risk than at one time they thought. On the whole there has been a marked relaxation in tension.

Hand over to CR Security Forces: going well; advanced cadres have now arrived. The French have picked the best of Cameroonian Officers, both in the army and gendarmes. "David Fraser speaks well of them."

Return of Cameroonians serving in the Nigerian Army: Five officers and 120 men have agreed to take their discharge from the Nigerian Forces. Still not known how many will join the CR Army.

Establishment of SC Police Force: thought that some ninety per cent of Cameroonians serving in the Nigerian Police will agree to transfer which will bring total to about the strength in August 1961. The Guards have done a first-class job training the 150 men. Four expatriate officers might be prepared to stay on.

Agency Services: the PTT have worked out arrangements whereby postal services will be able to function after the 30th September. Pilotage and maintenance of navigational aids agreed with Government of Nigeria pending take-over by the Republic. Labour and prisons also should be able to continue.

Expatriate Staff: it is hoped that about sixty expatriate staff in total will stay on.

General: many problems remain and no time available to solve them before 1st October but SC should be functioning at take-over and danger of collapse averted.

Among documents of interest that I retained with my personal papers was a note of the special security arrangements laid down for the visit to Buea of His Excellency President Ahidjo over the night of 14th June 1961. The president was to spend the night as the guest of the commissioner at the Schloss. Although intelligence had no specific warning of an attempt upon the president's life, it was considered that such an attempt was neither impossible or unlikely. From the president's arrival until his departure his personal security was to be the responsibility of a named superintendent of police.

The president's suite of Rooms at the Schloss was to be thoroughly searched an hour before his arrival at the airport and again fifteen minutes before HE's anticipated arrival at the Schloss. The airport buildings were to be searched twice before HE's arrival and departure and the building put under special surveillance. A police NCO, together with a small posse of police constables were to be solely responsible for the security of HE's personal luggage from the arrival of the aircraft to the handing over to HE's authorised staff at the Schloss. The airport crowd and the routes to be followed by HE were patrolled by plain-clothes members of Special Branch with instructions to report the presence of any non-southern Cameroonian or any other suspicious person.

Staff and guests at all receptions were to be issued with passes valid for one occasion only. An officer was put in charge of each precautionary measure. Although the definitive document was issued by Special Branch I detected, in its comprehensiveness and quiet competence, Mike Cartlidge's hand, he having just returned from leave.

It is tedious to go further into the mechanisms of protection. The point is that on all of the president's visits to Buea we, that is the British administration of the SC, genuinely tried to make him feel welcome and we were determined to protect him to the height of our ability. He was a friendly and dignified personality with the impeccable manners of his Fulani ancestors. He was a pleasure to deal with and the last thing we wanted was for ill to come to him.

On the last day of all—the 30th September 1961—the plan was for the Fields to depart for Lagos on a British destroyer whence they would fly on to London. President Ahidjo planned to arrive by air at Tiko after the Fields' departure and take over the territory from me in a midnight ceremony to be held in Buea.

As Kat and I were to fly to Jos at first light on 1st October, neither of us slept on the night of the 30th September. I grappled with the draft of a telegram for Eastwood reporting Field's departure and Ahidjo's take-over which Balmain in his brand new capacity of HM Consul would kindly encode and dispatch for me.

The afternoon of 30th September had been exceptionally brilliant. There weren't many days in the year Ambas Bay could be like that. But I for one—and I think others of my colleagues as well—felt that the beauty of the scene was an ironic comment on what we'd been up to rather than a sign of approbation for what we'd done. Maybe we'd let "these nice little people down" to use Foley Newns' words and one day would rue it.

We'd come to the end of a pretty sorry saga. We had—obedient to orders—given away what once we'd been charged with constructing. On the other hand none of us felt competent to question the orders emanating from cabinet level; our experience had always been that such orders, based upon all the facts, were correct, infallible.

My head full of such conflicts I found drafting what might have been a relatively straightforward telegram late that night desperately difficult. I felt that some of the "Whitehall Warriors", as we referred facetiously to our London colleagues, were treating the whole matter too casually by half. Most of them seemed incapable of understanding that our role had been a painful one.

The other day, when drafting this passage, I used the thirty-year rule to look out the CO file bearing my telegram. It seemed to have been virtually ignored. A junior officer had commented, "Mr Milne appears to have been reading Kipling," and, "What criticisms?"

As to criticisms, how could he ignore two years or more of Hansard and folios of press cuttings? He was right about my reading Kipling, though. I had, but only some 10,000 words—*The Maltese Cat*, probably the best *polo* story ever written.

The telegram must have tested the new consuls' cipher arrangements for it was not dispatched until 4th October 1961. It read as follows:

HM Consul Buea to Foreign Office. Following for Eastwood Colonial Office from Milne dated 1st October.

Field and Mrs Field embarked on HMS *Diana* at 3.30 p.m. yesterday after a moving and impressive ceremony on Bota Wharf. Guard of Honour was provided by Cameroon Republican Army and Grenadiers. Foncha and Ministers together with large numbers of prominent persons and personal friends of the Fields were present. Seldom can Ambas

Bay have appeared more beautiful. There was brilliant sun, blue sea and a cool breeze. Great skyscapes over partially obscured Cameroons Mountain provided magnificent backcloth and away to the West Fernando Po stood out beneath a girdle of cloud of great beauty. Whatever the criticisms of our recent policy towards the territory it cannot be denied that the departure of Her Majesty's Representative was a dignified occasion set in a scene of true splendour.

2 President Ahidjo's aircraft landed punctually at five p.m. He was welcomed by Guard of Honour provided by Grenadiers and Cameroon Army. The President and his suite were accommodated in the Lodge. He had previously informed Foncha that it would not be appropriate for the latter to move in until his departure today. I gave a dinner party for him at the Lodge and subsequently we adjourned to the Mountain Hotel where some 200 guests had been invited. Midnight was recorded by a twenty-one gun salute. I read my message to Foncha and King delivered Her Majesty's message. Lastly, Ahidjo broadcast to the Nation.

3 The President appeared happy to accept his position as my guest until midnight and in fact expressed a preference to travel in my official car with the Union Jack flying not only from Tiko to Buea but also from the Lodge to the Mountain Hotel. If the primary object of his visit was to divert limelight from Foncha this was successfully achieved.

4 Although there were large numbers of persons at the airport and on the roadside en route to Buea, the traditional palm and flower decorations were conspicuously missing and there was little show of enthusiasm; the tone was one of silent acceptance rather than of welcome or jubilation. Probable reason for scarcity of palm leaves and flowers was failure of government party to carry out the necessary organisation.

5 My wife and I propose to fly to Jos this morning and onwards to United Kingdom 4th October.

APPENDIX ONE

Nigerian and British Cameroons Constitutional Changes, 1914 to 1961

(The numerous Nigerian and British Cameroons constitutions became known by the name of the governor-general, governor or secretary of state who introduced them.)

Prior to 1st January 1914 Nigeria was administered as two protectorates. The two were merged on 1st January 1914 under Sir Fredrick Lugard with the personal title of Governor-general. He was assisted by two lieutenant governors. The colony of Lagos was placed under an administrator until 1916 when it became subject to the control of the Lieutenant-governor of Southern Nigeria.

In 1922 the British Cameroons (part of the former German colony of Kamerun) was added to Nigeria for administrative purposes, a portion to each Protectorate.

Sir Hugh Clifford, Governor of Nigeria at the time, introduced the 1922 **constitution** which created a legislative council for the colony of Lagos and the Southern Provinces. The council had forty-six members ten of whom were Nigerian, three were elected from Lagos, one from Calabar by adult suffrage and the remainder nominated. The governor retained executive authority for the Northern Provinces. The council only legislated for the Southern Region and Lagos. The annual budget which included Northern Provinces expenditure was, however, passed by the council. The chief commissioner, NP (the title of lieutenant-governor was changed to chief commissioner in 1933) was an ex-officio member of the council and commercial and mining interests were also represented. The constitution provided for an Executive Council to advise the governor.

The Richards Constitution was introduced by Sir Arthur Richards in 1946. It provided a central legislative council consisting of sixteen official members and twenty-eight unofficial members in the ratio of four elected to twenty-four nominated or indirectly elected. The north was represented by two officials, the chief commissioner and one resident, and by nine of the twenty-four unofficial members.

Nigerians were in a majority in both the legislative and Regional councils.

The constitution divided the country into three Regions with Regional Houses of Assembly. The Southern Cameroons under British trusteeship formed, for the purposes of the constitution, part of the Eastern Region.

The Western and Eastern Regional Council were represented in the Central Legislative Concil by two officials each and by six and five nominated officials respectively. Calabar was to have one elected member. Three unofficial members, either Nigerian or European, were to represent shipping, industry and commerce, banking and mining in the Legislative Council. The governor of Nigeria was to preside over the Central Legislative Council and the native authorities. The functions of Regional Councils included the debating of motions and resolutions, and the discussion of bills before submission to the Central Legislative Council and the scrutiny of estimates of expenditure.

The intention was that the Richards Constitution should remain in being for nine years, subject to limited reviews after three and six years. The election of only four members by adult suffrage was severely criticised.

The Macpherson Constitution

Sir John Macpherson, who became governor in 1948, proposed shortly after his arrival that constitutional changes to the Richards Constitution should be made not at the end of nine years but in the second three-year period which started at the beginning of 1950. A process of a wide consultation was set in motion and a report published in October 1949. A drafting committee then met and on 9th January 1950 the Macpherson Constitution emerged. It provided for a ministerial system of government at both the Regional and Central levels. The Central Legislative House was to be called the House of Representatives and the Central Executive Council was to be known as the Council of Ministers. The House of Representatives was to have 136 members; sixty-eight to be chosen by the "Joint Council" of the Northern Region, thirty-one by the Western House of Assembly, three by the Western House of Chiefs and thirty-four by the Eastern House of Assembly. Not more than six special members were to be appointed by the governor to represent communities not otherwise adequately represented.

The Council of Ministers was to consist of the governor as president, six ex-officio members and twelve ministers, four of whom were to be from each Region. It was prescribed that "the Council of Ministers shall be the principal instrument for policy in and for Nigeria and shall perform such duties and exercise such functions as may from time to time be prescribed by the British governor."

Political parties emerged to contest elections which were held in 1951. In the north the Jami'yar Mutanen Arewa (Union of Peoples of the North)—renamed the Northern Peoples Congress (the NPC)— won control and by virtue of the NPC membership of the House of Representatives won in that house also. The AG (Action Group) won in the Western Region and the NCNC (National Council of Nigeria and the Cameroons) in the Eastern Region.

The Lyttelton Constitution

Constitutional conferences were held in London in 1953 and in Lagos in 1954. As a result a **Federal form** of constitution (the Lyttelton Constitution) was introduced on 1st October 1954. Lagos was detached from the Western Region and became Federal Territory. The Southern Cameroons was also detached from the Eastern Region. The governor of Nigeria was re-designated the governor-general and the lieutenant-governors of all the Regions (except in the case of the Southern Cameroons) became governors of their respective Regions. The Southern Cameroons, being Trusteeship Territory, was placed in charge of a commissioner. Membership of the House of Representatives was increased to 184 of which ninety-two were to be elected from the Northern Region and forty-two each from the Eastern and Western Regions; six were elected from the Southern Cameroons and two from Lagos. Not more than six special members of the House of Representatives were to be appointed by the governor-general to represent communities not otherwise adequately represented. Members of the House of Representatives were to be elected directly from the Federal Constituencies which corresponded with the administrative divisions of the country; they would no longer be members of the Regional Houses of Assembly. Federal ministers from each Region were to be appointed on the recommendations of the leader of the party securing the most seats in each Region in the federal election or of the leader of the party with an overall majority in the House of Representatives. Each Region was given powers to make its own laws without the approval of the federal government.

There was, however, "an exclusive list" of matters reserved for the federal government. There was also a "concurrent list" of subjects on which both governments could legislate, although it was laid down that in the event of a conflict the federal law would prevail. The regional governments were to be headed by the premier but regional governors retained the right to veto bills which they considered were not in the public interest.

The governor-general presided over the Federal Council of Ministers which included the chief secretary, the financial secretary and the attorney-general as ex-officio members. Ex-officio members were removed from Regional governments.

The British government during the Constitutional Conference gave an undertaking to grant internal self-government to any Region that desired it.

The conference also provided for separate judicial systems for each Region and for a federal supreme court to supersede the West African Court of Appeal. Each Region was to have its own high court, with separate high courts for Lagos and the Southern Cameroons.

The Federal Supreme Court was to settle disputes between any Region and the Federation.

Each Region was to have its own public service and its own commodity marketing board; funds of the old marketing boards (which handled specific commodities) were to be shared by the new regional boards.

The Lyttelton Constitution came into force on 1st October 1954. Al Haji Ahamadu Bello, leader of the NPC became premier of the Northern Region; Chief Obafemi Awolowo leader of the AG, became premier of the WR; Dr Nnamdi Azikiwe, leader of the NCNC, became premier of the Eastern Region and Dr Emanuel Endeley, leader of the KNC, became leader of government business in the SC House of Assembly.

Self-government and Minorities

Another Constitutional conference was held in London in May/June 1957 to examine the matter of self-government and the fears of minorities.

It was agreed to grant the requests of the Eastern and Western Regional governments for internal self-government. It was also agreed that the Eastern Region should have a House of Chiefs in addition to a House of Assembly (with powers similar to the Western House of Chiefs) and that the Southern Cameroons be raised to the status of a Region with its own premier.

Membership of the House of Assembly was also increased to 320 single member constituencies. MHR were to be elected by universal adult suffrage in the E and W Regions, Lagos and the Southern Cameroons, and by adult male suffrage in NR.

It was decided to establish a second federal legislative house to be called the senate, composed of twelve members from each Region and the Southern Cameroons, four members from Lagos and four special members appointed by the governor-general.

It was also agreed that the office of prime minister of the federation should be created and ex-officio officers should be removed from the Council of Ministers. The prime minister should be free to recommend to the governor-general the appointment of minister of any member of the H of R.

Independence for Nigeria was proposed for a date not later that 2nd April 1960.

The ER and WR became self-governing on 8th August 1957.

On 2nd September 1957 Alhaji Abubakar Tafewa Balewa was appointed Nigeria's first prime minister. He immediately formed a national government of six NCNC ministers, four from NPC and two from AG and one from KNC. The PM explained why he formed a national government: he regarded the period before independence as a "national emergency" and wished to demonstrate to the world that Nigerians were united and could work together.

On 27th September 1957 the British government appointed Sir Henry Willink to chair a commission of inquiry into the fears of Nigerian minorities. It recommended on 30th July 1958 that the setting up of new states would create problems as great as those it sought to eliminate. The commission felt that the fears of minorities could best be protected at the federal level. It recommended the formation of special areas and minority areas. The recommendations were accepted by all other than the WR government.

The resumed Constitutional Conference was held in London in Sept/Oct 1958. Independence for Nigeria was recommended for 1st October 1960.

Federal elections were held in December 1959. NPC secured 148 seats all in the NR. The NCNC-NEPU Alliance secured eighty-nine seats and the AG and allies seventy-five seats. The NPC and NEPU formed a coalition government with Alhaji Abubakar Tafewa Balewa as prime minister and the AG in opposition. Dr Azikiwe resigned as PM, ER, and became President of the senate in Lagos preparatory to becoming the first governor-general after independence. Dr M I Okpara succeeded Dr Azikiwe in the ER.

Appendix Two

Abbreviations

ADO	Assistant District Officer
AG	Action Group
ALCAM	Assemblée Legislative Du Cameroun
ALNK	Armée Liberation National Kamerun (Military wing of UPC)
AO	Administrative Officer
AOC	Air Officer Commanding
ARCAM	Assemblée Représentative Du Cameroun
CC	Chief Commissioner
CCC	Cameroons Commoners Congress
CCP	Cameroons Commoners Party
CFU	Cameroons Federal Union
CDC	Cameroons Development Corporation
CIP	Cameroons Indigenes Party
CO	Colonial Office
CRSF	Cameroons Republic Security Force
DO	District Officer
ER	Eastern Region
ERDC	Eastern Region Development Corporation
ERFC	Eastern Region Finance Corporation
ERPDB	Eastern Region Produce Development Board
FRC	Federal Republic of Cameroons
GPS	Global Positioning System
HMSO	Her Majesty's Stationary Office
KNC	Kameroun National Congress
KNDP	Kameroun National Democratic Party
KPP	Kameroun People's Party
LEDB	Lagos Executive Development Board
MRH	Member House of Representatives
MHA	Member House of Assembly
NAB	National Archives Buea

NCNC	National Council of Nigeria and the Cameroons
NEMCO	Nigerian Engineering & Manufacturing Co Ltd
NEPU	Northern Elements Progressive Union
NIP	National Independence Party
NKDP	Northern Kameroun Democratic Party
NPC	Northern Peoples Congress
NR	Northern Region
OK	One Kameroun Party
OPPO	Oil Palm Production Officer
PRO KEW	Public Records Office Kew
RC	Republic of Cameroun
RWAFF	Royal West African Frontier Force
SASP	Senior Assistant Superintendent of Police
SDO	Senior District Officer
SPO	Senior Police Officer
S of S	Secretary of State
UNIP	United National Independence Party
UPC	Union Des Population Du Cameroun
WGS	Windermere Grammar School
WR	Western Region

Index